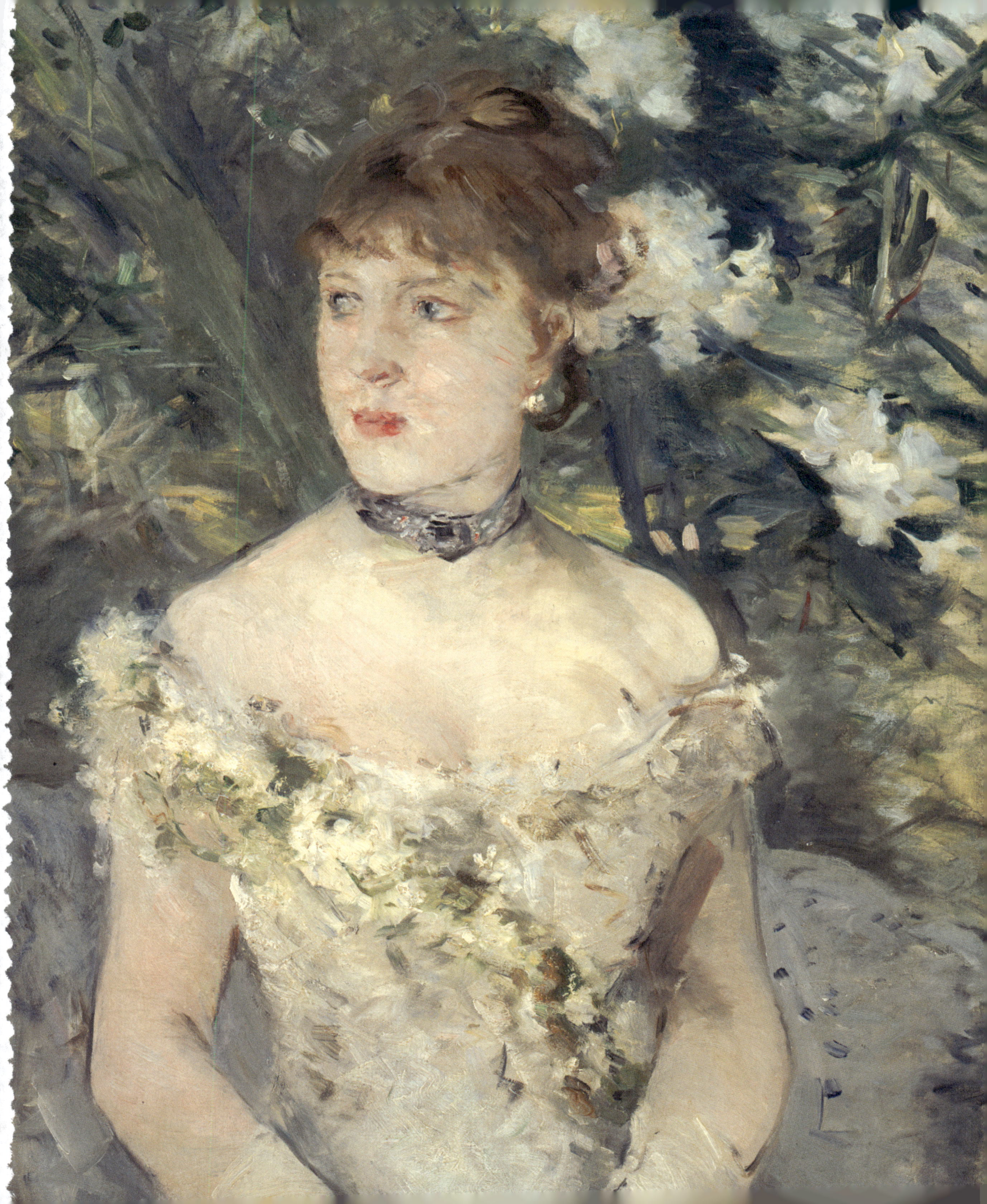

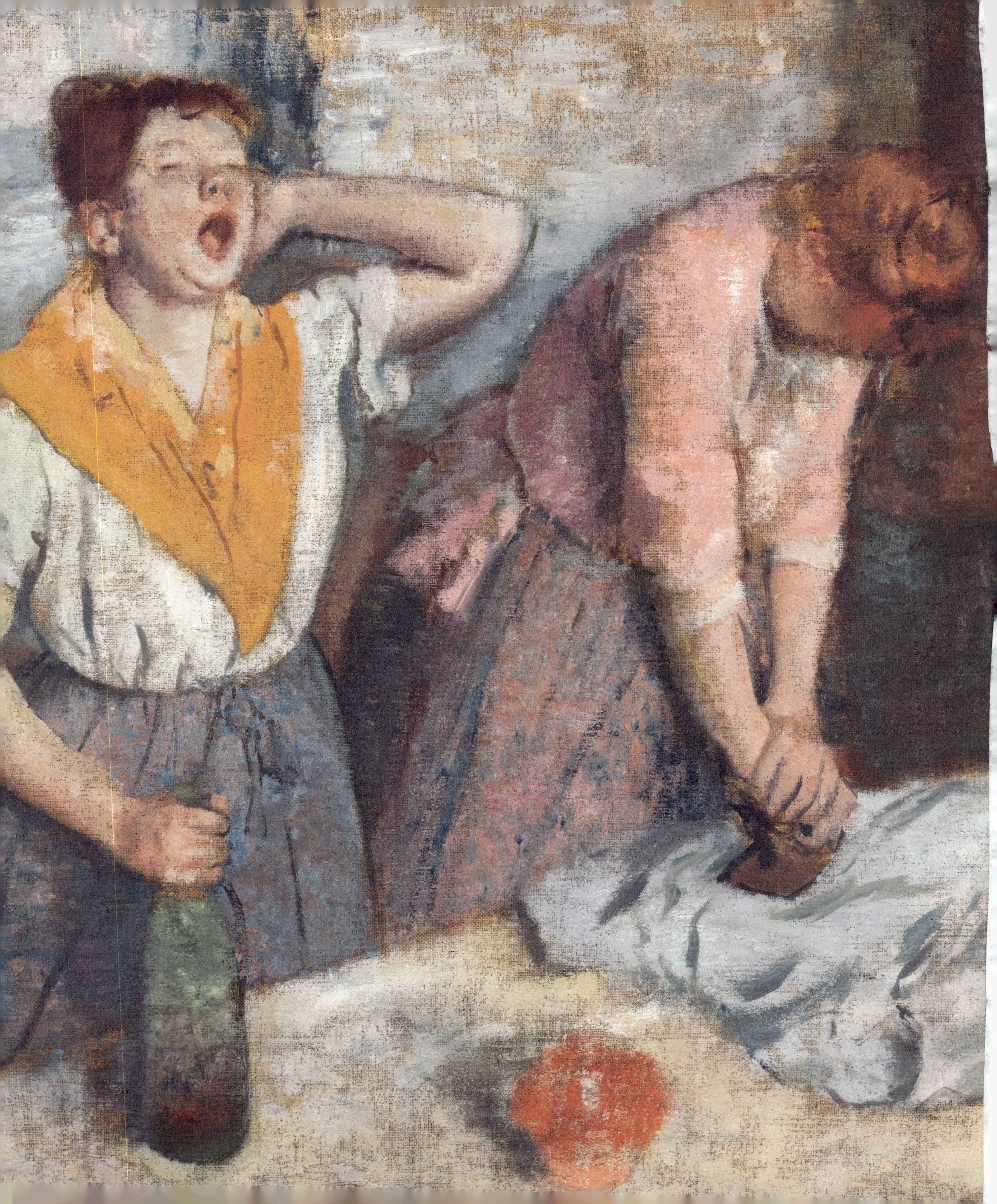

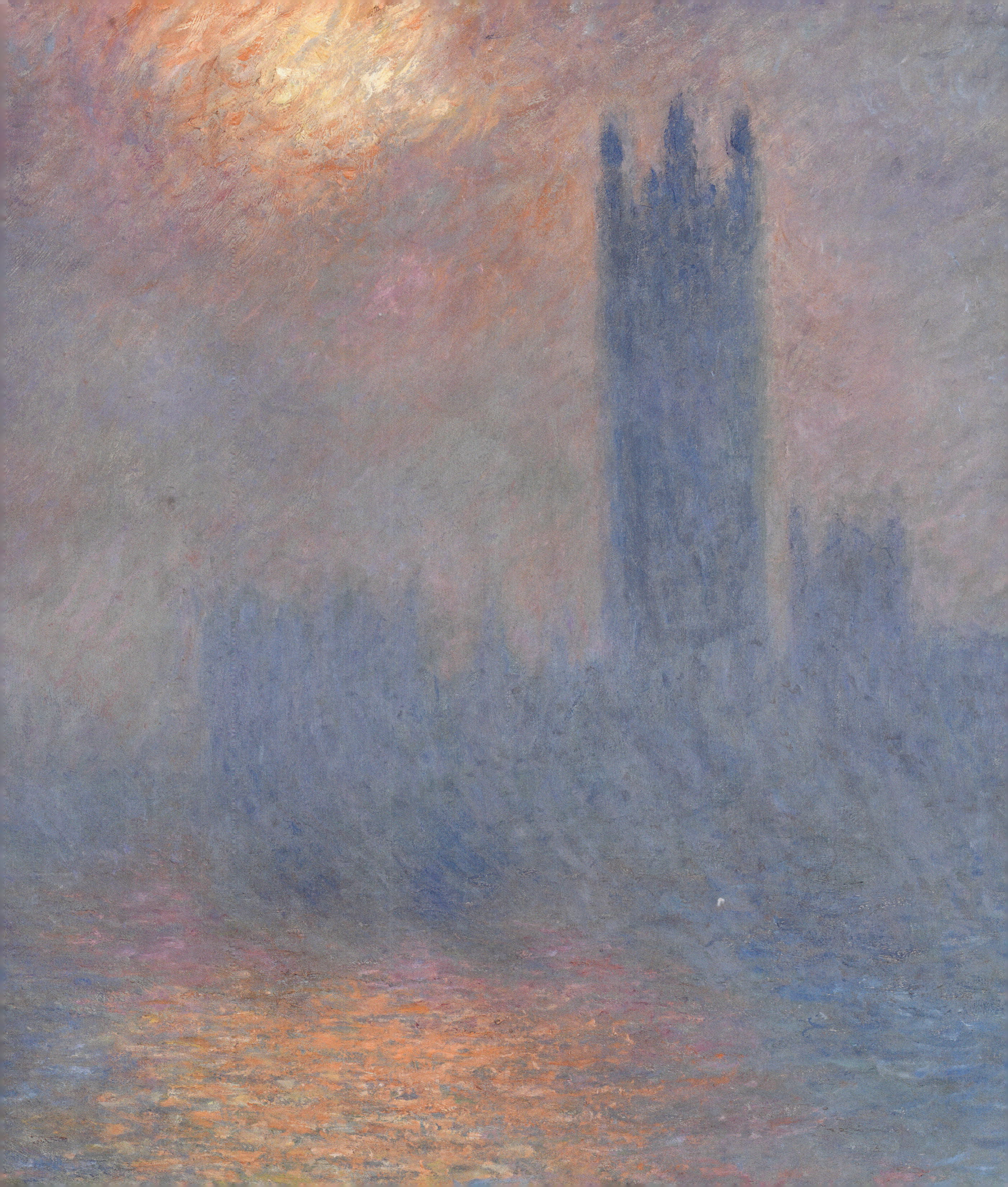

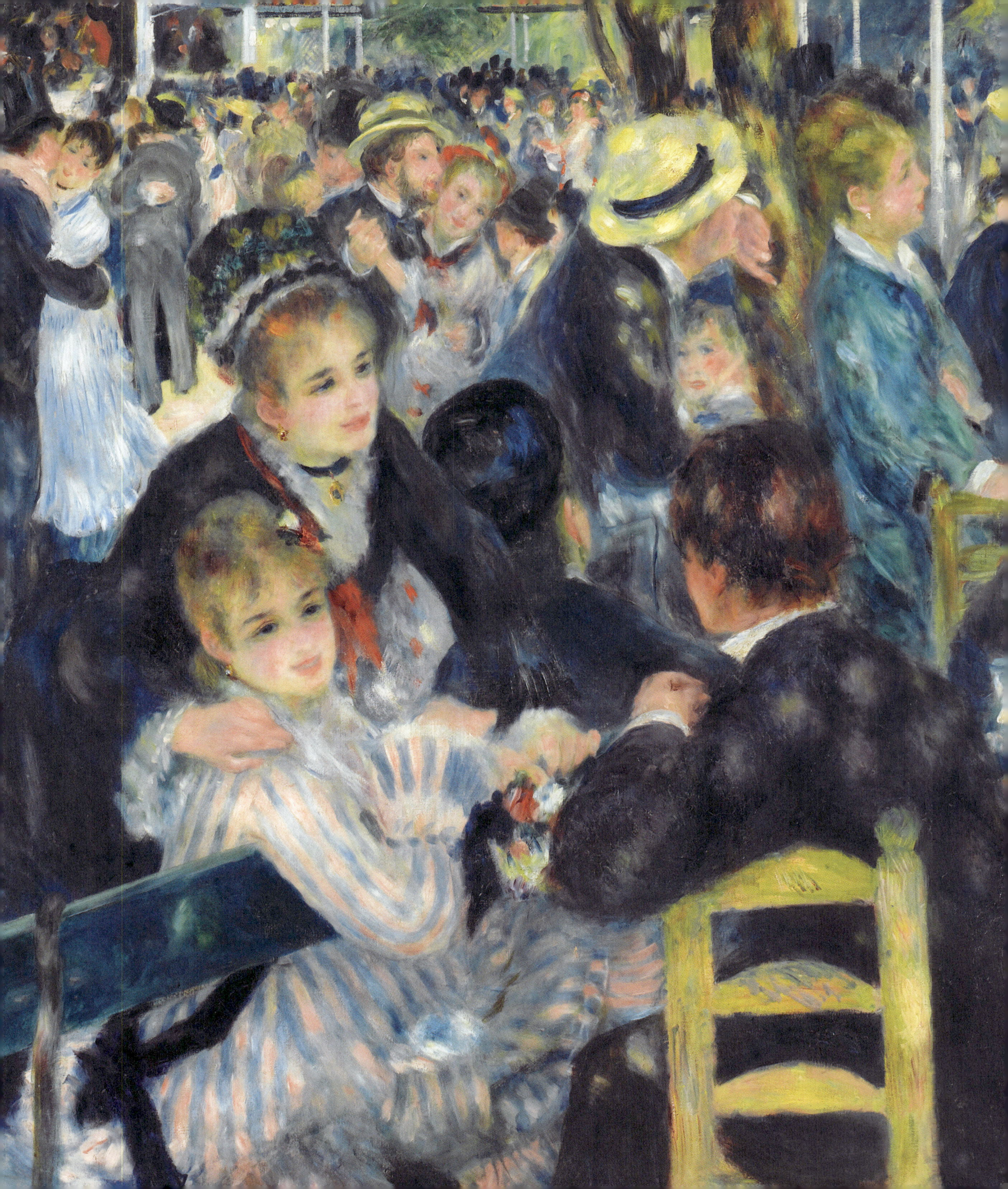

Impressionism
MUSÉE D'ORSAY

Edited by Paul Perrin,
Director of Curatorial Affairs and Collections at the Musée d'Orsay

with François Blanchetière, Caroline Corbeau-Parsons,
Stéphane Guégan, Leïla Jarbouai, Sylvie Patry,
Isolde Pludermacher, Anne Robbins, Marie Robert,
Jean-Rémi Touzet, and Bénédicte Trémolières

MASTERPIECES
ARTISTS
THEMES
KEY DATES

Musée d'Orsay

Flammarion
PARIS • SINCE 1875

Contents

The Musée d'Orsay's Impressionist Collection

It is a great pleasure for the Musée d'Orsay to be publishing a richly illustrated volume specifically devoted to its collection of Impressionist works, for the very first time. Renowned as both the most extensive and the most popular Impressionist collection in the world, it attracts several million visitors per year into the former Gare d'Orsay—the railroad-station building that is the museum's home. The property of the French Nation and State, the collection has been placed in the Musée d'Orsay's care as the national museum that displays art from the period 1848–1914 and holds works by artists who were born between 1820 and 1880—that is, after the period represented at the Louvre, and before that of the Musée National d'Art Moderne.

Definitions of "Impressionism" and of "Impressionist" artists have varied ever since the movement first received its name, in the press in 1874. Do these terms apply only to the artists who took part in one of the new independent group exhibitions that were organized in Paris in eight editions, between 1874 and 1886? Or to the first artists who painted genuine *plein-air* paintings that were not just studies, seeking to express their "impression" or "feeling" of the subject, and of the spectacle of modern life, through their rapid, loose brushwork, and with a palette of light, bright colors that could convey the radiance of light and the play of colored glints that it casts? Or more broadly, to any artist who had gravitated around these exhibitions, or experimented with this technique, at any point in their career? Was Impressionism a French style or an international trend? A movement that existed only in painting, or also in sculpture, music, and the applied arts? Formed in response to aesthetic, historical, national, or indeed ideological factors, the definitions and "canons" have been far from neutral in what they have included or excluded.

For this book, we have decided to focus on the artists who, with only a few exceptions, were born between the early 1830s and the early 1840s, worked in France, and either participated in most of the group's exhibitions, or were pivotal to the invention of the new style and iconography that Edmond Duranty named "*La Nouvelle Peinture*" (the New Painting) in the booklet that accompanied the 1876 exhibition. Some of them are often considered as mentors, precursors, or youthful companions (Jongkind, Boudin, Manet, Bazille), others as pillars of the group and of the *plein-air* aesthetic, even if their work later developed in different artistic directions (Pissarro, Cézanne, Sisley, Monet, Morisot, Guillaumin, Renoir). Still others embody more the aspect of naturalism, being more attached to the figure, draftsmanship, and working in the studio (Bracquemond, Degas, Caillebotte, Cassatt, Gonzalès). Added to these are a few younger artists who would later represent neo-Impressionism or post-Impressionism, having worked under the Impressionists' influence and exhibited alongside them at the start of their careers (Gauguin, Seurat).

The history of how these national collections of Impressionist works came together cannot be summarized within just a few lines, but suffice to say that the Orsay's collection was built up over more than

120 years (key stages of this story are laid out on pp. 230, 252 and 266), making it not only the most extensive but also the oldest Impressionist collection. Between the 1890s and today, numerous purchases, but above all gifts, bequests, and more recently transfers in lieu of estate tax, have been patiently gathered through generations of donors (the artists themselves, their models and the first collectors and dealers of Impressionism, then their heirs, and new generations of collectors throughout the twentieth and twenty-first centuries) and dedicated curators (first at the Musée du Luxembourg, then at the Louvre, the Musée du Jeu de Paume, and finally the Musée d'Orsay), all driven by the same passion and ambition. The Musée d'Orsay's collection is therefore not the result of a single collection being gifted, nor of a single collector's taste, but is an accumulation of dozens or even hundreds of different gazes and acts of generosity. Hence it stands as a genuinely collective undertaking, a body of work that is also a public asset available to all French people and, more broadly, to all lovers of Impressionism worldwide.

What is also special about this collection is how, in its own unique way, it tells the story of the relationship between a country—France—and what is probably the most significant artistic current of its history, which gradually became a strong marker of its cultural identity (the museum's masterpieces have long been part of French people's "collective imagination") and a tool for diplomatic outreach and cultural "soft power." But rather than being limited to this national dimension, over the course of time the collection has genuinely become a global heritage treasure. Housed here in the heart of Paris, the city where Impressionism was born, and overlooking the Seine, the river that these artists so loved, it is admired and disseminated the world over.

Today, the Musée d'Orsay's "Impressionist" collection consists of around 500 paintings (including those by artists such as Boudin, Manet, Guillaumin, and Marie Bracquemond), constituting about ten percent of all the paintings held at the museum. It also includes 150 pastels, some 1,500 other works on paper (in addition to the almost 6,000 drawings and watercolors from Boudin's studio collection), nearly 400 letters (including more than 160 signed by Monet), and around 80 sculptures (mostly by Degas). The most significant sets of paintings are those by Monet (87), Renoir (81), Cézanne (57), Sisley (47), Pissarro (46), and Manet (38). While the Musée Marmottan Monet in Paris has more Monet canvases, and the Barnes Foundation in Philadelphia holds more works by Renoir and Cézanne, the French national collections have the distinction of being more diverse and of representing the entirety of these artists' careers. The museum is also home to the world's largest set of works by Degas: 43 paintings, 48 pastels, almost 500 drawings, around 80 sculptures, about 20 photographs, and numerous archive documents. Some 200 Impressionist works are permanently on display in the Musée d'Orsay's galleries, while many others are on long-term loan to regional museums across France or circulate in temporary exhibitions. Each year, the collection continues to grow through the acquisition of significant works, filling gaps in its holdings—particularly with regard to women artists—and strengthening its areas of excellence.

To date, no publication has ever featured so many works from this collection (more than 250), bringing together all the artists (with works by women artists featuring prominently) and covering all techniques, notably including works on paper (but excluding the art of printmaking, with works created using this technique by Cassatt, Degas, Morisot, Pissarro and Renoir being preserved at France's national library, the Bibliothèque Nationale). In its own way, this book takes up the overriding thread of the museum's displays, but enriches it considerably through a diverse array of thematic, chronological, and monographic approaches. It allows us to retrace the whole history of the movement, while highlighting certain masterpieces and the collections' strong points. For example, for each of the group's eight exhibitions, the museum has several of the works that were presented, reproduced in this volume. The museum is also home to some of the most substantial sets of works painted by Monet in Argenteuil or Vétheuil, of Degas's depictions of dancers, and of Cézanne's still lifes.

Written by the Musée d'Orsay's team of specialists, this book—just like the collection—is the product of a collaborative effort and a range of viewpoints. The outcome of decades of research, studies of individual works, exhibitions, restorations, purchases, and archival or documentary finds, it aims to communicate the current state of knowledge, which—again like the collection itself, and the museum's displays—will constantly continue to grow and evolve.

Paul Perrin
Curator in Chief and Director of Curatorial Affairs
and Collections at the Musée d'Orsay

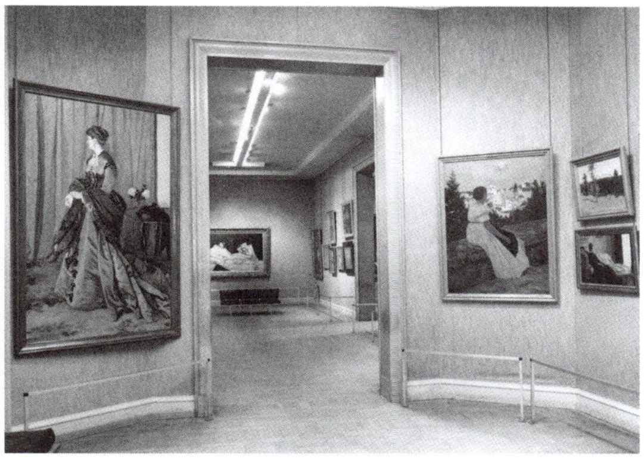

Paintings by Manet and Impressionist artists as presented in the Jeu de Paume gallery between 1947 and 1986.

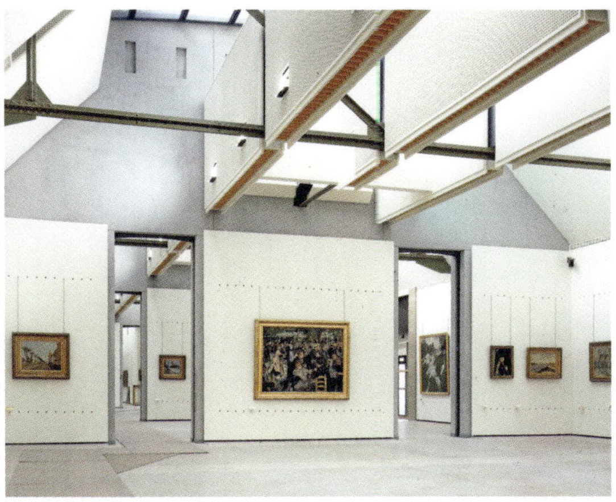

The "galerie des hauteurs" (upper-level gallery), as curated by Gae Aulenti at the opening of the museum in 1986.

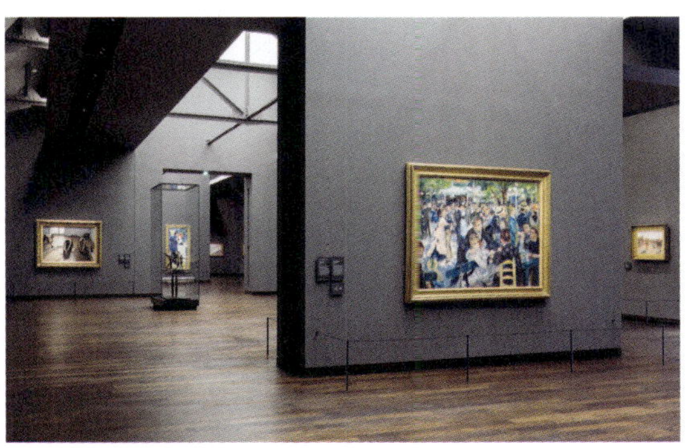

The new "galerie des impressionnistes," as reimagined by the architect Jean-Michel Wilmotte in 2011.

1861

The beginnings of friendship between Monet, Renoir, Sisley, and Bazille

Between 1860 and 1863, Alfred Sisley, and then Auguste Renoir, Frédéric Bazille, and Claude Monet, all joined the Paris studio of the Swiss painter Charles Gleyre, which offered sessions painting or drawing live models to young artists who were still training, as well as some masterclasses. Sisley, whose father was a British merchant, abandoned his business studies to focus on painting. Renoir, the son of a tailor and a seamstress, swapped painting on porcelain for high art. Bazille, from an upper-class family in Montpellier, was juggling medical studies with a painter's vocation. As for Monet, he was no longer a beginner, having already worked at Martin-François Suisse's informal art school, the Académie Suisse, where he had met Camille Pissarro, and had learned much from Johan Barthold Jongkind and Eugène Boudin. Monet only attended Gleyre's studio to please his father, who was still reluctant to see him embark on this career.

The four young men soon became friends, and would go out to paint together on site (notably in the forest of Fontainebleau: see p. 24). They left Gleyre's studio between 1863 and 1864 but remained close. Bazille rented an apartment-cum-studio with Monet on Rue de Furstenberg, and later let Renoir, who was penniless, share his studios on Rue Visconti between 1867 and 1868, then on Rue La Condamine until 1870. As Bazille wrote to his parents in January 1867: "I don't think I've mentioned to you yet that I'm putting up one of my friends, a former student at Gleyre's, who has no studio himself at the moment. His name is Renoir, and he's very hard-working. He's working from my models, and even helps me out with paying their fees."

When models were lacking, the two men turned to each other to paint portraits. Renoir's portrayal of Bazille at his easel, working on *Still Life with Heron* (1867; Musée Fabre, Montpellier), is natural and affectionate, his tall body curved in concentration. A short while later, Renoir struck a pose himself for his friend, sitting in an office armchair. Sisley was nearby, and also took advantage of the studio to paint his own version of the still life with heron. After moving back to Normandy, Monet regularly returned to Paris and used Bazille and Renoir's studio to store some of his paintings. We can see one of the snowy landscapes he painted near Honfleur on the wall in the background.   P.P.

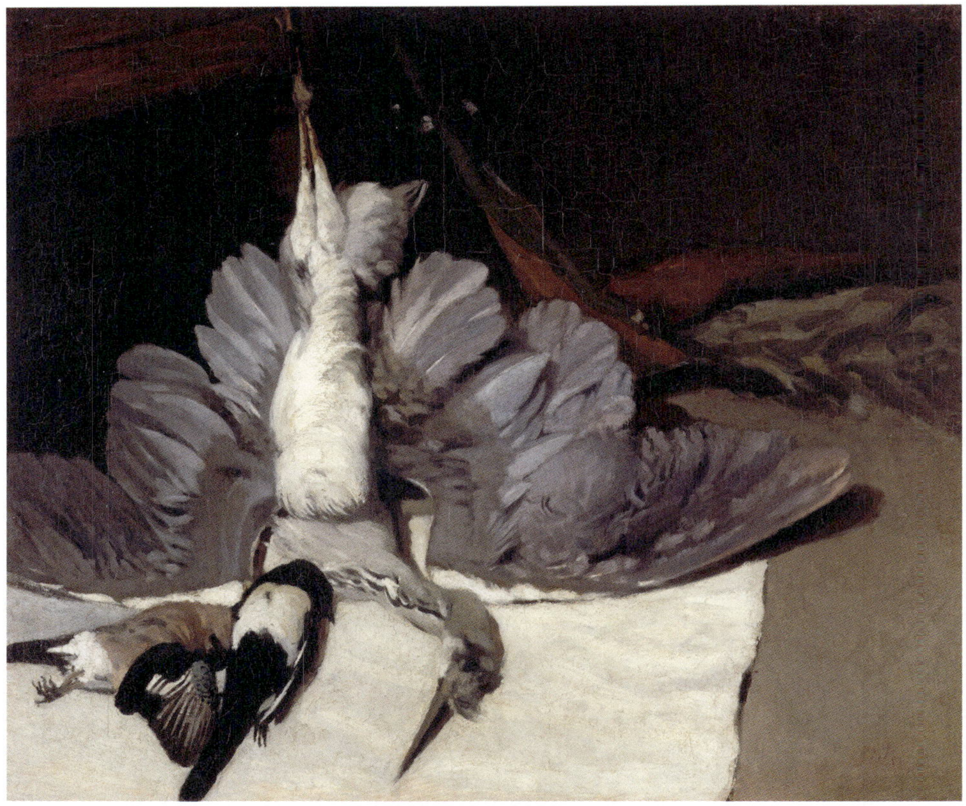

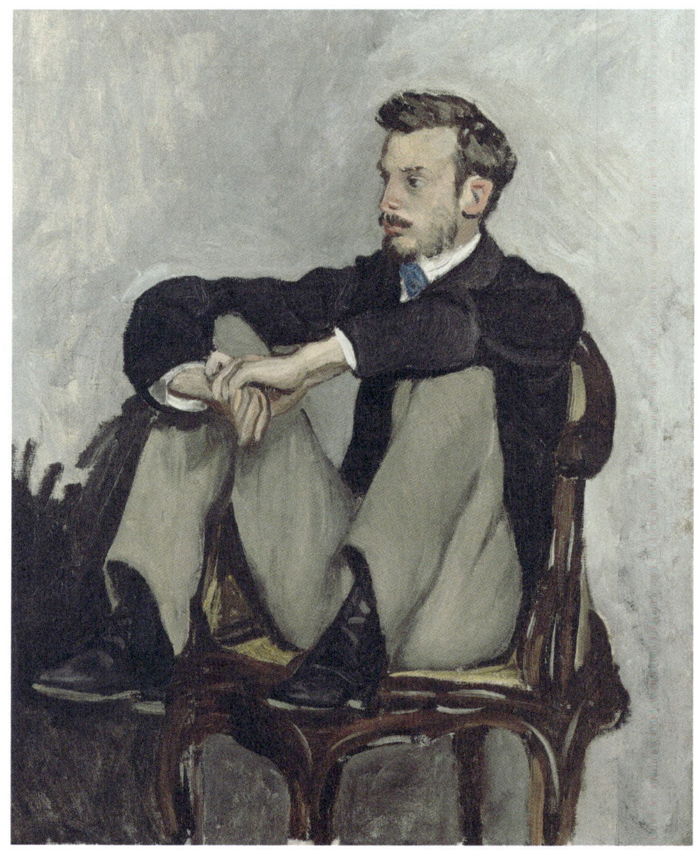

1 Top: Alfred Sisley, *Le Héron aux ailes déployées* (*The Heron with Outstretched Wings*), 1867
Oil on canvas, 31 ½ × 39 ⅜ in. (80 × 100 cm)

2 Bottom: Frédéric Bazille, *Pierre Auguste Renoir*, c. 1867–1869
Oil on canvas, 24 ⅛ × 19 ¹¹⁄₁₆ in. (61.2 × 50 cm)

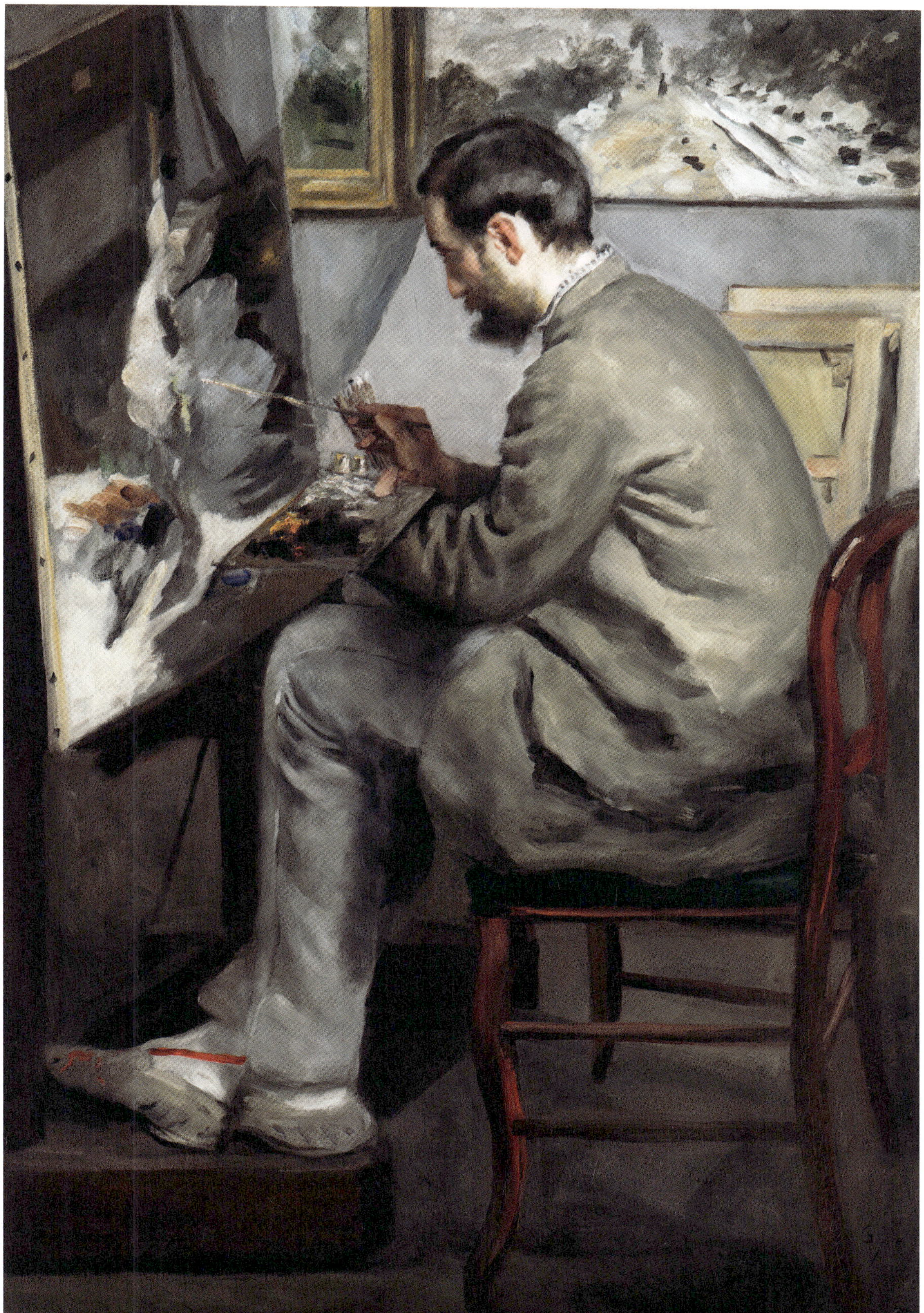

3 Auguste Renoir, *Frédéric Bazille*, 1867
Oil on canvas, 41 5⁄16 × 28 15⁄16 in. (105 × 73.5 cm)

1863

The Salon des Refusés

Composed of painters from the Académie des Beaux-Arts and led by Émilien de Nieuwerkerke, director-general of the imperial museums, the Salon jury of 1863 proved extremely severe. Of five thousand submitted works, more than half were rejected. Appalled at what they saw as arbitrary verdicts, the artists protested so vehemently that Emperor Napoleon III took an unexpected and radical decision. After coming to view the rejected paintings himself to form an opinion, he offered the "excluded" artists the chance to exhibit, leaving the public to judge the legitimacy of their claims. This "Salon des Refusés" took place in other rooms within the same building—the Palais de l'Industrie—where the official exhibition was held, separated from it only by a turnstile. It opened shortly after the main Salon, and had its own separate catalog and entrance fee.

The "counter-exhibition" was an instant success, attracting hordes of intrigued visitors: "People were filing in like they do in London to Madame Tussaud's Chamber of Horrors." Art critics' reactions were mixed: some found the exhibition "sad and grotesque," while others underlined the usefulness of "maintaining a free display" and wrote detailed accounts of it.

Among the hundreds of paintings on show, some, such as Jongkind's *Ruins of the Château de Rosemont*, did not look radically different from the ones at the official Salon. On the other hand, "the major work of the exhibition"—Édouard Manet's *Le Déjeuner sur l'herbe*—caught everyone's eye, arousing scorn and indignation. Initially titled *Le Bain* (*Bathing*), this ambitiously large painting flouted all the traditional codes in terms of technique, iconography, and most of all the treatment of the female nude. Along with James Abbott McNeill Whistler's *Symphony in White, No. 1: The White Girl* (1861–1863, 1872; National Gallery of Art, Washington, D.C.), it sparked heated debate that harked back to "the good old days of Romanticism," and offered Manet his first "*succès de scandale*," bringing him recognition as the leader of the "new way of painting." I.P.

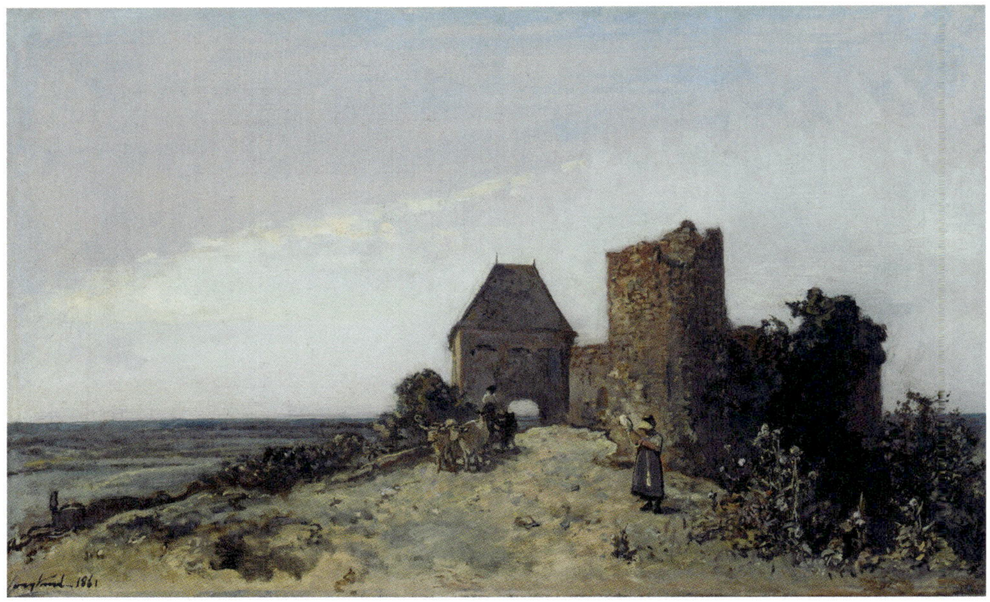

4 Johan Barthold Jongkind, *Ruines du château de Rosemont* (*Ruins of the Château de Rosemont*), 1861
Oil on canvas, 13 ⅜ × 22 ¼ in. (34 × 56.5 cm)

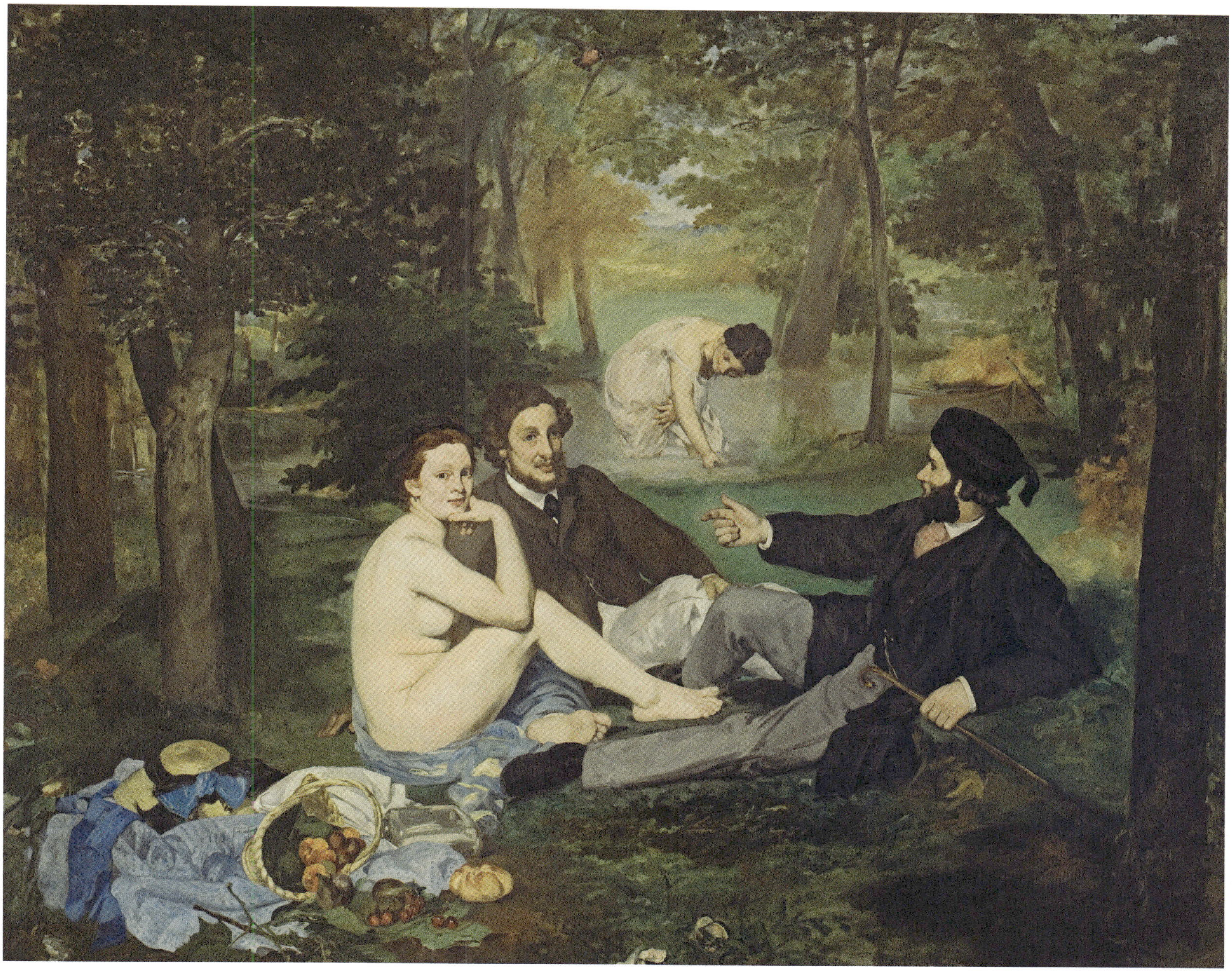

5 Édouard Manet, *Le Déjeuner sur l'herbe* (*Luncheon on the Grass*), 1863
Oil on canvas, 81 ½ × 104 5/16 in. (207 × 265 cm)

Édouard Manet
Olympia

Accepted at the 1865 Salon, *Olympia* sparked a momentous scandal. Visitors were first outraged by the chosen subject: a naked prostitute, whose maid is bringing her a bouquet sent by a client. The scene is represented at a scale usually reserved for history painting. Manet had two models pose, both of whom also appear in other works of his: Victorine Meurent for Olympia, and Laure for the maid. The courtesan's cold, confrontational gaze, her hand resting on her pubis, and the presence of a black cat, were all judged ugly, inept, and vulgar. *Olympia* was so glaringly different from all previous nudes that no critics commented on the parallels with Titian's *Venus of Urbino* (1538; Uffizi, Florence), which Manet had copied in Florence as a young man. While the two do present some striking similarities, the trivial *Olympia* could not in all decency be compared to a Renaissance Venus embodying ideal beauty—even if Titian's painting would itself have been inspired by a Venetian courtesan.

It was not just the subject, but also the technique that threw the critics. The colors are applied in large flat areas, resulting in a "ghastly cacophony" that accentuates the harsh treatment of the light. The modeling and perspective are simplified throughout, provocatively reinforcing the outline of the hand, which is not so much concealing as emphasizing her pubic area. This unprecedented artistic treatment made *Olympia* a genuine feat of painting, which Émile Zola celebrated as such. The canvas remained in Manet's studio until, following his death, it was purchased for the Louvre's collection by public subscription in 1889–1890, Monet having led the fundraising initiative. I. P.

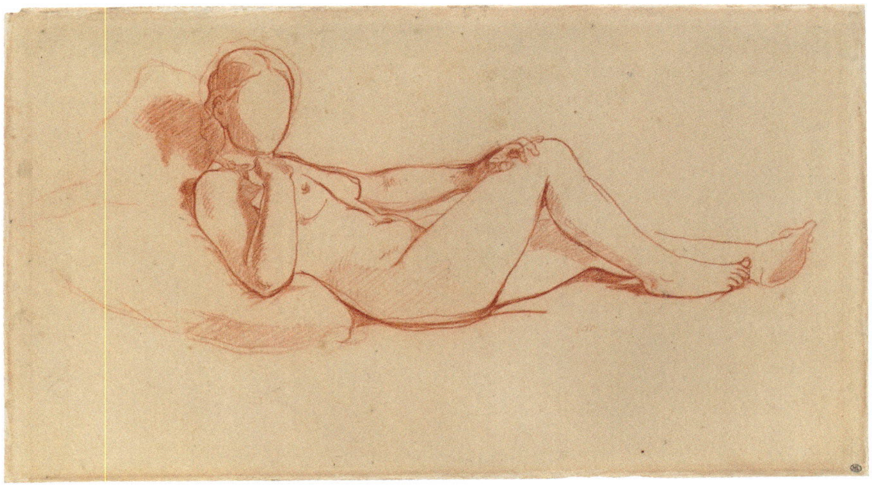

6 Édouard Manet, Study for *Olympia*, 1862–1863
Red chalk on paper, 9 ¾ × 17 15/16 in. (24.7 × 45.6 cm)

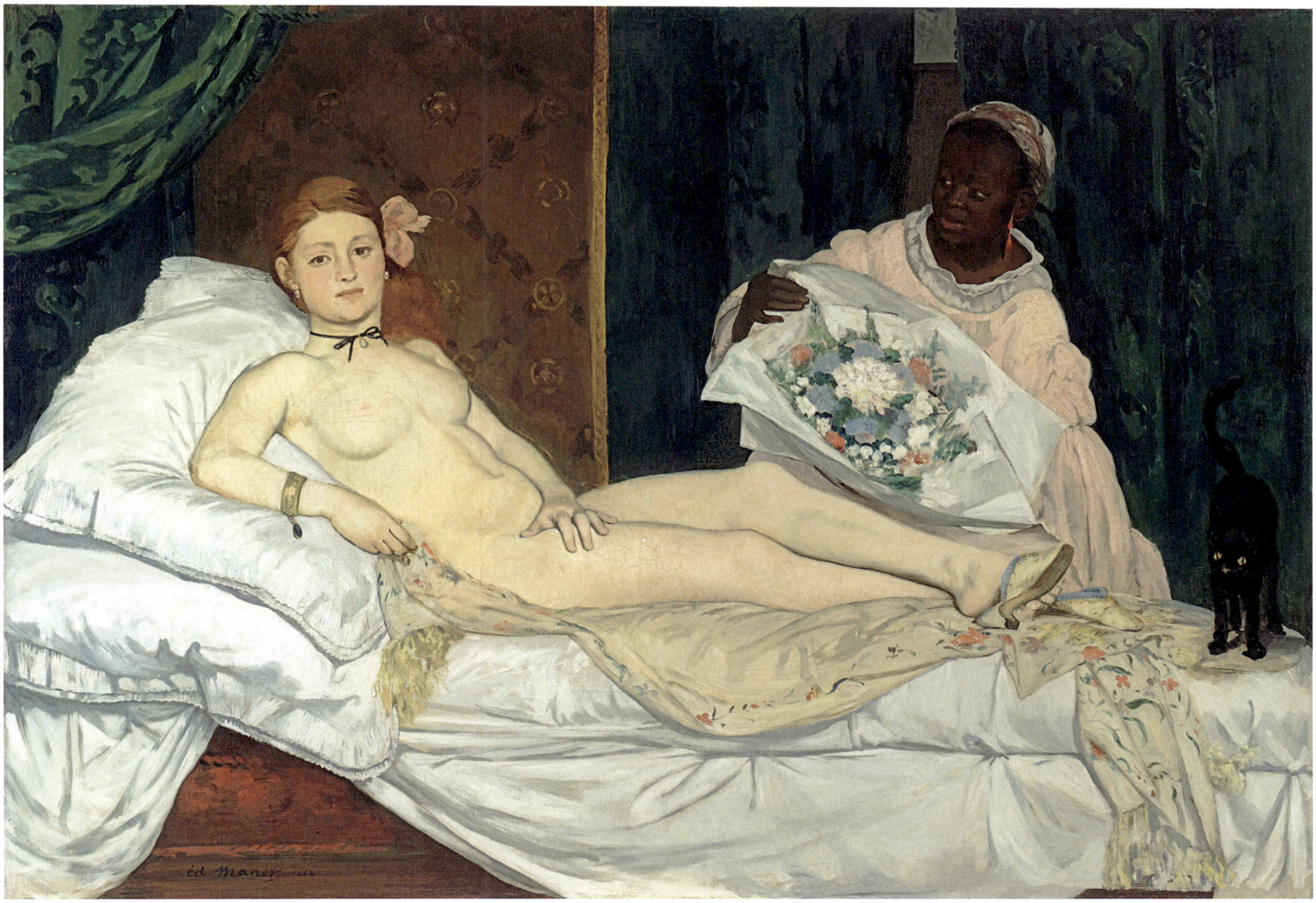

2 Édouard Manet, *Olympia*, 1863–1865
Oil on canvas, 51 ⅜ × 75 3⁄16 in. (130.5 × 191 cm)

Henri Fantin-Latour *Homage to Delacroix*

"Eugène Delacroix had the merit of being stirred by the feverishness of his time": so wrote Théophile Gautier on the death of the great painter and master colorist, who was laid to rest in mid-August 1863. Whether addressing literary subjects, religion, the East, or current political affairs, Delacroix had brought a new note of truth to his lyrical paintings. Young painters, from Manet's circle to Paul Cézanne, displayed their admiration for him in various ways, from simple citation to posthumous tributes. The canvas that Henri Fantin-Latour exhibited at the Salon of 1864 is a combination of both. He had attended Delacroix's funeral and been appalled at the lack of warmth in the press obituaries and official discourse. This affront needed to be remedied by a display of generational solidarity through a sort of secular apotheosis. The reparative work portrays a group of critics and artists whom Fantin-Latour had to paint separately. The Delacroix self-portrait around which we see them gathered never existed, but is drawn from a famous photograph of the late master. Despite these various devices, his 1864 *Homage* comes across as a believable scene showing a close-knit circle. Identifiable from left to right are Louis Cordier, Edmond Duranty, Alphonse Legros, Fantin-Latour himself, Whistler, Champfleury, Manet, Albert Balleroy, Charles Baudelaire, and Félix Bracquemond. The fact that the new Realist generation followed in Romanticism's footsteps was not always understood. And yet, to Renoir and Cézanne just as much as to Manet and Whistler, Delacroix was the daring colorist who had established self-expression and the personal interpretation of reality as golden rules. S.G.

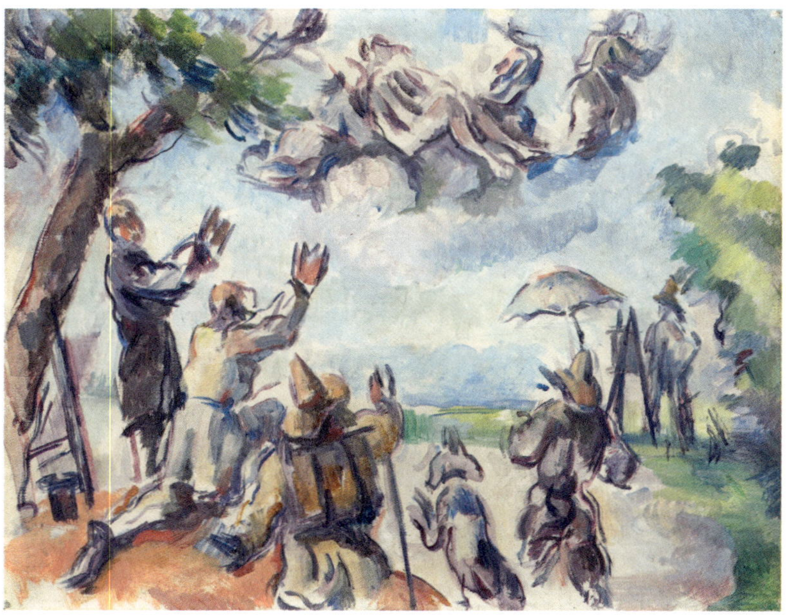

8 Paul Cézanne, *Apothéose de Delacroix* (*Apotheosis of Delacroix*), 1890–1894
Oil on canvas, 10 ⅝ × 13 ¾ in. (27 × 35 cm)

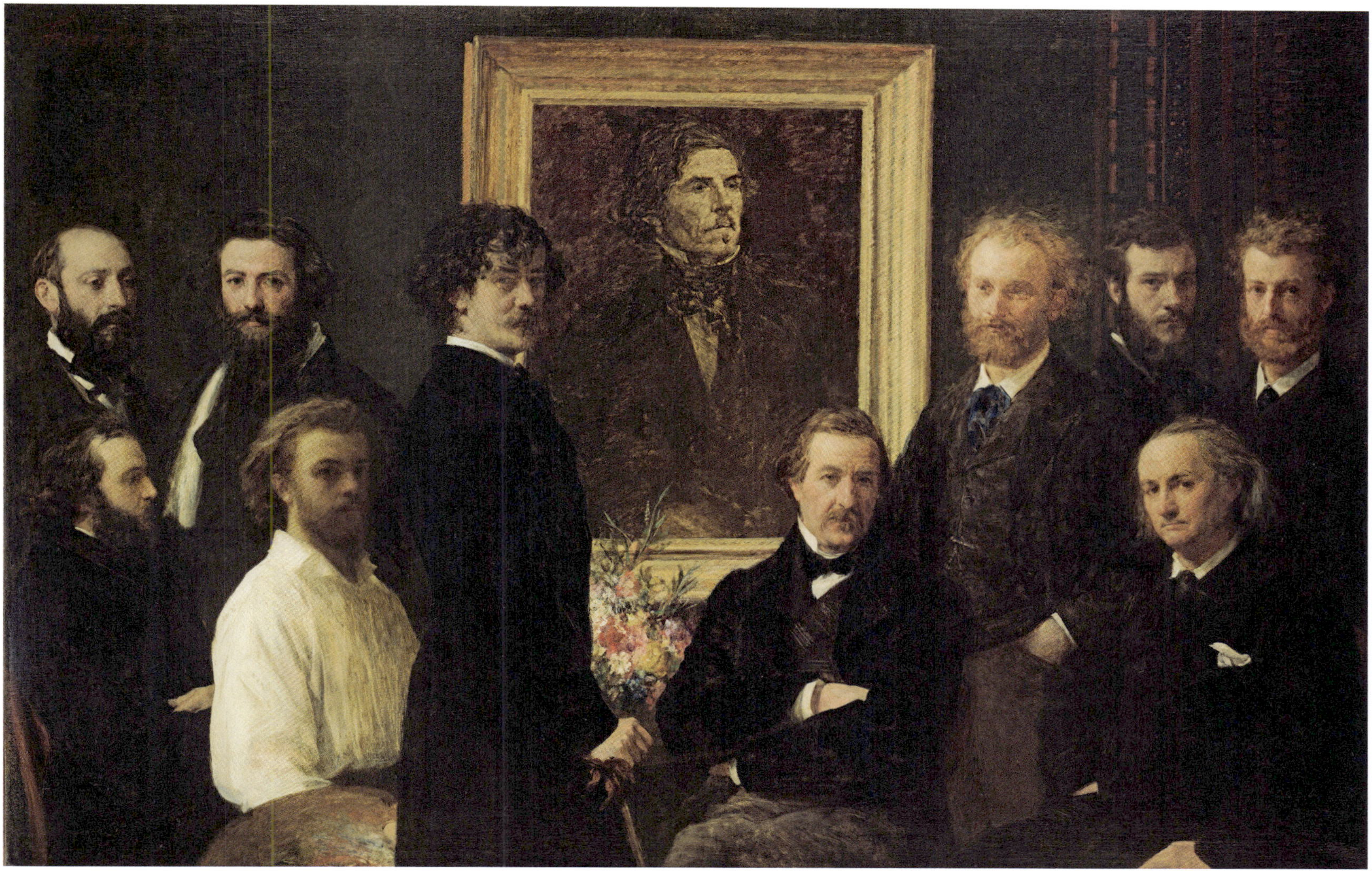

9 Henri Fantin-Latour, *Hommage à Delacroix* (*Homage to Delacroix*), 1864
Oil on canvas, 63 × 98 7⁄16 in. (160 × 250 cm)

History paintings

Some of the protagonists of the "New Painting" maintained a distinct, inventive attachment to traditional themes of history and the Bible. Edgar Degas, for instance, never disowned his early paintings of antique subjects in classical-style compositions. Some even featured in the so-called "Impressionist" exhibitions. This was not the case for *Semiramis Building Babylon*. A long frieze influenced by Gustave Moreau and Pierre Puvis de Chavannes, it also recalls frescoes by Piero della Francesca, which an awe-struck Degas had encountered in Arezzo shortly beforehand. However, his boldness never extended as far as offering a fresh approach to religious painting, unlike Manet. At the Salons of 1864 and 1865, as well as showing paintings of bullfighters and his *Olympia* (p. 17), Manet astounded his contemporaries with two unorthodox representations of Christ. He turned to El Greco, Zurbarán, Velázquez, and Goya as antidotes to the Second Empire's religious art. Brought up a Catholic, though not a believer himself, he tackled the subject of the Redeemer without any firm prospect of being redeemed. Reflecting St Paul's New Testament writings, his gut-wrenchingly realistic *The Dead Christ with Angels* (1864; Metropolitan Museum of Art, New York) makes us witnesses to Christ's return to life; the Musée d'Orsay holds a preparatory watercolor for the 1866–1867 etching. Cézanne too explored religious themes in the 1860s and 1870s. His *Mary Magdalene* and *Christ in Limbo* were originally both part of the same work, which he executed as a mural at the Jas de Bouffan, his family's manor house near Aix-en-Provence. Quoting both Domenico Fetti and Sebastiano del Piombo, their mixture of Italianism and Post-Tridentine pathos was intended to be striking. Likewise raised as a Catholic, Cézanne starkly combines a vision of the Magdalene, weeping over Christ's empty tomb, and an evocation of Jesus, between the Crucifixion and the Resurrection. This bears echoes of Manet, who had always fascinated Cézanne, as evidenced by his *A Modern Olympia* (p. 96), exhibited in 1874. Three years later, he produced one of his many works on the theme of the trials of St Anthony (*The Temptation of Saint Antony*, c. 1877; Musée d'Orsay, Paris), a sensual, angst-ridden meditation on the power of carnal desires. S.G.

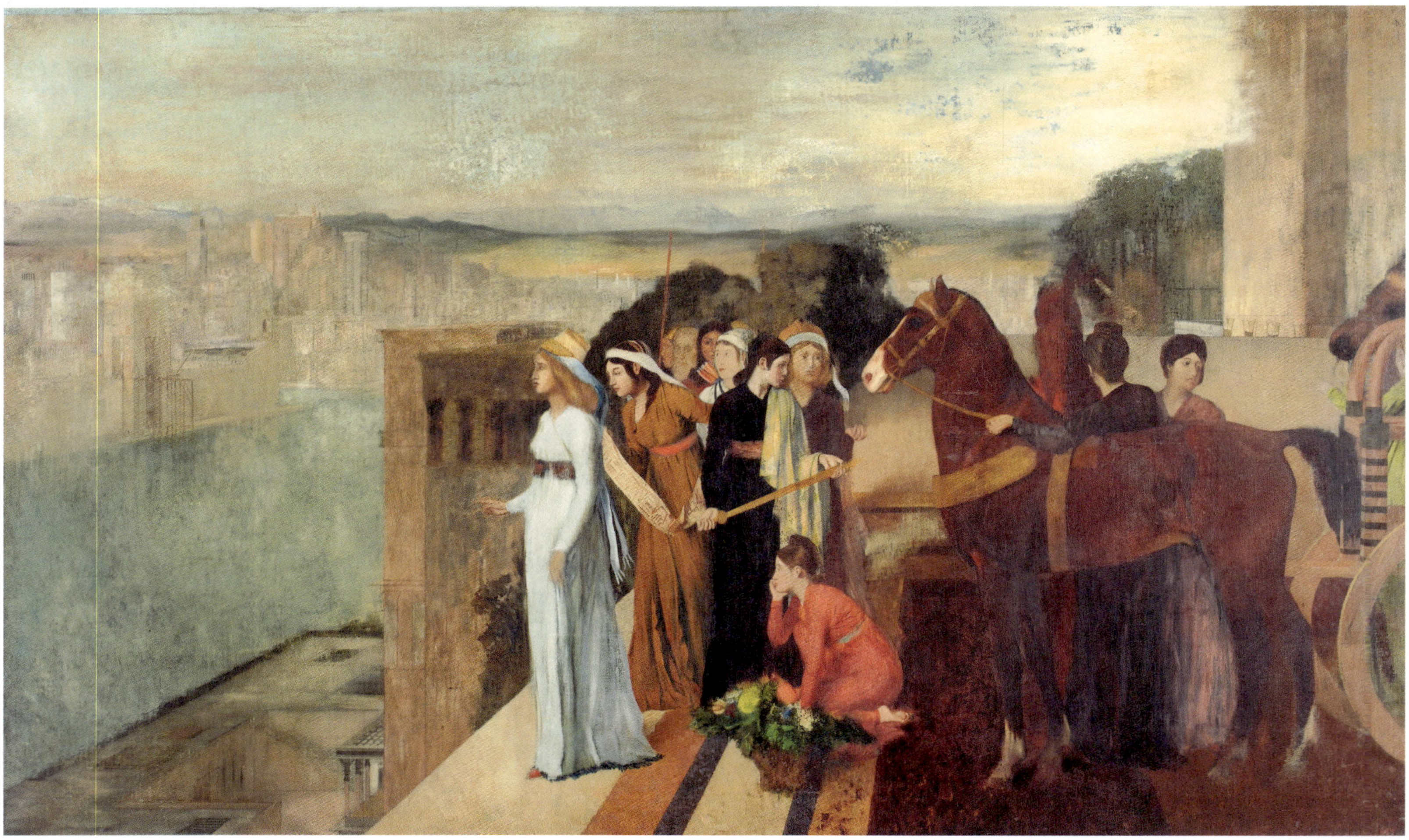

10 Edgar Degas, *Sémiramis construisant Babylone* (*Semiramis Building Babylon*), 1861
Oil on canvas, 59 ⅝ × 101 $^{9}/_{16}$ in.
(151.5 × 258 cm)

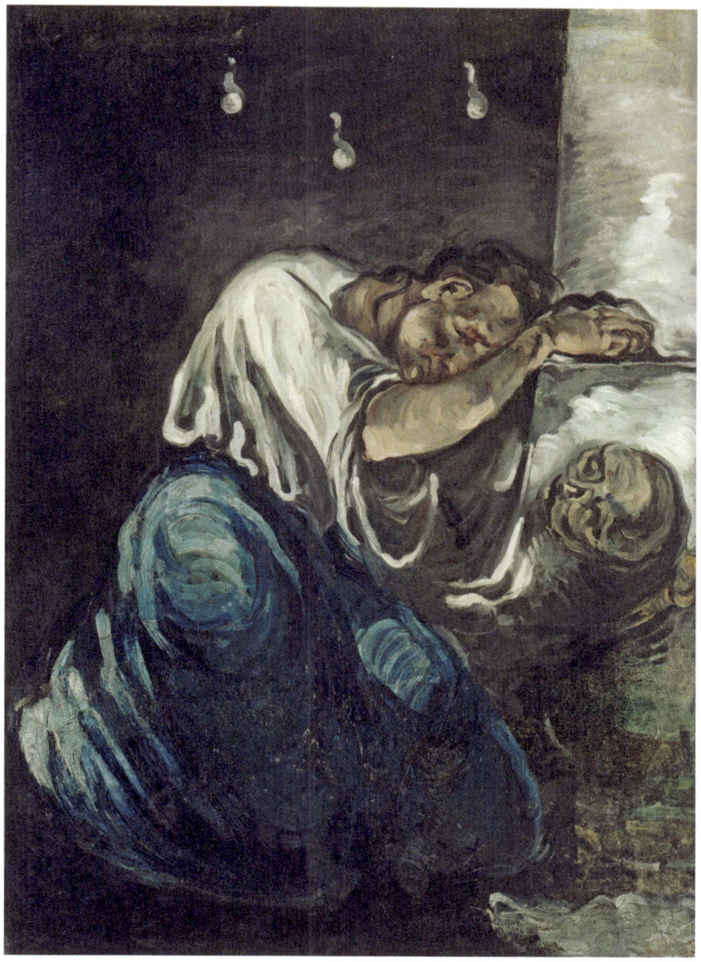

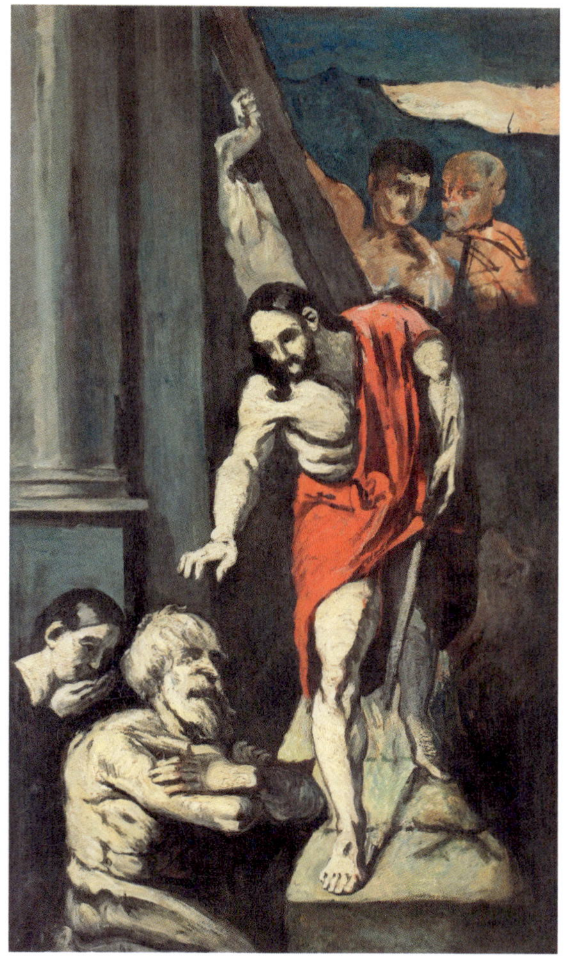

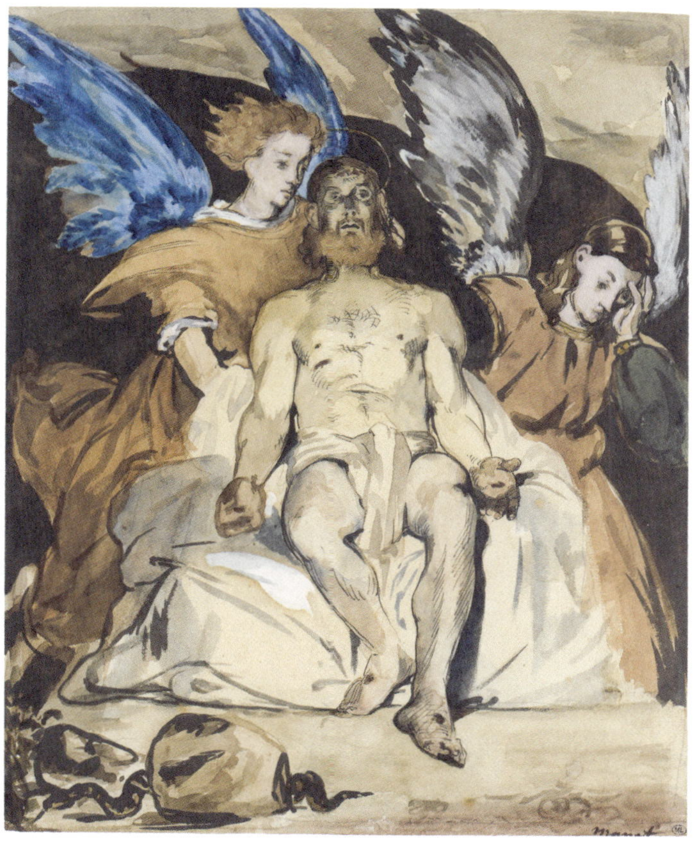

11 Top, left: Paul Cézanne, *La Madeleine* (*Mary Magdalene*), c. 1869
Oil on plaster transferred onto canvas, 66 ⅛ × 49 ¾ in. (168 × 126.4 cm)

12 Top, right: Paul Cézanne, *Le Christ aux limbes* (*Christ in Limbo*), c. 1869
Oil on plaster transferred onto canvas, 66 5⁄16 × 39 9⁄16 in. (168.5 × 100.5 cm)

13 Bottom: Édouard Manet, *Le Christ aux anges* (*The Dead Christ with Angels*), c. 1865–1867
Watercolor, pen and India ink, gouache, and graphite on paper, 12 13⁄16 × 10 ⅝ in. (32.5 × 27 cm)

Edgar Degas
Scene of War in the Middle Ages

Presented as a pastel at the 1865 Salon, where Degas was exhibiting for the first time, this mysterious work was met with indifference from critics and public alike. It was the artist's last effort in the domain of history painting, a genre that his friend Gustave Moreau had set out to thoroughly reform. The two had met in Italy in the late 1850s, when they shared a taste for dark subjects and an aesthetic inspired by quattrocento Italian frescoes.

This scene of rare brutality shows armed men on horseback violently attacking young women whose clothes have been ripped off. The women's bodies, stripped naked, are represented in poses that bear no resemblance to the ones adopted in traditional academic nude paintings. Numerous preparatory sketches evidence the depth of the effort Degas invested in depicting these brutalized women. Neither these studies, nor the desolate landscape where the silhouette of a church is visible in the background amid burning buildings, allow us to pinpoint the picture's subject. It does not appear to refer to any specific historical episode. Also known as *Les Malheurs de la ville d'Orléans* (*The Sufferings of the City of Orléans*), it has been suggested by art historian Hélène Adhémar that it may be an allegorical representation of violence from the American Civil War, which Degas had heard about from family members on his mother's side who lived in New Orleans. I. P.

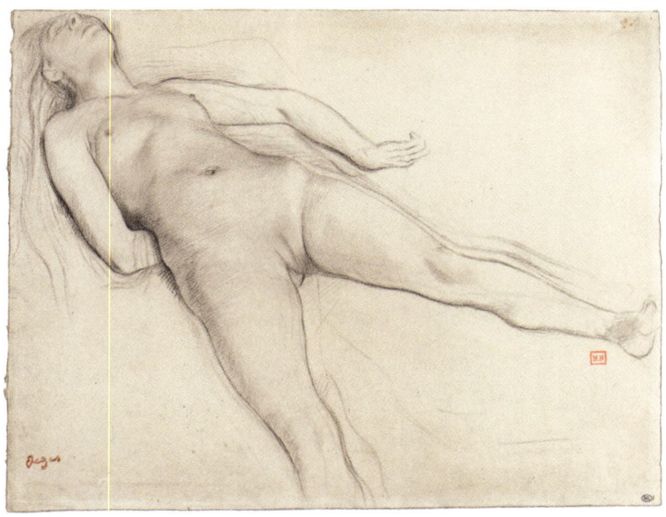

14 Edgar Degas, *Femme nue, couchée sur le dos* (*Nude Woman Lying on Her Back*, study for *Scene of War in the Middle Ages*), 1865
Black pencil on paper, 10 ½ × 13 15⁄16 in. (26.7 × 35.3 cm)

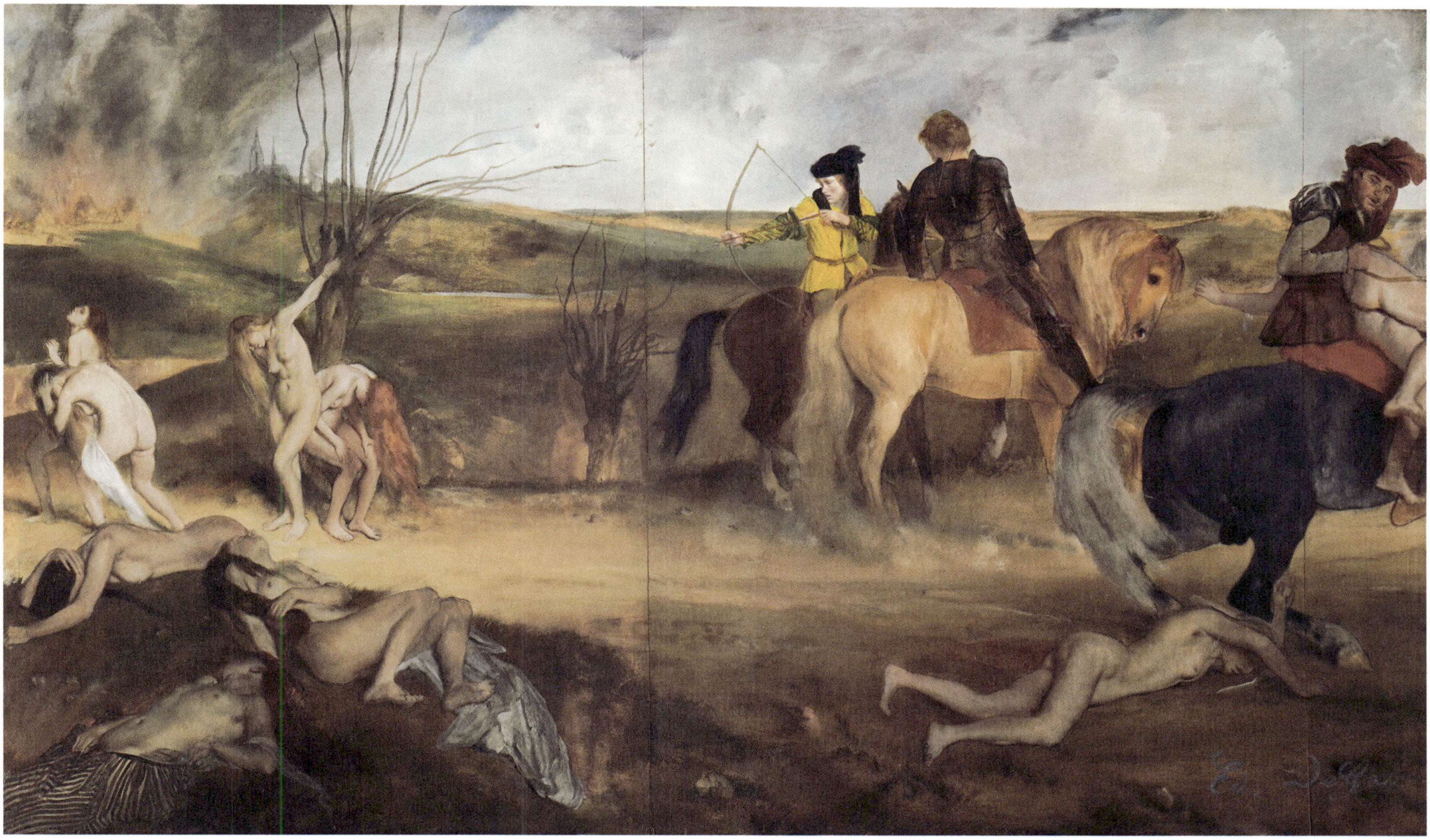

15 Edgar Degas, *Scène de guerre au Moyen Âge* (*Scene of War in the Middle Ages*), c. 1865
Turpentine-thinned oil on paper pasted on canvas,
32 ¼ × 58 7⁄16 in. (83.5 × 148.5 cm)

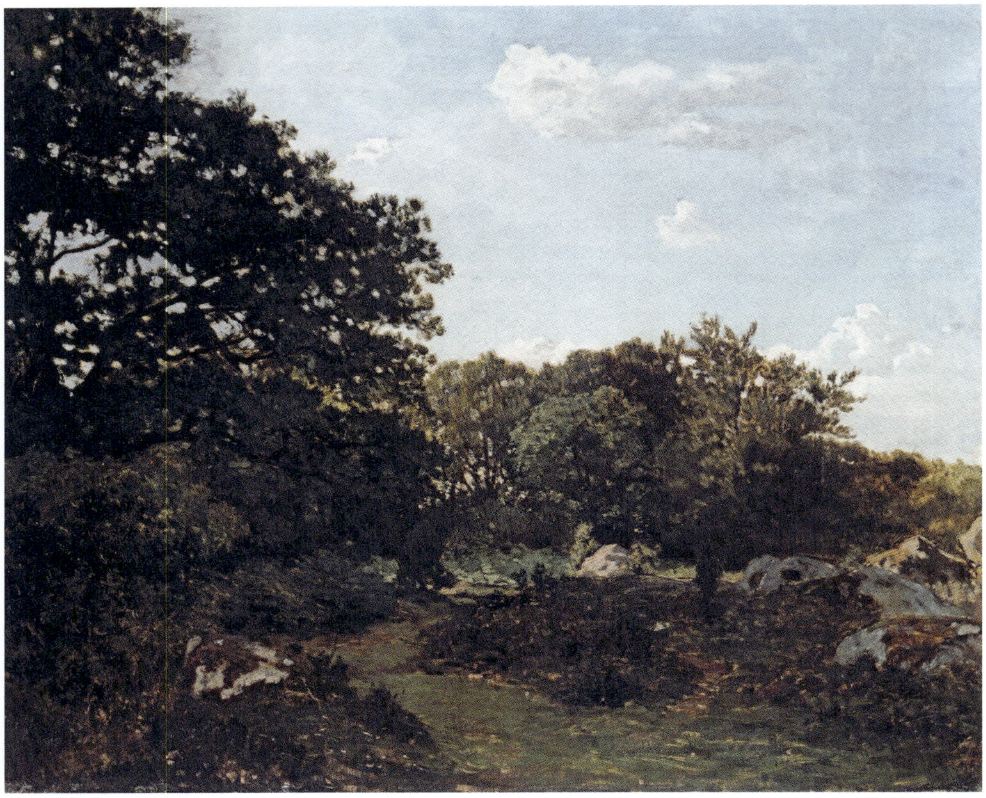

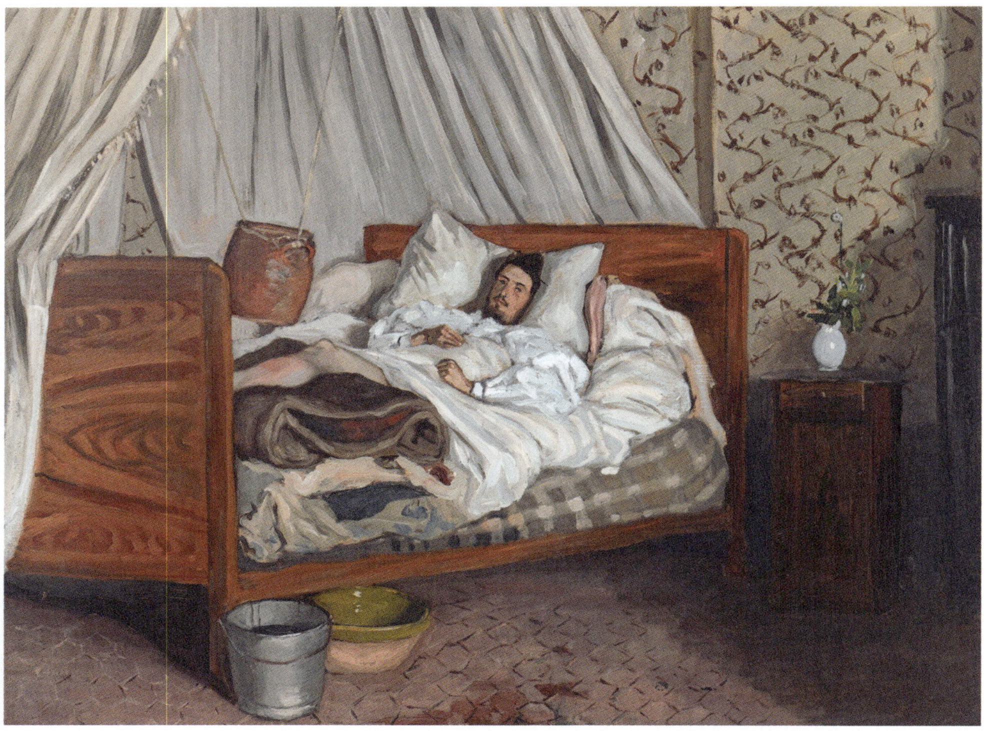

16 Top: Frédéric Bazille, *Forêt de Fontainebleau* (*Forest of Fontainebleau*), 1865
Oil on canvas, 23 ⅝ × 28 13⁄16 in. (60 × 73.2 cm)

17 Bottom: Frédéric Bazille, *L'Ambulance improvisée* (*The Improvised Field Hospital*), 1865
Oil on canvas, 18 ⅞ × 25 9⁄16 in. (48 × 65 cm)

1865

In the forest of Fontainebleau

Keen to paint on site, Monet—the most restless of the Gleyre studio set—took Bazille and some other friends (almost certainly Sisley and Renoir) to work in the Fontainebleau forest in the spring of 1863. Chailly, a village at the edge of the woods, was a fashionable destination for young landscape painters in the early 1860s. Théodore Rousseau and Jean-François Millet had gone to live in nearby Barbizon, and Camille Corot, whom the new generation considered the great master of landscape, also regularly visited the forest. More broadly, Fontainebleau landscapes had by then become ubiquitous at the Salon.

Similarly to the previous generation's landscape painters, the future Impressionists would take their easels with them to make initial studies *en plein air*, with a view to creating more ambitious compositions when back in the studio. But they saw these places differently than their predecessors, whose poetic or pantheistic visions invested the forest with sentiments. Like photographers at the time (such as Gustave Le Gray and Eugène Cuvelier), the younger painters would abruptly frame a particular spot in nature and simply set out to understand the light, tones, and contrasts, as we can see in Bazille's *Forest of Fontainebleau*. These studies gradually became compositions in their own right. The young painters also shifted away from the iconography of dark, mysterious woodland or people carrying bundles of firewood, to focus instead on light and to paint modern leisure activities. Monet's *The Pavé de Chailly*, for instance, provided the setting for the colossal *Luncheon on the Grass* (p. 31) that he painted in Fontainebleau in the summer of 1865.

For that painting, Monet had asked Bazille to come and pose for him. There was a reversal of roles when a leg injury saw Monet bedridden for several days at the Lion d'Or inn at Chailly. Recording this episode with a limited palette on a small canvas, Bazille's *The Improvised Field Hospital* indicates how he relished representing moments of stillness, as well as patterns and textures (floral wallpaper, terracotta floor tile, tartan mattress cover, etc.). From the midst of this modest but intimate setting, the motionless figure of Monet looks out at the viewer. P. P.

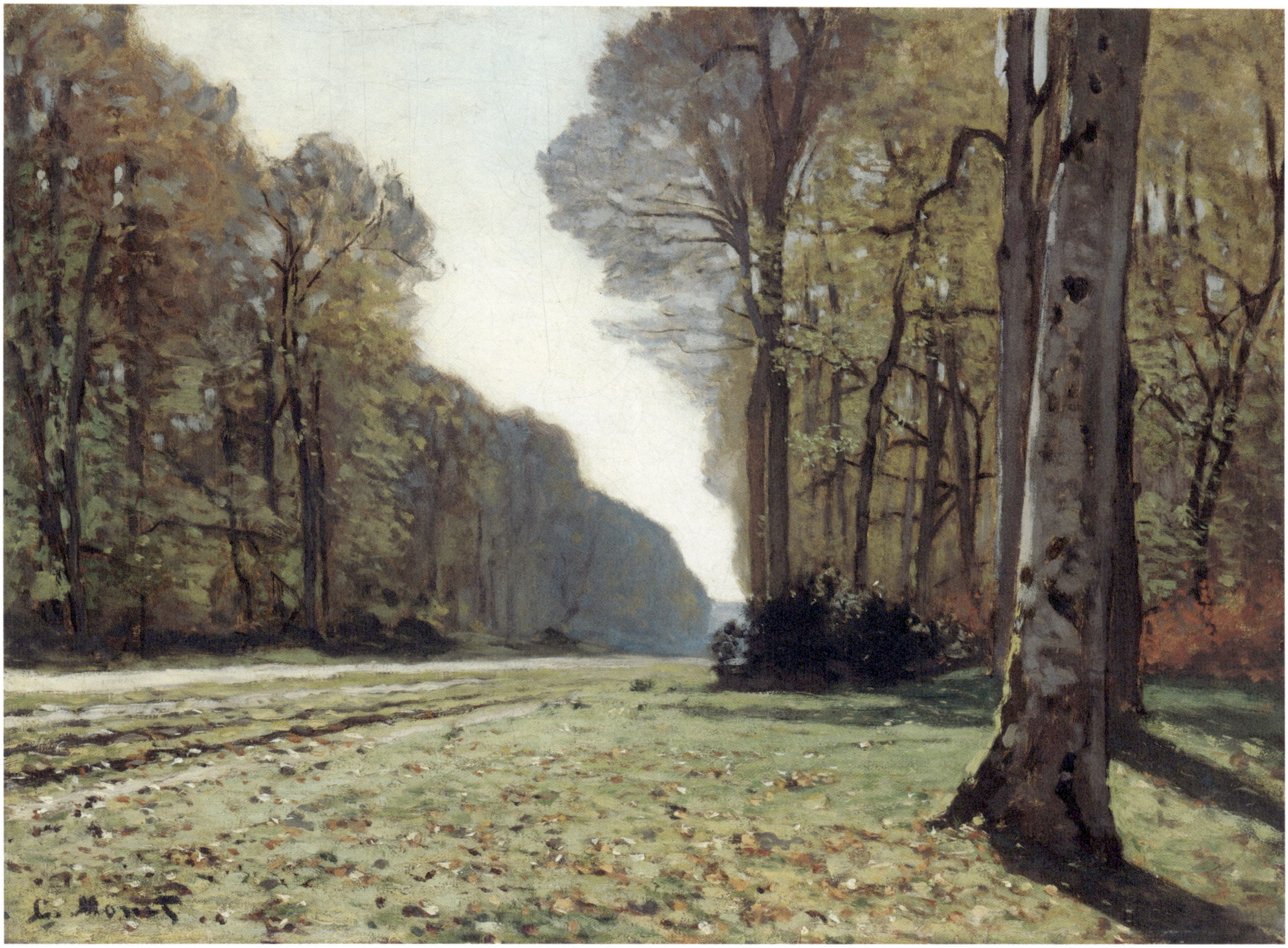

18 Claude Monet, *Le Pavé de Chailly*
(*The Pavé de Chailly*), c. 1865
Oil on canvas, 17 ⅛ × 23 ⅜ in. (43.5 × 59.3 cm)

Claude Monet
The Cart

Everything about this image speaks of the then-aging Barbizon School landscape painter Camille Corot's hold over nascent Impressionism: the cross-shaped composition; the perspective-deepening effect of the cart moving away from the viewer; the peaceful atmosphere; and the synthetic execution, also discernible in works from the mid-1850s by Charles-François Daubigny, also of the Barbizon School. As skillful portrayers of snowy landscapes, Monet and Sisley were no doubt drawn to white-themed works by painters and poets of the 1860s, from Whistler to Gautier. White became a color in its own right, particularly since, in terms of optical logic, it enhances the presence of blues—whether shadows or occasional glimpses of sky. When this painting entered the national collections and was first hung at the Louvre, Monet—now aged almost seventy-five and very proud of being represented in the Camondo collection—specified to the museum's directors that it was a "snow effect" view along the Trouville road at Honfleur, executed in 1865. The snow-covered roofs on the left are the thatches of the Saint-Siméon Farm, much celebrated by a circle of painters who were close to Monet: Constant Troyon and Gustave Courbet, Boudin, and Jongkind, as well as Corot and Daubigny. A local painter's correspondence later revealed the work to be two years younger. At a time when Monet was still participating in the official Salon, with varying degrees of success, its format was aimed more at art lovers than the State. S.G.

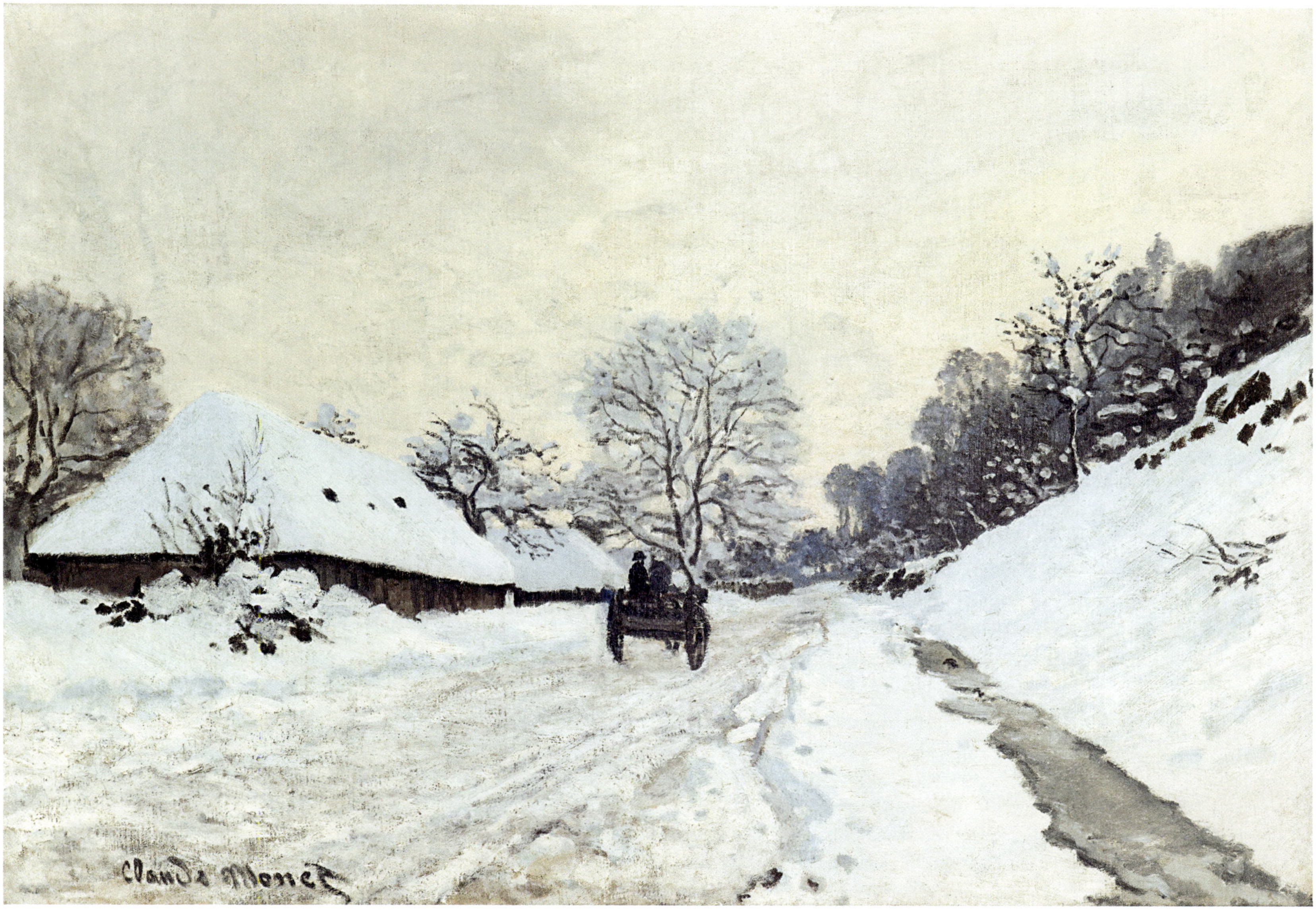

19 Claude Monet, *La Charrette. Route sous la neige à Honfleur* (*The Cart: Snow-Covered Road at Honfleur*), c. 1867
Oil on canvas, 25 9⁄16 × 36 5⁄8 in. (65 × 93 cm)

Claude Monet
The Magpie

Although extremely popular today, this work initially faced bitter criticism: according to Zacharie Astruc, it was one of the two paintings that were rejected by the Salon jury in 1869. The panoramic yet subtly nuanced view did, however, possess the requisite qualities for an exhibition painting. In letters to Bazille from the winter of 1868–1869, Monet admits how much he enjoys working around Étretat, where he was staying with his family at the time: "I go into the country which is so lovely here that I perhaps find it even more agreeable in winter than in summer; and naturally I'm working all the time, and I think this year I'm going to do some serious things."[1] In early January 1869, he wrote to his friend in his usual presumptuous tone, to order the pigments he needed for his snow effects: "Here are the colors I need: silver white ... a lot / ivory black ... a lot / cobalt blue ... a lot / Really go for it with the first four colors, they're the ones I need the most." In a reflection of these two letters, this painting was to turn out both serious and white. Echoing Japanese prints, Monet laid out his bright, frosty vision of the Normandy countryside vertically and horizontally. The bird that gives the work its name holds our gaze and lends a sense of suspense. Because it does not take long for this magpie, a representation of time, to disrupt the painting's magical serenity. S.G.

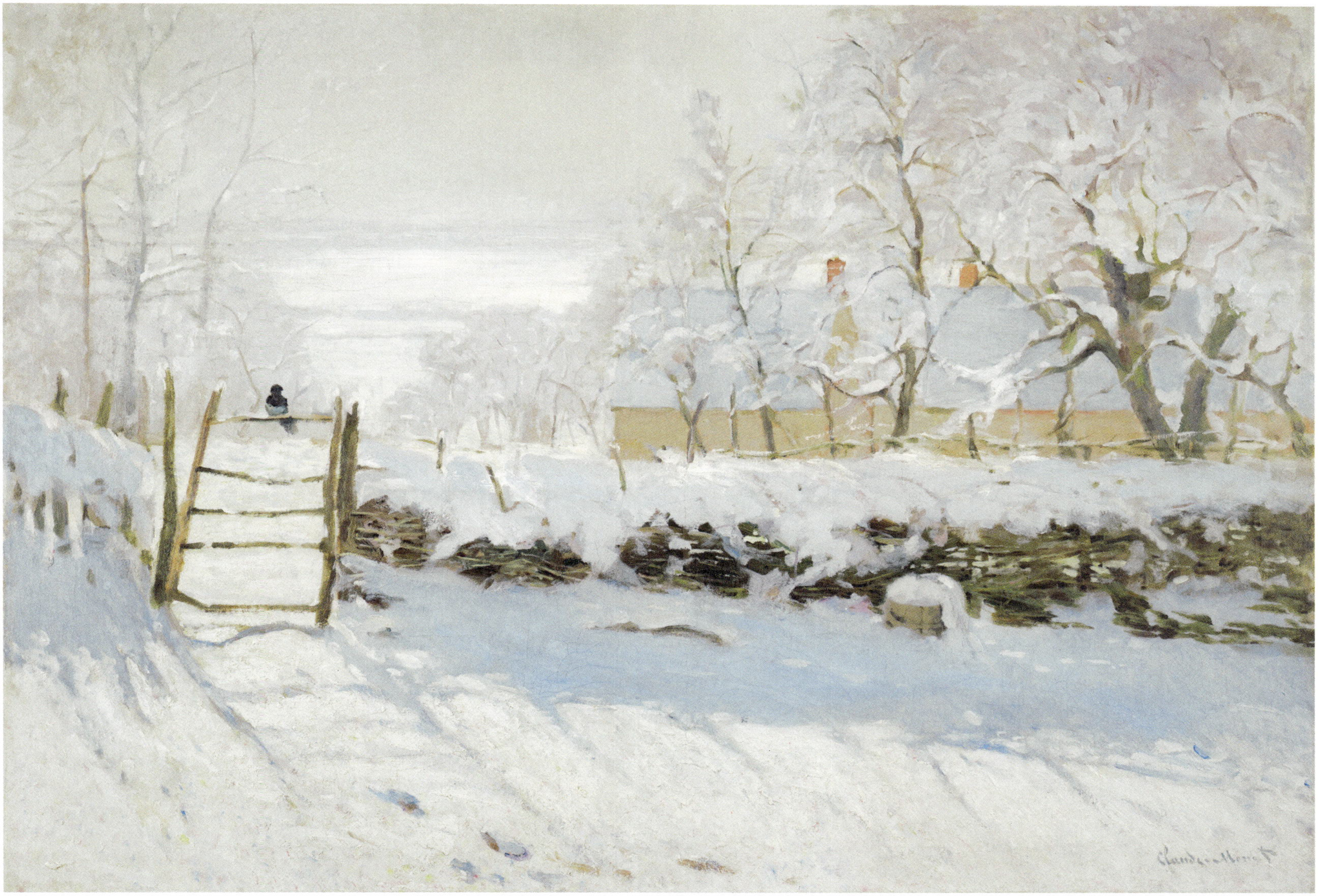

20 Claude Monet, *La Pie* (*The Magpie*), 1868–1869
Oil on canvas, 35 1⁄16 × 51 3⁄16 in. (89 × 130 cm)

Painting figures in sunlight

"The future of modern art, will it not lie in … the reality of people and their clothing transformed by the magic of light and shadow, by that sun that is a poem of colors dripping from the painter's hand?" noted the Goncourt brothers in their journal in 1861. The decade that had just begun would prove them right. Bazille, Monet, Renoir, and other young artists of their generation would develop a passion for realistic depictions of modern figures, often on large canvases, in landscapes that would gradually incorporate *plein-air* effects.

Bazille was thinking of "painting figures in the sunlight," as he wrote in 1863, from a very early stage, no doubt with Gustave Courbet's *The Meeting* (1854; Musée Fabre, Montpellier) in mind. Escaping from Paris's "indigestion of walls and streets," he took advantage of his stay at the family's house near Montpellier over the summer of 1864 to paint his fourteen-year-old cousin sitting on the garden terrace wall, overlooking the village of Castelnau. This large-format painting offered a new synthesis between figure, genre scene, and landscape, with the quality of the light very convincingly observed.

Monet was doubtless inspired by Édouard Manet (p. 15) when in 1865 he created a composition on the theme of the "*déjeuner sur l'herbe*"—a modern picnic set in the forest of Fontainebleau, for which his partner Camille Doncieux and Bazille served as models. Its originality lies in its subject matter and its enormous size, rivaling the Salon's largest history paintings, but also in the painting method. Based on smaller studies executed *en plein air*, it sets out to integrate attempts at new ways of capturing light, as well as sketchier brushwork. However, Monet never finished it and never exhibited it. By various twists of fate, the canvas ended up damaged and its artist decided to save only two fragments of it.

Although Monet generally did not manage to have his paintings shown at the Salon, Bazille's were regularly accepted there and commented upon, such as *Village View* (1868; Musée Fabre Montpellier), which prompted Berthe Morisot to write to her mother in 1869: "He is attempting what we have so often attempted: putting a figure outdoors; this time I think he has succeeded." P. P.

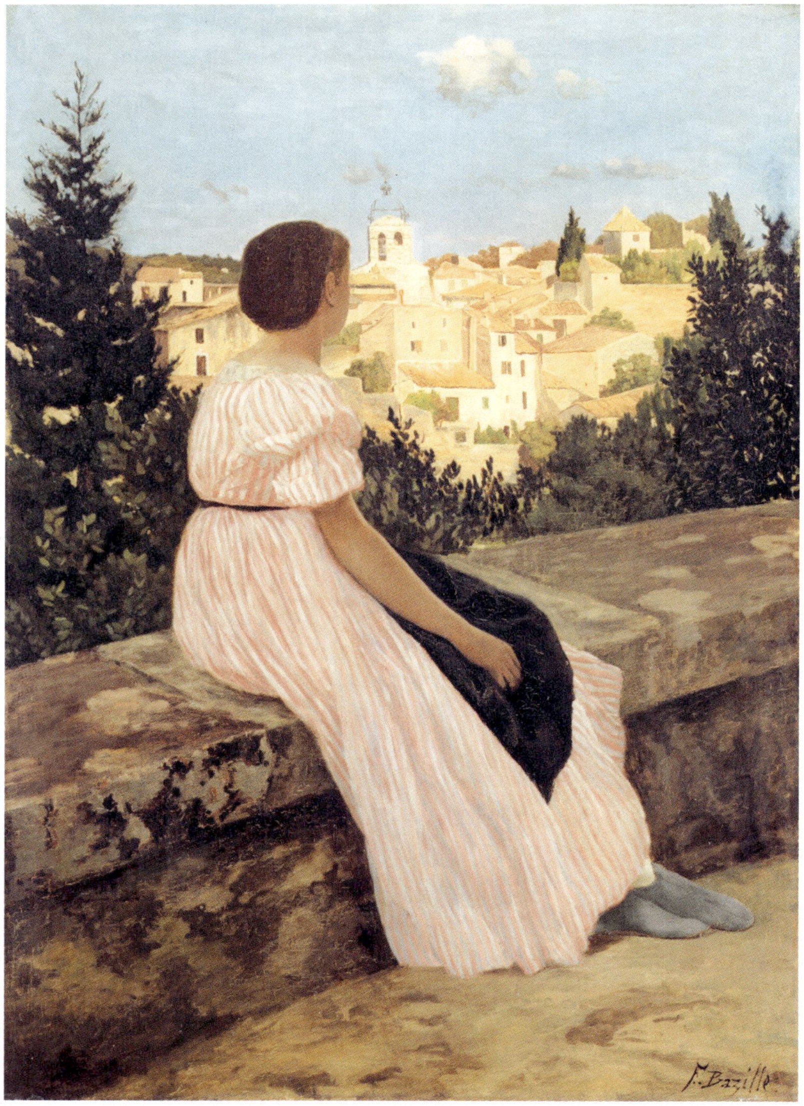

21 Frédéric Bazille, *La Robe rose* (*The Pink Dress*), 1864
Oil on canvas, 58 ¼ × 43 5⁄16 in. (148 × 110 cm)

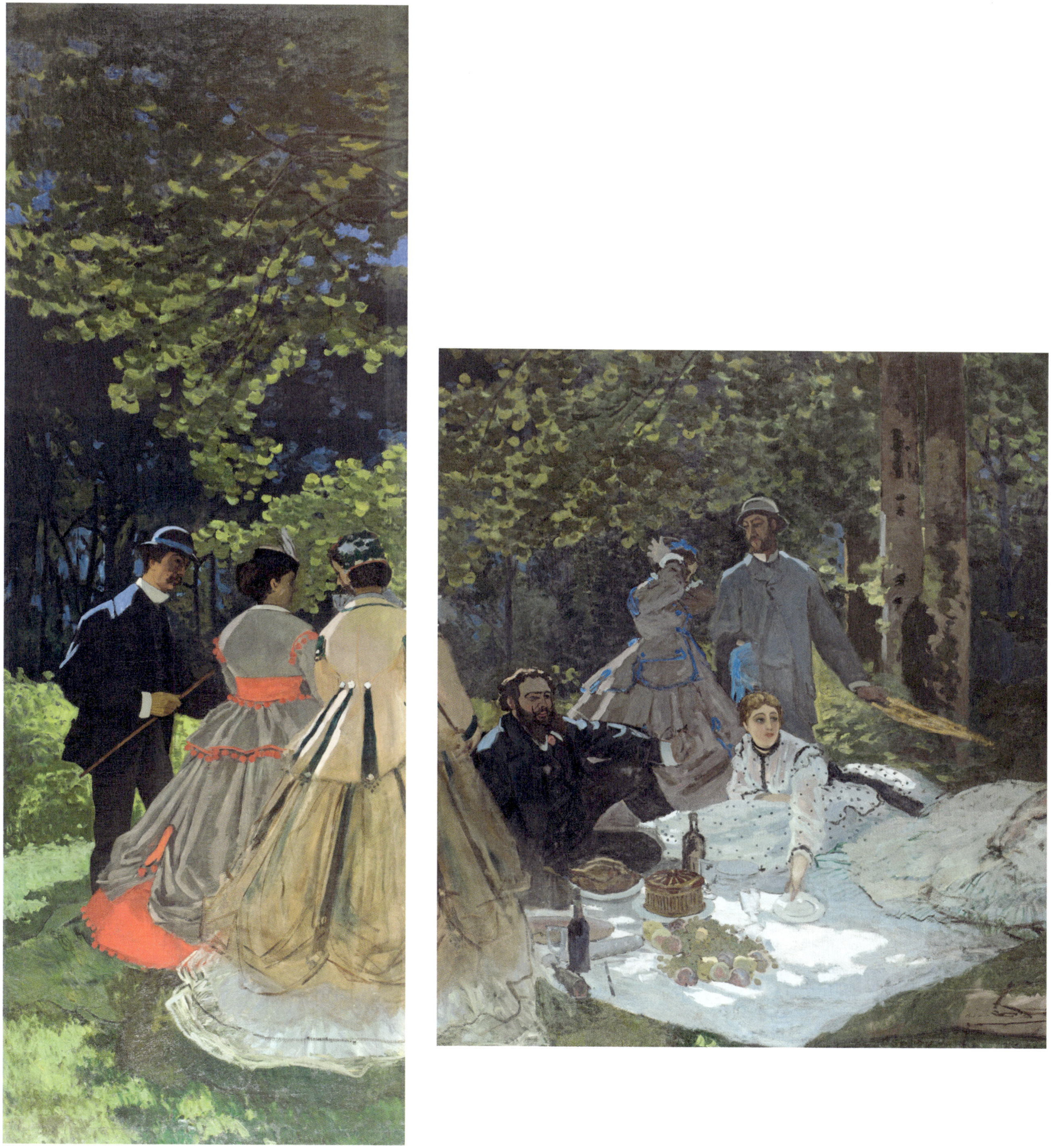

22 Claude Monet, *Le Déjeuner sur l'herbe* (*Luncheon on the Grass*), 1865–1866
Oil on canvas, 164 ½ × 59 in. and 98 × 85 ¾ in.
(418 × 150 cm and 248.7 × 218 cm)

Claude Monet
Women in the Garden

Encouraged by the positive reactions to his first successful Salon submissions, Monet planned to send an ambitiously large painting—a near-life-size image of elegant young women walking through a flower-filled garden—to the 1867 edition. With his partner Camille Doncieux, he rented a small house at Ville-d'Avray, not far from Paris. It was there that he began work on this monumental painting. Doncieux was also his favorite model, and she posed for the three figures to the left, amid blossoming bushes and flowerbeds. Monet was familiar with the challenges of working from life, outdoors, on a very large canvas, having already attempted it the previous year with his *Luncheon on the Grass* (p. 31): a colossal canvas that he never managed to finish. To avoid having to change his viewpoint, he had "a sort of trench dug in the grass, to gradually lower his canvas into the ground when painting its upper part."[2] He started the painting *en plein air*, but completed it elsewhere, in Honfleur, after moving there a few months later. In early 1867, the finished work was brought to Paris to be submitted to the Salon jury. Perplexed by the artist's bold brushstrokes and by the portrayal of such an ordinary subject at heroic dimensions, the jury rejected it. Yet Monet had admirably met the challenge of painting a large-format *plein-air* scene. The light—sharp, dazzling, and reflected by the gleaming white of the summer dresses—contrasts with the large puddle of bluish-gray shadow on the ground and the intense greens of the foliage. Seduced by these bright, radical, harmonious combinations, and by the artist's agile brush, Zola observed that "Monet has a very particular love of nature, which the hands of men fashion into modern styles," and commented that "To dare attempt such a tour de force, one must especially love one's own time."[3] A. R.

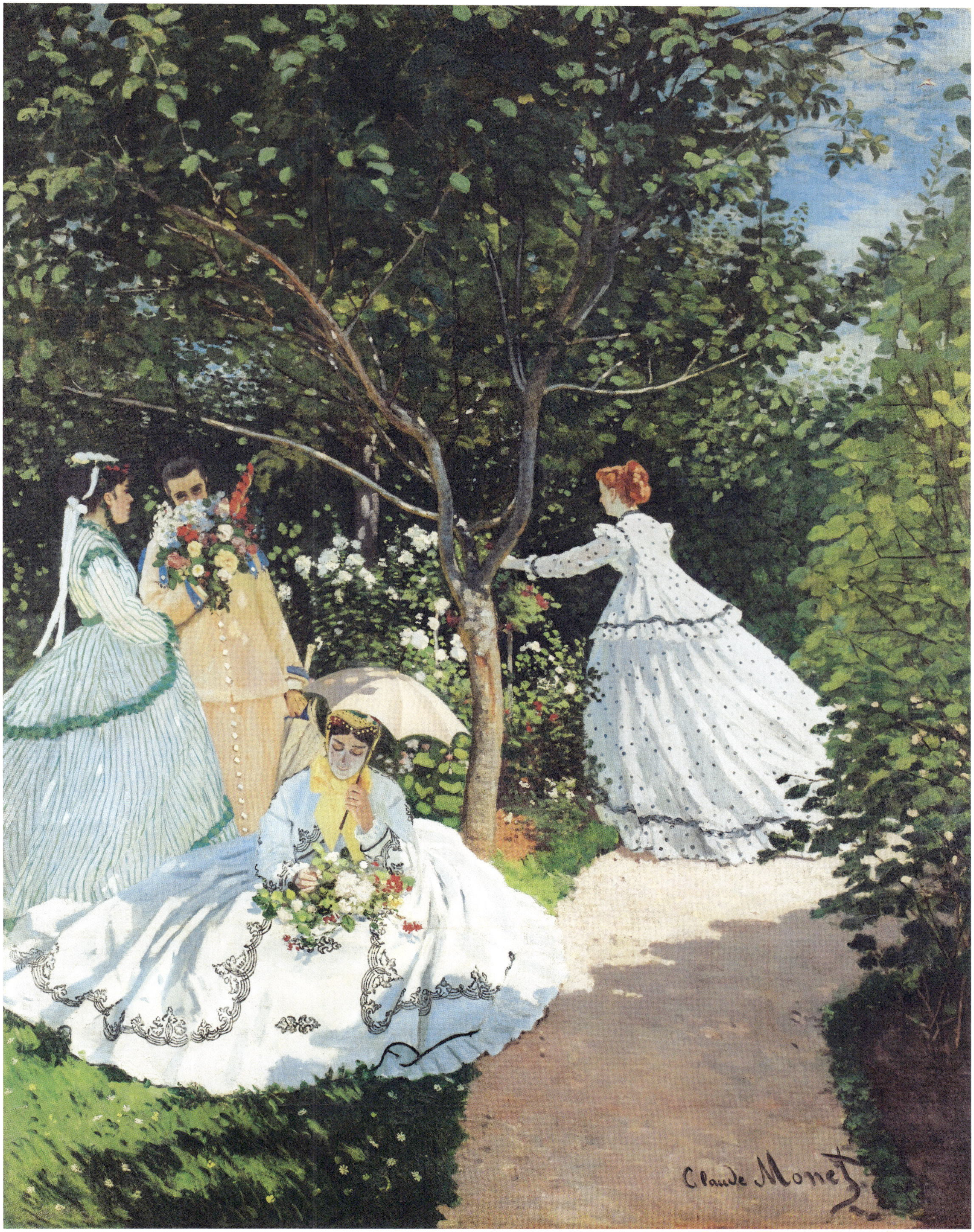

23 Claude Monet, *Femmes au jardin* (*Women in the Garden*), c. 1866
Oil on canvas, 100 ⅜ × 80 ¹¹⁄₁₆ in. (255 × 205 cm)

Frédéric Bazille
*Portraits of the *** Family*

In the summer of 1867, Bazille made a start on a new large-format painting of figures outdoors. This time he took his family as the subject, having his relatives pose on the terrace outside their country house near Montpellier. His parents, Camille (who owned the property) and Gaston (who managed the surrounding vineyards), are seated on the bench on the left. Bazille gives the best place, at the very center, to his young cousin Thérèse des Hours, who had already sat for him (p. 30). Each summer, the Bazille and des Hours families would get together for Gaston's birthday. In 1867 they were also celebrating the marriage of another cousin, Pauline des Hours, to a rich banker (the couple are arm in arm under the tree), and the engagement of Bazille's brother Marc (perched on the terrace wall). Bazille's painting was therefore a commemorative portrait of a proud, prosperous family of bourgeois Protestants.

The carefully considered, frieze-like composition, which Bazille developed through several drawings, is inspired as much by Monet (*Women in the Garden*, p. 33) as by the Renaissance tradition of family portraits, English eighteenth-century "conversation pieces," and contemporary photographic portraits (which he may have used as an aid). However, it was the first family portrait in French history to be painted out of doors. Partially executed from life, in the shade of a large chestnut tree, it boldly and faithfully conveys the brightness of the colors and the meticulously observed effects of sunlight and contrasts. Bazille maintained a precisely drawn approach for the figures, while the landscape is more loosely sketched. He finished the painting in his Paris studio during the winter, and it was accepted at the Salon in 1868. It was exhibited under the unusual title with three asterisks.

With this work, Bazille paid homage to his family while remaining detached from it and wondering where he now stood within it: still single, having left for Paris and given up on studying medicine so that he could pursue a career as a painter. At the last minute, he slipped himself into the composition, on the far left, behind his uncle.   P. P.

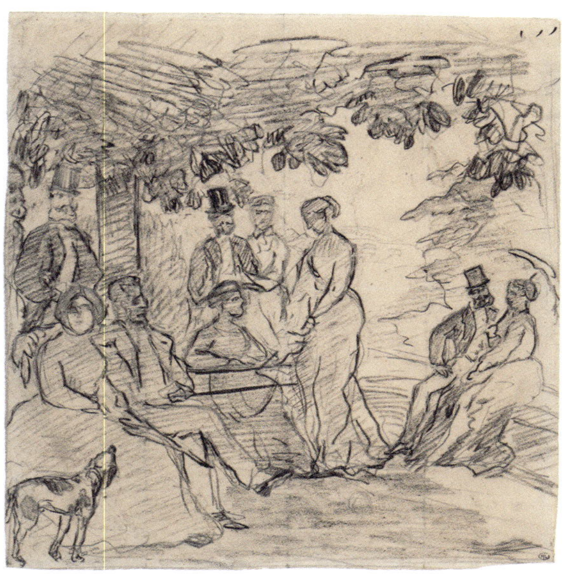

24 Frédéric Bazille, Study for *Portraits de la famille**** (*Portraits of the *** Family*), 1867
Black pencil, charcoal, and graphite on paper, 11 ⅞ × 11 13⁄16 in. (30.1 × 30 cm)

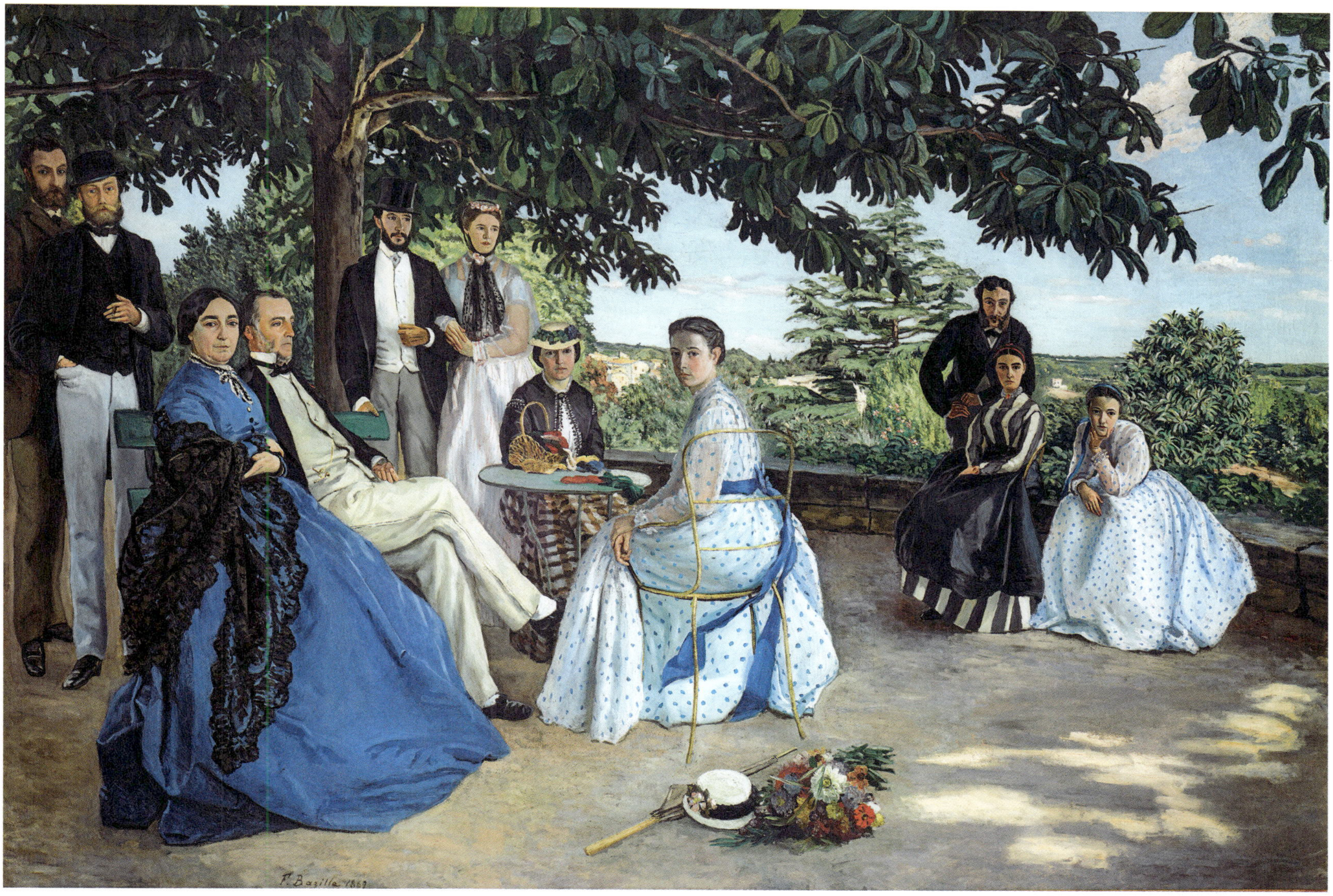

25 Frédéric Bazille, *Portraits de la famille**** (*Portraits of the *** Family*), also known as *Réunion de famille* (*Family Gathering*), 1867–1868
Oil on canvas, 59 13⁄16 × 90 9⁄16 in. (152 × 230 cm)

1867

The Manet exhibition on Avenue de l'Alma

In 1867, Paris hosted its second Exposition Universelle, which opened on April 1 at the Champ de Mars and included an international art exhibition. A few months earlier, having "little confidence" in the jury of the official exhibition, and encouraged by the laudatory article on him that Zola had published in the *Revue du XIXe siècle* after visiting his studio, Manet decided to organize a solo exhibition for himself. He wrote to Zola: "I have at least forty-odd pictures I can show, and have already been offered sites in very good locations near the Champ de Mars. I'm going to go all out, and with the support of people like you, it should be a success."[4] This bold course of action indicated parallels between Manet and Courbet, who had organized his own solo exhibition outside of the 1855 Exposition Universelle and did the same again in 1867.

With financial support from his mother, Manet had some temporary structures installed at the corner of Avenue Montaigne and Avenue de l'Alma, much smaller than Courbet's set-up. His exhibition opened there on May 24, with a fifty-centime entry charge. It featured around fifty of Manet's paintings, including *Lola de Valence*, *A Lady at Her Window*, and *The Fifer*—the latter having been rejected by the previous year's Salon jury—along with some etchings. It was accompanied by a catalog in which an anonymous text set out its motivation: "Since 1861, Mr. Manet has exhibited or attempted to exhibit his work. This year he has decided to present a retrospective exhibition of his work directly to the public.… It is a vital matter, a *sine qua non* for an artist to be able to exhibit his work, since after repeated viewing, surprise and even shock will give way to familiarity."[5] Despite Manet's efforts, the exhibition did not achieve the success he had hoped for, either in the press or among the public. This flop no doubt contributed to his continuing determination to show at the Salon, which he would be constantly seeking to conquer from the inside, while refusing to exhibit alongside the Impressionists. I.P.

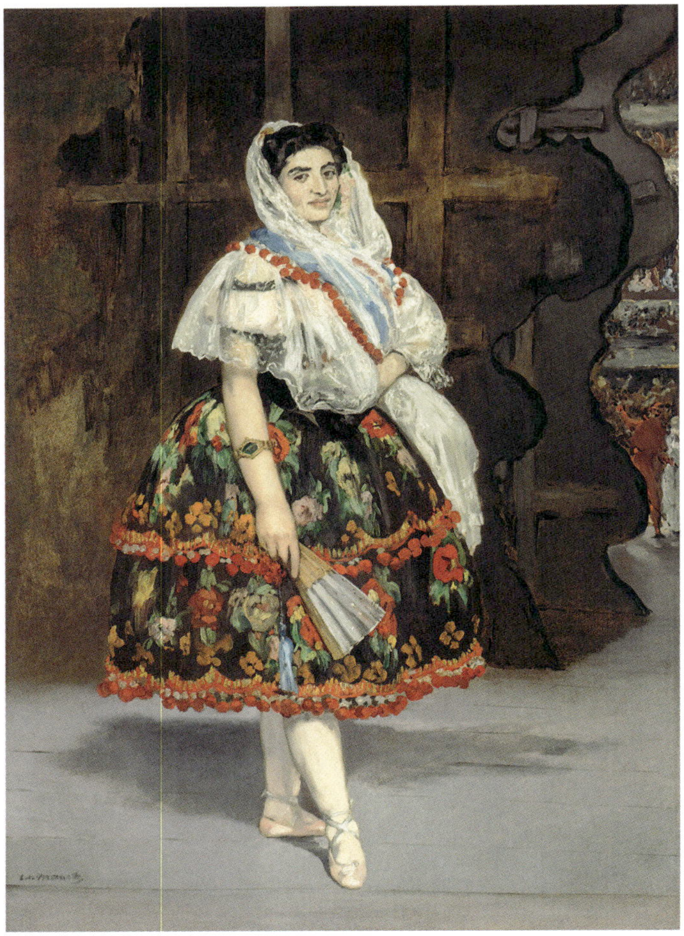

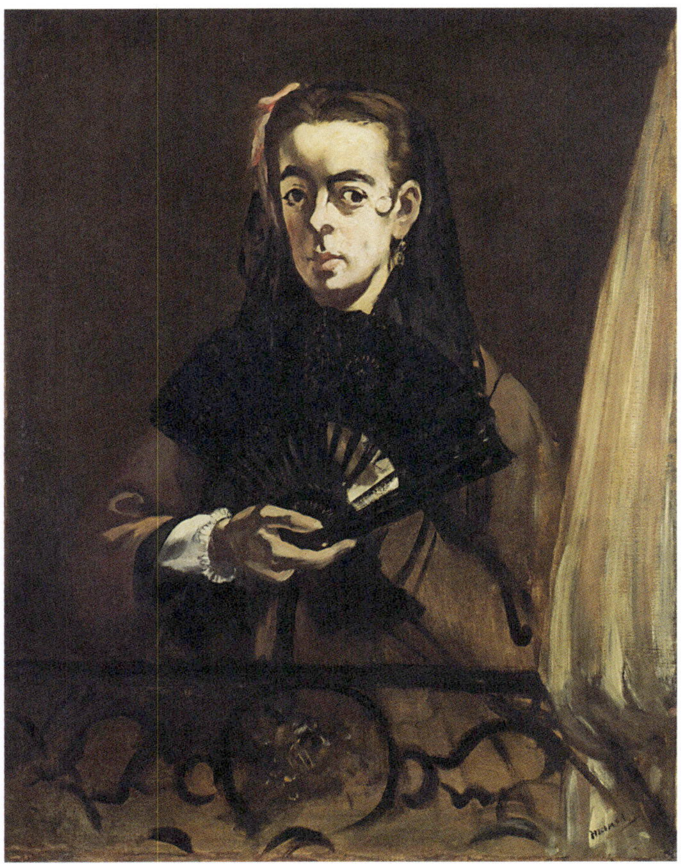

26 Top: Édouard Manet, *Lola de Valence*, 1862
Oil on canvas,
48 7⁄16 × 36 ¼ in. (123 × 92 cm)

27 Bottom: Édouard Manet, *Une dame à sa fenêtre (étude)* (*A Lady at Her Window [Study]*), 1865. Oil on canvas, 36 ¼ × 28 15⁄16 in. (92 × 73.5 cm)

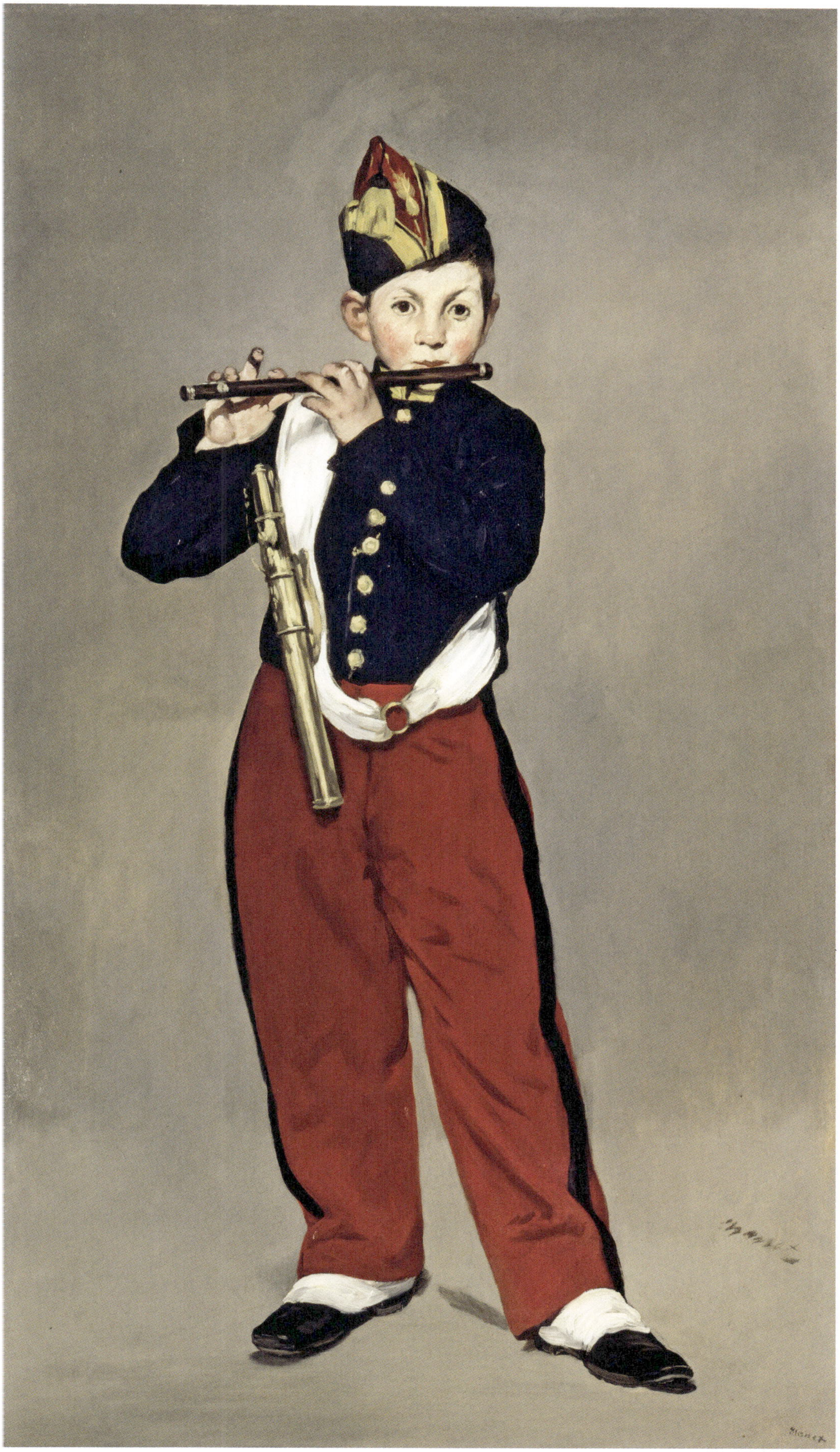

28 Édouard Manet, *Le Fifre* (*The Fifer*), 1866
Oil on canvas, 63 3⁄16 × 38 3⁄16 in. (160.5 × 97 cm)

Édouard Manet
Émile Zola

In his account of the Salon published in *L'Événement* in 1866, Zola expressed his indignation at the jury's rejection of the two works that Manet had submitted: *The Fifer* (p. 37) and *The Tragic Actor (Rouvière as Hamlet)* (1866; National Gallery of Art, Washington, D.C.). This bold stand led to his resignation from the journal, and earned him gratitude from Manet, who declared himself "proud and happy" to have been "championed by a man of [his] talent."[6] It was the publication of this article that spurred the two to meet, and a firm friendship ensued. This portrait tribute, which Manet showed at the Salon of 1868 before giving it to its sitter, is evidence of that.

Although Zola adopts the classic pose of a man of letters, sitting at his desk with a book in his hand, he did not pose at his home, but in Manet's studio—the painter's space becoming the writer's. The interior setting is meticulously put together: it includes a print after Velázquez's *The Feast of Bacchus* (1628–1629; Museo del Prado, Madrid)—Manet regarded Velázquez as "the painter of painters"—along with a Japanese print and folding screen, Zola considering the "strange elegance" and "wonderful patches of color" in Japanese art to be similar to Manet's "simplified painting."[7] On the right, the artist's signature forms part of the title of the sky-blue pamphlet on the desk, which was written and published by Zola in 1867 at the time of Manet's solo exhibition. In it, Zola predicts that "fate has no doubt already designated a future place in the Musée du Louvre for *Olympia* and *Le Déjeuner sur l'herbe*." The black-and-white reproduction of *Olympia* (p. 17) affixed to the board on the wall in the portrait appears to indicate her gratitude through her insistent gaze, which is oriented in a different direction than in the painting itself. I. P.

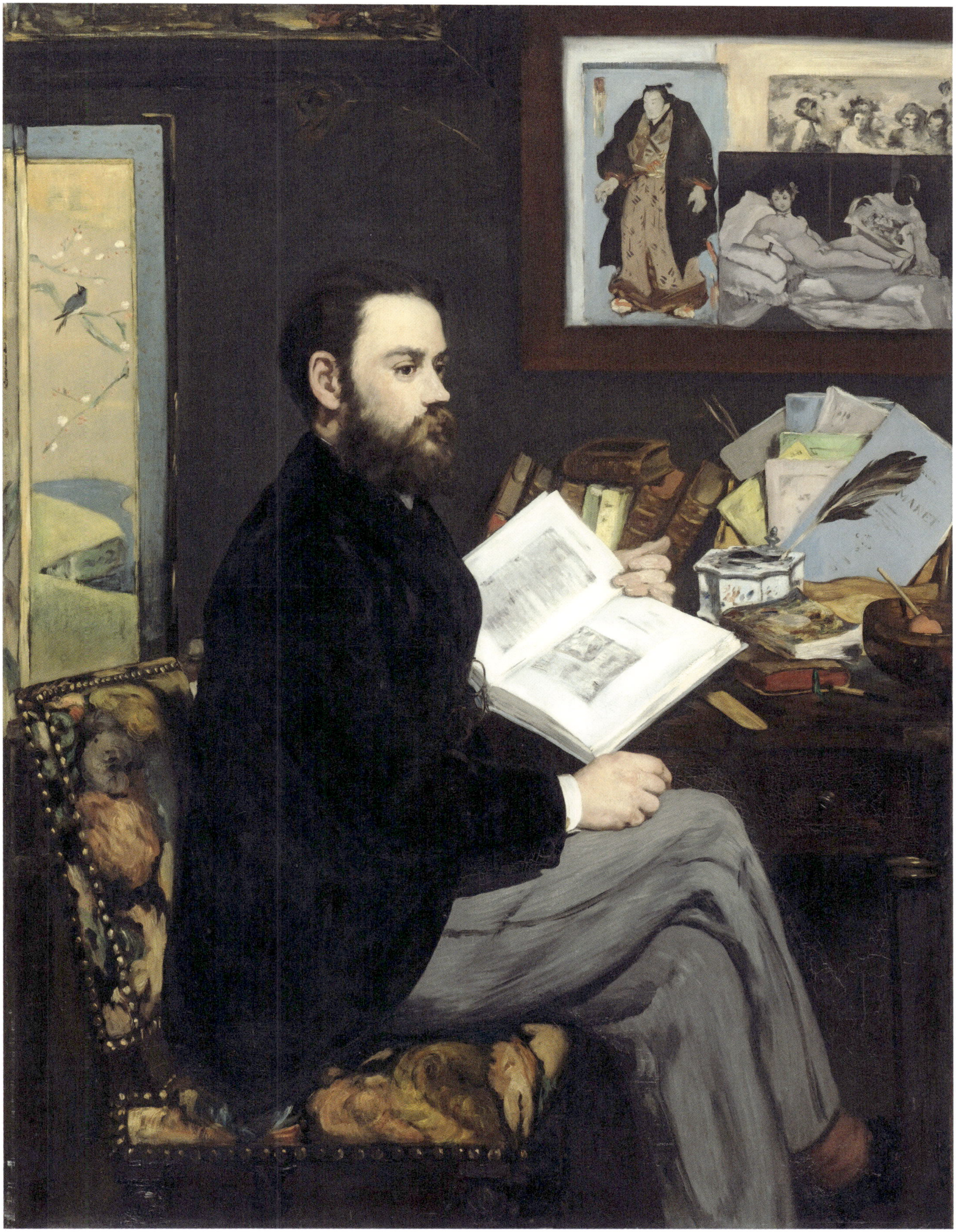

29 Édouard Manet, *Émile Zola*, 1868
Oil on canvas, 57 ½ × 44 ⅞ in. (146 × 114 cm)

Still lifes

Because of the realism it demands and the attention it affords to humble everyday objects, still life was one of the genres that the protagonists of the "New Painting" practiced the most. By depicting a quarter of meat in place of the usual piece of game—the latter being seen as more genteel—Monet provided a sort of manifesto for this mid-1860s anti-idealization. On top of the affront posed by the beef, his highly focused image also features a garlic, another indicator of working-class cuisine. More broadly, the Second Empire saw a revival of the still-life manner pioneered in the eighteenth century by Jean-Siméon Chardin, with the Louvre's expanding collections a contributing factor. In his own unique way, Manet associated himself with this movement, while always ensuring that any gustatory suggestions in his works remained subordinate to a dramatization of the elements depicted. His ventures in this domain were by no means unsuccessful: Zola wrote in 1867, "The most outspoken enemies of Manet's talent agree that he paints inanimate objects very well."[8] Yet some of them do not hesitate to offer a darker slant on still life's traditional oscillation between *memento mori* and *memento vivere*. One such work is the very strange *Eel and Red Snapper*, which homes in on a bloody fish, a somber eel, and a menacing knife. The image's underlying violence is typical of the uneasiness that Manet liked to provoke. In contrast, how cheery the asparagus from his final years appears, at a time when the illness that was taking hold of him prompted some unexpected bursts of good health! This last asparagus is a quintessential example of his art. The floating signature, comprising simply his initial, confirms its purpose as a gift for a friend. Manet had just sold *A Bunch of Asparagus* (1880; Wallraf-Richartz Museum, Cologne) to Charles Ephrussi, who had paid him a thousand francs for it—more than he had been expecting. The artist therefore sent the collector an additional asparagus, along with the note: "There was one missing from your bunch." S.G.

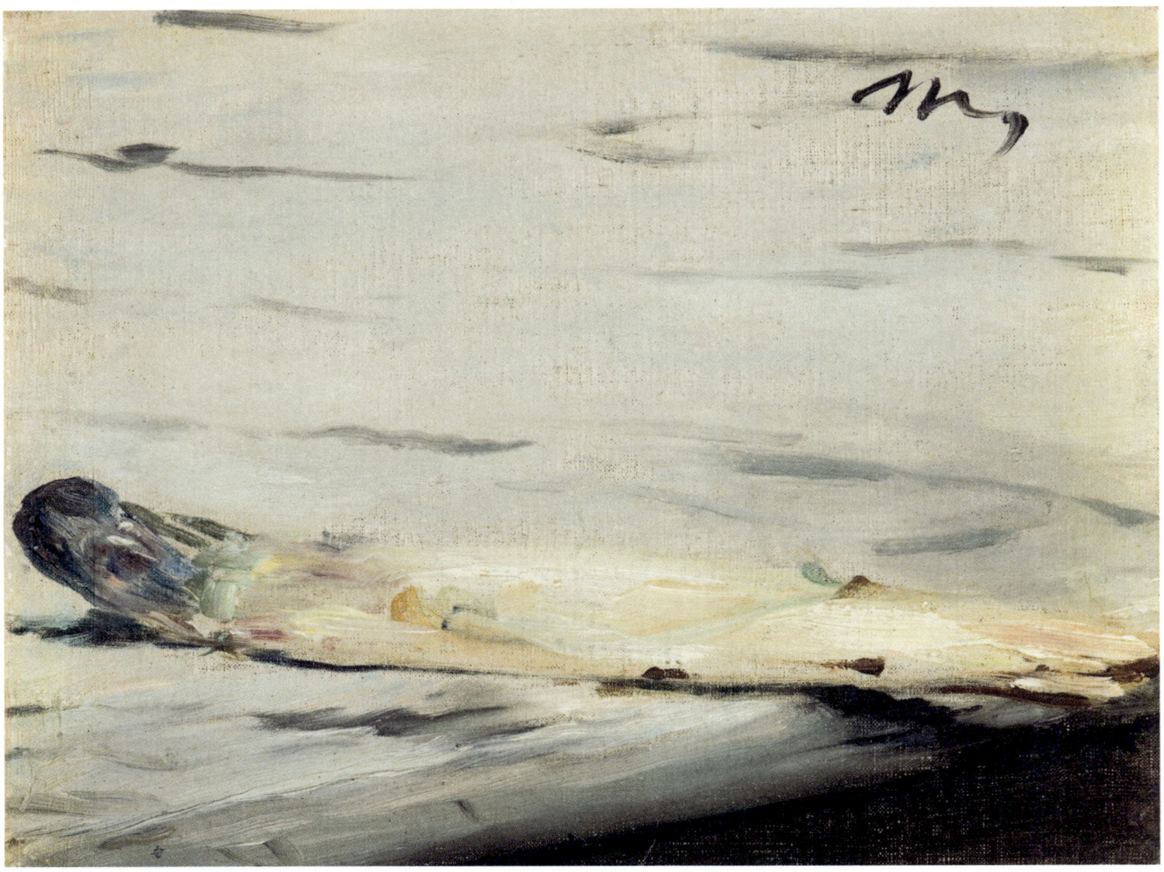

30 Édouard Manet, *L'Asperge* (*Asparagus*), 1880
Oil on canvas, 6 ⅝ × 8 ⅝ in. (16.9 × 21.9 cm)

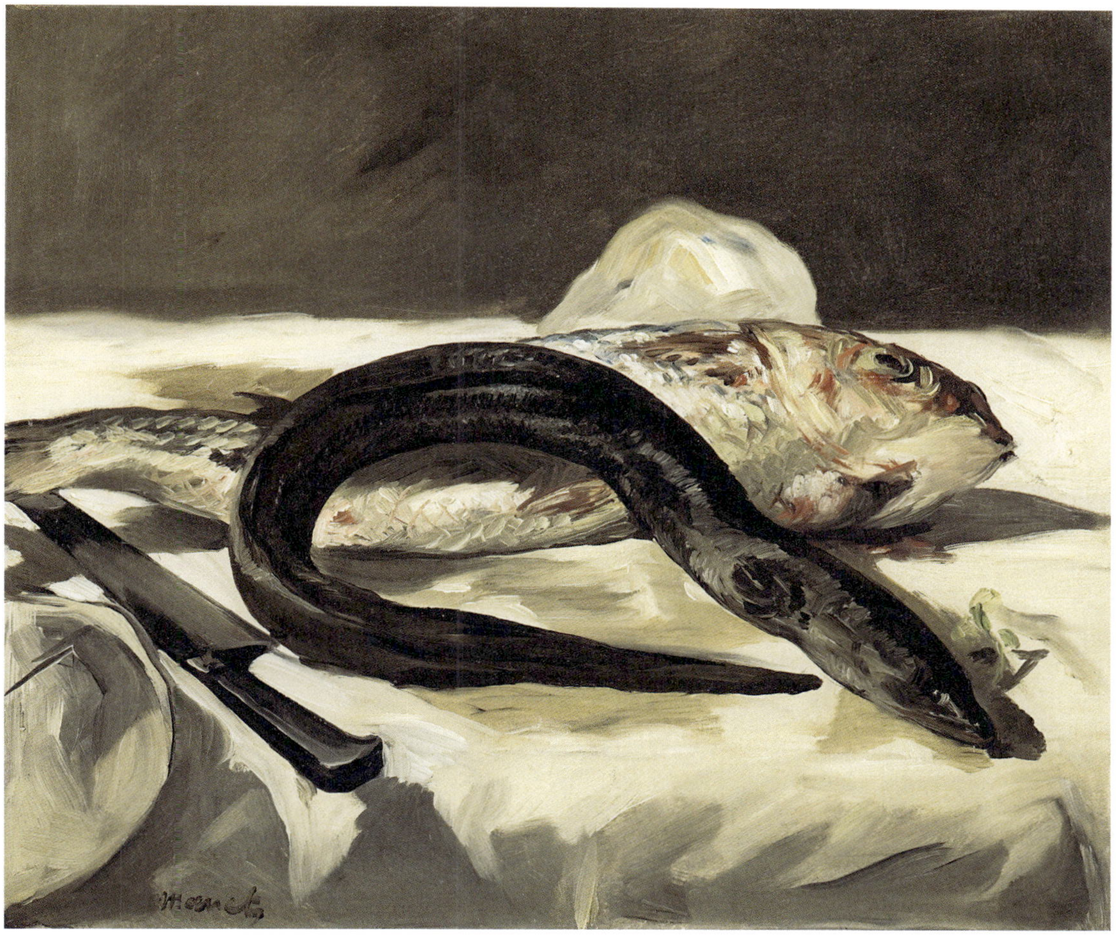

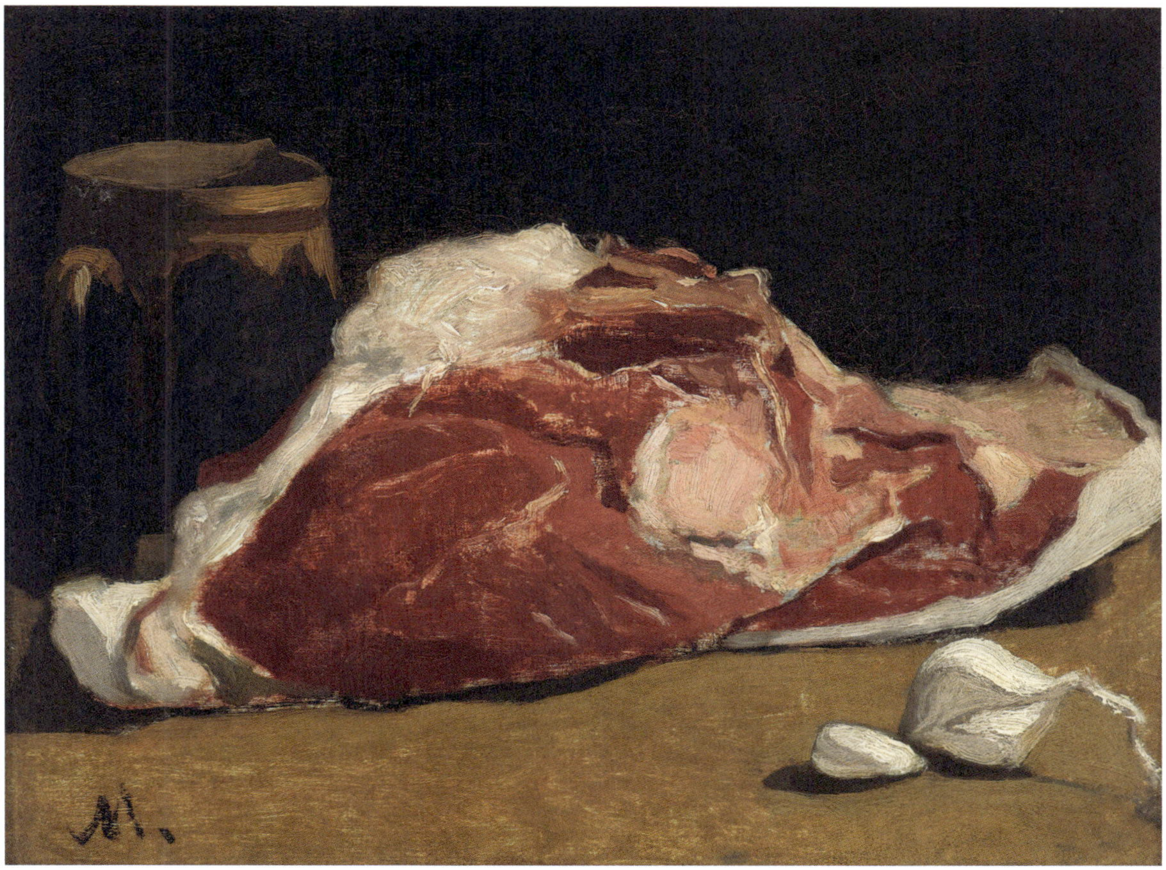

31 Top: Édouard Manet, *Anguille et rouget* (*Eel and Red Snapper*), 1864
Oil on canvas, 14 15⁄16 × 18 1⁄8 in. (38 × 46 cm)

32 Bottom: Claude Monet, *Nature morte: le quartier de viande* (*Still Life: The Quarter of Meat*), c. 1864
Oil on canvas, 9 7⁄16 × 13 in. (24 × 33 cm)

Flowers

While fruit and vegetables nourish us physically, flowers lend us only the fading charm of their uselessness. This is not much, and yet it is a lot, because they remind us that we do also need beauty. Manet, who was a friend of Monet's and of the poet and critic Stéphane Mallarmé's, shared their passion for flowers and for their many symbolic meanings. In the aftermath of the scandal that erupted around *Le Déjeuner sur l'herbe* (p. 15), the left side of the composition of which is dotted with flowers, he decided to produce still lifes, including bouquets and bunches of blooms. His passion for peonies came about quite suddenly. With their plump form and frothy petals, these very short-lived flowers offer a perfect illustration of our transient existence. In March 1865, after selling a small sketch of the sort that he would normally give away, Manet wrote to Baudelaire: "I've recently had quite a surprise. Mr. Ernest Chesneau bought a picture from me, two flowers in a vase, a little thing I showed at Cadart's, perhaps it will bring me luck."[9] At the end of his life, Manet pushed this aesthetic of "nothingness" to the extreme; underlying it was his profound emotion in the face of life's fragility. There is more exuberance and less melancholy in the flower paintings of Renoir and Monet, who himself shared that exuberance with Gustave Caillebotte. Both men were particularly fond of chrysanthemums and of how their explosive form offers the potential for visual saturation. They seem even to demand compositional asymmetry, as is the case in Monet's 1878 canvas. The motifs in the background introduce a subtle questioning of the decorative purpose of flowers, which here is indicated twofold. Unlike these artists, Cézanne rarely turned to floral subjects without assigning them a tighter ornamental gravity and a more assertive structural rigor, as demonstrated by *The Blue Vase*. A common theme running through the critical response to the Impressionists was their equal treatment of beings and things. Well, here Cézanne brings more nuance to the flowers and apples than to the rest of the canvas. Life prevails, even if it is discreet. S.G.

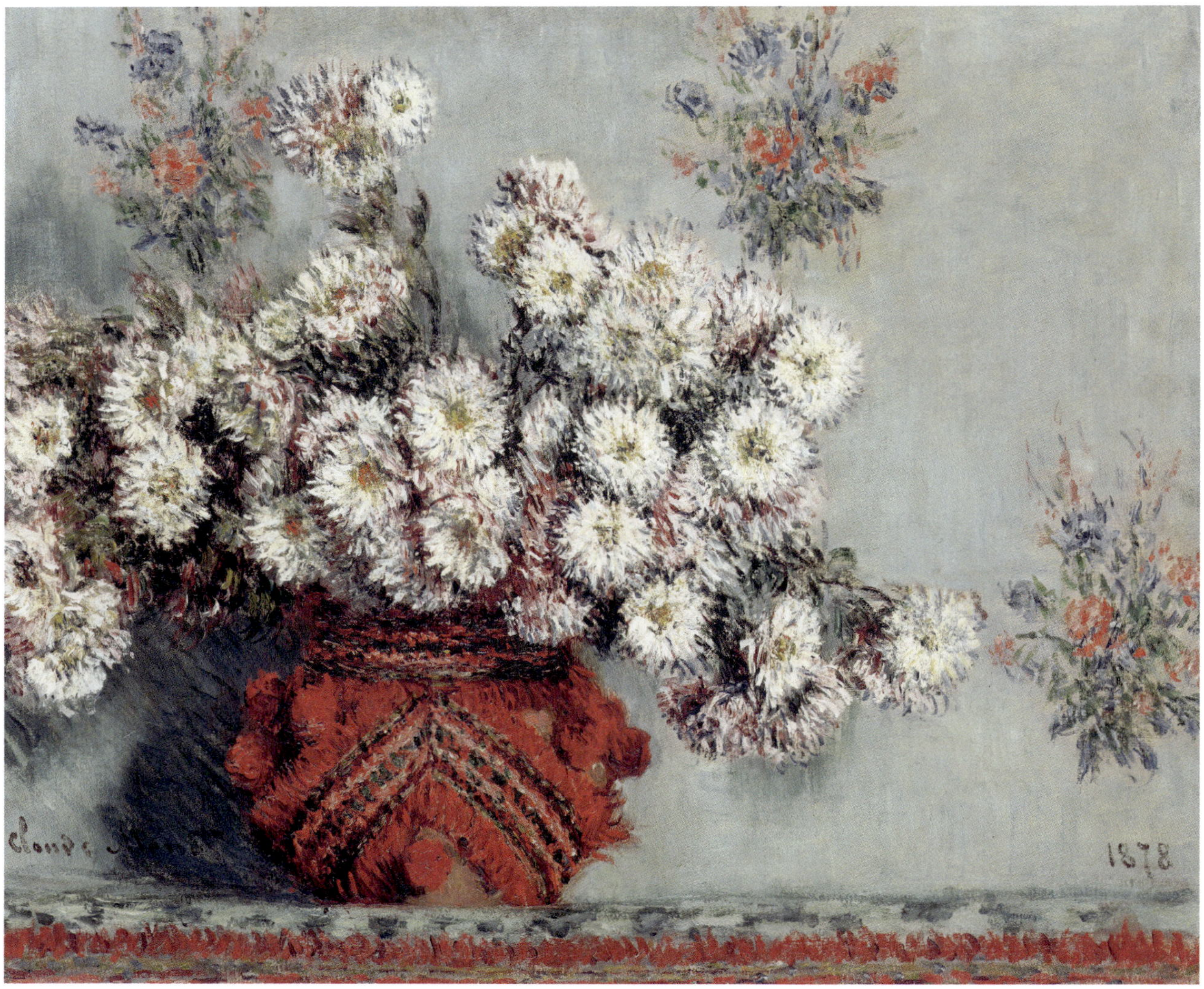

33 Claude Monet, *Chrysanthèmes* (*Chrysanthemums*), 1878
Oil on canvas, 21 ⅜ × 25 ¹¹⁄₁₆ in. (54.3 × 65.2 cm)

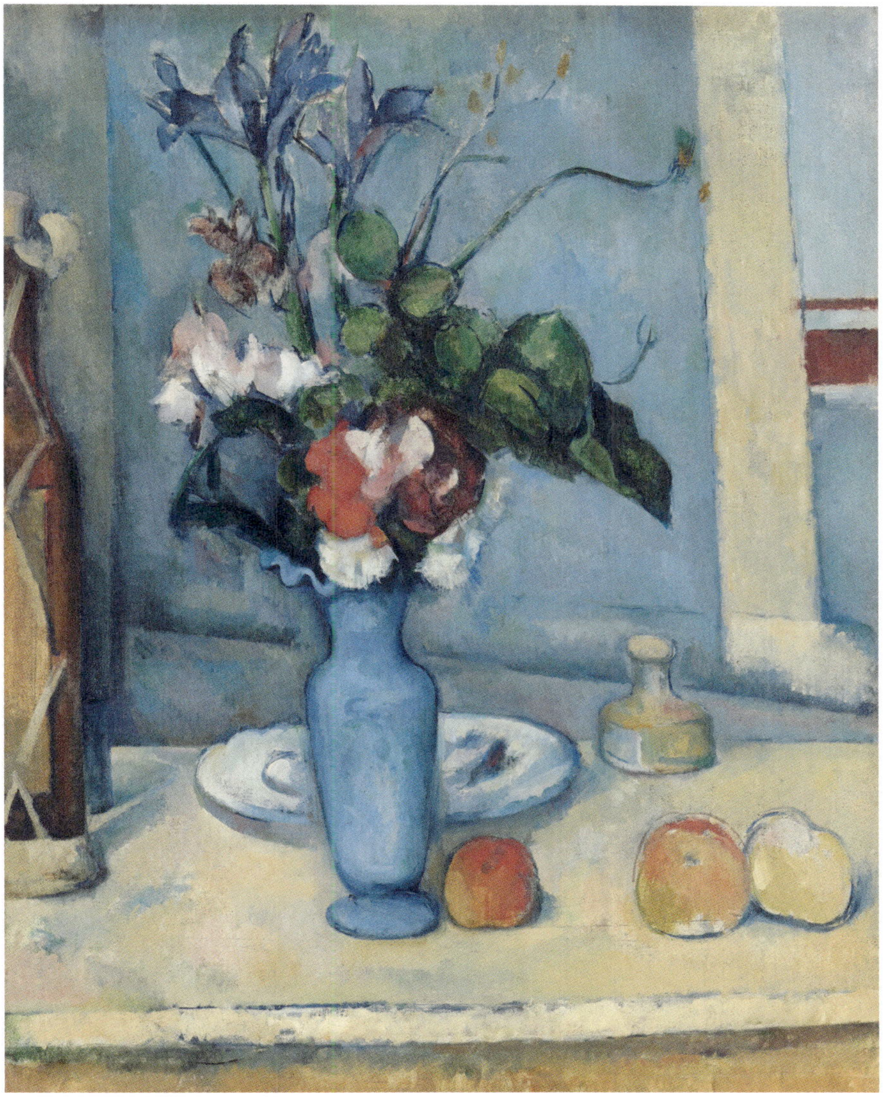

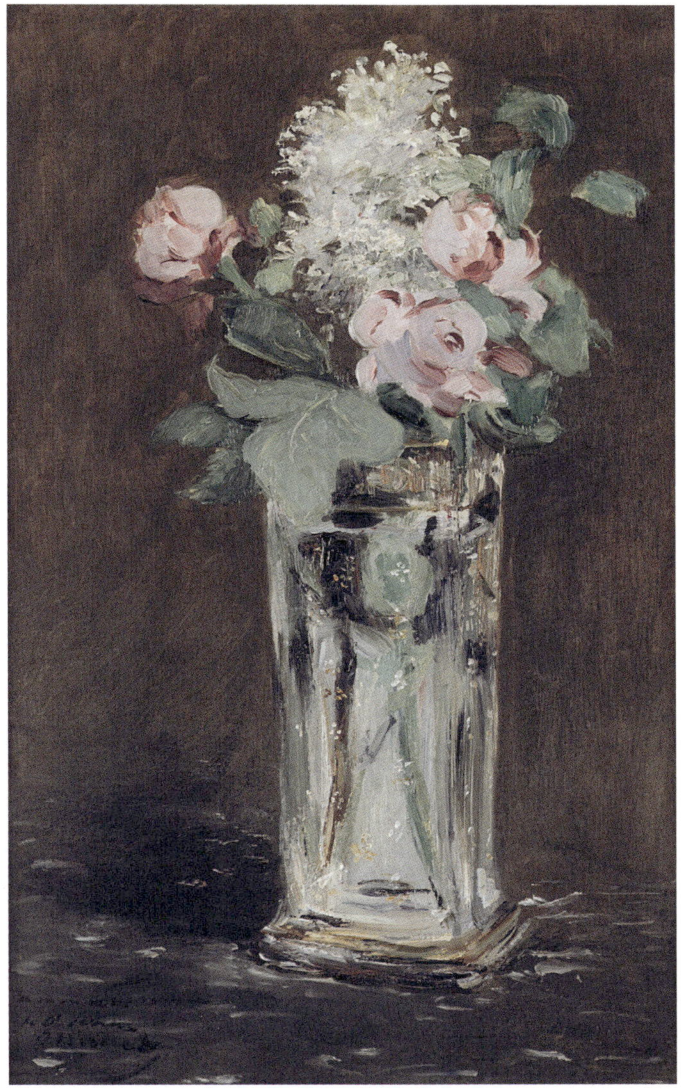

34 Left: Paul Cézanne, *Le Vase bleu* (*The Blue Vase*), 1889–1890
Oil on canvas, 24 ⅛ × 19 ¹¹⁄₁₆ in. (61.2 × 50 cm)

35 Right: Édouard Manet, *Fleurs dans un vase de cristal* (*Flowers in a Crystal Vase*), 1882
Oil on canvas, 21 ⁷⁄₁₆ × 13 ¾ in. (54.5 × 35 cm)

Édouard Manet
Peonies

One fifth of all of Manet's paintings comprises still lifes that alternately feature fauna, the marine world, and flora. Still-life painting stemmed from a tradition dating back to antiquity, which had recently been brought back to the attention of painters due to contemporary excavations at Pompeii. Flowers left a major mark on Manet's output in the mid-1860s, when he was struggling to sell his large figure paintings, and in the early 1880s, when the paralysis brought on by his illness forced him to reduce the scale of his work. Various compositions of peonies, painted in 1864 and described by Adolphe Tabarant as "delicate and powerful," remind us of how careful Manet was to avoid conventional formulas and to counter the melancholic sentiment of ephemerality through an impression of concentrated life or latent tragedy. Peonies were exotic flowers that had only recently begun to be imported. We know that Manet soon developed a passion for them, so much so that he grew them himself. In the canvases brought together here, the presence of shears suggests that the flowers have just been cut, or even that the bouquet is coming together before our very eyes. Elsewhere, the peonies are hung on a wall, like Chardin hares or Christ on a cross, or are laid out like a dead matador—because Manet's still lifes are in dialogue with his history paintings, and draw from them a particularly poignant dramatization of accident. Meanwhile, his more decorative and more Second Empire *Vase of Peonies on a Pedestal*, exhibited in 1867, charms us with its white and red explosion of petals, some full of life, others already having dropped, as little notes of elegant sadness. S.G.

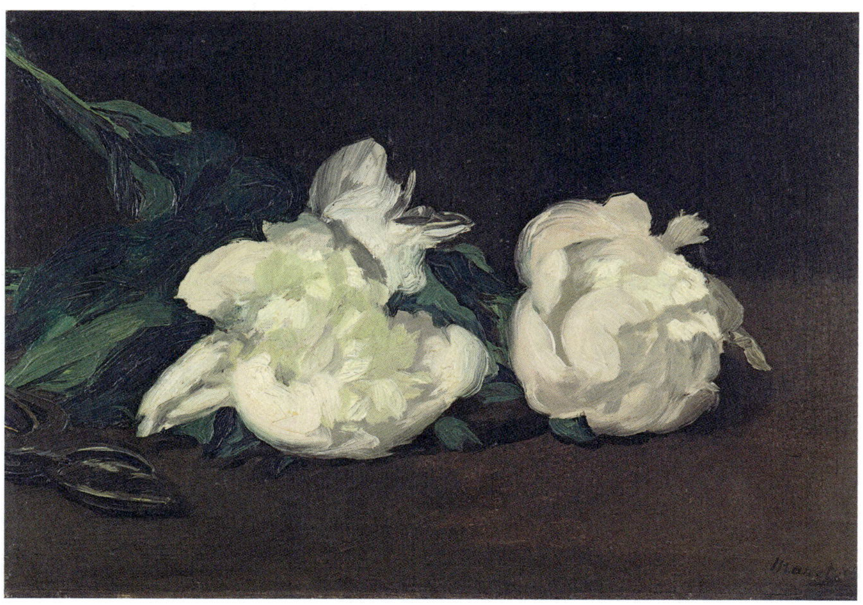

36 Édouard Manet, *Branche de pivoines blanches et sécateur* (*Branch of White Peonies and Shears*), 1864
Oil on canvas, 12 × 18 5⁄16 in. (30.5 × 46.5 cm)

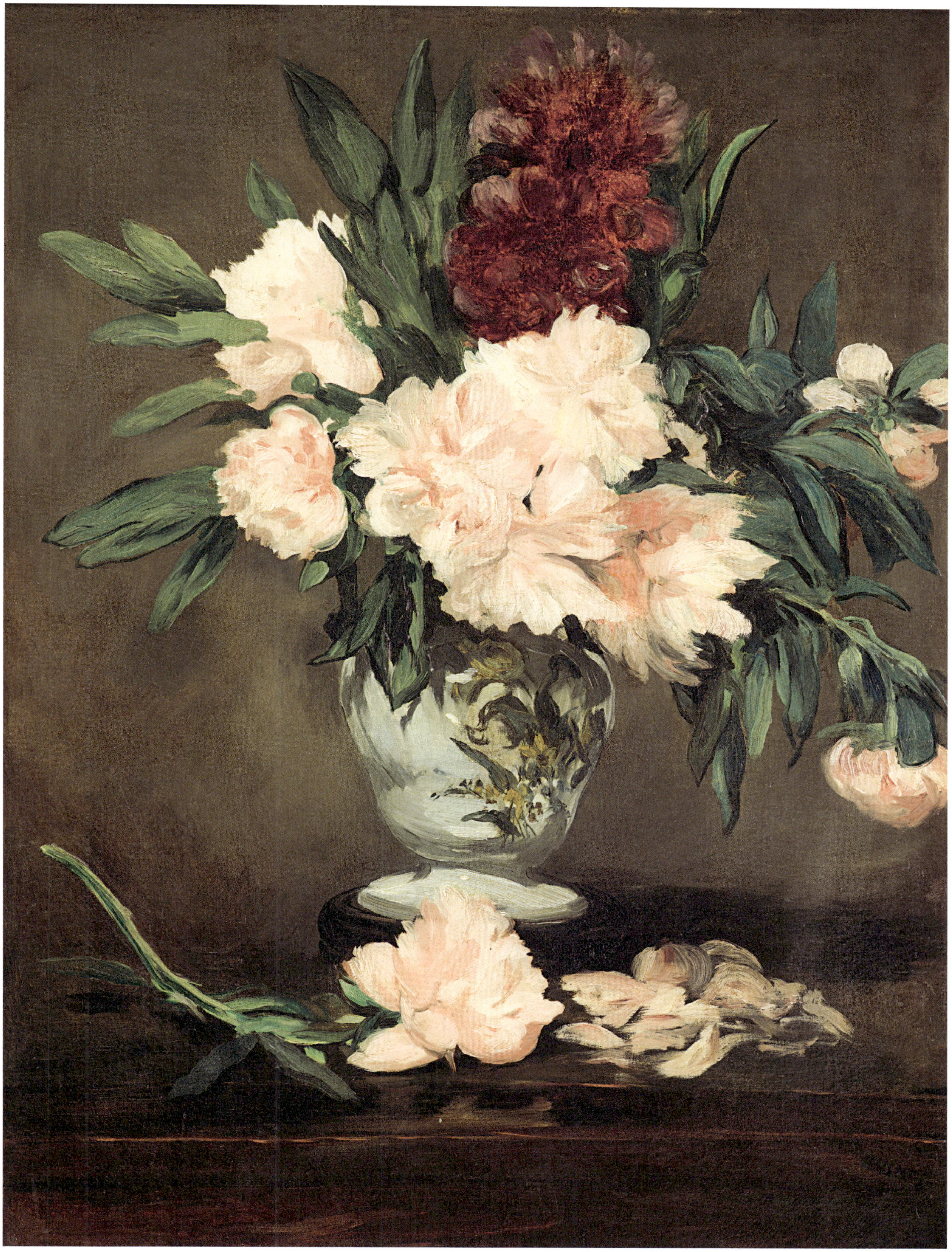

37 Édouard Manet, *Vase de pivoines sur piédouche* (*Vase of Peonies on a Pedestal*), 1864
Oil on canvas, 36 ¾ × 27 $^{9}/_{16}$ in. (93.3 × 70 cm)

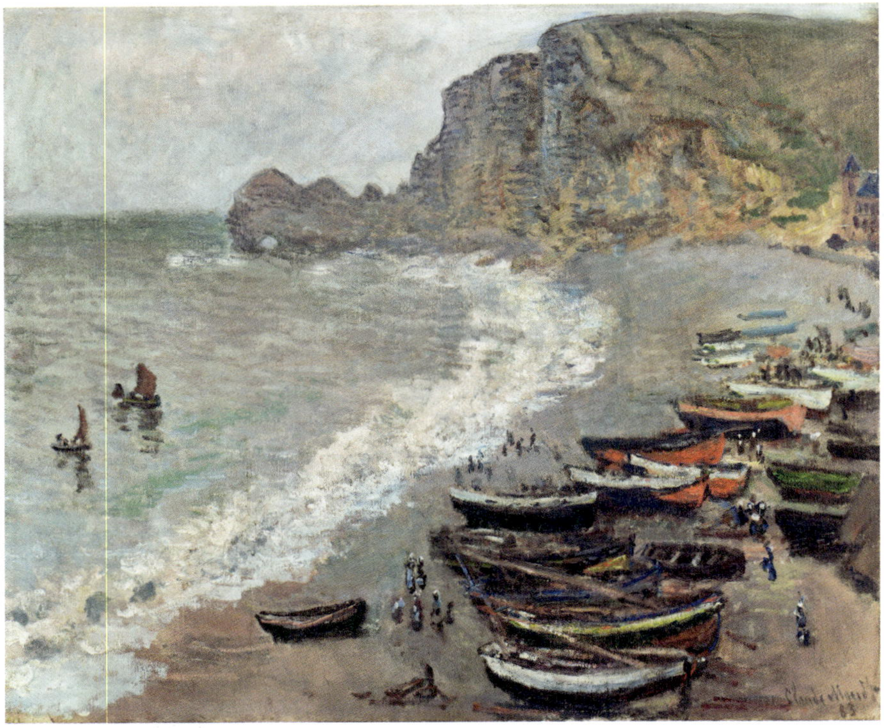

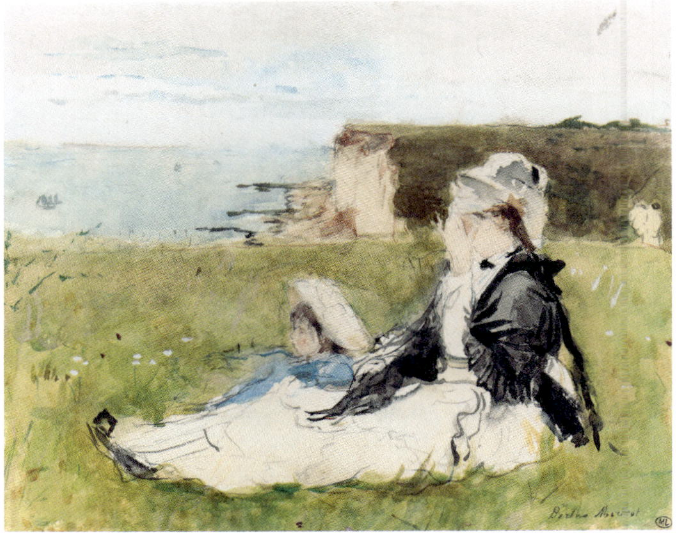

38 Left: Claude Monet, *Étretat: la plage et la porte d'Amont* (*Étretat: The Beach and the Porte d'Amont*), 1883
Oil on canvas, 26 × 31 15⁄16 in. (66 × 81.2 cm)

39 Right: Berthe Morisot, *Sur la falaise* (*On the Cliff*), 1873
Watercolor heightened by gouache over pencil lines on paper, 7 1⁄16 × 9 1⁄16 in. (18 × 23 cm)

The seaside

The appeal of the seaside and the development of activities associated with it had a profound impact on the "New Painting," which recorded this new taste for the sea, and drew a contrast with the unhealthiness of urban life. That said, it did not necessarily set out to extol sea bathing, however conducive it may have been to shifting people's attitudes to their bodies and the elements. Essentially, Impressionism kept well within the bounds of propriety that characterized the upper-class circles who feature in Eugène Boudin's beach paintings. Thanks to the seasonal influx that the railroad sparked and made possible, Boudin transposed Parisian society to Normandy—from Trouville to Honfleur (where he was born). In the early 1860s, his windswept scenes bathed in coastal light were all the rage, and were even exhibited at the Salon. Finely attired ladies and gentlemen engage in distinguished conversation, or look out dreamily toward the infinite horizon of the sea, which becomes as much a theater as the painting itself. Boudin was well aware that his clients expected him to pay attention to fashion trends. Chaste descendants from eighteenth-century *fêtes galantes*, his "*petites poupées*" (little dolls) sum up the touristy atmosphere and its pervasive poetry (p. 49). Through their rejection of any narrative, these works stand apart from traditional genre scenes and make flux or the void the very subject of the painting. In capturing unposed depictions of high society, the medium and the brush become lighter. Monet acknowledged his indebtedness to Boudin, who was one of his mentors. His painting, with its ever more fleeting quality, offers abundant confirmation of this, whether portraying fishermen at work, or the leisurely high-society lifestyle amid the grand hotels with their flapping flags—pointers to the Normandy coast's international character. While Manet went more to the Pas-de-Calais area in the period of the Second Empire, Morisot and her close circle were active participants in the heyday of the beaches to the west of Le Havre. Degas was likewise drawn to this area. S.G.

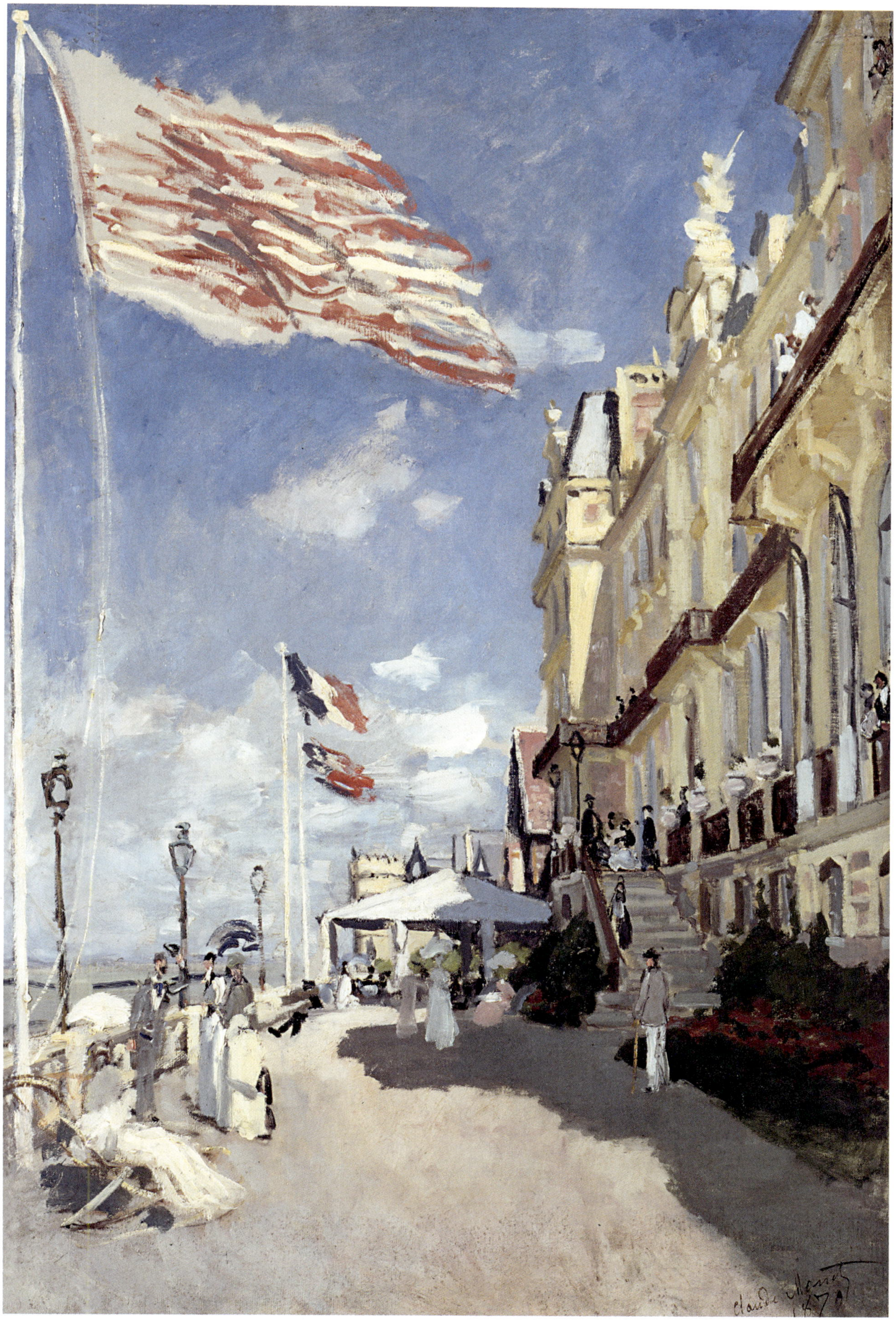

40 Claude Monet, *Hôtel des Roches Noires, Trouville*, 1870
Oil on canvas, 31 ⅞ × 22 13⁄16 in. (81 × 58 cm)

Eugène Boudin
The Beach at Trouville

In 1861, at the age of thirty-seven, Eugène Boudin moved away from his native Normandy to live permanently in Paris, hoping to launch his artistic career. There, he became part of a circle of painters that included Troyon, Courbet, and the young Monet, whom he introduced to landscape painting. These artists, along with the poet Baudelaire, whom he had met in Honfleur, admired the convincingness and virtuosity with which he portrayed the "beauty of meteorological phenomena" and the "prodigious magic of air and water."

His artistic activity was split between the coasts of Normandy and Brittany, where he worked from life, and Paris, where he resumed work on his studies in his studio. To expand his clientele, he abandoned his early practice of marine painting, and turned instead to a genre that he invented himself: beach scenes. In these, he represented the elegant milieu of Second Empire society that would install itself in Trouville and Deauville for the bathing season. His "little dolls," as he called them, earned him considerable success at the Salon and among collectors. The paintings display a mixture of his knowledge of landscape and his interest in "the people and things of [his] time"—a focus he shared with the Realist artists who were part of his social circle.

It was his studies in oil and pastel, more than his most "finished" canvases, that garnered the admiration of the Impressionist artists. He exhibited with them only once, in 1874. After his death, Monet declared: "If I have become a painter, I owe this to Eugène Boudin and no other." I. P.

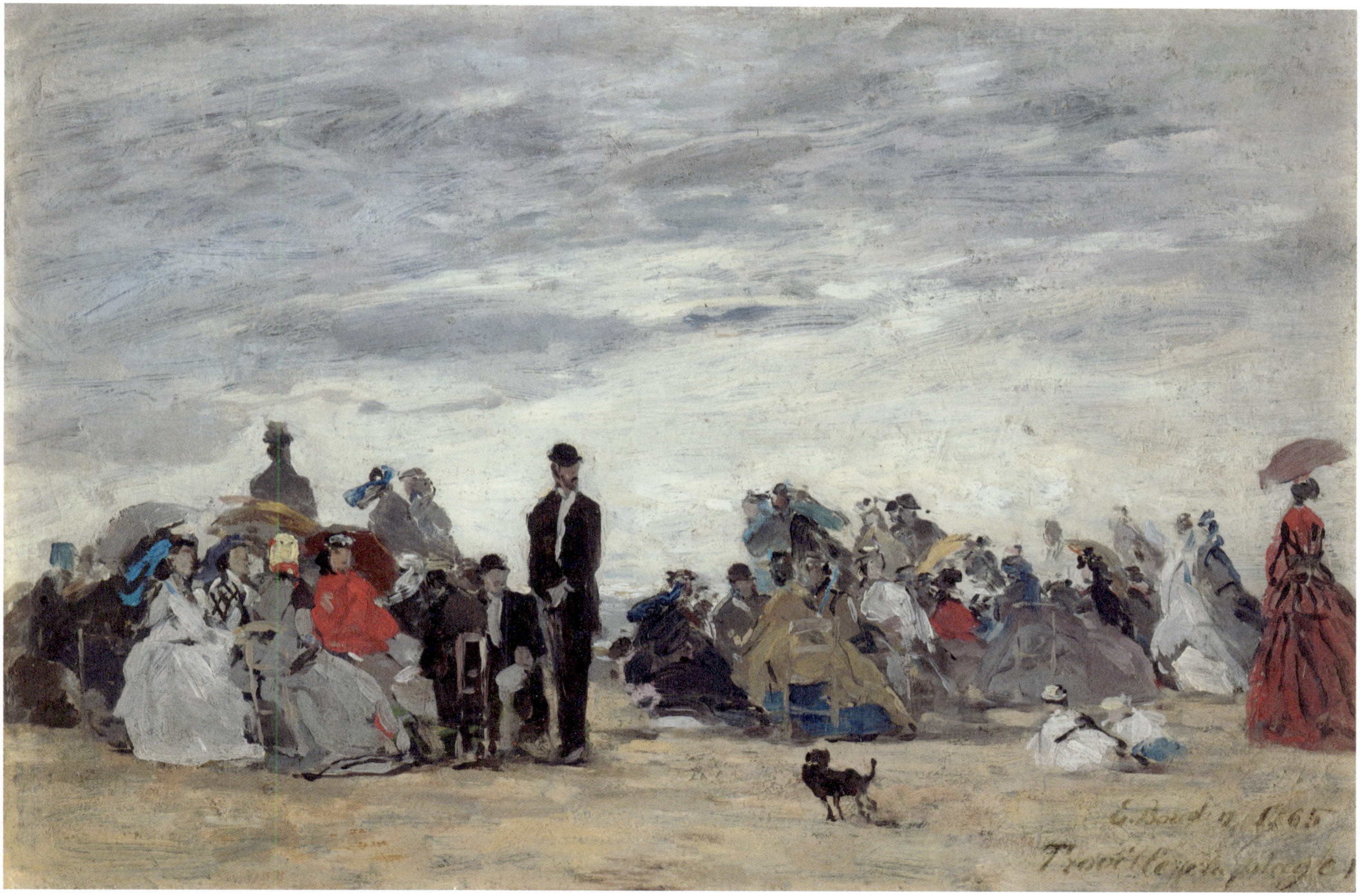

41 Eugène Boudin, *La Plage de Trouville* (*The Beach at Trouville*), 1865
Oil on board, 10 ⁷⁄₁₆ × 15 ⁷⁄₈ in. (26.5 × 40.3 cm)

Johan Barthold Jongkind
In Holland, Boats near the Mill

Boasting a prestigious provenance—having belonged to the collector Isaac de Camondo—this painting dates from the turning point in Jongkind's work that occurred under the Second Empire. Jongkind trained in the Netherlands and moved in 1846 to Paris. There, he became a pupil of the marine painter Eugène Isabey and of François Édouard Picot, who instilled the teachings of post-Davidian painting in all his students, from Gustave Moreau to William Bouguereau. After making his Salon debut in 1848, Jongkind was awarded a third-class medal there four years later. He then moved back to the Netherlands, before returning to France in the early 1860s. It was then that he joined forces with Édouard Manet, Félix Bracquemond, and others to set up the Société des Aquafortistes (Society of Etchers). In a critical review of the etching revival published in April 1862, Baudelaire makes a point to mention "the charming, ingenuous Dutch painter" and "the plates to which he confided the secret of his dreams, unique summaries of his painting, sketches that any art lover accustomed to deciphering the painter's soul through his swiftest scribbles will be able to read." Notable for his cloudy landscapes, he returned to the Salon in 1864, a few months before he met the young Monet, probably in Honfleur, where Boudin had encouraged him to come to paint. "From that day on, he was my true master, and it was he who definitively trained my eye," Monet would write of the brilliant Dutch painter, the drizzly magic of whose dynamic views created a dialogue between traditions ranging from Claude Lorrain and Joseph Vernet to the entirety of Northern art.   S.G.

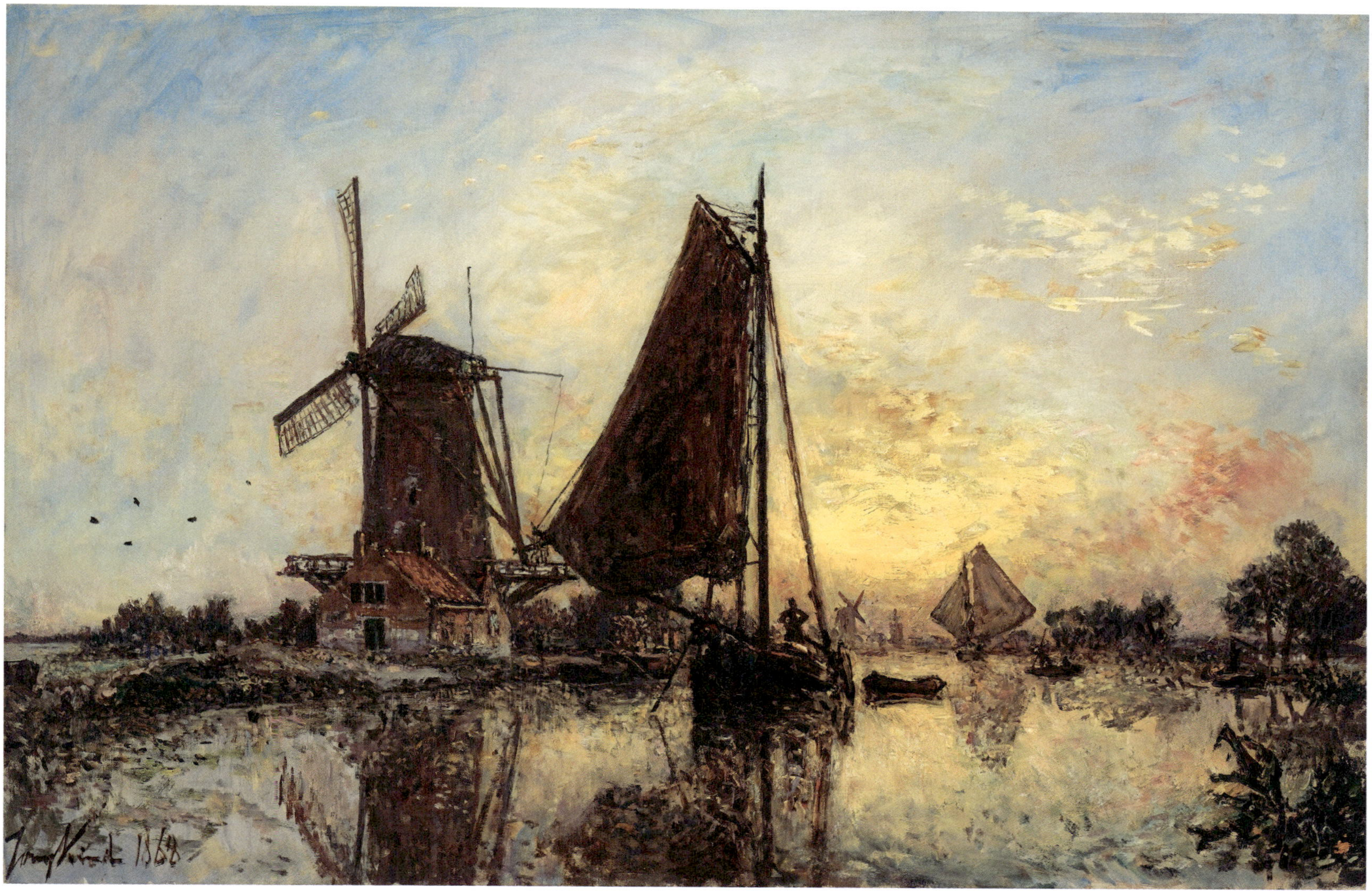

42 Johan Barthold Jongkind, *En Hollande, les barques près du moulin* (*In Holland, Boats near the Mill*), 1868
Oil on canvas, 20 11⁄16 × 32 in. (52.5 × 81.3 cm)

Edgar Degas
Beaches

Degas's art is widely believed to have resisted the craze for *plein-air* work that swept through French landscape painting from the late eighteenth century onward. A stickler for line, Degas would not lower himself to the atmospheric effects practiced by his contemporaries. He was essentially a stranger to Impressionism, intractable in his rethinkings of the then-aging neoclassical painter Jean-Auguste-Dominique Ingres. And yet he had practiced *plein-air* painting as a young man in Italy, in that spirit of the neoclassical landscape painters Pierre-Henri de Valenciennes and Camille Corot that the Morisot sisters—Berthe and Edma—so loved. Indeed, it was probably they who enticed him away from Paris in the summer of 1869 to stay between Dives-sur-Mer and Villers-sur-Mer, near Houlgate, where the Morisot family had a house. This time by the sea spawned a series of pearly pastels, which he kept for the rest of his life and which bear no hint of regret at having left Paris. Like his rivals, Degas places the emphasis on the feeling of vastness. Beaches, cliffs, and the sea itself draw us into the infinite bliss of total surrender to the world. His youthful Italian views herald this taste for pure landscapes. Degas certainly drew a clear distinction between landscapes devoid of any human presence and the opposing view of sailboats and walkers, the Normandy coast's new consumers. Also notable is his frequent use of colored papers as a base—well suited to the subtle tonal nuances that modern marine painting called for. From then on, Degas's magic derived largely from how he bathed his paintings in color and light. S.G.

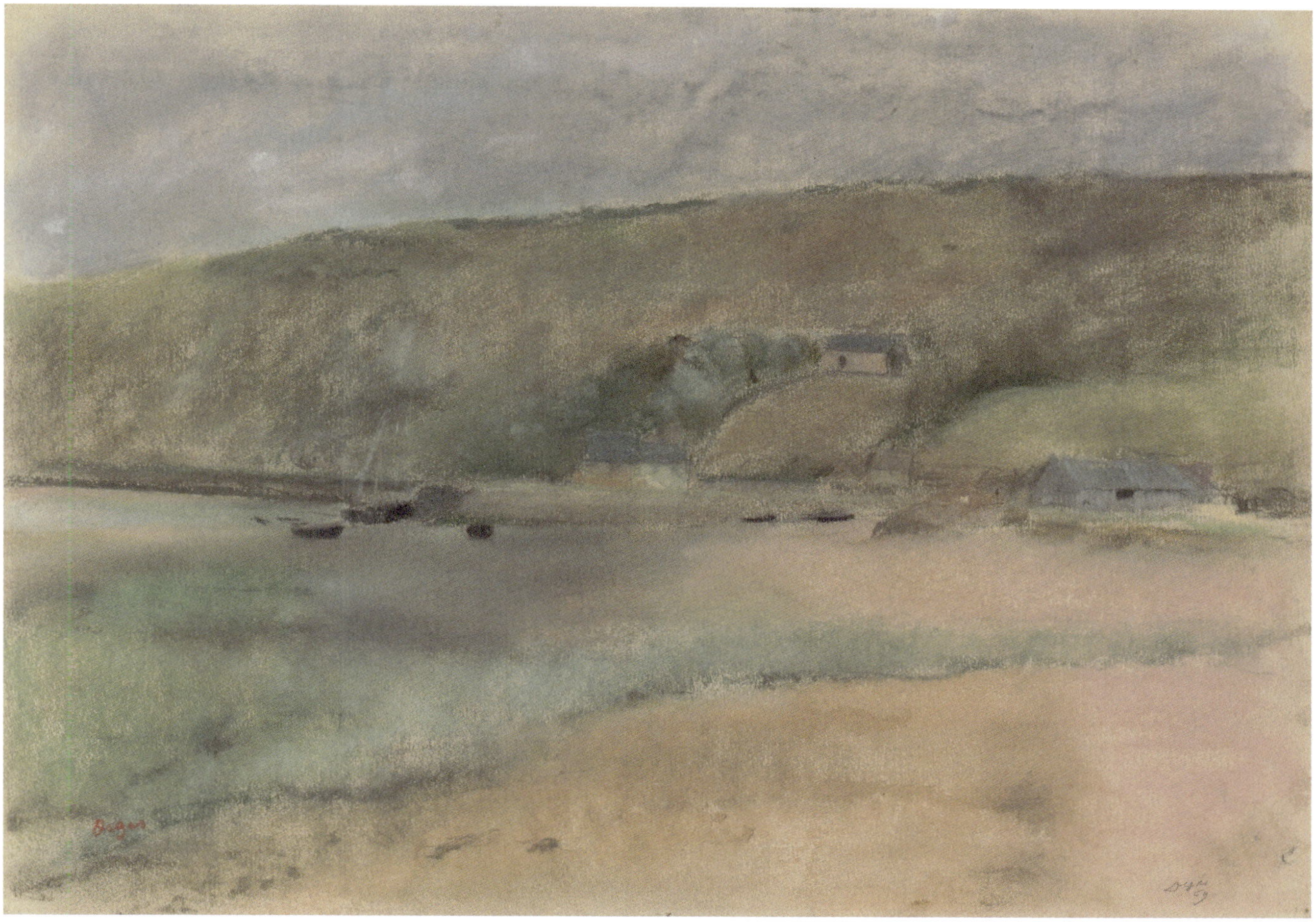

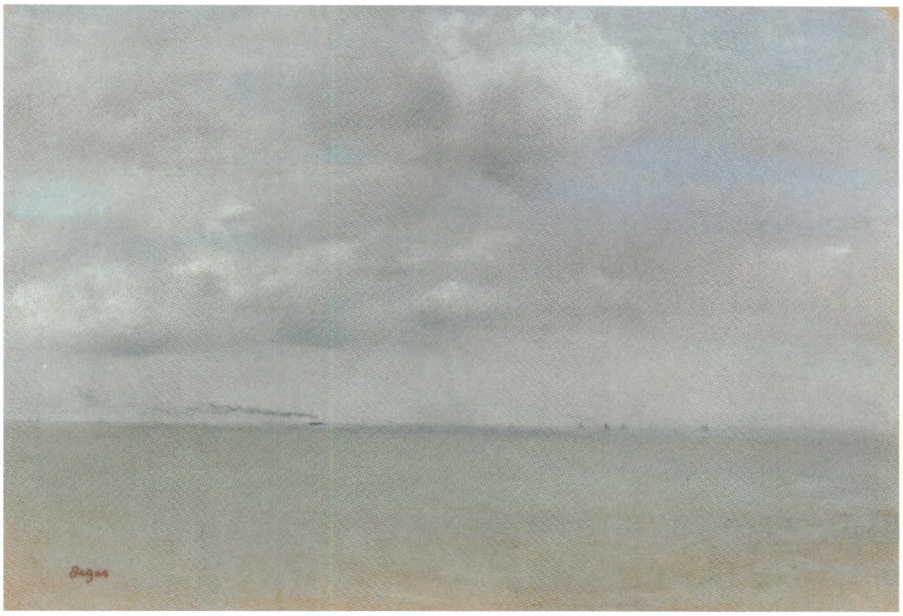

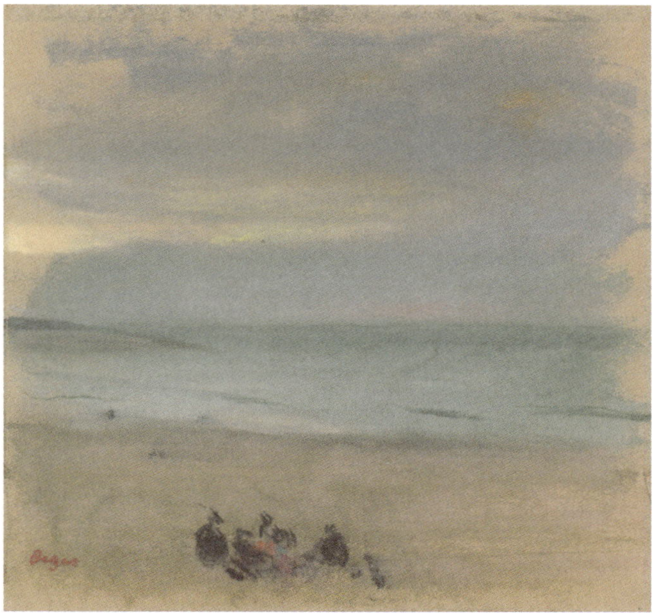

43 Top: Edgar Degas, *Falaises au bord de la mer* (*Cliffs at the Seaside*), 1869
Pastel on gray paper,
12 ¾ × 18 7⁄16 in. (32.4 × 46.9 cm)

44 Bottom, left: Edgar Degas, *Marine* (*Seascape*), 1869
Pastel on buff paper,
12 ⅜ × 18 7⁄16 in. (31.4 × 46.9 cm)

45 Bottom, right: Edgar Degas, *Marine* (*Seascape*), 1869
Pastel on paper,
9 7⁄16 × 10 ⅜ in. (24 × 26.3 cm)

Édouard Manet
On the Beach

In the summer of 1873, Manet spent several weeks at Berck-sur-Mer, on the Opal Coast of northern France, with his family. He painted a number of pictures there, including *On the Beach*, which he probably executed *en plein air*, as suggested by the sand present in the paint layer. His subject and technique are comparable to those of the future Impressionists, although he would never exhibit with them. The figures, treated in a monumental way that accentuates their stillness, are deeply absorbed in reading or daydreaming, and barely pay any attention to one another. Manet depicts his wife, Suzanne, in a gray dress, her eyes protected from the sand by a veil worn over her hat. Next to her is Eugène Manet, the artist's brother, in a pose similar to the one he adopted in *Le Déjeuner sur l'herbe* (p.15). The rendering of the water is extremely accurate, with swift brushstrokes of blue, green, and yellow, heightened with white. Manet was intimately acquainted with the sea, having sailed to Brazil when he was a young naval apprentice, before he devoted himself to an artistic career. The high position of the horizon, and the composition of horizontal strips punctuated by the geometrically shaped sails of boats placed rhythmically across the water's surface, together give a Japanese feeling to the painting. One of its former owners was the fashion designer Jacques Doucet, who in the 1920s had the Art Deco red-and-black lacquer frame made for it that is still associated with the painting today. I.P.

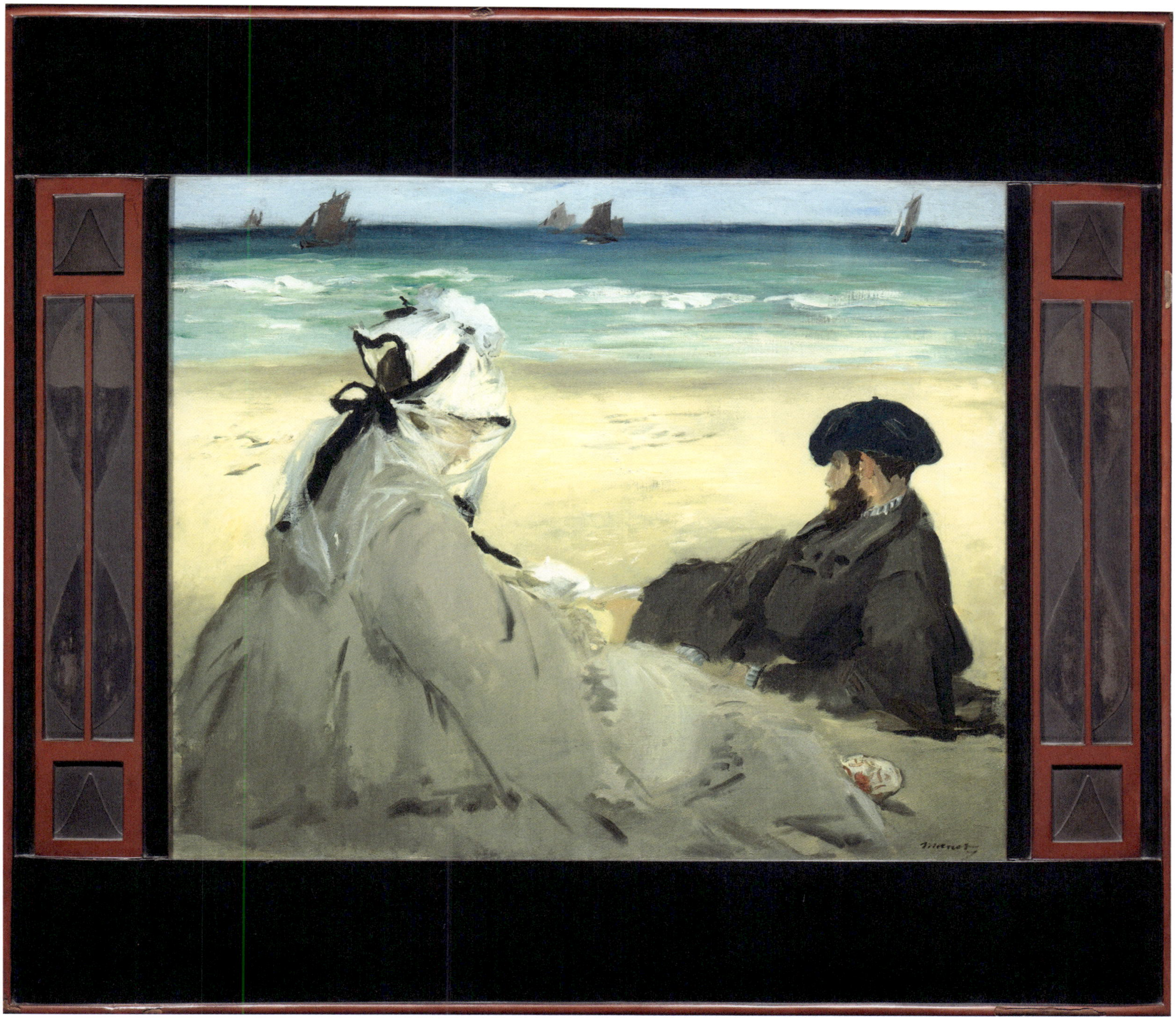

46 Édouard Manet, *Sur la plage* (*On the Beach*), 1873
Oil on canvas, 23 ⅝ × 28 15⁄16 in. (60 × 73.5 cm)

Impressionist portraits

Landscapes and portraiture were the predominant genres in late nineteenth-century exhibitions, and soon also in photography studios. Their prevalence speaks to the decline of religious faith and the irresistible rise of individualism, not to say narcissism. Portraits were after all intended to immortalize their sitters, both in terms of their social rank and their personality, by flattering them to some degree or another. Throughout the nineteenth century, middle-class clients and the old and new aristocracy drove considerable demand, as if increasing social equality were spurring a need for them to distinguish themselves.

Impressionist artists would sometimes act as society portraitists. Marguerite Gaudibert and her husband were members of Le Havre high society, and part of the milieu from which Monet's first collectors were recruited. We sense that he devoted as much attention to the silk dress and the cashmere shawl as he did to giving his elegant sitter an air of nobility. She turns her face from us, all too happy to show off her exquisite taste. Madame Georges Hartmann commissioned portraits of the same type from Renoir (Musée d'Orsay, Paris), who additionally made sure to underline the fact that her husband was a music publisher.

The well-documented canvas, with its free brushwork, reminds us how crucial it had then become for portraits to be situated within their sitters' domestic or professional context. Making every element speak of the present, of physiology or fashion, became the paramount concern. Shown at the Impressionist exhibition of 1879, *Portraits at the Stock Exchange* presents the banker Ernest May, a pioneering early collector of Degas, as deeply immersed in his financial business. Speculation is portrayed through the reality of the constant flow of information that it involves. Conversely, what Caillebotte records when he paints his friend Henri Cordier—an eminent specialist and teacher of Eastern languages in Paris—is the solitude of the researcher, surrounded by the scholarly journals and books hoarded in his study. S. G.

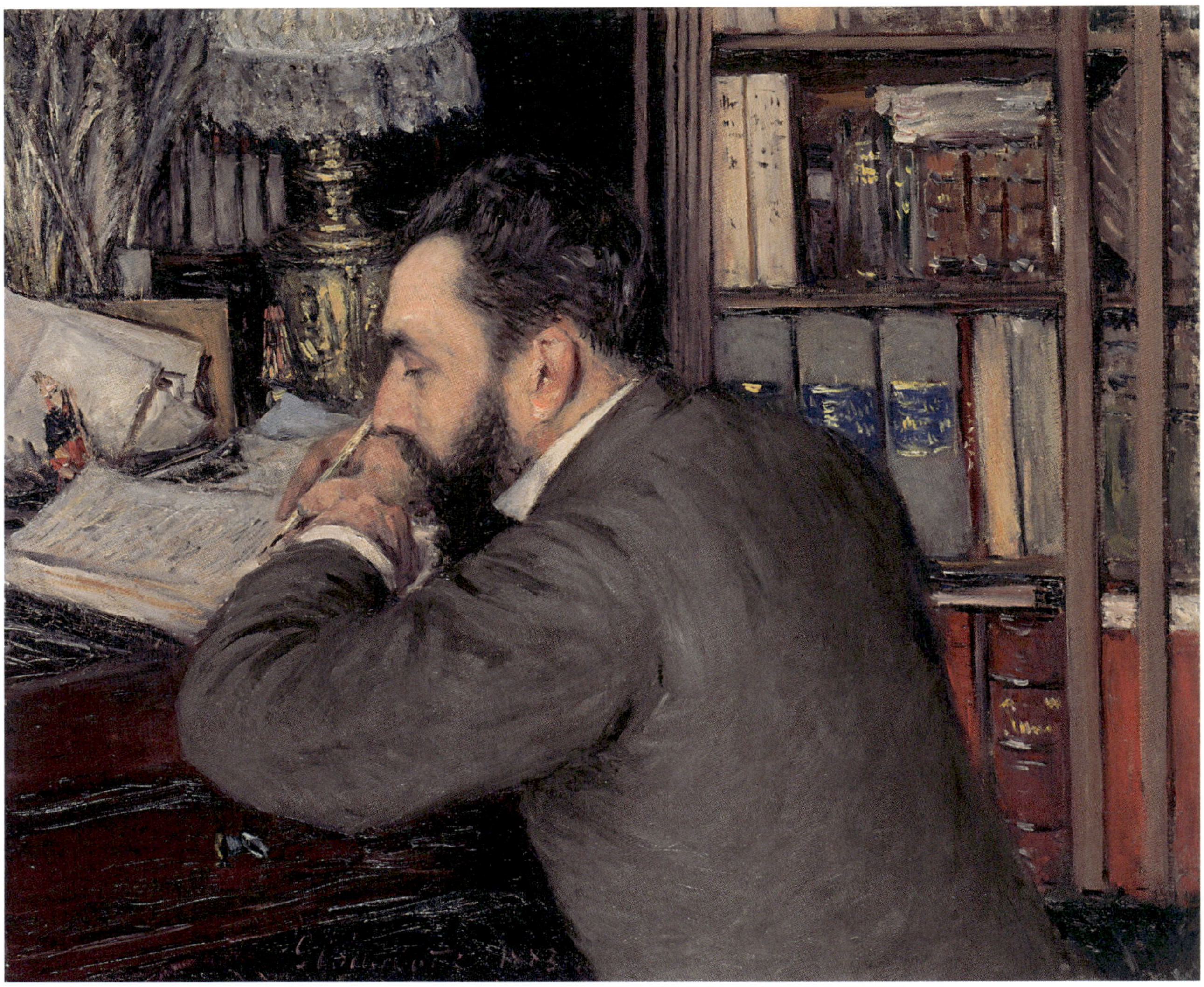

47 Gustave Caillebotte, *Henri Cordier*, 1883
Oil on canvas, 25 9⁄16 × 32 1⁄16 in.
(65 × 81.5 cm)

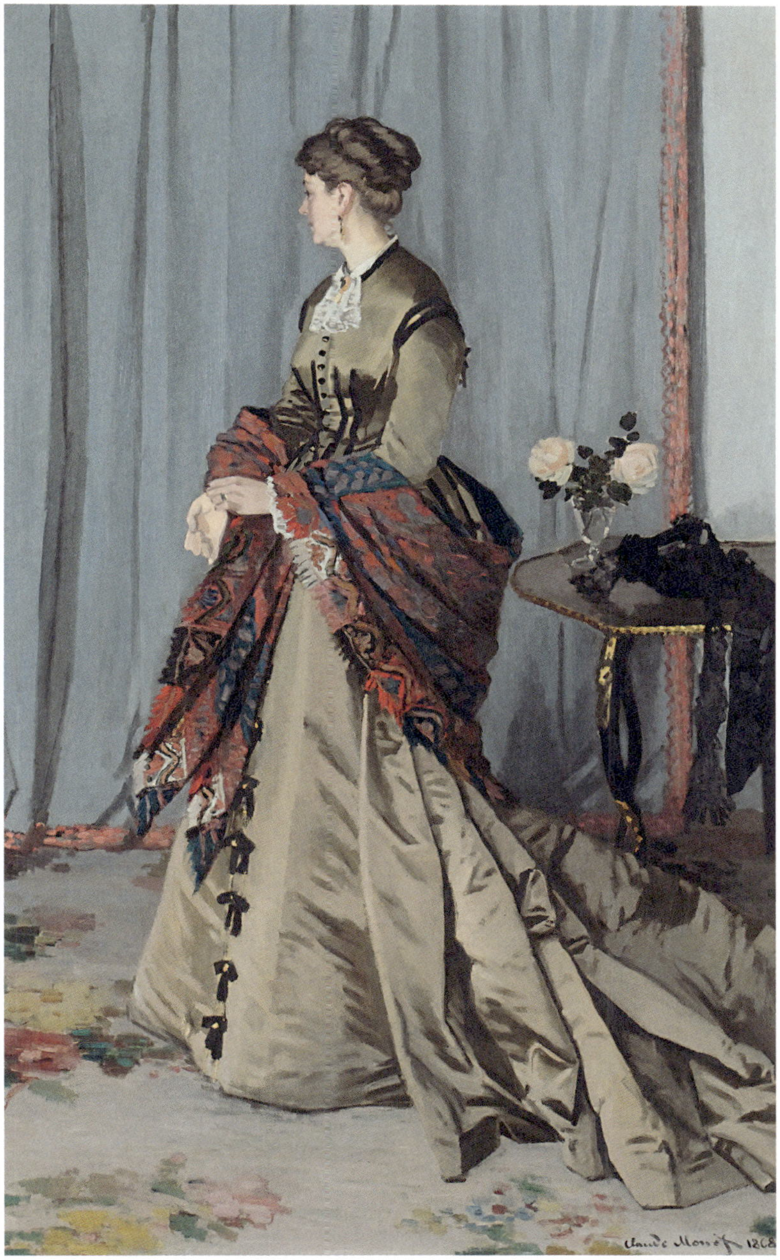

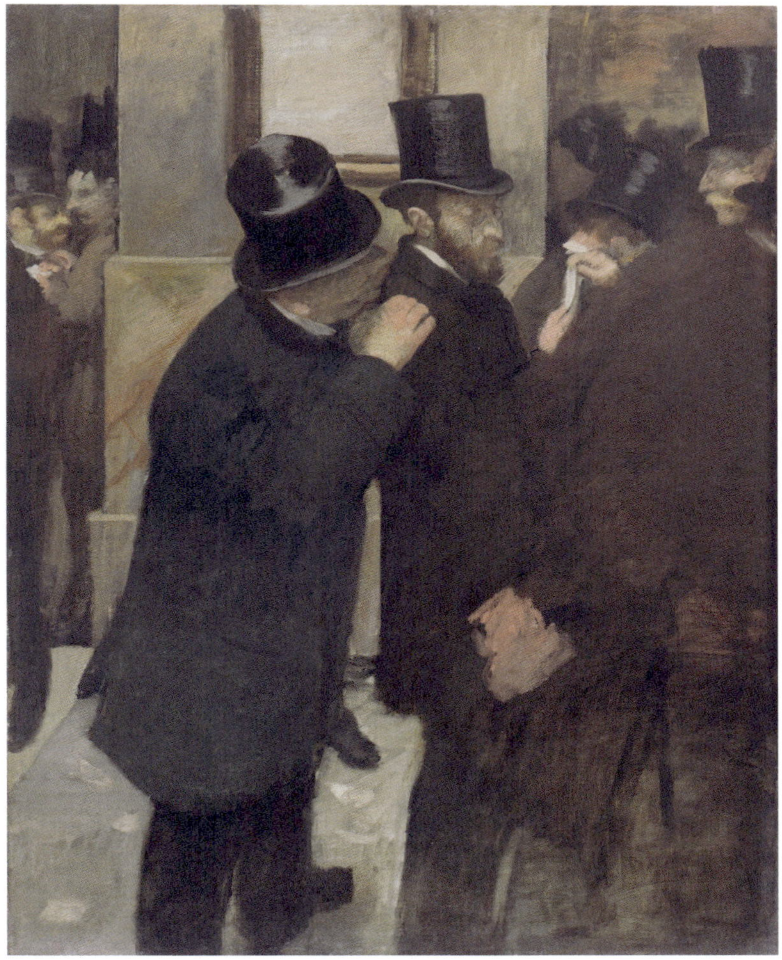

48 Left: Claude Monet,
Madame Louis Joachim Gaudibert, 1868
Oil on canvas, 85 ¼ × 54 ½ in. (216.5 × 138.5 cm)

49 Right: Edgar Degas, *Portraits à la bourse*
(*Portraits at the Stock Exchange*), 1878–1879
Oil on canvas, 39 ⁹⁄₁₆ × 32 ¹⁄₁₆ in. (100.5 × 81.5 cm)

Edgar Degas
Family Portrait

Held up today as one of the fifteen or twenty finest paintings of the entire French School, this portrait remained unsold until after Degas's death. He made the sketches for it in Italy, where he spent much of the 1850s. It portrays his paternal aunt Laura, his cousins Giovanna and Giulia, and his uncle baron Gennaro, exiled from Naples for having taken part in the revolutionary events of 1848 and continuing to push for Italian unification. The lady of the house is shown in mourning dress, following the death of her father, Degas's grandfather. The numerous preparatory sketches indicate what an ambitious undertaking it was; Degas did not complete it until some ten years later. The simplicity of its title belies its aristocratic gravitas and its mixture of charm and solemnity. Worthy of Van Dyck or Holbein, the vast canvas did not appear at the Salon until 1867, and even then without success. A cross between a society portrait and a history painting, it remains fascinating to this day: the painter's aunt, somber and noble, has her two daughters close to her, but is set apart from her husband, a more silent presence with his back to the viewer. The father and mother do not look at each other, and nor do their two daughters. It is a very strange image, a total contrast to the post-revolutionary iconography of the bourgeois nuclear family which was based on an accepted patriarchy and a display of sentiment. Only Giovanna and her timid smile are addressed at the Salon's visitors, who were given no keys to the psychologically incomprehensible composition. The frisky little dog lends a mysteriously mischievous note, although without remotely lightening the atmosphere. S.G.

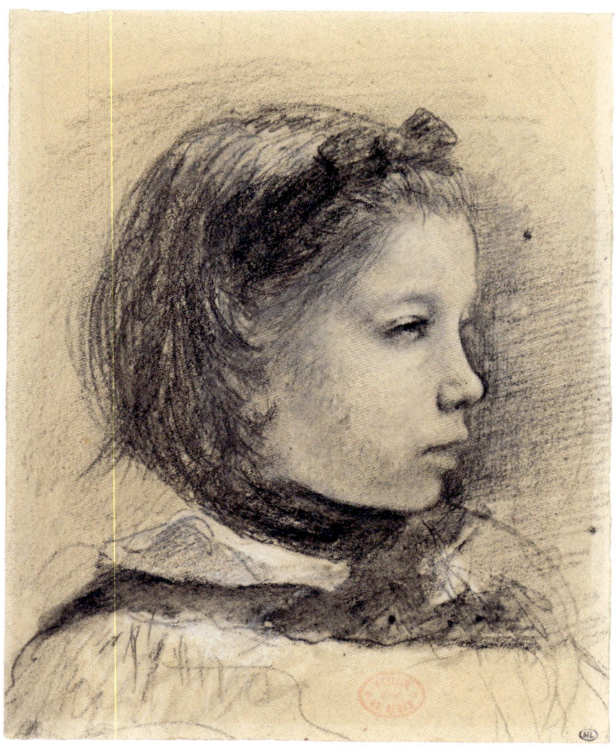

50 Edgar Degas, *Portrait de Giulia Bellelli* (*Portrait of Giulia Bellelli*), c. 1858
Black pencil, gray wash, turpentine, and white highlights on cream paper, 9 5/16 × 7 3/16 in. (23.6 × 19.6 cm)

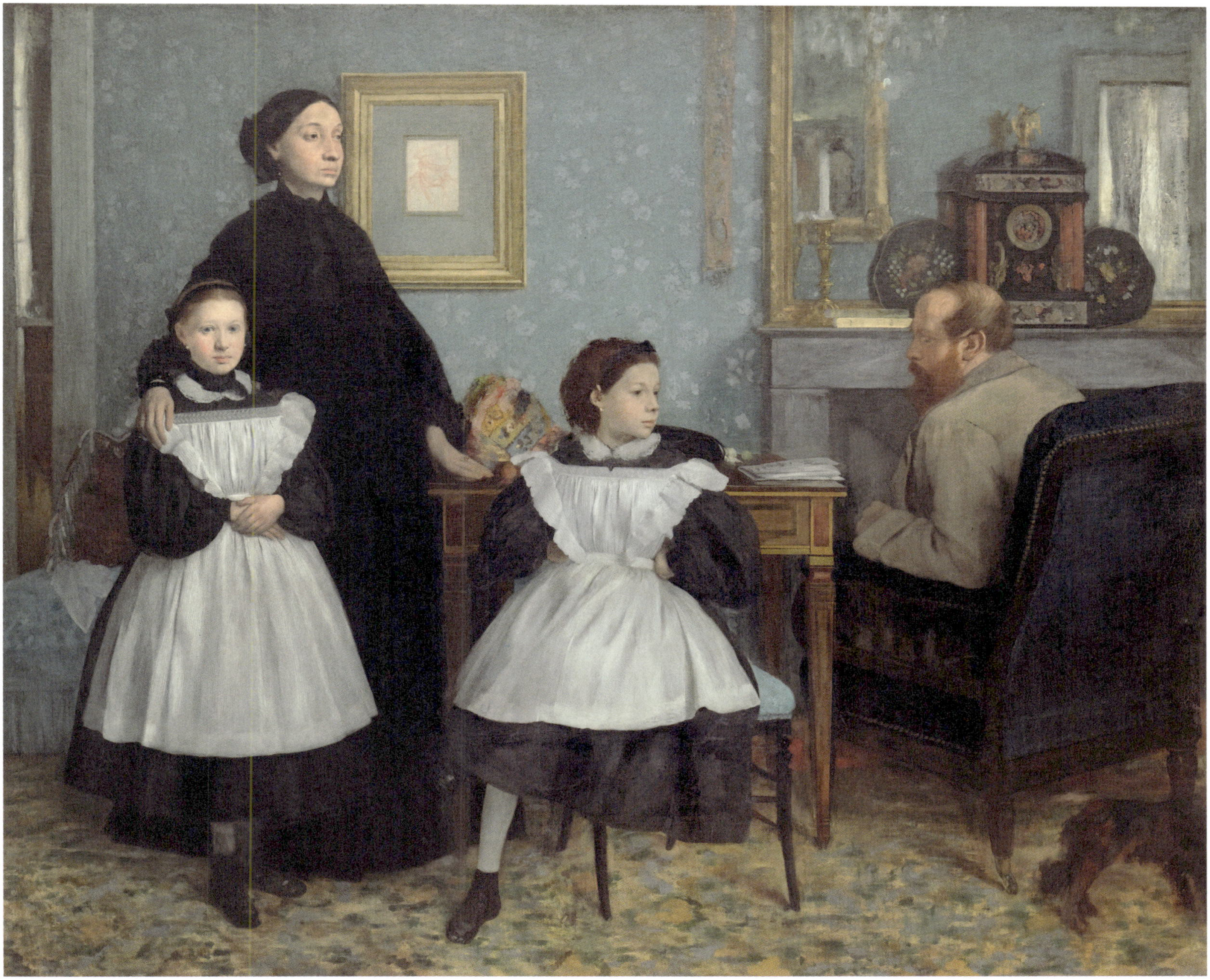

51 Edgar Degas, *Portrait de famille* (*Family Portrait*),
also known as *La Famille Bellelli* (*The Bellelli Family*), 1858–1869
Oil on canvas, 79 ⅛ × 98 ¼ in. (201 × 249.5 cm)

Edgar Degas
The Orchestra of the Opéra

One of Degas's favorite themes took pictorial shape at the very end of the Second Empire, as if he sensed that the "imperial party" was nearing its end. A music lover who mingled with musicians and fellow enthusiasts, he was a regular at the opera house on Rue Le Peletier, until it burned down in 1873. This painting was probably commissioned by the bassoonist Désiré Dihau, its central figure; it remained in his family's ownership for many years. The composition does not reflect the position he would have been assigned in the orchestra pit. The French national museums acquired the work from Dihau's daughter in 1935, through a special financial arrangement in recognition of its historical importance. Art-historical criticism has viewed Degas's decisive step here in various ways, most often celebrating the fact that he had at last turned away from traditional subjects and embraced aspects of specifically modern life. His notebooks contain countless musings on the aesthetic path that he decided to take in the late 1860s. In them, we read of his desire to "make portraits of people in familiar and typical poses, and especially to give their faces the same expressive possibilities that are given to their bodies."[10] But his quest for truth and modernity did not lead him to the realism of Courbet's followers. The painting is highly composed, with strong and expressive draftsmanship, organized into a geometrical interlocking of spaces that would eventually bring clusters of colorful tutus exploding into the spotlight. S. G.

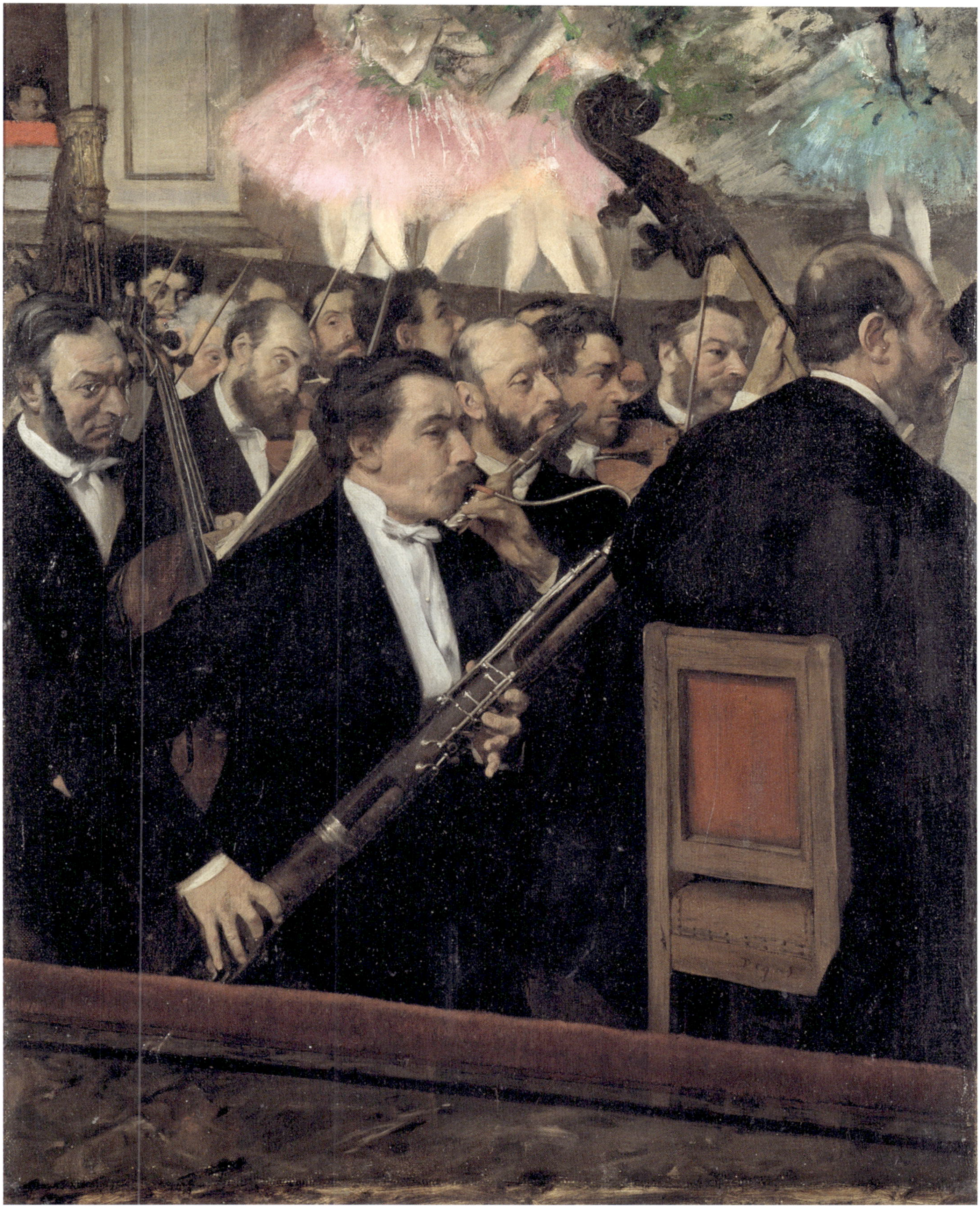

52 Edgar Degas, *L'Orchestre de l'Opéra*
(*The Orchestra of the Opéra*), c. 1870
Oil on canvas, 22 5⁄16 × 18 1⁄8 in. (56.6 × 46 cm)

Édouard Manet
The Balcony

Painted in the winter of 1868–1869, *The Balcony* was the last of a cycle of Manet's work that focused on Spanish or religious themes. He had recently got to know Morisot, whose alluring personality was certainly a contributing factor. We see her here commanding her new friend's brush for the first time. Resting her forearm on the garish green metal railing, she lets her beautiful, dark eyes wander askance—a true "femme fatale," as she said herself. The other two figures, who are looking in different directions, reinforce the overall tone of an elegant social milieu. The man, identifiable as the landscape painter Antoine Guillemet, strikes a distinguished pose as he smokes his cigarette; a young woman, the violinist Fanny Claus, is either putting her gloves on or taking them off, an eminently sensual gesture. Goya had already associated the theme of the balcony with female seduction—not necessarily positively—and had likewise kept the balcony's fixtures hidden, so that it aligned with the picture plane. Manet loved to play with perspectives and with moments frozen in time. The press in 1869 declared its repugnance at the colors and brushwork: "The coloring, at once pallid and garish, produces an effect on the eye akin to that of a rasping saw on the ear," wrote *La Gazette de France*. Morisot responded to Monet's detractors with irony: "As always, his paintings create the impression of a wild or even slightly unripe fruit. I find them far from displeasing." On Manet's death, *The Balcony* entered the collection of Caillebotte, himself a painter of frozen and sometimes unsettled moments. S.G.

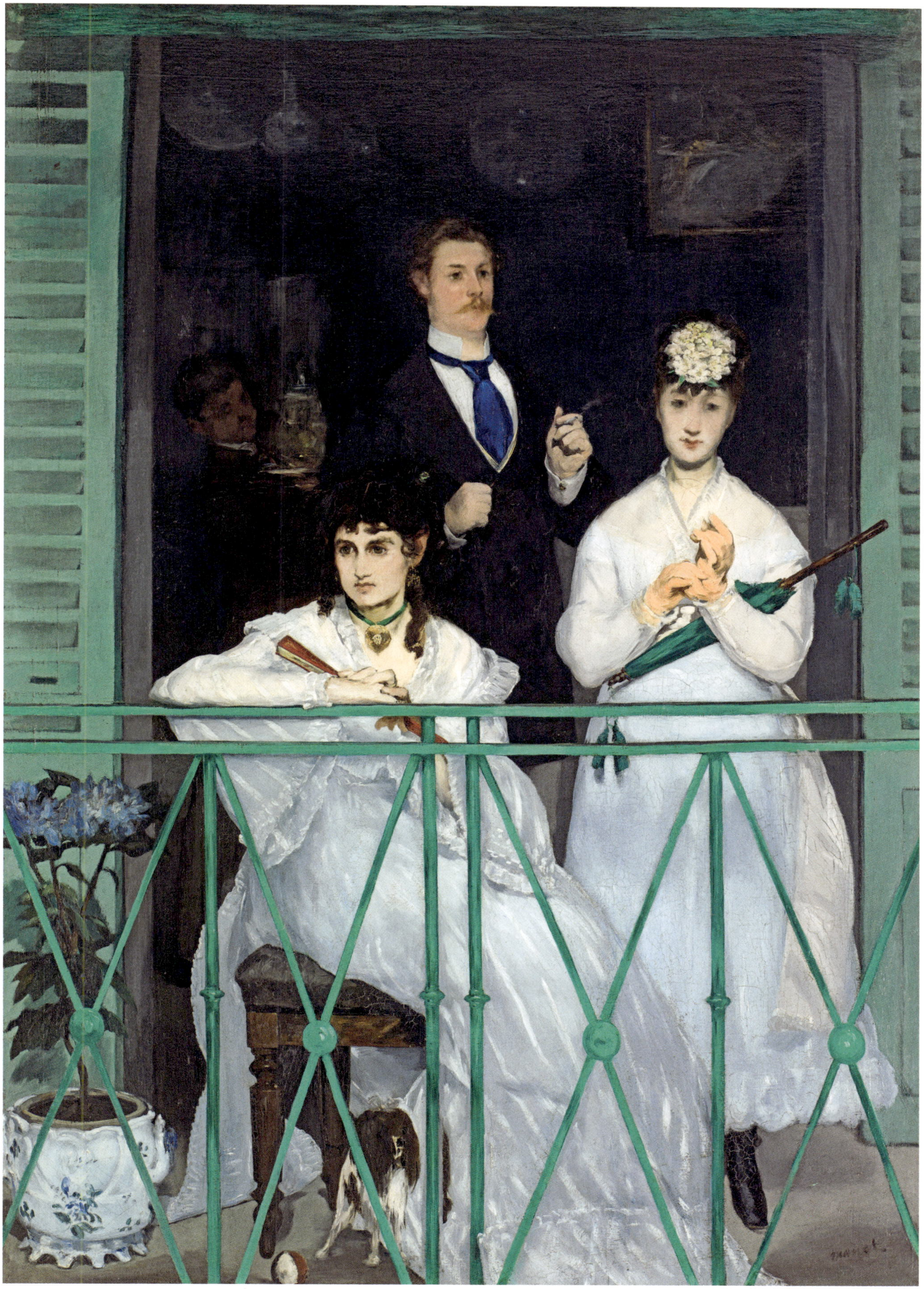

53 Édouard Manet, *Le Balcon* (*The Balcony*), 1868–1869
Oil on canvas, 66 15⁄16 × 49 3⁄16 in. (170 × 125 cm)

Paul Cézanne
Achille Emperaire

Long ridiculed by critics and ostracized by museums, Cézanne's early style was re-evaluated in the late 1980s. These unique paintings—some extremely dark, others intensely Venetian—graphically portray scenes of rape, brutal murder, orgiastic banquets, or frenzied sea bathing. It is difficult to compare them to anything else, other than to cite some of the painters whom the young artist from Aix-en-Provence admired: Delacroix, Courbet, Zurbarán, Tintoretto, and early-1860s Manet. "We are striding at pace toward Manetism,"[11] wrote Marius Roux, a friend of Cézanne's, in 1868. Scorning "commercial painting" and its deplorable details, he raised the stakes by betting on fully frontal compositions, implacable realism, and underlying irony. Everything was pushed "to the extreme," as the novelist and journalist Émile Zola, another friend of his, wrote. Cézanne did not have to go against his own nature to produce such an image of Achille Emperaire, a painter he knew who was part of the circle of Baudelairean poets that these spirited artists attracted. Intended for the Salon of 1870, where it was rejected, the portrait makes no attempt to conceal the sitter's dwarfism, nor the incongruity of his attire, which perhaps refers to a portrait of Napoleon I, "the emperor," that Ingres painted in 1806. It should be seen as a satirical nod to Napoleon III. Cézanne's republican leanings burst into view after the fall of the Empire and the rebirth of Marianne, the national personification of the French Republic, on September 4, 1870. S.G.

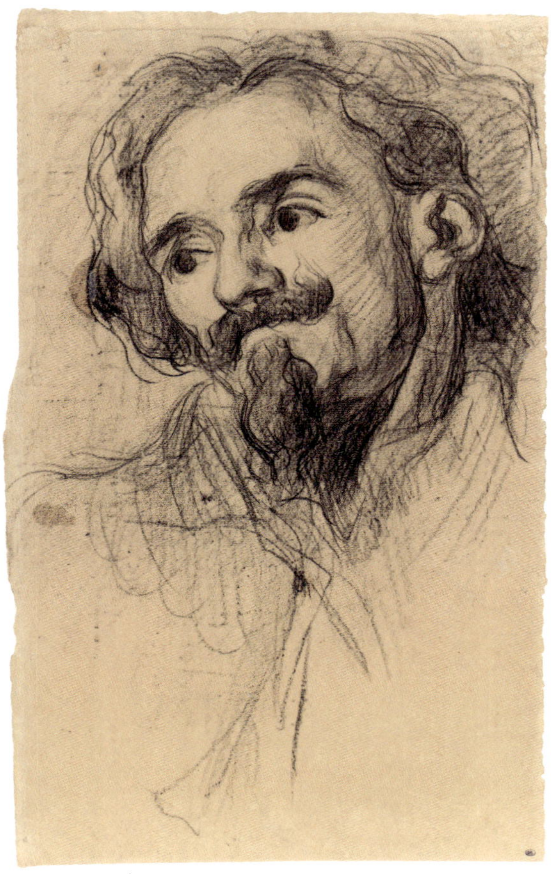

54 Paul Cézanne, *Portrait d'Achille Emperaire* (*Portrait of Achille Emperaire*), c. 1867–1870
Charcoal and graphite on mounted buff paper, 19 × 12 ⅛ in. (48.2 × 30.8 cm)

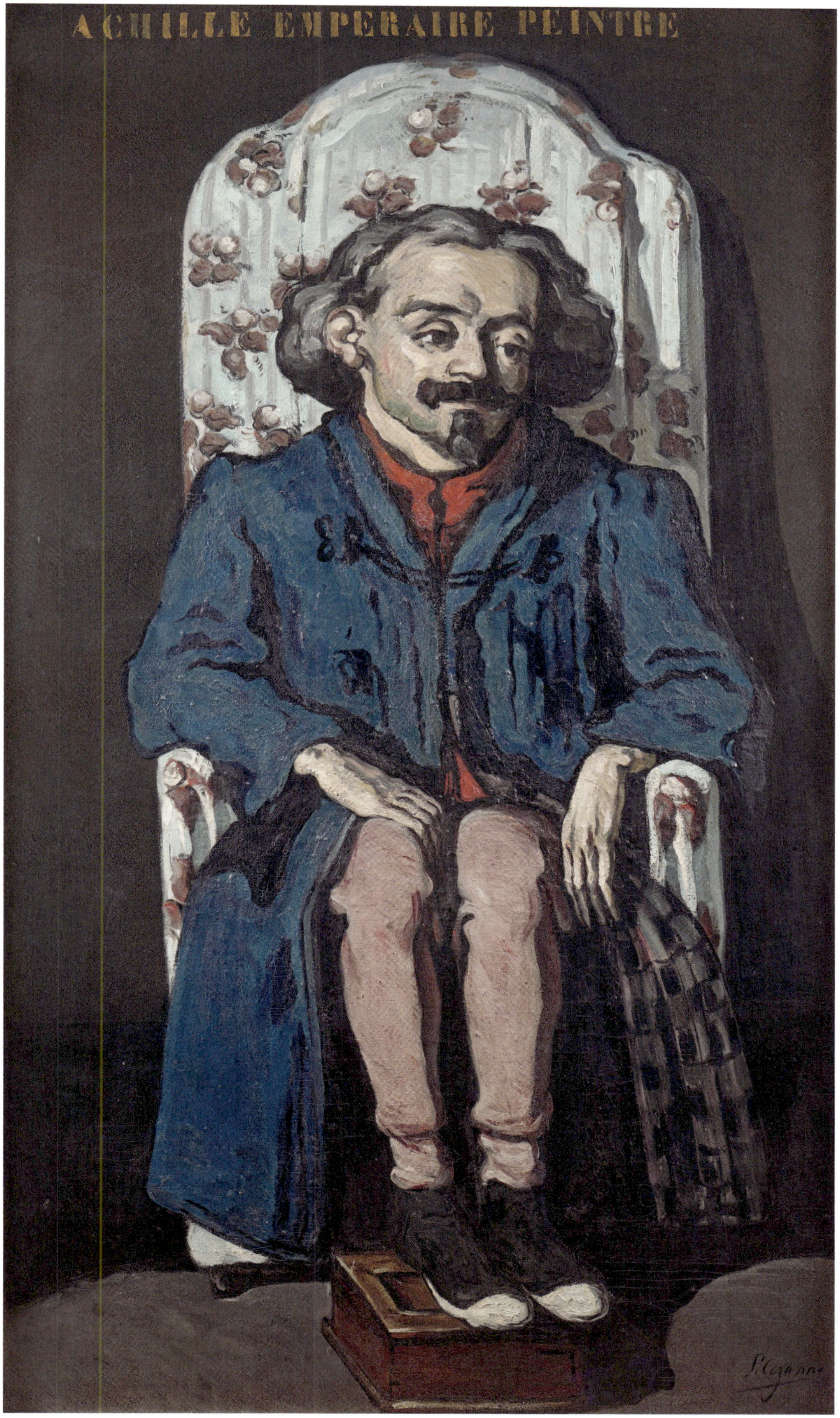

55 Paul Cézanne, *Achille Emperaire*, 1867–1868
Oil on canvas, 79 ⅛ × 47 ⅝ in. (201 × 121 cm)

Henri Fantin-Latour
A Studio at Les Batignolles

Shown at the 1870 Salon, the painting was likened by some to a rather stiff group photograph, and by others to the specifically Nordic tradition of male gatherings. Ever since the late eighteenth century, images of artists' studios or of artists gathered together had been signaling their increasing freedom from the old system of patronage. Courbet's *The Painter's Studio* (1855; Musée d'Orsay, Paris), powerfully proclaimed this too. Fifteen years later, it was the turn of the new generation of Realists. The 1870 painting was undertaken following the 1865 Salon, where Manet and Fantin-Latour—the former with his *Olympia* (p. 17), the latter with *The Toast!*—had both fallen flat.

Fantin-Latour hesitated over the painting's composition and whom to depict in it. Any female figures disappeared from the preparatory drawings at a fairly early stage. The final painting extols the authority that Manet had acquired in that late Second Empire period. Jesus amid his disciples, sneered a caricature. Manet holds sway in the center, his face bathed in light. He is shown in action, brush and palette in hand—a nod to Velázquez and his *Las Meninas*. Zacharie Astruc, whose portrait he is painting, dutifully holds his pose. Behind Manet we can recognize Otto Scholderer, a German painter who admired Courbet. Then come Renoir (wearing a hat), Zola, the Wagnerian writer and musician Edmond Maître, and lastly Bazille and Monet (at the back). The atmosphere is a contrasting mixture of monastic fervor and individual solitariness. "Each of them," wrote the art critic Philippe Burty at the time, "is immersed in his own thoughts." We know today that not all of "Manet's friends" admired him quite as much as Fantin-Latour did. S.G.

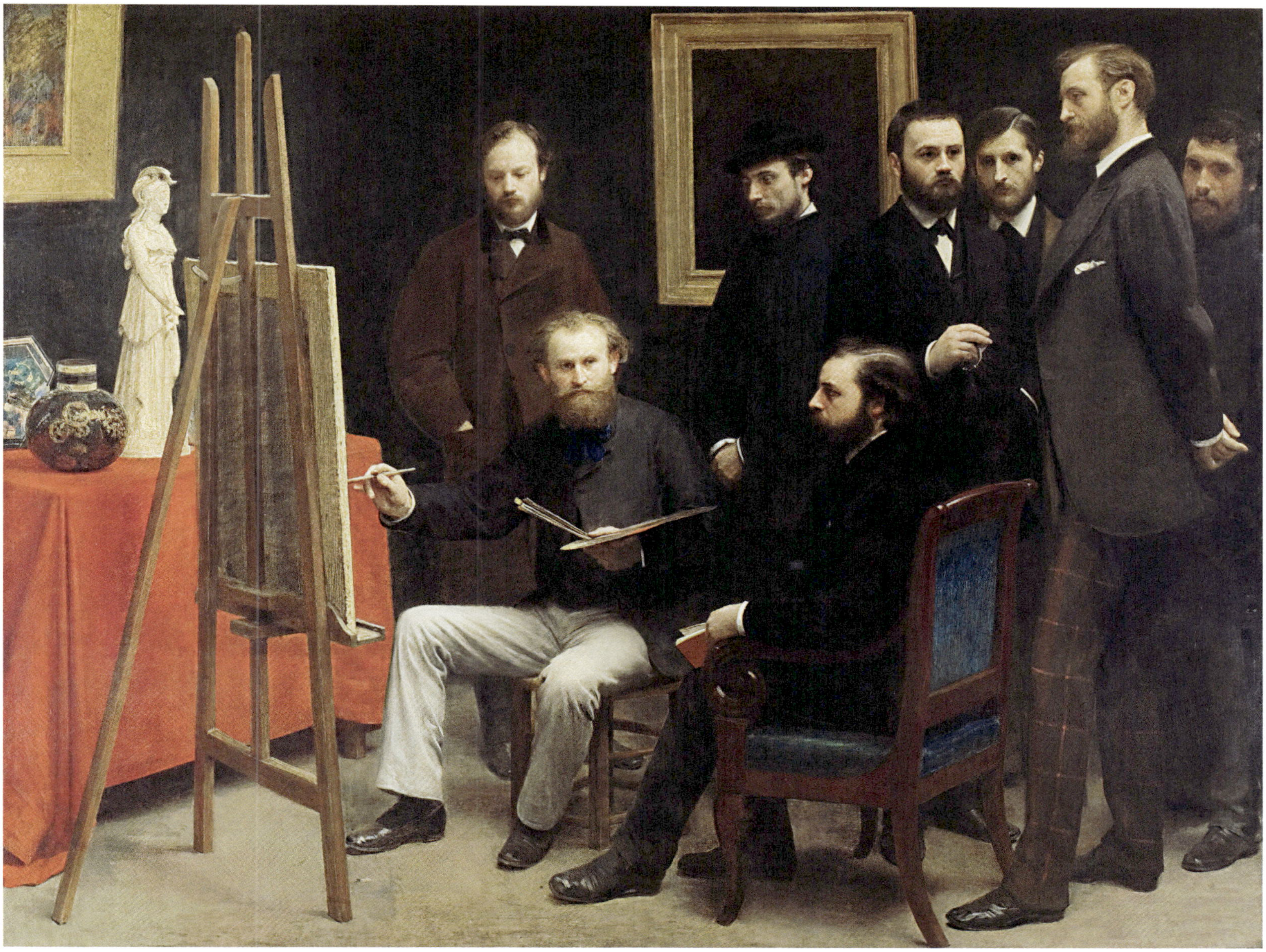

56 Henri Fantin-Latour, *Un atelier aux Batignolles* (*A Studio at Les Batignolles*), 1870
Oil on canvas, 80 5⁄16 × 107 11⁄16 in. (204 × 273.5 cm)

Frédéric Bazille
Bazille's Studio

Since his arrival in Paris, Bazille had persistently asked his parents for a studio to work in. Between 1863 and 1870, he occupied six of them. Three of these spawned interior views that are also inverted self-portraits—manifestoes of this new life as an artist, which Bazille so cherished. In early 1868 he set himself up along with Renoir in a new, more spacious studio in the Batignolles neighborhood, which was undergoing a major metamorphosis at the time. It was not far from the Café Guerbois, where the whole Realist avant-garde would get together: Fantin-Latour, Degas, Manet, plus the writers Zola, Astruc, and Duranty.

In response to Fantin-Latour's *A Studio at Les Batignolles* (p. 67), over the winter of 1869–1870 Bazille painted a view of his studio, this time featuring the cheerful presence of his friends. The tall central figure of Bazille was painted by Manet, the younger generation's mentor. Standing with Bazille, looking at the painting on the easel, are Manet himself and perhaps Monet or the critic Zacharie Astruc. Edmond Maître is playing the piano, while Renoir, partway up the stairs, is talking to a man below who may be Sisley or Monet. The studio is very simply furnished: a Voltaire armchair, a piano, and of course canvases by Bazille and Renoir, constitute the young men's only treasured possessions. Many of the paintings on the studio's walls were rejected by the jury of the Salon, but this little group of rebellious bohemian artists liked to define itself by its independence from institutions and prevailing tastes. The modern studio was a place not just for working but also for exhibitions, socializing, forming an artist "collective," and, clearly, subject matter for paintings, with the particular challenge of representing an interior with daylight flooding in through a large studio window.

In April 1870, Bazille moved to a new studio in the same building as Fantin-Latour's, on Rue des Beaux-Arts. This time he was the sole occupant. In August that year, against the wishes of his family and friends, he signed up to fight in the Franco-Prussian War. He was killed at Beaune-la-Rolande on November 28, aged twenty-eight. P. P.

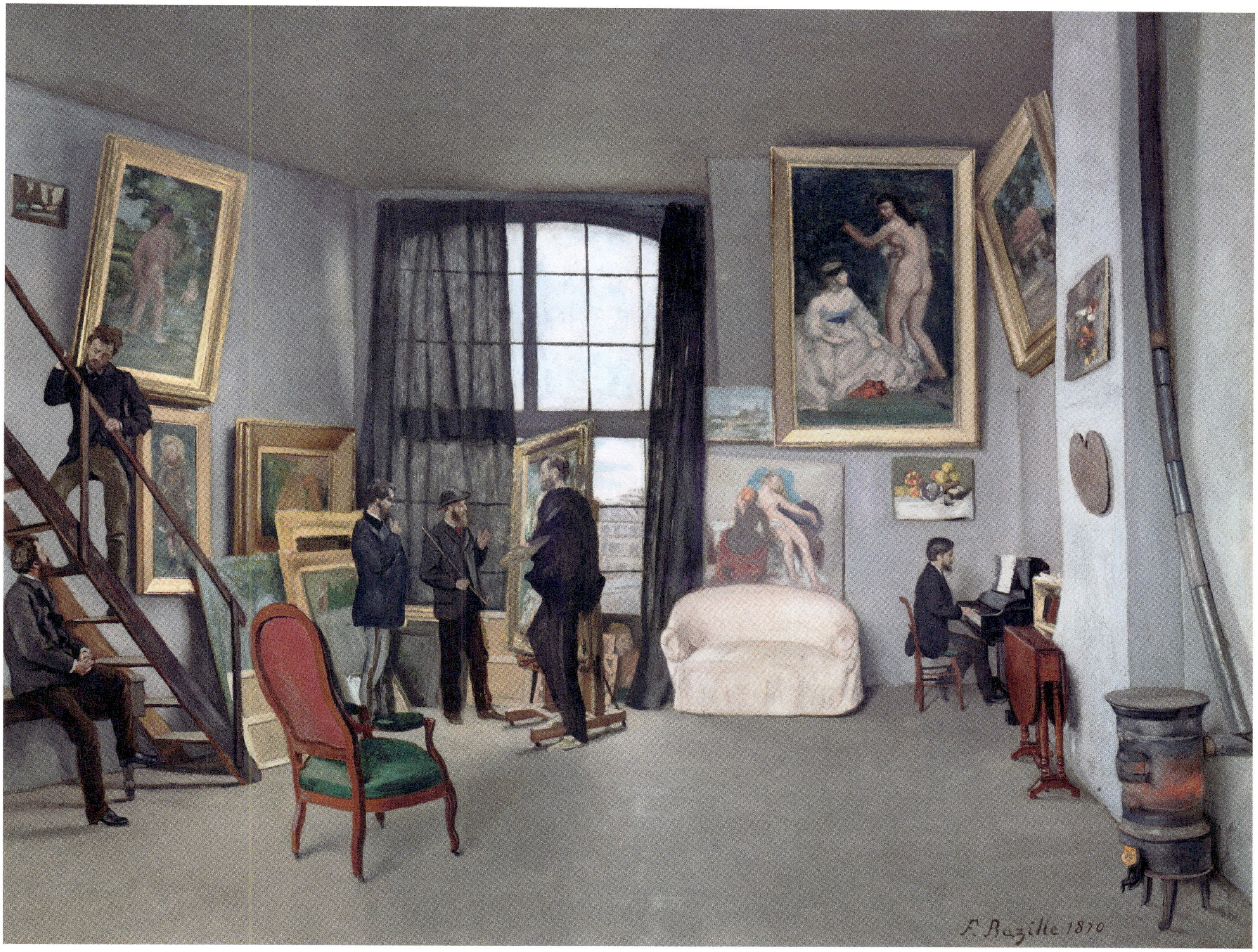

57 Frédéric Bazille, *L'Atelier de Bazille* (*Bazille's Studio*), also known as *L'Atelier de la rue La Condamine* (*The Studio on Rue La Condamine*), 1869–1870
Oil on canvas, 38 9/16 × 50 3/8 in. (98 × 128 cm)

1870

War and exile

The Franco-Prussian War of 1870–1871, culminating in France's humiliating defeat, profoundly shook the country. Napoleon III surrendered at Sedan on September 2, 1870; two days later, the Third Republic was proclaimed and a Government of National Defense was formed. While some artists remained in Paris and joined the National Guard, such as Manet, and others enlisted and fell as heroes on the front, like Bazille who died aged twenty-eight, many took the path of exile. Among them was Monet, who fled to London sometime between mid-September and early October 1870 to avoid conscription. He was joined there by his wife Camille Doncieux and their three-year-old son, Jean. In early December, Pissarro also arrived in London, with his partner Julie Vellay and their two children, their house in Louveciennes being occupied by Prussian troops. Most of Pissarro's works, and some of Monet's, were destroyed there. Sisley's house in Bougival met the same fate in the autumn of 1870, and the bulk of his oeuvre was unceremoniously destroyed by the Prussians.

Being in such dire straits, Monet produced only two paintings during his stay in London. However, he also met the art dealer Paul Durand-Ruel there, he too having fled France. This encounter proved pivotal, and likewise for Pissarro, as Durand-Ruel was to become the Impressionists' main supporter. One of the very few paintings that testify to Monet's period in exile is *Meditation: Madame Monet on the Sofa*, which shows Camille in their Kensington apartment. A fan, a Japanese vase, and a painting glimpsed at the center constitute the simple décor of their temporary residence. Cold light infuses the scene and highlights the young woman's forlorn expression as she sits there lost in thought, her hands resting around a London guidebook in her lap. In May 1871, Monet left London for the Netherlands, not returning to France until October or November. Excited by the Dutch countryside, he painted no fewer than twenty-four landscapes of Zaandam, including this view of the Zaan flanked by picturesque green houses, with the church and the city hall in the distance—a painting that Durand-Ruel bought from him and which made its way into Étienne Moreau-Nélaton's collection. The impact of the war was a subtext of Monet's depictions of the reconstruction of the Pont d'Argenteuil, the original bridge having been destroyed by bombing in 1870. C.C.-P.

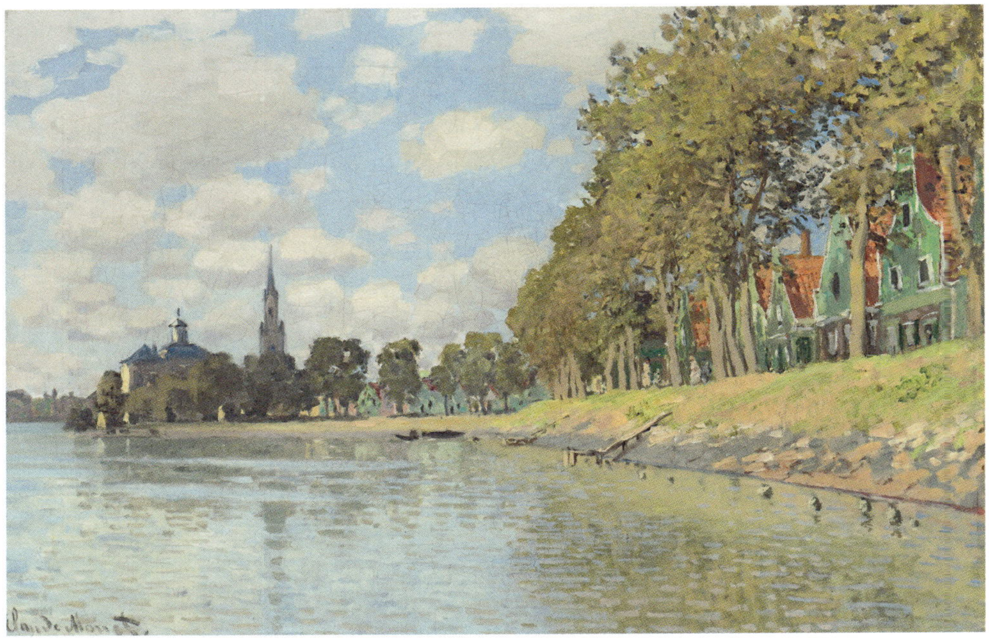

58 Claude Monet, *Zaandam*, 1871
Oil on canvas,
18 13/16 × 28 3/4 in. (47.8 × 73 cm)

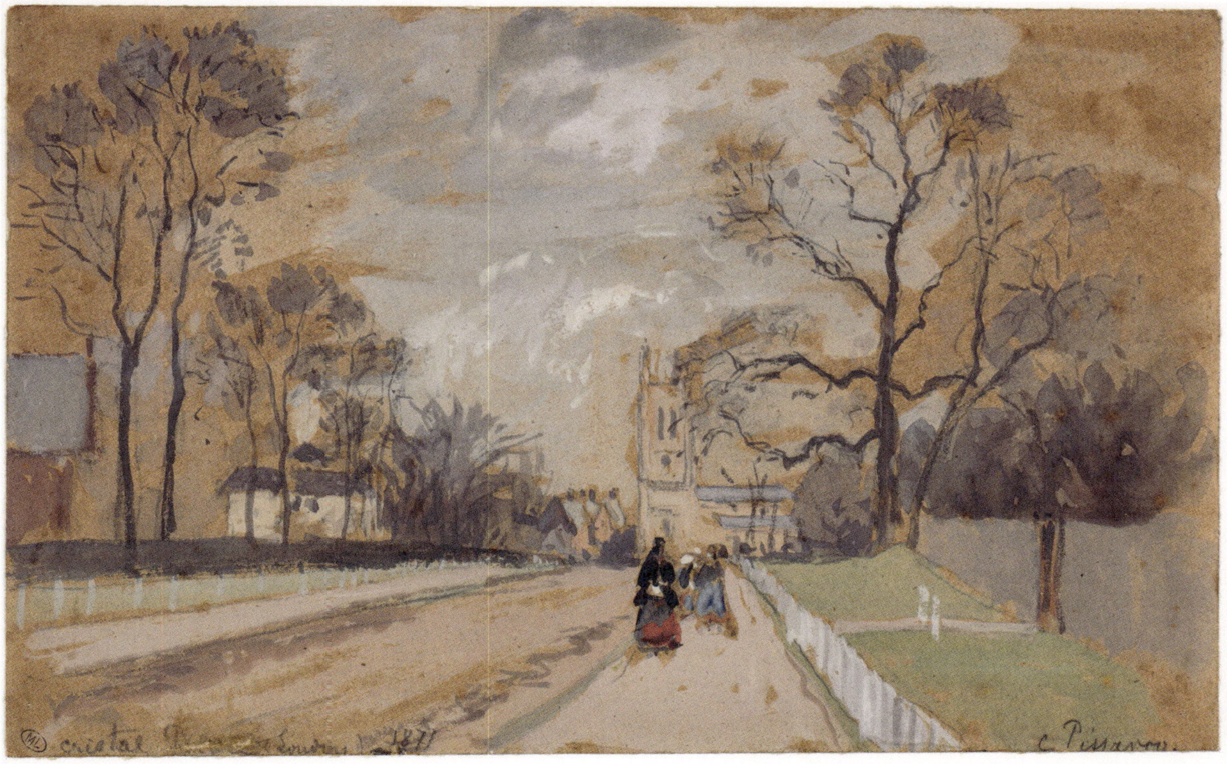

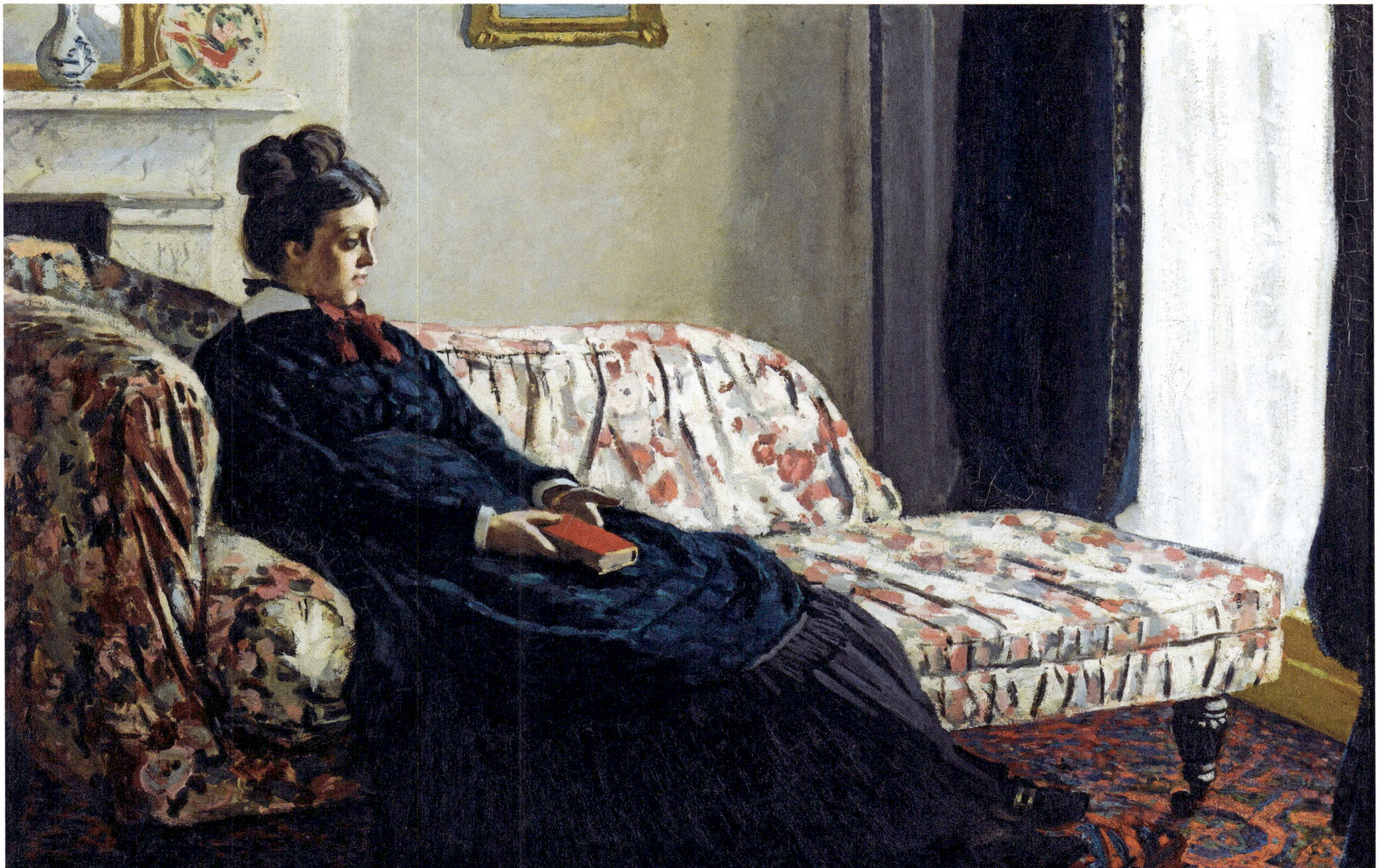

59 Top: Camille Pissarro, *La Route de Sydenham, Londres* (*The Avenue, Sydenham, London*), 1871
Gouache over pencil lines on paper, $5\frac{7}{8} \times 9\frac{11}{16}$ in. (15 × 24.6 cm)

60 Bottom: Claude Monet, *Méditation. Madame Monet au canapé* (*Meditation: Madame Monet on the Sofa*), c. 1871
Oil on canvas, $19 \times 29\frac{5}{16}$ in. (48.2 × 74.5 cm)

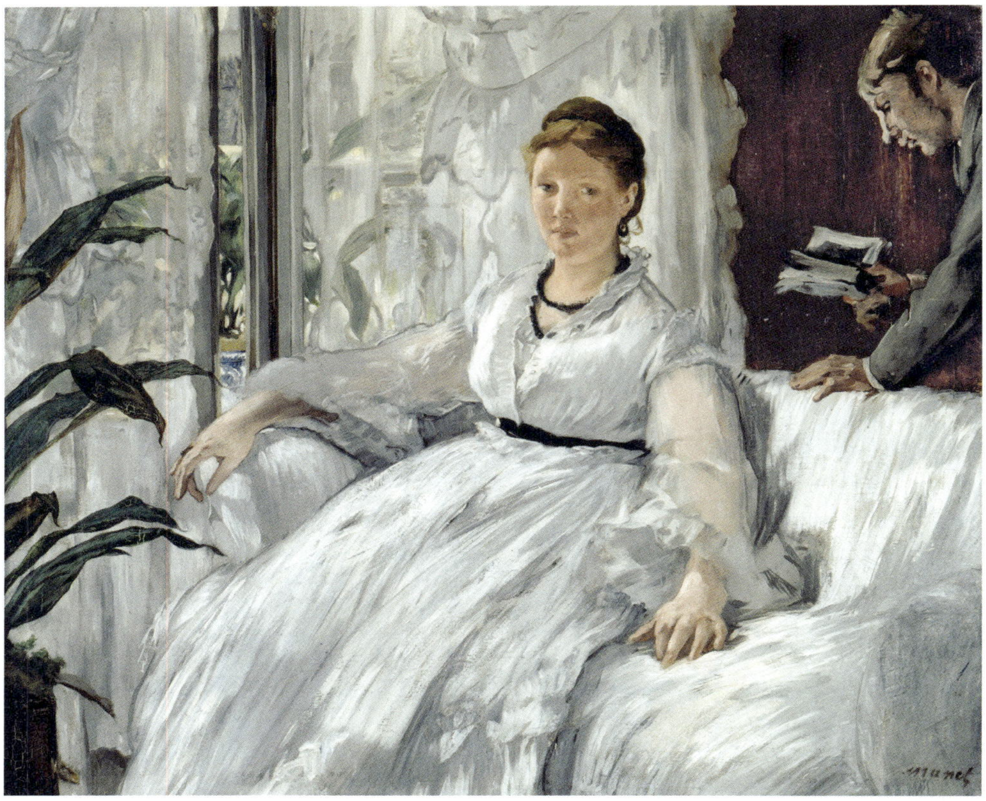

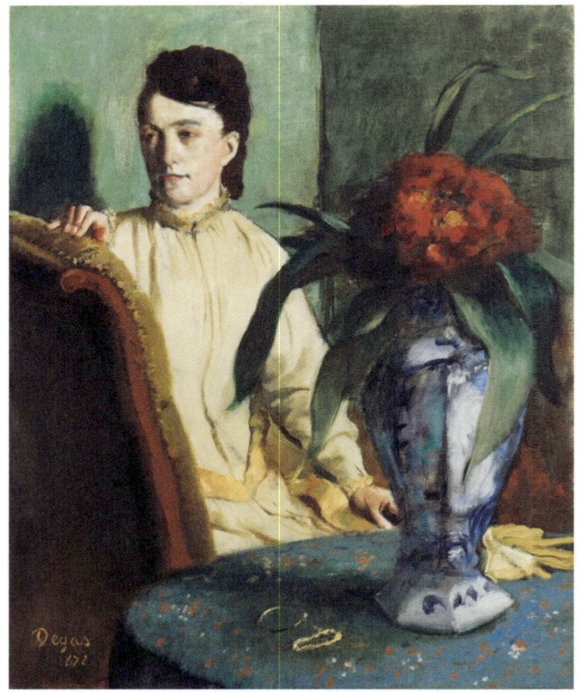

61 Left: Édouard Manet, *La Lecture* (*Reading*), 1865–1873
Oil on canvas, 24 × 28 13/16 in. (61 × 73.2 cm)

62 Right: Edgar Degas, *La Femme à la potiche* (*Woman with Porcelain Vase*), 1872
Oil on canvas, 25 9/16 × 21 1/4 in. (65 × 54 cm)

Private moments

The “New Painting” movement extensively recorded the private sphere, and in doing so helped elevate this major phenomenon of post-revolutionary France. From the time of the Directory government in the late 1790s, artists started to focus on scenes of domestic contentment and chronicling family life. There was therefore some continuity through to Manet, Degas, and Morisot, who also were all connoisseurs of eighteenth-century art, and who notably examined the status of women in the middle classes—lower and upper—from which they themselves originated. Manet’s marriage to his brothers’ former piano teacher, Suzanne Leenhoff, constituted a revolt against his native milieu, even though they had waited until after his father’s death. Painted two years later, *Reading* endows Suzanne with beauty and nobility, presenting her like a Renaissance princess, dressed in white chiffon and wearing a wedding ring. Léon, their son, whom he added around 1872, leans toward her ear, as if he has just read a passage that he is keen to share with his mother. In that year, Degas was staying with members of his mother’s side of the family in New Orleans and producing a series of portraits with his distinctive approach that refuses to flatter either the sitter or their domestic setting in any way. The one shown here may be of Estelle Musson, a cousin of his, who was still single at the time. Wearing a beige house dress with golden trim, she is seated in the background of the painting, looking over the back of her armchair which Degas uses to indicate unease, further reinforced by her awkward facial expression. Shadow competes with light, and openness with sadness. Despite the light enlivening the pair of gloves and the discreet pieces of jewelry on the table, the whole confirms the painter’s commitment to his disdain for conventional prettiness. The young woman whom Morisot observes powdering her face is completely different. With brushwork inspired by Fragonard, the painting, which was exhibited in 1880 at the fifth Impressionist exhibition, fondly enfolds its subject in milky-white tones and subtle fragrances. S.G.

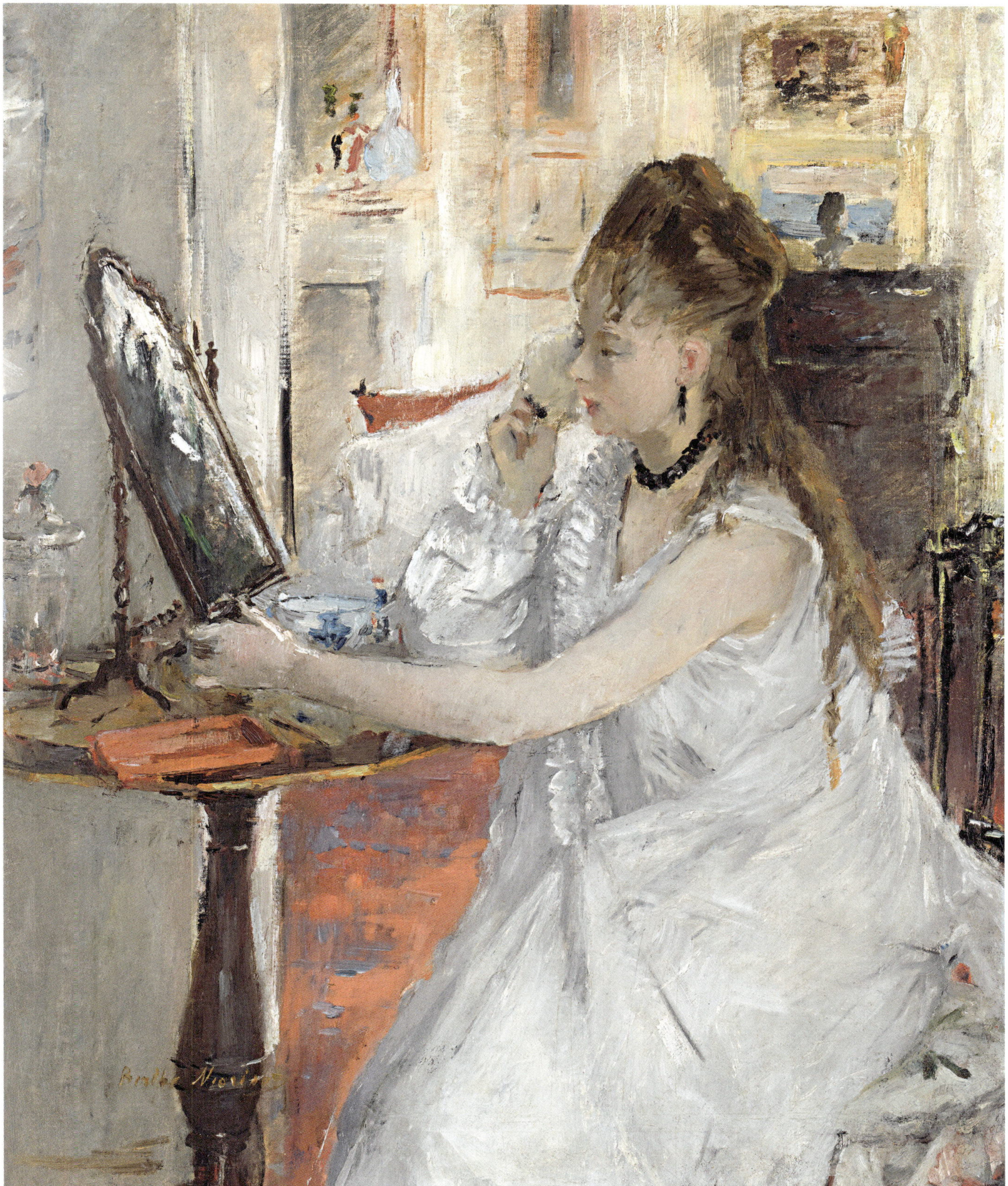

63 Berthe Morisot, *Jeune femme se poudrant*
(*Young Woman Powdering Her Face*), 1877
Oil on canvas, 18 ⅛ × 15 ⅜ in. (46 × 39 cm)

Édouard Manet
Berthe Morisot

Édouard Manet and Berthe Morisot got to know each other through the musical soirées that served as key opportunities for France's nineteenth-century elites to socialize fairly freely. People of both sexes from the same milieu would form firm friendships and perhaps develop romantic attachments—reciprocated or otherwise. We sense that Manet, who married in late 1863, was playing with fire here. It was around then that Tiburce Morisot moved into a house on Rue Franklin with his wife and their four children; at that stage, the surrounding sixteenth arrondissement had not undergone major urbanization. He was a senior adviser to the Cour des Comptes (France's State auditing body), and had a studio built for Edma and Berthe, who received a good training and made their Salon debut in 1864. It was Fantin-Latour who introduced Manet to the sisters, on encountering them one day in the Louvre. Berthe Morisot's correspondence provides extensive evidence of how close the two became. Manet, nine years her elder, was generous with both advice and introductions to art-world contacts. Their undoubtedly strong mutual attraction is evident in *The Balcony* (p. 63). Morisot embodies the status and seductiveness of the depressive Parisienne, being one herself, in around a dozen more intimate paintings that show her sporting Spanish-style dress (fan, uncovered hair) or in a spirit of melancholy ranging from wistful to devastated. She does not act as a model, striking a pose; it is Morisot herself, and her changing moods, that Manet is observing. He plays on her coquettishness, and captures her somewhere between her self-perceived ugliness and the clearly irresistible charm that he sees in her. Her gaze from behind her fan is a metaphor for this visual flirtation. Commenting on *Berthe Morisot with a Bunch of Violets*, Paul Valéry describes a "big-eyed face with a vaguely fixed expression that appears deeply distracted and in a sense offers a *presence of absence*." Manet's painting is suffused with this. S.G.

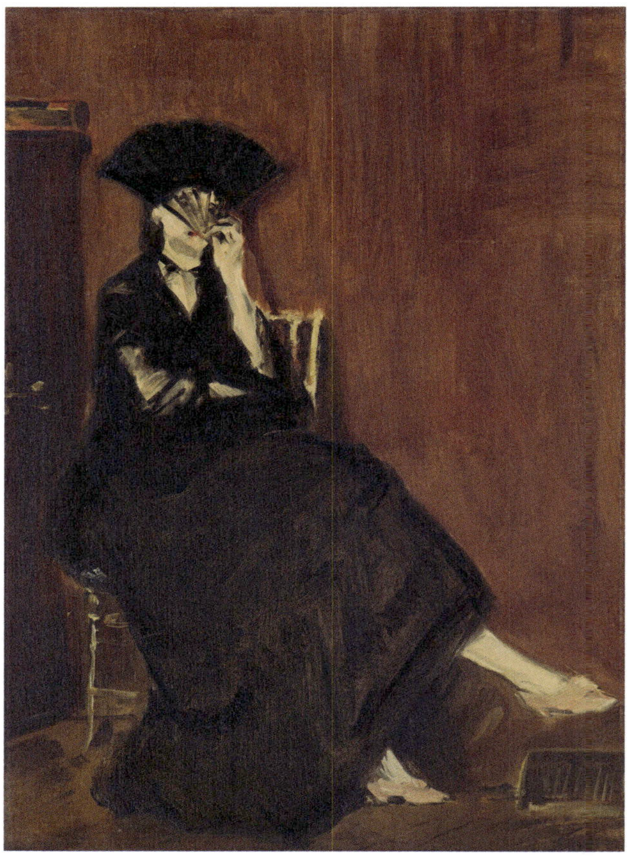

64 Édouard Manet, *Portrait de Berthe Morisot à l'éventail* (*Portrait of Berthe Morisot with a Fan*), 1874
Oil on canvas, 24 3/16 × 19 7/8 in. (61 × 50.5 cm)

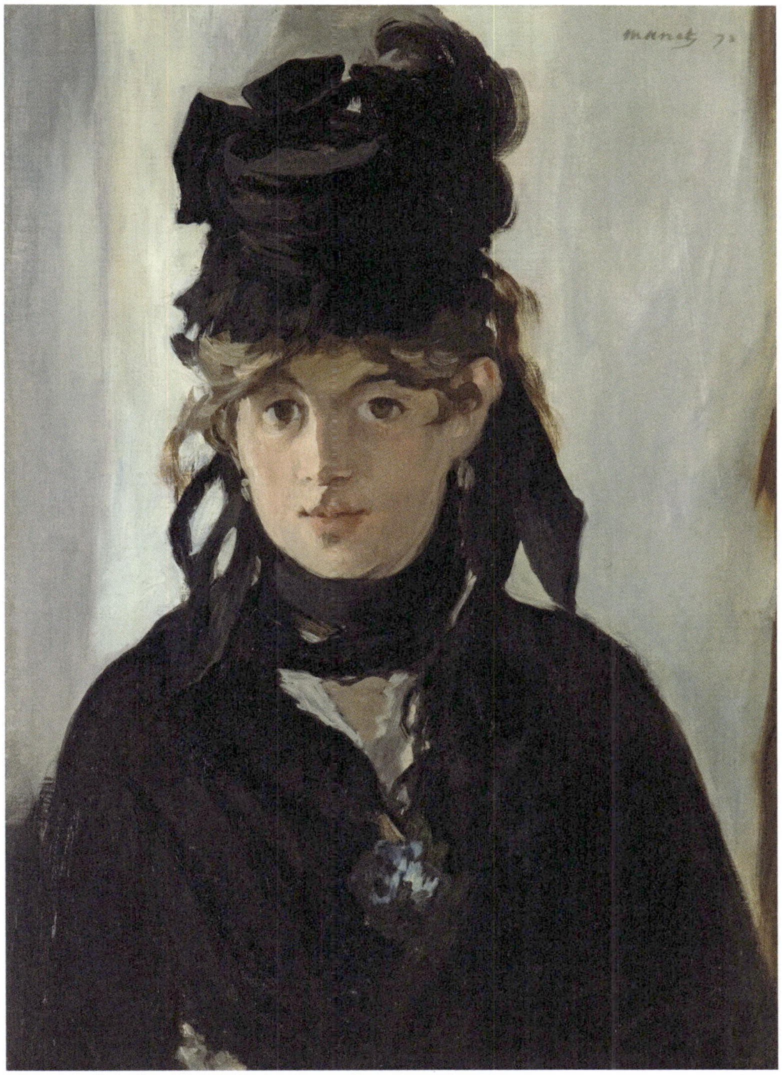

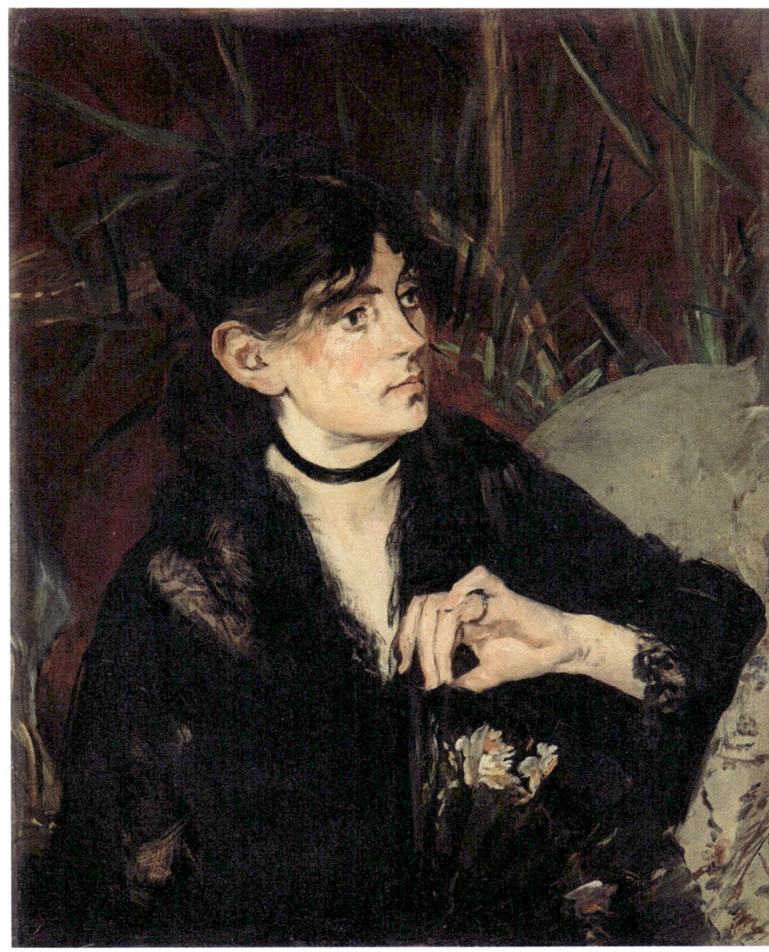

65 Left: Édouard Manet, *Berthe Morisot au bouquet de violettes* (*Berthe Morisot with a Bunch of Violets*), 1872
Oil on canvas, 21 ⅞ × 15 15⁄16 in. (55.5 × 40.5 cm)

66 Right: Édouard Manet, *Berthe Morisot à l'éventail* (*Berthe Morisot with a Fan*), 1872
Oil on canvas, 23 ¾ × 17 13⁄16 in. (60.4 × 45.2 cm)

Berthe Morisot
Portrait of Madame Edma Pontillon

Edma Pontillon, Berthe Morisot's elder sister, had received art training under Joseph Guichard and then Camille Corot, like Berthe. Unquestionably talented, she had exhibited her canvases at the Salon every year from 1864 until 1868 alongside her sister. However, she had given up any aspirations to an artistic career after her marriage to the naval officer Adolphe Pontillon in 1869 and the birth of her first child, Jeanne, in 1870.

Morisot produced this pastel the following year, when Edma was housebound shortly before the birth of her second daughter, Blanche (p. 79). The portrait constitutes a very rare depiction of a pregnant woman within the history of Western art in the second half of the nineteenth century. The young woman's rounded belly, which is barely noticeable at first due to her black dress (a fashion that women adopted in their droves after the heavy losses suffered through France's crushing defeat in the Franco-Prussian War), is however emphasized by Edma's hands, which rest over her unborn child.

This was the third of almost two hundred pastels that Morisot produced. Even so, it already reveals her at ease with the medium, and shows her ability to create varying effects with it. Here, she used it wet and thickly for Edma's face and employed a brush to work on the floral motifs of the couch. As for the background, it is treated as a flat plane of color, in pale gray—an approach that her friend and future brother-in-law Édouard Manet also favored. C. C.-P.

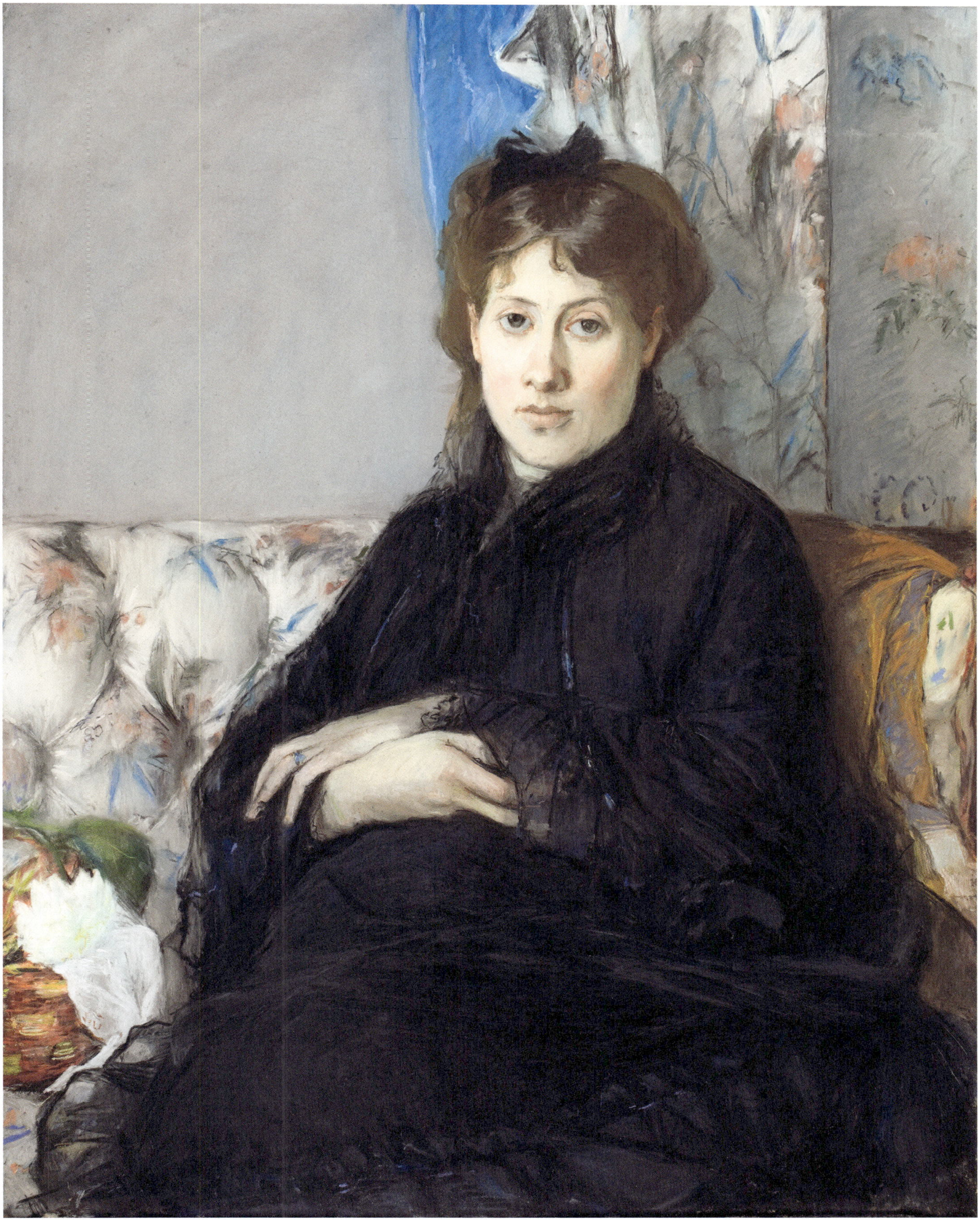

67 Berthe Morisot, *Portrait de Madame Edma Pontillon, née Edma Morisot, sœur de l'artiste* (*Portrait of Madame Edma Pontillon, née Edma Morisot, the Artist's Sister*), 1871
Pastel on paper, 32 1⁄16 × 25 7⁄8 in. (81.5 × 65.8 cm)

Berthe Morisot
The Cradle

The young woman who is attentively keeping watch over her sleeping baby here is none other than Morisot's sister, Edma Pontillon (p. 77). This autobiographical dimension indicates the close bond between the two sisters, who had made their artistic debuts together in the 1860s; it also reveals the heavy restrictions that society placed on women in the nineteenth century, expecting them to limit their lives to domesticity and family life. Marriage and motherhood effectively sounded the death knell of Edma's career, while notions of propriety drove female painters to derive most of their subject matter from the private sphere. Here, Morisot presents a scene from modern life that is typical of the "New Painting," better known from 1874 under the label "Impressionist." It was in that year that a group of artists, including Morisot, organized an independent exhibition where they asserted their desire to paint their contemporaries and capture moments that were a world apart from the artifice of studio stagings. *The Cradle*, which was well received at that first Impressionist exhibition, sums up these new ambitions. Beyond this, the sense of melancholy that the painting exudes also subtly interrogates the ambivalence of the maternal bond, between protectiveness and distance. S. P.

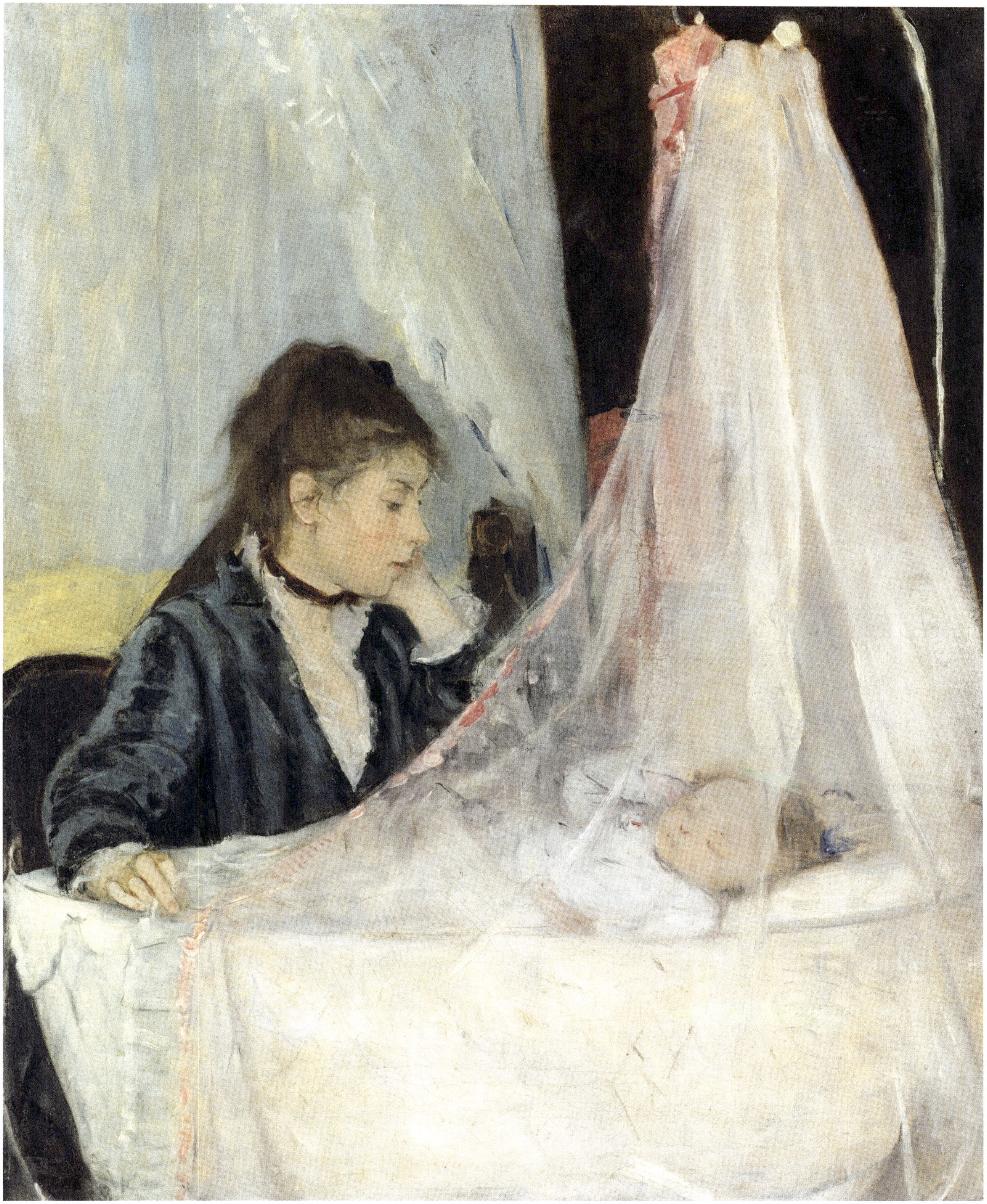

68 Berthe Morisot, *Le Berceau* (*The Cradle*), 1872
Oil on canvas, 22 1⁄16 × 18 5⁄16 in. (56 × 46.5 cm)

Eva Gonzalès
The Pink Morning Gown

Born in Paris, Eva Gonzalès grew up in a refined intellectual milieu. Her mother was French and her father, from Monaco, had Spanish roots. Having first trained under the high-society portraitist Charles Chaplin, she went on to become Manet's first "official" student. She distinguished herself through her portraits and interior scenes, and often used family members as models, including her mother but most often, as here, her sister Jeanne, also an artist. In 1879, Eva married Henri Guérard, who likewise appears in some of her works. She died young, aged just thirty-six, from an embolism after the birth of her first child, Jean.

In this pastel, Gonzalès adopts a color range of pearly grays, pale pinks, and whites: a particular favorite of hers. Her "master," Manet, also favored this palette, although, with the exception of one 1874 work (*Portrait of Madame Édouard Manet on a Blue Sofa,* p. 83), he did not take up this medium until later, no doubt having learned himself from Gonzalès's pastels. Jeanne is portrayed here in a pink negligee, looking at a litter of puppies in their basket. Through her remarkably skillful blending, Gonzalès makes the light from the window a palpable presence as it falls on the young woman at her dressing table, just waking up. This treatment contrasts with the strong, confident contours of her sister's figure and hands, in black and sienna pastel.

This work met with an enthusiastic reception when she exhibited it at the Salon in 1874, the year of her twenty-fifth birthday and of the first Impressionist exhibition. Like Manet, she refused to take part in these independent events. C. C.-P.

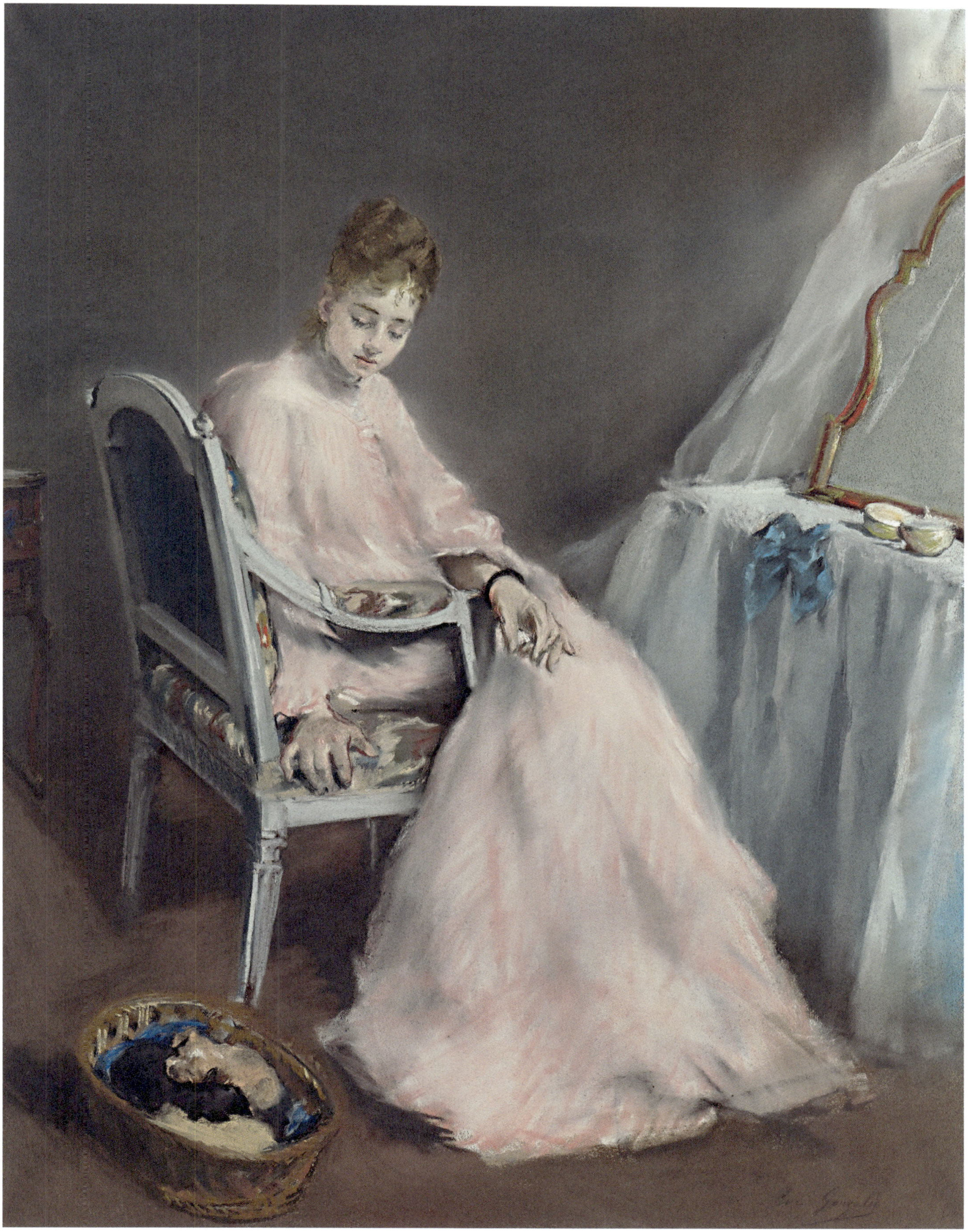

69 Eva Gonzalès, *La Matinée rose* (*The Pink Morning Gown*), 1874
Pastel on paper and stretched canvas, 36 15⁄16 × 29 1⁄4 in. (93.8 × 74.3 cm)

Édouard Manet
Madame Manet on a Blue Sofa

This unusual pastel portrays Manet's wife, Suzanne Leenhoff, reclined on a sofa in the small salon at Rue de Saint-Pétersbourg, where the couple lived between 1872 and 1878. It is Manet's first known pastel, and already displays a mastery of this demanding technique, which he adopted extensively from 1879, using it almost exclusively for his female portraits. Here, he plays with its powdery texture to depict the French-blue velvet of the sofa and to bathe his sitter in light. Her pose mysteriously evokes his *Olympia* (p. 17), although Manet's intentions in this reference to his famous nude remain unclear. Suzanne is depicted lying stiffly in her voluminous clothes, looking directly at the painter, just like Victorine Meurent does in *Olympia*.

After Manet's death, this pastel belonged to Degas, one of his favorite works in his extensive collection. Degas liked to stay in contact with his close friends' wives, and had owned several portraits of Suzanne Leenhoff. The critic Arsène Alexandre described him as having been "restlessly excited, like a young man is about his first experiences of love"[12] when he acquired this one. C.C.-P.

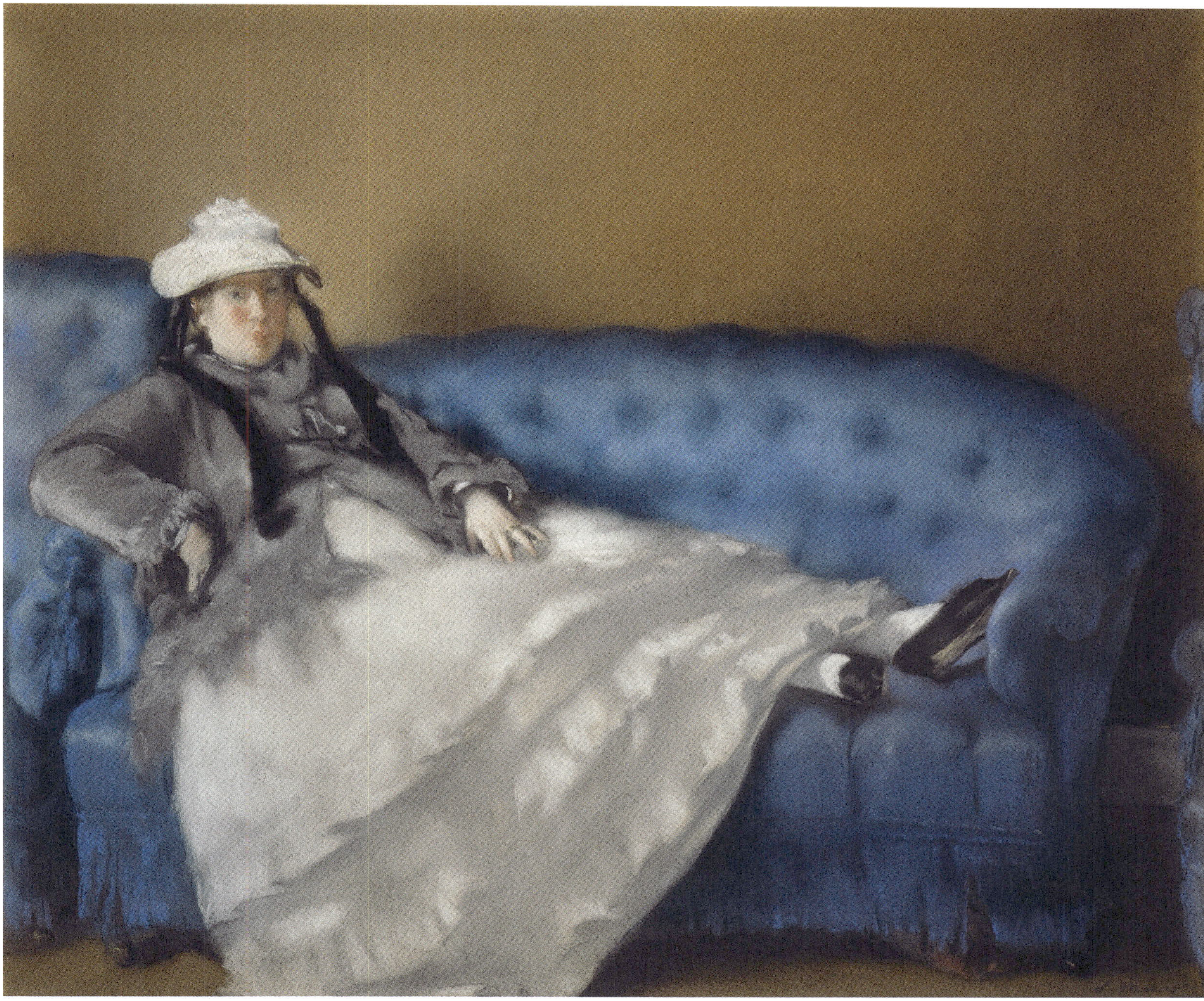

70 Édouard Manet, *Portrait de Madame Édouard Manet sur un canapé bleu* (*Portrait of Madame Édouard Manet on a Blue Sofa*), 1874
Pastel on tan paper mounted on canvas, 19 5/16 × 23 5/8 in. (49 × 60 cm)

Pastels

Pastel found a new momentum and became a favorite experimental medium for the Impressionists. The artists of the second half of the nineteenth century saw it as a way of depicting light, the moment, and the energy of the sensory world, without the constraints of oil painting. With its dry, direct, spontaneous technique, pastel allowed them to capture the changing tones of the sky or the softness of skin, on the spot. As such, it was a perfect match for the Impressionists' quest for visual sincerity and immediacy.

Eugène Boudin, whose ability to "sketch the beauty of the weather" was praised by Baudelaire in his account of the 1859 Salon, was one of the first to understand that pastel could mimic the weightlessness of air and the shifting nature of clouds. His sketches in this medium directly inspired Monet, who found in it an ideal instrument to convey the fleeting reality of atmospheric phenomena, as he did in London, capturing the effects of fog on the Thames. Pissarro also used pastel for his landscapes, while Renoir and Manet (p. 83) embraced it for portraits.

Degas, for his part, found that the versatility of pastel made it the perfect fit for his constant desire to experiment, and he adopted it almost exclusively from the late 1880s (p. 237). He overlayed, scraped back, moistened, and mixed pastel with other techniques, often obtaining the same density as a painting. In his female nudes, the material seems to pulsate (p. 220 and p. 223). His friend and fellow artist Mary Cassatt also accorded pastel a prominent role in her work, making the most of the swift execution that it allows: she sketched women and children, her favorite subject (pp. 225, 255), in an approach that is at once spontaneous, personal, and tangible.

Pastel thus embodied the very essence of the Impressionist spirit—the marriage of pure color with immediate sensation—offering these artists another way to make color resonate on the paper's surface. C. C.-P.

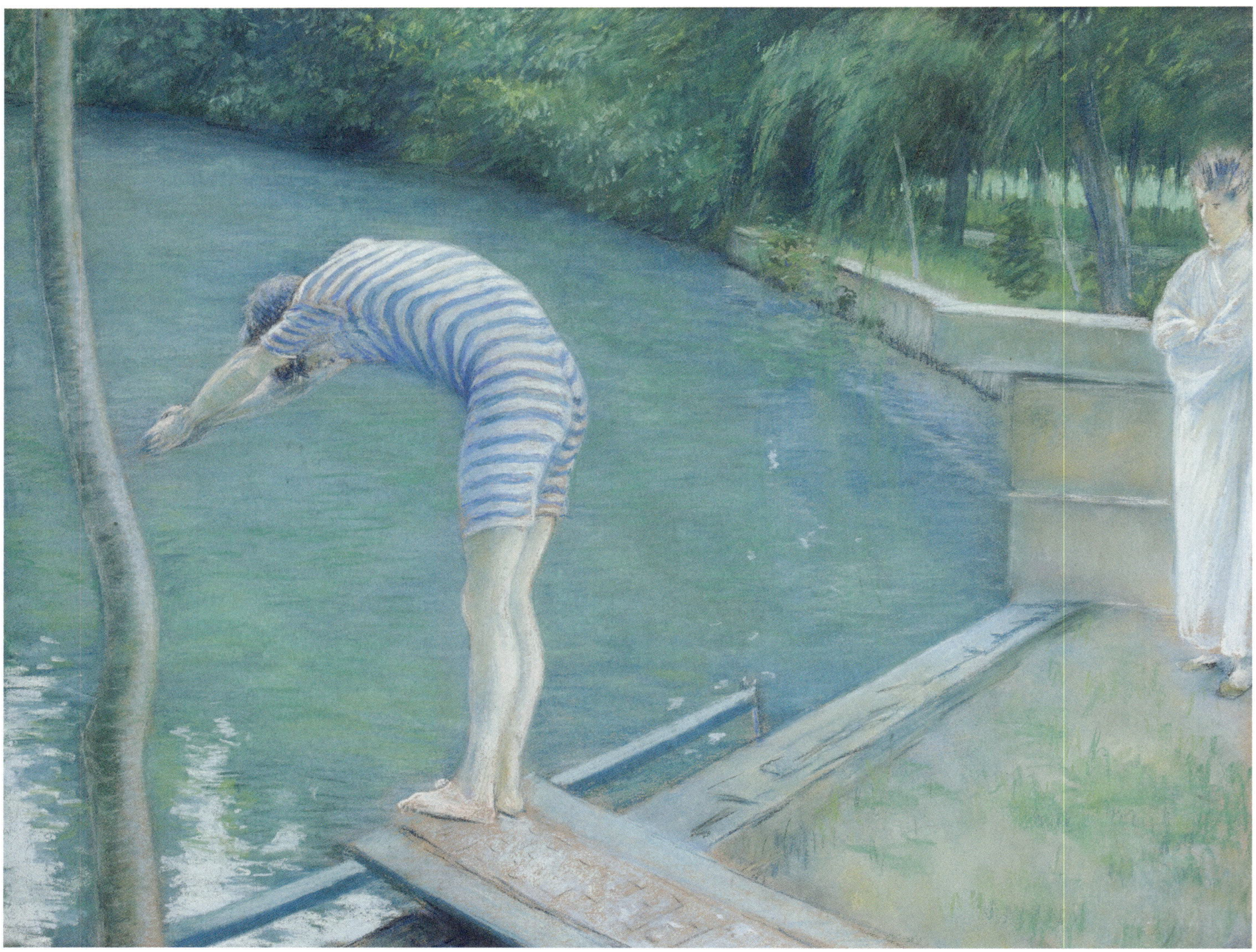

71 Gustave Caillebotte, *Le Nageur* (*The Swimmer*), 1877
Pastel on paper, 27 3⁄16 × 34 13⁄16 in. (69 × 88.5 cm)

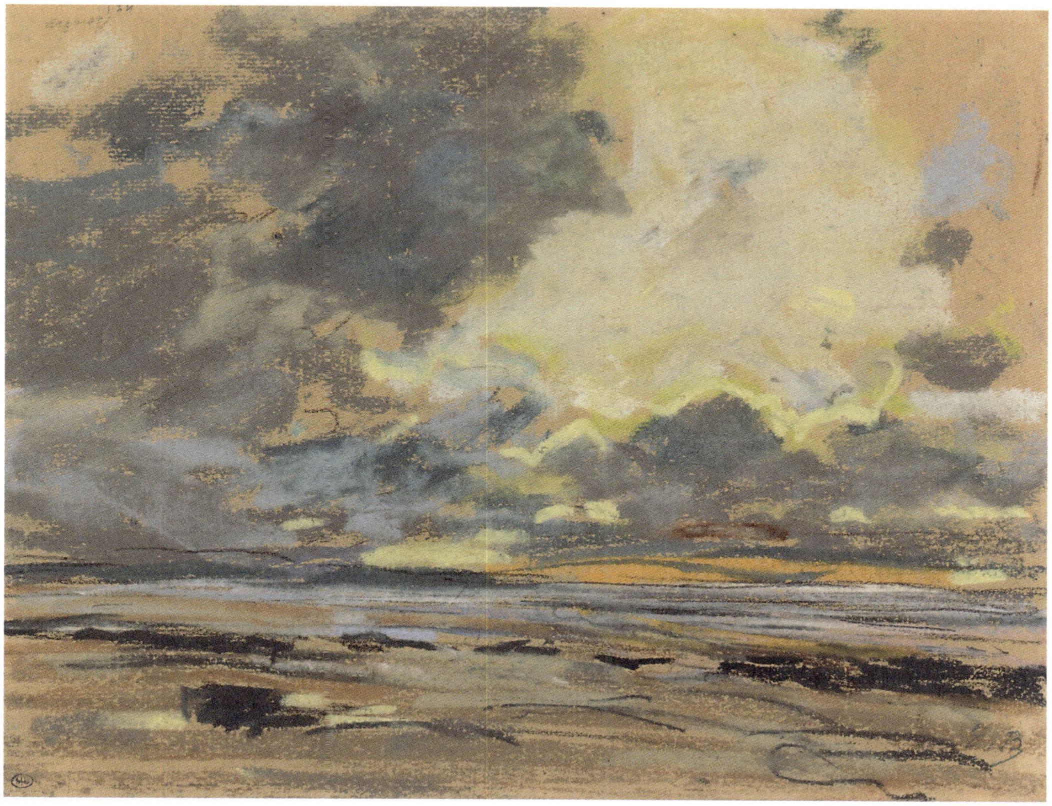

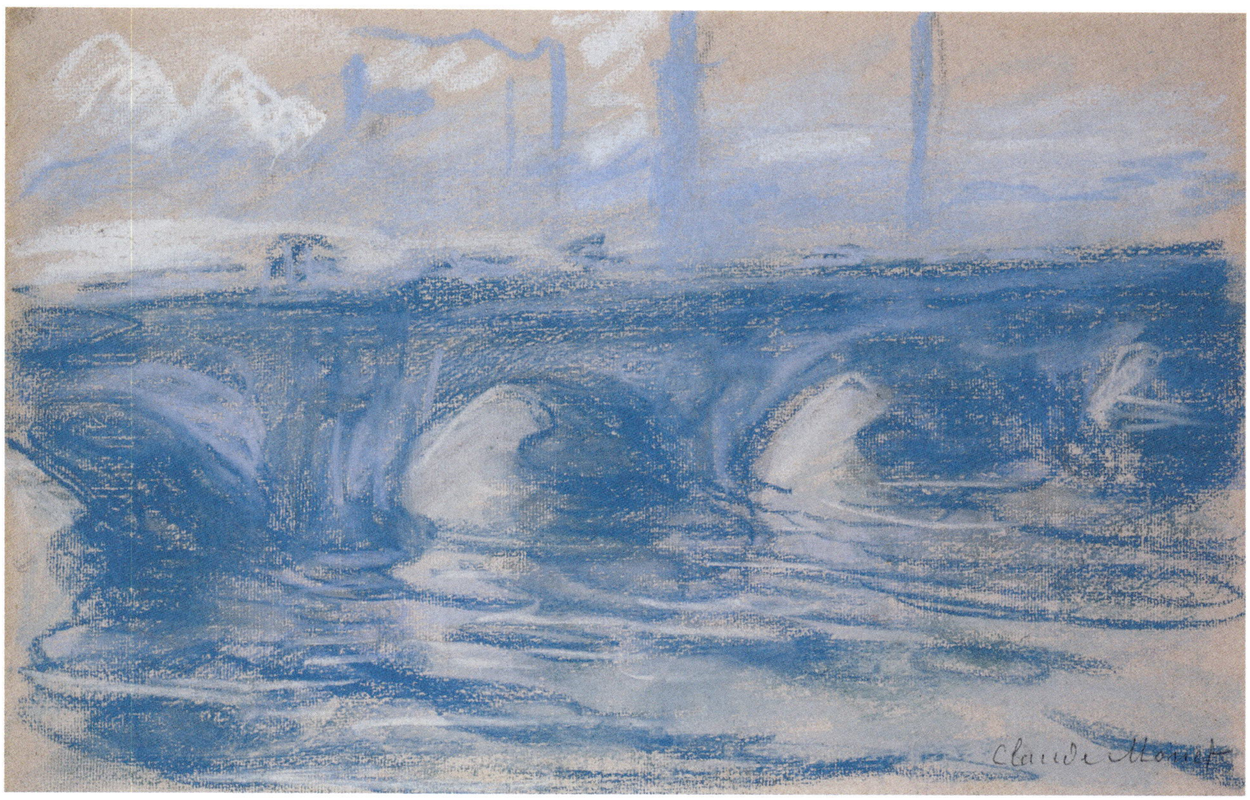

72 Top: Eugène Boudin, *Soleil couchant ou ciel d'orage* (*Setting Sun or Stormy Sky*), c. 1859–1860
Dry pastel on cream laid paper,
8 7⁄16 × 11 5⁄16 in. (21.5 × 28.7 cm)

73 Bottom: Claude Monet, *Le Pont de Waterloo à Londres* (*Waterloo Bridge, London*), c. 1899
Pastel on pinkish-beige paper,
12 5⁄16 × 19 1⁄8 in. (31.3 × 48.5 cm)

Claude Monet
Apartment Interior

This subtly psychological virtuoso masterpiece is best referred to by its original title—the one used when it was shown at the third Impressionist exhibition in 1877 along with thirty other works by Monet—which translates as *Apartment Interior*. The mention of an "interior" rather than a "corner" of the apartment (as it is sometimes also known) indicates a dual intention and almost a dual intrusion. Our gaze is drawn in by the work's optical construction, which Louis Leroy described as "exaggerated" perspective when it was first presented to the public. Monet had been reproached for not knowing the techniques of his trade, but here he demonstrates the opposite—so much so that another critic, writing anonymously in *La Petite Presse*, fairly questioned why the painting had not featured in the official Salon. The same writer commented on being struck by the mastery of the play between foreground, middle ground, and background, and of the light that floods in from the window at the far end, growing brighter as it extends into a foreground that is deliberately overloaded with potted plants and long drapes; the whole is conducive to the desired effect of a grand, almost baroque doorway. Painted in Argenteuil and with the figures discernible as Monet's wife Camille and their son Jean, the canvas also fulfils a second ambition: to remind the viewer that the Impressionists were not penniless daubers, and that they sought to paint and enchant the class they came from. In 1877, as the exhibition brochure indicated, this masterpiece was already owned by Caillebotte, adding to its credentials. S.G.

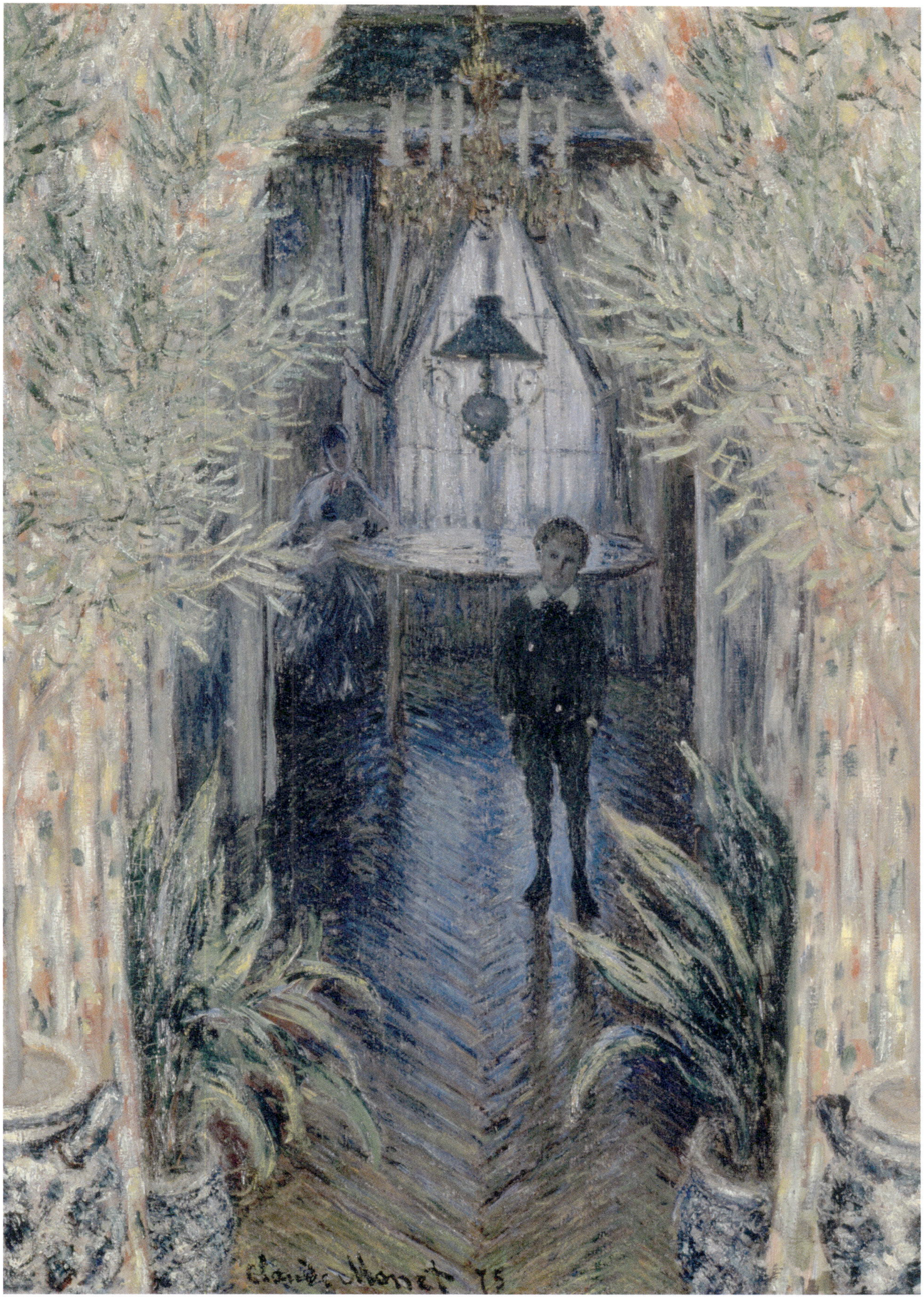

74 Claude Monet, *Intérieur d'appartement* (*Apartment Interior*), also known as *Un coin d'appartement* (*Corner of an Apartment*), 1875
Oil on canvas, 32 1/16 × 23 5/8 in. (81.5 × 60 cm)

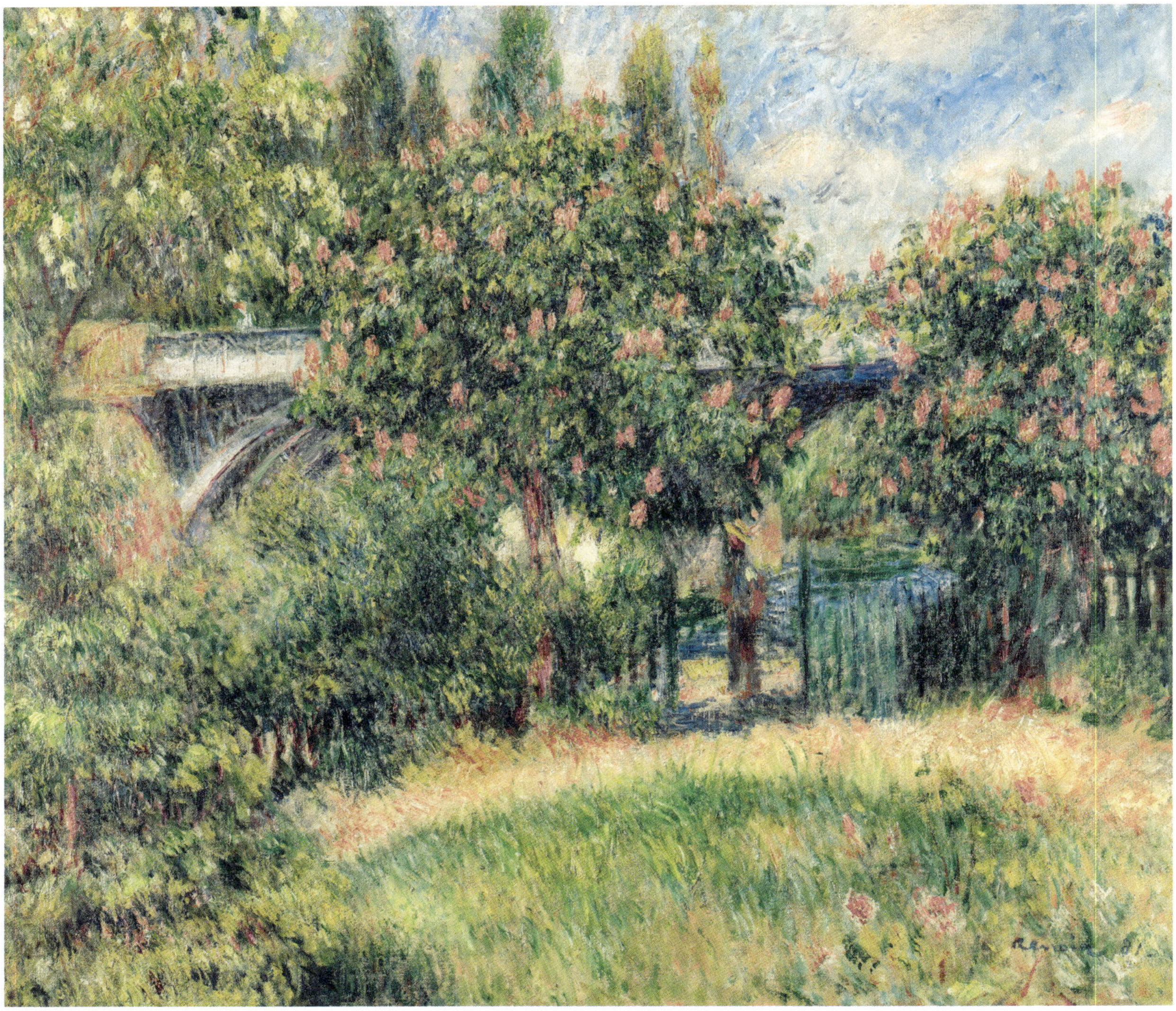

75 Auguste Renoir, *Les Marronniers roses* (*Red Horse-Chestnut Trees*), also known as *Pont de chemin de fer à Chatou* (*Railway Bridge at Chatou*), 1881
Oil on canvas, 21 7⁄16 × 25 13⁄16 in. (54.5 × 65.5 cm)

Argenteuil and the leafy suburbs

The cradle of Impressionism followed the meanders of the Seine, from Pontoise, some 20 miles (30 kilometers) north-west of the capital, via Chatou and Louveciennes, to Paris itself. The movement's artists were often guests in these communities of the then still-green region encircling the city. For their urban-dwelling clientele, who lapped up their images, they were also the ambassadors and pictorial chroniclers of this other world where modern leisure activities were thriving. The railroad that enabled the regular weekend exodus itself became a central or peripheral subject for the artists, who made use of it in every sense. The fact that they more often depicted its bridges than its locomotives, coaches, and cars confirms that the potential for people to move around appealed to them more than the machinery or the Age of Steel that it symbolized. The resulting images refrain from displaying the consequences of this new development in Paris's surroundings, preferring—with only rare exceptions—to ignore the heavy presence of new and particularly polluting industries, which were booming along the riversides. While Monet and Renoir are considered to have definitively invented Impressionism at La Grenouillère near Croissy-sur-Seine, Argenteuil was the new movement's unparalleled stronghold. Monet lived there in the aftermath of the 1870–1871 Franco-Prussian War, the wounds from which pepper much of his output. His *The Dock at Argenteuil* radiates the sweetness of re-established peace, the tensions of the time a world away. The same can be said of Sisley's paintings, although the temporary bridge in his eponymous picture exudes the memory of the destruction wrought by that war. His *Chemin de la Machine, Louveciennes* (1873; Musée d'Orsay, Paris) is filled instead with memories of the Ancien Régime, including the Château de Madame du Barry, among other things. In Renoir's *Red Horse-Chestnut Trees*, which belonged to Caillebotte, resplendent nature, presented through a scattering of short brushstrokes, masks the rail tracks that connected Chatou to the capital—symbolic in itself! S.C.

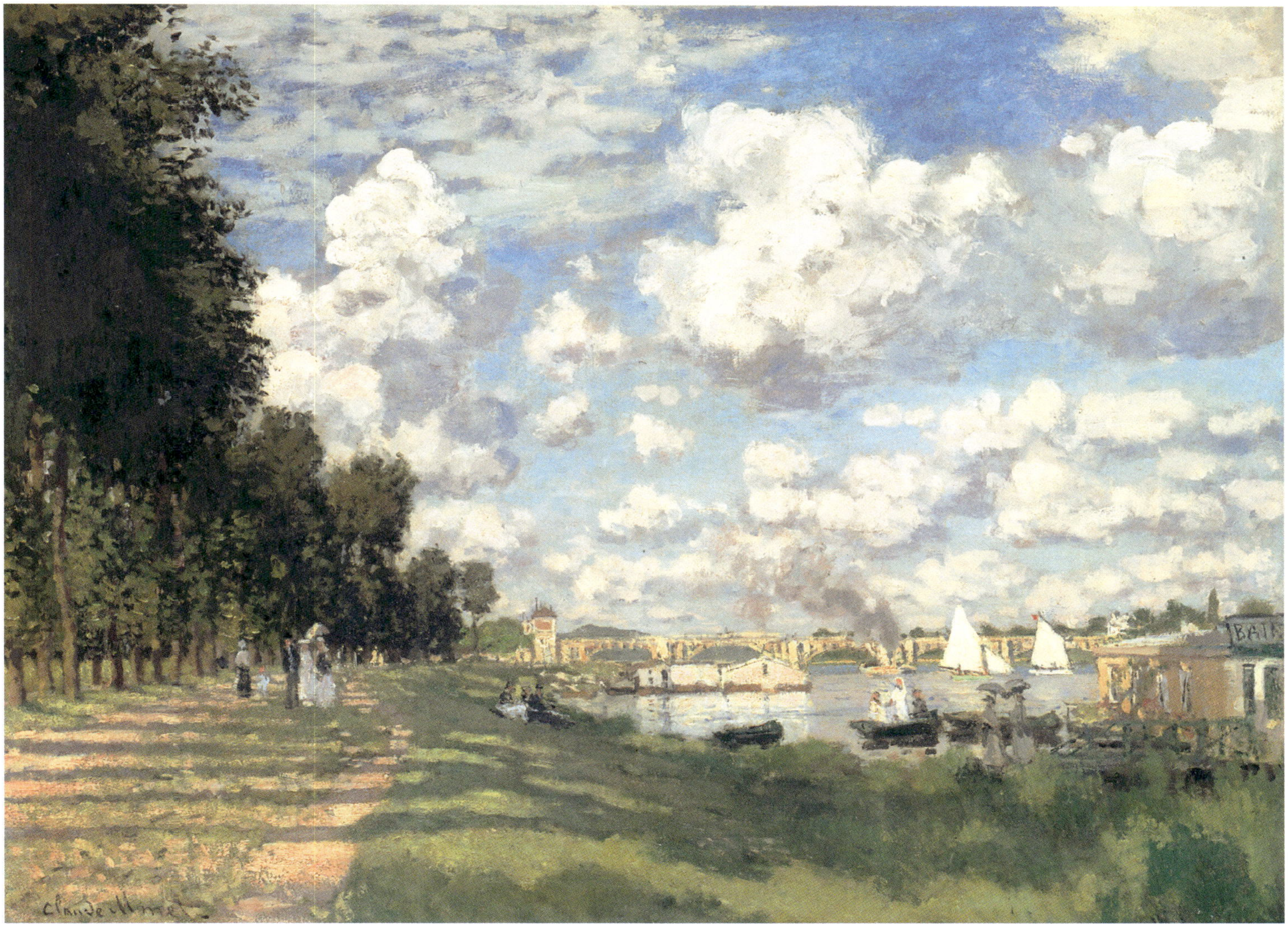

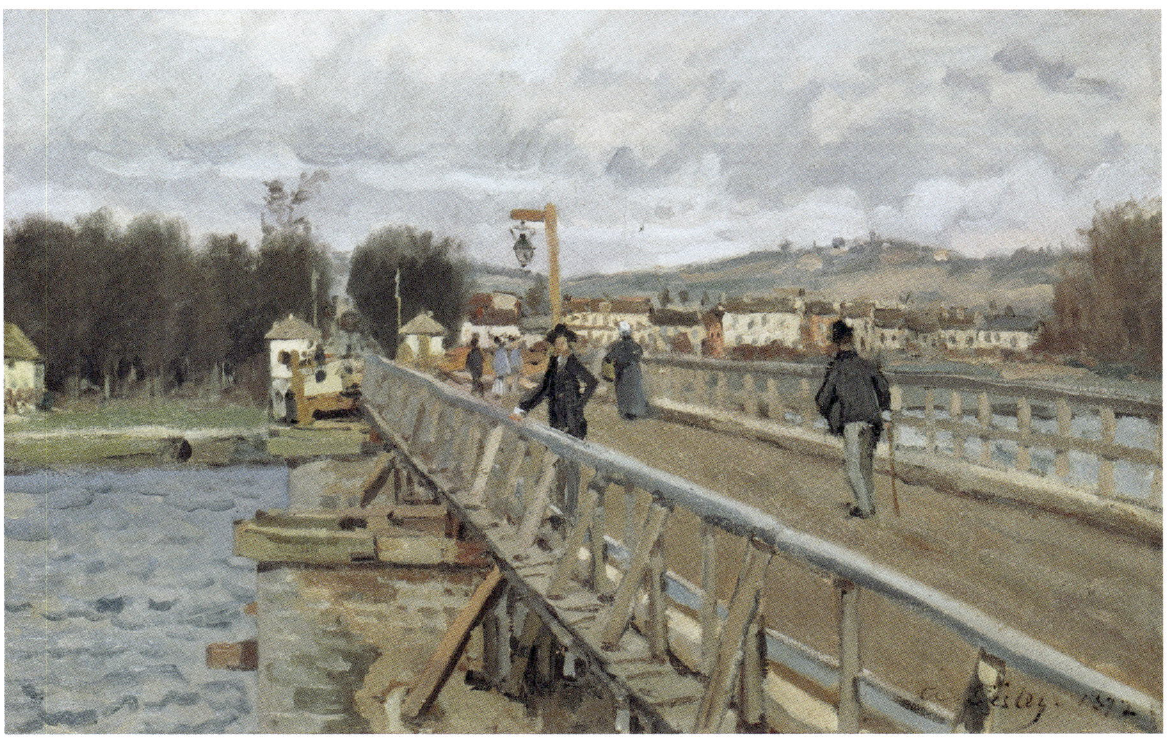

76 Top: Claude Monet, *Le Bassin d'Argenteuil* (*The Dock at Argenteuil*), c. 1872
Oil on canvas, 23 ⅝ × 31 ⅞ in. (60 × 81 cm)

77 Bottom: Alfred Sisley, *Passerelle d'Argenteuil* (*Footbridge at Argenteuil*), 1872
Oil on canvas, 15 ⅜ × 23 ⅝ in. (39 × 60 cm)

Claude Monet
The Railway Bridge at Argenteuil

The Franco-Prussian War of 1870–1871 destroyed many of the bridges in the outskirts of Paris, and their reconstruction under the Third Republic was symbolic of the sense of national renaissance that took hold across all sectors, including in Impressionist painting. Monet, who had not taken part in the fighting, associated himself with this iconography of reparation, in all senses of the word. The strong diagonal that cuts across the composition derives from similar ideas. We are propelled across the river and, more than the train itself, which is reduced to the tops of the coaches and the smoke from the locomotive, it is the bridge that plays the canvas's starring role. Erected on sturdy piers, the metal bridge materializes as an allegory of the new era, and heralds the series inspired by Paris's Pont de l'Europe and its environs. On that subject, the canvas is clearly a harbinger of the bridges that Caillebotte, who admired Monet, began painting in the summer of 1875. Also not to be forgotten is a renowned precedent, Joseph Mallord William Turner's *Rain, Steam, and Speed—The Great Western Railway* of 1844 (National Gallery, London), a manifesto of the Age of Steel ahead of its time, which Félix Bracquemond transposed into an etching that he exhibited in 1874, at the first Impressionist exhibition. In symbolizing the reconstruction of Argenteuil, Monet's painting was on a par with the history painting of its day. Its owners, Adolphe Moreau and Étienne Moreau-Nélaton, were no doubt aware of that. S.G.

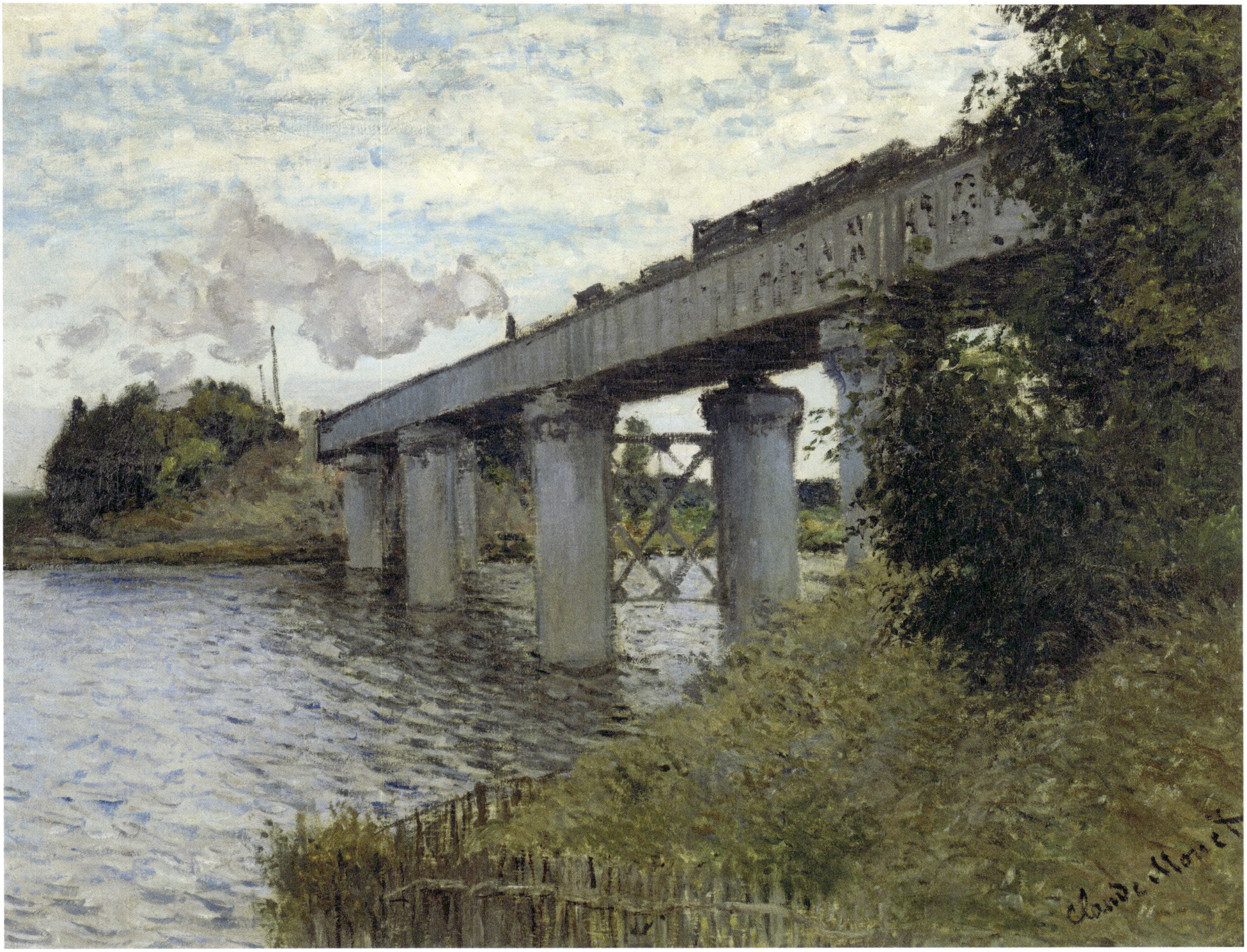

78 Claude Monet, *Le Pont du chemin de fer à Argenteuil* (*The Railway Bridge at Argenteuil*), between 1873 and 1874
Oil on canvas, 21 ¼ × 27 15/16 in. (54 × 71 cm)

Camille Pissarro
Port-Marly

Of the six paintings that Pissarro showed in 1879 at the Impressionist group's fourth exhibition, he was particularly fond of this small canvas. Painted on his return from England, where he had gone into self-imposed exile during the 1870–1871 Franco-Prussian War, it retains the solid construction and impasto that Zola had so appreciated in the late Second Empire period. It borrows extensively from Corot, such as in the female figure in working clothes, alone on the left, and the repeated diagonals which energize the space and draw our gaze toward the scene in front of her. The rows of trees, following through from one riverbank to the other, contribute to this dynamic construction of the space. As the main element in Pissarro's eyes, the floating washhouse naturally occupies the center of the canvas, in line with his often-stated commitment to traditional practices. The counterpoint presented by the factory glimpsed in the distance, with its smoking chimney, cannot be accidental. Besides, Pissarro has aligned it with the washhouse, as if wanting to set up a contrast between two worlds and perhaps between the blackness of the fuel and the cleanness of the laundry. In 1879, the work was well received for its simultaneously pensive and active suburban rusticity. One critic described it as a solace from what was then being produced, and found in it "the qualities [of his] earlier paintings." When negotiations with the State over the Caillebotte bequest were underway, Pissarro ensured that this work was selected, on the basis of its being "quite advanced, and from a date that would otherwise be lacking in the collection."   S.G.

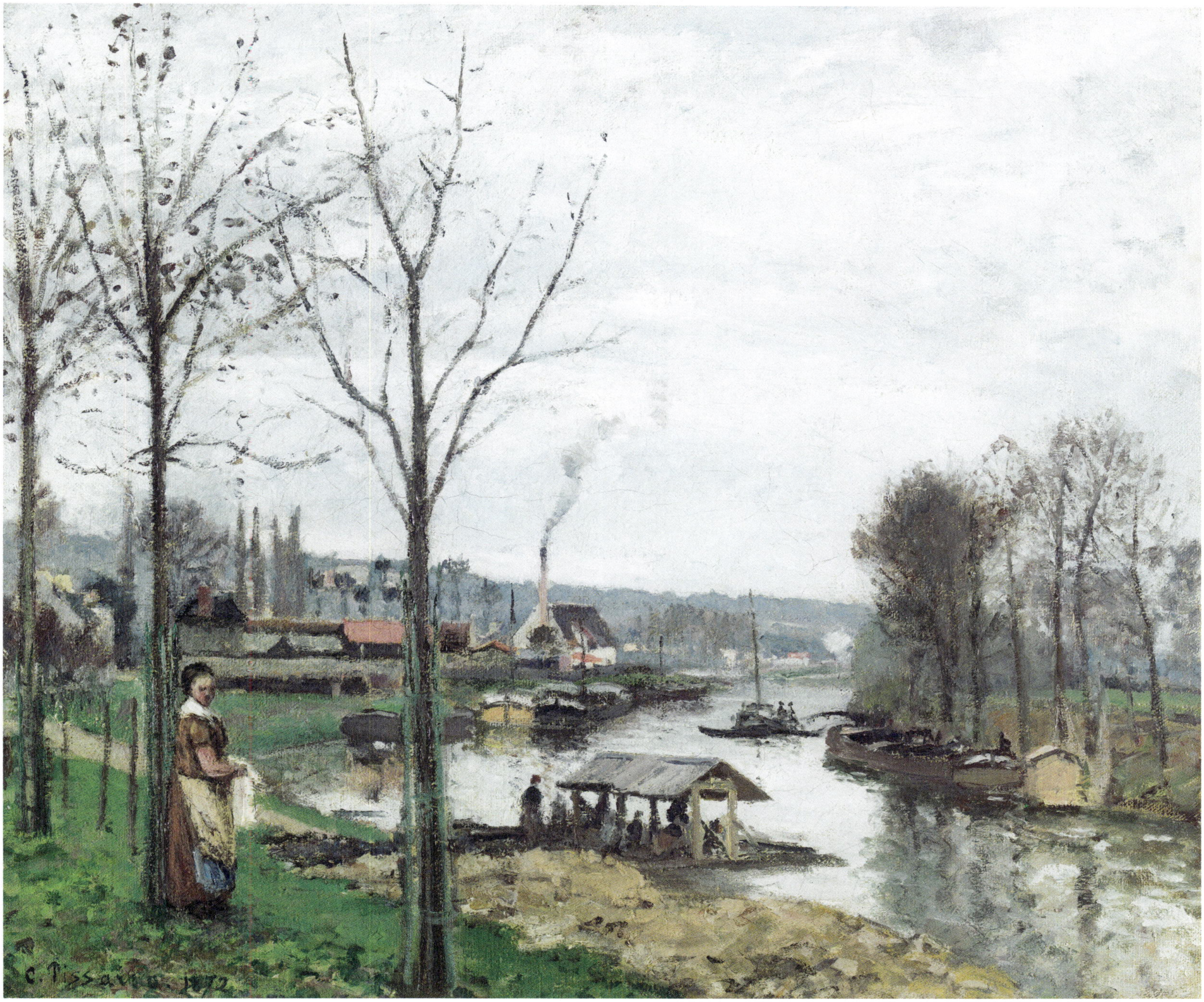

79 Camille Pissarro, *Port-Marly*, 1872
Oil on canvas, 18 5/16 × 22 1/16 in. (46.5 × 56 cm)

Alfred Sisley
The Flood at Port-Marly

It was not only press illustrations and popular color prints that lingered over the damage caused by the Seine bursting its banks in March 1876, with images like the one showing Marshal Patrice de Mac Mahon—then president of the Third Republic—and his wife attending to victims of the disaster. Sisley was already familiar with the theme, having depicted it in 1872, and so returned to it, once more steering clear of any sense of dramatization. This did not mean he was indifferent to the subject, or that he saw it only as a pretext to paint the myriad glints of the rising river's surface, in a very humid atmosphere. Both his *The Flood at Port-Marly*, which was well received when shown at the second Impressionist exhibition and which is more classical in its composition and technique, and his *The Bark during the Flood, Port-Marly* treat the dramatic events with a sense of distance, but without negating them. One 1876 critic however did not grasp this: "*The Flood at Port-Marly* has a ring of truth about it; the pale tones of the inn, with the water lapping at its base, are very true to life. But why does this bright, sunny flood scene come across as so fresh and cheery? It is not remotely distressing, and we would be only too happy to go to this inn to eat some fried goujons fished from just under the window." On the contrary: through his self-imposed restraint, Sisley is pointing the finger at human vulnerability and the fragility of French society in those times of supposed progress. The two canvases are typical of the artist's diffuse, flowing, slightly misty manner of painting. S.G.

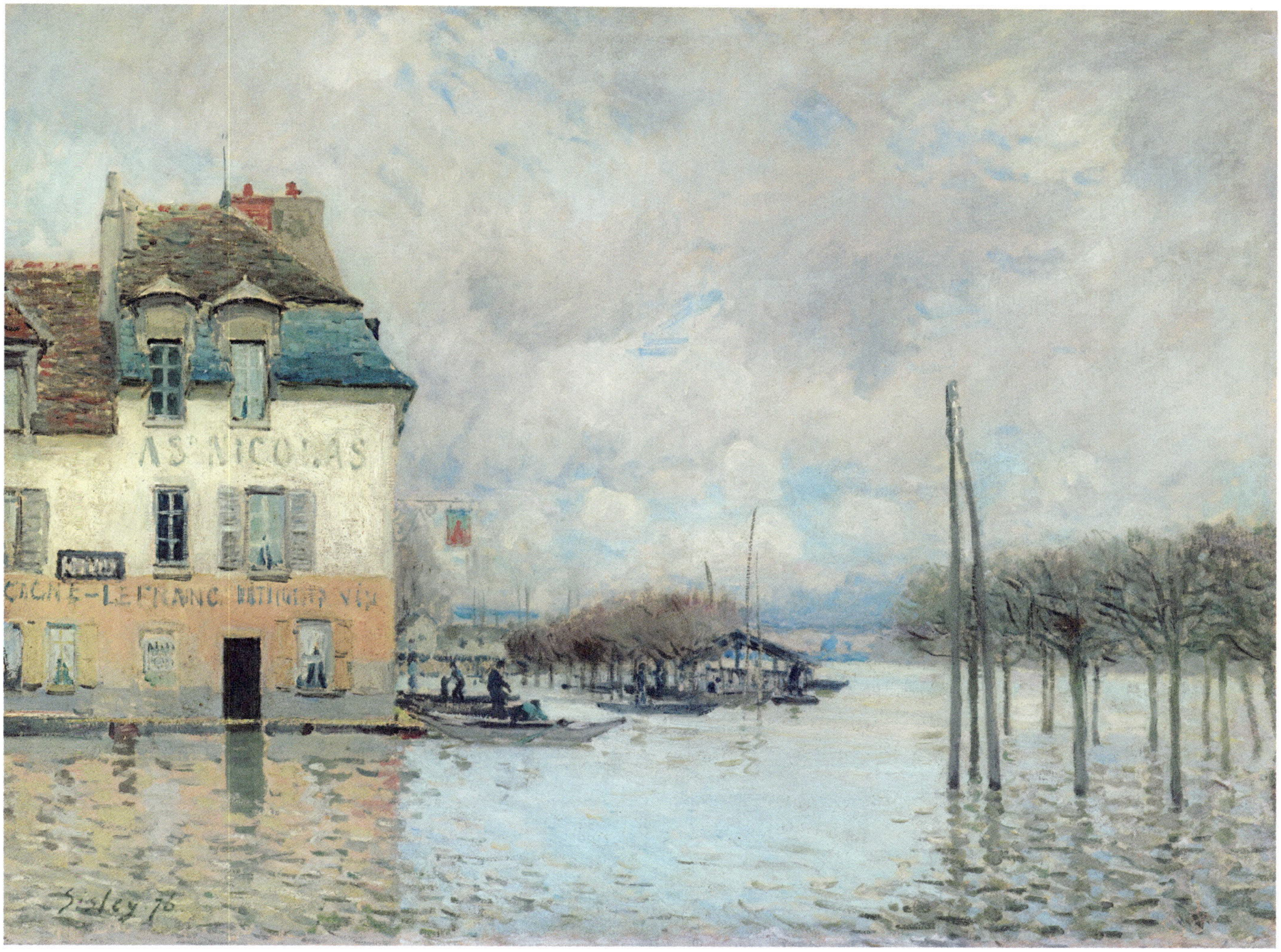

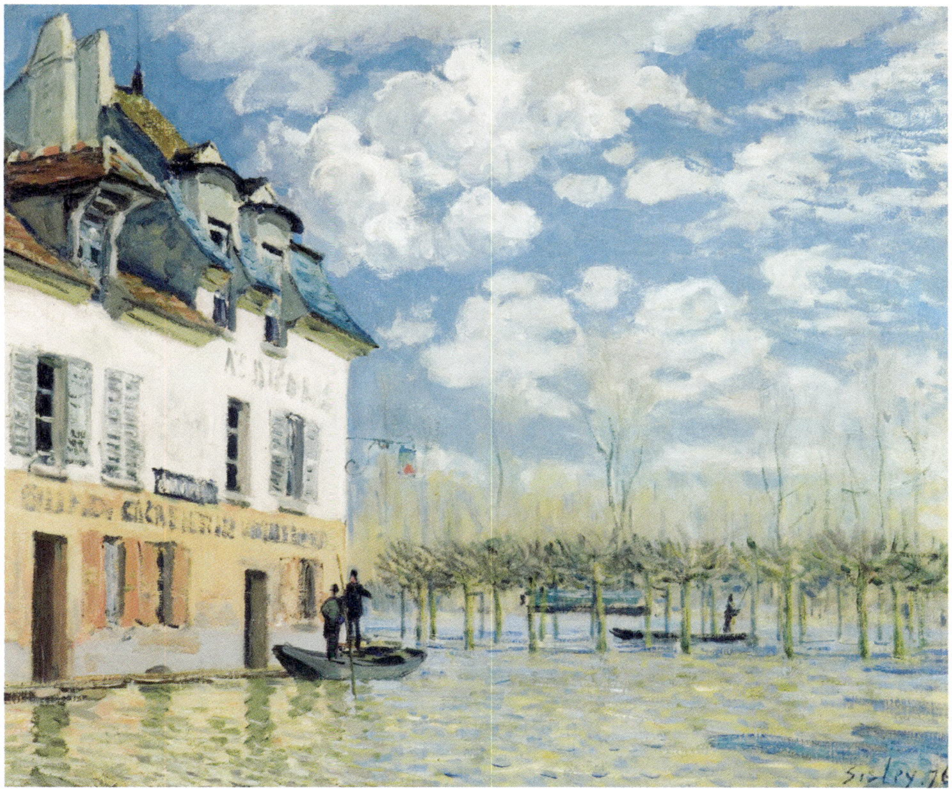

80 Top: Alfred Sisley, *L'Inondation à Port-Marly* (*The Flood at Port-Marly*), 1876
Oil on canvas, 23 5⁄8 × 31 7⁄8 in. (60 × 81 cm)

81 Bottom: Alfred Sisley, *La Barque pendant l'inondation, Port-Marly* (*The Bark During the Flood, Port-Marly*), 1876
Oil on canvas, 19 13⁄16 × 24 in. (50.4 × 61 cm)

1874

The first Impressionist exhibition

The Impressionist movement emerged over the course of eight independent exhibitions held in Paris in the 1870s and 1880s. They were organized by artists who joined forces to directly present their works to the public, outside the official circuit—without being judged by a jury, and with no gallery or dealer as a go-between. These painters, who soon became known as "Impressionists," had met in the 1860s. Although they came from a wide range of backgrounds, nearly all of them had started out at the Salon. Their approach to painting was radically new, representing scenes from modern life, or spirited landscapes painted on the spot that replicate the feeling of being outdoors. Repeatedly rejected by the Salon, they sought other means to market their work, and by 1867 they were contemplating the idea of exhibiting as a group. The Franco-Prussian War and the Commune delayed their plans, but in 1873 they set up a subscription-based association, with the aim of organizing their own exhibition to display their works as they pleased.

This opened on April 15, 1874, in a space they had hired for the occasion: the former studio of photographer Nadar, fashionably located on Boulevard des Capucines in Paris's second arrondissement. The show had thirty-one participants, only nine of whom are considered Impressionists today: Monet, Pissarro, Sisley, Renoir, Morisot, Boudin, Guillaumin, Degas, and Cézanne. To make the venture more financially viable, other, more traditional artists were also included. As a result, the displays were eclectic to say the least, with a variety of styles and subjects. Having no artistic manifesto, the exercise aimed solely to get their work seen and sold. It was a commercial failure: only a handful of works found buyers. But the event did not go unnoticed. The public were struck by the pale tones and swift brushwork that this core group of innovative artists were using. Their radicalism was broadly subjected to scorn. One critic, Louis Leroy, coined the scathing adjective "Impressionist" when describing Monet's *Impression, Sunrise* (1872; Musée Marmottan Monet, Paris)—a sketch-like view of the port at Le Havre whose subject he found impossible to make out. It was this insult that gave the new school of painting its name. A. R.

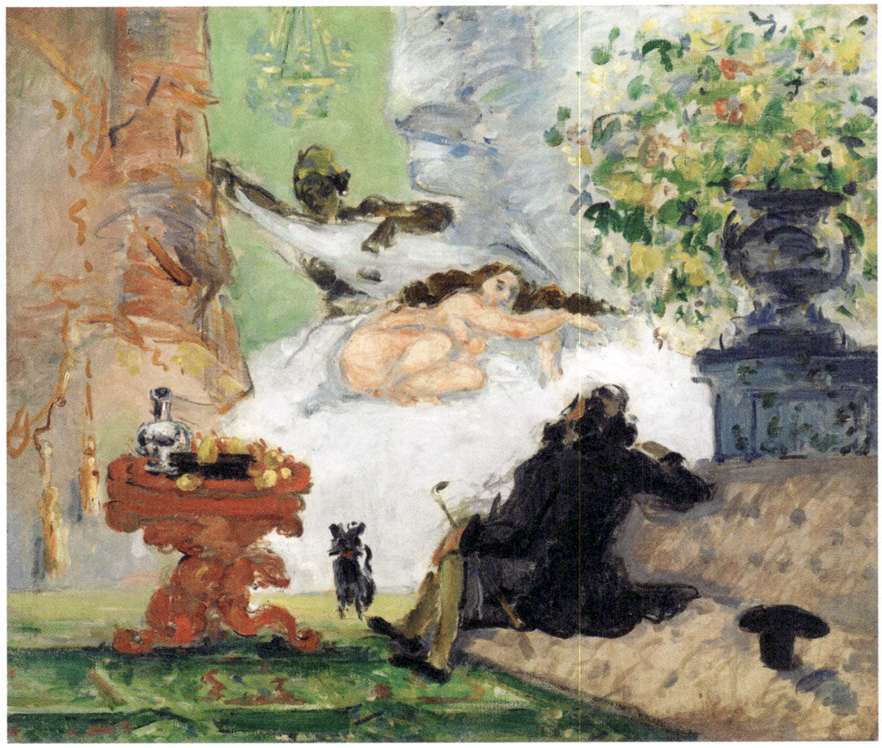

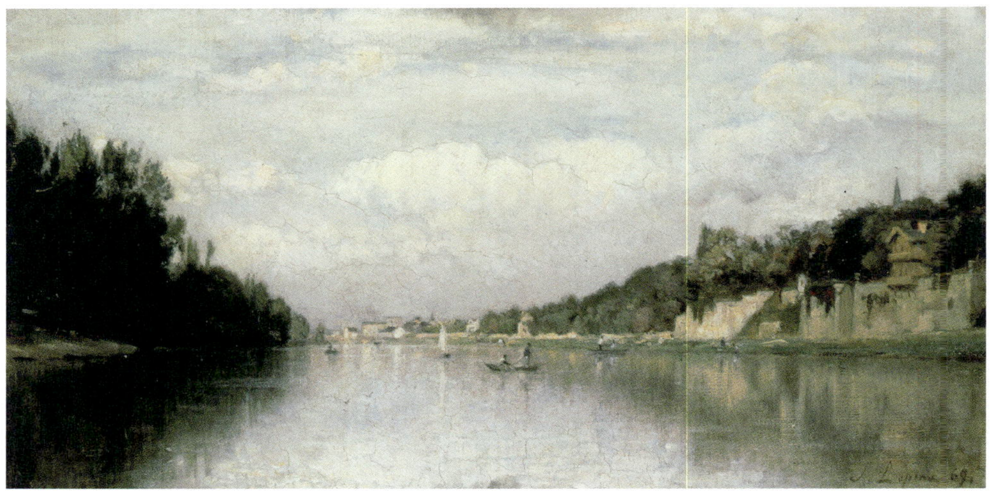

82 Top: Paul Cézanne, *Une moderne Olympia* (*A Modern Olympia*), 1873–1874
Oil on canvas, 18 3/16 × 21 7/8 in. (46.2 × 55.5 cm)

83 Bottom: Stanislas Lépine, *Paysage* (*Landscape*), 1869
Oil on canvas, 11 13/16 × 22 13/16 in. (30 × 58 cm)

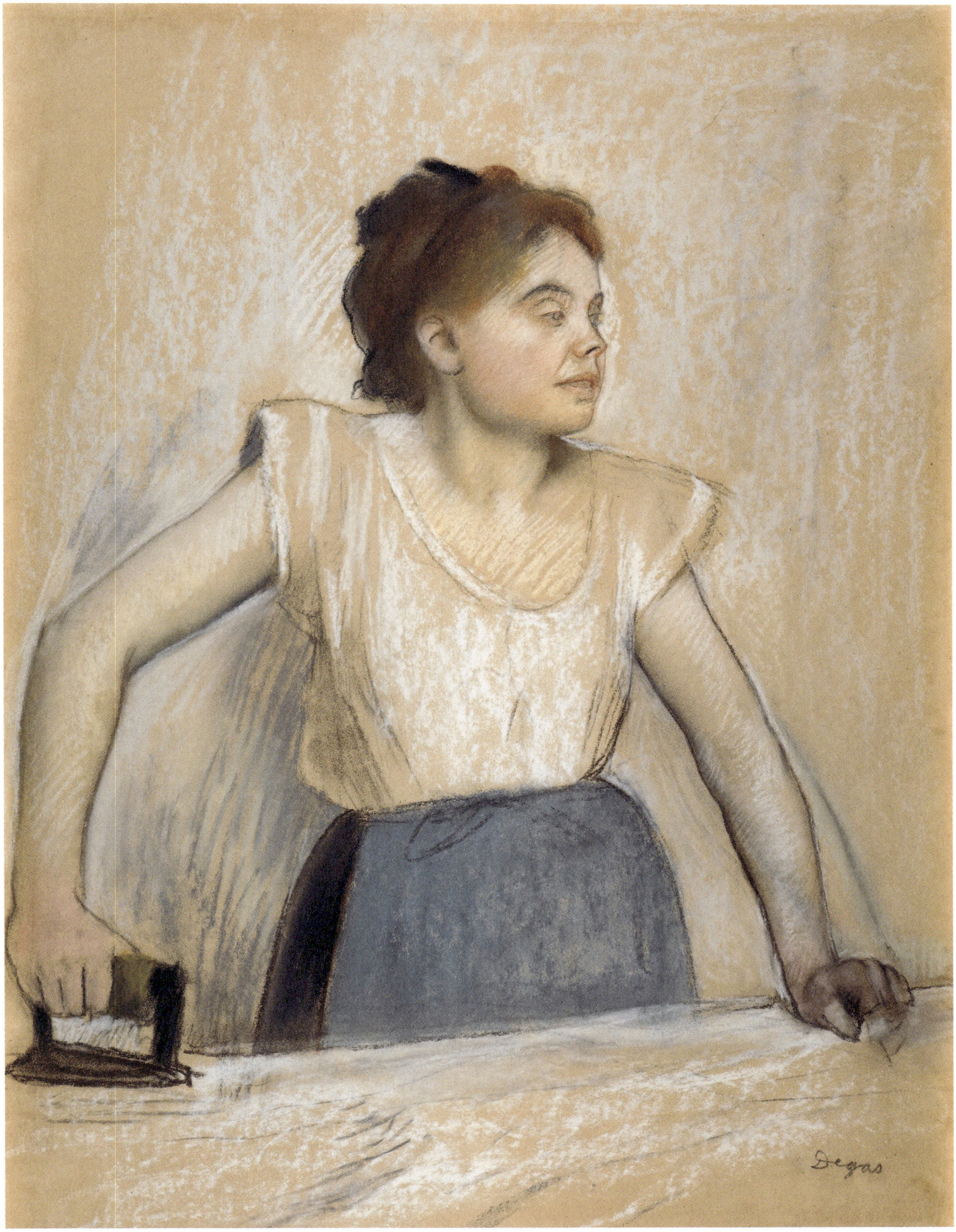

84 Edgar Degas, *La Repasseuse* (*Woman Ironing*), 1869
Charcoal, white chalk, and pastel on paper,
29 ⅛ × 24 in. (74 × 61 cm)

Claude Monet
Poppies

Back in France after a period of voluntary exile in London during the Franco-Prussian War of 1870–1871 and the subsequent Paris Commune, Monet moved to Argenteuil, about a twenty-minute train ride from the Gare Saint-Lazare. By the winter of 1871 he was "well settled there and seem[ed] very keen to establish himself," as his friend Boudin noted on January 2, 1872. Those years in Argenteuil certainly gave his art a new impetus. The small suburban town offered him plenty of subjects to paint, all very much of their time: bridges being rebuilt, popular regattas, neat gardens, and the countryside a stone's throw away, which attracted an influx of walkers from the capital. There, Monet painted his *Poppies*, an eminently modern landscape. His by-then wife Camille and their son Jean, followed by another woman and child, are strolling across the sloping field, through grass so high that the little boy is only just visible. Above this recently created hill (an embankment resulting from new development works in the then fast-expanding town), clouds blow swiftly by, enhancing the sense of pictorial depth as they go. Monet was a strong believer in *plein-air* painting, and chose the spot for his easel from which he could best capture the ambient light and the atmospheric nuances. His rapid, fragmented brushwork and the bright tones recreate "the clarity of [his] first impression"[13] of this landscape, dominated by the radiant colors of the poppies that seem to be bursting into bloom on the canvas's surface.

It was also when living in Argenteuil that Monet helped organize the first Impressionist exhibition, which opened in the spring of 1874 and where he showed this painting. His work was ridiculed by the critics, but more perceptive visitors found this "stroll through the grass that cheerfully mingles the women's flowery hats with the red poppies in the wheatfields"[14] particularly charming. As the critic Jules-Antoine Castagnary summarized, writing about this "new way of seeing nature": "It's lively, it's nimble, it's fresh: it's ravishing."[15] A. R.

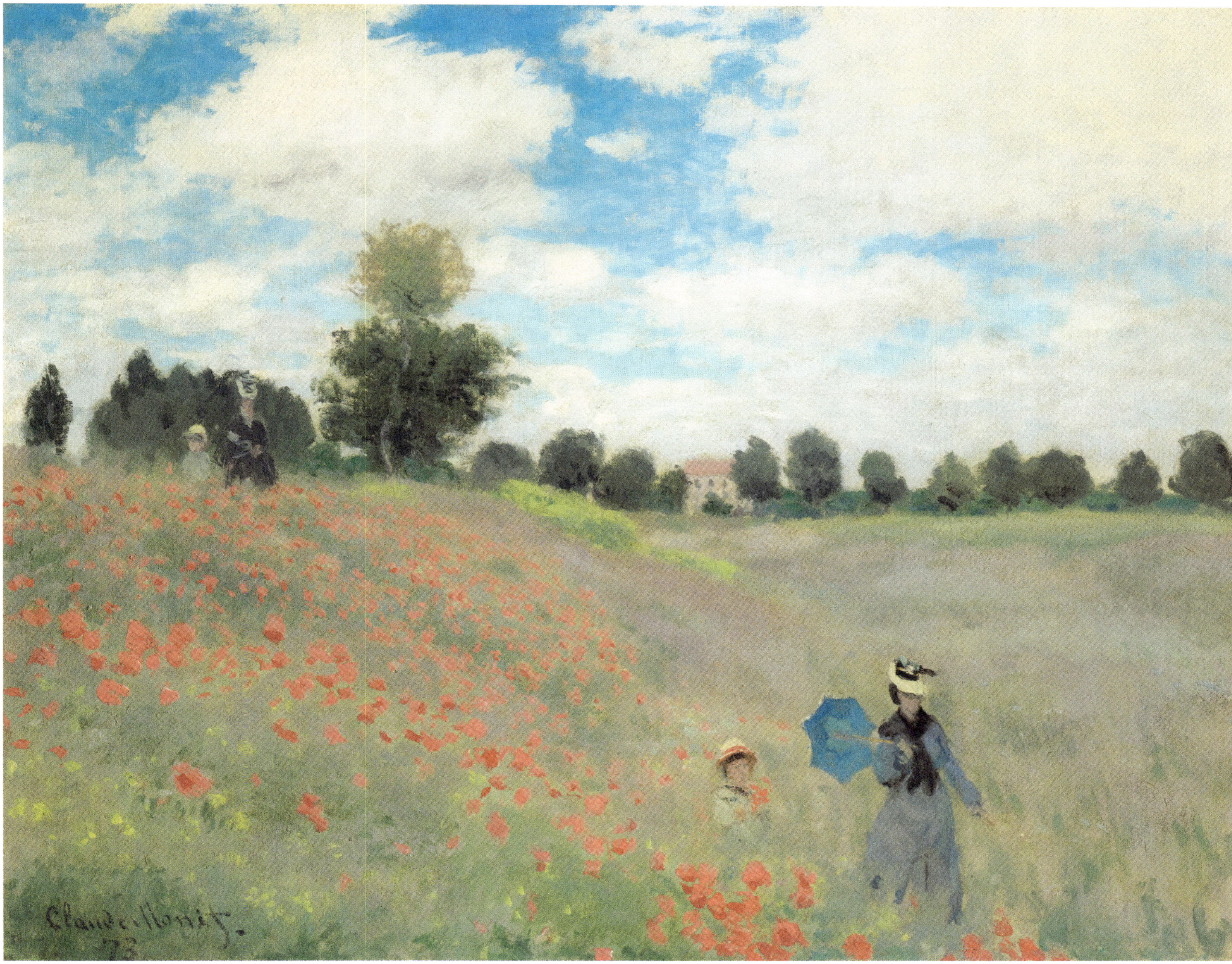

85 Claude Monet, *Coquelicots (Poppies)*, 1873
Oil on canvas, 19 11⁄16 × 25 11⁄16 in. (50 × 65.3 cm)

Paul Cézanne
The House of the Hanged Man

In late 1872 Cézanne moved to Auvers, in the countryside north-west of Paris, not far from Pontoise where his friend and fellow artist Pissarro lived. The two often got together to paint on location, side by side. At a curve in one of Auvers's steep lanes—Rue du Four—looms a tall, white house with a somber-sounding name (*pendu* meaning "hanged man") which, however, is more likely to derive from that of a former resident, a man from Brittany called Pen'du. This view of the village is typical of the new manner that Cézanne developed in these pivotal months. Solidly constructed around the diagonals of the pitched roofs and the paths that slope steeply upward or plunge down into the village center, the image retains the powerful rawness of Cézanne's early paintings. But here, thick paint (partly applied with a palette knife) is combined with more lightly applied areas of brushwork in paler, almost silvery tones, such as in the distance. The atmosphere is that of a late winter's day, with whiffs of mossy stone, earth, and damp thatch. Cézanne must have been pleased with his picture, as he agreed to exhibit it three times—an unusual decision for an artist whom the critic Téodor de Wyzewa described as "convinced that his painting was awful." It was thus displayed at the first Impressionist exhibition where, despite being mocked in the press, it was one of just a handful of works (out of more than a hundred on show) to find a buyer. This proved Pissarro right, as he had predicted in September 1872 that, with his Auvers landscapes, Cézanne would "astonish" those who had been "too quick to condemn him."[16] A.R.

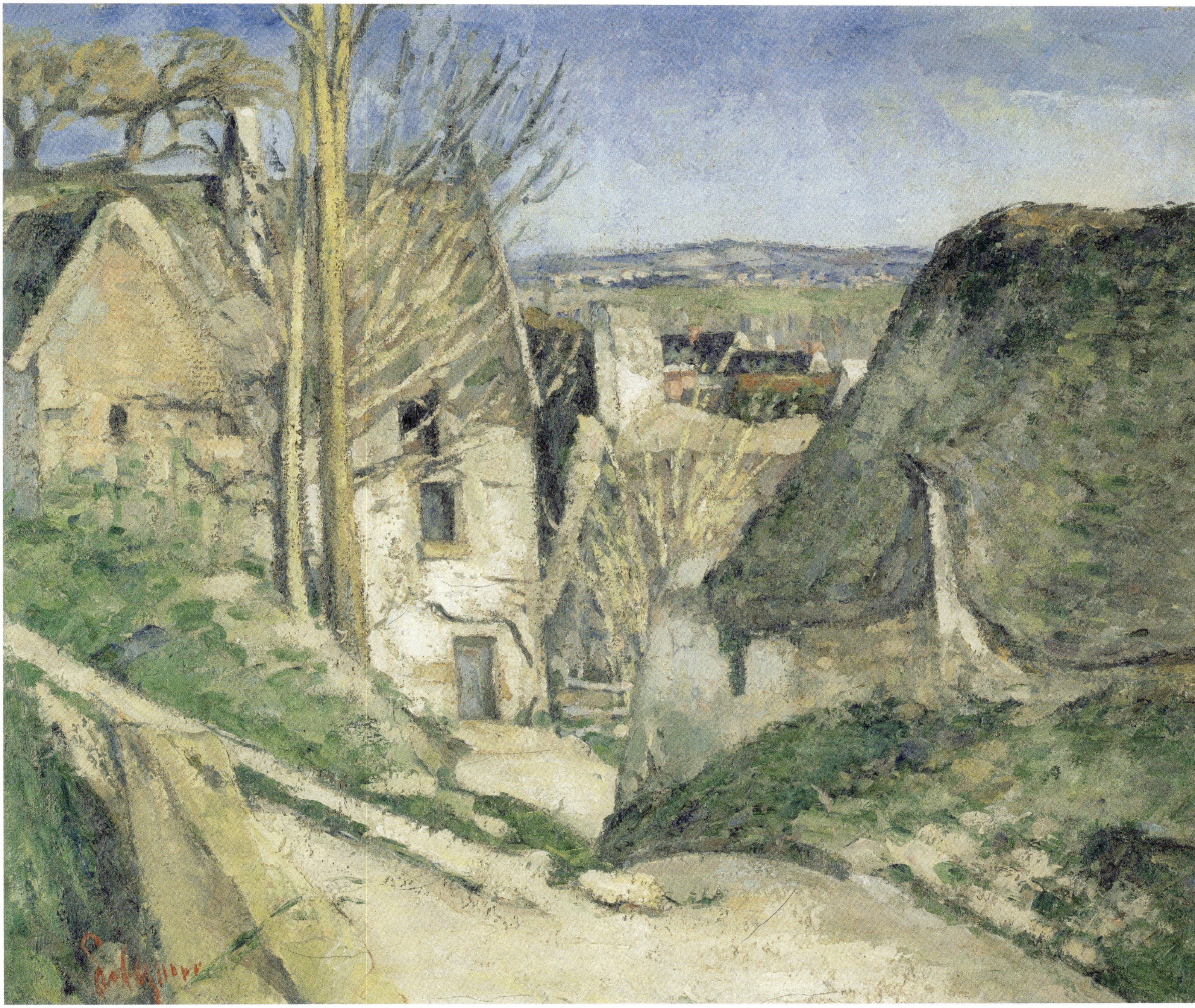

86 Paul Cézanne, *La Maison du pendu, Auvers-sur-Oise* (*The House of the Hanged Man, Auvers-sur-Oise*), 1873
Oil on canvas, 21 ⅞ × 26 ⅛ in. (55.5 × 66.3 cm)

Armand Guillaumin
Setting Sun at Ivry

This was without doubt the weirdest and perhaps one of the most disturbing paintings to have appeared at the first Impressionist exhibition, where two other, less fiery canvases by Armand Guillaumin were also shown. Despite the prominence of the industrial suburb shown, the subject is nonetheless conventional, but its treatment turns other artists' previous efforts to capture sunsets—from Claude Lorrain or Camille Corot to the protagonists of the "New Painting"—on their head. As the sun disappears beneath the horizon, it not so much fades away as sets the sky ablaze, with flames flickering from ochre to red. The green and violet of the foreground lead into the pyrotechnic display beyond. Drawn to the work in 1874, Marc de Montifaud, a woman writing under a male pseudonym, underlined the work's throbbing intensity. Other writers at the time were sufficiently well-informed to recognize Guillaumin as one of the movement's initiators, and not an extremist follower of it—for Impressionism had its sages and its fanatics, the former sometimes resistant to the latter. By then a friend of Courbet's for some twelve years, Guillaumin had studied at the Académie Suisse and was soon admitted to paint alongside Pissarro, but the juries of the 1861 and 1863 Salons could not fathom his work. In the latter year, the rejected artists, including himself, formed a separate group, with Napoleon III's authorization. Ten years later, Guillaumin participated in another Salon des Refusés and perhaps naturally became one of the founders of the Société Anonyme des Artistes Peintres, Sculpteurs, Graveurs, etc. (Society of Painters, Sculptors, Engravers, etc.) that formed the basis for the 1874 exhibition. He went on to take part in five of the seven Impressionist exhibitions. In 1881, the critic Joris-Karl Huysmans was won over by this "ferocious colorist," showering him with praise. It cannot be said that art history as it stands today treats him so well. S.G.

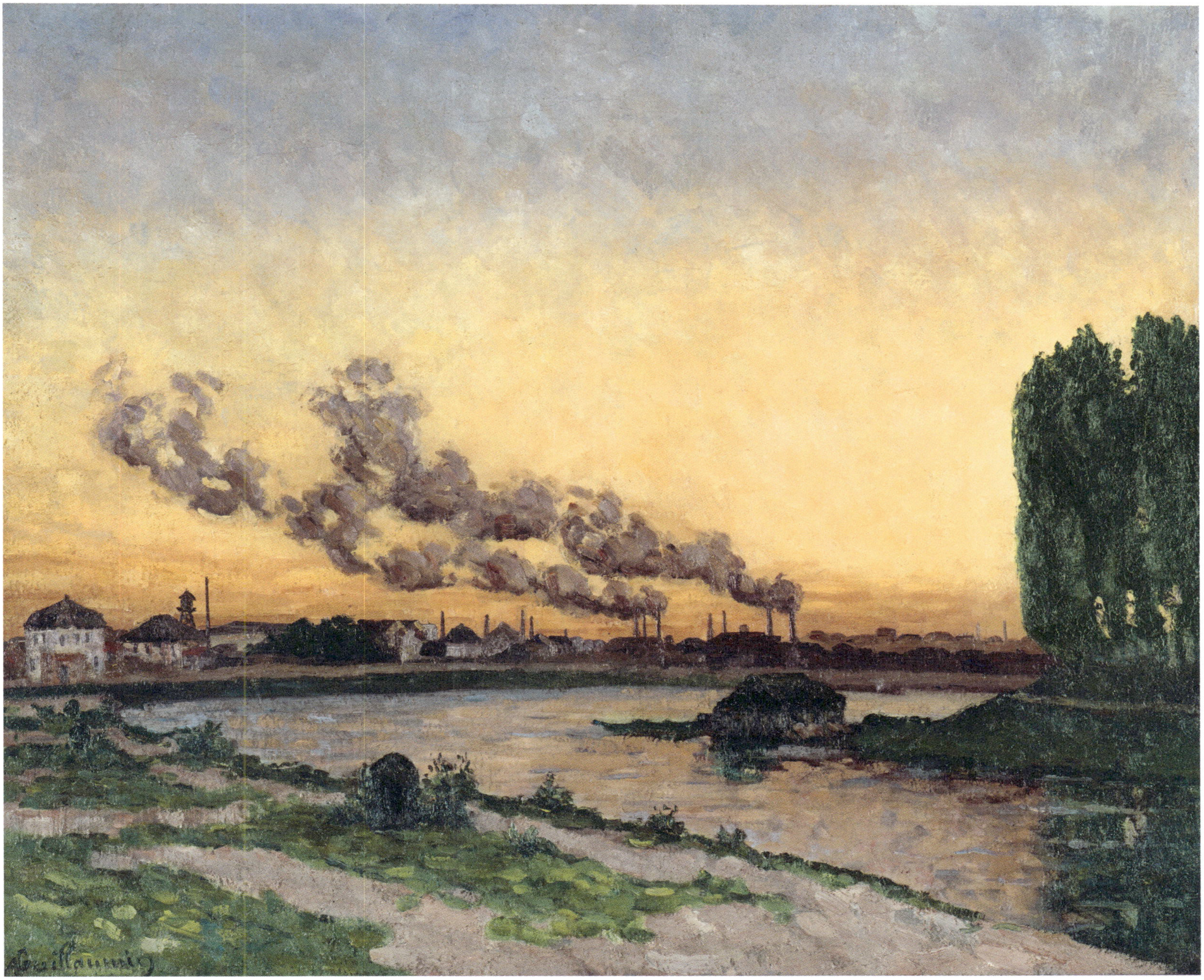

87 Armand Guillaumin, *Soleil couchant à Ivry* (*Setting Sun at Ivry*), 1873
Oil on canvas, 25 9⁄16 × 31 7⁄8 in. (65 × 81 cm)

Countryside

Ever-increasing numbers of painters moved away from the city in the nineteenth century, and not only for aesthetic reasons. Financial concerns were often a deciding factor, but the choice also stemmed from social and political convictions, with artists professing a clear aversion to technicalism and labor, which they considered dehumanizing. This was notably true of Camille Pissarro, who was born in the Caribbean and encountered rural communities at an early age. Greatly influenced by Corot, Daubigny, and above all their fellow Barbizon School founder Jean-François Millet, he sought to express a balanced way of living that Zola attempted to define in 1868 when writing about him: "This is the modern countryside. We sense that man has passed through, digging up the soil, slicing up the land, saddening the views.... Out of the ordinary reality, the painter's temperament has drawn a true poem of life and strength."[17] Pissarro paints not virgin nature but the union between humanity and the environment from which we draw our subsistence, a harmony that Paris's green outskirts created for a time. His painting dances to the rhythm of the seasons, with people gathering wood in winter, then tending the earth as it is reborn in the spring, all in a dense, organic style. Although less left-wing and more urban, Berthe Morisot and Auguste Renoir lent their brushes to the beauty of the countryside and rustic escapes. Very few of Renoir's landscapes are without any human presence or narrative potential. In this orchard, painted in Louveciennes in the summer prior to the first Impressionist exhibition, three figures are going about their business. One woman is walking away from us carrying a bundle of wood, while another, dressed identically, is picking fruits that are already ripe in what could well be a sunny September. The light is again the crowning glory, taking possession of the forms and giving them a deliciously melting quality. This feeling of being softly enveloped combines with the composition's pronounced asymmetry, which recalls some Barbizon School arrangements. The English pear tree's size and natural vigor bring a sense of energy to the foreground. S.G.

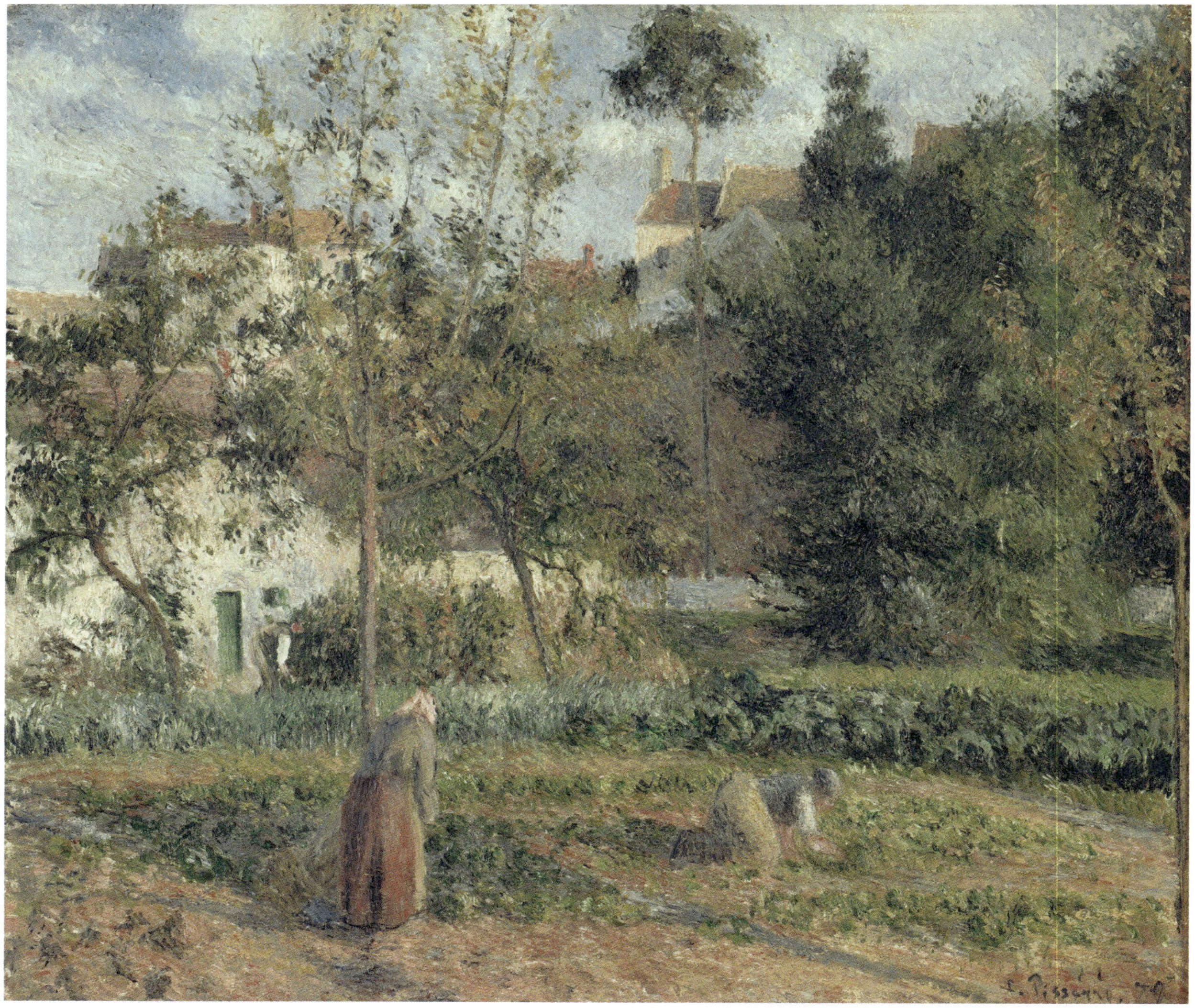

88 Camille Pissarro, *Jardin potager à l'Hermitage, Pontoise* (*Vegetable Garden at L'Hermitage, Pontoise*), 1879
Oil on canvas, 21 ⅝ × 25 $^{13}/_{16}$ in. (55 × 65.5 cm)

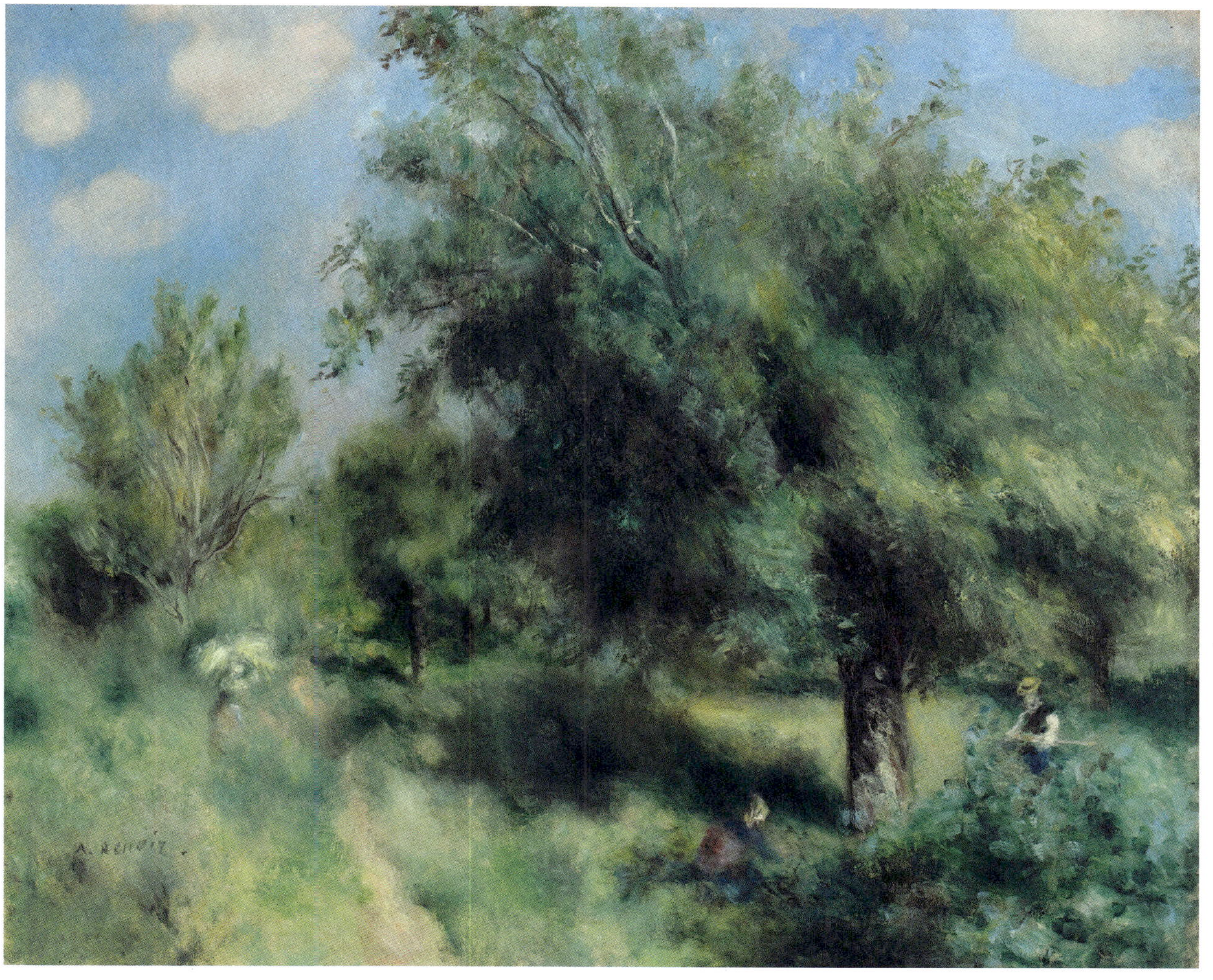

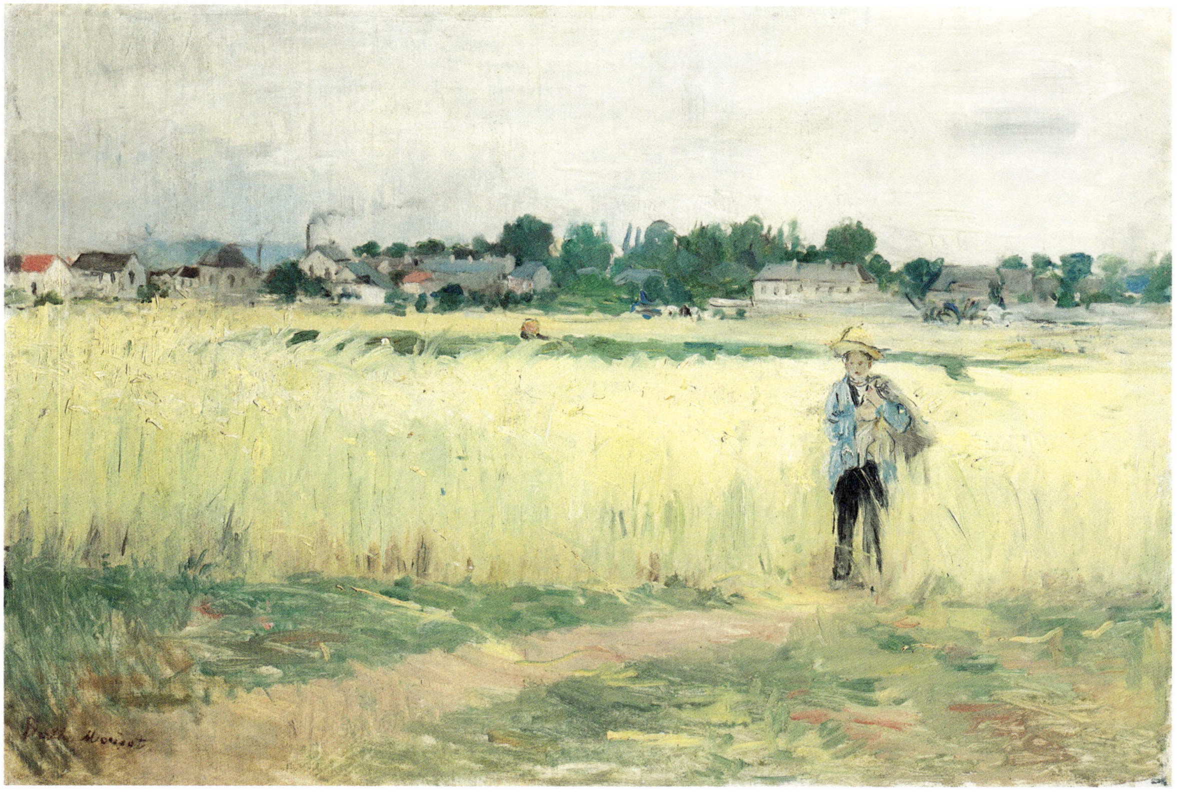

89 Top: Auguste Renoir, *Le Poirier d'Angleterre* (*The English Pear Tree*), c. 1873
Oil on canvas, 26 3⁄16 × 32 1⁄16 in. (66.5 × 81.5 cm)

90 Bottom: Berthe Morisot, *Dans les blés* (*In the Wheatfields*), 1875
Oil on canvas, 18 5⁄16 × 27 3⁄16 in. (46.5 × 69 cm)

Camille Pissarro
Hoarfrost

It was a quick and easy journey from Pontoise's L'Hermitage neighborhood to Ennery, where Pissarro found the subject for this painting. One of five he showed at the first Impressionist exhibition, it was also among those that prompted the critic Louis Leroy to comment sarcastically about the group, citing its lumpy paint treatment and its obvious myriad glints and shadows. The work was also criticized for ignoring standard compositional rules, in favor of a de-hierarchized tabular presentation: "It has neither head nor tail, neither top nor bottom, neither front nor rear." Other critics rallied in favor of Pissarro's style and technique, which still closely mimicked Millet's example. The man carrying the bundle of wood, seen from behind and leaning on a stick so as to inspire greater empathy, makes no attempt to conceal Pissarro's debt to his master. Writing in *La République française*, Philippe Burty likened *Hoarfrost* to Millet's best works, albeit with some reservations regarding its lack of finish. Millet was a skilled portrayer of wintry landscapes, although his were often more desolate. Here, in contrast, the winter sunlight reigns supreme as we witness the melting of the morning frost. Not all critics understood the ghostly ballet of the tall trees outside the frame, even those who complimented the painting's silent synthetic power. Courbet's friend Jules-Antoine Castagnary, for example, did not grasp why Pissarro was forcing the public to imagine elements that he was content merely to suggest, forgetting that even realism is an intellectual exercise.   S.G.

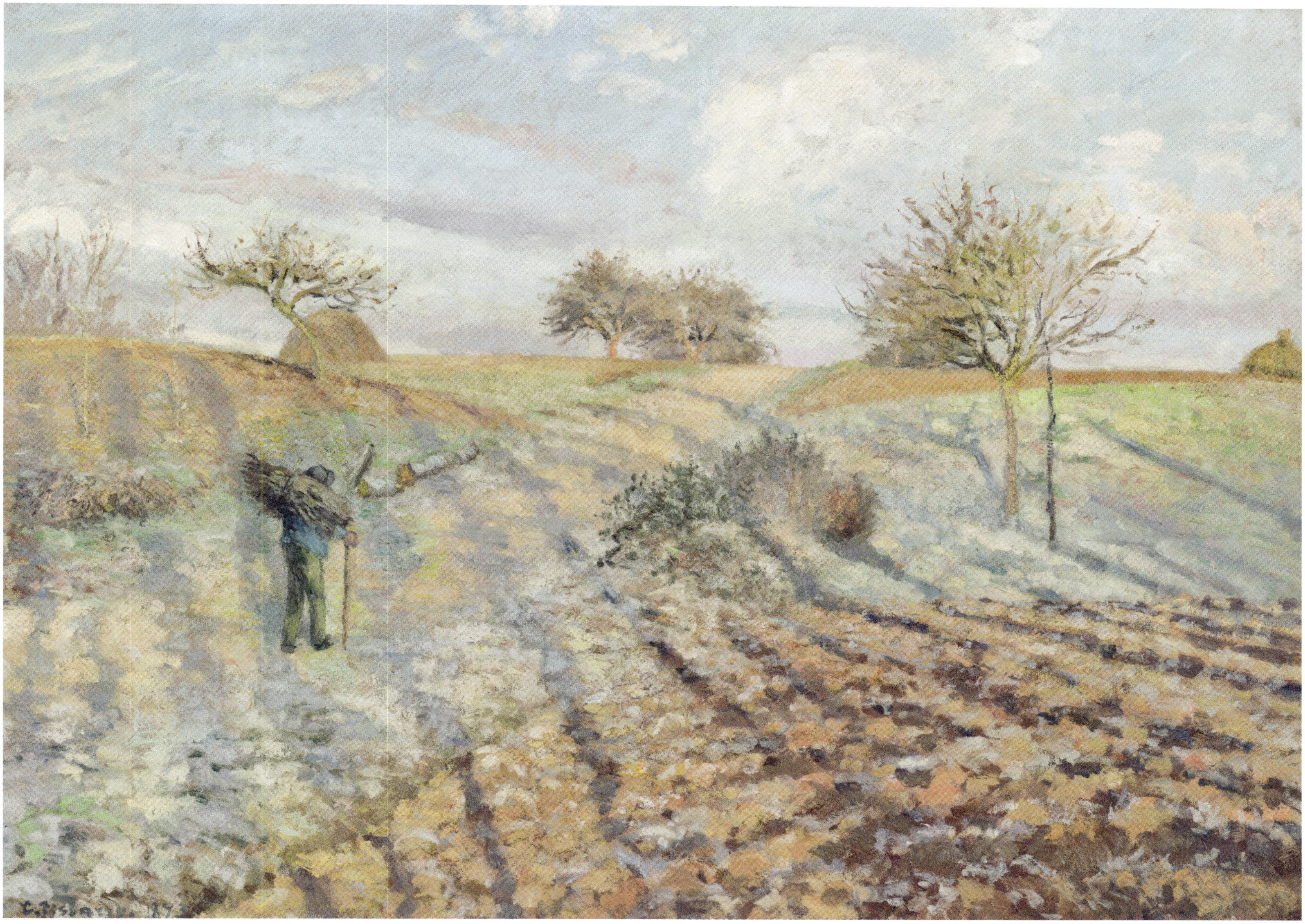

91 Camille Pissarro, *Gelée blanche (Hoarfrost)*, 1873
Oil on canvas, 25 13⁄16 × 36 11⁄16 in. (65.5 × 93.2 cm)

Camille Pissarro
The Côte Saint-Denis at Pontoise

Pissarro lived in Pontoise between 1866 and 1868, and again from 1872 until 1882. It therefore goes without saying that its sights became associated with the years when Impressionism was coming into its own. At the time, Pontoise was on the rise both demographically and economically. Pissarro himself avoided living in its town center, preferring the outlying neighborhood of L'Hermitage. The row of houses in this picture, which was one of the artist's favorites, had already appeared in a canvas painted around 1867 (now in a private collection). Rising up in the background is the hill known as the Côte Saint-Denis, with its cereal crops. The appearance and effect of this picture, painted ten years later, at a time when winter had stripped the trees and converted the surrounding fields into furrows, are very different. A curtain of tall trees forms a screen that occupies the foreground, through which we glimpse a group of houses nestled together, devoid of any human presence, so as to emphasize their protective permanence. The reddish browns of the palette, which offer a counterpoint to the few green accents, dominate the canvas with a rich, vibrant touch. The work, which belonged to Caillebotte, was widely acclaimed when it appeared at the third Impressionist exhibition, in 1877: the critic Amédée Descubes wrote at the time, "A lovely painting, a little house hidden in the forest; I was struck by the steadiness and simplicity of the brushwork." He could also have highlighted its beautiful winter light. S.G.

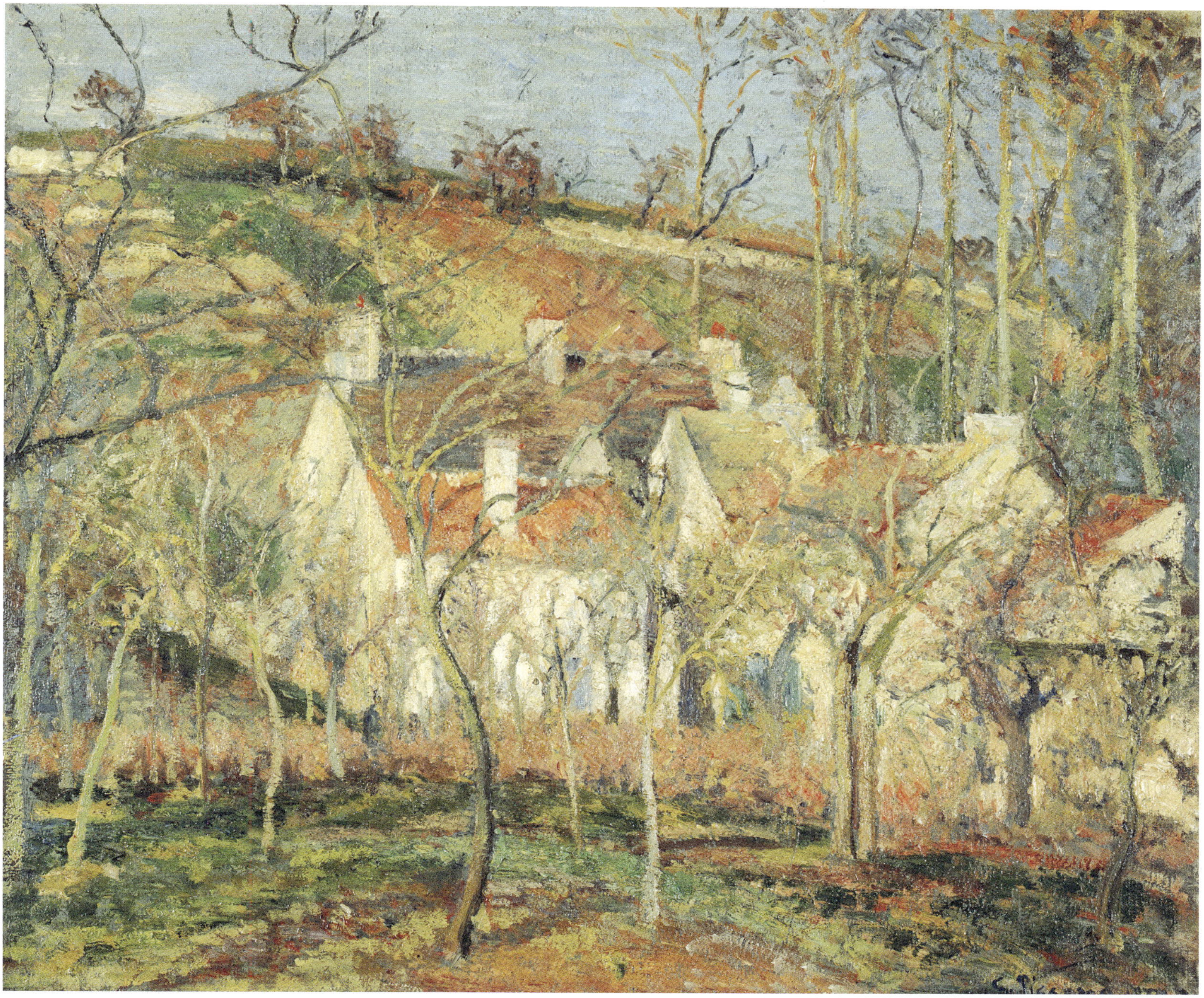

92 Camille Pissarro, *Côte Saint-Denis à Pontoise* (*The Côte Saint-Denis at Pontoise*), 1877
Oil on canvas, 21 ⁷⁄₁₆ × 25 ¹³⁄₁₆ in. (54.5 × 65.6 cm)

Finished and unfinished

From close up, Impressionist brushstrokes look like juxtaposed, fragmented, chaotic blotches. It is only on moving away from the canvas that motifs become distinguishable and forms fall into place. Still, these strokes are not all alike: each painter's individual manner of placing these colored marks on the canvas is recognizable, sometimes constant, sometimes varied. There is very little resemblance, for example, between Monet's broad, spaced-out brushstrokes when painting *The Regatta at Argenteuil* and Renoir's light, vibrant ones in *Path Rising into Deep Grass*, even though the two had been so close just a few years earlier when painting together on the island at La Grenouillère. And it is hard to see a connection between Cézanne's precise, clearly defined brushstrokes when painting *The Poplars* and Morisot's flowing, evanescent ones when representing two girls on a bench in the Bois de Boulogne. In 1874, critics reporting on the first Impressionist exhibition already noted the painters' different use of paint, while recognizing what their output had in common: that is, the same "casualness," the same "embryonic" look, in contrast to the smooth paintings of academic painters where the subject is immediately identifiable. So it was not the form of the brushstrokes that united these painters, but rather the unfinished aspect that shows their shared desire to represent the light at a specific moment, and the fleetingness of feeling. To paint diffracted light, blurred outlines, and the shifting, fluid nature of air and water, what could be more fitting than these spaces between the brushstrokes and this absence of blending, which do not delimit contours and which fragment lines. And with this aim in mind, what could be more apt than to leave voids, to end the gesture at the point where the feeling of a moment disappears. Unfinishedness, represented through the techniques of spacing out brushstrokes and leaving areas unpainted, no longer came across as pictorial cluelessness but rather as the impossible, poetic harnessing of the ephemeral. B.T.

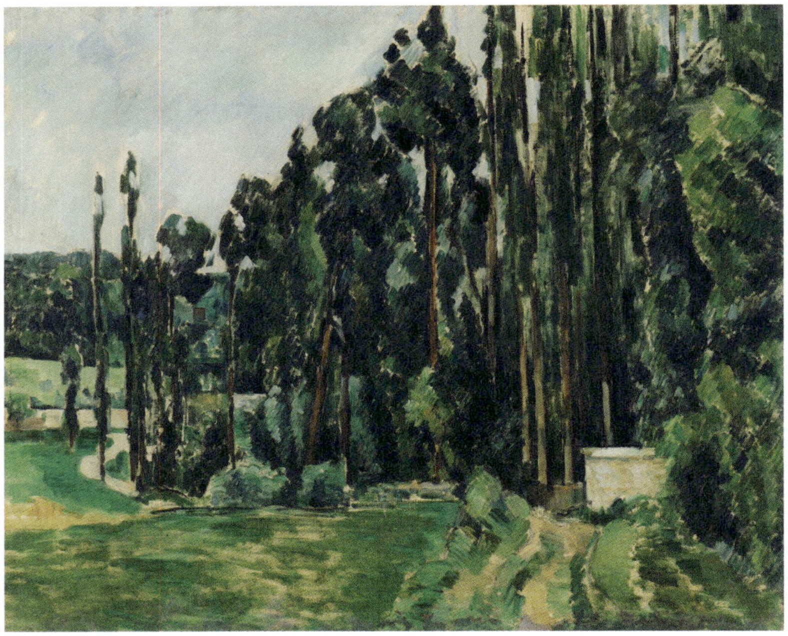

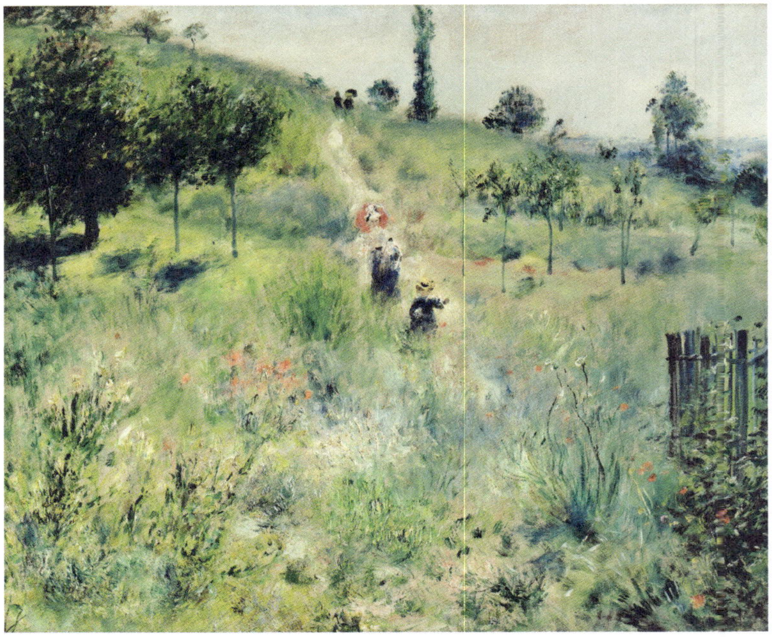

93 Left: Paul Cézanne, *Les Peupliers* (*The Poplars*), 1879–1880
Oil on canvas, 25 9⁄16 × 32 1⁄16 in. (65 × 81.5 cm)

94 Right: Auguste Renoir, *Chemin montant dans les hautes herbes* (*Path Rising into Deep Grass*), c. 1875
Oil on canvas, 23 5⁄8 × 29 1⁄8 in. (60 × 74 cm)

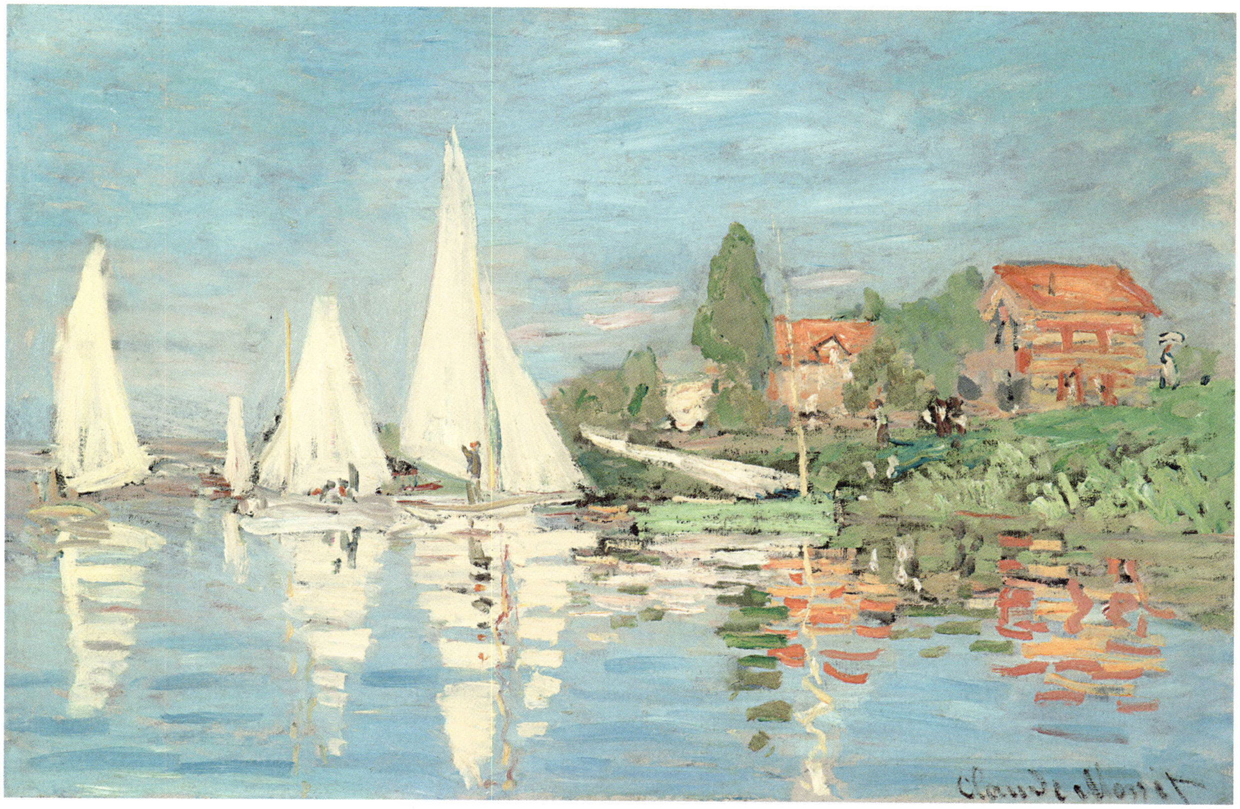

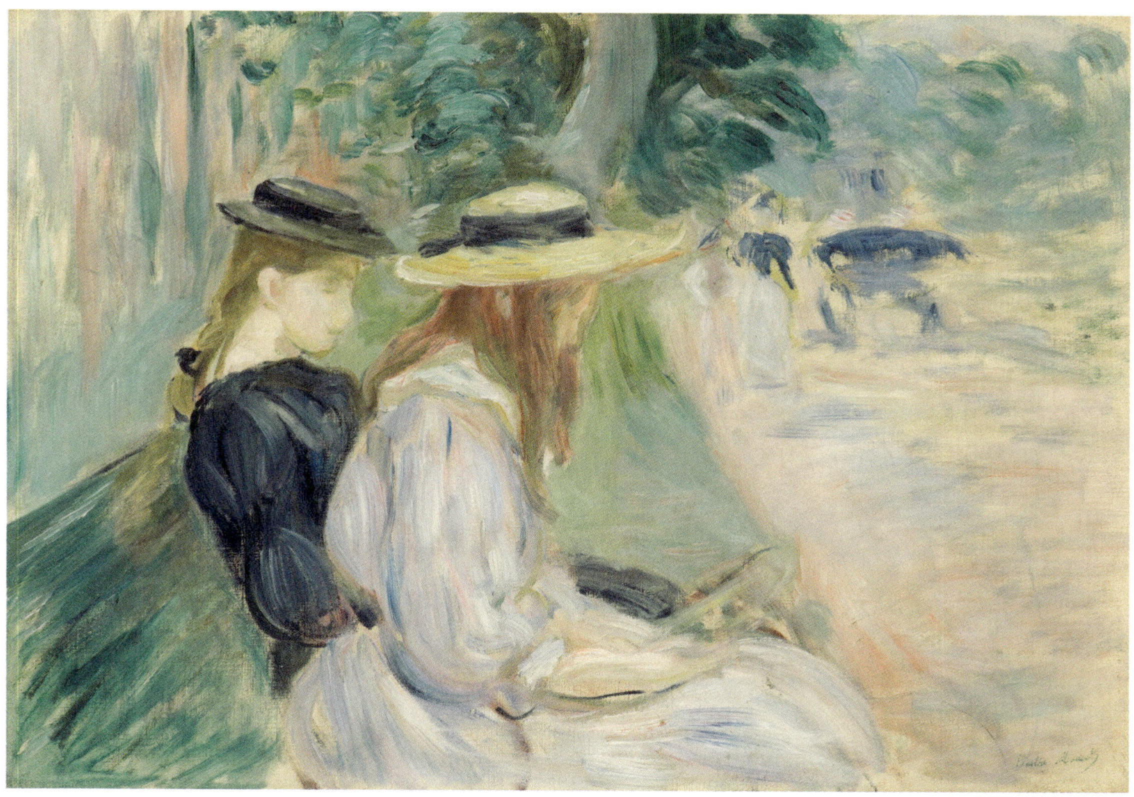

95 Top: Claude Monet, *Régates à Argenteuil* (*The Regatta at Argenteuil*), c. 1872
Oil on canvas, 18 ⅞ × 29 ⅝ in. (48 × 75.3 cm)

96 Bottom: Berthe Morisot, *Sur un banc au bois de Boulogne* (*On a Bench in the Bois de Boulogne*), 1894
Oil on canvas, 15 1⁄16 × 21 ¾ in. (38.2 × 55.3 cm)

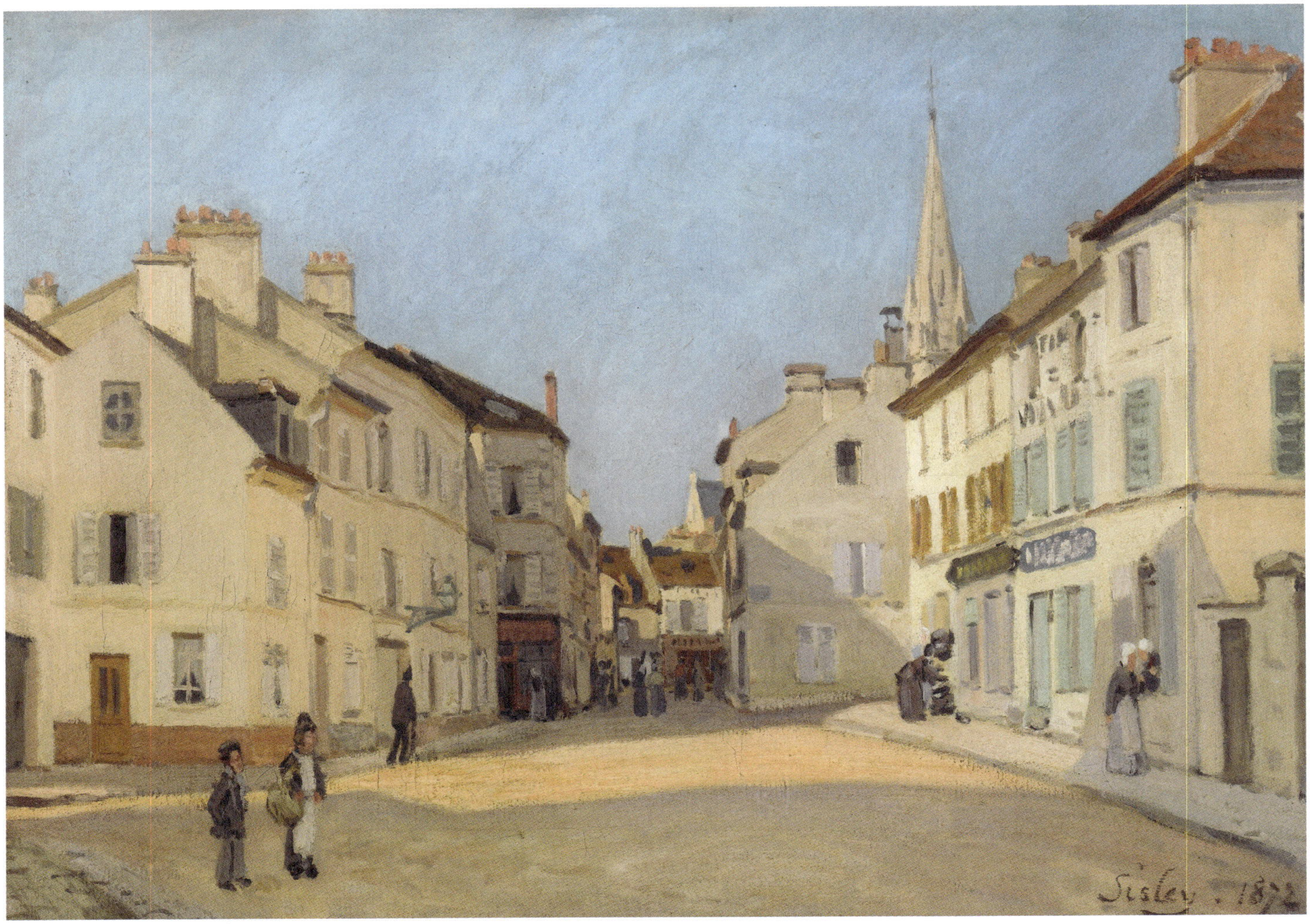

97 Alfred Sisley, *Rue de la chaussée à Argenteuil* (*Rue de la Chaussée at Argenteuil*), 1872
Oil on canvas, 18 5⁄16 × 25 15⁄16 in. (46.5 × 66 cm)

Colors, light, and shadow

Regardless of the subject matter, whether landscapes, portraits, or street scenes, for the Impressionists, light was not simply a piece of theoretical data that they could adapt or modify in order to bring out an element of their composition according to codes that had been in place since the Renaissance. They saw and painted the sunlight that suffused their entire chosen subject: the parts in direct light, those in shade, and the omnipresent glints and reflections. The question was how they should go about translating light's all-encompassing presence into color.

Following in Corot's footsteps, they devoted themselves to discerning the distribution of light and shadow according to a value scale, from the lightest to the darkest; but they took this much further than he had. The Impressionist painters sought to transpose these values into a range of colors that shared the same luminosity: in bright atmospheres, they chose pure colors; in hazier ones, they would mix all their colors with the same quantity of white. In this transposition of values to hues that shared the same level of brightness, the relationship between warm and cool, as well as contrasts between complementary colors and gloss effects, were also taken into account. The cold, blueish shadows of Sisley's *Rue de la Chaussée at Argenteuil* alternate with the warm tones of the ground and the house without presenting any glaring contrasts, sharing the same intensity of light, to render the saturated atmosphere of summer. This alternation of warm and cold colors is even more pronounced in Renoir's *Algerian Landscape: The Ravine of the "Femme Sauvage,"* where the pure blue of the shadows and the white flashes of light are equal in strength. In *The Seine at Vétheuil, Sun Effect After Rain*, Monet plays with reflections of the sky in the water. His vibrant brushstrokes distributed across the canvas are unified in tone, and give an effect of coolness and of how a landscape sparkles after rain. B. T.

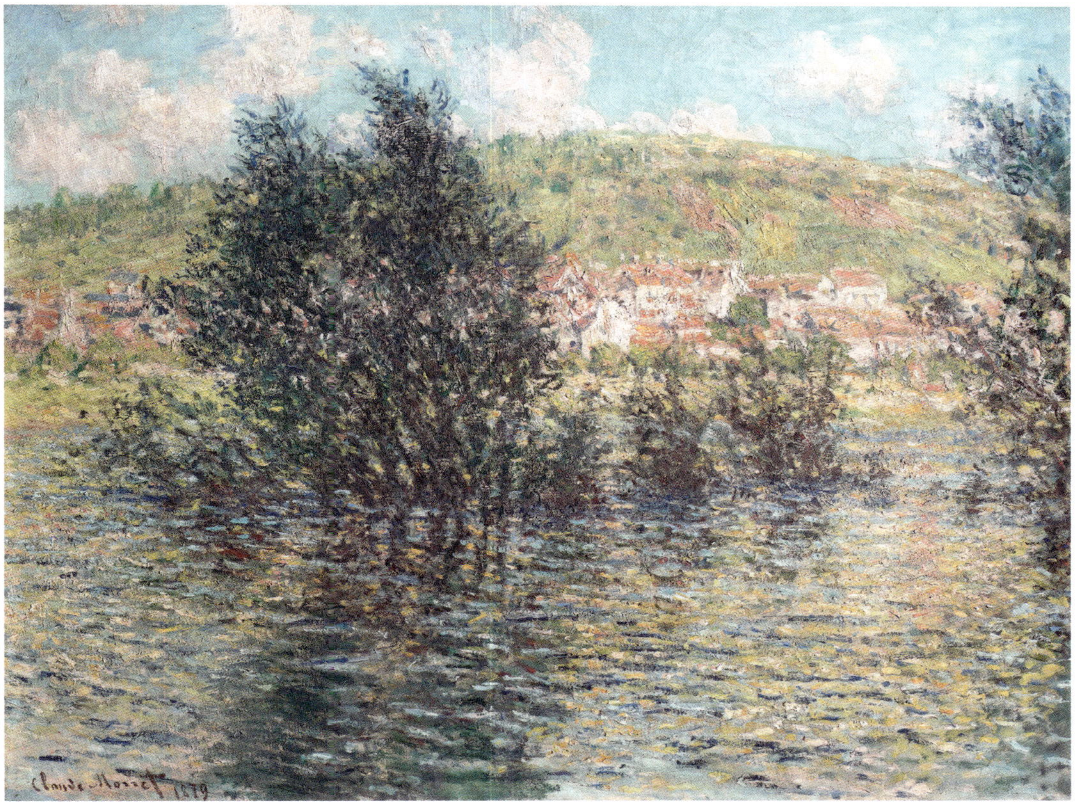

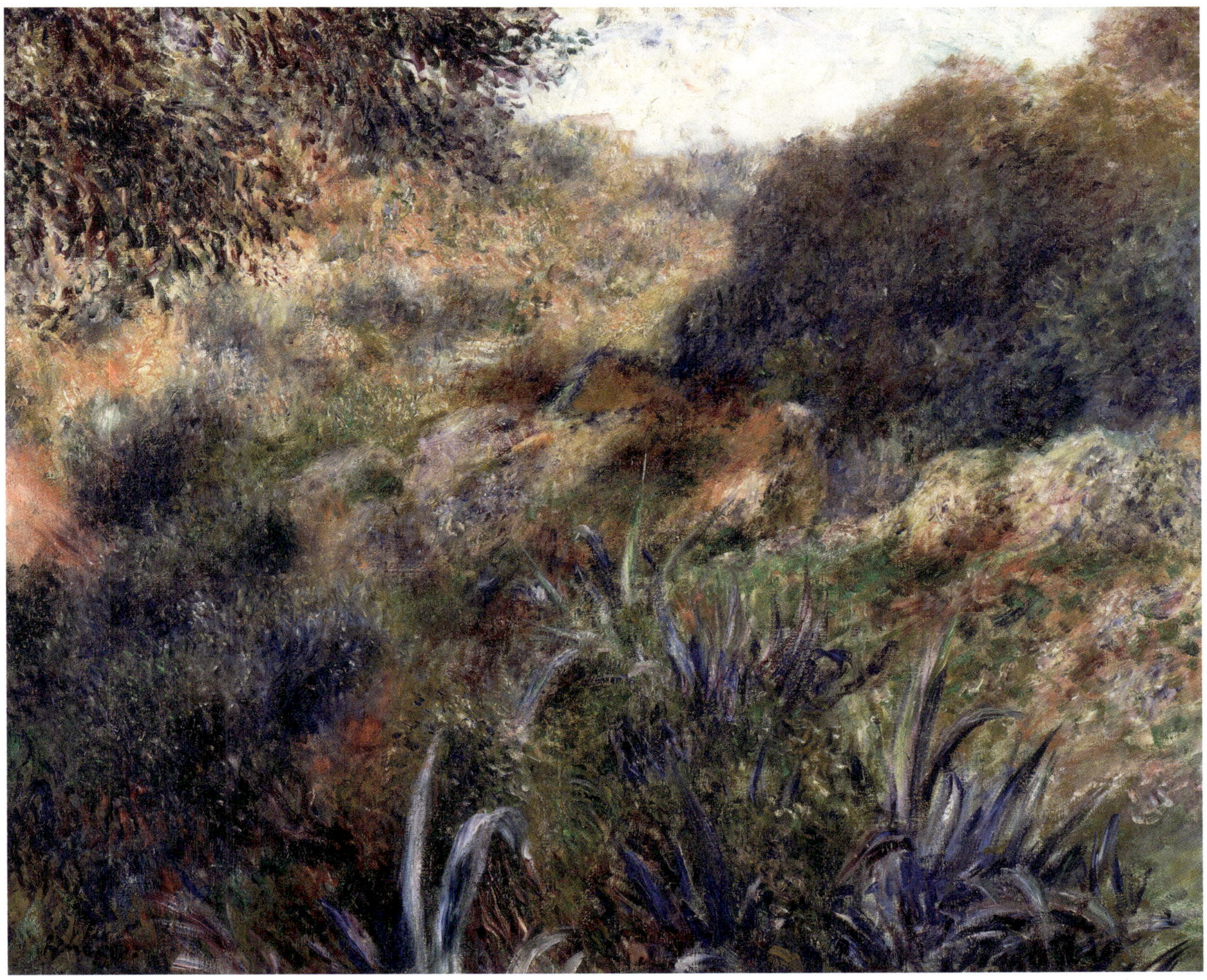

98 Top: Claude Monet, *La Seine à Vétheuil, effet de soleil après la pluie* (*The Seine at Vétheuil, Sun Effect After Rain*), 1879
Oil on canvas, 23 13⁄16 × 32 1⁄16 in. (60.5 × 81.5 cm)

99 Bottom: Auguste Renoir, *Paysage algérien, le ravin de la femme sauvage* (*Algerian Landscape: The Ravine of the "Femme Sauvage"*), 1881
Oil on canvas, 25 9⁄16 × 32 1⁄16 in. (65 × 81.5 cm)

1876

The second Impressionist exhibition

Although the Impressionist exhibitions had been envisaged from the outset in 1874 as annual events, the second one did not take place until the spring of 1876, postponed due to "various obstacles." More often than not, the Impressionists's art was still derided. In March 1875, Monet, Renoir, Morisot, and Sisley organized a public auction of their works at the Drouot auction house. The catastrophic results of this sale—and the "ridiculous kerfuffle" of how it unfolded—put them off repeating the exhibition experiment too soon. When the group decided in early 1876 to come together again to show their work, it was on the same principles as the first group initiative: each participating artist would contribute to the rental costs of the exhibition space. This time the venue was three rooms of a gallery on Rue Le Peletier. The gallery was that of Paul Durand-Ruel, who had been supportive of them for several years and took the risk of buying large numbers of their works. The show opened on April 1. The works were presented in a carefully orchestrated display, shown off in sumptuous frames. The group had shaken off its fringe of more minor artists, and was now condensed down to "the new school of painting" and their "innovative works." All of them were trying to consolidate their position in the Paris art world. The loss of some was compensated for by the arrival of an important new recruit: Gustave Caillebotte (invited by Renoir and by Henri Rouart, a collector and artist who was an engineer by trade). Like the others, Caillebotte was trying to circumvent the Salon's censorship of style and subject matter, and among the paintings he showed was *Floor Scrapers* (p. 121), which had been rejected by the Salon jury the previous year.

Each exhibiting artist showed a well-rounded, carefully chosen selection of works, fully representative of "*La Nouvelle Peinture*" (The New Painting)—which was the title of a brochure of their art, published by the critic Edmond Duranty for the occasion. The exhibition itself was titled simply "*2e exposition de peinture*" (Second painting exhibition). While it had not yet adopted the "Impressionist" moniker, the participating painters were "steadily flying their flag," as Duranty wrote. A. R.

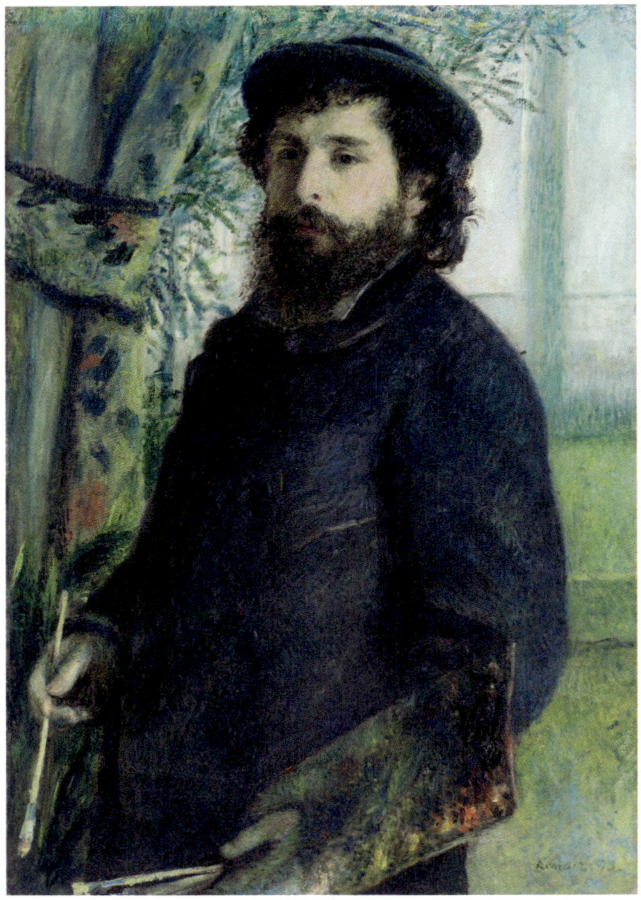

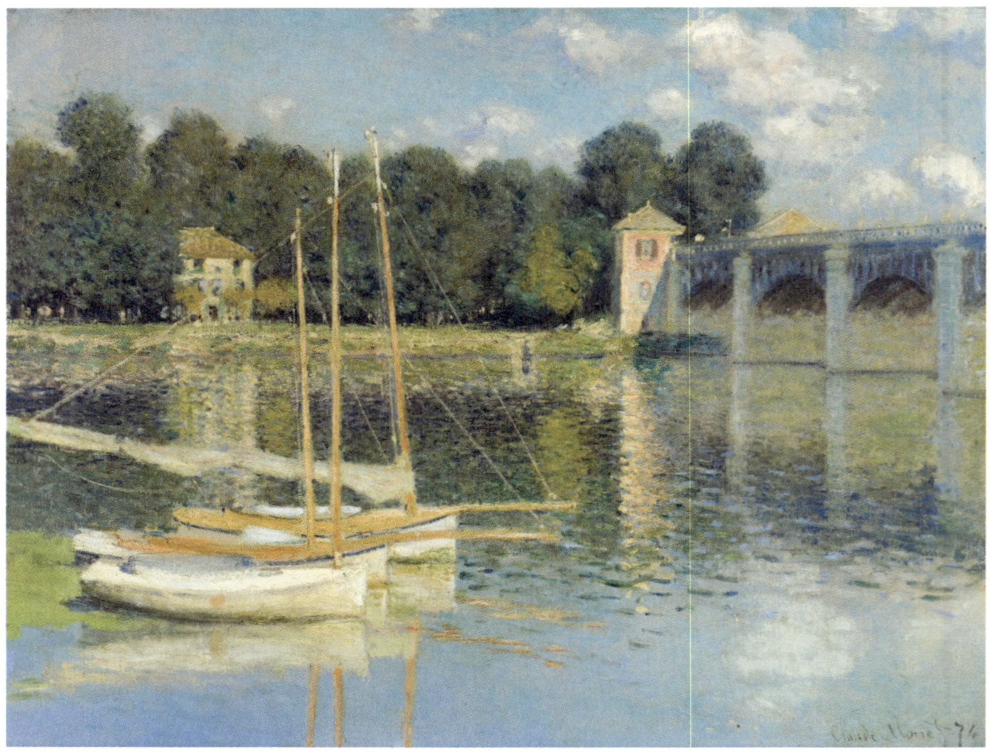

100 Top: Auguste Renoir, *Claude Monet*, 1875
Oil on canvas, 33 1/16 × 23 13/16 in. (84 × 60.5 cm)

101 Bottom: Claude Monet, *Le Pont d'Argenteuil* (*The Argenteuil Bridge*), 1874
Oil on canvas, 23 3/4 × 31 1/2 in. (60.3 × 80 cm)

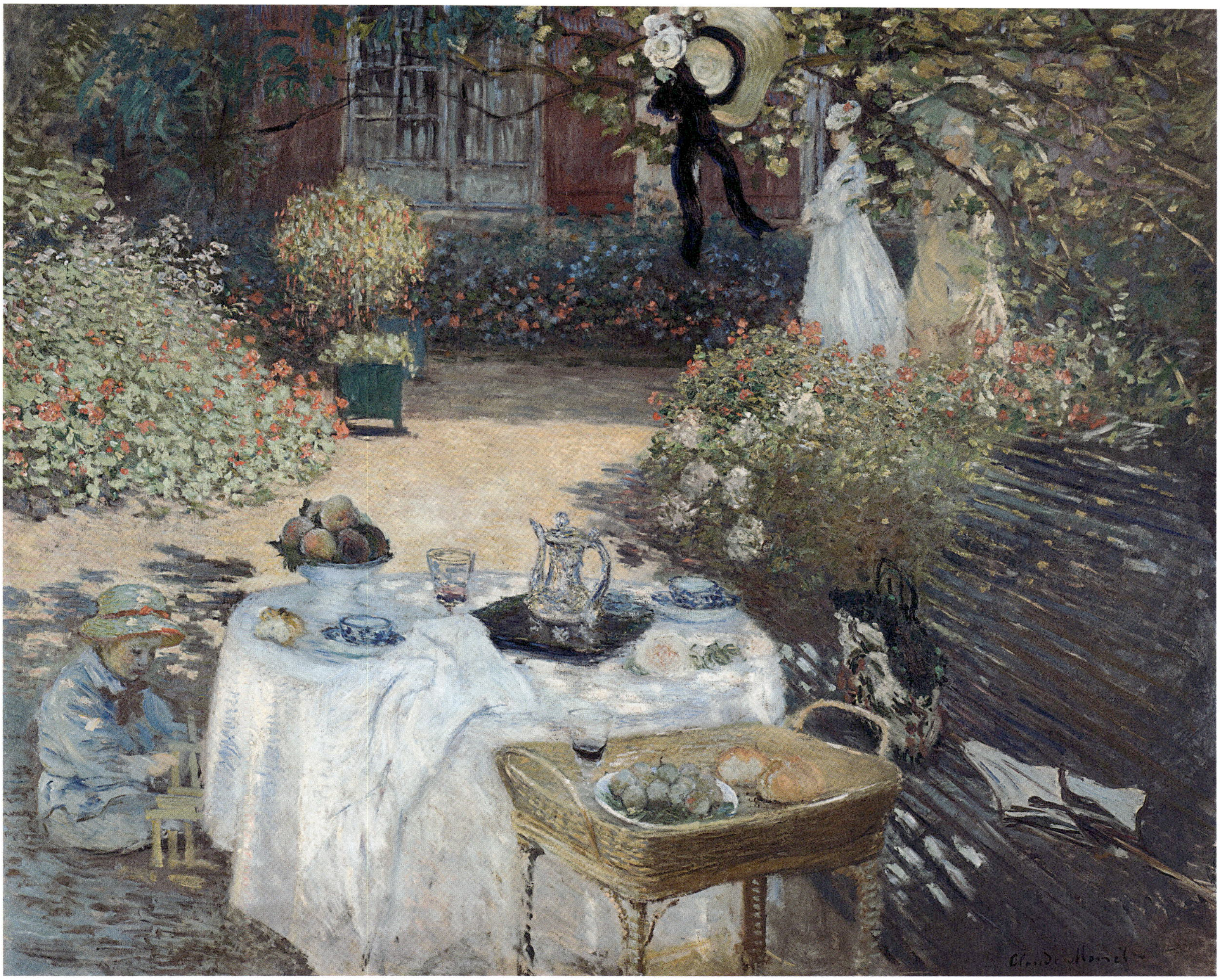

102 Claude Monet, *Le Déjeuner. Panneau décoratif* (*The Luncheon: Decorative Panel*), c. 1873
Oil on canvas, 63 × 79 ⅛ in. (160 × 201 cm)

Auguste Renoir
Torso, Sunlight Effect

Renoir's *Torso, Sunlight Effect* marks a crucial stage within both the history of nudes and the context of the painter's career. For the first time, he painted a nude entirely *en plein air*, and applied the principles of Impressionist aesthetics, as they were defined in those years, to the flesh: fluid brushstrokes applied rapidly *alla prima*; dissolved forms and contours; vivid colors; plays of light that filters through greenery and creates colorful glints; and the abandonment of "local color" and black. It was one of very few genuinely Impressionist nudes to have been painted at the time, and was the first to be shown to the public and critics, in 1876 at the second Impressionist exhibition. Its strictly experimental character is clearly indicated through Renoir's having given it the title *Étude* (*Study*), just as Monet had chosen the term "impression" in 1874 for his sunrise over the port of Le Havre (*Impression, Sunrise*).

The work drew some positive critical reactions, but also virulent attacks from more conservative writers. Albert Wolff, in the newspaper *Le Figaro*, took offence: "Try to explain to Mr. Renoir that a woman's torso is not a mass of decomposing flesh, with purplish-green marks that denote a corpse in a state of total putrefaction!"[18] Several other commentators and caricaturists took up the image of "gamy flesh"[19] to bolster their criticism of Renoir for straying from the conventions that governed representations of the female nude and thereby assaulting the very symbol of beauty and the ideal in art.

For Renoir, on the contrary, the painting sought to revitalize a longstanding tradition—that of Giorgione, Titian, Rubens, Boucher, and Fragonard—which he had long admired at the Louvre. The sense of plenitude that radiates from the woman's flesh and from the fusing of the figure and the landscape, made possible by Renoir's particularly energetic brushwork in this picture, no doubt also evidences the artist's dream of a return to nature, embodied by the female figure. P. P.

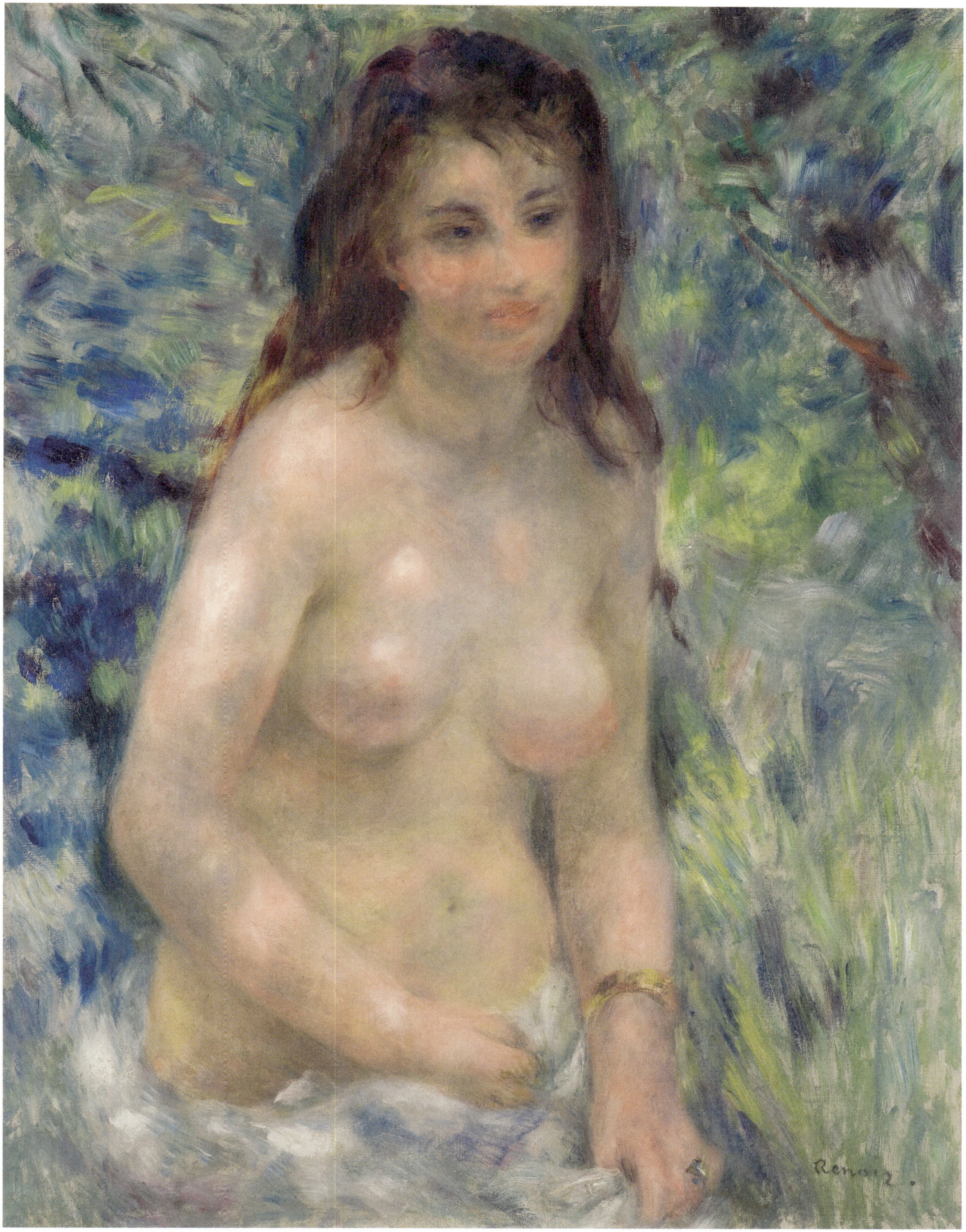

103 Auguste Renoir, *Étude* (*Study*), also known as *Torse, effet de soleil* (*Torso, Sunlight Effect*), c. 1876
Oil on canvas, 31 7/8 × 25 9/16 in. (81 × 65 cm)

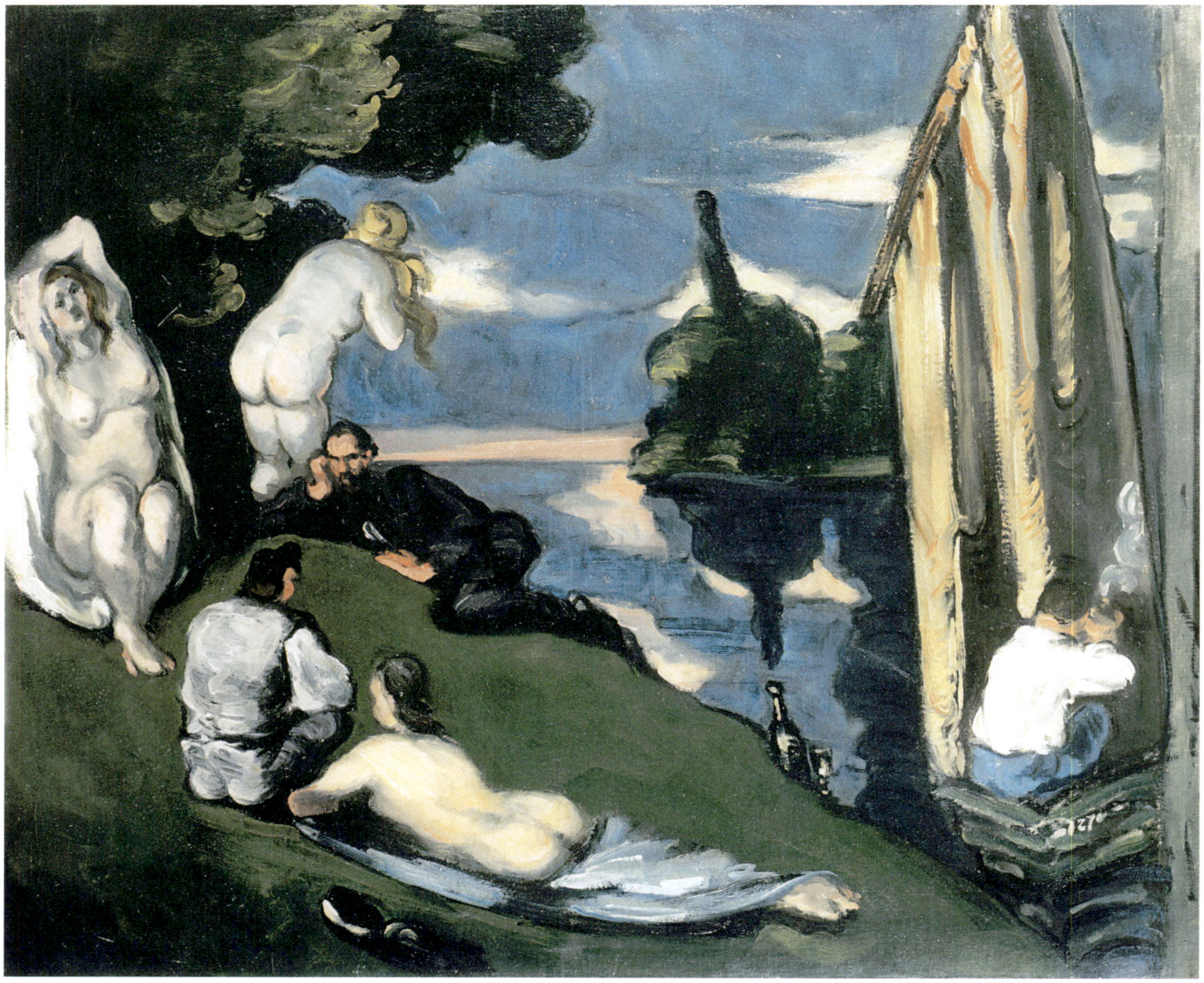

104 Paul Cézanne, *Pastorale (Pastoral)*, 1870
Oil on canvas, 25 9⁄16 × 32 1⁄16 in. (65 × 81.5 cm)

Modern nudes

Of all the genres, the nude was without doubt the one that was the most shielded from being redefined by the "New Painting." Ever since the Renaissance, it had been central to instruction in the art of drawing, the purpose of which was purportedly to celebrate the most beautiful things that divine creation had to offer. By dissociating ideal beauty from imperfect flesh, and by establishing statuary as a model for painting, a fixed aesthetic ideal developed, which was perpetuated through copying models from antiquity. Anything that might serve as a reminder of the human figure's naturalness, starting with body hair, was proscribed.

The Romantics had already been criticized for not sufficiently ennobling their anatomies. Courbet's and Manet's approach was more radical, given their affinity with Venetian and Nordic masters, while the Second Empire encouraged the widespread proliferation of the female nude, pure in form though impure of thought. The Salon's mythological paintings gave way to figures in a state of undress captured in real-life situations, from getting washed to engaging in modern leisure pursuits, and from prostitution to the domestic interior. At the 1877 Impressionist exhibition, Guillaumin, who was close to Pissarro and Dr. Gachet, showed *Reclining Nude*, a dreamy, working-class paraphrase of the earlier *Olympia* (p. 17); the Japanese-style fan here serves as the equivalent to Manet's black servant girl. Renoir is unequalled in the collective consciousness where images of naked women are concerned His hundreds of bathing women, usually detached from the urban setting, testify to this, with a pastoral theme that links his work to that of his friend Cézanne. *Boy with a Cat* is even more bizarre. Deliberate ambiguity had been part of Renoir's training under Charles Gleyre, a leading figure of the 1840s–1860s neo-Greek movement. Odalisques and Adonises, sometimes feminized, were passed down from master to pupil. While the canvas echoes Manet in its palette and sharp lighting, this boy and this rapturous cat, which seems to have come straight out of Lewis Carroll, appear intentionally provocative for any viewer, regardless of their gender. S.G.

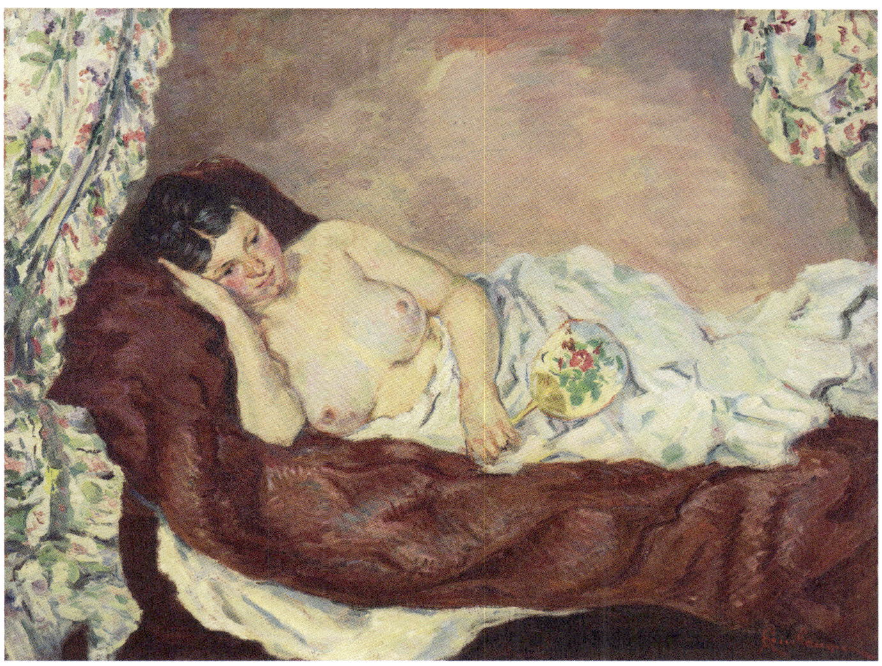

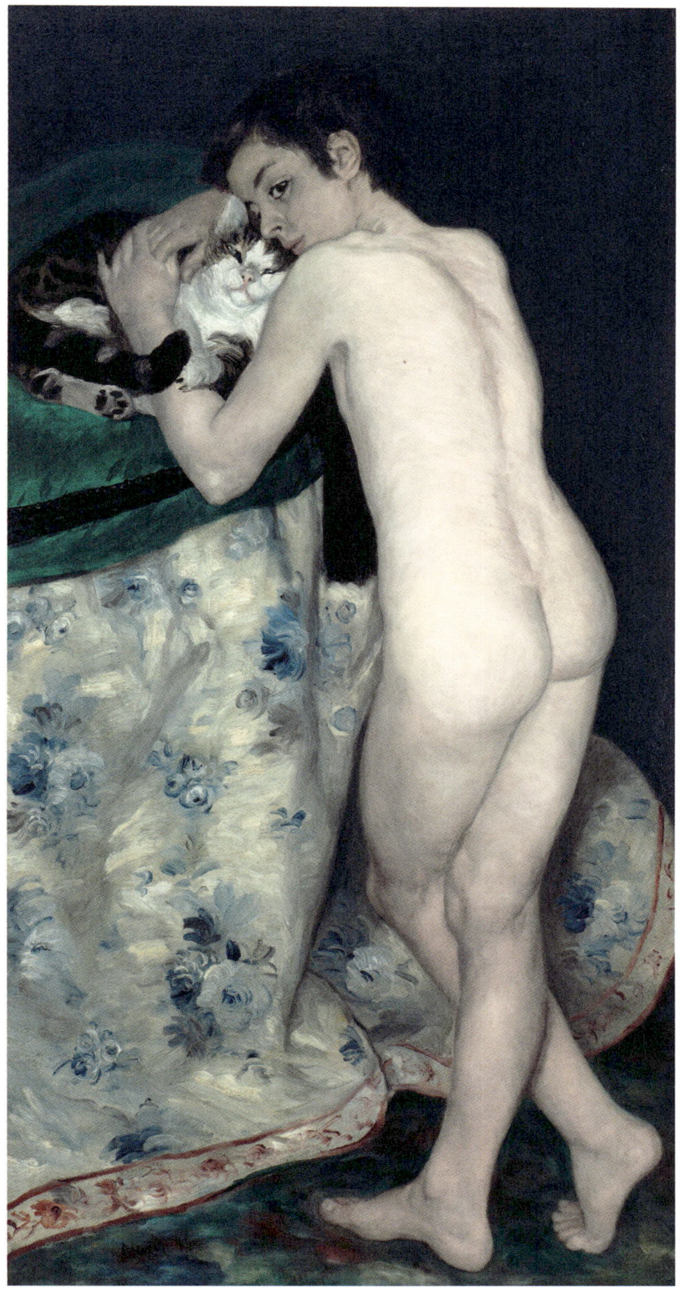

105 Left: Armand Guillaumin, *Femme nue couchée* (*Reclining Nude*), c. 1877
Oil on canvas, 19 5⁄16 × 25 9⁄16 in. (49 × 65 cm)

106 Right: Auguste Renoir, *Le Garçon au chat* (*Boy with a Cat*), 1868
Oil on canvas, 48 5⁄8 × 26 in. (123.5 × 66 cm)

Gustave Caillebotte
Floor Scrapers

Caillebotte here transports us into the upper stories of the *hôtel particulier* that his family built at the end of the Second Empire at the corner of Rue de Miromesnil and Rue de Lisbonne, in the midst of Paris's upmarket new districts. Before his father died, he had paid for a room there to be fitted out as his son's painting studio, and that may be where we find ourselves, observing from a slightly raised viewpoint. With the light flooding in so sublimely, the heightened perspective effect, and the trio of tradesmen hard at work, the painting established Caillebotte's style and name, as the oversized signature confirms. The actions are precise, the poses balanced, the glances very human. He does not overexaggerate the men's muscles. And the rhythmic harmony of the three bodies is reminiscent of *The Gleaners* painted in 1857 by Millet (Musée d'Orsay, Paris), whom Caillebotte greatly admired. Lastly, the subject offers an echo of the French nation's reconstruction after the terrible year of 1870–1871. Despite all this, the jury of the 1875 Salon still found the canvas unacceptable; indeed, they were very hostile to all forms of realism. But the rejection in 1875 paved the way for triumph in 1876, when Caillebotte, already close to Degas, chose to exhibit with the Impressionists. In the journal *Le Rappel*, the poet Émile Blémont, who was close to Mallarmé, exclaimed on seeing the painting: "It is astounding in its truthfulness, its sense of life, and its simple, honest intimacy." Apart from Pissarro's countryfolk and Degas's laundresses, it is true that Impressionist iconography avoided agricultural labor and the urban working class. S.G.

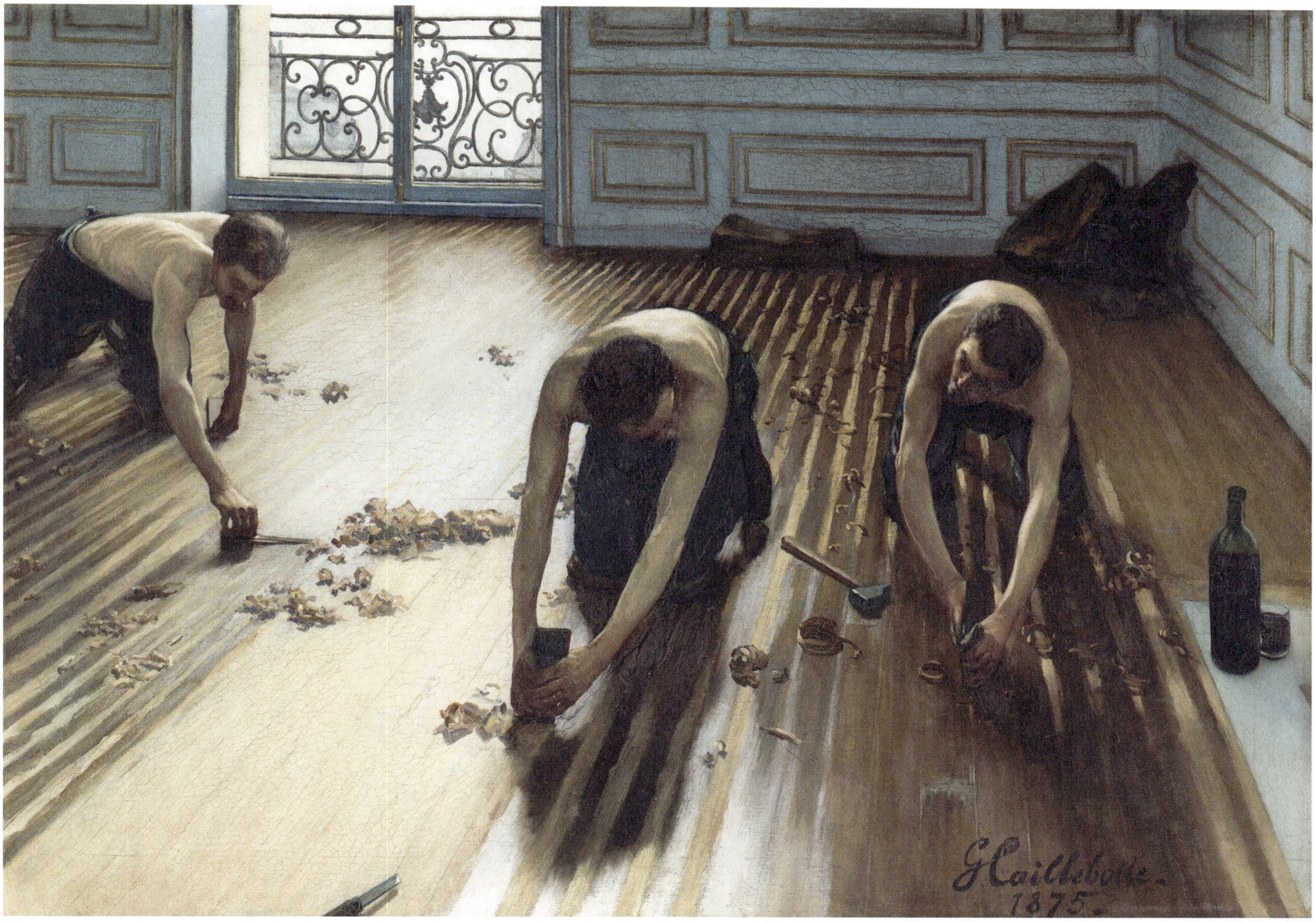

107 Gustave Caillebotte, *Raboteurs de parquets* (*Floor Scrapers*), 1875
Oil on canvas, 40 $\frac{3}{16}$ × 57 $\frac{7}{8}$ in. (102 × 147 cm)

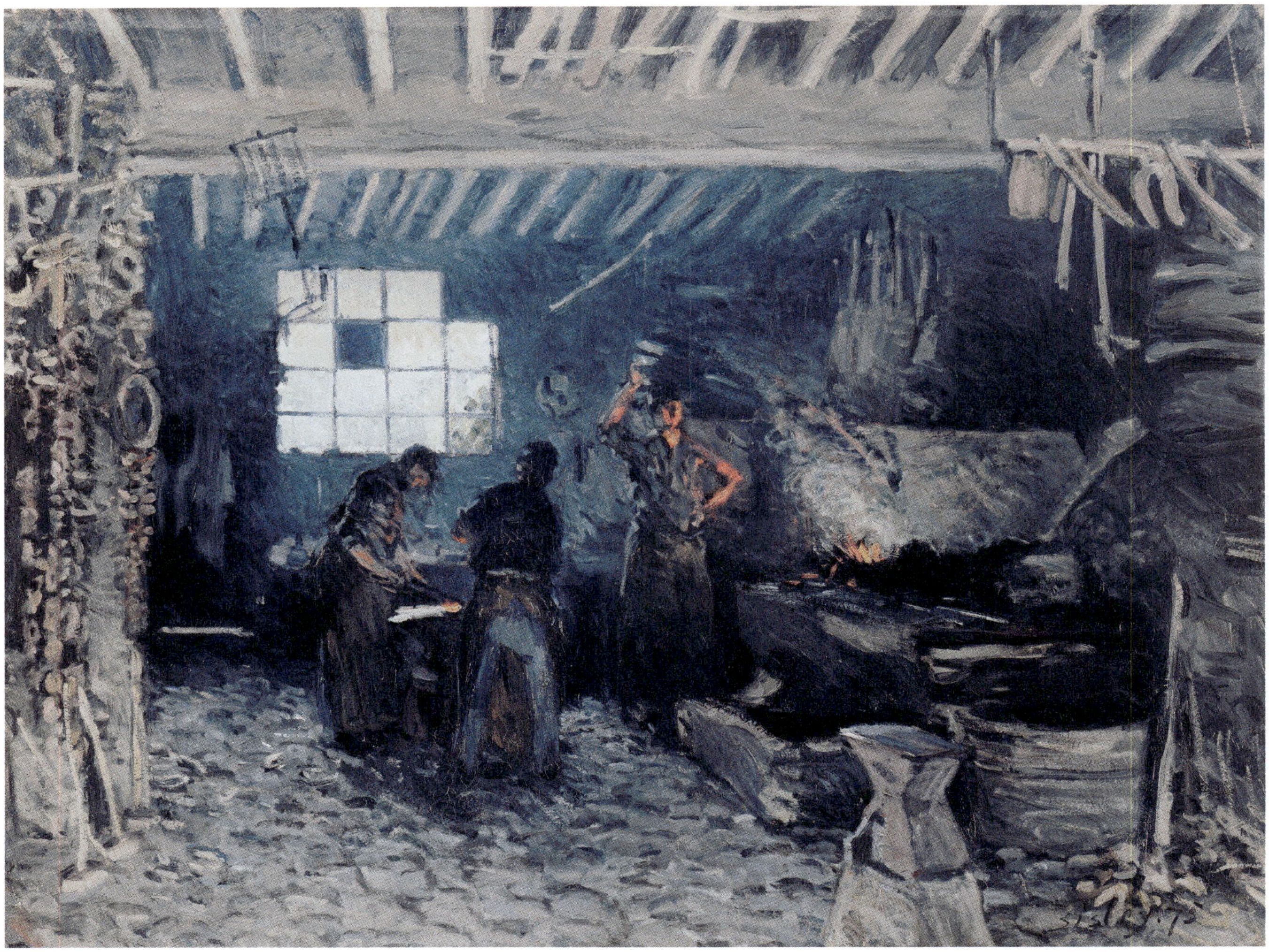

108 Alfred Sisley, *La Forge à Marly-le-Roi* (*The Forge at Marly-le-Roi*), 1875
Oil on canvas, 21 ⅝ × 28 ¾ in. (55 × 73 cm)

Painting workers

After viewing the first Impressionist exhibition, Philippe Burty—who supported the group from 1874—immediately admitted in the London press to feeling a sense of relief. According to his review, these secessionists with their bright, effusive paintings displayed no regrettable trace of any social, political, or even "human" concerns. Their work set out solely to be pleasing to the eye. Of course, this was not the full story. Burty's statement was certainly indicative of the rarity of Impressionist images of manual labor, these artists being more focused on representing contemporary leisure and the domestic sphere than the world of factories; but this only makes the exceptions more interesting. *Unloading the Coal*, shown at the 1879 Impressionist exhibition, belonged at the time to Charles Hayem, who was close to the politician Léon Gambetta, and whose wealth had come from the clothes industry.
In that year when political radicals came to power in France, he no doubt saw an ideological dimension in this vision of goods handling, with both its human quality and the mechanical nature of the repeated gestures. Despite its obvious Japonism, the canvas is arranged in response to its subject's demands: the stone-and-iron bridge supplants the spectacle of nature, and its arch frames the workers' robotic ballet. At the gateway to Paris and across the river from Asnières, Clichy was already covered with polluting factories and chimneys. Such eloquent images of coal-fueled manufacturing, a characteristic feature of the 1830s–1870s industrial boom, are few and far between. Compared to this painting, which one contemporary described in 1894 as "infernal," Sisley's forge conveys a feeling of rural craft practice, the Marly-le-Roi farrier's world, and of the poetic, mysterious nocturnes of his eighteenth-century compatriot Joseph Wright of Derby. A rectangle inside a rectangle encircled in blue shadows and glowing red sparks, the scene in no way suggests that this trade is alienating.
On the contrary: the anvil in the foreground has a proud look about it, and the patched-up window at the back indicates that productivist madness has no place here. S.G.

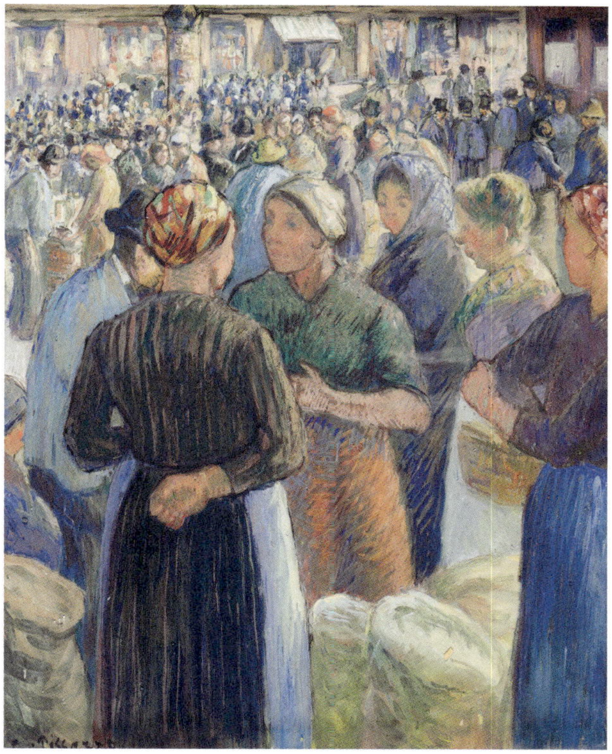

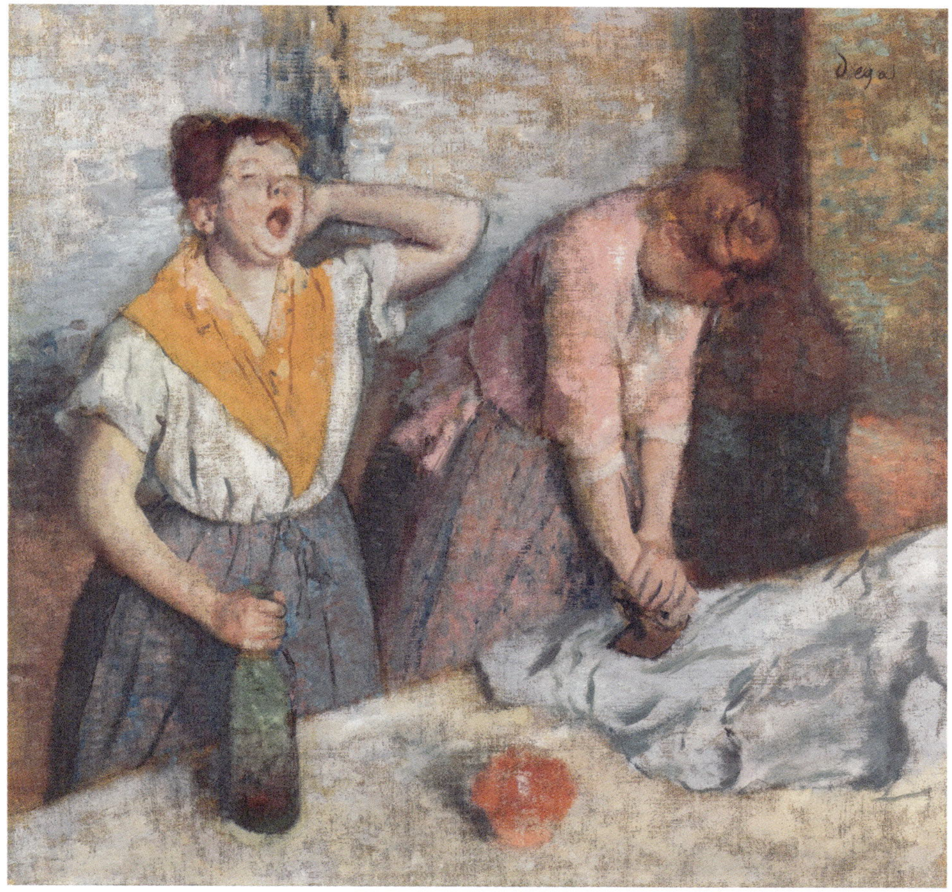

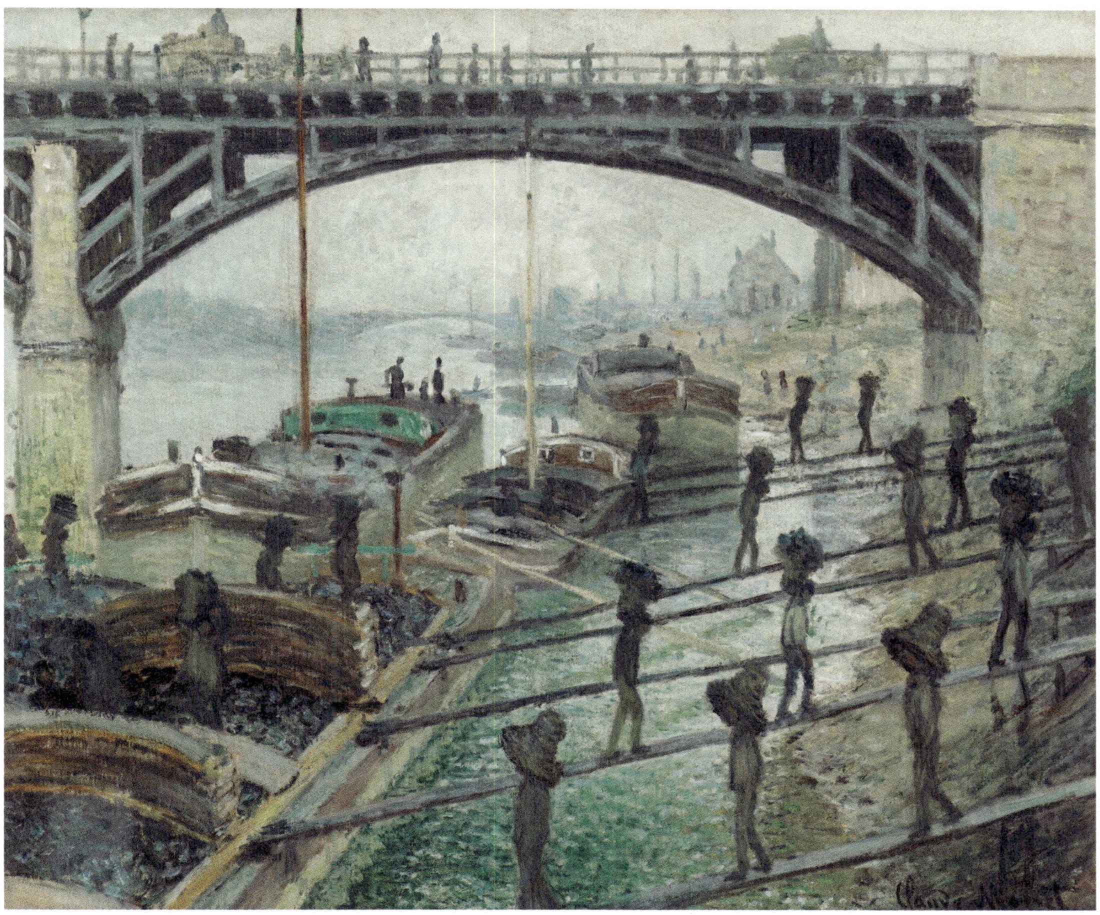

109 Top, left: Camille Pissarro, *Marché à Gisors* (*Market at Gisors*), 1890
Gouache over charcoal lines on canvas, 18 ⅛ × 14 15⁄16 in. (46 × 38 cm)

110 Top, right: Edgar Degas, *Repasseuses* (*Women Ironing*), between 1884 and 1886
Oil on canvas, 29 15⁄16 × 32 1⁄16 in. (76 × 81.4 cm)

111 Bottom: Claude Monet, *Les Déchargeurs de charbon* (*Unloading the Coal*), c. 1875
Oil on canvas, 21 ¼ × 25 13⁄16 in. (54 × 65.5 cm)

Impressionist gardens

The depiction of so-called "ornamental gardens" was a key component of Impressionist iconography. Ever more popular in the nineteenth century thanks to the flourishing of the middle classes, vacations, and leisure, these places where nature was tamed and on a human scale were now accessible to a generation of painters who, favoring outdoor scenes, picked their subjects from what they saw around them, in Paris and neighboring areas. Stripped of any religious or moral symbolism, the Impressionist garden was first and foremost a protected private space, a piece of nature laid out by city-dwellers purely so that they could enjoy the spectacle of it.

Monet, who moved to a house in Argenteuil with his wife and son in the early 1870s, took his own garden as a subject, painting it in different weathers over the course of the spring ("gray weather," shown here, and "in the sun," in a version held at the Pushkin State Museum of Fine Arts, Moscow). In the shade of a tall, blossoming lilac tree, two women and a man are sitting on the grass, chatting. The composition is especially typical of Impressionist garden paintings, with the greenery occupying almost the entire space (there is very little sky), the absence of any real effect of perspective or depth, and the framing of the landscape with no sense of either a center or an edge, giving the impression that it continues beyond the frame.

From the 1880s, a passion for horticulture (enabled by their financial means) set Caillebotte and Monet apart from the other Impressionists. Both became genuine painter-gardeners, Caillebotte establishing his flower-filled garden at Petit-Gennevilliers while Monet created his at Giverny, and they used these artificial landscapes as subject matter for their paintings. Caillebotte's compositions are often highly structured and emphasize contrasts between light and shade, between solid and void, and between the lushness of the vegetation (in this case, great swaths of sunflowers) and the rigid geometry of pathways or architecture. In Monet's case, the architecture (his own house, visible here in the background) is completely obscured behind the luxuriant flowerbeds (rows of irises) and an interweaving arrangement of bright, rapidly applied colors that fills the whole canvas. P.P.

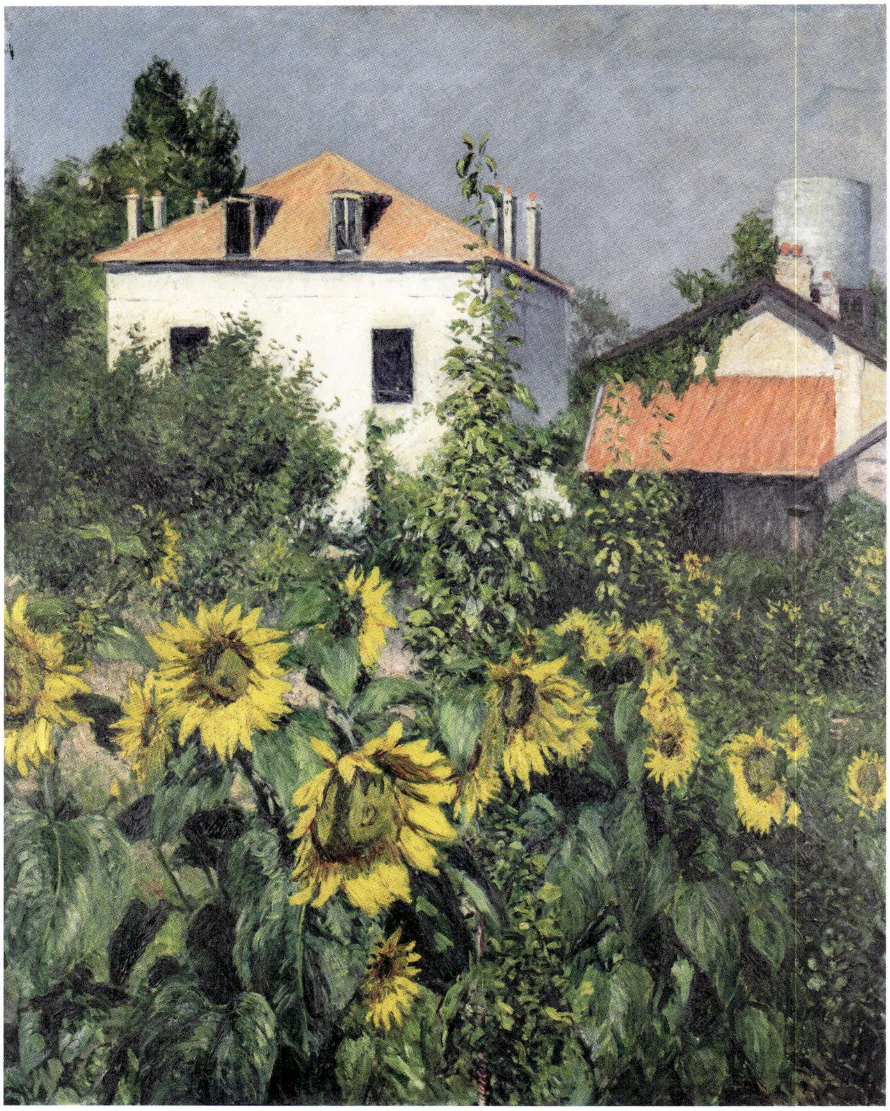

112 Gustave Caillebotte, *Les Soleils, jardin du Petit-Gennevilliers* (*Sunflowers, Garden at Le Petit-Gennevilliers*), c. 1885
Oil on canvas, 51 ⅜ × 41 ⅝ in. (130.5 × 105.8 cm)

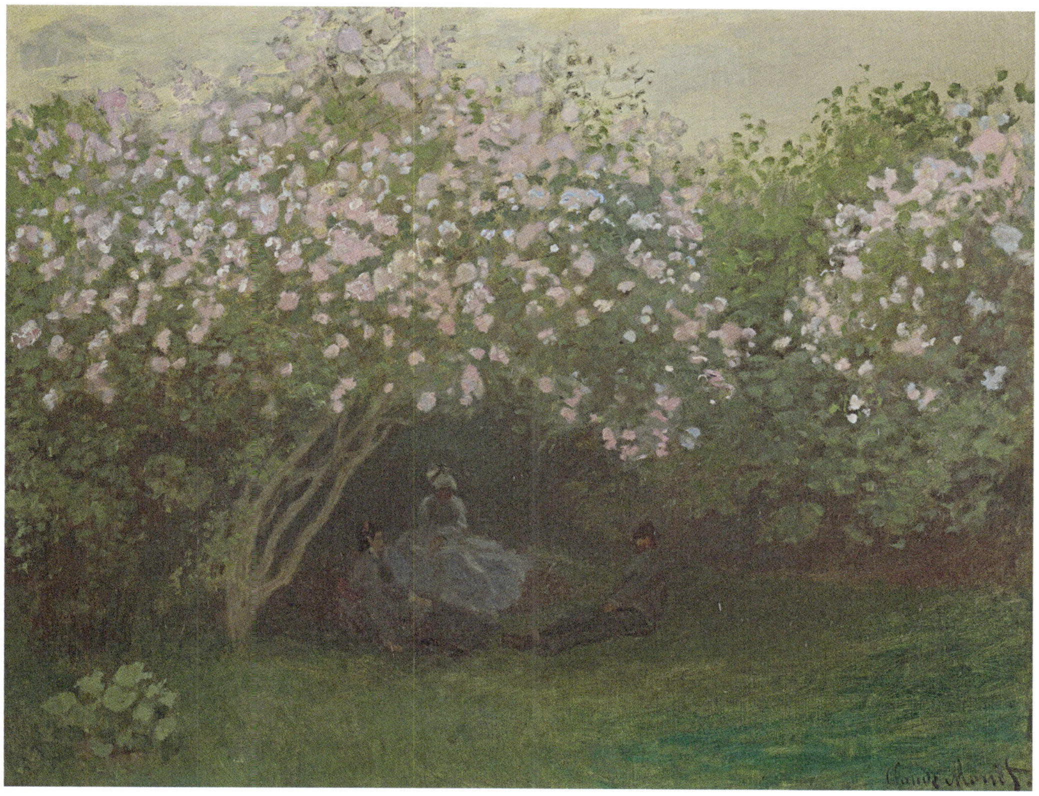

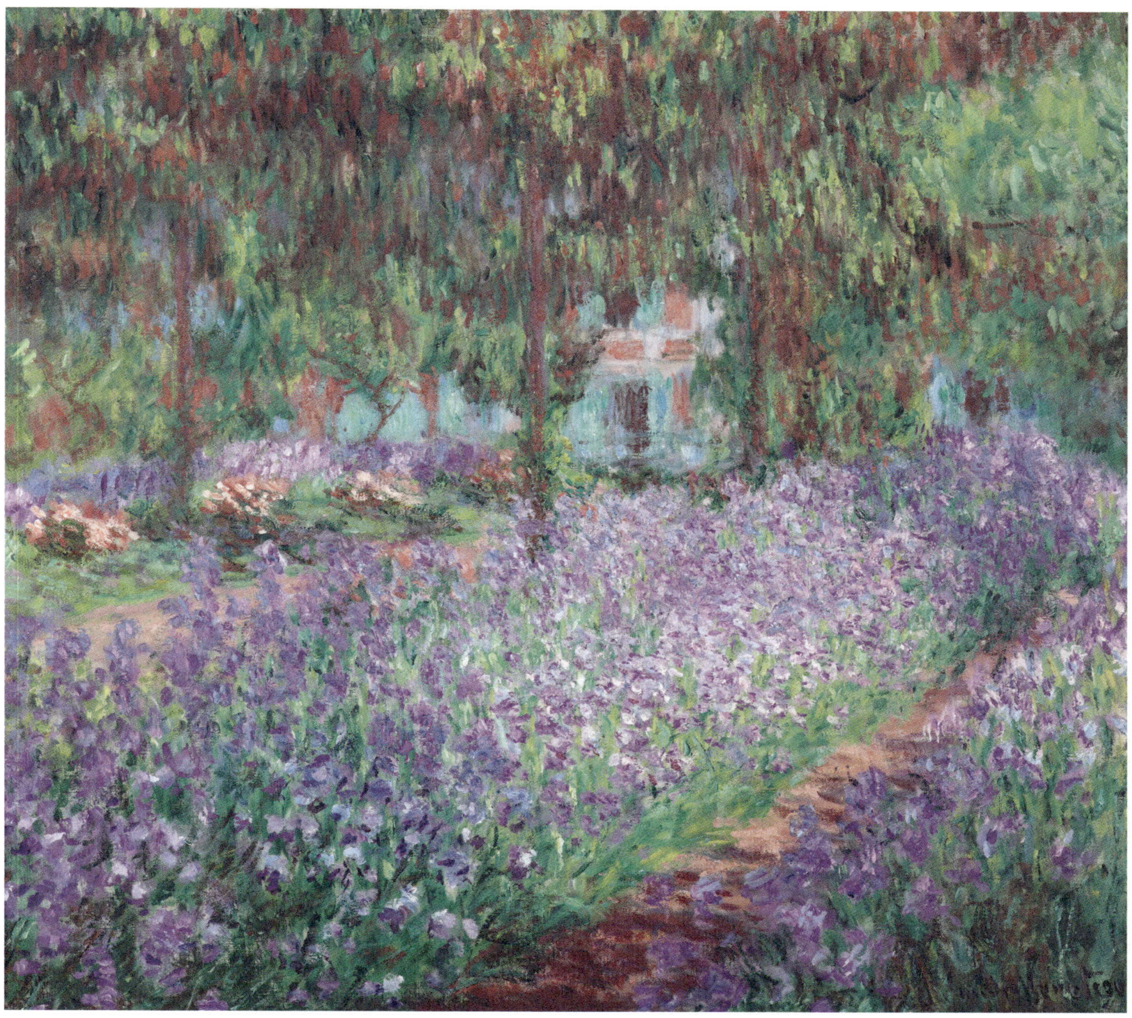

113 Top: Claude Monet, *Lilas, temps gris* (*Lilacs, Gray Weather*), 1872–1873
Oil on canvas, 19 ¾ × 25 ¹¹⁄₁₆ in. (50.2 × 65.2 cm)

114 Bottom: Claude Monet, *Le Jardin de l'artiste à Giverny* (*The Artist's Garden at Giverny*), 1900
Oil on canvas, 32 ⅛ × 36 ⁷⁄₁₆ in. (81.6 × 92.6 cm)

Berthe Morisot
Chasing Butterflies

Painted in the summer of 1874, this picture seems to resonate with Gérard de Nerval's poem *Les Papillons* (*Butterflies*), which sings the praises of these "fluttering stemless flowers" while reflecting on the mournful fate of their being caught in nets. Inextricably linked to "glorious summer,"[20] as celebrated in the poem, butterflies symbolize freedom, lightness, and ephemerality. Here, Morisot is celebrating the carefree nature of child's play: she paints her two little nieces in an outdoor setting where their mother, the artist's sister, Edma, holding a net, wants them to have fun chasing butterflies. The two children however seem otherwise occupied, or to be taking a break from their game. The artist focuses our attention on Edma, who faces us, motionless and pensive. This was one of the last times that Edma would pose for her sister. She is dressed in a light muslin dress, which may be a relaxed, intimate dress (as in Monet's *The Balcony*, p. 62) or a *robe de promenade* (walking dress), which would be worn in the countryside on hot days. We are in the garden of Edma's in-laws' property at Maurecourt, near Paris. Morisot transcribes a scene from modern life, a moment of leisure during the holidays, typical of the bourgeois lifestyle that developed during the nineteenth century. This refreshing, lush garden is also the pretext for an array of greens that emphasize the few small areas of blue sky, as well as the blacks and whites of the clothes, dotted with light. Morisot's brushwork is confident, precise, and swift, in tune with the fleetingness of the moment she captures, and with the brevity of the summer and childhood, both of which will pass. S. P.

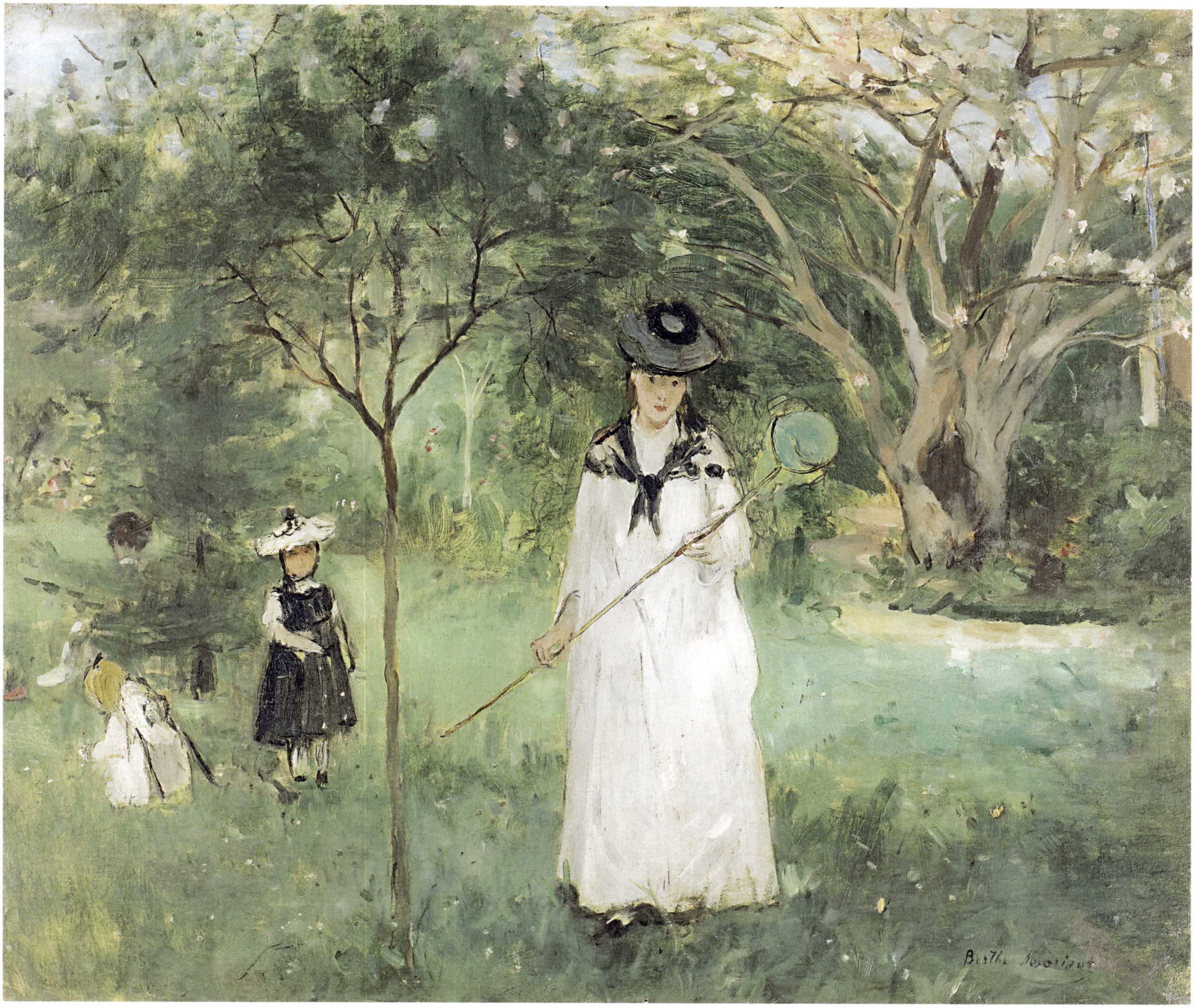

115 Berthe Morisot, *Chasse aux papillons* (*Chasing Butterflies*), 1874
Oil on canvas, 18 ⅛ × 22 1/16 in. (46 × 56 cm)

Auguste Renoir
The Swing

Above a garden path, in the shadow of some trees, a young woman is standing on a swing while a man speaks to her. Next to them, another man is standing behind one of the trees, and a child looks on. In the background, another group likewise seems to be in conversation. According to Georges Rivière, a very close young friend of Renoir's, the girl on the swing may be Jeanne, a sixteen-year-old seamstress from a working-class Montmartre family; the models for the men are the painter's friends. The canvas was painted in the neglected garden of the house that Renoir was renting temporarily, in 1876, on Rue Cortot in Montmartre, to paint *Dance at the Moulin de la Galette* (p. 137). Although the scene looks banal at first glance, Renoir elevates it through a palette of pale but bright colors, including for the shadows, and a very bold play of "blotches" of sunlight filtering through the foliage.

Renoir showed both of these works at the Impressionist group's third exhibition, in 1877, which also featured Monet's *Gare Saint-Lazare* series (p. 135), Caillebotte's large street scenes, and Degas's shadier depictions of entertainment (p. 141). Unlike these three, Renoir had little interest in Haussmannian Paris, industrial modernity, or nocturnal pleasures. He focused instead on public dance halls, suburban guinguettes, and gardens, favoring a cheery, working-class, bohemian vision of the modern world that was made up of flirting couples, chatting friends, and convivial moments. He admired eighteenth-century French artists' *fêtes galantes*, and brought them up to date in his own way, steering clear of pastiche.

At the 1877 Impressionist exhibition, the painting was criticized extensively for the "fatty blotches"[21] that seem to be spattered all over it, but Georges Rivière was more enthusiastic: "Not since Watteau have we seen charm similar to that exuded by *The Swing*. Something of the *Voyage to Cythera* is recognizable in it, but with a specifically nineteenth-century note." P. P.

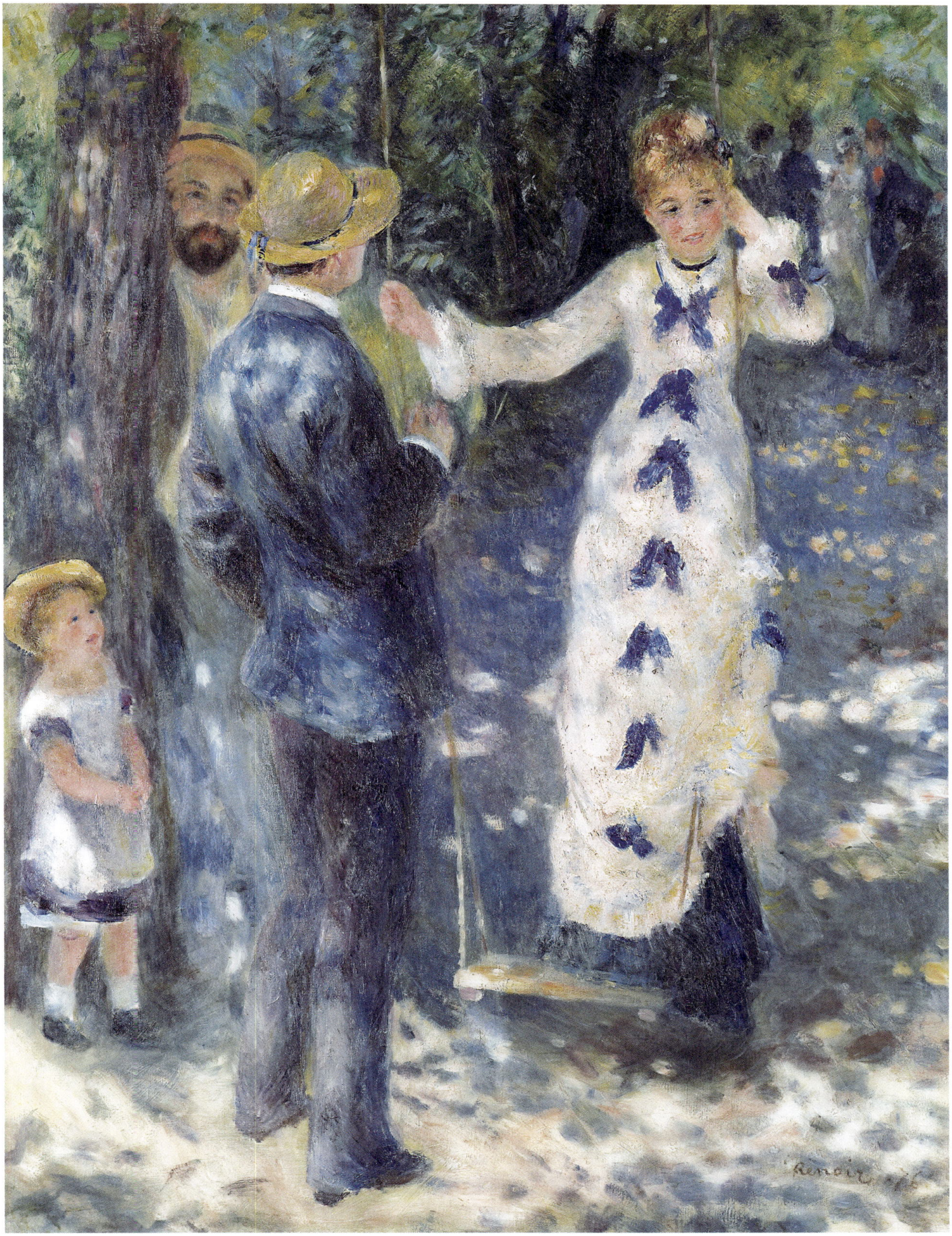

116 Auguste Renoir, *La Balançoire* (*The Swing*), 1876
Oil on canvas, 36 ¼ × 28 ¾ in. (92 × 73 cm)

Claude Monet
The Turkeys

This painting is surprising for its almost square format, its brushwork, and its subject, which is unusual to say the least. Monet places us at eye level with a disorderly gaggle of meandering turkeys. The critic George Moore, who saw the painting in 1877, records his stupefaction: "Then we stood and screamed at Monet.... We stood before the 'Turkeys,' and seriously we wondered if 'it was serious work.'"[22] Our gaze is led upward in a zigzag, from the birds, in the lower reaches of a vast garden, standing in fresh grass and bathed in shadow, up to the façade of a fine country residence that looms up between large trees. This building, the Château de Rottembourg (at Montgeron, south-east of Paris), not only features in the painting, but was its intended destination. Its then owner was the businessman and patron Ernest Hoschedé (one of Monet's first collectors), who commissioned the artist to paint four decorative panels for the main reception room. Monet was put up on site for several months, and produced landscapes inspired by these grounds and a local woodland. This painting stands out for its bold treatment, dominated by the patches of white that constitute the birds, with their agitatedly applied brushwork. Determined to prove his skills as a painter-decorator, Monet displayed this large canvas at the third Impressionist exhibition, where he gave it the title *Décoration non terminée* (Unfinished decorative scheme). The turkeys were ridiculed in the French press as "turkey in cream sauce," "piled up on top of each other," and "gobbling away on the garish green grass." Hoschedé went bankrupt the following summer, and it is not clear whether the panels were ever installed. But with this flock of hefty birds, Monet shook the conventions of decorative painting to the core. A. R.

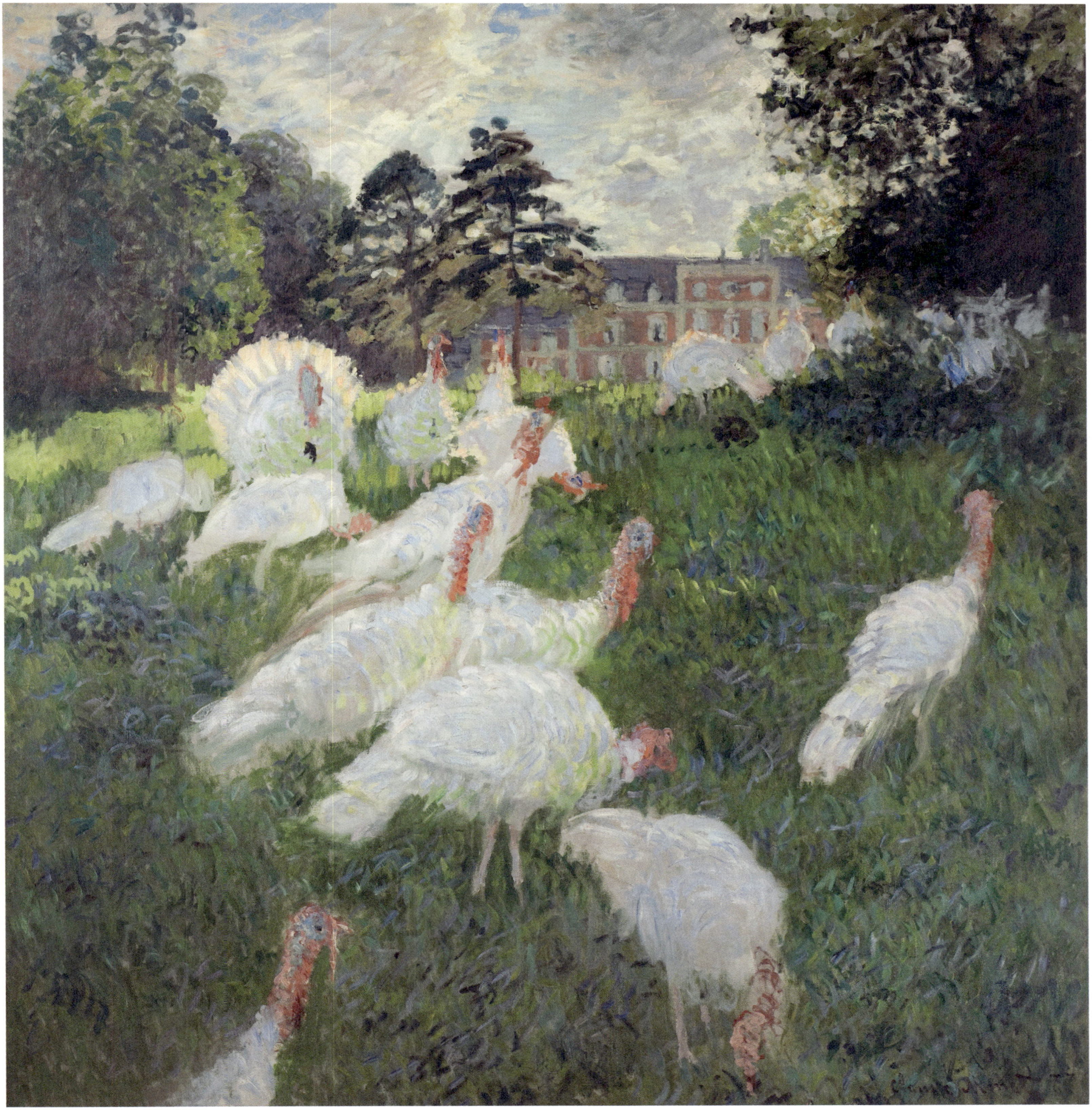

117 Claude Monet, *Les Dindons* (*The Turkeys*), 1877
Oil on canvas, 68 ½ × 67 15/16 in. (174 × 172.5 cm)

1877

The third Impressionist exhibition

Of all the eight independent exhibitions organized between 1874 and 1886, the third, in the spring of 1877, is considered to have been the most "Impressionist." It was the first to be called as such, appropriating what had started out as a journalist's jeer—the term coined in 1874 to denigrate a Monet seascape that the writer judged slapdash. In April 1877, the Impressionists turned the insult on its head and made it their slogan, emblazoning it at the entrance of their exhibition. "A sign informs us that what is inside is new art," noted one journalist. They also made it the title of a journal that accompanied the show: *L'Impressionniste*, a long-planned project, of which four issues were published that month.

Caillebotte poured himself into organizing the exhibition, and also supported it financially. "The exhibition will happen, it has to happen," he wrote to Pissarro a few weeks before it. A huge, empty apartment with an abundance of natural light was rented in a newly built block at 6 Rue Le Peletier. The works—for the first time mostly paintings—were put in rich frames. With the group reduced to just the few practitioners of the "New Painting," joined by Cézanne and Guillaumin (both of whom had skipped the 1876 exhibition), the third Impressionist exhibition was also the most homogeneous. As the critic Théodore Duret later commented, "They [had] all fully flourished." The exhibited works testify to this, displaying a unity of theme and of style that had reached its peak: brilliantly rendered scenes of modern life, such as Renoir's *Dance at the Moulin de la Galette* (p. 137) and Degas's *In a Café* (p. 139), and landscapes that evidence remarkable technical mastery. More favorably received than the previous editions, the exhibition proved a success and even brought in some revenue, so that all the participants not only recouped their expenses, but also made a modest profit.

Among the six works that Caillebotte exhibited was the striking, monumental *Paris Street; Rainy Day* (1877; Art Institute of Chicago). He not only showed his own paintings but also lent works by others, alongside fellow collectors of the Impressionists (Ernest Hoschedé, Georges Charpentier, Georges de Bellio), as well as buying a good number to add to his collection. Many of these would later become part of France's national collection, through his bequest to the State that is held and displayed today at the Musée d'Orsay. A. R.

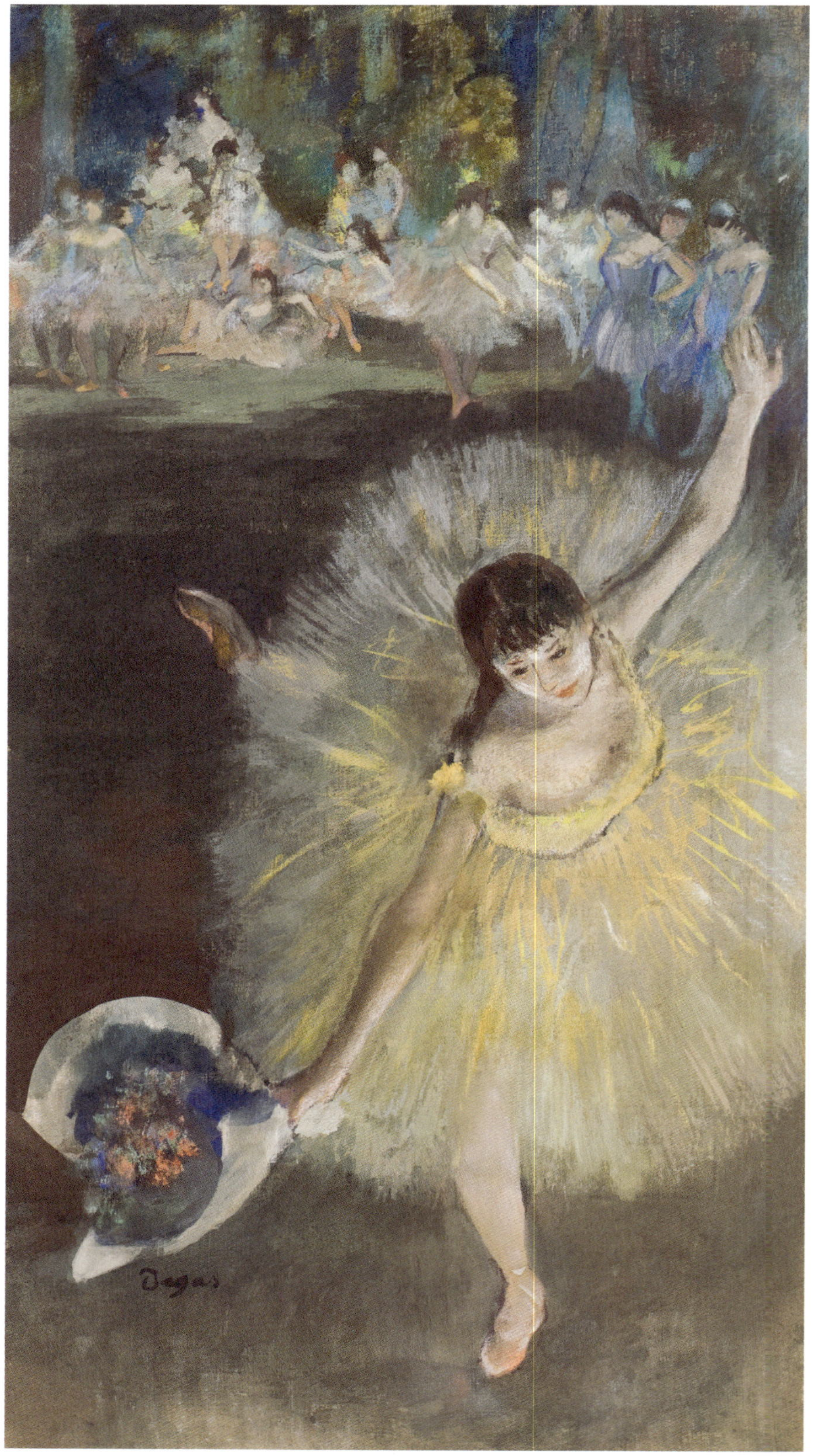

118 Edgar Degas, *Fin d'arabesque* (*Finishing the Arabesque*), 1876–1877
Turpentine-thinned oil and pastel on canvas,
29 9/16 × 14 15/16 in. (67.4 × 38 cm)

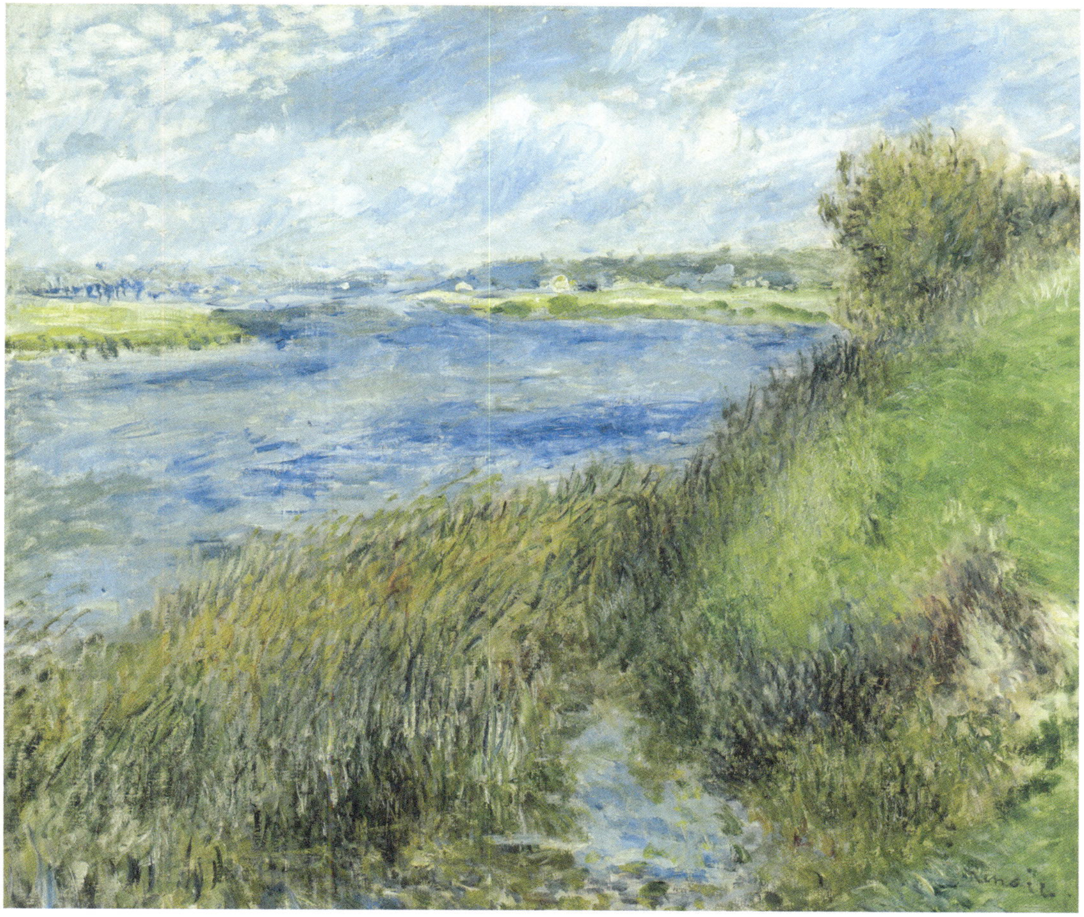

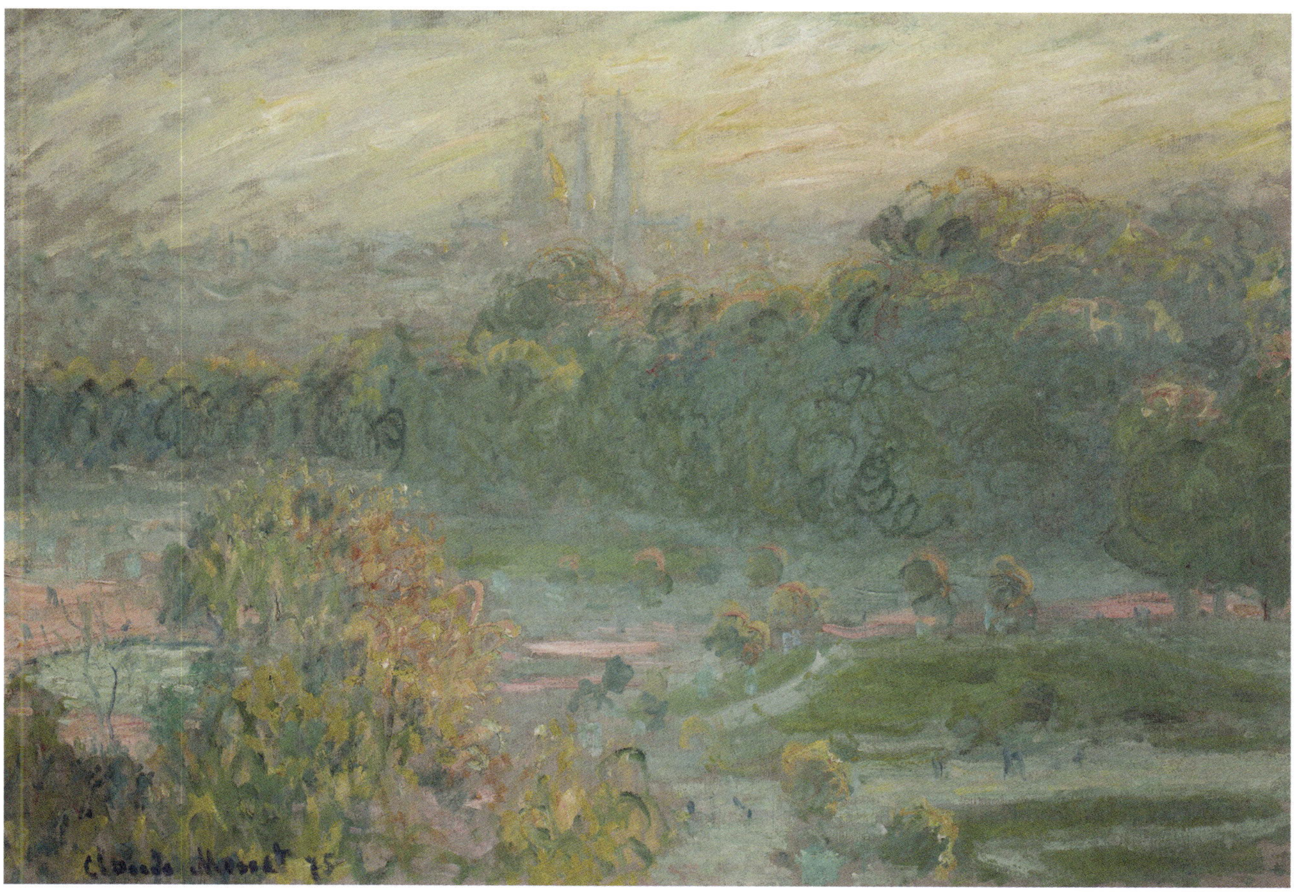

119 Top: Auguste Renoir, *La Seine à Champrosay* (*The Seine at Champrosay*), 1876
Oil on canvas, 21 ½ × 26 in. (54.6 × 66 cm)

120 Bottom: Claude Monet, *Les Tuileries; esquisse* (*The Tuileries: Sketch*), c. 1876
Oil on canvas, 19 ¹¹⁄₁₆ × 29 ¾ in. (50 × 75.5 cm)

Claude Monet
The Gare Saint-Lazare

"I've got it! The Gare Saint-Lazare! I'll show it just as the trains are starting, with smoke from the engines so thick you can hardly see a thing. It's a fascinating sight, a regular dream world"[23]: this is how Jean Renoir records Monet's enthusiastic outburst to his father Auguste, at a point when Monet had already been very familiar with the Saint-Lazare railroad station for quite some time. The station connects Paris with Normandy, but also with Argenteuil, where the painter moved in the early 1870s. Using vocabulary such as "fascinating" and "dream world" to describe an ordinary, polluted utilitarian building is certainly surprising. Monet was effectively glorifying one of the symbols of nineteenth-century modernity and, for some, of its industrial ugliness. Especially since he shows the station—which served France's first railroad line from 1837—in its then-current state of development, remodeled by the engineer Eugène Flachat with its huge glass roof, multiple platforms, the metal bridge of Place de l'Europe, and the apartment buildings overlooking the bridge, which were completed in 1872. To show the site in the most comprehensive manner, Monet secured permission to set up his easel in the station, placing us on the same level as the passengers and railroad workers, face to face with three locomotives and engulfed in the smoke. He produced twelve paintings inspired by this station, and showed seven or eight of them at the third Impressionist exhibition. Visitors were struck by the subject, the unprecedented repetition effect, and the atmospheric treatment of the light and the swirling steam. At the time, the novelist Émile Zola, who would take the railroad as his subject for *La Bête humaine* (*The Beast Within*), hailed Monet as one of the artists who had succeeded in "finding the poetry of the railroad stations, like their fathers found that of the forests and rivers." In his eyes, "That is where painting lies."[24] S.P.

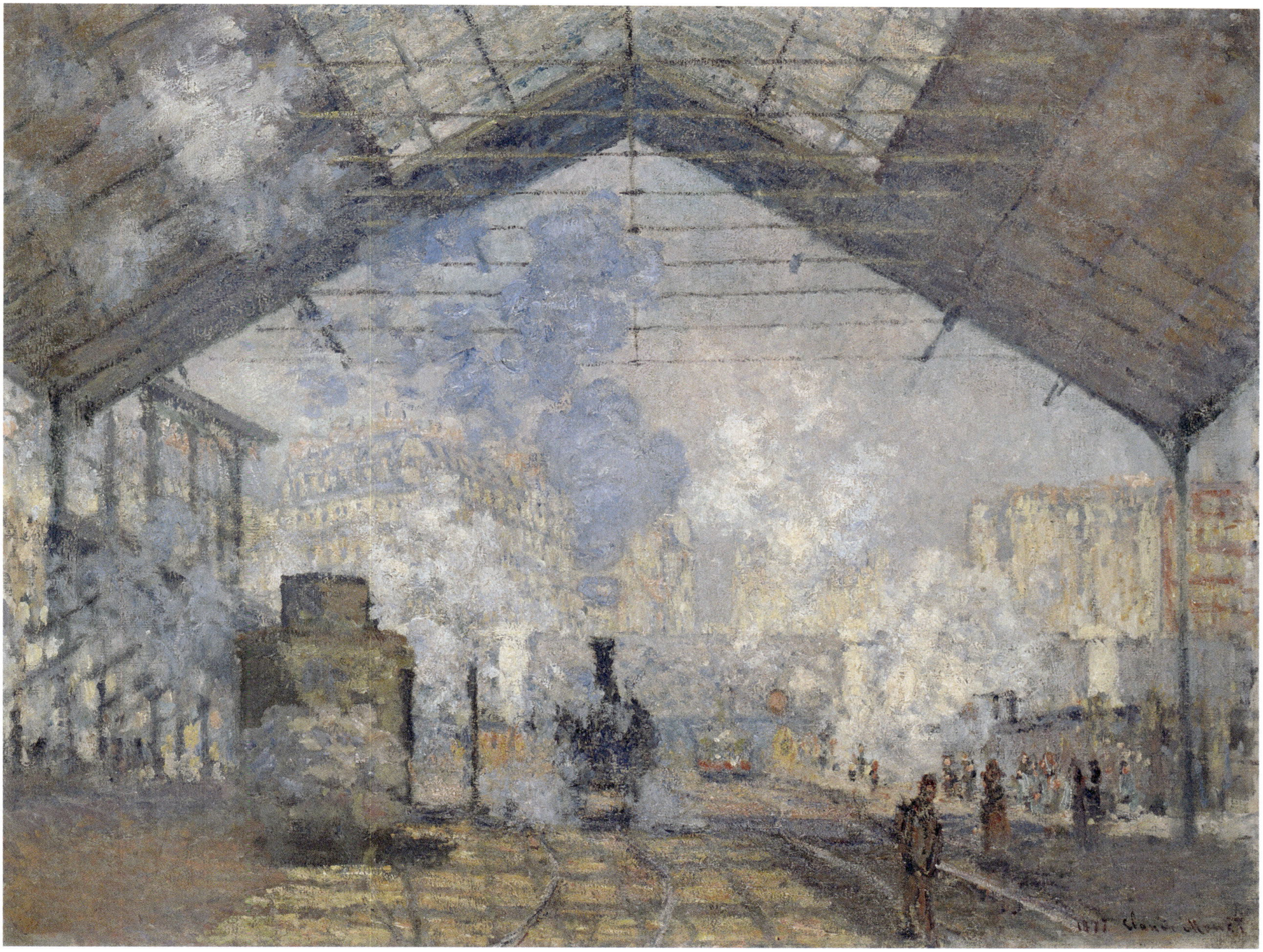

121 Claude Monet, *La Gare Saint-Lazare* (*The Gare Saint-Lazare*), 1877
Oil on canvas, 29 ½ × 41 5⁄16 in. (75 × 105 cm)

Auguste Renoir *Dance at the Moulin de la Galette*

At the time it was painted, *Dance at the Moulin de la Galette* was Renoir's most ambitious composition, conceived as a true manifesto for the 1877 Impressionist exhibition. It shows a guinguette in Montmartre, a former village that had been absorbed into Paris as its eighteenth arrondissement. A restaurant with space for live music and dancing, the Moulin de la Galette was founded by the Debray family in the early 1830s, and was among the capital's last outdoor dancing venues.

To take in the whole scene and build up a dense, lively tableau, Renoir chose to paint from a slightly raised position, on a stairway leading to one of the eponymous mills (*moulins*). From there he had a view down over the crowd, the outdoor space with its acacia trees, tables, and benches, and the covered dance hall with the orchestra platform at the far end. The composition is particularly complex, deploying multiple groups of figures throughout its depth, but the whole is brought together by the predominantly blueish palette, the spots of light filtering through the foliage, and the loose, fluid brushwork that seems to connect the people with one another. Glances, gestures, and continuity between forms all enhance this sense of general cohesion. Edmond Renoir, the artist's brother, stressed that his sibling was not aiming simply to represent the dance in an objective way, but to understand it and melt into it: "Mingling with the swirling motion of this mass merriment, he conveys its frenzied movement with astounding gusto."

Renoir chose this Sunday dance because it took place in the daytime, offering ideal conditions for working outdoors, and because it attracted an unpretentious, bohemian, family-oriented crowd that he could identify with. Empathizing with the subject, he set out to show these residents in a favorable light, unlike other artists who preferred to underline the darker aspects of working-class life. The models for the male figures were friends of his—artists, writers, and journalists—while he had young working-class women from Montmartre pose for the female ones. The painting celebrates the beauty of life, flirting, a "certain camaraderie" (according to his friend Georges Rivière, who appears in the foreground) between the men and women and across different social classes, and the type of resilience that the people of Paris displayed after the traumas of the 1870–1871 war and the Commune. "Noise, laughter, movement, sunshine, in a youthful atmosphere: such is Mr. Renoir's *Dance*.... It is a page of history," summarized Rivière. P.P.

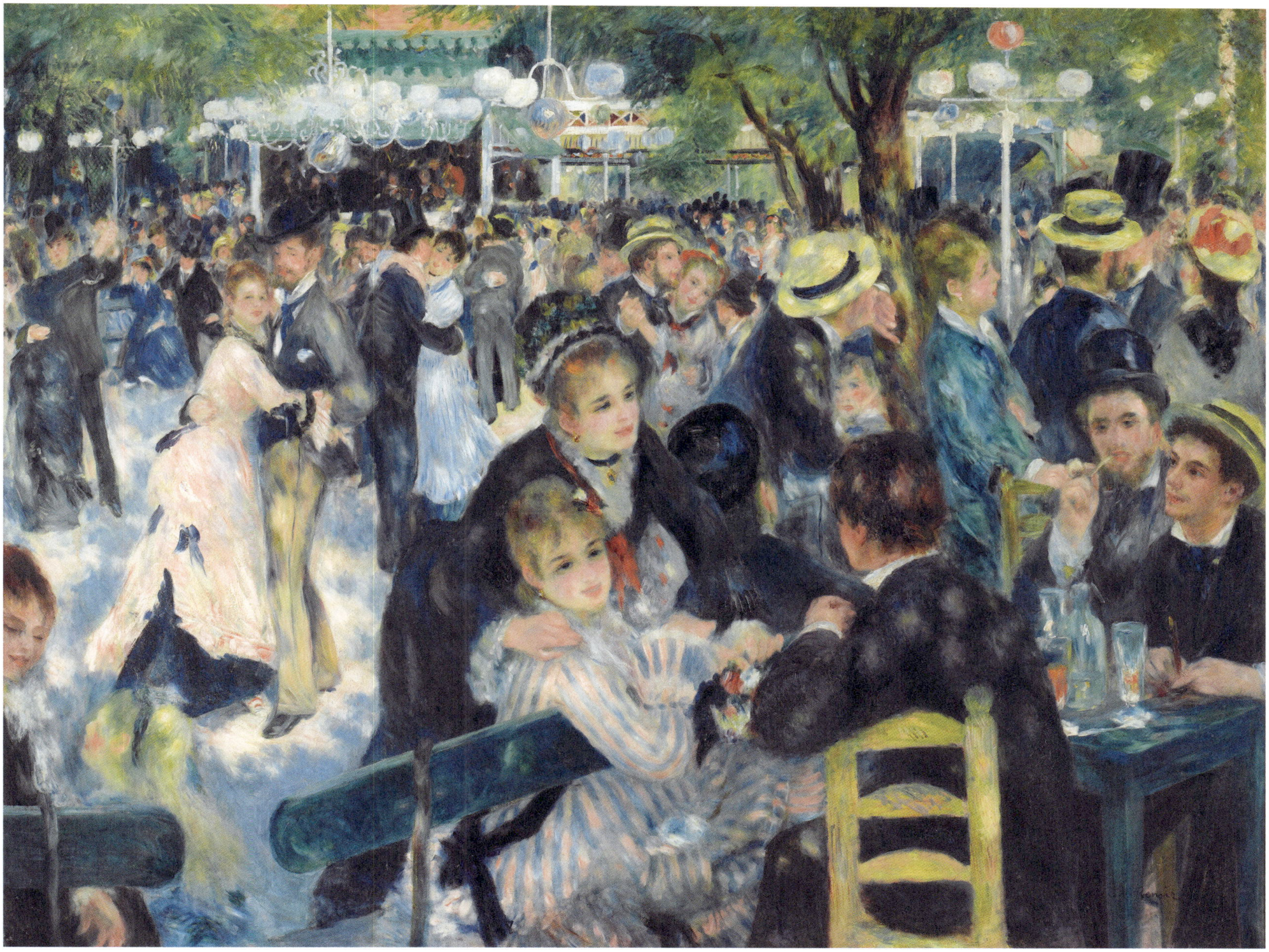

122 Auguste Renoir, *Bal du Moulin de la Galette* (*Dance at the Moulin de la Galette*), 1876
Oil on canvas, 51 ¾ × 69 ½ in. (131.5 × 176.5 cm)

Cafés

As compact settings for accessible enjoyment, the possibility of intoxication, or solitary reverie, cafés can fairly be likened to the poetics of modern paintings, which were determined to open up "another world" within the real world. Both symbolically and in reality, the café was one of the most important "modern" places: the enclosed space where a culture of pleasure and debate was developed and experienced, the two going hand in hand since the seventeenth century. As well as being a "salon of democracy," it was equally always an enclave where people could let their destinies and their dreams of a different life converge. These simulated snapshots playing on encounters between different sexes and social types achieved their fullest manifestation in the hands of Degas and Manet. The former's *In a Café* swiftly kills off any idealized vision of its theme. Long believed to have been exhibited in 1877 at the third Impressionist exhibition, we now know that the work of that title listed in the exhibition booklet was only a summary sketch. Degas may well have witnessed such scenes; here, he has the actress Ellen Andrée and the painter and printmaker Marcellin Desboutin pose together, their supposed relationship deliberately left unclear. A glass of absinthe stands in front of the woman, and a glass of beer in front of the man. Degas clearly indicates the third character in this Parisian moment: alcohol, its pleasures, and its less happy consequences. The two customers seem to be ignoring or unaware of one another, each lost in their own thoughts.

Cafés, brasseries, and performance spaces became more of a focus for Manet after 1870. These open social settings obliged him to master effects of gas lighting and the specific glare of the stage. Ultimately it was all about conveying the way the perception of modern life shakes up traditional rules of perspective and composition. What is Manet's charming waitress looking at as she serves the beer with a deftness that he ennobles? The new economy of framing is accompanied by more striking colors and brushwork. Caillebotte echoes Degas's title but removes all female presence from his picture. While he retains the note of shadiness, he lets the reflections repeat to infinity, along with a sense of magic. S. G.

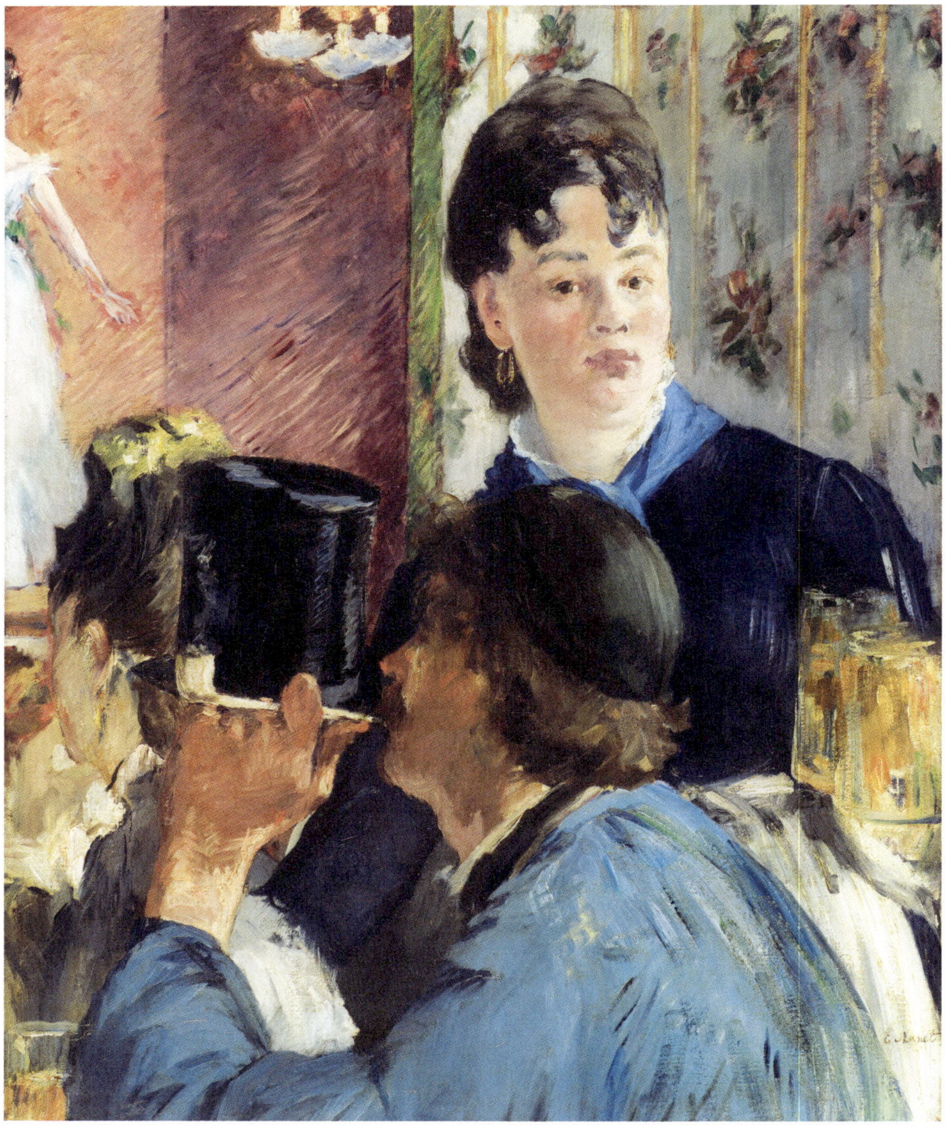

123 Édouard Manet, *La Serveuse de bocks* (*The Beer Waitress*), 1878–1879
Oil on canvas, 30 5⁄16 × 25 3⁄8 in. (77 × 64.5 cm)

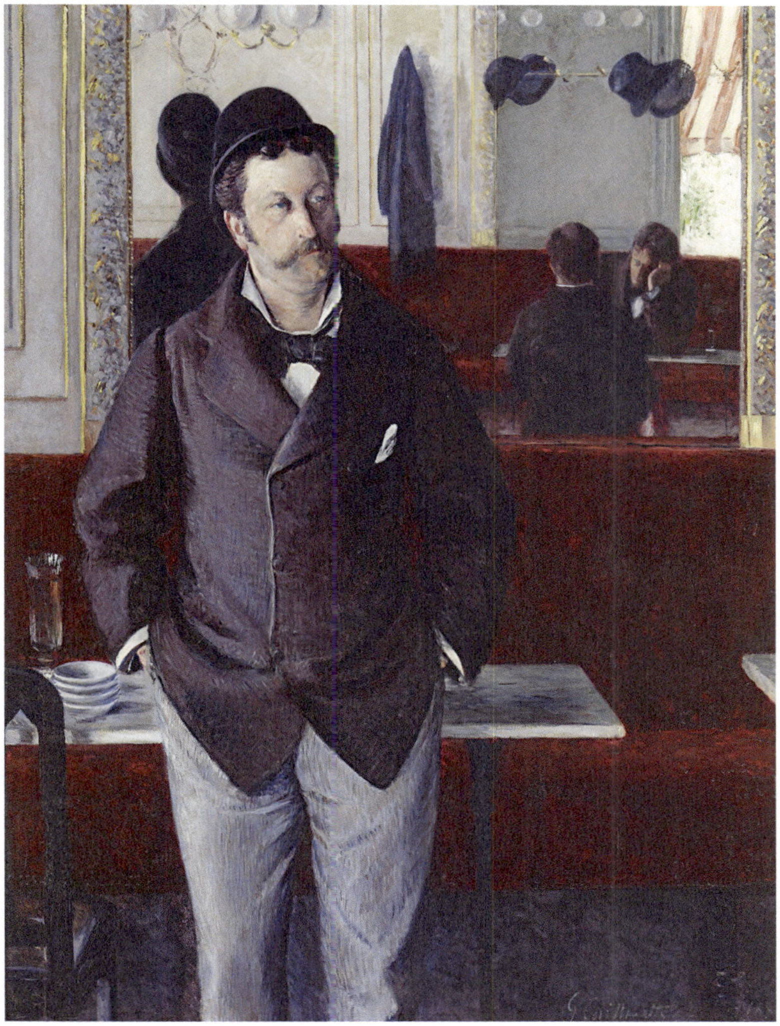

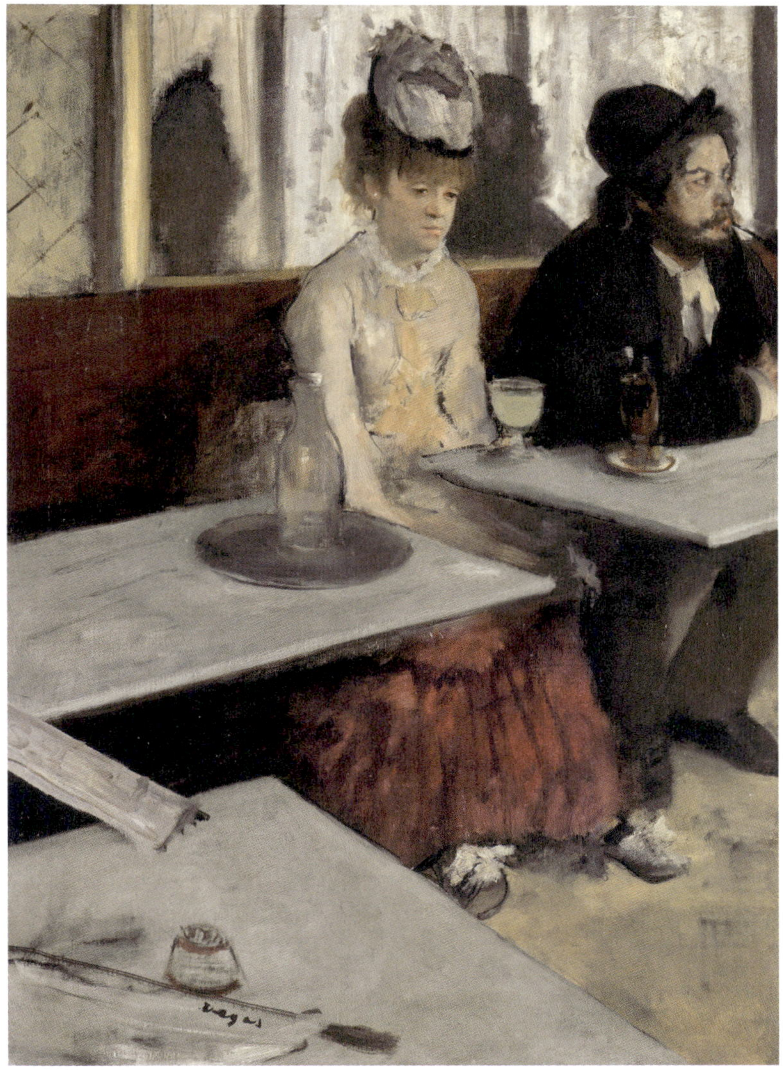

124 Left: Gustave Caillebotte,
Dans un café (*In a Café*), 1880
Oil on canvas, 61 × 45 ¼ in. (155 × 115 cm)

125 Right: Edgar Degas, *Dans un café* (*In a Café*),
also known as *L'Absinthe* (*The Absinthe Drinker*), 1875–1876
Oil on canvas, 36 ¼ × 26 ¹⁵⁄₁₆ in. (92 × 68.5 cm)

Edgar Degas
Women on a Café Terrace in the Evening

This pastel was executed on a monotype, which Degas described as a "drawing in greasy ink and printed." He started to work on it in the mid-1870s. Monotypes are a hybrid of drawing and printmaking. Contrary to what their name suggests, they were sometimes printed twice or even three times. Here, Degas uses the medium's gray, abstract, expressive masses to form a matrix, with parts left blank, as the background to his nocturnal scene.

The work depicts a group of sex workers sitting on the terrace of a café on Boulevard Montmartre, chatting together between tricks. One of the women adopts a provocative attitude, with her thumbnail pressed against her teeth. All of the women have receding chins, which Degas associated with depravity. He represented them in a frieze arrangement, with a tight compositional framing, structured by the café's columns in front of its window pane, giving the impression the women are encaged. The pastel's bright tones emphasize their heavy makeup and garish hats.

Degas creates an innovative, subtle interplay of artificial light, the women all being lit both from the interior and by the streetlamps. The pastel would feature at the third Impressionist exhibition, in 1877. C.C.-P.

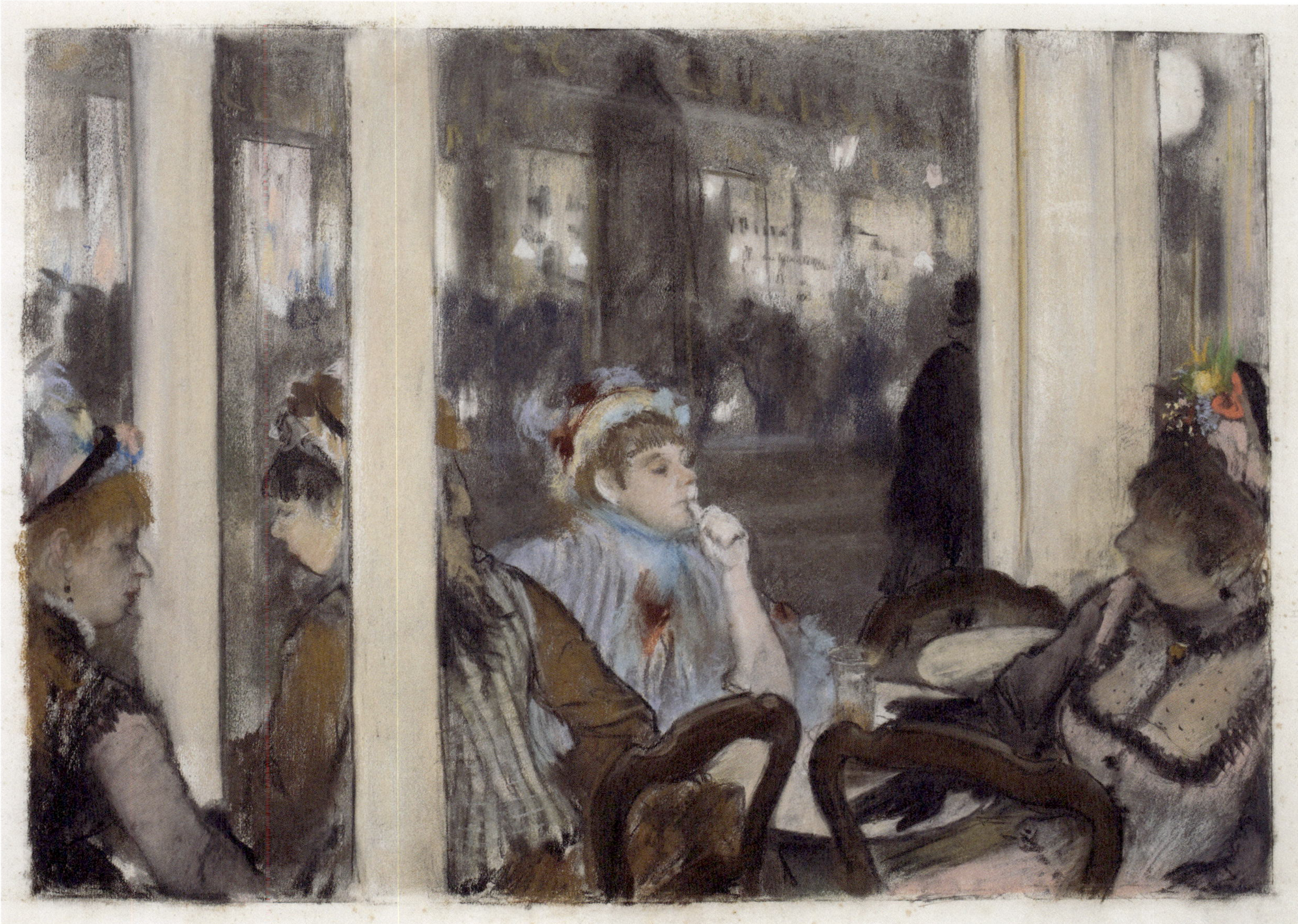

126 Edgar Degas, *Femmes à la terrasse d'un café, le soir* (*Women on a Café Terrace in the Evening*), 1877
Pastel on monotype on paper, 16 ⅛ × 23 ⅝ in. (41 × 60 cm)

Edgar Degas
At the Ambassadeurs Café-Concert

Manet and Degas were both part of the café-concert generation: a flurry of these establishments sprung up in Paris at the time of Louis-Philippe, after 1830, moving into working-class neighborhoods and thriving thanks to the areas that were undergoing urbanization, such as the Champs-Élysées. There, the opening of the café-concert Les Ambassadeurs in the early 1870s topped off the transformations hastened by Georges-Eugène Haussmann's urban renewal program. It had a mixed audience, and some of its singers—such as Mademoiselle Bécat, a particular favorite of Degas's—became genuinely famous through their performances. A string of cheeky songs and satires on the news would ring out from the stage, which was miraculously transformed by gas lighting. The venue was surrounded by trees, and the hall itself, with its constant comings and goings, offered endless diversion. It was a shady form of entertainment, heavily monitored by the police. Degas had to turn to very different techniques of both printmaking and drawing to give a complete idea of it. This 1885 pastel overlays and enhances what is his largest acid etching, produced five or six years earlier. We emerge from the dark of night, drawn in to a very new outburst of color. The viewpoint, which is also highly original, places us behind the stage and the singer, who is cut off just below the knee. Is she taking her bow, or just coming to the end of her act? Seated to left and right, her workmates wait their turn. Other stationary elements, in contrast, accentuate the impression of movement, such as the two insistent verticals, especially the tree trunk. In his pre-cinematographic gusto, Degas often made use of similar Japanese-inspired effects to structure the space. S.G.

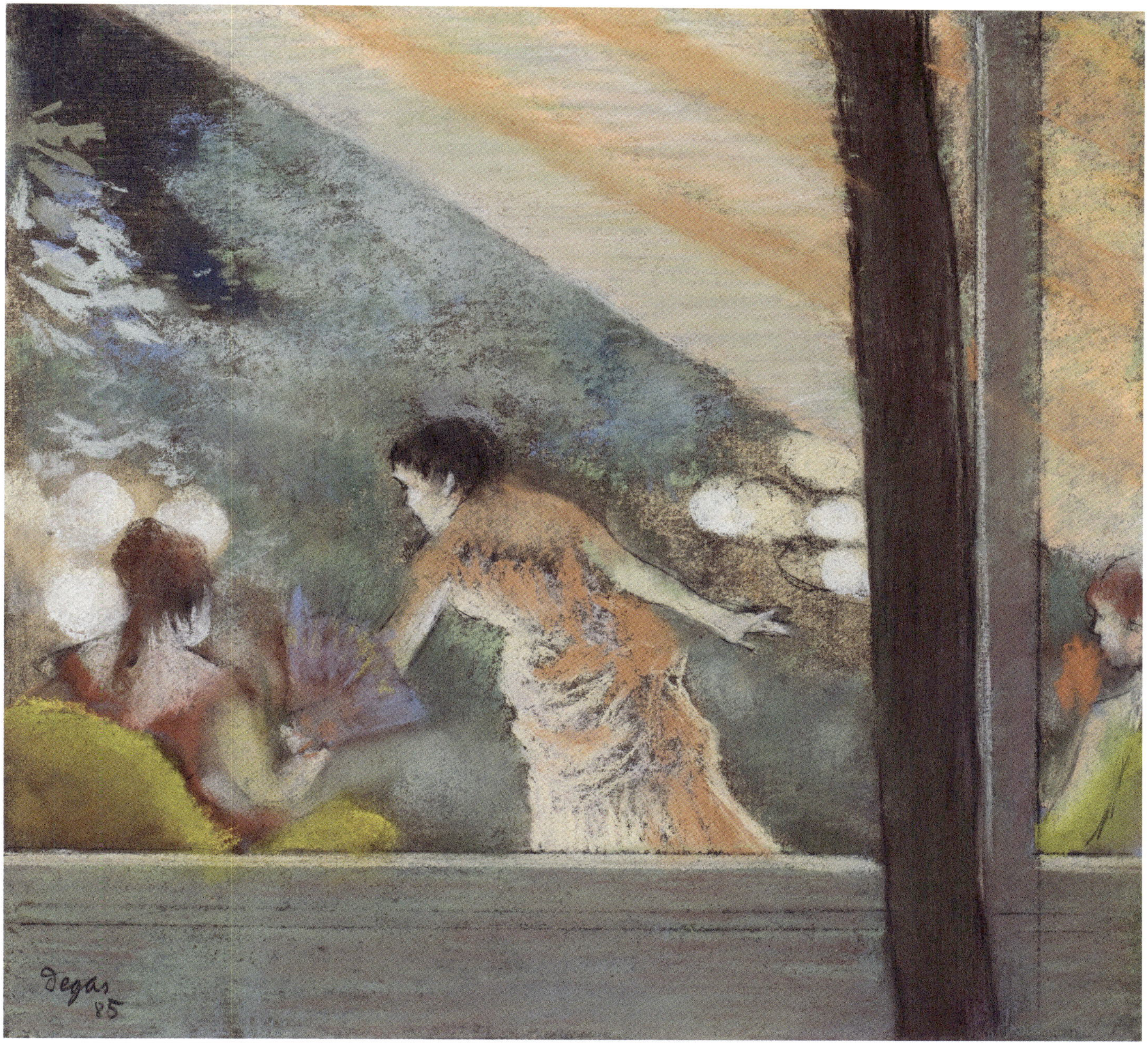

127 Edgar Degas, *Au café-concert des Ambassadeurs (At the Ambassadeurs Café-Concert)*, 1885
Pastel on monotype etching on paper, 10 7⁄16 × 11 5⁄8 in. (26.5 × 29.5 cm)

Degas and the stage

An opera and dance enthusiast, Degas always found stimulation for his artistic imagination in the theater arts, from genteel choreography to café-concert licentiousness. A successor to and collector of Honoré Daumier's prints, his "cinematic eye" led him to break movement down and to stretch the expressiveness of gestures and faces. He was particularly fond of the ballet world, observing dancers both in class or rehearsal and on stage as they strove to achieve the correct movement, defy gravity and space, and exceed the audience's expectations. He tiptoed into this theme in the early 1870s, as a sideline to his views of orchestras. Constructed on an ascending diagonal, as if the ballerina is acknowledging the audience just after landing from a leap, *The Star*, also called *Ballet* or *Dancer on Stage*, accords the floor its full importance, to paraphrase Paul Valéry. The painting seems to have been among the seven works on this subject that Degas showed as a group at the third Impressionist exhibition. Precise and poetic in equal measure, they caught the critics' eyes: "What are thoroughly good are Mr. Degas's *Dancers*. In these admirably rendered studies we find blurred outlines, fluidity, movement, spontaneity, and confidence. We have heard the name Goya mentioned with regard to these *Dancers*," we read in *Le Petit Moniteur universel*. Caillebotte, who had lent three other works on paper to this group exhibition, seems to have acquired this unique pastel as soon as it was unveiled to the public there. The pastel *Chorus* again brings us to the front of the stage, near the footlights which light up the faces from underneath, exaggerating their features to the extreme. Some of their mouths are wide open, dismissing the decorum of classical painting. In 1877, the press was not sure how to respond, except by pulling out the old argument of ugliness: "Are these hideous singers, bawling at the top of their voices, quite true to life?!" The music-hall performers whom Degas depicted with such great care, relishing their irresistible pantomime and gift of the gab, were also subjected to sarcasm. Here again, Daumier is never far away.   S.G.

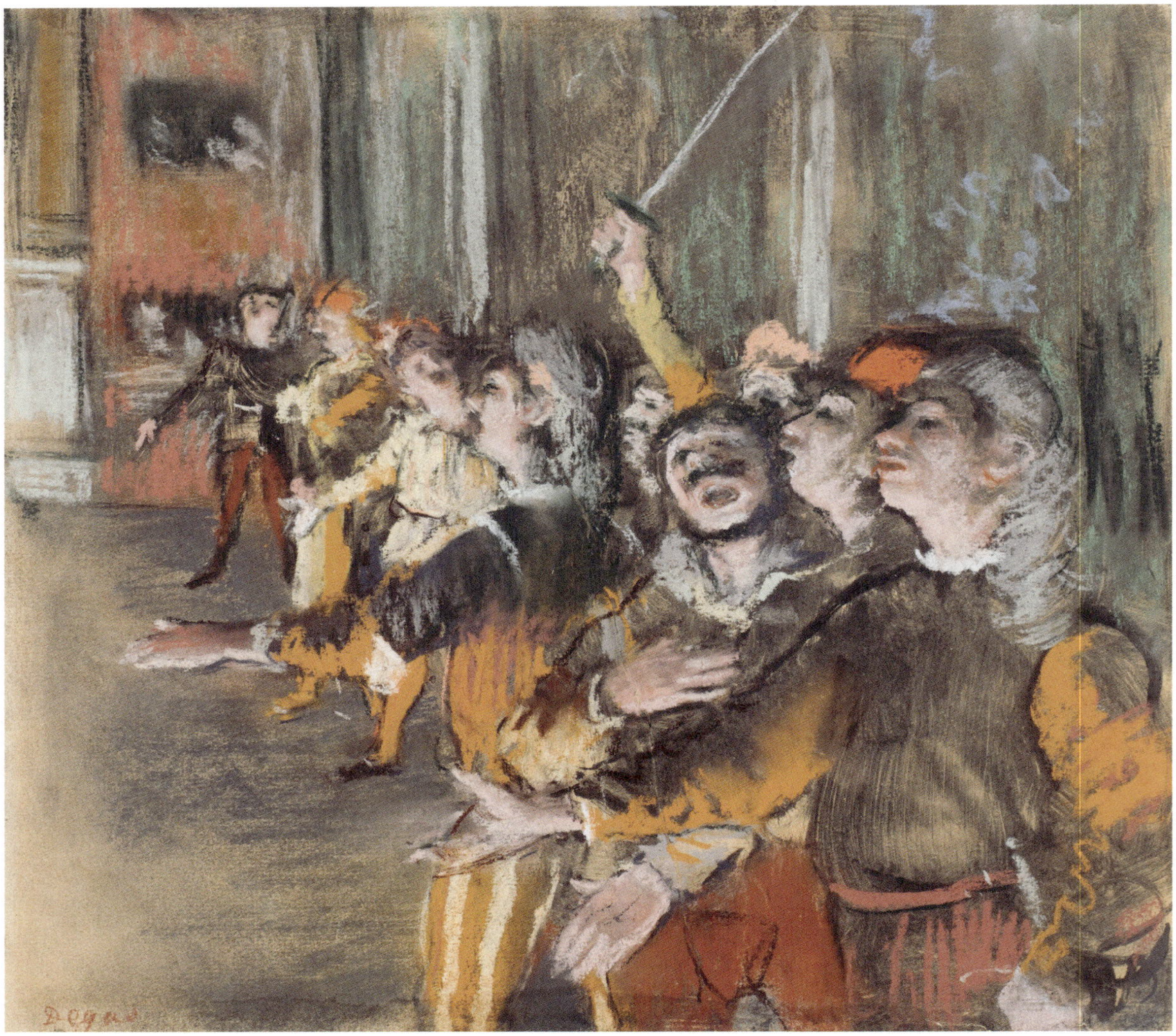

128 Edgar Degas, *Choristes* (*Chorus*), 1876–1877
Pastel on monotype on paper, 10 11⁄16 × 12 11⁄16 in. (27.1 × 32.3 cm)

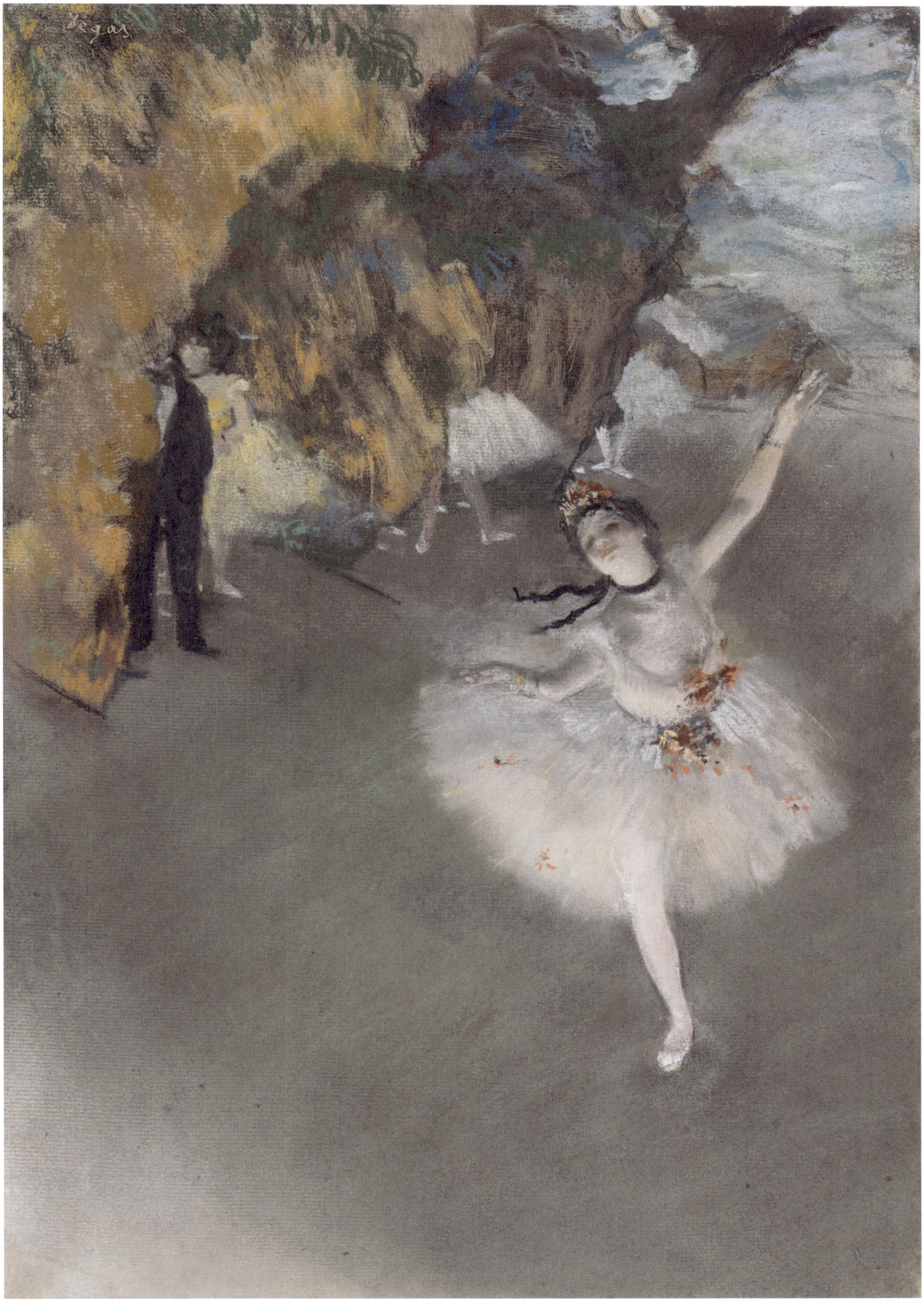

129 Edgar Degas, *Ballet*, also known as *L'Étoile*
(*The Star*, or *Dancer on Stage*), c. 1876–1877
Pastel on monotype on paper, 23 × 16 9⁄16 in. (58.4 × 42 cm)

Edgar Degas *Dancers*

Degas had a deep fascination with the Paris Opéra, which started in the 1860s and lasted the rest of his life. On stage and backstage; the music and the dance; the young female dancers' world that sometimes intermingled with that of the *abonnés* (wealthy male subscribers to the Paris Opéra)—it all offered him a wealth of subjects to tirelessly explore the limitless variety of this enclosed microcosm. He first painted dance classes in the early 1870s. These works quickly found buyers in Paris and England, such as the baritone and collector Jean-Baptiste Faure. Despite their charm, they are by no means facile, but rather evidence the very rigorous approach that Degas took to his work. He never resorted to executing multiple copies of a successful image, but would endlessly rework his compositions, as examinations have revealed. He meticulously observed not only the young dancers' movements as they worked, but also the postures they adopted when relaxing during a pause. Additionally, he was interested in how their bodies related to the space around them, favoring highly original viewpoints and framings. Despite their realistic appearance, these scenes were recomposed from memory, based on studies of dancers who had posed for him in his studio. The setting is usually the opera house on Rue Le Peletier, which he remained very attached to even after it burned down in 1873 (the Palais Garnier opera house did not open until 1875). Degas, not without a touch of mischief, confessed to the role that imagination played in this section of his output: "I have done so many of these dance examinations without having seen them that I am a little ashamed of it." I. P.

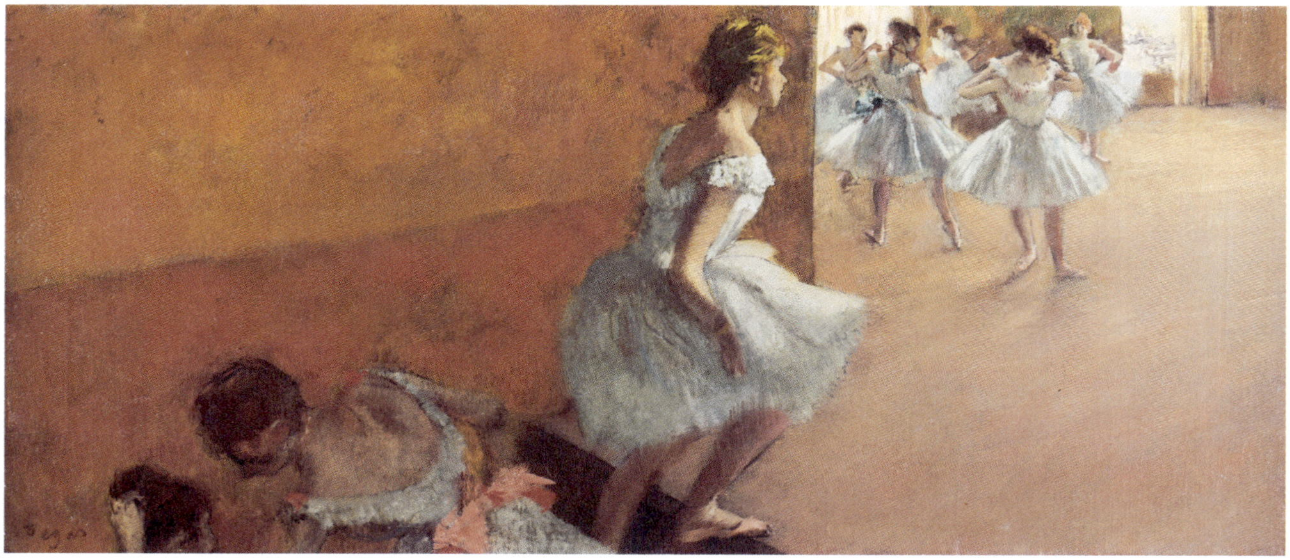

130 Edgar Degas, *Danseuses montant un escalier* (*Dancers Climbing the Stairs*), 1886–1890
Oil on canvas, 15 ⅜ × 35 ¼ in. (39 × 89.5 cm)

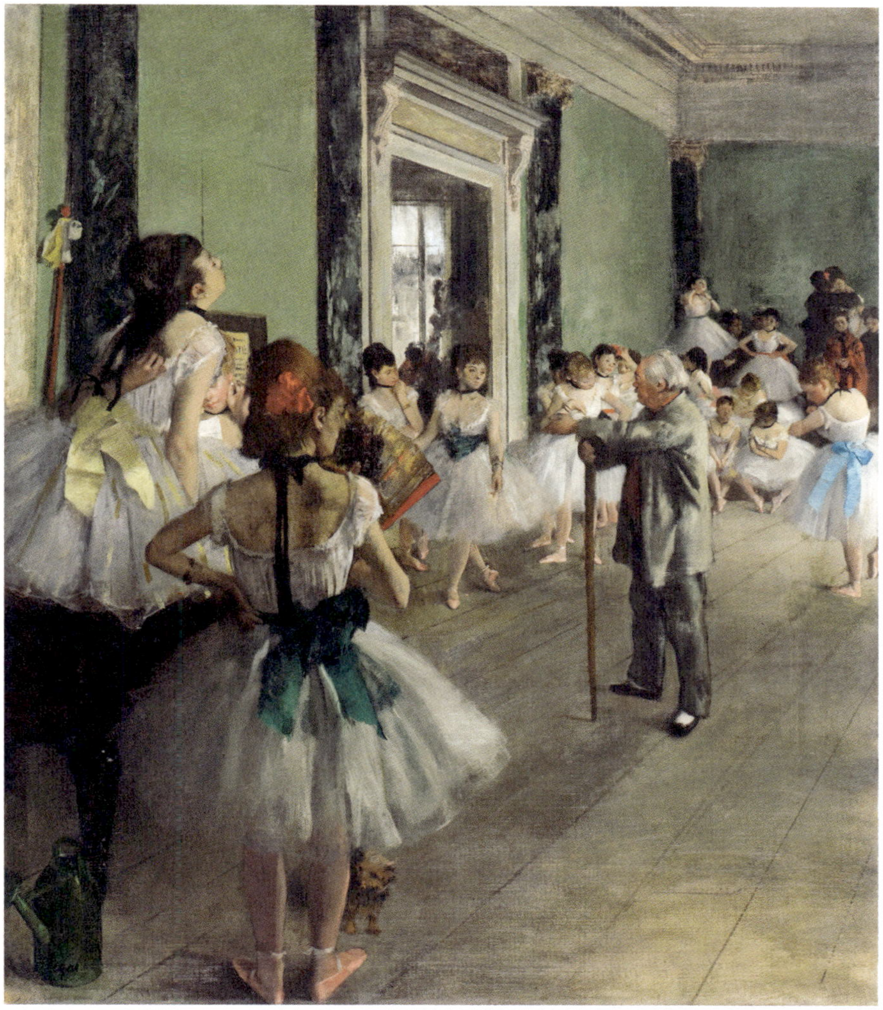

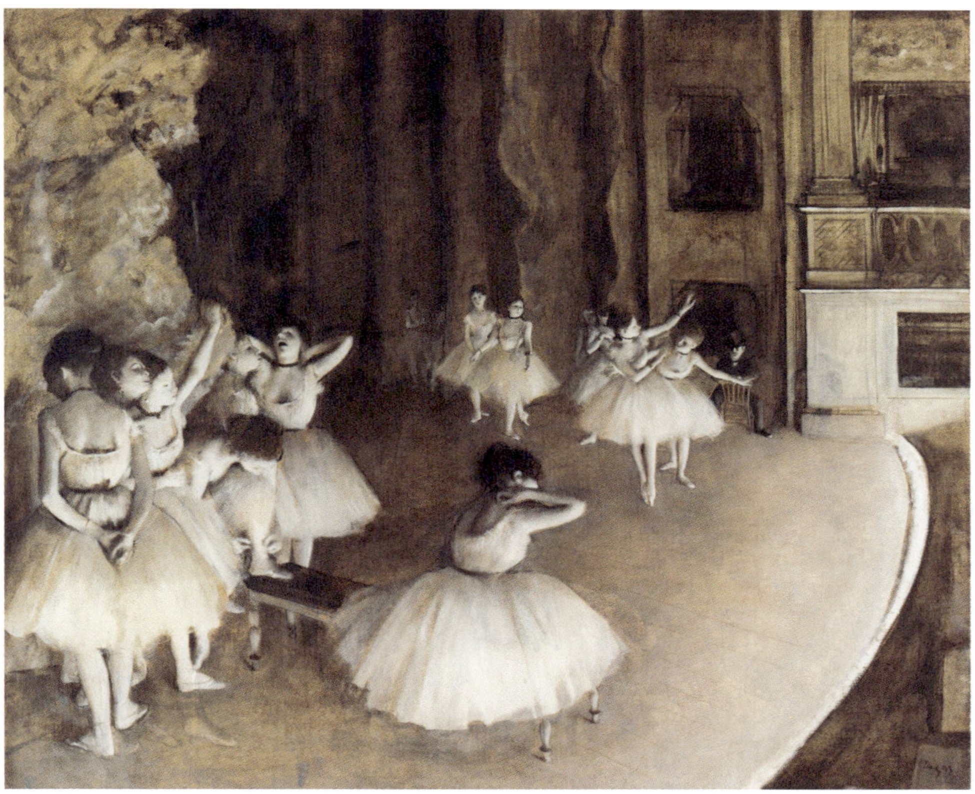

131 Top: Edgar Degas, *La Classe de danse* (*The Dance Class*), 1873–1876
Oil on canvas, 33 11⁄16 × 29 ½ in. (85.5 × 75 cm)

132 Bottom: Edgar Degas, *Répétition d'un ballet sur la scène* (*Ballet Rehearsal on Stage*), 1874
Oil on canvas, 25 9⁄16 × 32 1⁄16 in. (65 × 81.5 cm)

Degas's drawings

Drawing was the only means of expression that Degas faithfully embraced throughout his life. One of the nineteenth century's greatest draftsmen, he was recognized as such during his lifetime and regularly exhibited drawings, notably at the Impressionist exhibitions. It was the sales of his studio contents, in 1918–1919, that revealed the full scope of this aspect of his work to the public, with more than a thousand sheets representing every drawing technique, along with dozens of sketchbooks.

In the 1850s and 1860s, Degas studied masters of drawing in France and Italy. He produced several portraits of his close circle, including of his youngest brother, René. In one of these, showing him aged nine or ten, the boy is drawn in graphite with red chalk on pink paper. The use of blending creates a hazy *sfumato* effect inspired by Italian Renaissance masters, and especially by Leonardo da Vinci.

From the 1870s, drawing took on a very broad meaning in Degas's work, where painting, sculpture, and printmaking came together. He drew with brush and ink on intense blue, green, and pink colored papers. His dancer seen from behind, on pink paper, was shown in 1876 at the second Impressionist exhibition, and he chose to have it reproduced in a selection of his drawings published by Michel Manzi in 1894. After passing through several illustrious collections, the drawing entered Isaac de Camondo's, thanks to whom the Musée d'Orsay today holds a large number of Degas's works.

Keen to achieve an expressive, synthetic realism, Degas never stopped studying the nude, and especially focused on it in the years around 1880. He produced wax sculptures of dancers, horses, and female nudes to check the accuracy of his drawings. L. J.

133 Left: Edgar Degas, *Portrait de René de Gas (Portrait of René de Gas)*, c. 1855–1856
Graphite on paper, 11 13/16 × 9 1/16 in. (30 × 23 cm)

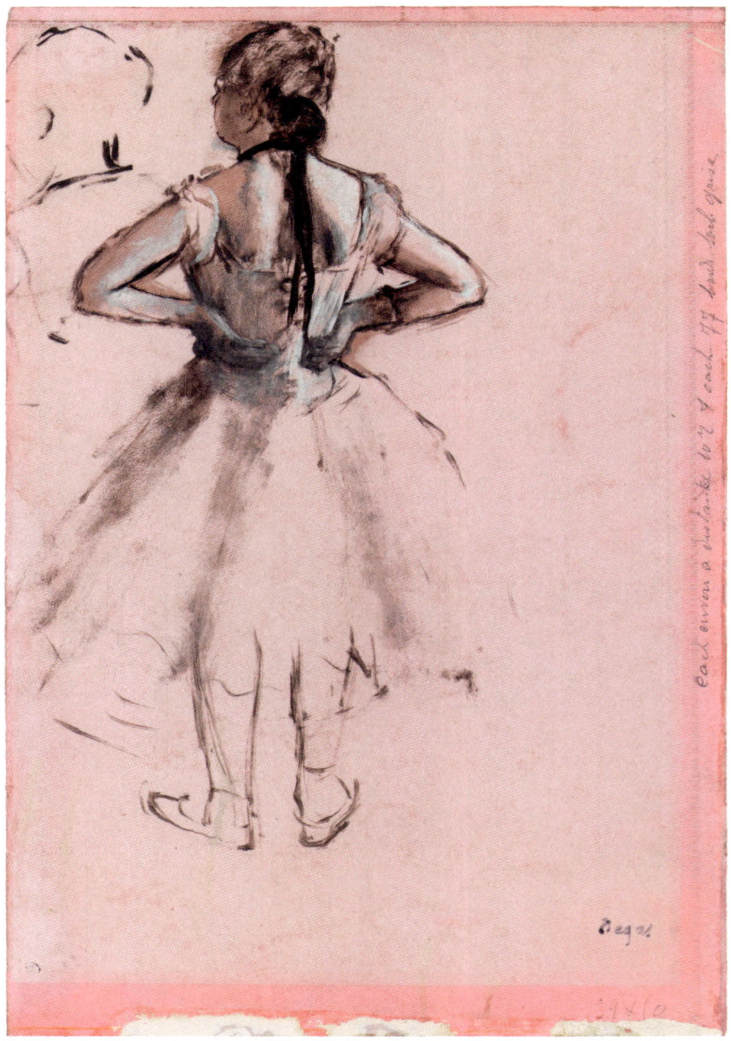

134 Right: Edgar Degas, *Danseuse, vue de dos, les mains sur les hanches (Dancer, Hands on Hips, Viewed from Behind)*, c. 1873
Turpentine-thinned oil heightened with white on pink paper
14 ½ × 10 ⅛ in. (36.8 × 25.7 cm)

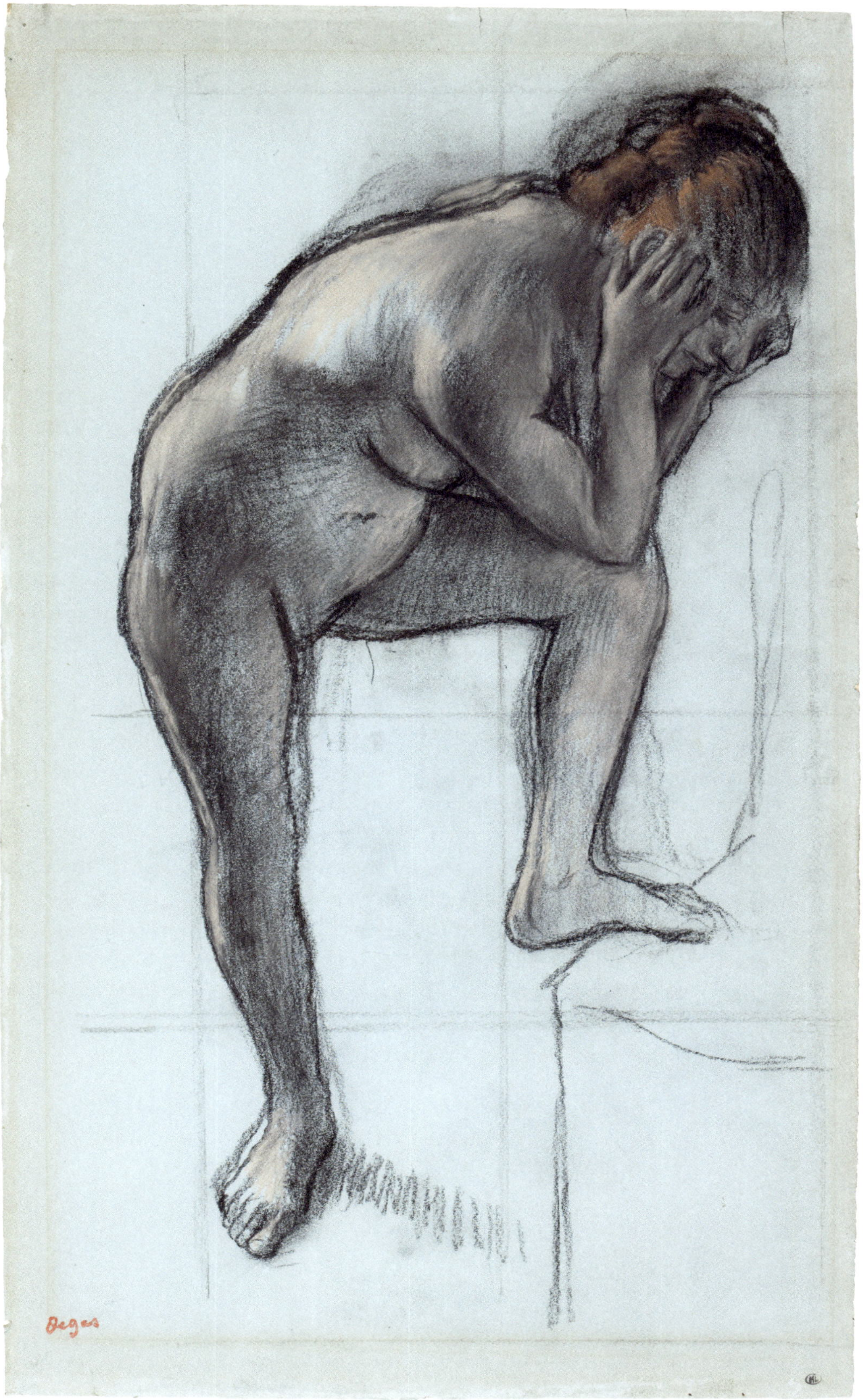

135 Edgar Degas, *Femme nue debout*
(*Standing Female Nude*), 1880–1883
Pastel and charcoal on blue-green paper,
19 ½ × 12 1⁄16 in. (49.5 × 30.7 cm)

Edgar Degas
The Racecourse

There was a crossover between the boom in horse racing and the aspirations of modern Parisian society in the 1860s, and Manet and Degas were good examples of this overlap. Degas was a skilled horseman, friendly with breeders, and possessed a deep knowledge of horses and of the artists who shared that knowledge, from Théodore Géricault to Ernest Meissonier. Memories of his copies after Benozzo Gozzoli and Paolo Uccello mingled with influences from across the English Channel. Degas focused in particular on the moment before the race starts: the psychological challenge faced by the jockeys; the delicate dance of the mounts, whose necks curve so elegantly as they paw the ground; the slenderness of their legs; the bright ripple of their coats. A higher grace, which also derives from the subtlety of the pigments, emanates from *The Parade*: the internal dynamic of the lines, especially in the play between posts and factory chimneys, invests the scene with a slow kinetic quality. *The Racecourse: Amateur Jockeys near a Carriage* was sketched out in 1876 but delivered much later to the baritone Jean-Baptiste Faure. While claiming to need to "see the *Races* again in the field" in order to keep his client waiting, Degas was careful to depict the scene just as he saw it. The women in the back of the carriage do not appear to be members of high society. The composition pulsates in all directions, and the riders create an effect of oscillation as they pass each other. Although Degas did know of chronophotography by this time, he still references the flying gallop pose, and accentuates its springing effect through the framing. The man sporting a hat, on the right, could have stepped right out of Caillebotte's *Boating Party* (p.161). S.G.

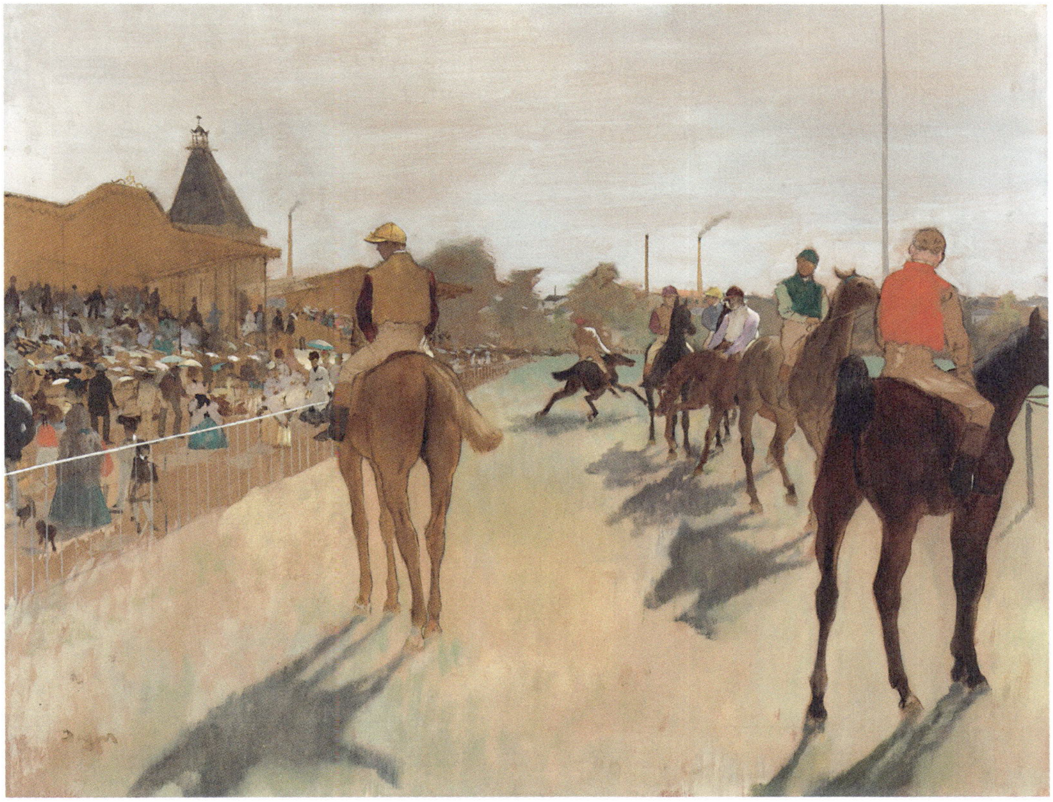

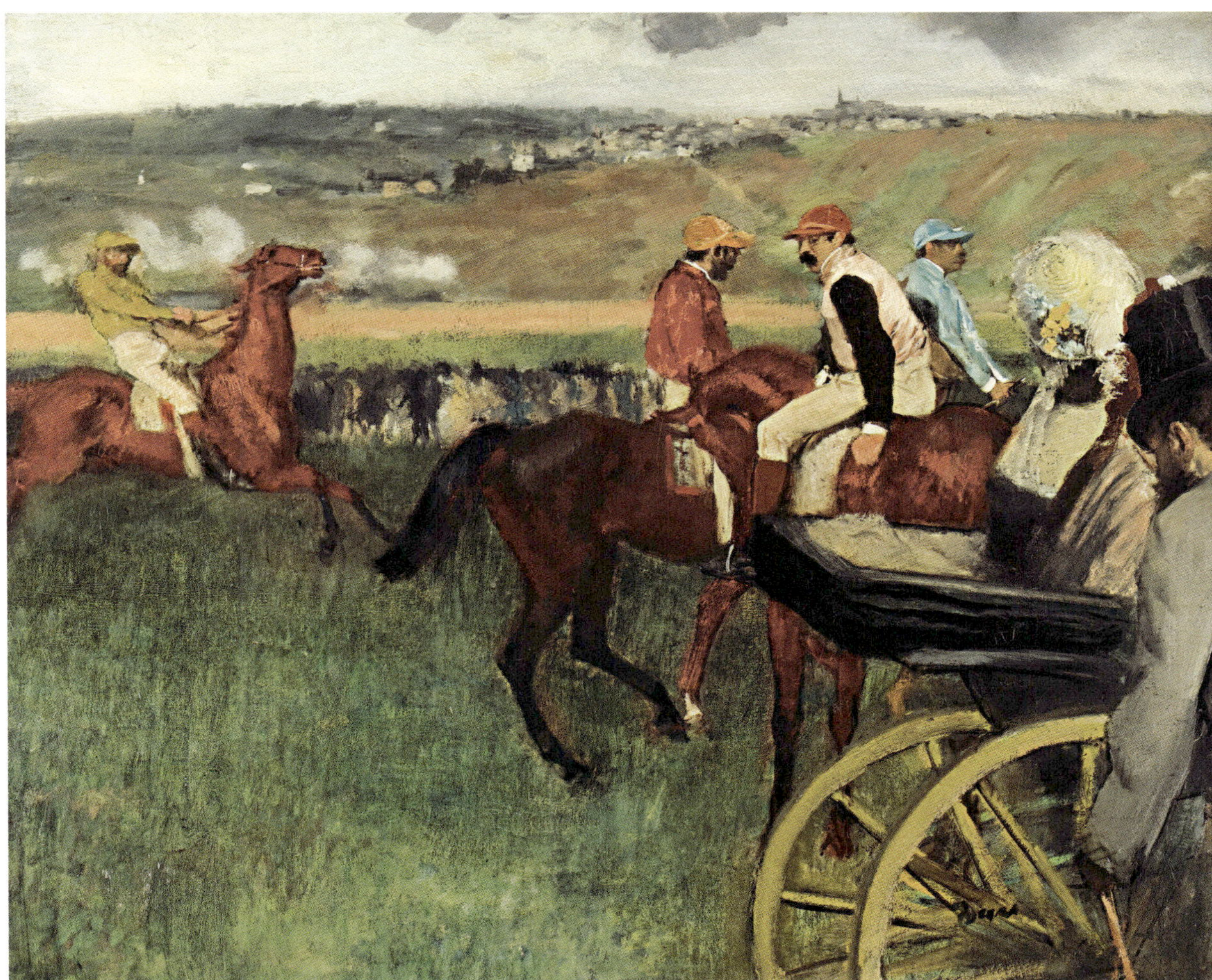

136 Top: Edgar Degas, *Le Défilé* (*The Parade, or Racehorses Before the Stands*), 1866–1868
Oil on paper mounted on canvas, 18 ⅛ × 24 in. (46 × 61 cm)

137 Bottom: Edgar Degas, *Le Champ de courses. Jockeys amateurs près d'une voiture* (*The Racecourse: Amateur Jockeys near a Carriage*), 1876–1887
Oil on canvas, 25 11⁄16 × 31 15⁄16 in. (65.2 × 81.2 cm)

Japonism

In the early 1860s, a small group of writers, art lovers, and painters developed a passion for Japanese art, examples of which (mainly contemporary *ukiyo-e* prints and small modern crafted objects) arrived in Europe following the signature of the treaties that forced Japan to open up to Western trade. Édouard Manet was one of these, and traces of this interest can be found particularly in his portrait of Émile Zola (p. 39) and in *The Fifer* (p. 37). Zola observed that the latter painting is "interesting to compare … with Japanese prints, which resemble it in their strange elegance and wonderful patches of color."[25] Manet also collected fans, which he put on display in his studio, pinning them to a wall hanging that was itself Japanese and which is very visible in his portrait of Nina de Callias. Here, it is more a case of a taste in ornaments, a new exoticism, rather than a deep assimilation of Japanese aesthetic principles.

Other Impressionists were similarly partial to these accessories, notably Degas and Pissarro, who showed multiple designs for fans at the 1879 exhibition. Degas's, with their emphasis on asymmetry and playing with the void, owe much to Far Eastern aesthetics. The technique—ink wash on silk—is also inspired by Chinese and Japanese painting, and allowed him to achieve almost calligraphic refinement. In his paintings of racecourses (p. 151) and nudes at their toilet (p. 152), Degas also incorporated a tendency toward dynamic compositions that recalls the prints he collected.

Monet likewise amassed a large collection of prints over the course of his life, seeing them as a different way to view nature, in an echo of his own approach. Ultimately, these images shaped the way he saw things himself. Hence, during a trip to Norway in 1895, he wrote: "It looks just like Japan, which is not unusual in this country, in fact … I am doing a mountain that you can see from everywhere here and it makes me think of Fuji-Yama."[26] The snowy silhouette of Norway's Kolsås Mountain is indeed reminiscent of some of Hokusai's depictions of Japan's sacred mountain. P. P

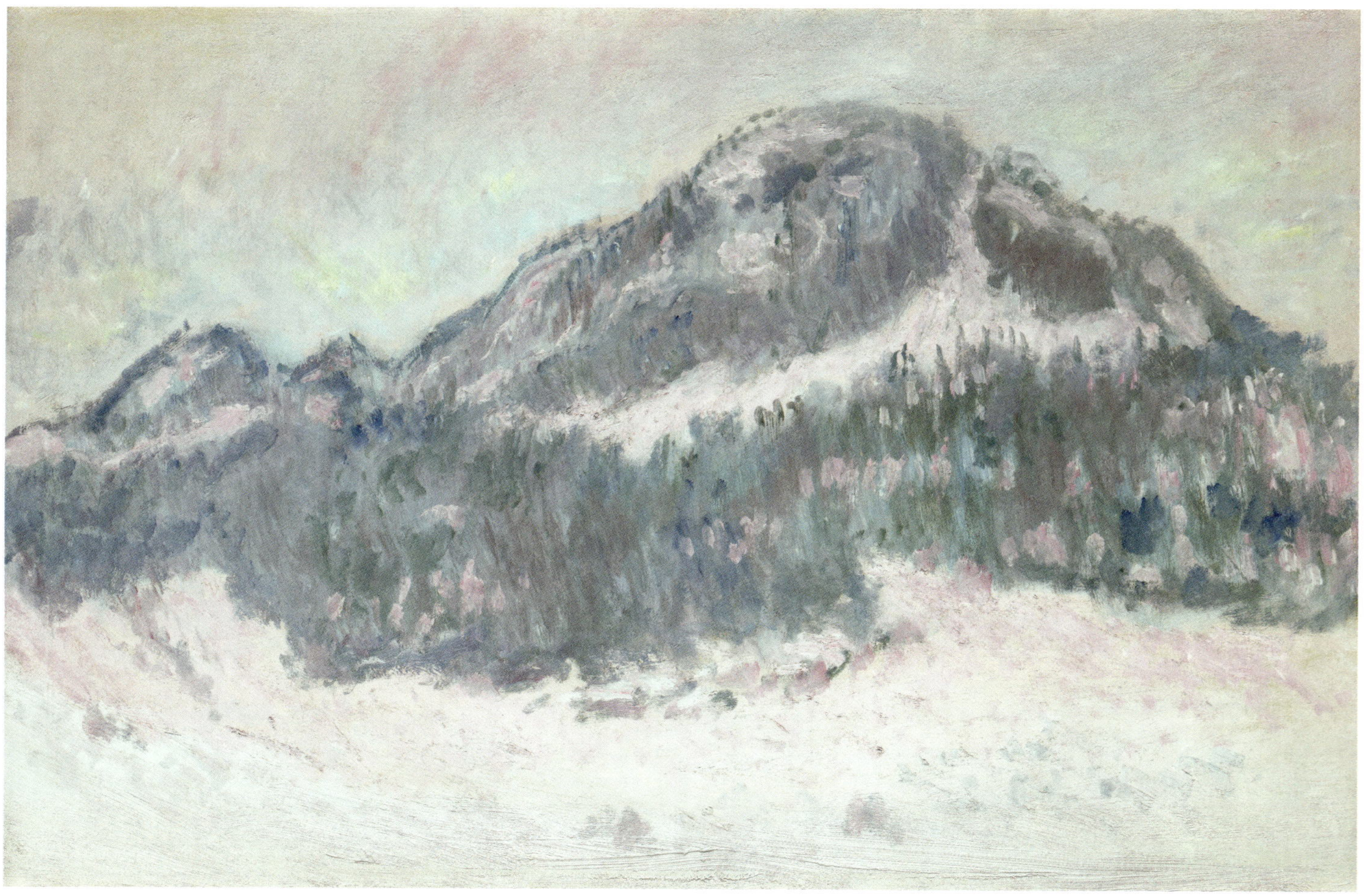

138 Claude Monet, *Le Mont Kolsaas en Norvège* (*Kolsås Mountain, Norway*), 1895
Oil on canvas, 25 13/16 × 39 9/16 in. (65.5 × 100.5 cm)

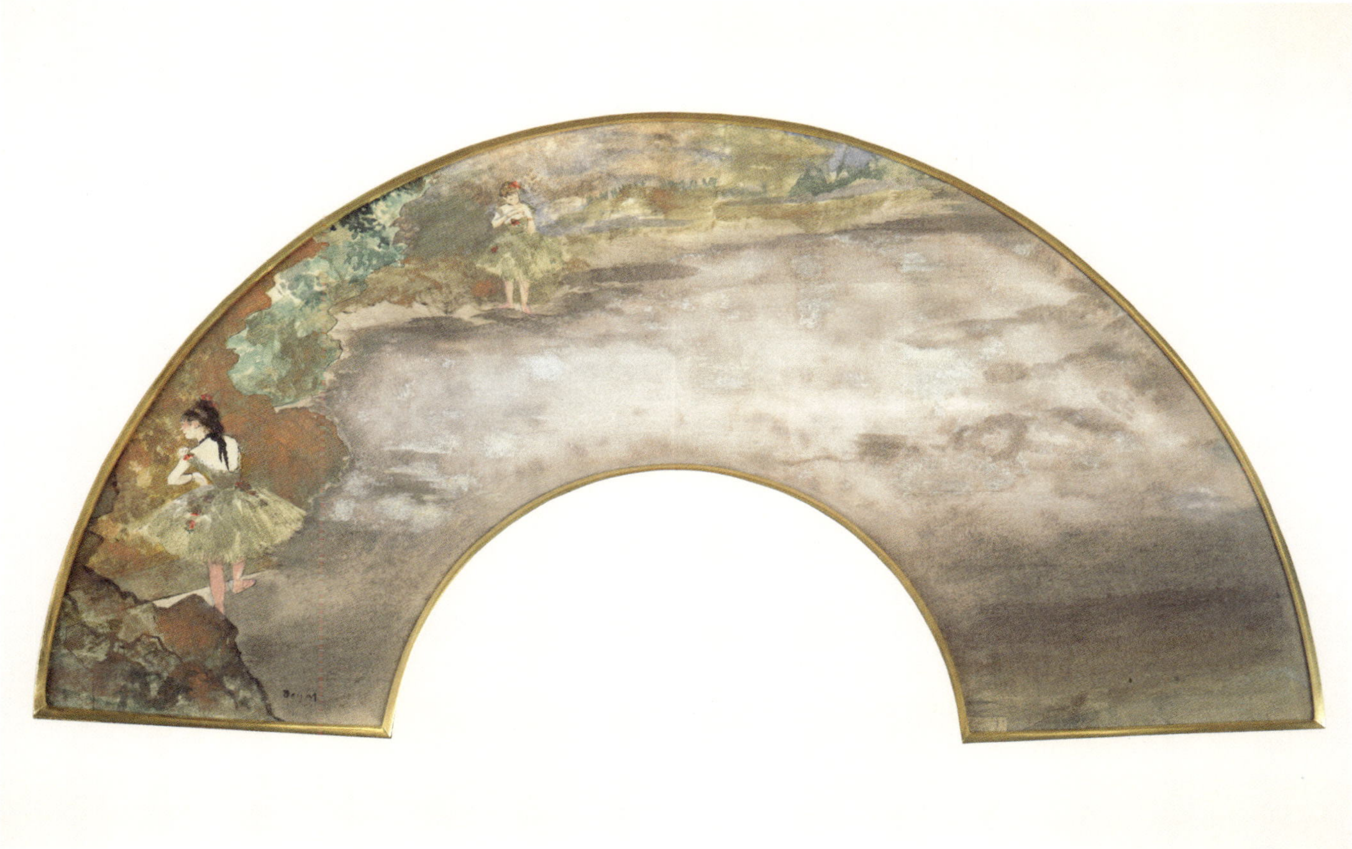

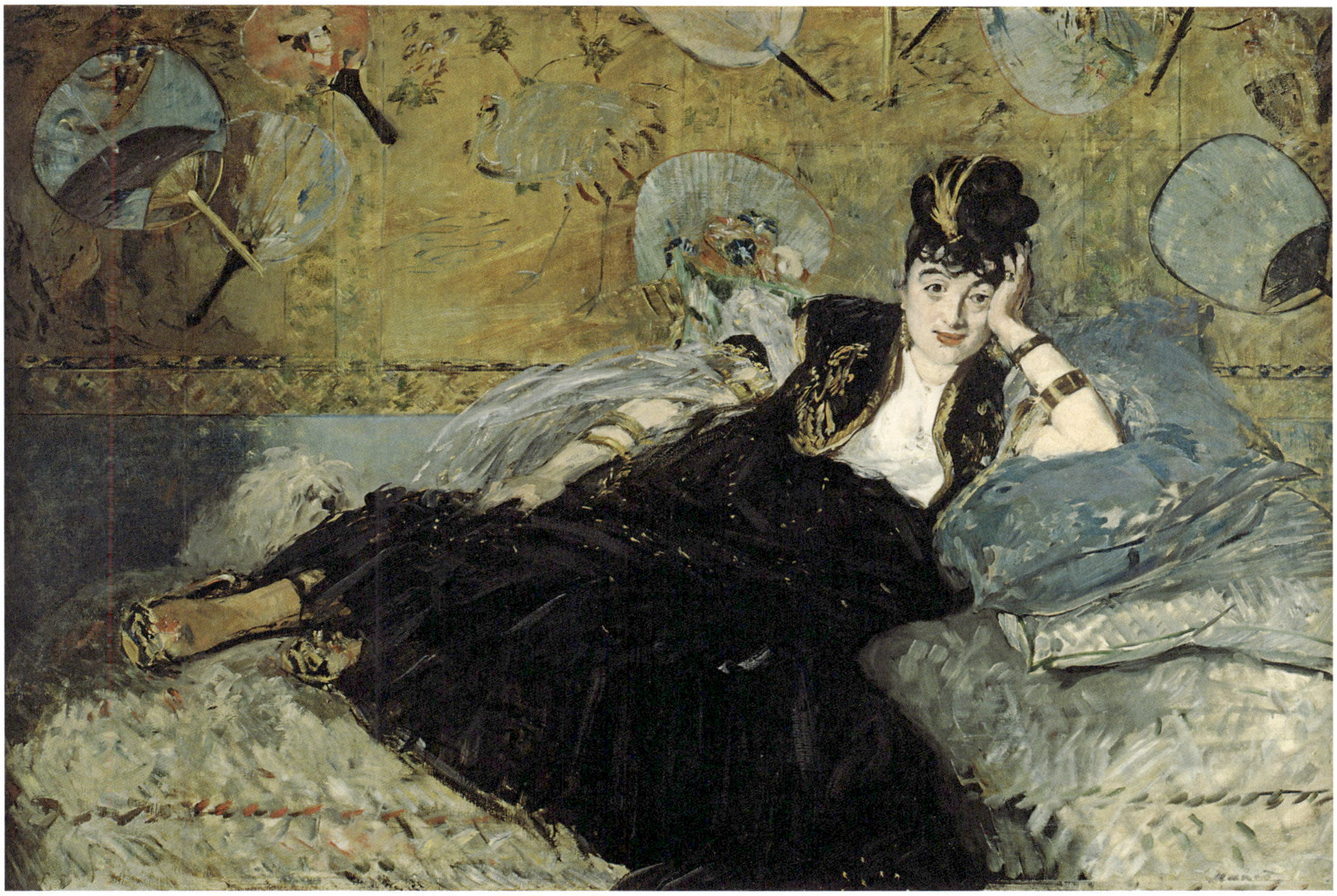

139 Top: Edgar Degas, *Deux danseuses* (*Two Dancers*), 1878–1879
Fan; watercolor heightened with gold and silver
on cream silk laid on card, 11 × 22 13⁄16 in. (28 × 58 cm)

140 Bottom: Édouard Manet,
La Dame aux éventails (*Lady with Fans*), 1873
Oil on canvas, 44 ½ × 65 9⁄16 in. (113 × 166.5 cm)

Paul Cézanne
The Gulf of Marseille

After working extensively at Auvers-sur-Oise in the early 1870s, often alongside Pissarro, Cézanne returned to Provence, and in particular to L'Estaque, in April 1876. This industrious and indeed pre-industrial port town near Marseille had served as a refuge for him when he had fled the outbreak of war in 1870. No sooner had he returned to his native South than he sketched two small seascapes for Victor Chocquet, "red roofs over the blue sea." In a famous letter to Pissarro, dated July 2, 1876, he emphasizes the effects of the "terrifying" summer sun that seems to turn "objects" into "silhouettes"—something that strikes him as "the opposite of modelling." Even more than these canvases, those from 1878–1879 feature accentuated surface effects while still adhering to an impression of perspectival depth. Cézanne never aimed for the fixed, synthetic flatness of the playing card, however much the twentieth-century avant-gardes liked to assert this. For proof, we need only examine his painterly touch in the subtle auras and three-dimensional accents, such as the factory chimney. The Mediterranean Sea, supported by a plunging diagonal, asserts itself in all its majesty, to the point of pushing back the horizon line and rivaling some of Poussin's paintings. The jewel of Caillebotte's collection, this "magnificent southern seascape," as described by Gustave Geffroy, was relegated to the upper levels of the Musée du Luxembourg on the opening of the new Impressionist gallery there in 1897.   S. G.

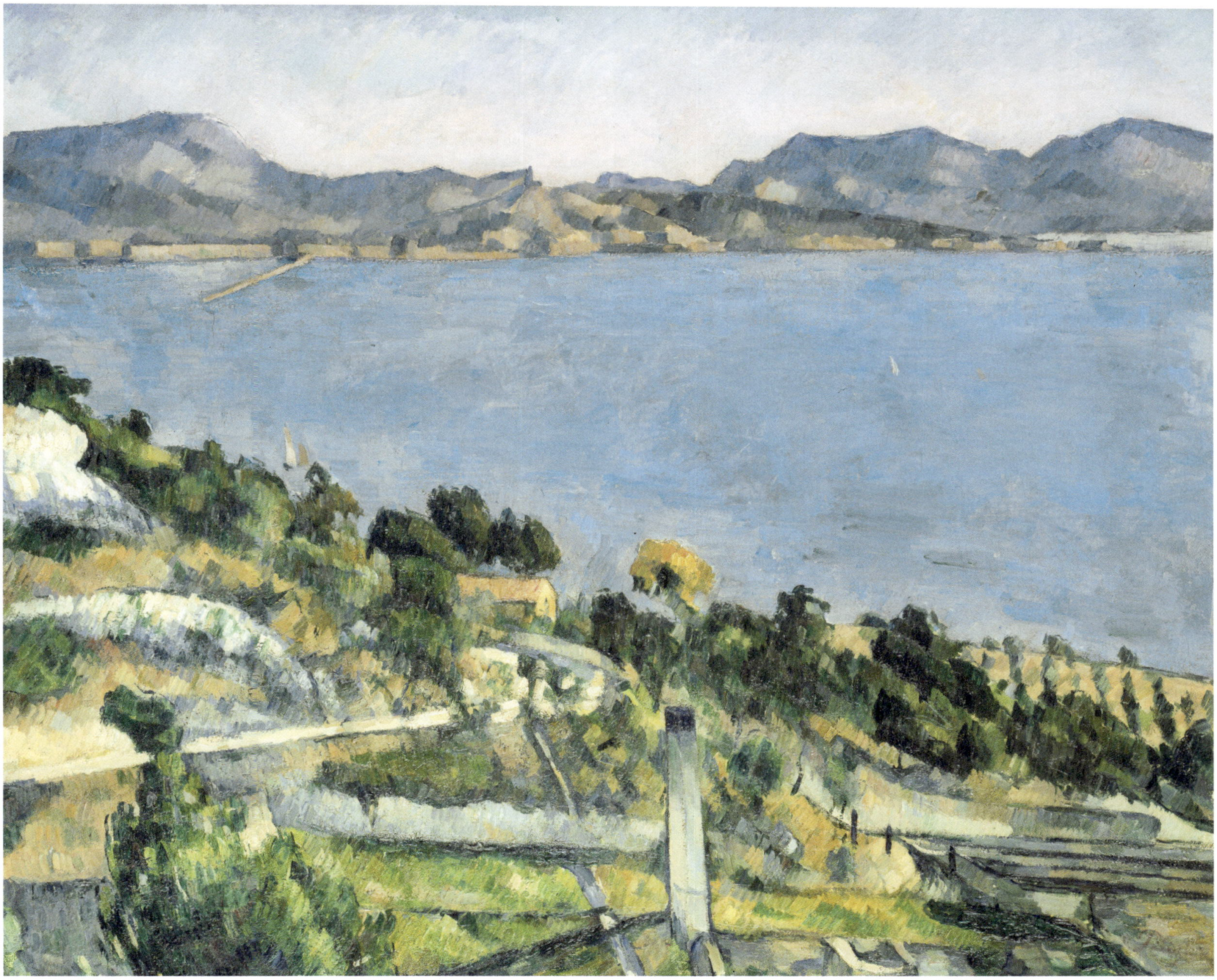

141 Paul Cézanne, *Le Golfe de Marseille vu de l'Estaque*
(*The Gulf of Marseille Seen from L'Estaque*), 1878
Oil on canvas, 23 7⁄16 × 28 ¾ in. (59.5 × 73 cm)

Paul Cézanne
The Bridge at Maincy

In early 1879, as preparations were underway for the fourth Impressionist exhibition, Cézanne decided to try his luck with the Salon, and opted not to exhibit with his "independent" fellow artists. That April, he left Paris and its usual hectic atmosphere to move to Melun, some 35 miles (60 kilometers) south-east of the capital. He worked there alone for almost a year, painting views of the town and surrounding countryside. In the nearby village of Maincy, he found a subject that inspired one of his most remarkable compositions: a bridge straddling the calm river Almont, surrounded by tall trees with dense foliage. This wood-and-stone structure is different in every respect from the metal bridges, emblematic of the modern world, which frequently appeared in his Impressionist friends' canvases. Cézanne places the footbridge parallel to the picture plane, bringing balance and stability to the composition. Having been introduced to *plein-air* painting several years earlier by his friend Pissarro, he brilliantly replicates the depth and coolness of this confined, damp, shady site. The strong, solid, "constructive" brushstrokes define the planes and volumes with perfectly mastered precision. Cézanne had taken the lessons of Impressionism on board, but transcended them, lending his painting an incomparable sense of harmony. A.R.

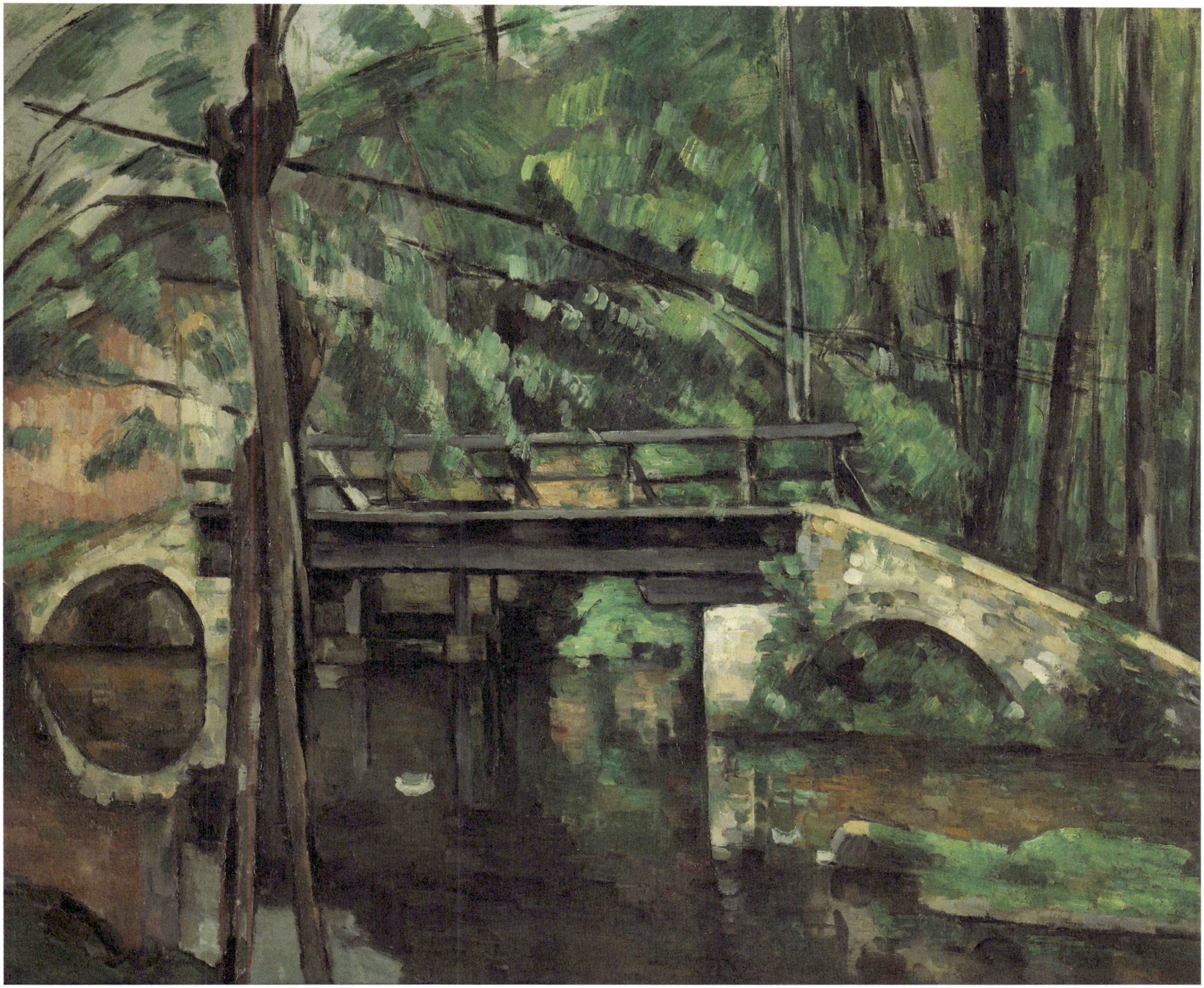

142 Paul Cézanne, *Pont de Maincy* (*The Bridge at Maincy*), c. 1879
Oil on canvas, 23 × 28 ½ in. (58.4 × 72.4 cm)

1879

The fourth Impressionist exhibition

The Impressionist adventure might have ended in 1879 had it not been for Degas's, Pissarro's, and above all Caillebotte's energetic commitment. For them, Monet's involvement was crucial. Without Renoir, Sisley, Morisot, and Cézanne, the group had become increasingly fragmented, making a fourth joint venture all the more important. Monet hesitated, then came round on his more convinced fellows' insistence, and ended up exhibiting nearly thirty works. Caillebotte was particularly determined that *Rue Montorgueil* (p. 163) be included, as a powerful expression of the political antagonism and exhilaration around the national festival of June 30, 1878—the date chosen to celebrate a Republic that was then torn between Mac Mahon's faithful and Gambetta's radicals. In a sign of the disagreements that had brought the Impressionists' group strategy to a state of gridlock, over a third of the fifteen exhibiting artists had not participated in any of the three previous exhibitions. The number was bolstered mainly by artists close to Degas, such as Jean-Louis Forain and the Italian painter Federico Zandomeneghi. Also significant was the presence of the American painter Cassatt, Degas's only student. Another woman notably joined the struggling enterprise: Marie Bracquemond, who exhibited paintings on faience, while her husband Félix sent in several etchings. These were not the only indications of the artists' shared wish not to be limited to easel painting. Degas, an aficionado of colorful frames, and Caillebotte showed some attempts at decorative mural painting. These two were responsible for some of the 1879 exhibition's masterpieces, from *Portrait of Friends on the Stage* to *View of Rooftops (Snow Effect)* and *Boating Party* (p. 161). Paul Gauguin joined at the last minute, exhibiting his very classical marble bust of his son Emil (c. 1877–1878; Metropolitan Museum of Art, New York). The press response was almost more negative than before. Albert Wolff's attack in *Le Figaro* set out to sow even more division in the group: "Manet is wrongly considered the leader of these Impressionists, but he alone is more talented than their entire little flock; he must not be mentioned here." Still, there were some enthusiastic voices, and between April 10 and May 11 the public flocked into 28 Avenue de l'Opéra, where the works had been carefully hung in an elegant apartment rented for the occasion. S.G.

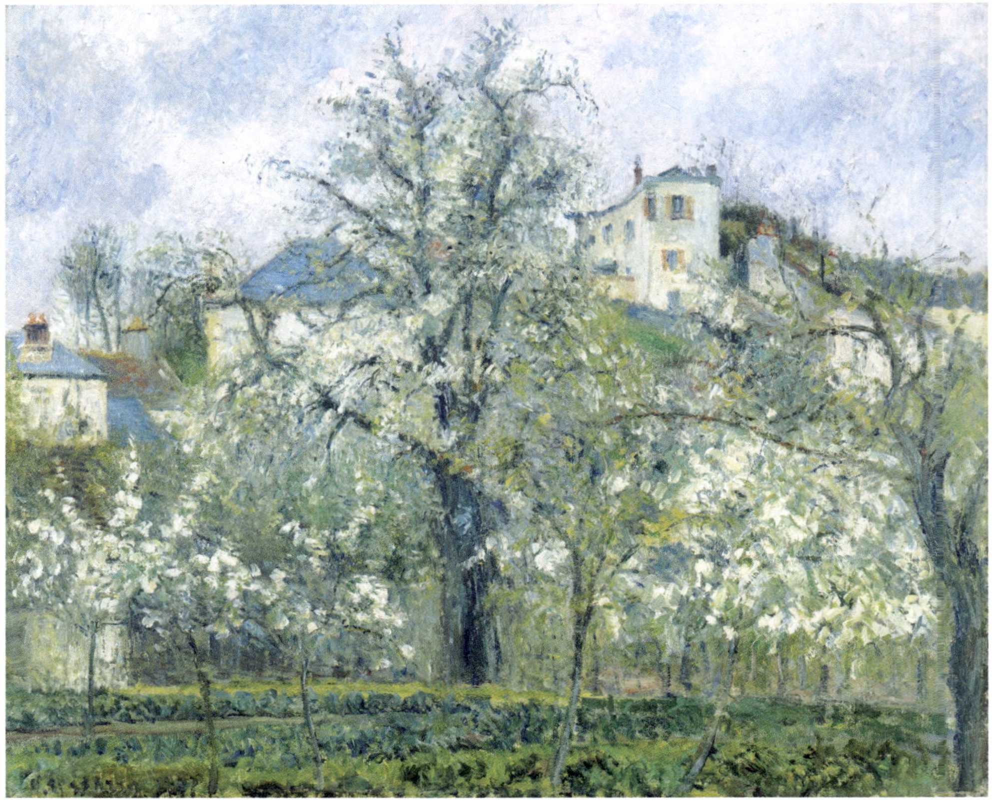

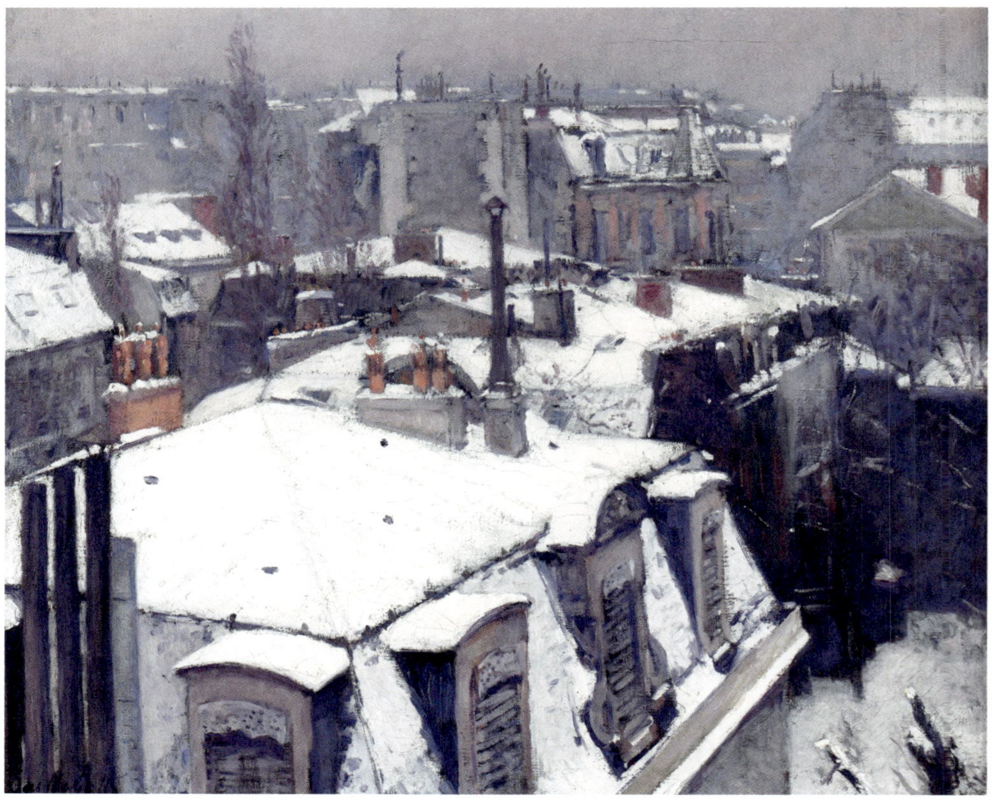

143 Top: Camille Pissarro, *Printemps. Pruniers en fleurs (Springtime: Plum Trees in Blossom)*, 1877
Oil on canvas, 25 13/16 × 31 7/8 in. (65.5 × 81 cm)

144 Bottom: Gustave Caillebotte, *Vue de toits (Effet de neige) (View of Rooftops [Snow Effect])*, 1878
Oil on canvas, 25 3/8 × 31 7/8 in. (64.5 × 81 cm)

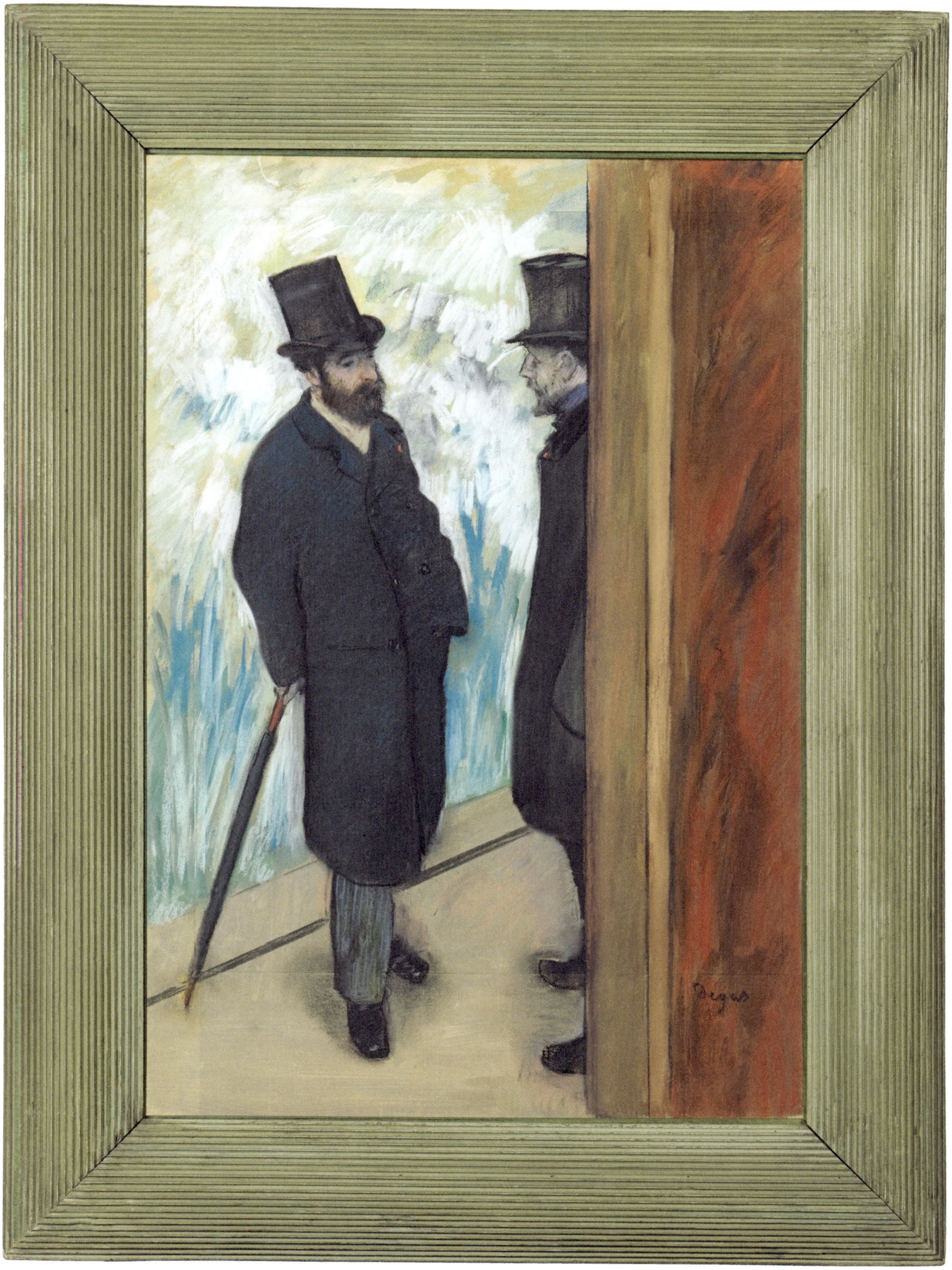

145 Edgar Degas, *Ludovic Halévy et Albert Boulanger-Cavé dans les coulisses de l'Opéra* (*Portrait of Friends on the Stage*, also known as *Portrait of Ludovic Halévy and Albert Boulanger-Cavé*), 1879
Tempera and pastel on paper, 31 ⅛ × 21 ⅝ in. (79 × 55 cm)

Gustave Caillebotte
Boating Party

Before becoming a keen sportsman himself and excelling at regattas, in the 1870s the young Caillebotte developed a passion for the world of boating—a very fashionable pursuit for Parisians since the middle of the century. Related to the development of the new culture of leisure, boating subjects had appeared in Manet's, Monet's, and Renoir's paintings from time to time, but Caillebotte brought them to a new level. Between 1877 and 1878 he devoted a major series of oils and pastels to the theme, depicting people boating on the river Yerres, which ran alongside the Caillebotte family's country estate in the town of the same name, south-east of Paris.

Always on the search for something new, he painted them from an increasingly surprising range of viewpoints, such as here, where he has placed himself inside the boat, facing the rower, to achieve an absolutely unprecedented effect of realism and immersion. Unlike Monet, who was mainly interested in landscape, or Renoir, who preferred to paint the world of freedom and merriment that boating men and women enjoyed, Caillebotte focused on the exclusively male side of the sport: the movements, the bodies in action. *Boating Party* is different from the other paintings in the series because here we have not a young sportsman in a white boating outfit, but an elegant (and as yet unidentified) Parisian, who has taken off his jacket but kept his top hat (a sign of dandyism?), rowing along in a simple pleasure boat.

The image exudes a sense of strength, confidence, and freedom, but also of mystery. The sketchy brushwork and light colors are reminiscent of *plein-air* painting, which Caillebotte was feeling more and more drawn to: he had been buying works from Monet, Renoir, and Pissarro since 1876. *Boating Party* is one of the paintings on the theme of nautical leisure pursuits that Caillebotte sent in 1879 to the fourth Impressionist exhibition, which he played a major part in organizing. Critics at the time considered him one of the group's most radical and provocative artists. P. P.

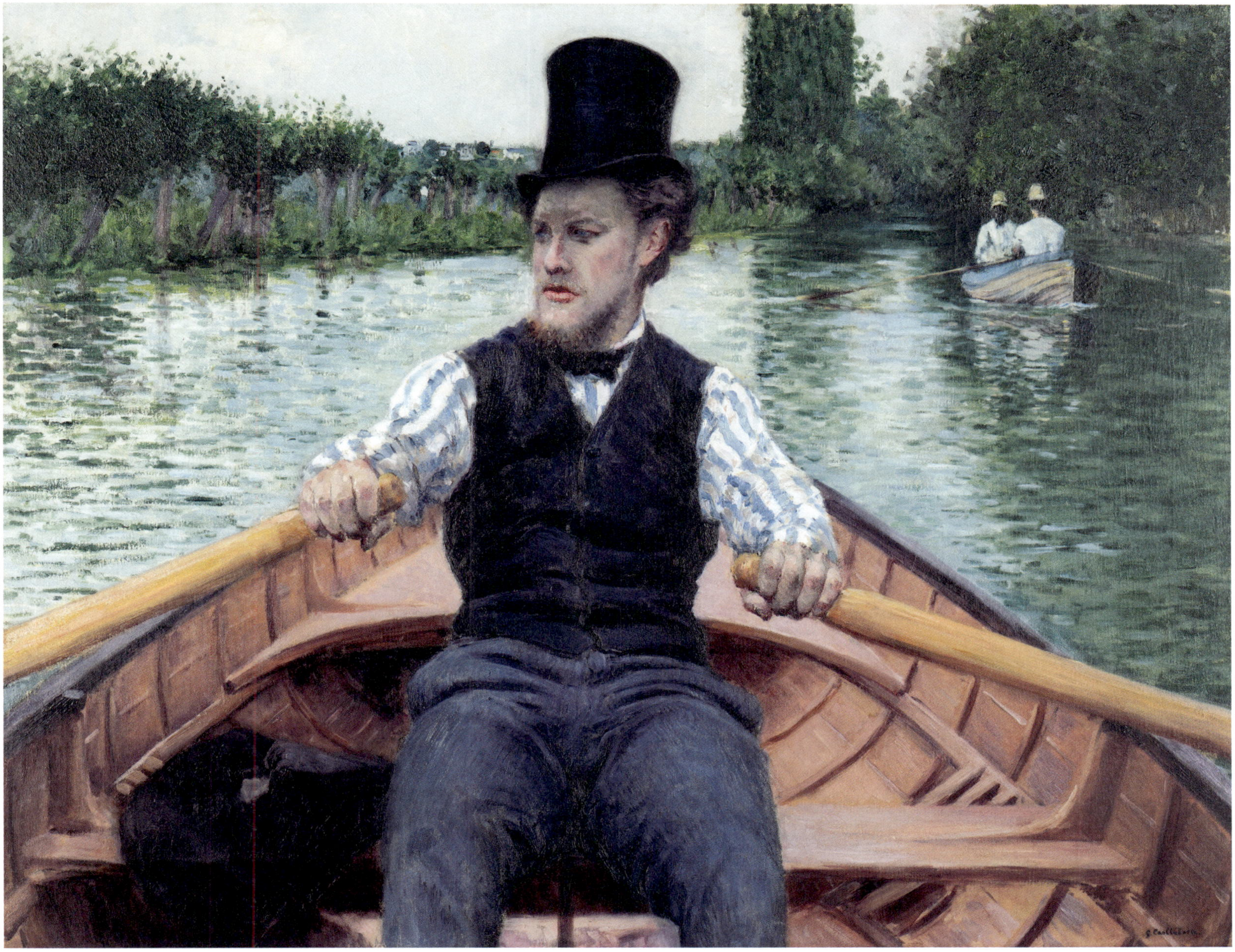

146 Gustave Caillebotte, *Partie de bateau* (*Boating Party*), c. 1877–1878
Oil on canvas, 35 ¼ × 45 15/16 in. (89.5 × 116.7 cm)

Claude Monet
Rue Montorgueil

As a new Exposition Universelle opened to the public in Paris in the spring of 1878, Marshal Mac Mahon's regime was already considerably weakened and the radical opposition was gearing up to overthrow it. A dispute arose around which date to choose for the French national day and the symbolic significance that should be associated with it, its aim being to assert the country's political stability based on the values of peace and labor. On the Republican side, the left was holding out for July 14, and the right for June 30. Monet, who supported the former faction, nevertheless decided to paint, from above, two streets in working-class areas of Paris decked in flags. In both *Rue Saint-Denis* (c. 1878; Musée des Beaux-Arts, Rouen) and *Rue Montorgueil, Paris: Festival of June 30, 1878* the paint itself appears jubilant, mirroring the tricolors and the hordes of celebrating people. Monet's choppy brushwork probably never served the subject matter's needs more than it does here, the moment and the group taking precedence over spatial precision and anecdotal detail. The capital's residents, regardless of their individual opinions, were responding en masse to the government's wish to see the city covered in blue, white, and red. It would therefore be inaccurate to see Monet as indifferent to the political connotation of the painting. The canvas was purchased on July 11, 1878, by Georges de Bellio, who already owned *Impression, Sunrise*. It would not have become one of the stars of the Impressionists' fourth exhibition had it not been for Caillebotte's insistence on the need to keep their shows alive, the group being ever-increasingly beset by conflict. S. G.

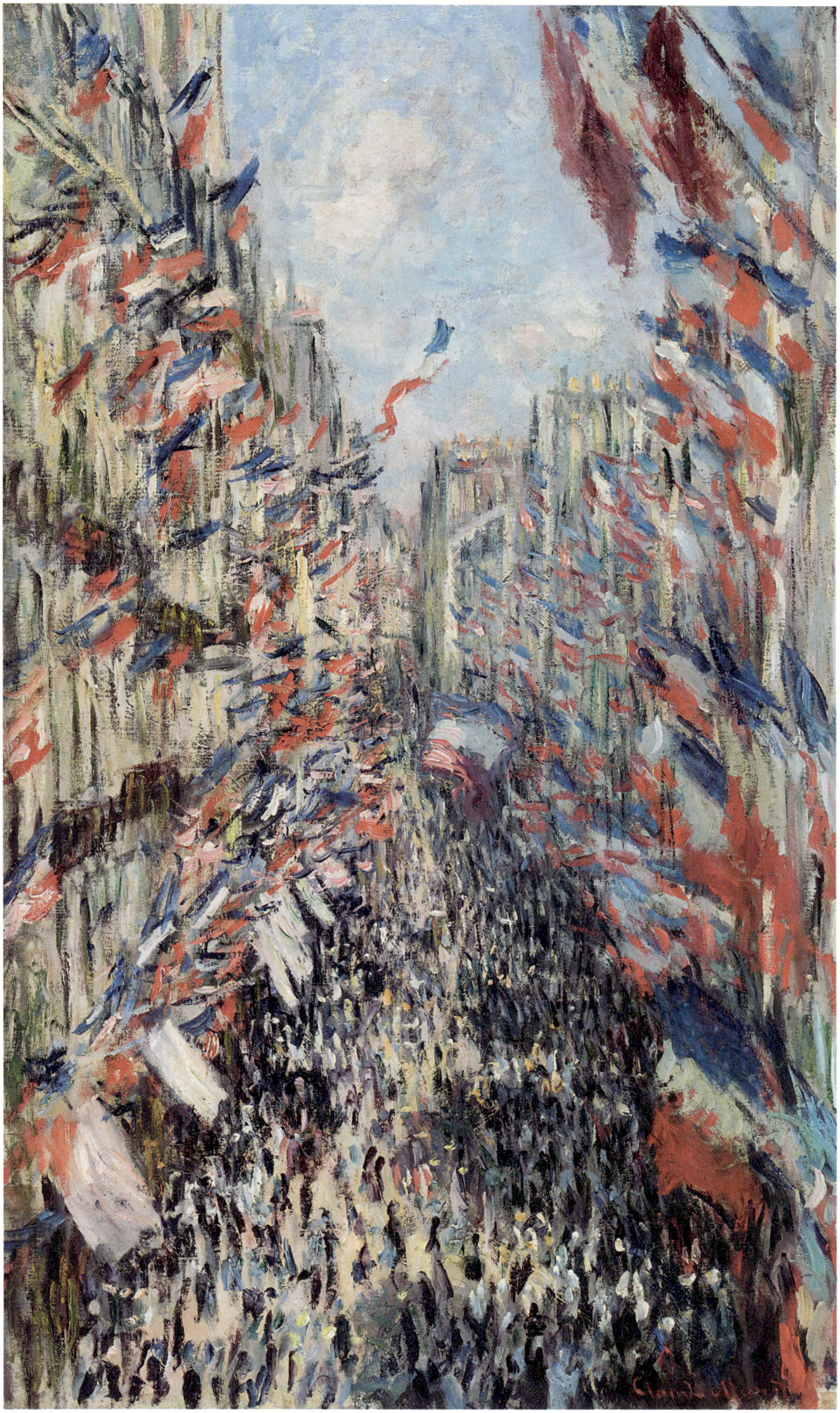

147 Claude Monet, *La Rue Montorgueil, à Paris. Fête du 30 juin 1878*
(*Rue Montorgueil, Paris: Festival of June 30, 1878*), 1878
Oil on canvas, 31 ⅞ × 19 ¹¹⁄₁₆ in. (81 × 50 cm)

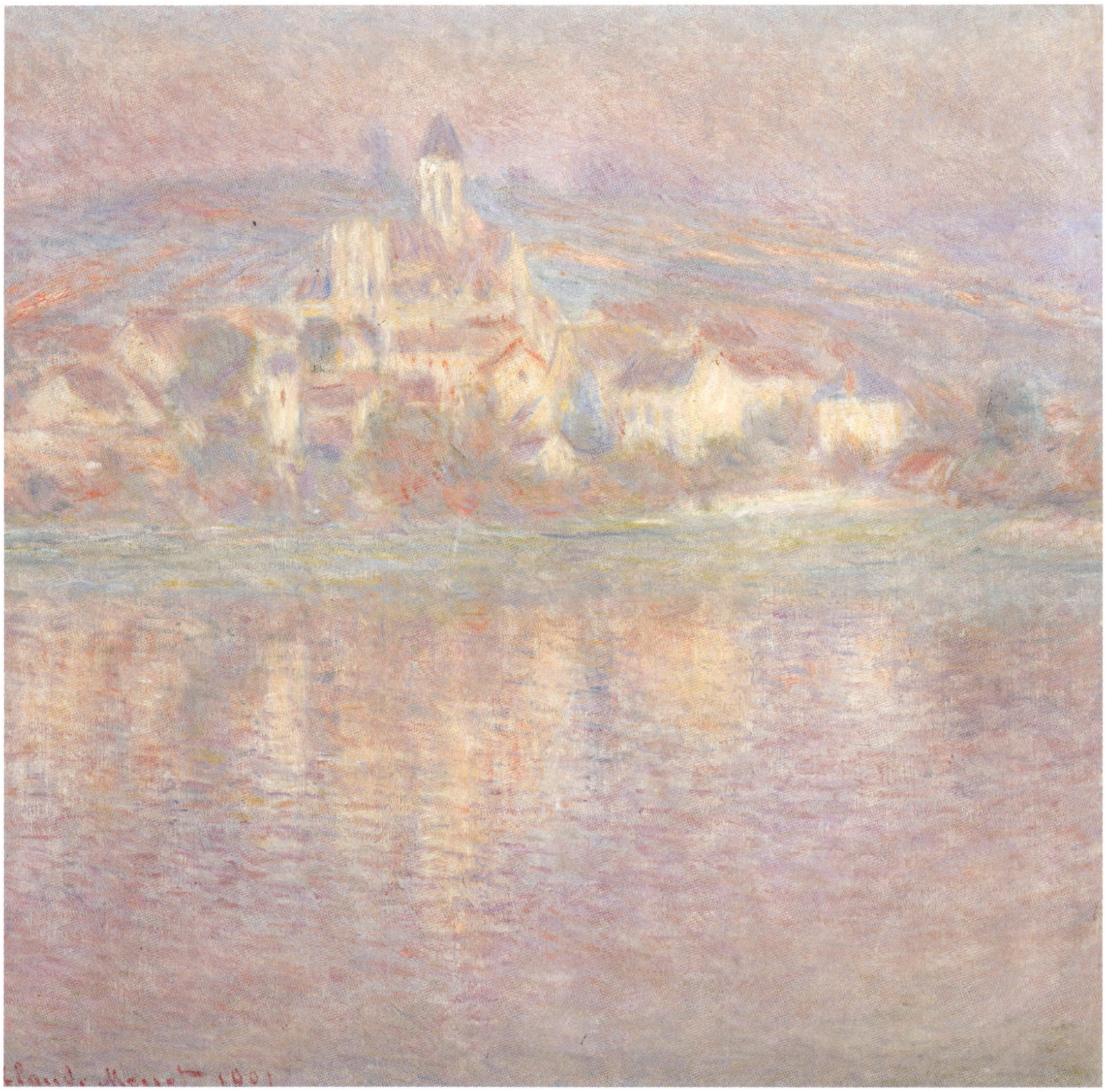

148 Claude Monet, *Vétheuil, soleil couchant* (*Vétheuil, Setting Sun*), c. 1900
Oil on canvas, 35 7⁄16 × 36 5⁄8 in. (90 × 93 cm)

Monet at Vétheuil

The three-and-a-half years that Monet spent in Vétheuil, some 40 miles (70 kilometers) west of Paris—from the summer of 1878 until December 1881—were undoubtedly among the darkest of his life. The art market was in crisis and the Impressionist exhibitions had not proved the commercial success that he had been banking on. Despite a devoted circle of enthusiasts, Monet wrote in April 1878: "We don't have a single cent in the home, not even anything to keep the pot boiling today."[27] The birth of his second son, Michel, was tragically followed by the illness and then, a year later, the death of his wife Camille (p. 167).

Despite this, it was a fruitful period for him artistically. As was his habit, he roamed around observing the village, and painted its huge, beautiful medieval and Renaissance church from different angles and in different weathers, notably when it was covered in snow. He also took an interest in the natural setting, and especially the Seine, which ran along the bottom of his garden and which he described to one journalist as his "studio." Among some 205 paintings that he produced at Vétheuil, one series stands out: the *Debacles*. After a winter that was so harsh that the Seine froze over in December 1879, the thaw caused major damage: blocks of ice were carried along by the water, destroying houses and vegetation. Monet, who had painted the snow and frost shimmering iridescent in the winter sunshine (p. 29), was suddenly taking on a topical subject that was front-page news. However, aside from a few fractured trees and the Seine flood, he kept quiet about the destruction and human drama, concentrating instead on light effects and reflections in the water. He painted some twenty canvases in which the Seine occupies the foreground: the swelling water and the ice contrast with the verticality of the few trees that remain standing as somber silhouettes along the riverbanks. The brushstrokes are nervous, cursive, and sometimes brightly colored. The arrangement on the canvas such as the motif of blocks of ice on the water's surface makes the *Debacles* forerunners of the *Water Lilies* series that he went on to paint at Giverny in the late 1890s (p. 263). He remained forever fond of Vétheuil, which was close to his house at Giverny, and he returned to the area and painted the village in summer 1901; Camille was buried there, and it inspired him to capture melancholic, meditative, almost dreamlike views from across the river. S. P.

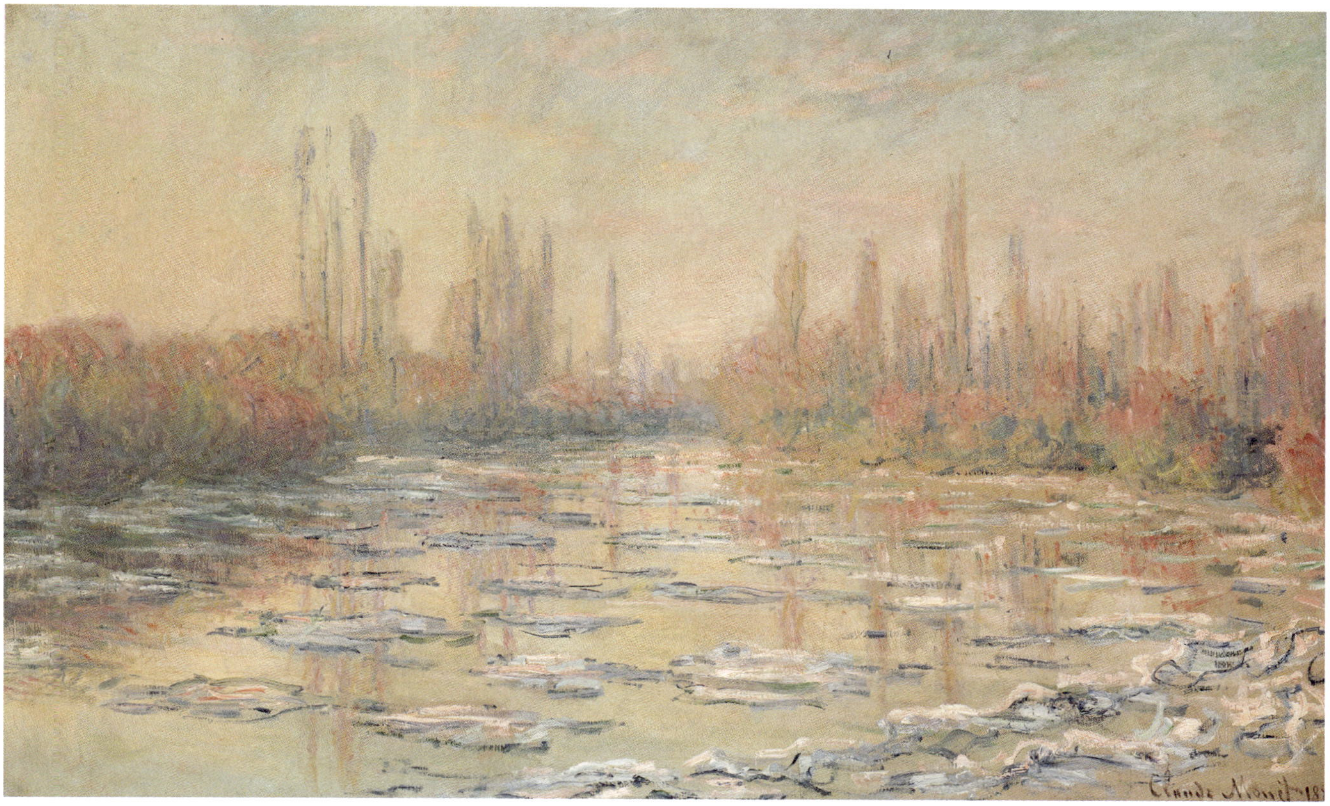

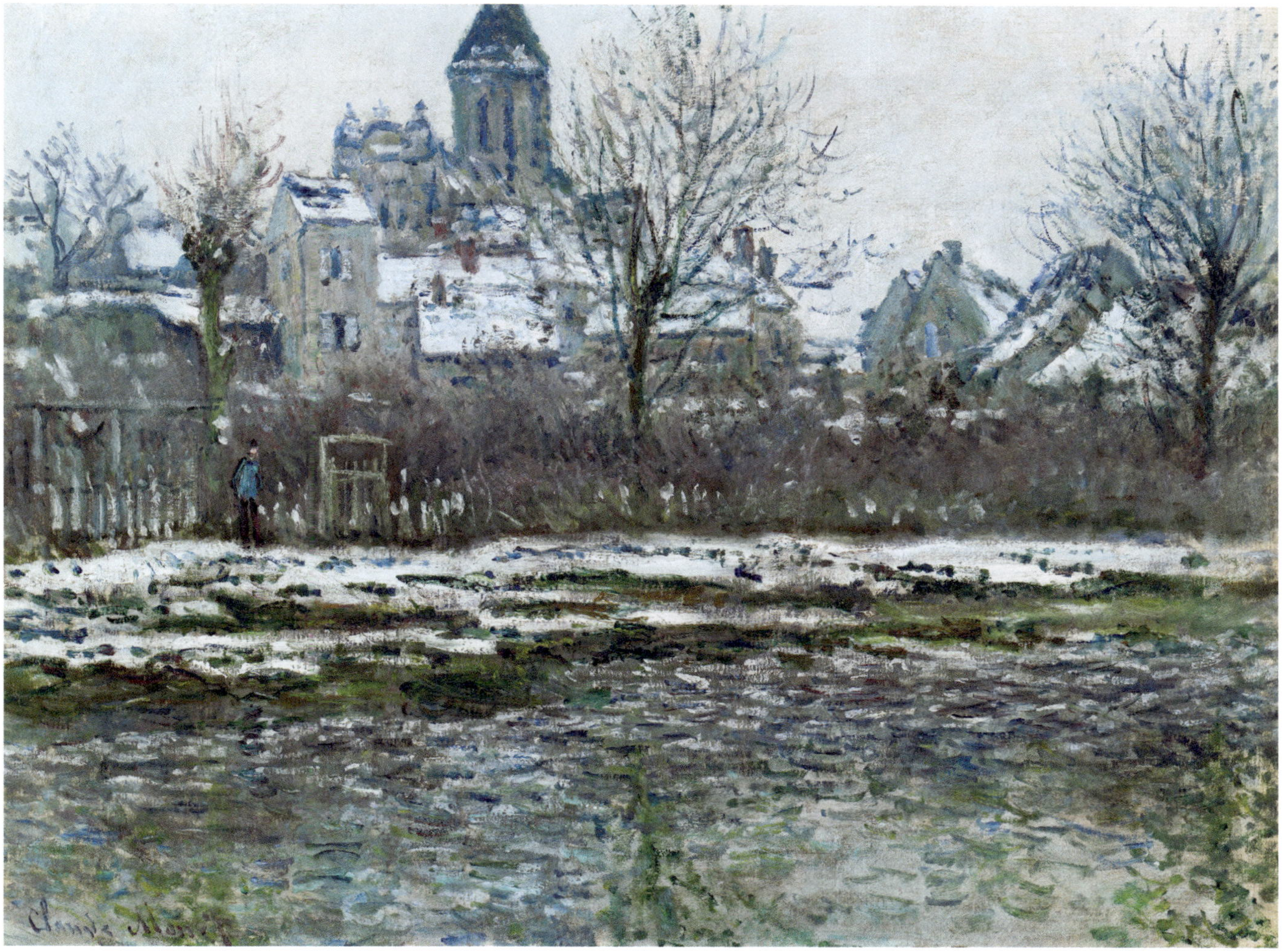

149 Top: Claude Monet, *Les Glaçons*
(*Ice Thawing on the Seine*), 1880
Oil on canvas, 23 $\frac{13}{16}$ × 39 $\frac{3}{16}$ in. (60.5 × 99.5 cm)

150 Bottom: Claude Monet, *Effet de neige à Vétheuil*
(*Snow Effect at Vétheuil*), 1878–1879
Oil on canvas, 20 $\frac{11}{16}$ × 27 $\frac{15}{16}$ in. (52.5 × 71 cm)

Claude Monet
Camille on Her Deathbed

At Vétheuil on September 5, 1879, at about 10.30 a.m., Monet's first wife, Camille Doncieux, lost her life to an agonizing cancer. She was only thirty-two. Devastated, Monet painted her one last time, recording the features of the woman who had been his companion, the mother of his two sons, and his favorite model since the 1860s. In producing this funerary portrait, he was conforming to a common nineteenth-century custom: the face of the deceased would be cast as a death mask, to preserve their memory. Photography also offered families and other loved ones countless funerary effigies, from its very earliest stages.

This final portrait was also an extreme artistic experiment, as Monet later testified with some guilt to his dear friend, the French prime minister Georges Clemenceau: "I caught myself watching her tragic forehead, almost mechanically observing the sequence of changing colors that death was imposing on her rigid face. Blue, yellow, gray, and so on."[28] Camille already seems far away. Her anguished, emaciated face, encircled in cloth, looks as though it is being carried along by the swell of a shroud, like the chunks of floating ice after the Seine disaster in the desolate landscapes that Monet painted a few weeks later. He never exhibited this very personal, autobiographical work, but kept it close as a memento that is at once an uncompromising image of death and a heartbreaking, poetic adieu. S.P.

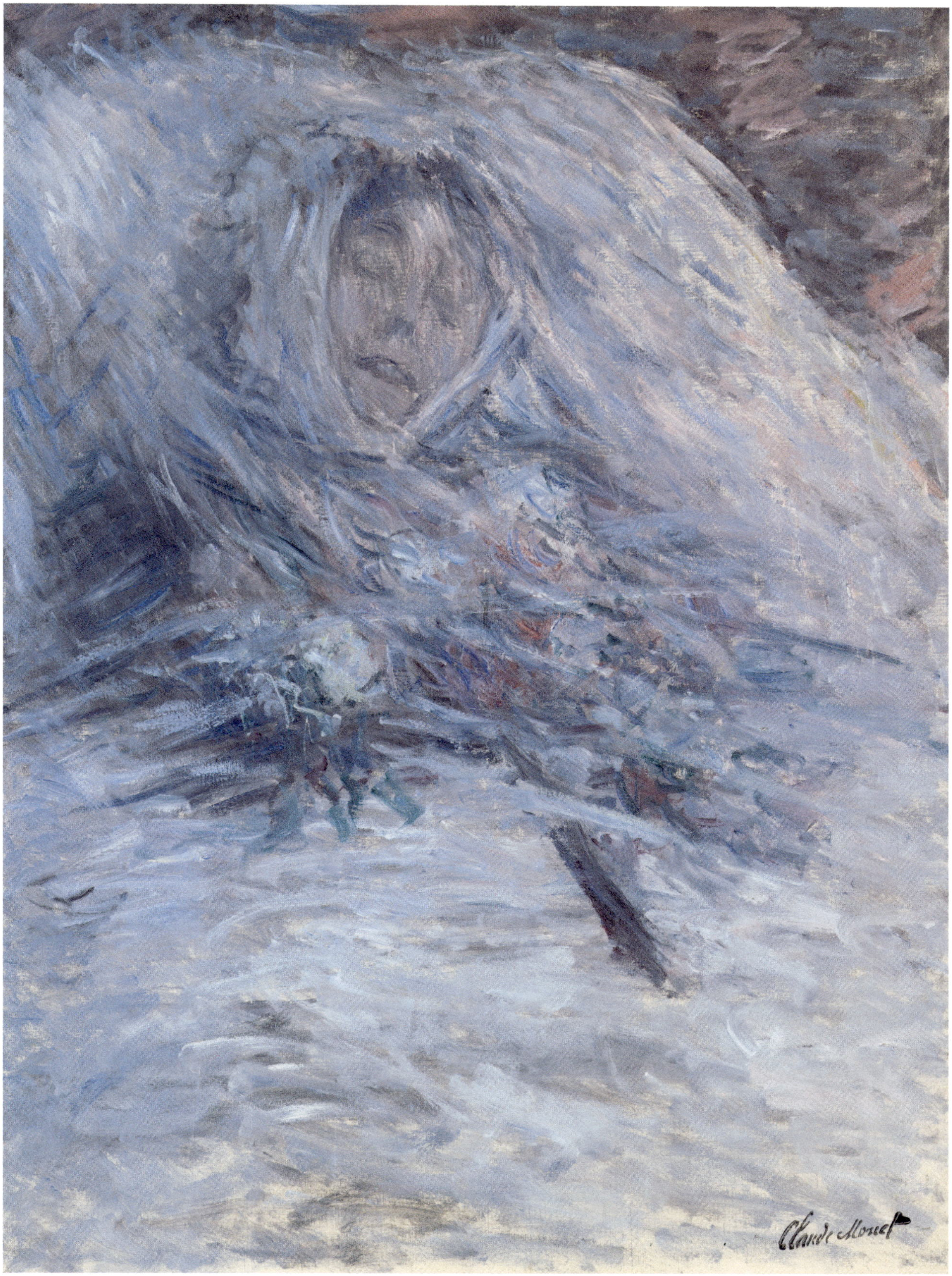

151 Claude Monet, *Camille sur son lit de mort* (*Camille on Her Deathbed*), 1879
Oil on canvas, 35 7/16 × 26 3/4 in. (90 × 68 cm)

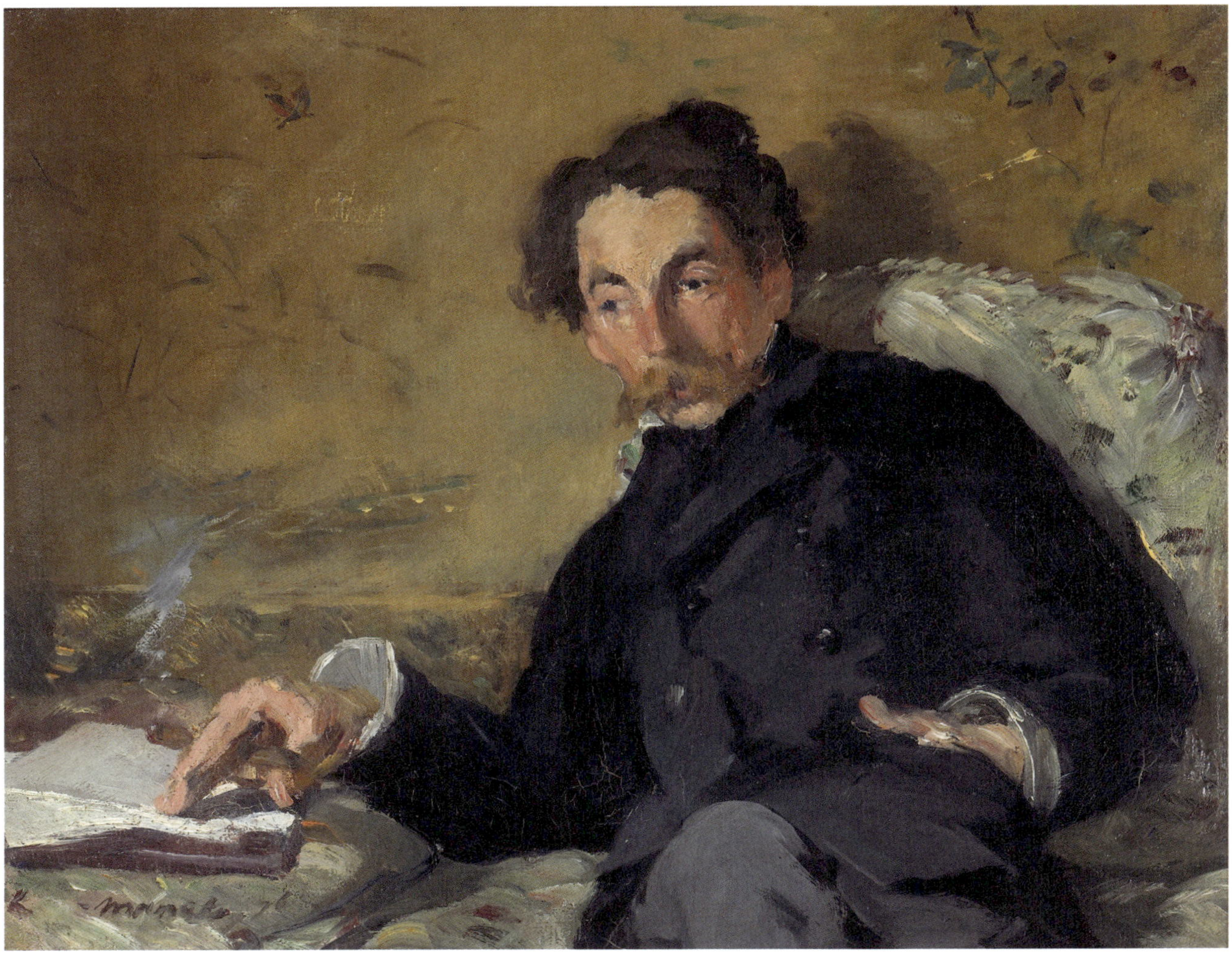

152 Édouard Manet, *Stéphane Mallarmé*, 1876
Oil on canvas, 10 11⁄16 × 14 1⁄16 in. (27.2 × 35.7 cm)

Artistic circles and supporters

Independent painters were in more vital need of support and advocates than those such as Alexandre Cabanel and William-Adolphe Bouguereau, who earned their living from State commissions or American collectors' munificence. Newspapers and journals extensively supported them. This is firstly true of Manet, who was much derided at the Salon and found little favor with the art market before the 1870s. The public-relations effort that his artistic choices and determination to exhibit at the Salon demanded was met by the best writers of the era: Zola, Baudelaire, Mallarmé, and Théodore de Banville. It was at Nina de Callias's republican literary and artistic salon that Mallarmé bonded with Manet, and he devoted two highly influential essays to him, in 1874 and 1876, when Manet was being rejected by the Salon. Two illustrated books sealed their friendship, which is immortalized in the Musée d'Orsay portrait. The poet's reverie and the cigar smoke, a common metaphor in modern poetry, suggest the unpredictable and random sources that inspired his dreamlike visions. Most of the Impressionists paid their debt to the critics and collectors who were committed to their cause by painting their portraits. Hence Renoir did not forget to thank the Charpentier family or Victor Chocquet. Cézanne, likewise, made sure to express his gratitude: in 1895, a very successful year for the Vollard gallery, he produced a portrait of Gustave Geffroy, a defender of Monet and Rodin. We glimpse one of the latter's statuettes in the painting, and the books, inkwell, and composition bear no small resemblance to Manet's *Émile Zola* (p. 39) and Degas's *Edmond Duranty* (1879; Burrell Collection, Glasgow). Geffroy, who had been won over by the eclecticism and anticlericalism of the Third Republic, soon pushed Cézanne to breaking point. The painting's unfinished state is in part due to this. As for politicians, who were also very useful, Manet was the only one to pay homage to those in his close circle, from Émile Ollivier to his great friend Antonin Proust, as well as Clemenceau, who was very close to his youngest brother, Gustave. He was glad when the Communards—supporters and participants of the Paris Commune—were granted amnesty, and painted a heroic portrayal of one of them: the journalist Henri Rochefort (p. 171). S. G.

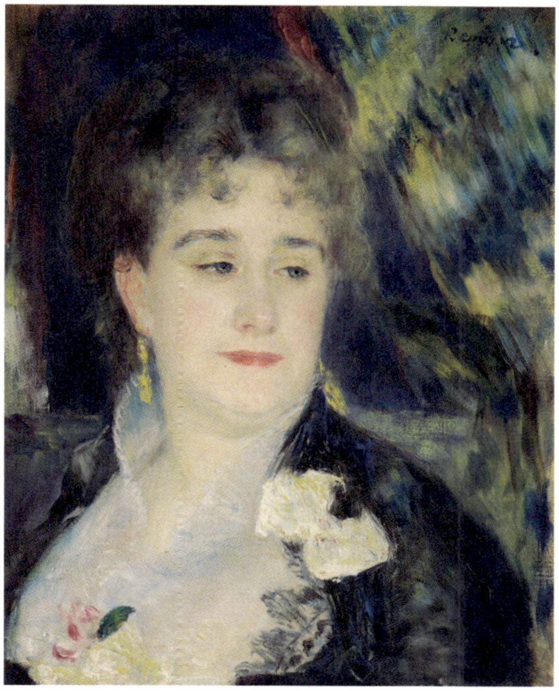

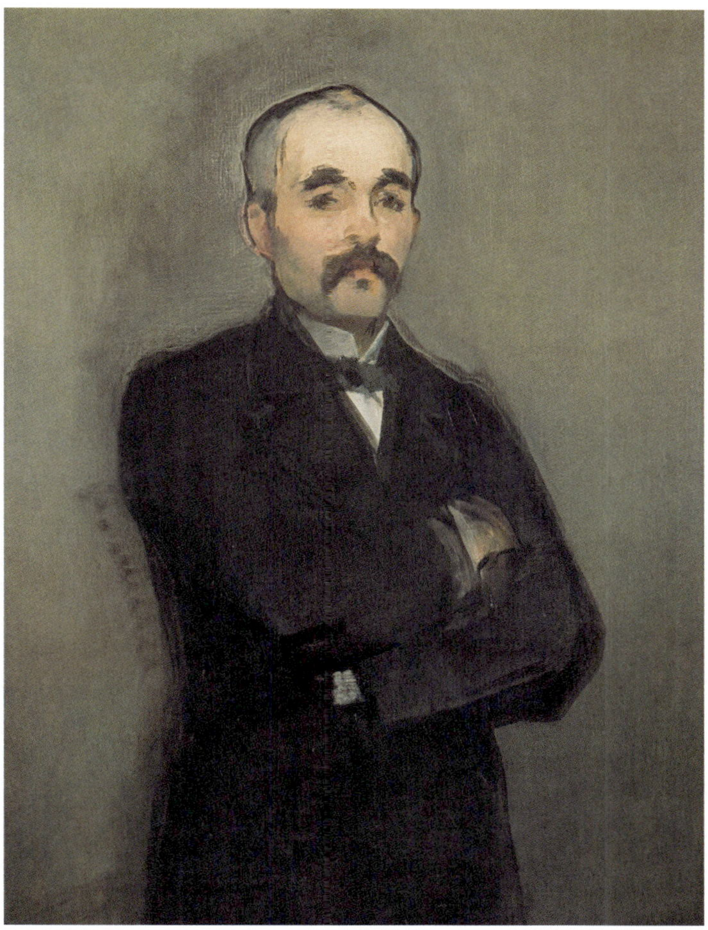

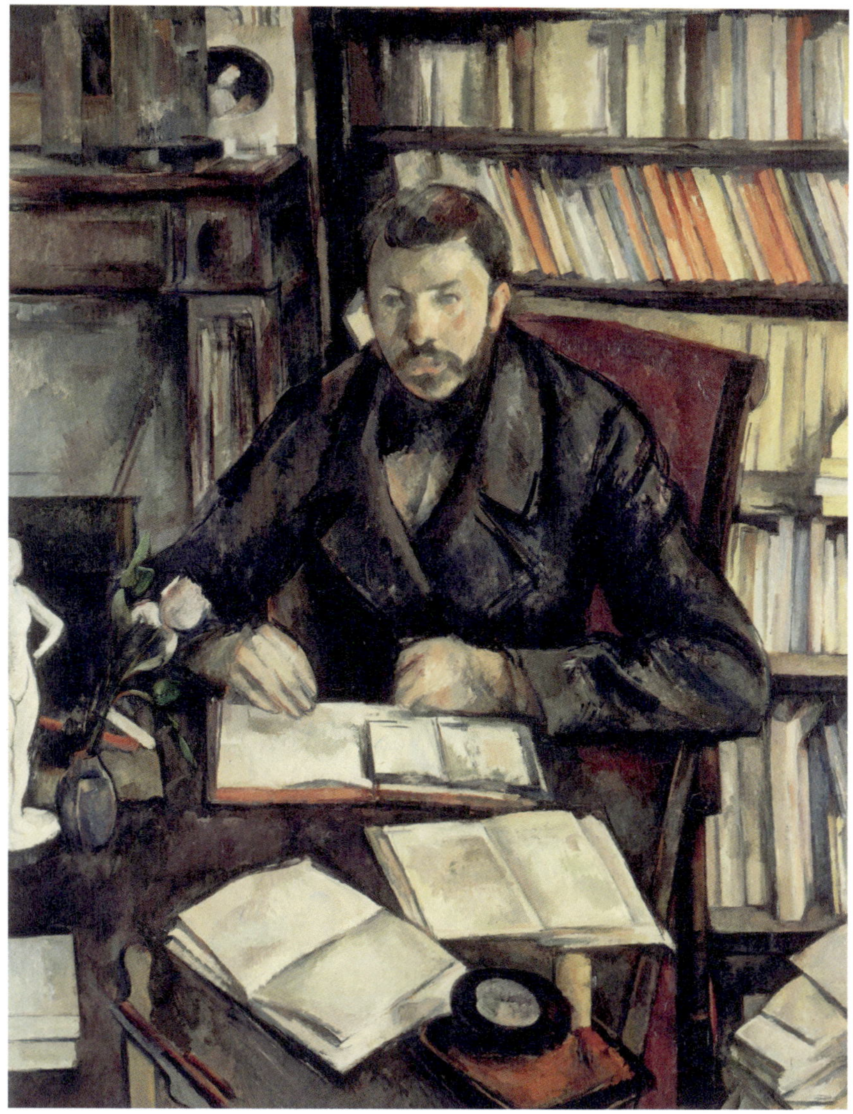

153 Top, left: Auguste Renoir,
Madame Georges Charpentier, 1876–1877
Oil on canvas, 18 ⅛ × 14 15⁄16 in.
(46 × 38 cm)

154 Bottom, left: Édouard Manet,
Georges Clemenceau, 1879–1880
Oil on canvas, 37 × 29 1⁄16 in.
(94 × 73.8 cm)

155 Right: Paul Cézanne,
Gustave Geffroy, 1895–1896
Oil on canvas, 46 1⁄16 × 35 ¼ in.
(117 × 89.5 cm)

Édouard Manet
Rochefort's Escape

Manet's paintings were very political, and he often took it upon himself to tackle topical subjects. He was close to the Republican opposition under the Second Empire, and also criticized Mac Mahon's regime after 1873. Records of a supervised public meeting held in Manet's studio in October 1877 have been found in the police archives. Two years later, a new era was opening up, with the election of Jules Grévy as head of state and the reform of the way the fine arts were administered, among other bodies. When amnesty was granted to the Communards, it offered Manet, already suffering from his final illness, the material for his last history painting. He had copied Delacroix's *The Barque of Dante* (1822; Musée du Louvre, Paris) in his youth, and now painted his own vision of Henri Rochefort's escape, for the Salon. Rochefort had been given a life sentence and transported to New Caledonia, from where he managed to flee in July 1874. He took refuge in London, and returned to Paris five years later. Through shared acquaintances acting as go-betweens, Manet persuaded him to agree to being painted. After extensive research into the circumstances of the escape, he started painting the large canvas that is now in Zurich, which would remain unfinished. When Monet saw it in his friend's studio, he described it as "thrilling." Inverting the scales of the central group and the marine element, the Musée d'Orsay canvas weaves together the ocean's emerald-green immensity and the adventurers' destiny, as uncertain as unfolding history. A variant of, rather than a sketch for, the Zurich canvas, this jewel of a painting has the delicate rawness typical of Manet's final flourishing. S.G.

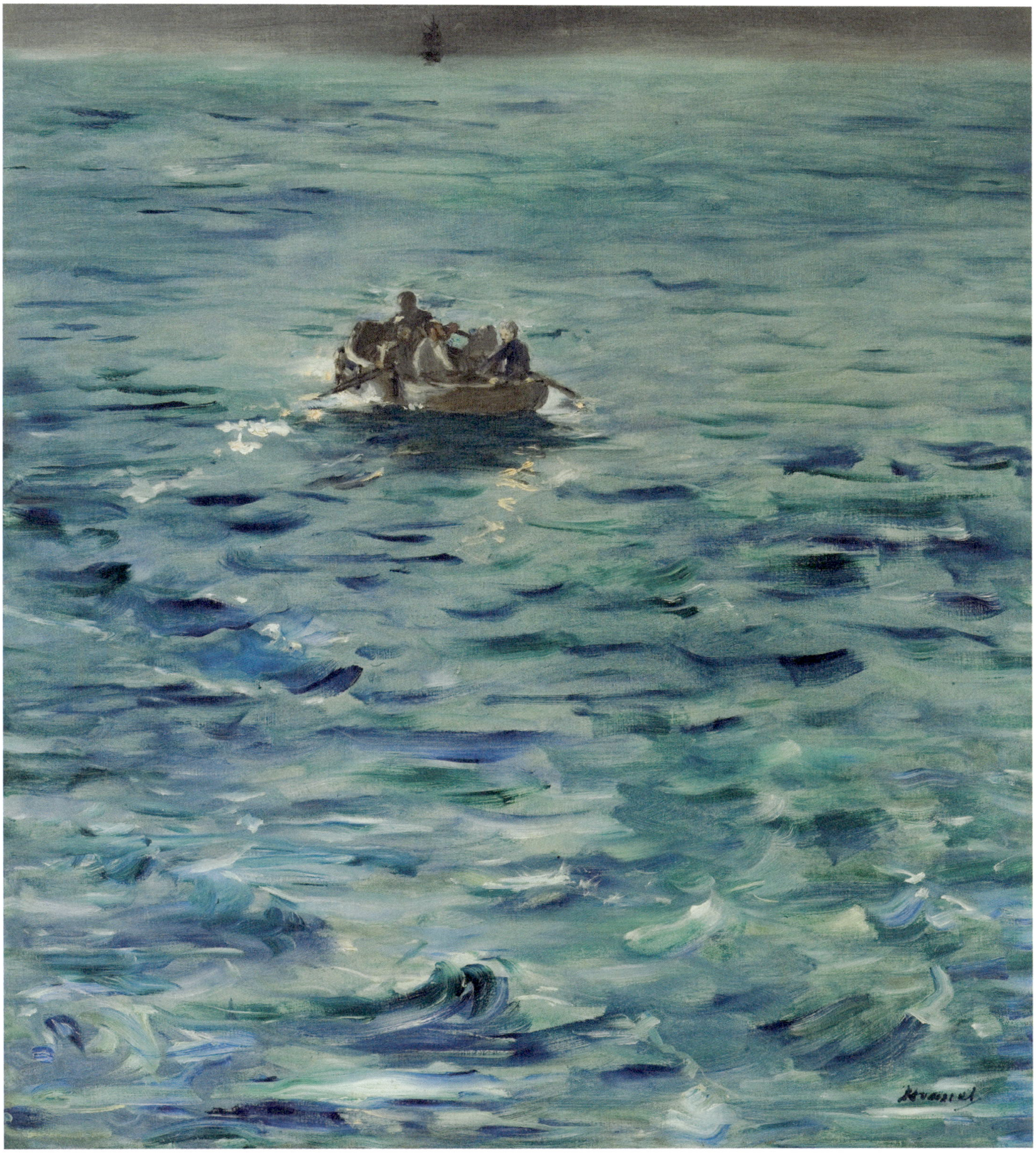

156 Édouard Manet, *L'Évasion de Rochefort* (*Rochefort's Escape*), c. 1881
Oil on canvas, 31 ⅛ × 28 ⅜ in. (79 × 72 cm)

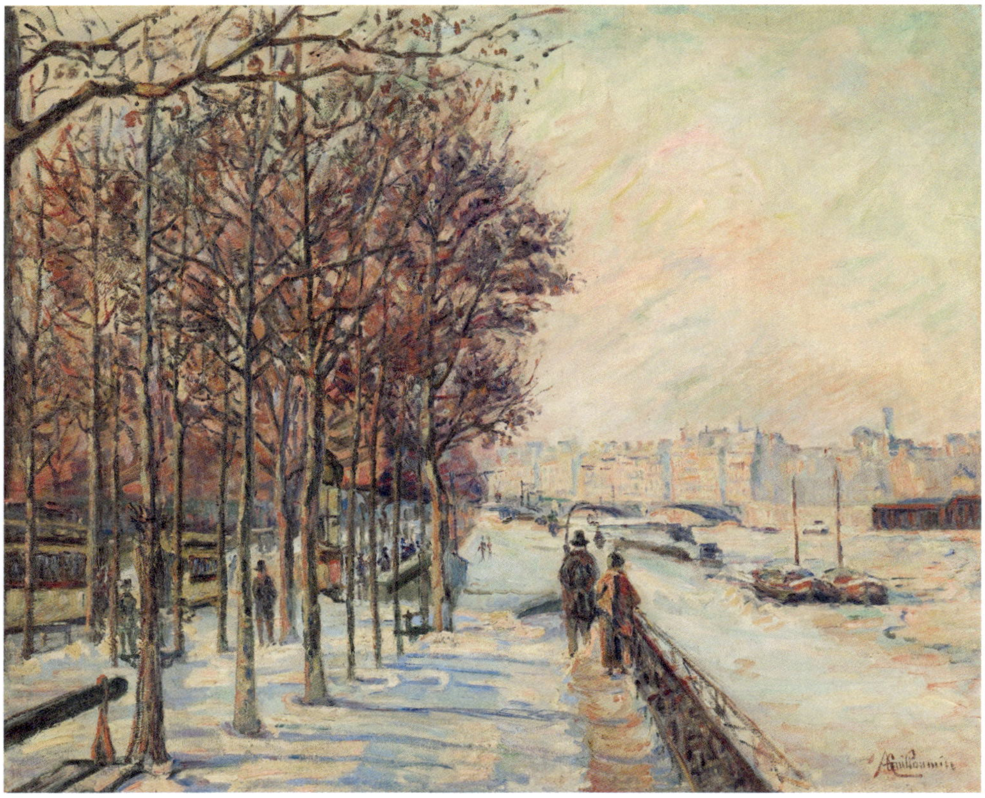

157 Armand Guillaumin, *La Place Valhubert* (*Place Valhubert*), c. 1880
Oil on canvas, 25 ⅜ × 31 ⅞ in. (64.5 × 81 cm)

1880

The fifth Impressionist exhibition

While Impressionism's destiny as a group enterprise seemed ever shakier, Caillebotte persevered. He judged Monet's involvement to be crucial, but Monet was drawn to the Salon and on March 8, 1880 informed the critic and collector Théodore Duret of his intention to return there. His letter to Duret, who thoroughly agreed with his decision, is very frank; only the "official" exhibition would open the doors of the top commercial galleries, exemplified in his view by that of Georges Petit. He obviously was not very proud of abandoning the Impressionists to their fate, but it was a matter of his career and survival. While Morisot came back to the fold in 1880, Monet, Renoir, Sisley, and Cézanne did not participate in the "fifth exhibition by a group of independent artists," as the posters billed it in red lettering on a green background. In any case, Morisot, who had returned, and Cassatt, who remained, had held their names back from the posters, in accordance with social convention. Without burning his bridges with Monet—although he did speak his mind to him about his desertion—Caillebotte agreed to exhibit with Degas's circle, notably including Jean-François Raffaëlli, whom he detested. Forain and Gauguin, with eight works, chose their side. The apartment that was to serve as an exhibition space, at the corner of Rue des Pyramides and Rue Saint-Honoré, in a desirable neighborhood, was rented from April 1 through 30. *In a Café* (p. 139) was Caillebotte's most significant contribution, while Degas went so far as to dig up a work from his early years that was rather lacking in atmosphere, *Young Spartans Exercising* (c. 1860; National Gallery, London). The critics commented on the defections and the presence of newcomers who, unlike Gauguin, did not always conform to the new aesthetic of transience. The rest of the year would confirm Caillebotte's opinion of Degas, who was opposed to the idea of Renoir or Monet rejoining the group, and would hear nothing of the reasons that had driven them to exhibit at the Salon. S. G.

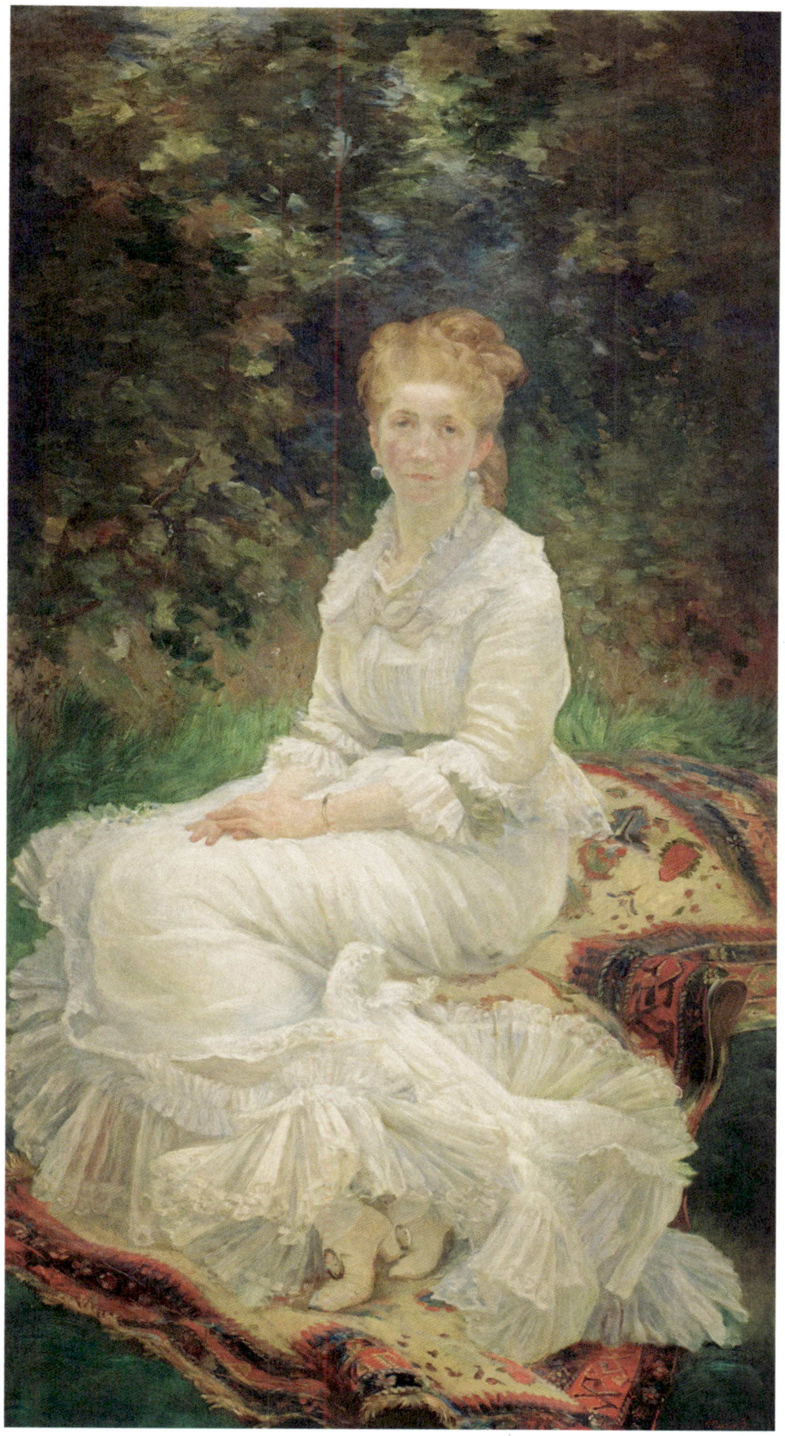

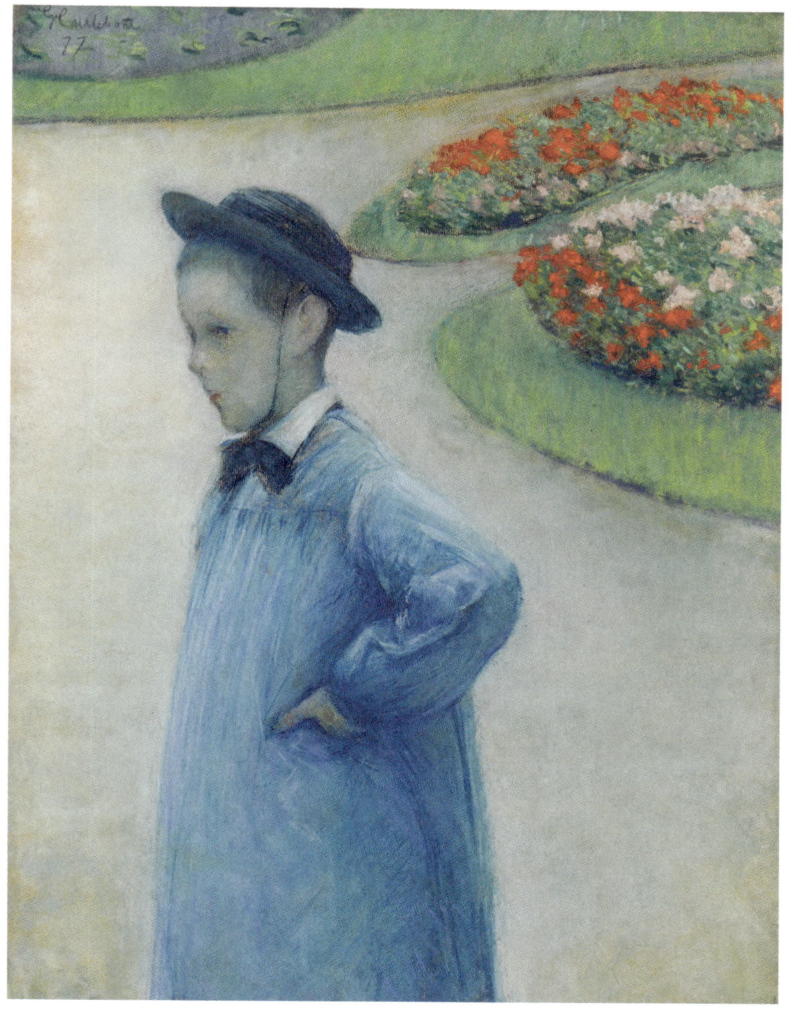

158 Left: Marie Bracquemond, *La Dame en blanc* (*The Lady in White*), c. 1880
Oil on canvas, 71 1⁄16 × 41 5⁄16 in. (180.5 × 105 cm)

159 Right: Gustave Caillebotte, *Portrait de Camille Daurelle dans le parc de Yerres* (*Portrait of Camille Daurelle in the Park at Yerres*), 1877
Pastel on paper, 28 ¾ × 23 ⅝ in. (73 × 60 cm)

Eva Gonzalès
A Box at the Théâtre des Italiens

Despite the persistence of certain prejudices at the time, some women who were linked in varying degrees to Impressionism succeeded in forging successful careers, their identity as artists fully recognized within their lifetime. Eva Gonzalès was born into the art world. Her father, Emmanuel, a renowned journalist and novelist, had started out in the most mainstream press in the mid-1830s. In 1865, Eva attended her first classes in drawing and painting, under Charles Chaplin, who at the time was painting in a very pretty neo-eighteenth-century mood. Then, thanks to the Stevens brothers, in late 1869 she came into contact with Manet, who agreed to give her advice and let her work in his studio on Rue Guyot. At the 1870 Salon, Gonzalès demonstrated her allegiance to the "New Painting" through a topically military-themed work, *Military Child* (1870; Musée de Gajac, Villeneuve-sur-Lot), a variation on Manet's *The Fifer* (p. 37). This obvious artistic kinship helps explain why her submissions to the 1874 Salon were turned down, Manet himself being largely excluded from it also. *A Box at the Théâtre des Italiens* demonstrates that she had fully signed up to Manet's style. The bouquet recalls his *Olympia* (p. 17), as does the black ribbon. Although the woman openly offers herself up to our gaze, there is nothing submissive about her, nothing of the flower about to be plucked. The fact that she is holding the opera glasses, underscoring her confident gaze and her right to a viewpoint, shakes up traditional theories of gender-based separation of roles. When the previously spurned painting ultimately reached the Salon's walls in 1879, five years after its initial rejection, it marked the beginning of a new phase in Gonzalès's career. Huysmans praised the canvas as "intrepidly painted" and having "a bitter, harsh flavor that is a welcome relief after the sickly-sweet offerings that we have just tasted." As if in a strange proof of her faithfulness to Manet, she barely outlived him; he died on April 30, 1883, and she on May 6, at Rue Bréda, in Paris's Nouvelle Athènes district where the "New Painting" reigned supreme. S. G.

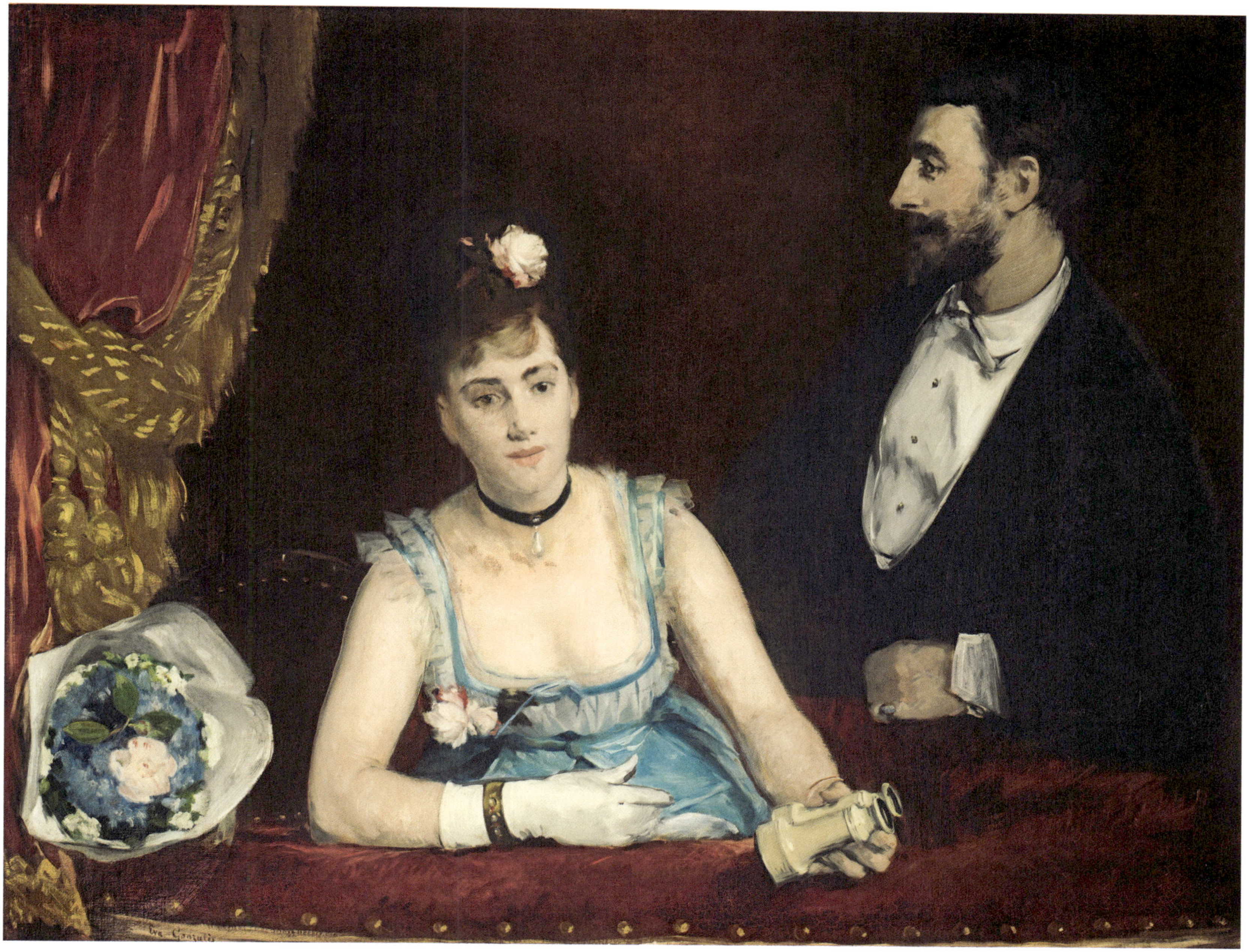

160 Eva Gonzalès, *Une loge aux Italiens* (*A Box at the Théâtre des Italiens*), c. 1874
Oil on canvas, 38 7/16 × 51 3/16 in. (97.7 × 130 cm)

Berthe Morisot
Young Woman in a Ball Gown

It is as if a magic wand had been waved over this painting by Morisot, which occupies a unique position in her career. When she returned to exhibiting with the Impressionists in 1880, after taking time off for her daughter's birth, she chose to show a series of half-length images of elegant young women, executed with a decisive, authoritative touch. The successful painter Giuseppe De Nittis bought this "study" on the spot stating that it had "a pleasing tonality." It then went to Théodore Duret, the great collector and historian of Impressionism, at whose home Mallarmé would come to admire it. Hence, when Duret sold off part of his collection, Mallarmé, who was also a friend of Morisot's, entreated the French State to purchase the painting. It was in this way that Morisot secured a place in the Musée du Luxembourg, Paris's contemporary art museum at the time, during her own lifetime.

This "portrait," as she defined it in 1880, seizes on the spirit of "modern life," Baudelaire's term to signify the shifts of his era. A young woman, whose identity remains unknown, is seated in what must be a winter garden, a fashionable space in upper-class residential architecture. In *Young Woman in a Ball Gown*, Morisot painted one of the most important rituals of social and high-society life in Paris for a young middle-class woman. She took advantage of the occasion to "grind flower petals onto her palette" and energetically apply a symphony of white on white, from the dress to the gloves, the settee, and the blooms—perhaps cattleya orchids—in the background. S.P.

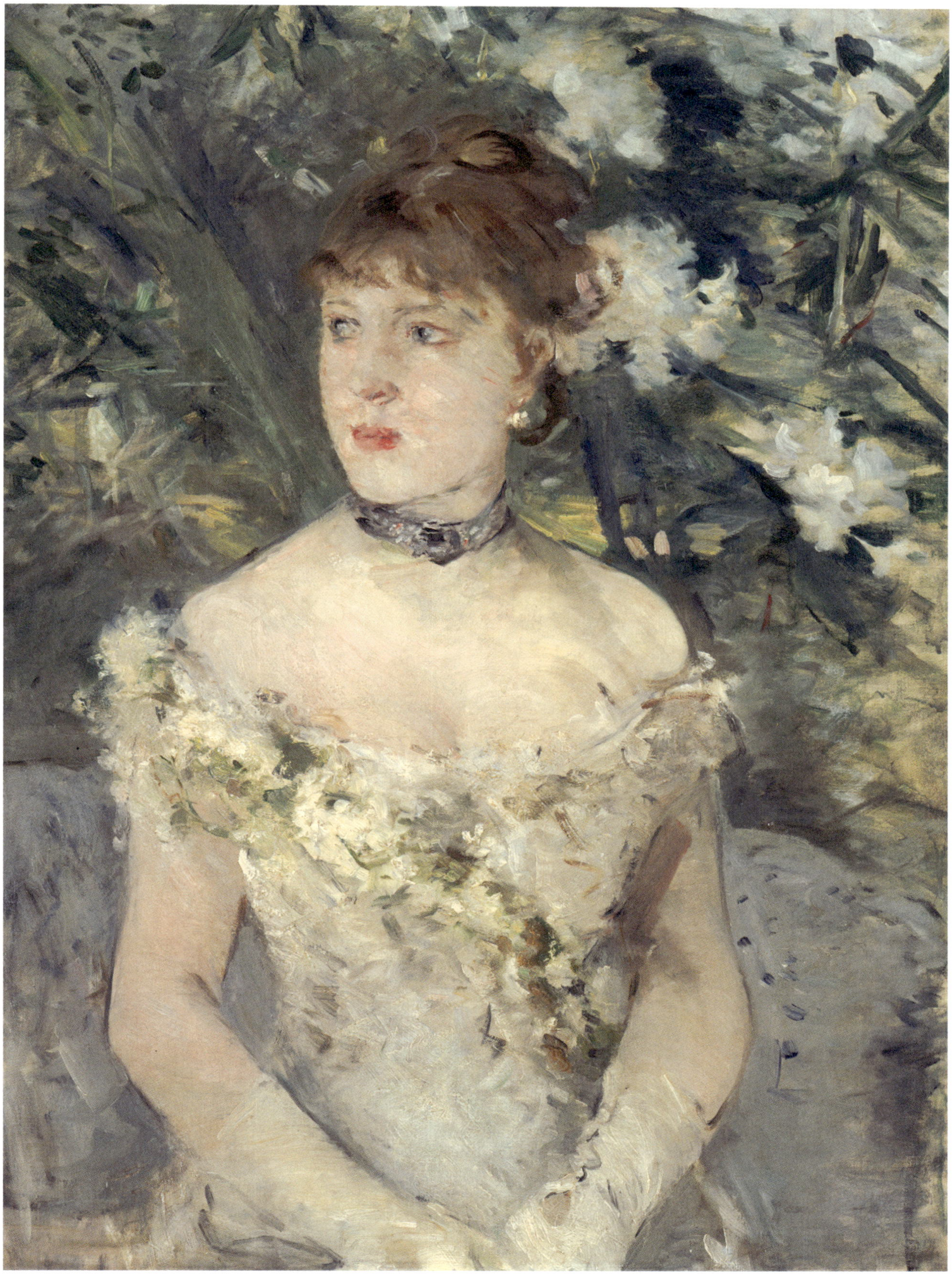

161 Berthe Morisot, *Jeune femme en toilette de bal* (*Young Woman in a Ball Gown*), 1879
Oil on canvas, 28 ⅛ × 21 ¼ in. (71.5 × 54 cm)

Mary Cassatt
Young Girl in the Garden

The American artist Mary Cassatt was born in Pennsylvania and moved permanently to France in 1871. Alongside Bracquemond and Morisot, she was one of Impressionism's "three great ladies,"[29] to quote the art critic Gustave Geffroy. She also played a key role in introducing American art lovers and collectors to the movement.

Her work is characterized by a bright, lively palette. Taking her family and close friends as models, her favorite subject matter was the human figure. In the painting *Young Girl in the Garden*, also called *Woman Sewing*, the depicted girl is very likely Susan, the cousin of Cassatt's housekeeper. She appears in several canvases from the 1880s, often depicted outdoors, as here. The background of lush greenery is structured around a path that forms a broad diagonal band which further projects the figure of the girl into the foreground. Without abandoning the precision of drawing, Cassatt here adopts a freedom in her brushwork to convey the transparency of the pale dress fabric, which is masterfully rendered through bluish touches in the vibrant light. The pink of the girl's plump cheeks echoes the hue of the geraniums around her. Cassatt exhibited the canvas at least four years after painting it, at the final Impressionist exhibition, in 1886. Geffroy then described her painting as "a sort of emanation of life, made of summer warmth and women's sensual fragrance. Those who claim that Impressionism is devoid of charm and delicacy should be brought to look at these canvases."[30] C.C.-P.

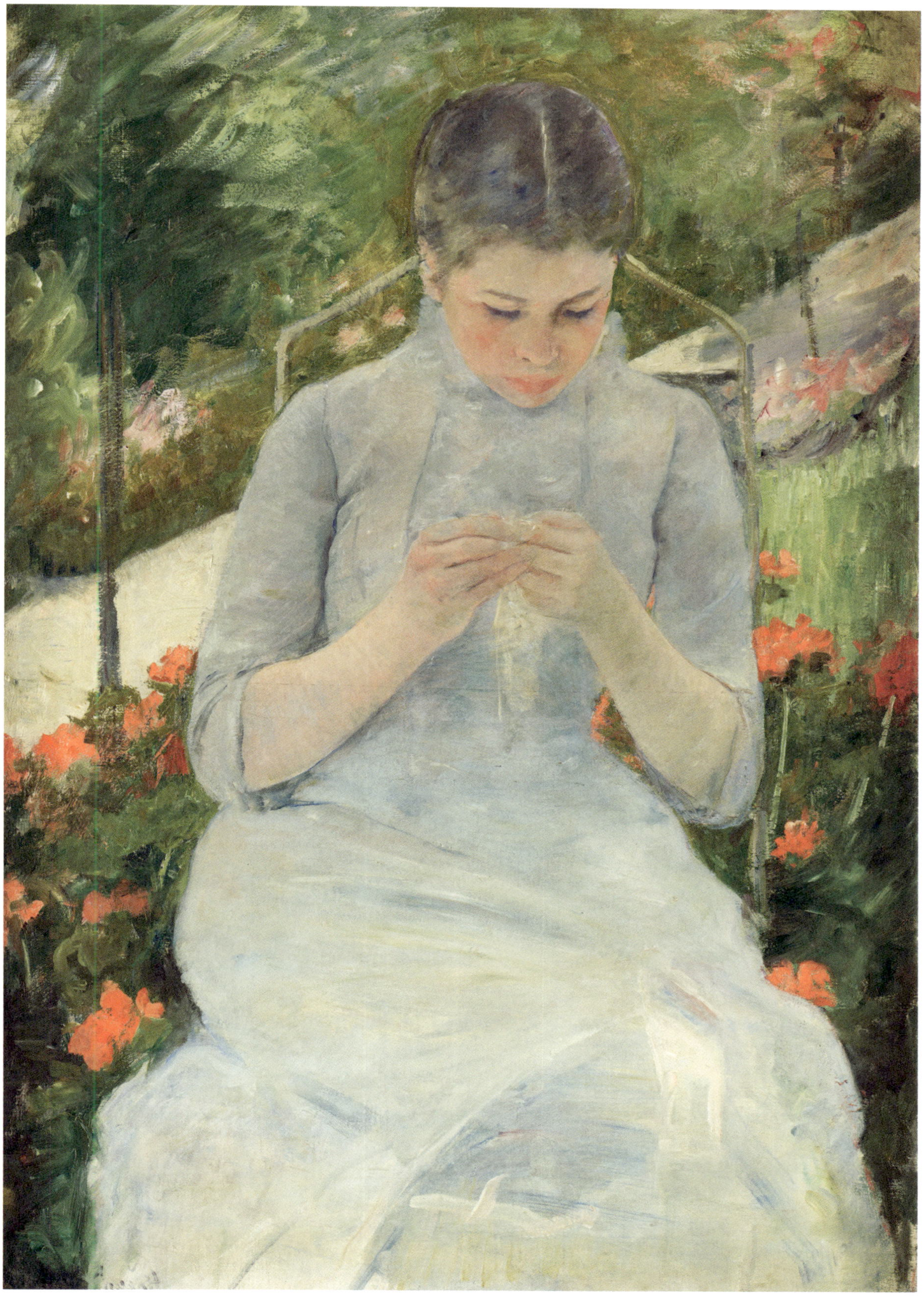

162 Mary Cassatt, *Jeune fille au jardin* (*Young Girl in the Garden*), 1880–1882
Oil on canvas, 36 7⁄16 × 25 9⁄16 in. (92.5 × 65 cm)

Camille Pissarro
The Shepherdess

Although, unlike Renoir and Monet, Pissarro had received no training in history painting, this did not deter him from producing paintings of figures, or works of a sentimental nature. Here again, his choices were influenced by the example of Millet, whose skill at depicting wistful young countrywomen remains unchallenged. This pedigree did not go unnoticed by the most observant visitors to the 1882 Impressionist exhibition, where Pissarro presented no fewer than thirty-six of his works to the public. The critic and art historian Ernest Chesneau, an often-reserved follower of independent painting, admitted the sense of relief he felt on seeing this successor of Millet's, whose "powerful vigor" and "perceptiveness" he praised. Philippe Burty, who was closer to the avant-garde, commented on how "charming" he found the young girl "playing dreamily with a green branch. Her body is very chastely suggested beneath the stiff fabric of her clothes." What Burty is implying in a roundabout way, and what historiography took some while to acknowledge, is the work's erotic potential: the picture's feeling of springtime and the central placement of the figure both lend themselves to the theme of nascent or rekindled love, as exploited in many Salon paintings. It is not surprising that Durand-Ruel, on the lookout for anything that could boost the market for Impressionism, included this work in the 1883 retrospective of its painter. S. G.

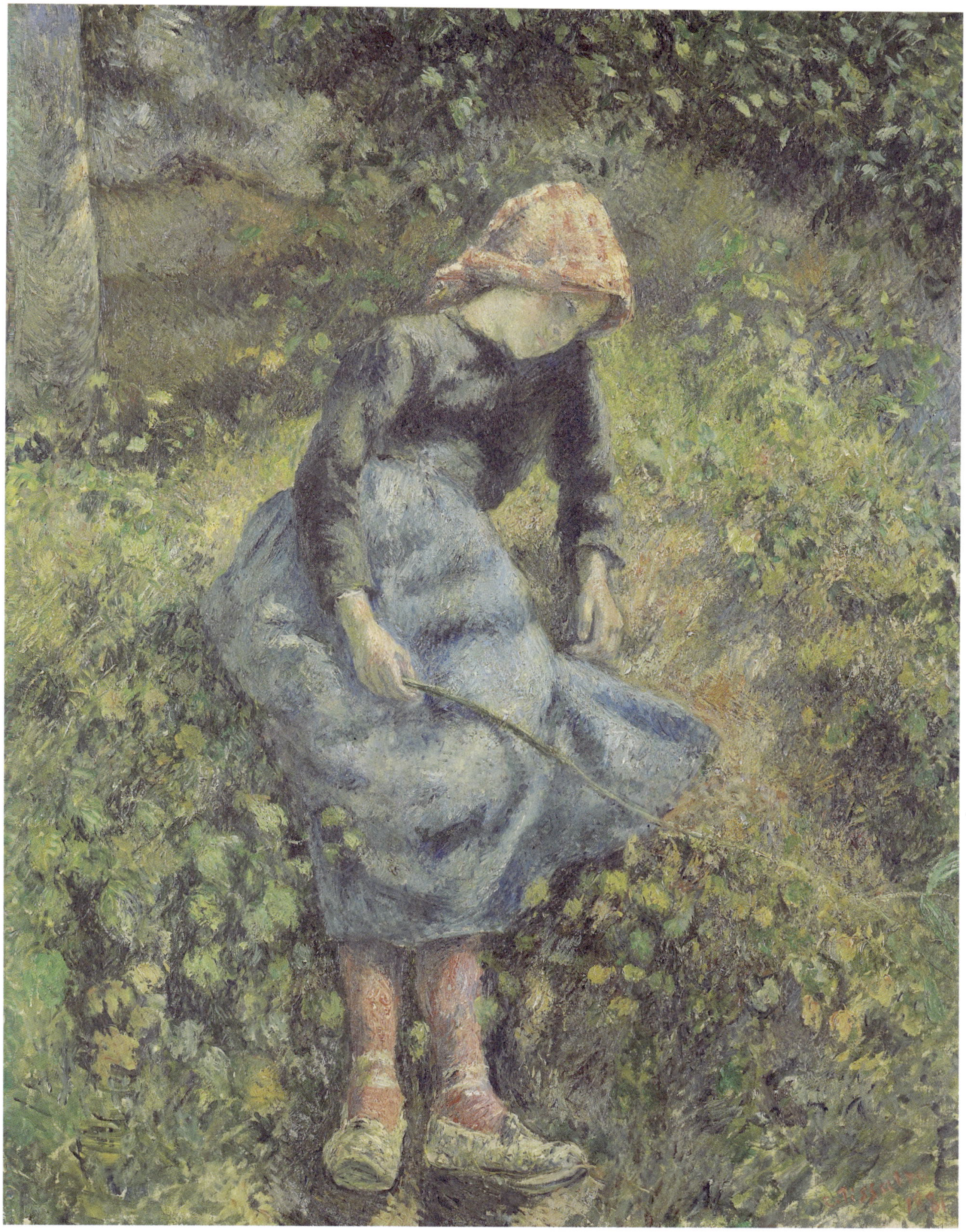

163 Camille Pissarro, *La Bergère* (*The Shepherdess*), 1881
Oil on canvas, 31 ⅞ × 25 ½ in. (81 × 64.8 cm)

1881

The sixth Impressionist exhibition

At the "sixth exhibition of painting," presented from April 2 through May 1, 1881, the work that caused the biggest stir was a totally unique sculpture, Edgar Degas's *Little Fourteen-Year-Old Dancer*. Announced in the catalog as a "wax statuette," she kept visitors waiting for two weeks before finally appearing in her display case, and sparked emotional reactions. About three feet (a meter) high, dressed in a fabric bodice, soft tulle tutu, and ballet slippers, and with real hair tied back in a silk bow, she blurs the boundaries between art and life. The very medium, wax, recalls the realistic statues that were displayed at funfairs or at Madame Tussaud's in London (Paris's Musée Grévin opened just the following year, in 1882), or anatomical models in medical museums. Her pose is relaxed, with no attempt to be elegant. The model was the young Marie Van Goethem, and Degas did not flatter her facial features, which he had studied through preparatory drawings. Her body is by no means perfect, and many critics berated her skinniness, her overly low hairline, and her "vicious" expression. Others, however, praised the artist's boldness and the sociological authenticity of his study. For behind the façade of this little corps-de-ballet trainee, anyone at the time could see a sordid reality that we would no longer guess at today: poverty, and the likelihood of resorting to prostitution to top up her low pay with a little extra money. In the same room, Degas showed two drawings each titled *Physiognomy of a Criminal*; he chose his model for the little dancer knowingly, and his handling of the impression she would give was deliberate. He liked to be provocative, and no doubt relished the fact that the work sparked so much emotion. He never exhibited it again, nor did he show the numerous little study models of dancers, women at their toilet, and horses, which he made in preparation for his paintings or simply for his own enjoyment. Following the discovery of these sculptures after Degas's death, more than seventy of them were cast in bronze by the Hébrard foundry, with varying quantities produced for each. F.B.

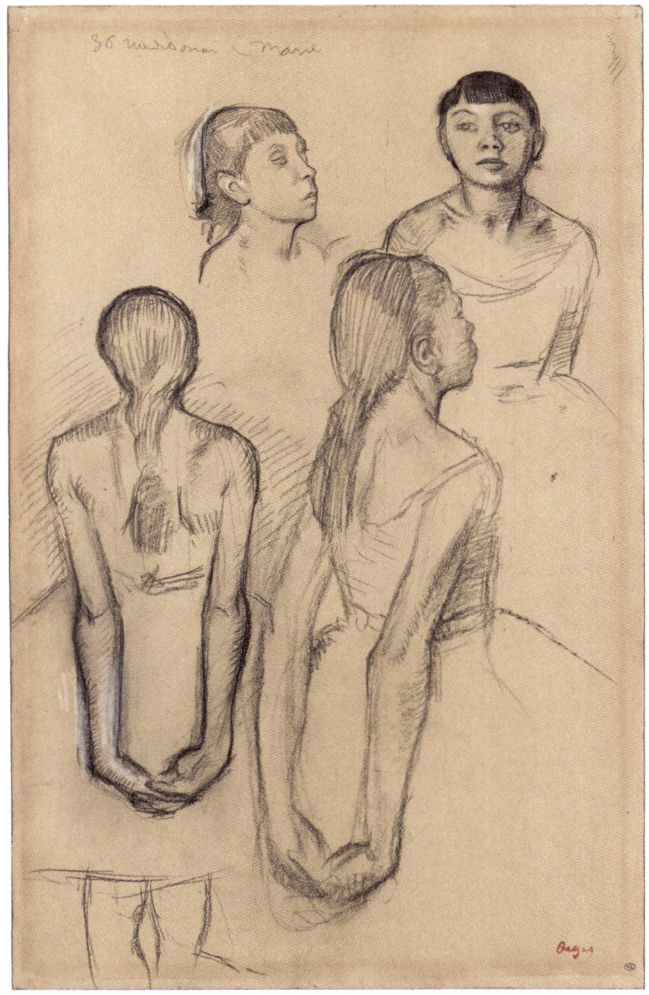

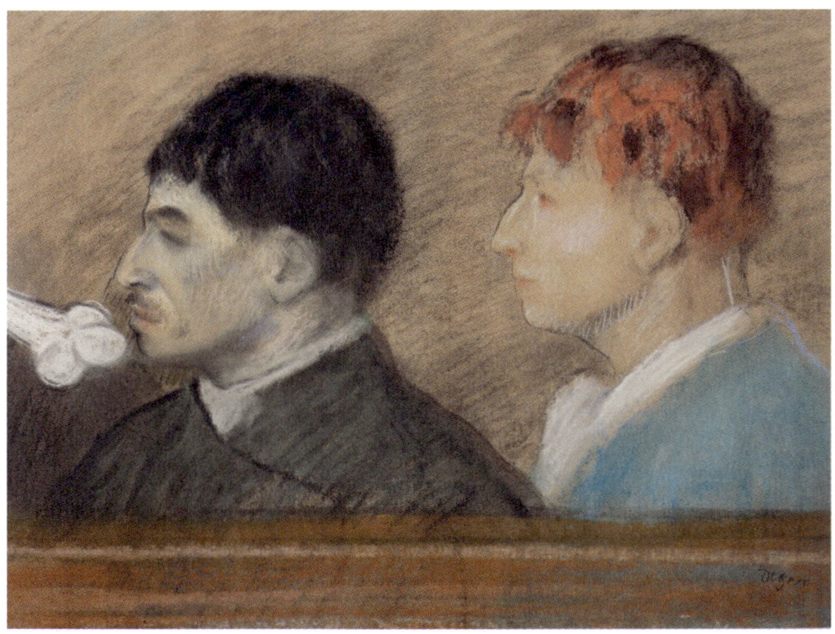

164 Top: Edgar Degas, *Quatre études d'une danseuse* (*Four Studies of a Dancer*), c. 1878–1879
Graphite with white highlights on pink paper,
19 5⁄16 × 12 5⁄8 in. (49 × 32 cm)

165 Bottom: Edgar Degas, *Physionomie de criminel* (*Physiognomy of a Criminal*), 1880–1881
Pastel and charcoal on paper mounted on artist's board,
18 13⁄16 x 24 14⁄16 in. (47.8 x 63.2 cm)

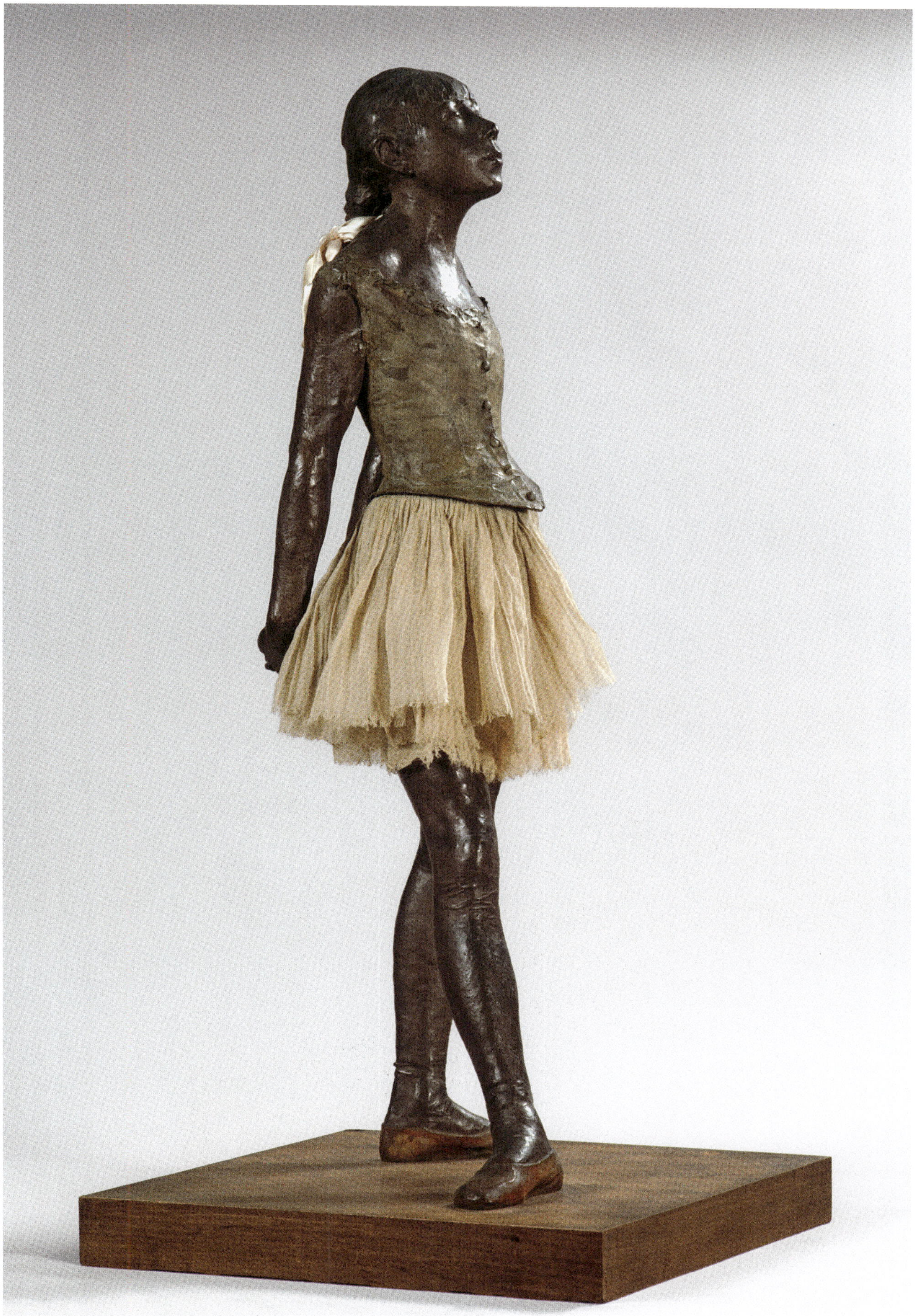

166 Edgar Degas, *Petite danseuse de quatorze ans* (*Little Fourteen-Year-Old Dancer*), between 1878 and 1881 (model), between 1921 and 1931 (bronze)
Patinated bronze, tulle tutu, satin ribbon, wooden base,
40 ⅞ × 19 ³⁄₁₆ × 19 ¹¹⁄₁₆ in. (103.8 × 48.8 × 50 cm)

Impressionism and sculpture

Is Impressionism compatible with sculpture? The answer comes down to definitions, and so needs to be given in several parts. Certainly sculptures were regularly shown in the group's exhibitions, starting in 1874 with several by Auguste Ottin, a sculptor who trained at the École des Beaux-Arts and won the Prix de Rome in 1836. However, on an aesthetic level, his sculptures have nothing in common with the canvases of Monet, Sisley, or Renoir. The works in marble and stoneware that Gauguin exhibited in 1879, 1880, and 1881 are fairly classical portraits, and his subsequent sculptures in wood or ceramic would take him along a completely different track, between Symbolism and a "primitivist" inspiration. As for Degas, he made a striking impression in 1881 with his *Little Fourteen-Year-Old Dancer* (p.183), which shares the same subject as many of his oil studies depicting the wings at the Paris Opéra. But can this work, based on copious studies and modeled with such great precision, be said to be Impressionist, in the sense by which the term is generally understood—that is, as an attempt to truthfully capture a specific moment in time? The dozens of small wax studies that the artist sculpted in the privacy of his studio are much more akin to this idea, but he did not consider them finished works, and never exhibited them. Renoir also tried his hand at modeling, at various periods, and especially toward the end of his life, when he was suffering from painful arthritis. At that point, the art dealer Ambroise Vollard sent a young sculptor along to him—Richard Guino, who was close to the famous French Catalan sculptor Aristide Maillol, and who helped Renoir give physical form to his ideas by translating his earlier paintings into three dimensions. Only one sculptor expressly invoked Impressionism: the Italian artist Medardo Rosso, present on the Paris art scene from the mid-1880s, who produced works that aimed to capture their subjects at a fleeting moment, such as *Impression from an Omnibus* (1884; destroyed). In his handling of wax and plaster, he sought to convey the shimmer of light on surfaces, especially in his portraits. F.B.

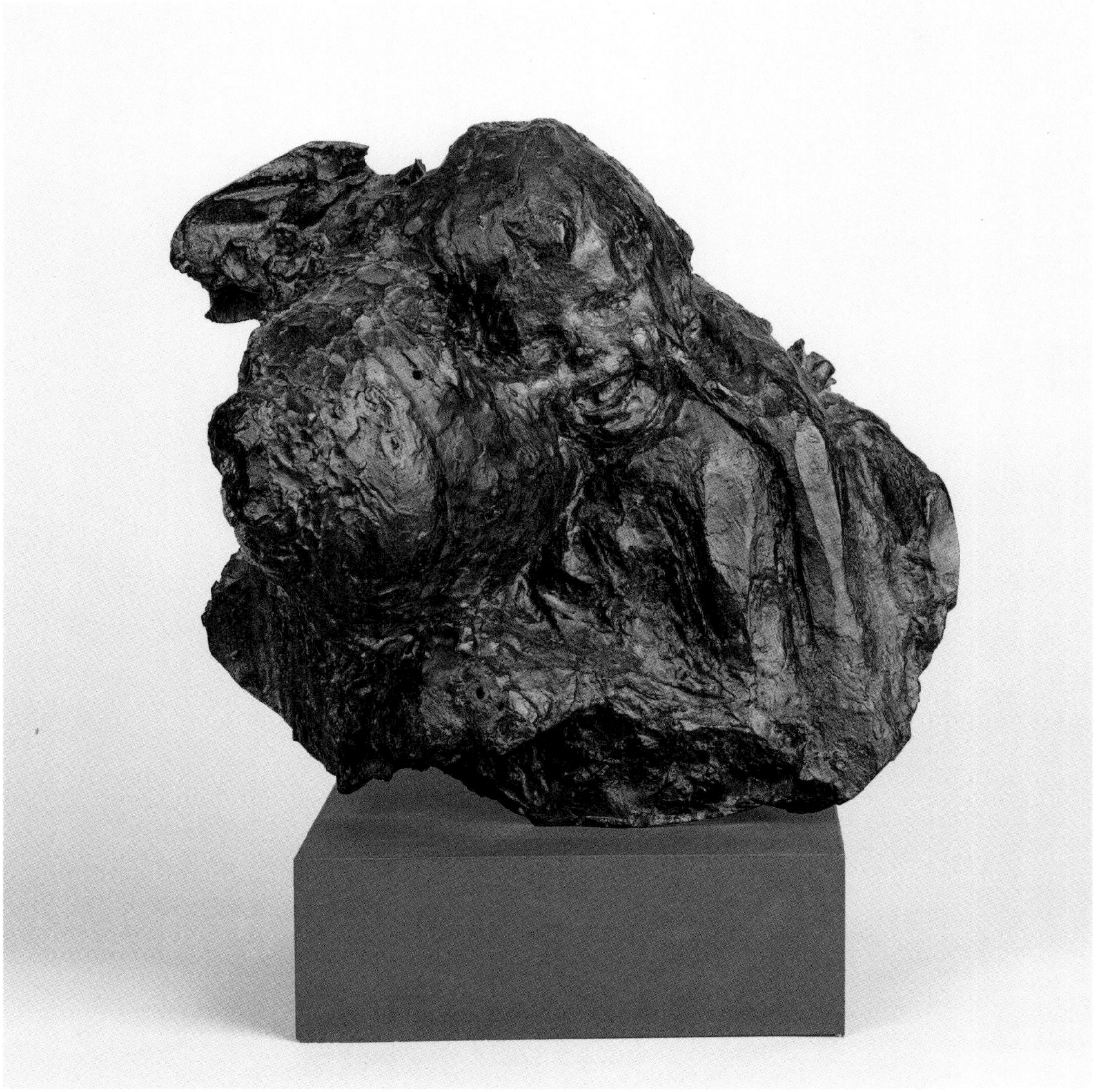

167 Medardo Rosso, *Aetas Aurea* (*The Golden Age*), 1886
Bronze relief, 19 11⁄16 × 14 7⁄8 × 10 7⁄16 in. (50 × 37.8 × 26.5 cm)

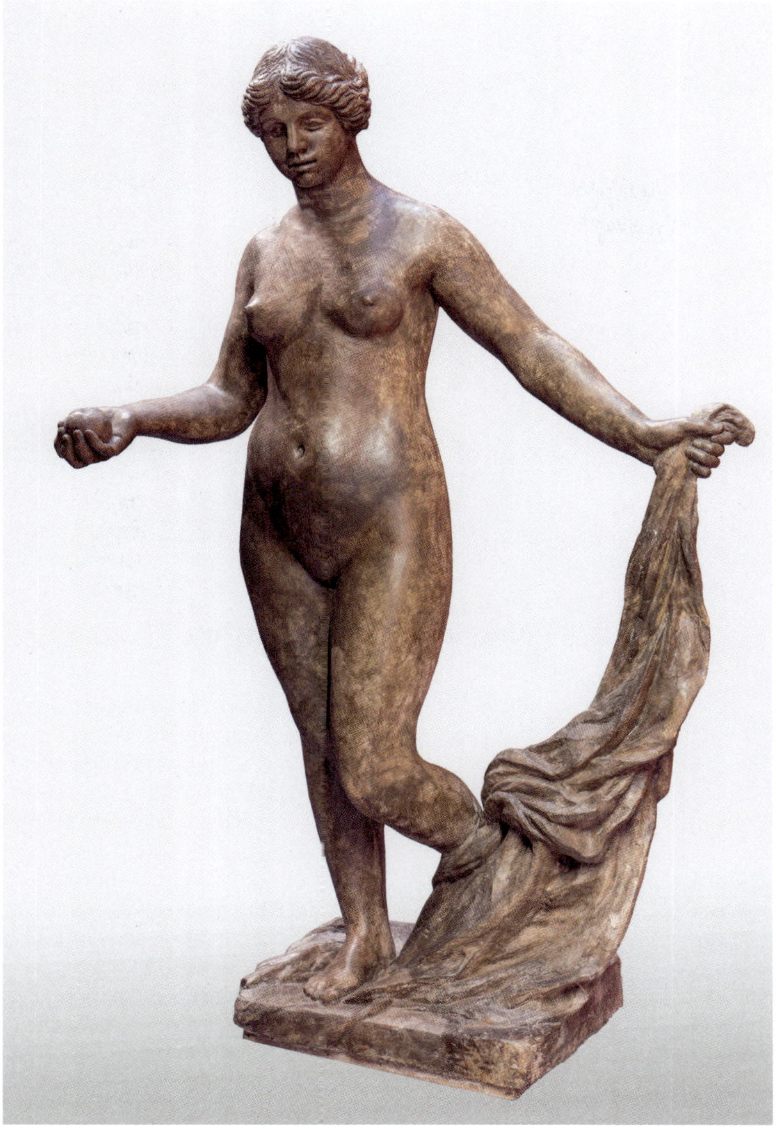

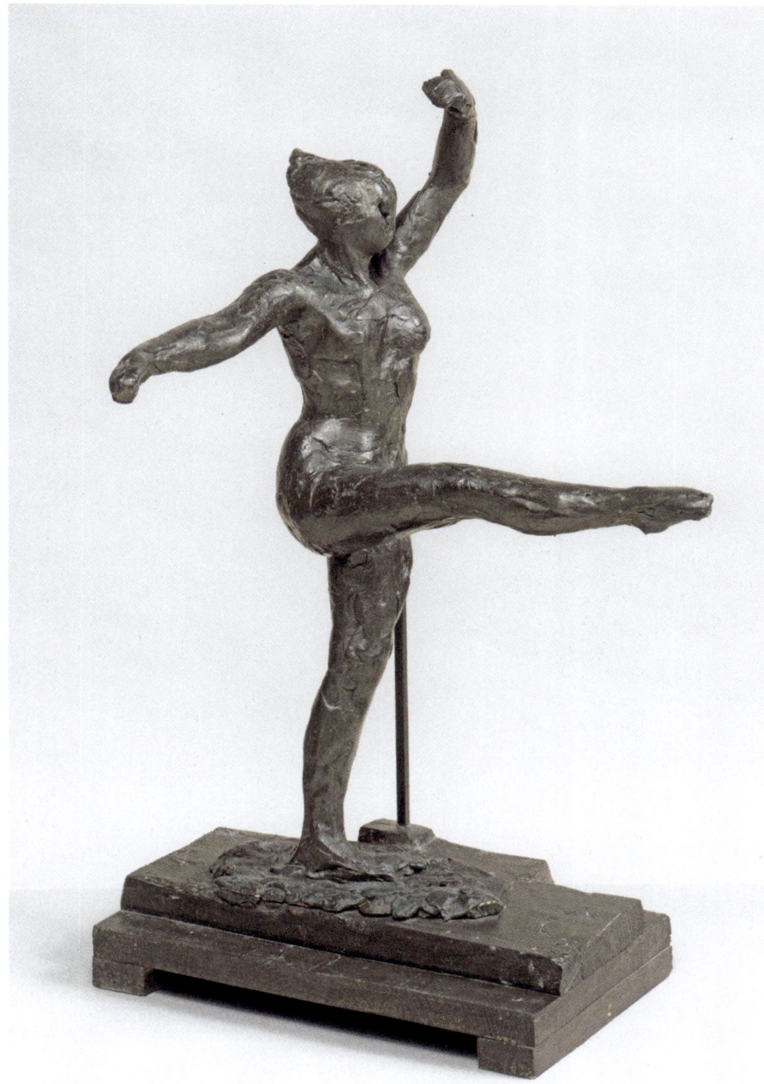

168 Left: Auguste Renoir, Richard Guino,
Venus victrix, between 1914 and 1916
Patinated shellac-sealed plaster,
75 9⁄16 × 52 3⁄4 × 28 3⁄4 in. (192 × 134 × 73 cm)

169 Right: Edgar Degas, *Danseuse, position de quatrième devant sur la jambe gauche, première étude* (*Dancer, Fourth Position on Left Leg, First Study*), between 1896 and 1911
Wax on wooden base, 16 1⁄8 × 10 1⁄4 × 9 13⁄16 in. (41 × 26 × 25 cm)

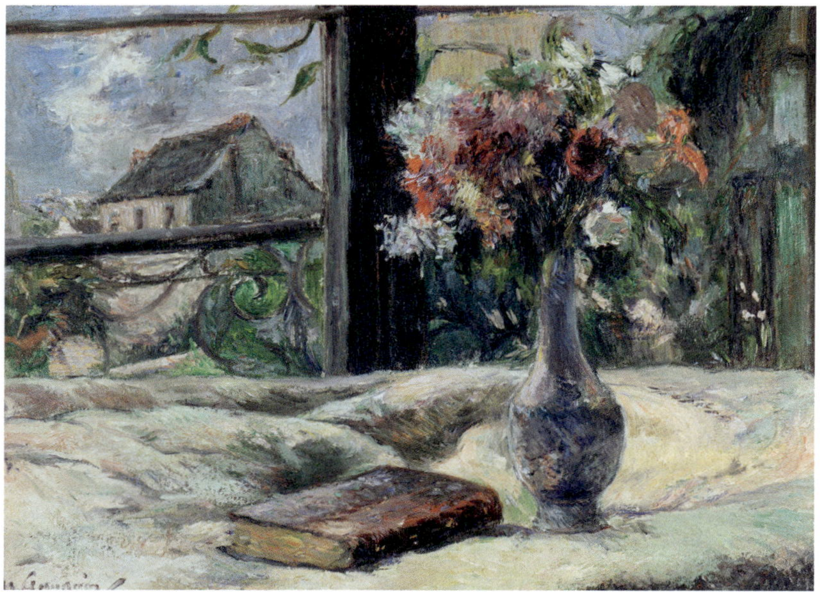

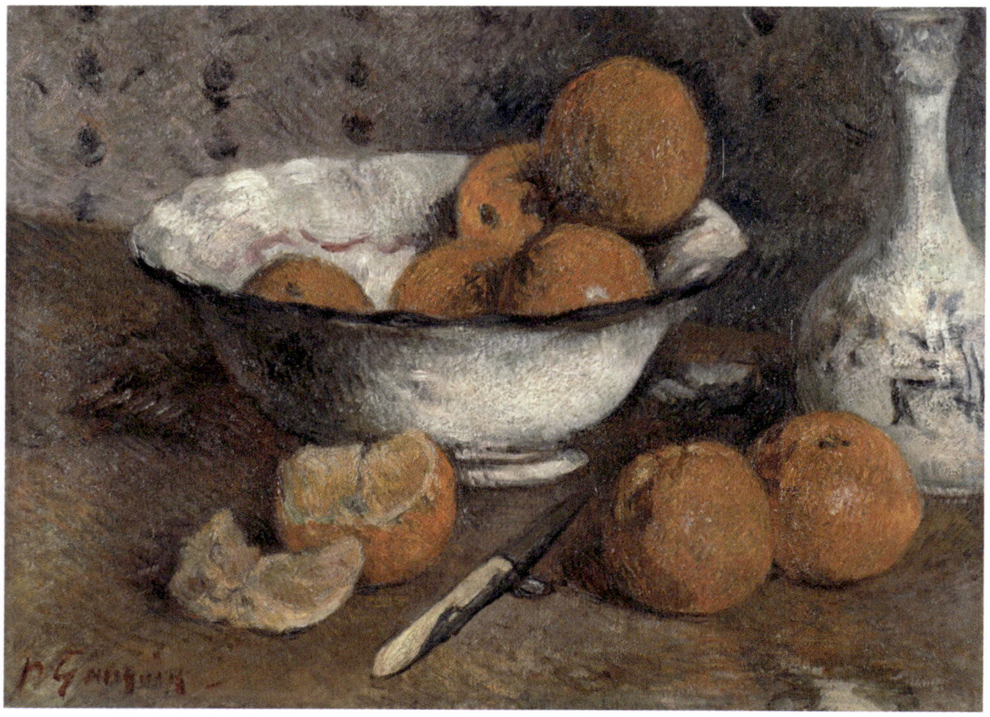

1882

The seventh Impressionist exhibition

Within the turbulent history of the Impressionist exhibitions, the seventh, organized after a hard-fought struggle, was undoubtedly the most similar to the one of 1877. Held from March 1 through 31, 1882, it welcomed back Renoir, Sisley, and Monet, on alternate display walls. Conversely, Raffaëlli having been ousted, Degas withdrew out of solidarity, as did Cassatt. Forain's absence completed the group's change of face; the number of exhibiting artists was reduced to just nine. Another distinctive aspect was their chosen venue: the rotunda at 251 Rue Saint-Honoré that housed the enormous Panorama de Reichshoffen, which depicted the soon-to-be-crushed heroism of the French cavalry at Wörth in Alsace during the Franco-Prussian War. The economic depression also played its role. Durand-Ruel, who had been severely affected by the banking crisis, invested all his energy into organizing an exemplary exhibition, meaning one where Monet and Renoir were well represented. As a means to this end, he was willing to sacrifice Caillebotte, whose extreme paintings he did not like. But Caillebotte threw himself into it just as much as Pissarro did. Alongside these two and Monet, Renoir, and Sisley, as already mentioned, Morisot, Guillaumin, and Victor Vignon also put their egos aside. Even Gauguin, who knew that Caillebotte did not particularly like him, was prepared to forego participating in the exhibition in order to make it possible. In the end, he did take part. Though the participating painters were small in number, each one flooded the space with work. But in Degas's absence, Caillebotte was the only one to challenge the dominance of landscape. Huysmans, in his review of the exhibition, thanked him for this, while lamenting the consequences of the internal quarrels: "From the viewpoint of contemporary life, this exhibition unfortunately could not be more perfunctory. No more dance halls or theaters, no more private interiors, no more girls or glimpses of the Folies-Bergère, no more downtrodden souls or common folk; only one note that absorbs all others: landscape." He concluded that the circle of modernism was shrinking. S.G.

170 Top: Paul Gauguin, *Nature morte. Vase de fleurs à la fenêtre* (*Still Life: Vase of Flowers at the Window*), c. 1881
Oil on canvas, 7 ½ × 10 ⅝ in. (19 × 27 cm)

171 Bottom: Paul Gauguin, *Nature morte aux oranges* (*Still Life with Oranges*), c. 1881
Oil on canvas, 13 × 18 ⅛ in. (33 × 46 cm)

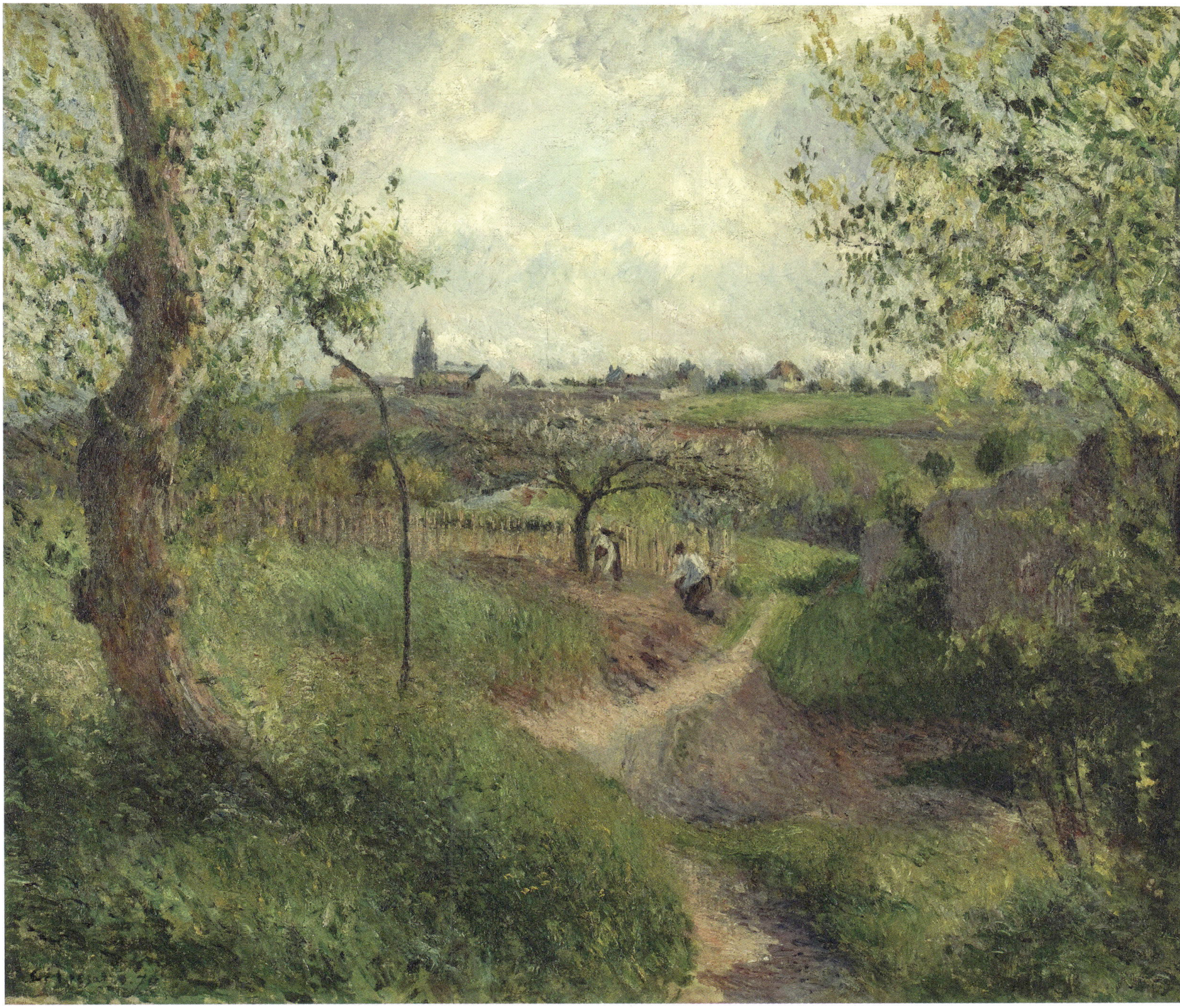

172 Camille Pissarro, *Le Chemin des Mathurins montant à travers champs, Pontoise* (*The Chemin des Mathurins in Pontoise, Climbing Through Fields*), 1879
Oil on canvas, 21 ¼ × 25 ⁹⁄₁₆ in. (54 × 65 cm)

Edgar Degas
At the Milliner's

Degas was passionate about female labor, the precision of women's gestures as they go about their work, their "naturalness" and "unposed movements."[31] At the first Impressionist exhibition, in 1874, he presented a pastel of a laundress ironing (p. 97). Female ballet dancers and washerwomen were other favorite subjects of his, which captured the essence of modern Parisian life and of the everyday experience of the working class.

Here, his focus is a milliner. We know that he liked to accompany his friend and fellow artist Cassatt on shopping trips, to observe "the milliner's gestures, the way her nimble fingers alight on a wing or a flower, the way she tilts her head appraisingly, presents a hat on her fist, or gently places it on the customer's head."[32]

As is often the case in his portrayals of milliners, Degas obscures part of the young woman's face, in this instance behind the hat that is presented on the turned-wood stand, as if to better showcase her precise gestures. On the left, her elegant customer studies her reflection in a mirror. Compositionally, the round shape of the polished timber table echoes that of the hats. The palette is warm, ranging from pink to golden yellow to brown. Degas fully demonstrates his mastery of pastel and his versatility in transferring the rich textures of the materials—feathers, fabrics, straw, and flowers—onto paper. C. C.-P.

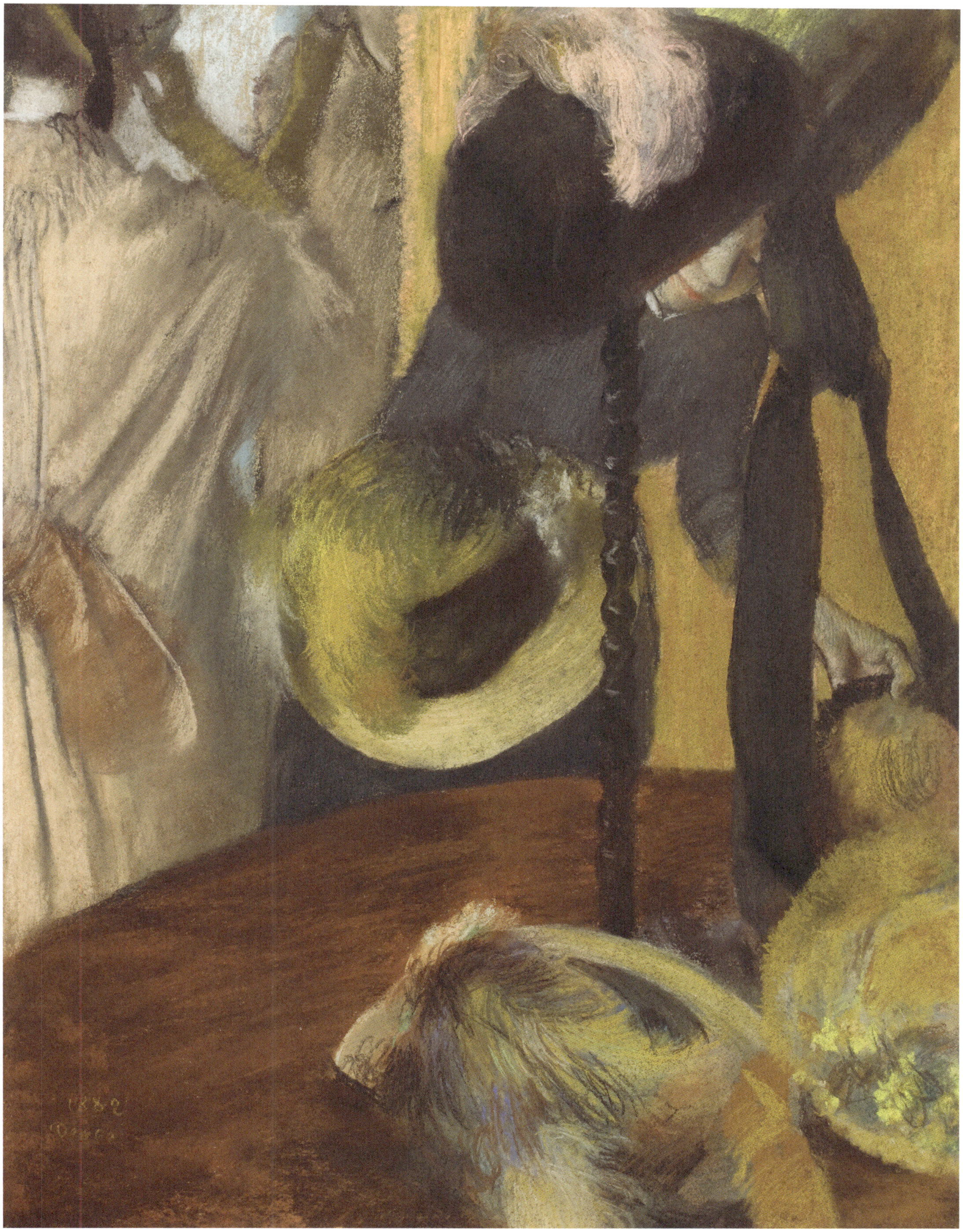

173 Edgar Degas, *Chez la modiste* (*At the Milliner's*), 1882
Pastel on paper, 26 ⅜ × 20 ½ in. (67 × 52 cm)

Auguste Renoir *Dances*

In late 1882, Renoir set about painting three monumental canvases on the theme of dance and the modern couple, which was among his favorite subjects. One of the compositions was a stand-alone painting titled *Dance at Bougival* (1883; Museum of Fine Arts, Boston), and the other two were a pair: *Dance in the Country* and *Dance in the City*. Despite their size and importance, they did not result in any private commissions, and were not shown at the Salon, but instead at Paul Durand-Ruel's commercial gallery.

In *Dance in the City*, the setting (a ballroom) and the protagonists' attire (tails and a ballgown) suggest that the waltz we are witnessing is taking place within a milieu of strict social codes. Meanwhile, the presence in *Dance in the Country* of a straw hat that has fallen on the floor, and of a napkin, a coffee cup, and a glass of liquor on a table, leads us to think that the couple have just finished their meal, the pull of the music having perhaps driven them to spontaneously get up and dance a polka. In *Dance in the City*, we are kept at a distance from the scene, whereas in *Dance in the Country*, the smiling young woman is looking directly at us, drawing us in to her joyful movement. The man posing in both paintings was one of Renoir's close friends, Paul Lhote, with whom he had just traveled to Algeria and Italy. The young woman in *Dance in the City* is the model and artist Suzanne Valadon, while it is Aline Charigot, Renoir's future wife, who strikes a pose for *Dance in the Country*.

This pair of canvases was the culmination of a process of ennoblement and heroizing of modern life, the couple, and love, which Renoir had embarked upon in the 1860s. For the first time in the history of art, an anonymous dancing couple was represented here on the same scale as history paintings or full-length state portraits. With their more precise draftsmanship and their monumental figures, these paintings bear witness to the evolution of Renoir's style, which in the early 1880s gradually moved away from Impressionism and toward a sort of classicism with a solidness of form. P. P.

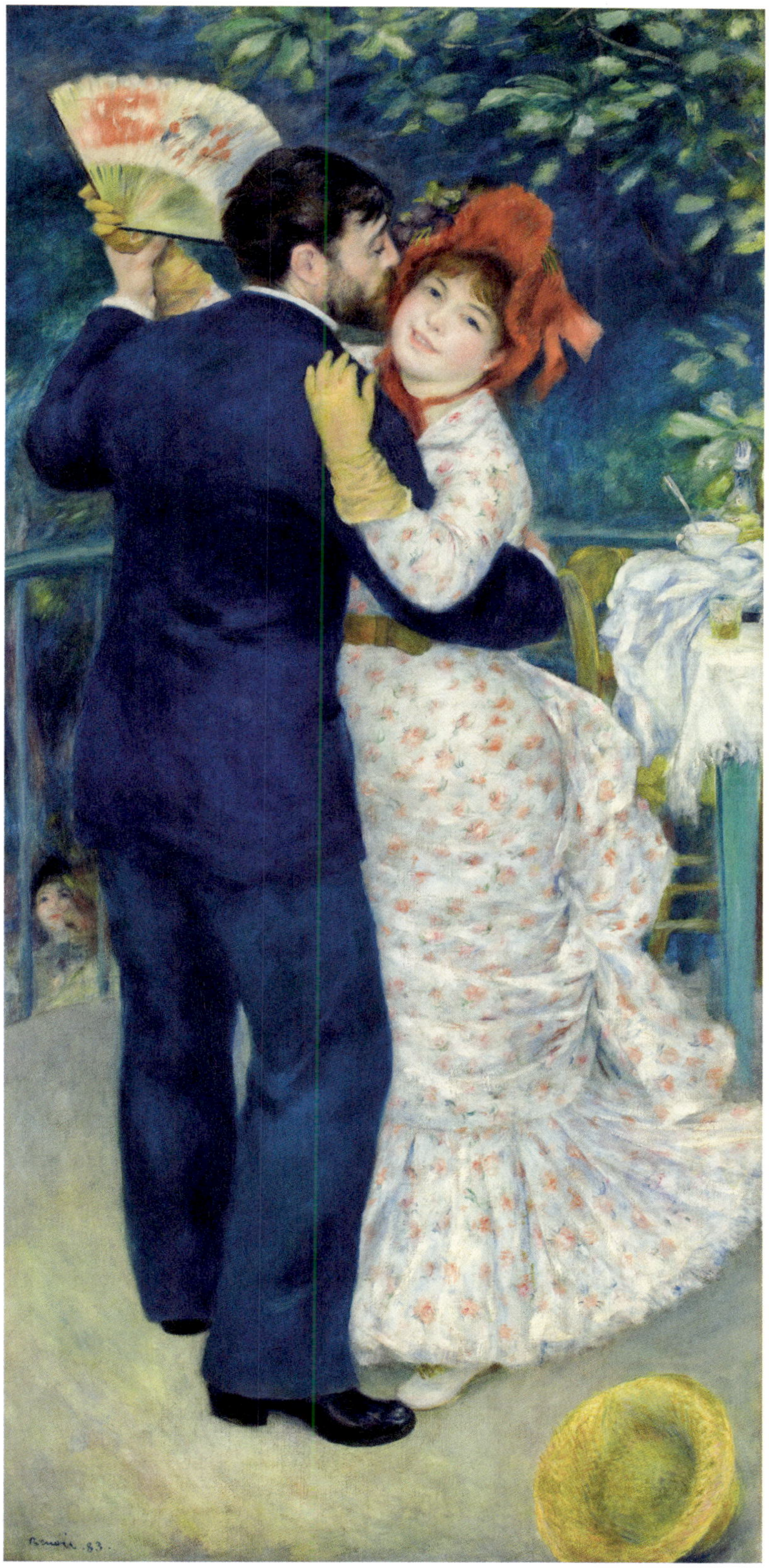

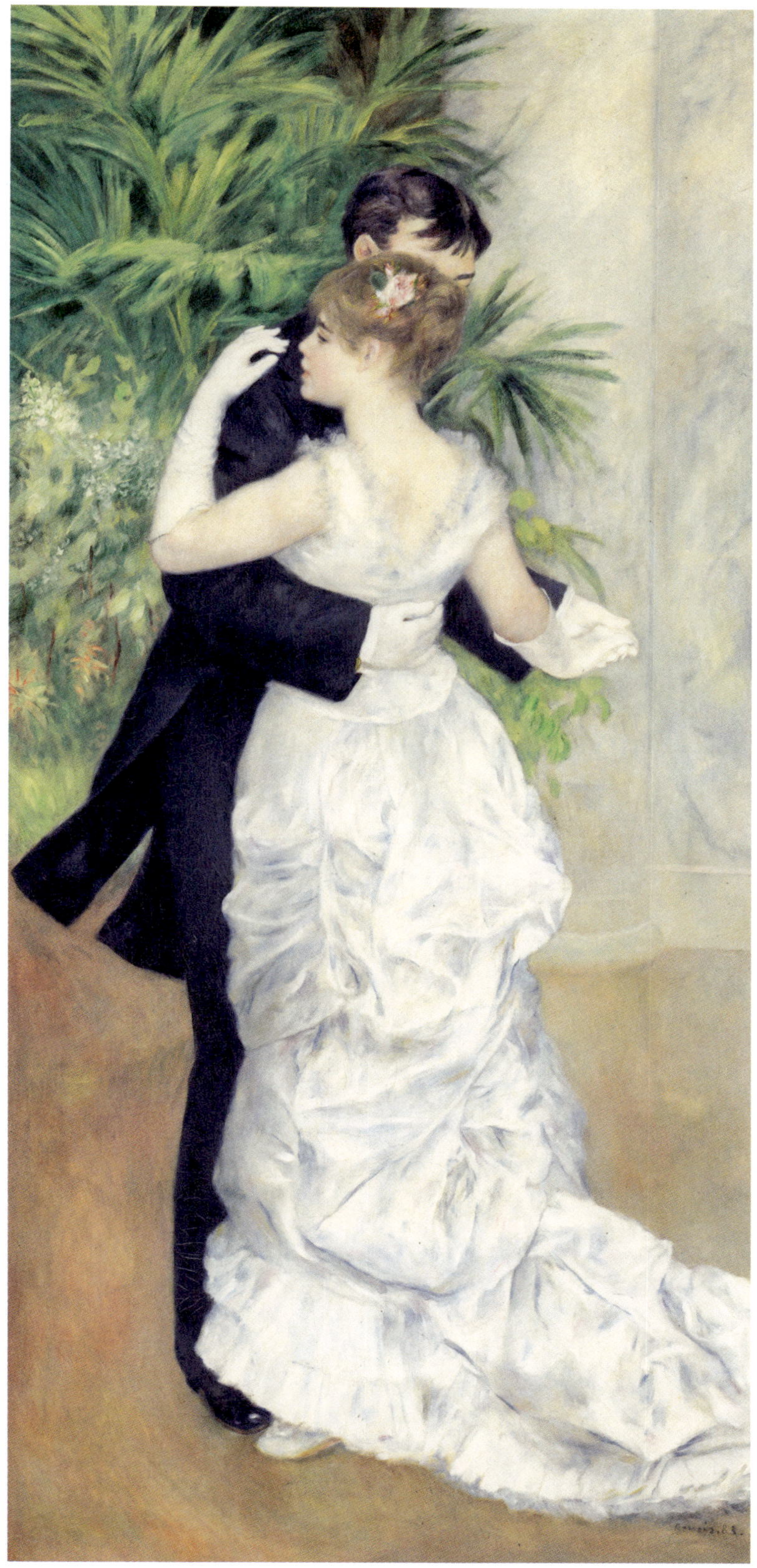

174 Left: Auguste Renoir, *Danse à la campagne* (*Dance in the Country*), 1883
Oil on canvas, 71 × 35 7⁄16 in. (180.3 × 90 cm)

175 Right: Auguste Renoir, *Danse à la ville* (*Dance in the City*), 1883
Oil on canvas, 70 ¾ × 35 1⁄16 in. (179.7 × 89.1 cm)

Claude Monet
Studies of a Figure in the Open Air

"On a sunny slope of which we see only the very top, with pink earth and scorched grass, up in the sky..., with white and pink clouds hurrying by..., a woman is walking, svelte, light, unpredictable, a gust of wind in the flowing muslin of her veil,... she seems to glide along, hovering over the grass. In her modernity, she has the distant grace of a dream, the unexpected charm of an ethereal apparition,"[33] wrote the art critic and novelist Octave Mirbeau, a close friend of Monet's. "Take a good look at her," he continues. The painter was effectively engaged in a return to figure painting, which he had somewhat neglected over the previous ten years in favor of landscapes. Here he paints one of his stepdaughters, Suzanne Hoschedé, walking on the banks of the Île aux Orties (Island of Nettles) at Giverny, not far from their house. The young woman is painted *sotto in sù*—observed from a low viewpoint—which enhances the decorativeness of these two parasol-holding women; facing opposite directions, they respond to each other as pendants. This framing also accentuates the impression of movement and fleetingness: Suzanne seems to loom up and then pass by, between presence and absence. The whole image quivers with life, and the mysterious figure is enveloped in air and light. S.P.

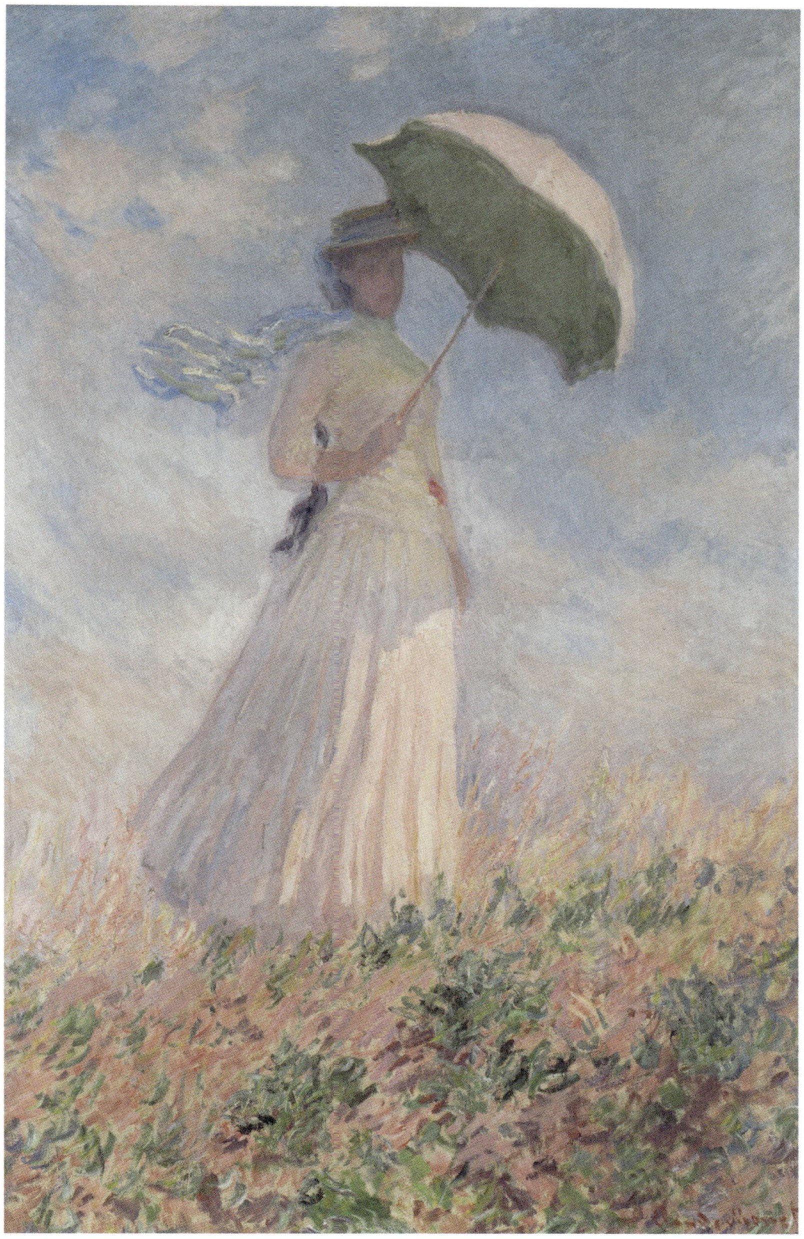

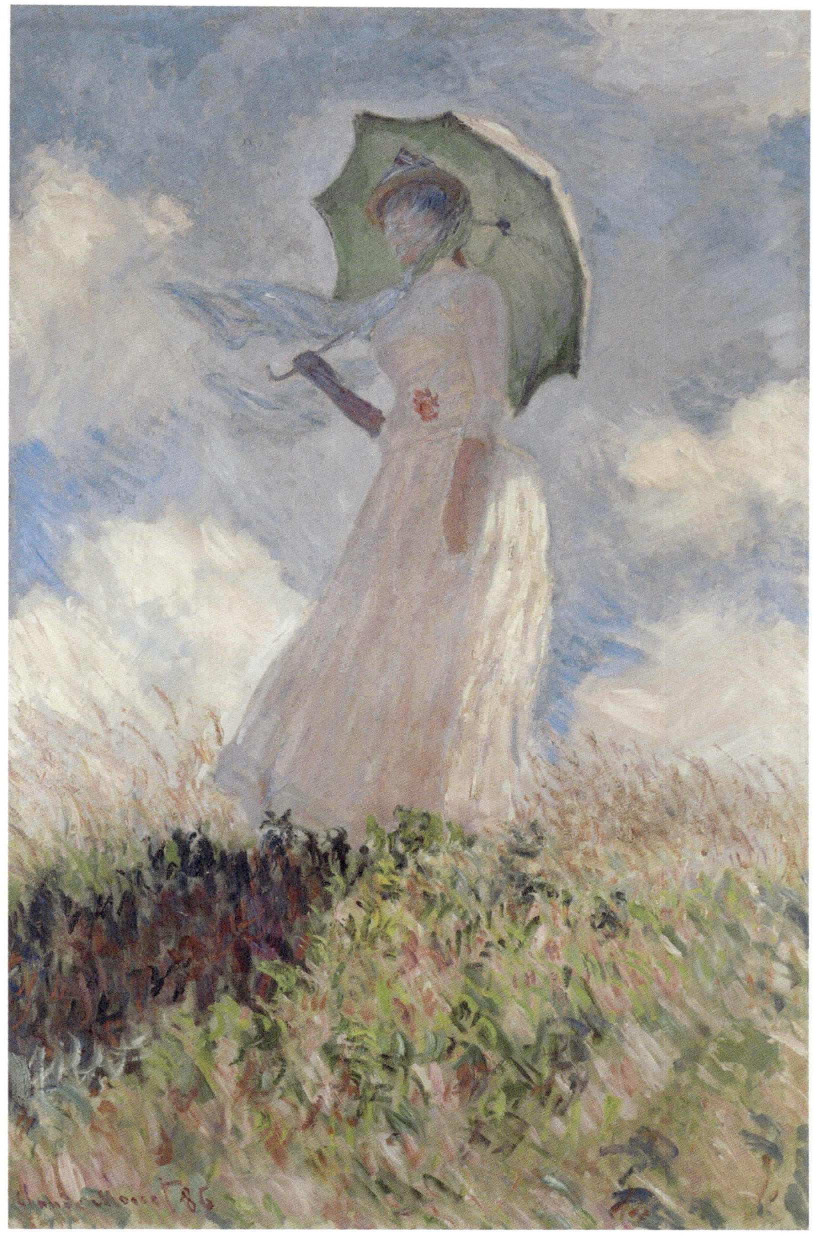

176 Left: Claude Monet, *Essai de figure en plein-air: femme à l'ombrelle tournée vers la droite* (*Study of a Figure in the Open Air: Woman with a Parasol Facing Right*), 1886
Oil on canvas, 51 ⅜ × 35 3⁄16 in. (130.5 × 89.3 cm)

177 Right: Claude Monet, *Essai de figure en plein-air: femme à l'ombrelle tournée vers la gauche* (*Study of a Figure in the Open Air: Woman with a Parasol Facing Left*), 1886
Oil on canvas, 51 9⁄16 × 34 15⁄16 in. (131 × 88.7 cm)

Marie Bracquemond
Three Ladies with Umbrellas

It was not until the mid-1980s that the etcher Félix Bracquemond's wife, whose work was halfway between Morisot's and Cassatt's, began to be rediscovered. The great critic Gustave Geffroy, who owned this painting, would have been surprised at how long this recognition was in coming, and how incomplete it remained. Born Marie Quivoron, the budding artist had received only brief training before placing herself under Ingres's wing, even though he paid scant attention to women painters' work. It was clearly not for nothing that the large portraits he produced under the Second Empire—where the clothes are as expressive as the faces and poses—became engraved on her memory as a teenager. At the Salon of 1857, she exhibited a first drawing that was quite close to Ingres's penetrating group portraits. In the early 1860s, she started to break free of this approach, increasingly distancing herself as the influence of the "New Painting," linked notably to Manet, took hold. Félix Bracquemond was close to that movement; she married him in 1869, but waited ten years before exhibiting her works alongside the Impressionists, whose ranks her husband joined in 1874. *Three Ladies with Umbrellas*, also known as *The Three Graces*, is a condensation of several characteristics of the new aesthetic, from frontal presentation to the luminous frisson of the clothes under a very blue sky. Monet, Renoir, and Caillebotte had invested the motif of the parasol or umbrella with a charm that was paradoxical, given that they all came across as sun-worshippers. The shadows are colored, as is the whiteness of the two dresses that delimit the canvas. The insistent seductiveness of the faces does not tip over into mawkishness, and nor does the nod to rococo painting. In 1893, Geffroy pointed out this sensual link to Louis XV's reign: "There is a kinship to the painting of the last century in the addition of a very lively feeling of modernity that is swift and straightforward in its originality; a continuation of art but without imitation."   S.G.

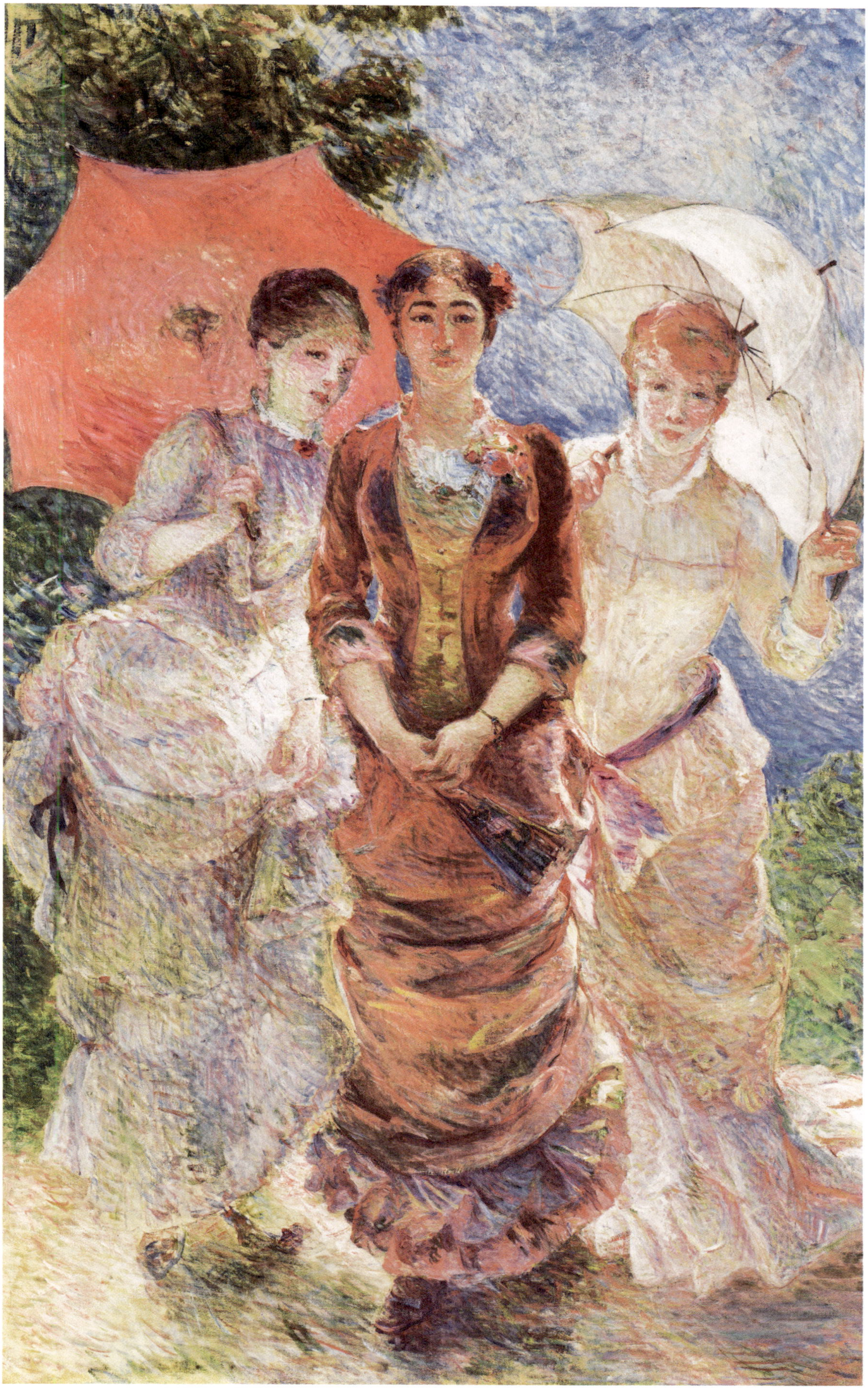

178 Marie Bracquemond, *Trois femmes aux ombrelles* (*Three Ladies with Umbrellas*), 1880
Oil on canvas, 55 ⅝ × 35 ¼ in. (141.3 × 89.5 cm)

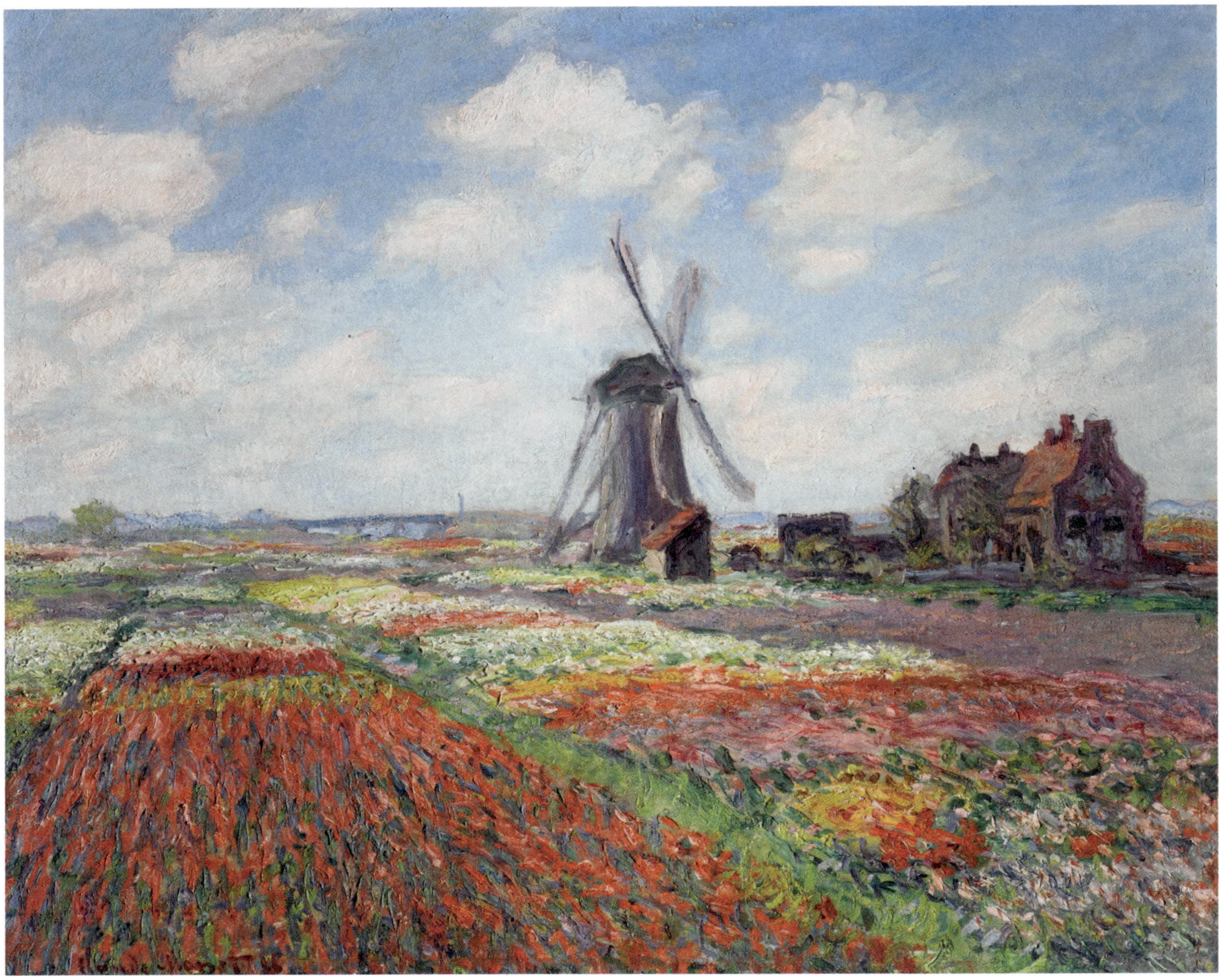

179 Claude Monet, *Champ de tulipes en Hollande* (*Field of Tulips in Holland*), 1886
Oil on canvas, 25 13⁄16 × 32 1⁄16 in. (65.5 × 81.5 cm)

The art of travel

While Impressionism is often linked to Japonism, the incursions of Manet, Monet, and Renoir into the terrain and market of travel painting, or even orientalism, are generally—and incorrectly—judged to have been negligible. Monet in fact looked back on his military service in Algeria with a sense of wonder, and took an interest in artists such as Charles-Théodore Frère and Eugène Fromentin. At the Salon of 1859, the ones who most attracted his attention were messengers from exhilarating Eastern horizons: "In all of these paintings, there is a grandeur, a warm light, plus the detail and the movement are beautiful." Renoir's first orientalist paintings follow in a vein that was begun by Delacroix and continued by many different artists, not all of whom ever visited North Africa. Renoir did, however; he first stayed in Algiers in the winter of 1881, and returned the following year. As he reached forty, he rekindled his interest in orientalism, at the same time as he was taking a break from the Impressionists. His lodgings were in the European part of Algiers, and he constantly returned there in his paintings. After all, he was addressing a public who were expecting him to conjure up different worlds, yet ones that were subject to their own world's authority. This is as true of the Sidi Abd al-Rahman al-Tha'alibi mosque, of which he painted the exterior, and its veiled women, as it is of the test garden, where he painted the extraordinary *Field of Banana Trees*, an ode to the fertility of the Algerian soil and therefore auxiliary to its colonization. Not long afterward, Monet went to the Italian town of Bordighera, which so captivated him that he stayed for several months in early 1884, meticulously seeking to capture the resprouting greenery, the warm air, and the dazzling blue of the sea. These paintings, with their broad brushstrokes, are also alive with notes of pink, blue, yellow, and orange. On his first visit to Venice, in late 1908, Monet was ripe for an even more intense artistic explosion. His other travels, including to Brittany, remind us that, for him, shifting geographies were a crucial tonic to the eye and the mind.   S.G.

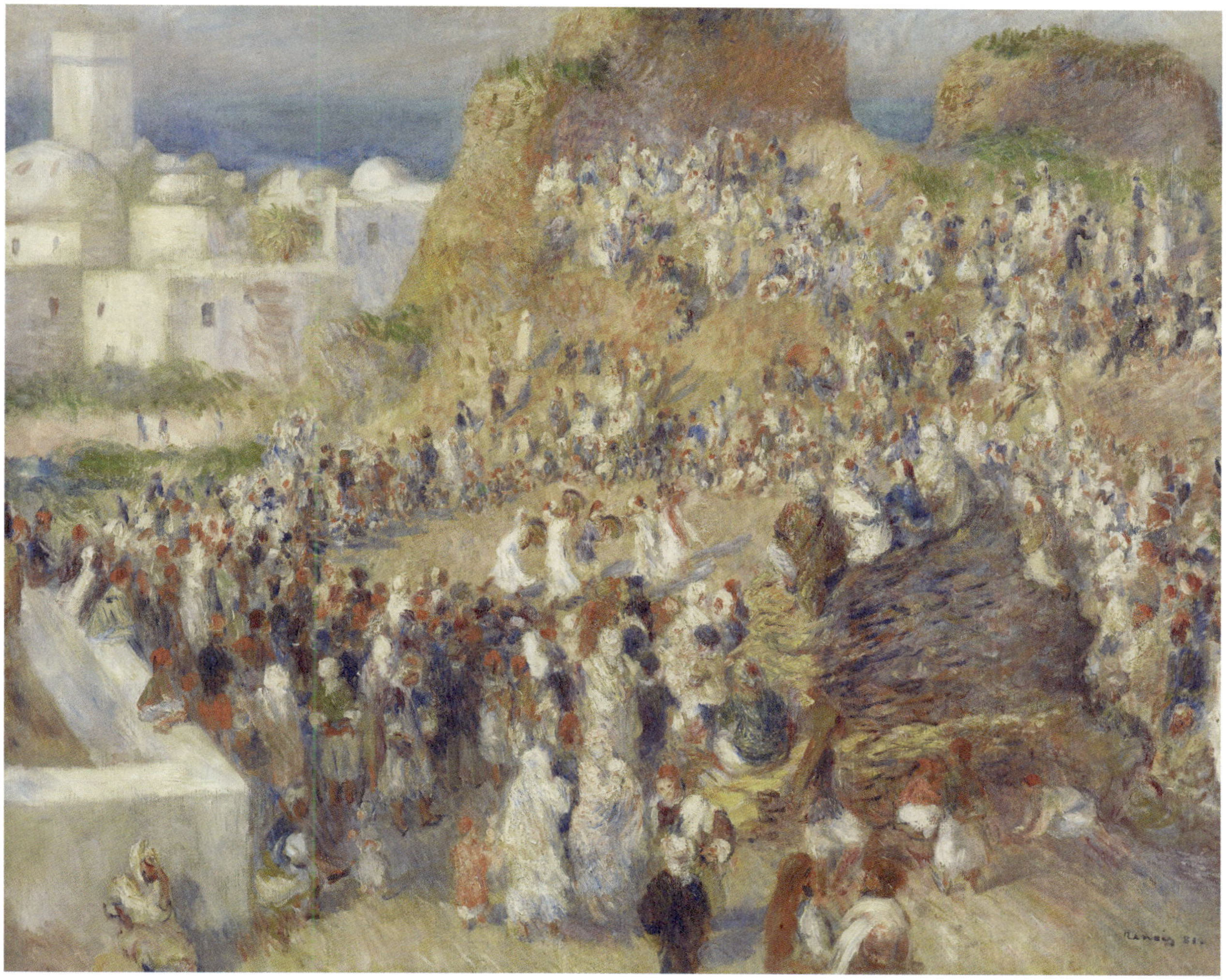

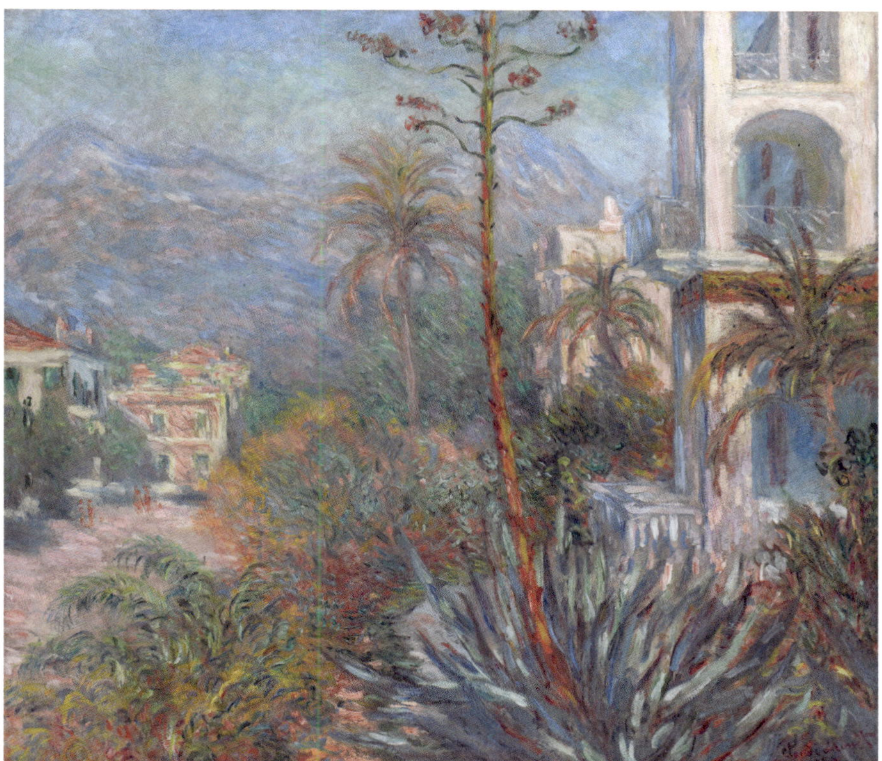

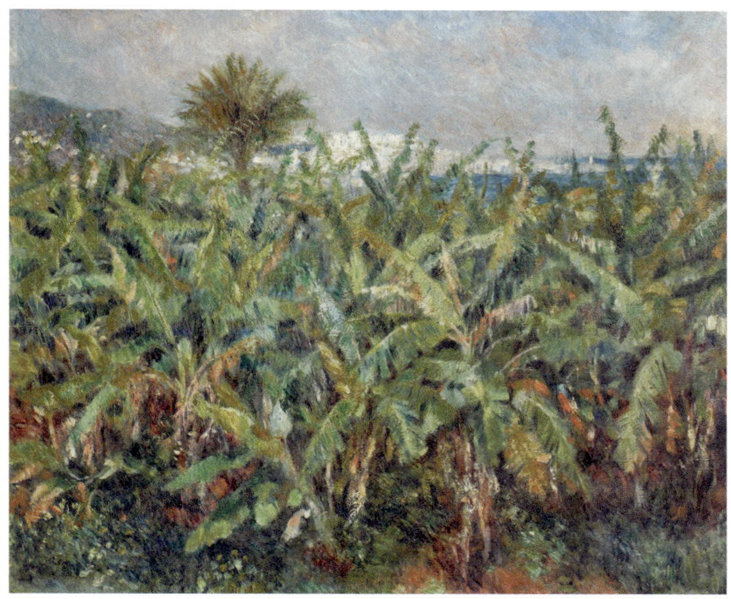

180 Top: Auguste Renoir, *La Mosquée* (*The Mosque*), 1881
Oil on canvas, 28 15⁄16 × 36 7⁄16 in.
(73.5 × 92.5 cm)

181 Bottom, left: Claude Monet, *Les Villas à Bordighera* (*Villas at Bordighera*), 1884
Oil on canvas, 45 7⁄8 × 53 3⁄4 in.
(116.5 × 136.5 cm)

182 Bottom, right: Auguste Renoir, *Champ de bananiers* (*Field of Banana Trees*), 1881
Oil on canvas, 20 1⁄16 × 24 13⁄16 in.
(51 × 63 cm)

Claude Monet
Belle-Île

Way out at sea off the southern coast of Brittany, Belle-Île-en-Mer and its inhospitable coastline inspired mixed feelings in Monet. He stayed there from September 12 through November 25, 1886, and immediately wanted to share his reactions on this first visit with friends back home. On October 11, he wrote to fellow painter Caillebotte, who was also one of his key collectors and confidants: "I am in a land that is magnificent in its wildness, a great pile of rocks and an incredible sea of colors; I am very excited, although I'm struggling quite a bit, because I was used to painting the Channel and of course I'd developed a routine, but the Ocean is something else entirely." The amount of time he devoted to exploring rugged and sometimes hazardous spots on this, the largest of Brittany's islands, indicates his need to break away from the tyranny of Impressionist spontaneity.

The Breton sequence, which came to its close in the year of the group's final exhibition, produced only five paintings. It was a turning point, as confirmed by the heightened synthesis of the forms and their severe arrangement, counterbalanced by recollections of those Japanese masters of printmaking, Harunobu and Hokusai. Plunging viewpoints, which raise the horizon line and enable the dark, luxuriant, partially submerged rocks to come into their own, are reminders of his working method: the site was so steep and dangerous that it made it almost impossible to get closer to the sea. The greens and blues, with their shifting materiality, magnificently envelop the predominant purple of the mineral mass, devoid of any human presence. Exactly how Monet liked his landscapes. S.G.

183 Facing page, top: Claude Monet, *Tempête, côtes de Belle-Île* (*Storm off the Belle-Île Coast*), 1886
Oil on canvas, 25 ¾ × 32 1⁄16 in. (65.4 × 81.5 cm)

184 Facing page, bottom: Claude Monet, *Les Rochers de Belle-Île, la Côte sauvage* (*The Rocks of Belle-Île: The Wild Coast*), 1886
Oil on canvas, 25 13⁄16 × 32 1⁄16 in. (65.5 × 81.5 cm)

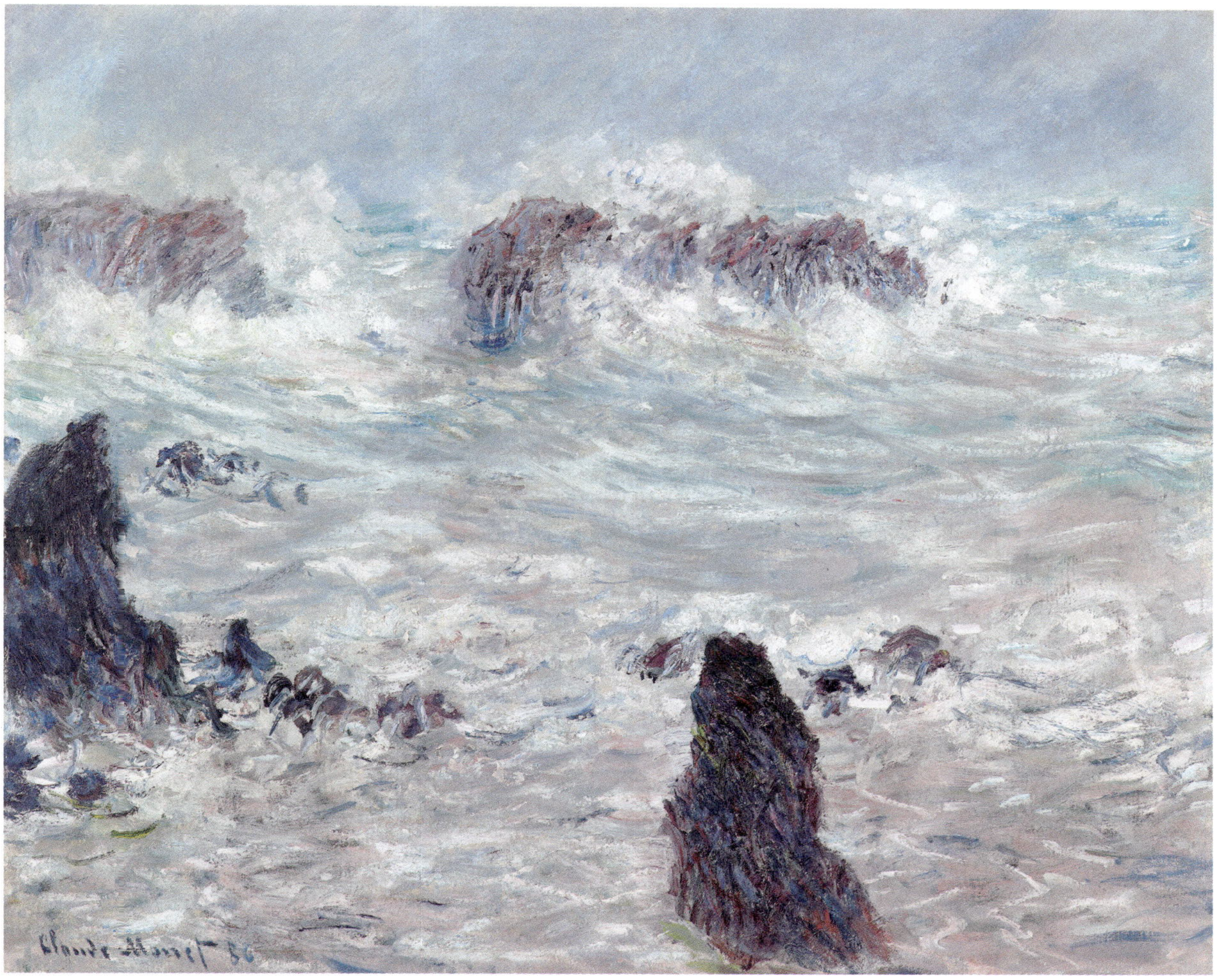
Claude Monet 86

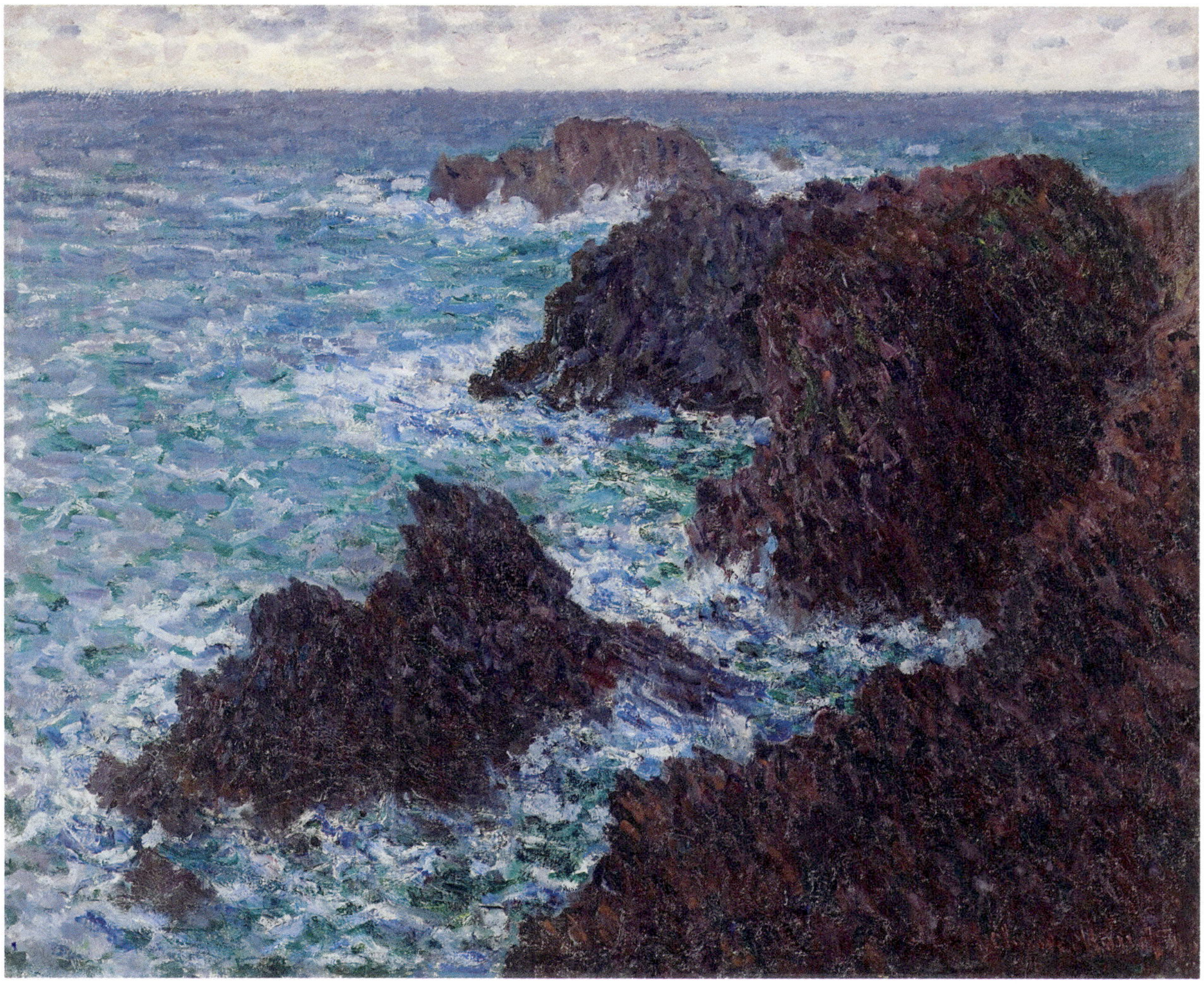

Auguste Renoir
Motherhood

At La Roche-sur-Yon, where he spent part of the summer of 1885, Renoir executed a series of drawings and paintings based around the image of his partner and future wife Aline Charigot breastfeeding their baby son Pierre, born on March 21. He had already displayed an interest in woman-and-child subjects for several years, no doubt with Renaissance examples in mind, and notably Raphael's paintings of the Virgin and Child, which he had admired in Italy in 1881. This was the first time he depicted the subject of breastfeeding, which was still rare in painting at a time when most women, especially those living in towns and cities, would entrust their babies to wet-nurses. For Renoir, the mother-and-child theme was a celebration of human bonds and of a sort of rural healthfulness (Aline was born in a small village in the Champagne region, to a winemaking family) at a time when urban life was seen more and more as a source of illness and "vice." With this painting, Renoir also recognized his family, both pictorially and symbolically (having not acknowledged the children he had had with Lise Tréhot, his partner in the 1860s); by orienting Aline's face and gaze toward the viewer rather than toward the child, the artist includes himself in the trio.

This work also bears witness to Renoir's efforts in the mid-1880s to break away from Impressionism, which he considered at a "dead end." Its composition was prepared and reworked through numerous large drawings in red and white chalk, which he used to adjust the arrangement of the figures and to perfect his sense of line. Dated 1885, the painting was no doubt a preliminary study for other, more finished works: the very dilute color is applied rapidly on a very smooth white primed ground, and a prior drawing is still visible. One of those other canvases, exhibited in 1886, prompted the critic Octave Mirbeau to write: "Take a good look at his woman and child, for the image's originality recalls the charm of the Primitives, the cleanness of the Japanese, and the mastery of Ingres."[34] P.P.

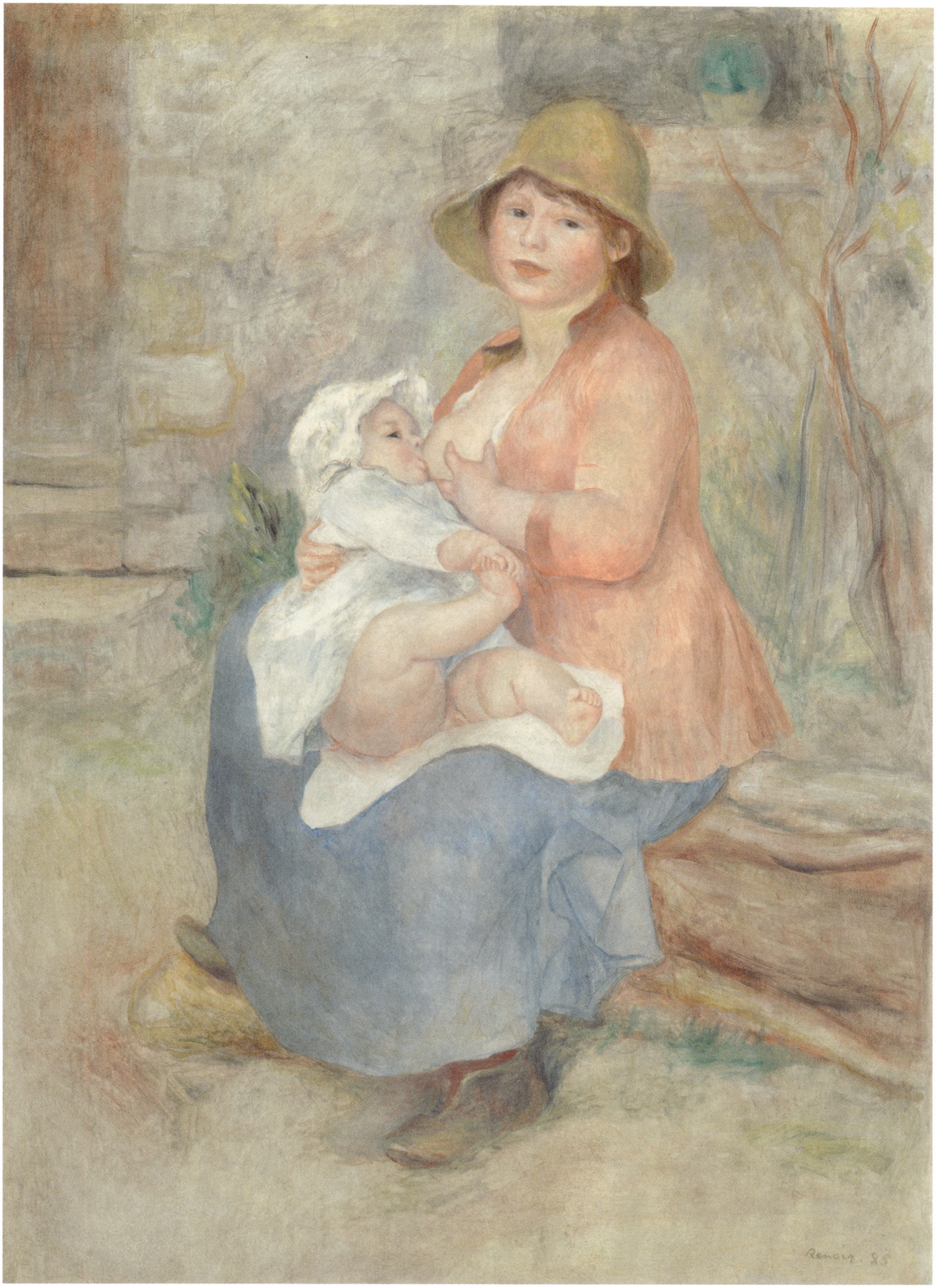

185 Auguste Renoir, *Maternité* (*Motherhood*), 1885
Oil on canvas, 36 ¼ × 28 ⅜ in. (92 × 72 cm)

Auguste Renoir
Three Bathers at the Water's Edge

Renoir practiced all forms of drawing, from preparatory studies to illustrations, watercolor sketches, and pastels. In 1883, following Manet's death, he confided to Ambroise Vollard that he felt he had "wrung Impressionism dry"[35] To escape from what he considered an "impasse," he set off for Italy to study Raphael—Ingres's favorite artist—and the paintings of Pompeii. Returning to studying the masters, he drew in order to master form and simplify volumes through line. For his *The Great Bathers* (1884–1887; Philadelphia Museum of Art), a painting that was shown at Georges Petit's commercial gallery in 1887, he made numerous preparatory studies, including this one, which is the largest and the closest to the finished painting. The composition is notably inspired by the bas-relief by François Girardon at Versailles titled *Nymphs Bathing* (1670–1671), the rococo painter François Boucher's *Diana Leaving Her Bath* (1742; Musée du Louvre, Paris), and Raphael's *Triumph of Galatea* (1513; Farnese Collection, Rome). The simultaneous use of black, red, and white chalk revives the *trois crayons* (three pencils) technique that was used extensively in the seventeenth and eighteenth centuries. This large study was preceded by an array of single-figure studies and sheets of multiple drawings, some details from which reappear in the painting. To avoid losing the lifelike impression that life-size imagery can offer, Renoir did not use the technique of squaring-up smaller drawings, preferring instead to make a full-scale drawing that could then be transferred onto the canvas. Seeking cleaner lines at that period in the 1880s, he drew the bathers' reclining bodies with precise, stylized strokes. He focused on linear balance and rhythm, with virtually no modeling. The artists he admired, such as Fragonard and Boucher, were particularly fond of red chalk—a stick of clay containing iron oxide and also known as sanguine—and the medium enabled Renoir to adopt a softer line than graphite or pen would allow, while its warm color suggests volume through light. L.J.

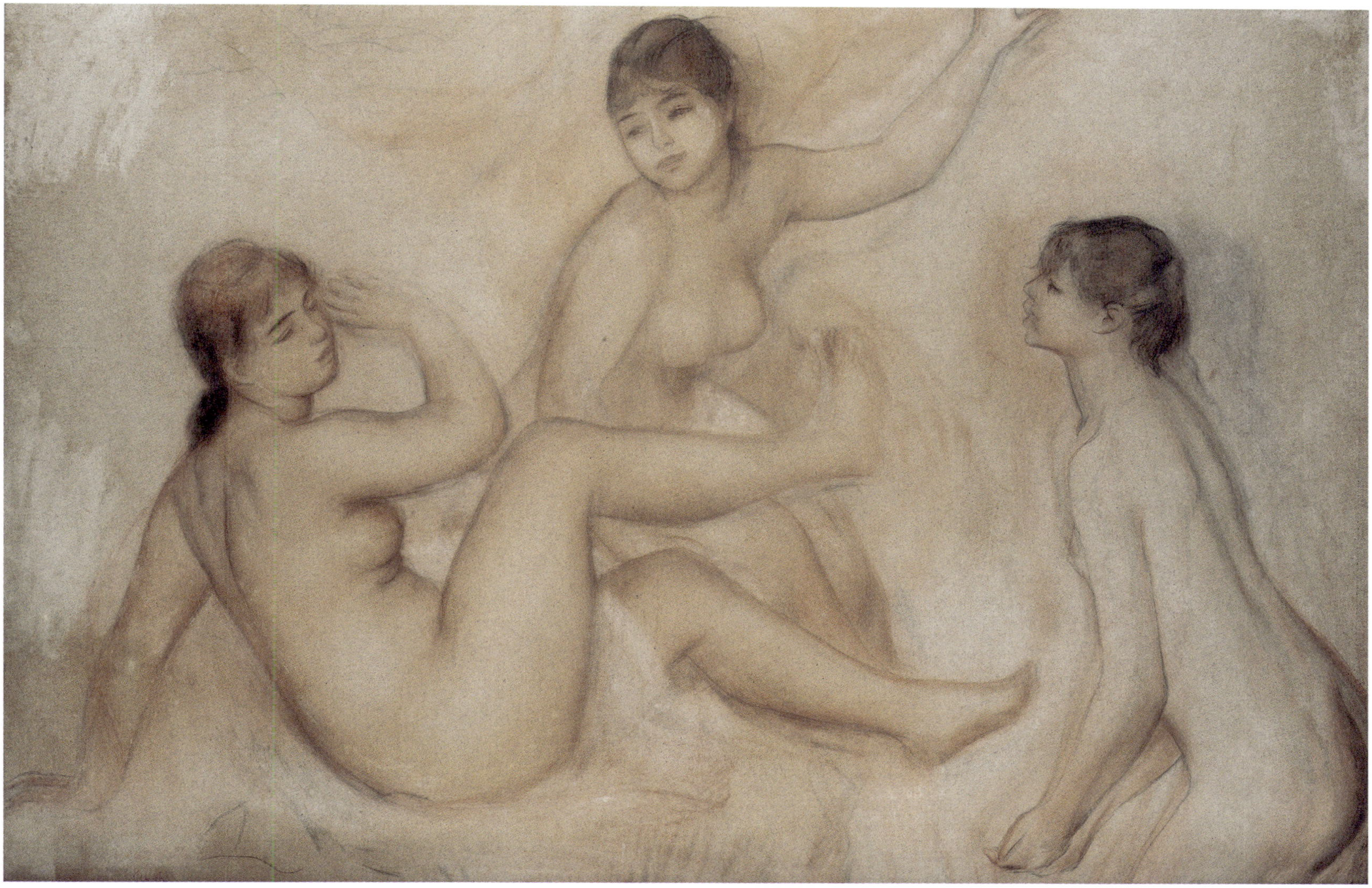

186 Auguste Renoir, *Trois baigneuses au bord de l'eau* (*Three Bathers at the Water's Edge*), study for *Baigneuses. Essai de peinture décorative* (*The Great Bathers*), c. 1886
Black pencil with white and red chalk highlights on paper, 42 ½ × 63 ¾ in. (108 × 162 cm)

Auguste Renoir
Julie Manet

Born the same year but to families of very different social status, Renoir and Morisot met in the late 1860s and both participated in the Impressionist group's first exhibition, in 1874. A genuine friendship sprung up between them, and was consolidated in the 1880s, when Renoir was regularly invited to the soirées organized by Morisot and her husband Eugène Manet (brother of Édouard) at 40 Rue de Villejust in Paris, as were Mallarmé, Degas, and Monet. Renoir became a close friend of the family, and it was he whom Berthe and Eugène thought of to paint the portrait of their only child, Julie, then aged nine.

Morisot was one of few people who liked Renoir's new, so-called "Ingresque" style—a more precise, more synthetic manner that was less reliant on the haphazard effects of *plein-air* painting. She particularly appreciated the drawings and works in red chalk that she had seen in his studio in 1886: "He is a first-rate draftsman ... I do not think anyone could go further in rendering form."[36] For this painting, with its particularly harmonious, balanced composition, Renoir left nothing to chance or to spontaneity, and made copious preparatory drawings. The paint is loosely applied, but the color is made especially opaque and matte through the addition of white. Julie Manet would later recall that Renoir worked "bit by bit, one day my head and a little of the background, another day my dress and the cat."

After Eugène's and then Berthe's early deaths, Renoir, who became a substitute father figure for Julie, kept watch over her and encouraged her to practice painting. She would keep this canvas for the rest of her life. P. P.

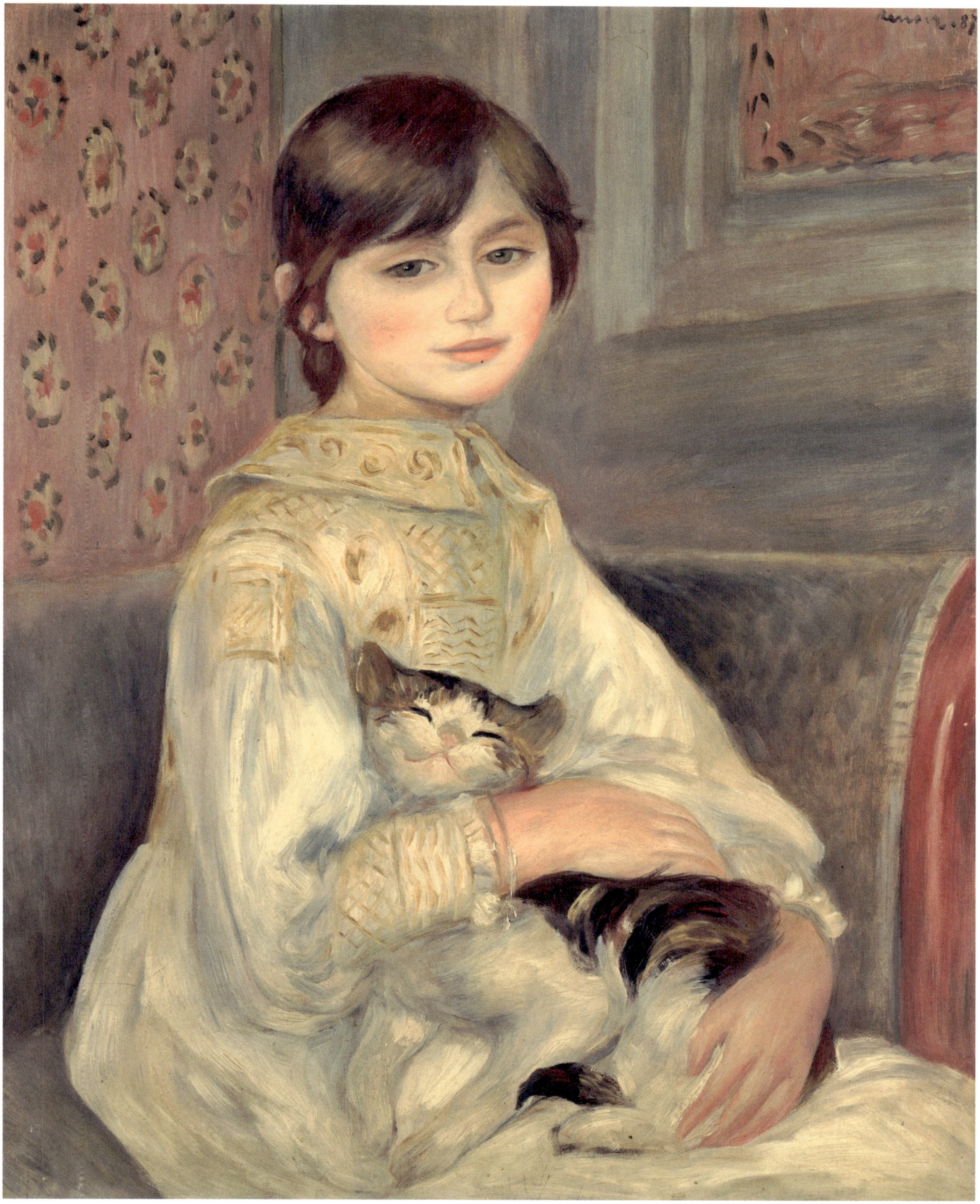

187 Auguste Renoir, *Julie Manet*, 1887
Oil on canvas, 25 13⁄16 × 21 1⁄16 in. (65.5 × 53.5 cm)

1886

The eighth Impressionist exhibition

The show brought together seventeen artists. Among them were Morisot, who provided much of the funding for it, and Degas, who played an essential role in its organization. Exhibiting alongside them were Cassatt, Gauguin, Guillaumin, Camille Pissarro and his son, Lucien, as well as Redon, Seurat, and Signac. A few big names, such as Monet, Sisley, Renoir, and Caillebotte, were conspicuous by their absence. Their reasons for not participating in the exhibition varied from aesthetic differences to loss of interest or disagreements regarding the direction the group was taking.

The exhibition's catalog and poster referred to it obliquely as "Eighth exhibition" without labeling it as "Impressionist," evidencing a shift in the group's self-awareness and in its public recognition. One of the show's defining aspects was the presence of artists who would soon be designated neo-Impressionists. Seurat, Signac, and the new pointillist technique were front and center.

The exhibition's layout itself reflected the tensions between the "old" and "new" participants: the neo-Impressionists' works were grouped together in the same room to take account of their formal coherence, and to spare confrontations and contrasts with the group's more traditional works. Seurat showed *A Sunday on La Grande Jatte* (1884; Art Institute of Chicago), an imposing work whose effect was judged to have been stifled by the small space in which it was displayed.

Among the "old" crowd, Morisot exhibited portraits and landscapes in a variety of techniques, displaying an ever-freer touch. Cassatt mainly presented works on the theme of childhood, and Degas, eighteen pastels of female nudes at their toilet, which are striking in their absence of idealization. Their flesh is rendered through superimposed energetic hatching and zigzags in pinkish but also yellow, green, and blue pastel, making them pulsate.

The eighth Impressionist exhibition revealed a dual rupture: between the traditional members of Impressionism and the newcomers, but also tensions between the desire for artistic permanence and the taste for experimentation. That 1886 event definitively marked the end of the adventure of collective exhibitions by the original group, while at the same time opening up new avenues in modern art. C.C.-P.

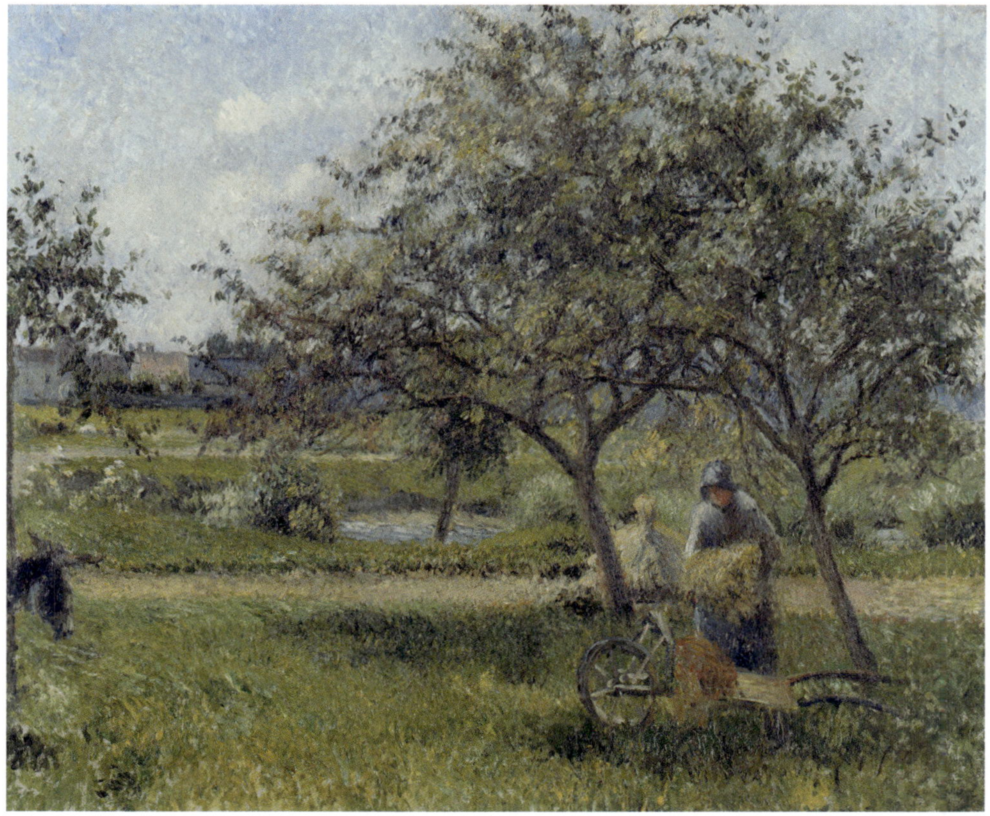

188 Camille Pissarro, *La Brouette, verger, le Valhermeil, Auvers-sur-Oise* (*Wheelbarrow in an Orchard at Le Valhermeil, Auvers-sur-Oise*), c. 1879
Oil on canvas, 21 ¼ × 25 $^9/_{16}$ in. (54 × 65 cm)

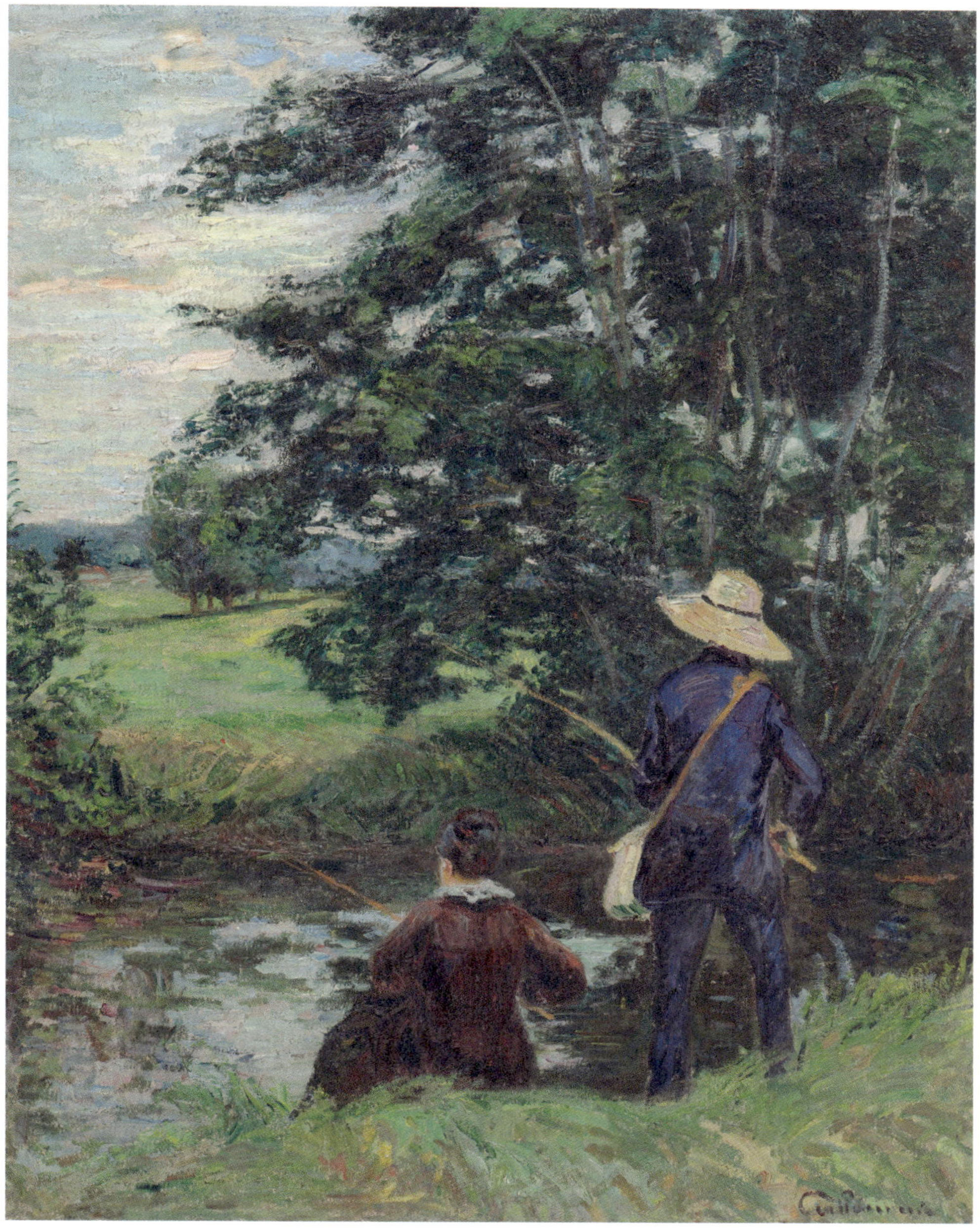

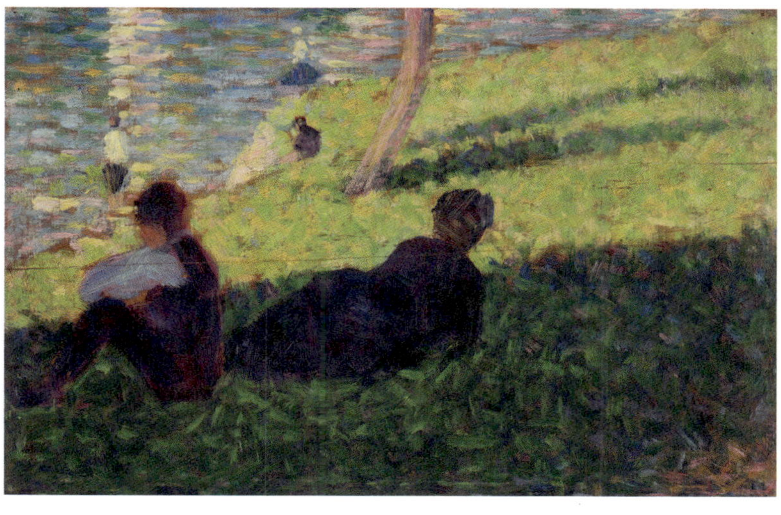

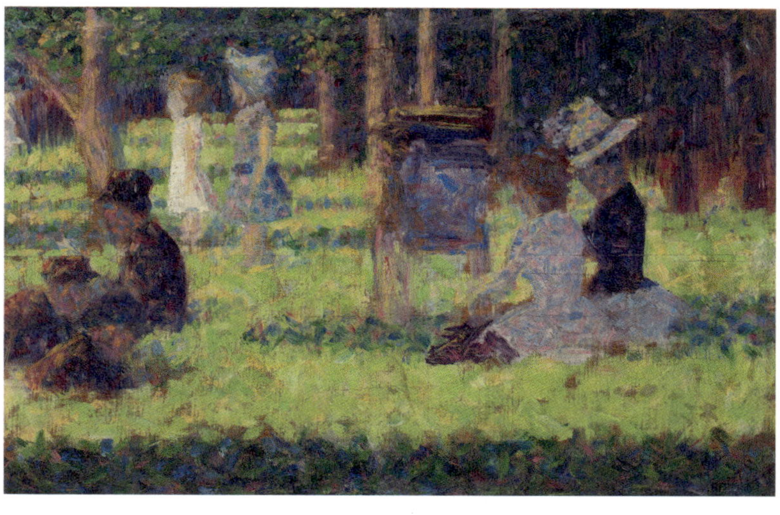

189 Top: Armand Guillaumin,
Les Pêcheurs (*Fishing*), c. 1885
Oil on canvas, 31 ⅞ × 26 in.
(81 × 66 cm)

190 Bottom, left: Georges Seurat, Study for
Un dimanche après-midi à l'île de la Grande Jatte
(*A Sunday on La Grande Jatte*), 1884
Oil on wood panel, 6 ⅛ × 9 13⁄16 in. (15.5 × 25 cm)

191 Bottom, right: Georges Seurat, Study for
Un dimanche après-midi à l'île de la Grande Jatte
(*A Sunday on La Grande Jatte*), 1884–1886
Oil on wood panel, 6 ¼ × 9 13⁄16 in. (16 × 25 cm)

Camille Pissarro
Woman in a Field

With very slow sales of paintings and with France's struggling economic situation, the first half of the 1880s was a materially difficult period. It also marked a shift in Pissarro's style, prompted as much by the reflections of the Pontoise group (along with Cézanne, Gauguin, and Guillaumin) as by Pissarro's own luminist experiments before he came over to Seurat's and Signac's neo-Impressionism in 1886. Four years earlier, he left Pontoise for nearby Osny before setting up home in Éragny-sur-Epte, some 25 miles (40 kilometers) further from the capital. He would live out the rest of his life there, in a house he bought in 1892. In a letter dated March 14, 1888, from Theo van Gogh—brother of Vincent—announcing that his employer, the Boussod, Valadon & Cie gallery, had sold one of Pissarro's paintings, Theo suggests he replace the work in question with *Le Paysage en plein soleil* (the landscape in full sunlight). His title is befitting of the painting's cheerfully agitated quality and the foreground's predominantly yellowish-green tones. Pissarro was classically trained, and uses the orchard's white wall, which runs parallel to the picture plane, to stabilize the image, while discreetly animating it with the figure who is walking toward us. The different zones interlock rather than creating a sense of depth. The second painting's visual arrangement is not greatly different other than in its reference to Manet's *Laundry* (1875; The Barnes Foundation, Philadelphia) and, beyond that, to Chardin. Pissarro uses the white laundry to carefully establish a rhythm, and also allows himself a tender note in the exchange of glances between the child and the woman—no doubt one of the artist's maidservants—the eloquence of whose gesture is reminiscent of Millet. S.G.

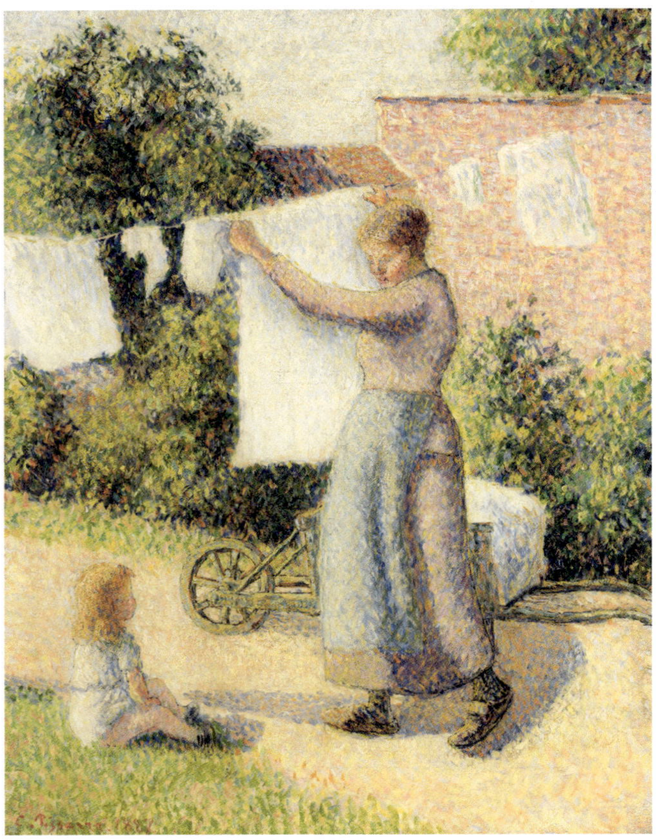

192 Camille Pissarro, *Femme étendant du linge* (*Woman Hanging Laundry*), 1887
Oil on canvas, 16 ⅛ × 13 in. (41 × 33 cm)

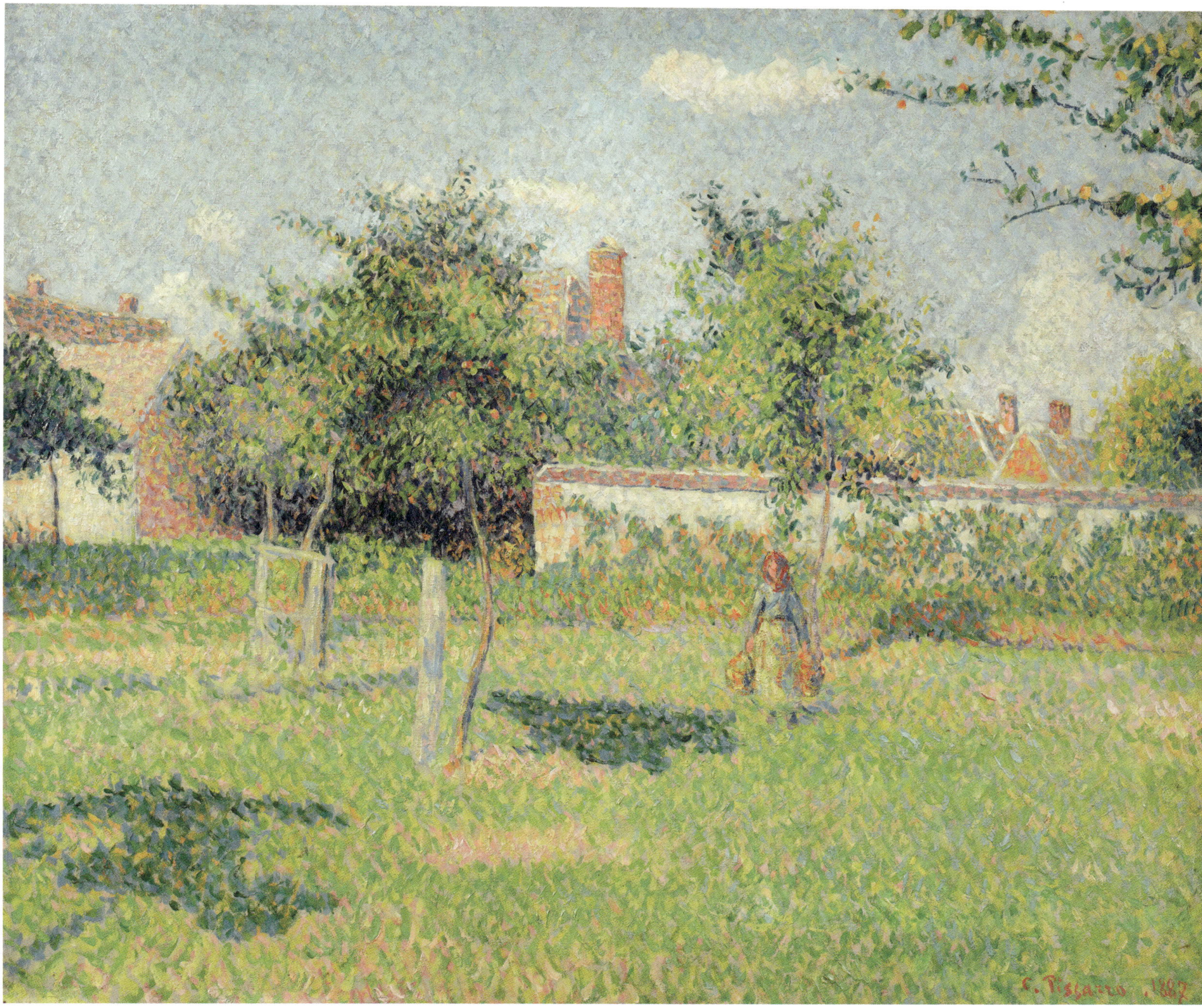

193 Camille Pissarro, *Femme dans un clos, soleil de printemps dans le pré à Éragny* (*Woman in a Field: Spring Sunshine in the Meadow at Éragny*), 1887
Oil on canvas, 21 7⁄16 × 25 5⁄16 in. (54.5 × 65 cm)

Camille Pissarro
Fields in the Sunshine

Pissarro met Monet during their time at the Académie Suisse, and was part of the Impressionist adventure from the very start. In 1885, through Guillaumin, he met Paul Signac, who in turn introduced him to Georges Seurat. He then experimented with the theory of contrasting colors, and with neo-Impressionist pointillism, in his own work. Thanks to him, Signac and Seurat participated in the final Impressionist exhibition, in 1886.

Pissarro was one of the Impressionists' most prolific draftsmen besides Degas. After traveling to Venezuela in 1853–1855, during which trip he filled up numerous sketchbooks, Pissarro studied landscape mainly through drawing with Corot. In the 1870s, under Millet's influence, he took an interest in figure painting. He also explored the possibilities of decorative formats such as fans, exhibiting twelve of these at the 1879 Impressionist exhibition. In 1886, he reinterpreted pointillism in his own way through "dot" drawings and a few watercolors. In his correspondence with his son Lucien, he mentions three of these. The sun-drenched fields in this picture are expressed by a succession of juxtaposed spots that vary in size and proximity and are applied fairly freely and unsystematically. The spacing between them conveys variations in light and leaves the paper ground extensively visible. The subtle balance between the colors and the white of the paper is fundamental to the watercolor. This sheet was not a preparatory sketch, but a finished work intended for sale.   L.J.

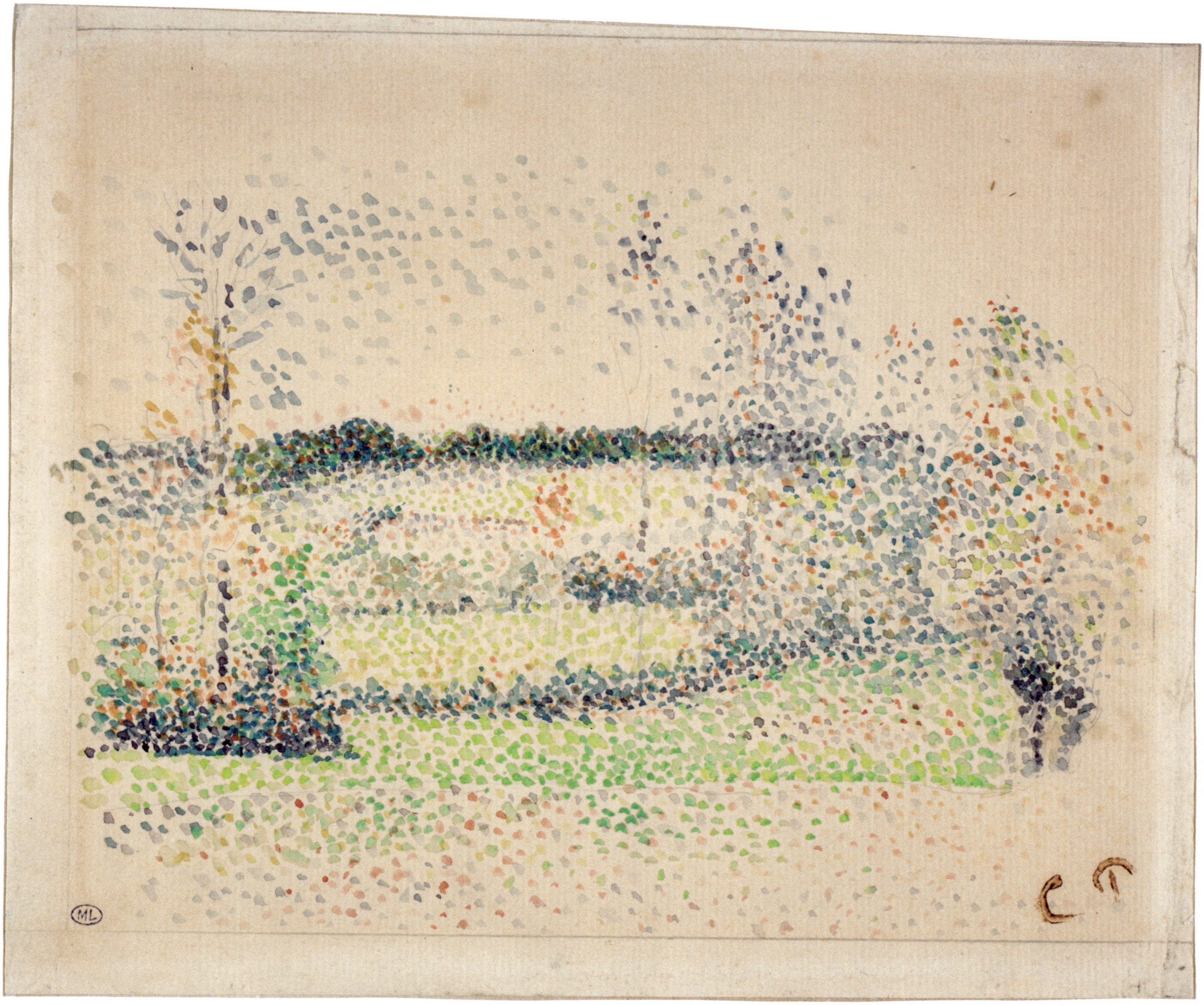

194 Camille Pissarro, *Champs au soleil* (*Fields in the Sunshine*), c. 1886
Watercolor over graphite sketch on paper, 7 1⁄16 × 8 5⁄8 in. (18 × 21.9 cm)

Watercolors

Lightweight, portable, and allowing subtle effects of light and spontaneity of gesture, watercolor was a medium and technique that the Impressionists relished, as Boudin and Jongkind had before them. Morisot practiced it throughout her career, and showed watercolors at all the Impressionist exhibitions with the exception of those in 1879 (where she did not participate), 1881, and 1882. She first tried her hand at the medium around 1865, working *en plein air* to paint studies from life at Beuzeval (now Houlgate) on the Normandy coast. She also used it for portraits set in interiors. Often works in their own right, her watercolors proved more swiftly successful than her oils. With *Young Woman in a Landscape*, for which her sister Edma was the model, Morisot set about tackling the subject of figures in the outdoors. Watercolor would enable her to capture a scene without making the child models pose for too long, in a vibrant light offered by the white of the paper, which contrasts with the greens.

Manet also practiced watercolor, for various purposes. His watercolors sometimes repeat his oil compositions, with a view to producing prints. In the years around 1870, he used the technique for on-the-spot sketches of skies and figures outdoors. In the summer of 1880, he sent letters embellished with watercolors to his friends Isabelle Lemonnier, Madame Guillemet, and Méry Laurent. His watercolors are like a pictorial equivalent of a Japanese haiku: he would precisely and succinctly paint items such as an almond, some plums, a watering can, or a cat, on a sheet of paper, sometimes accompanied by a text. *At the Café, Study of Legs*, painted in his garden at Bellevue, south-west of Paris, takes up a composition that he had already used to illustrate a letter to Madame Guillemet. He used tracing paper to repeat some of his compositions.

Cézanne, for his part, was considered the master of watercolor at the turn of the twentieth century. Paradoxically, he used it slowly, building up layers, to create effects of opacity and represent the permanence of things rather than their transience. He first exhibited watercolors in 1877, when he contributed three to the third Impressionist exhibition, two of which were titled *Watercolor: Impression after Nature*. His *Flower Pots* was probably painted in the greenhouse at the Jas de Bouffan, the property at the edge of Aix-en-Provence where he spent his winters in the 1880s. He set up the greenhouse as a studio, and arranged the objects for his compositions there, such as these pots of geraniums, with their tangle of flowers and leaves, rigorously arranged and represented in the Provençal late-winter light.   L. J.

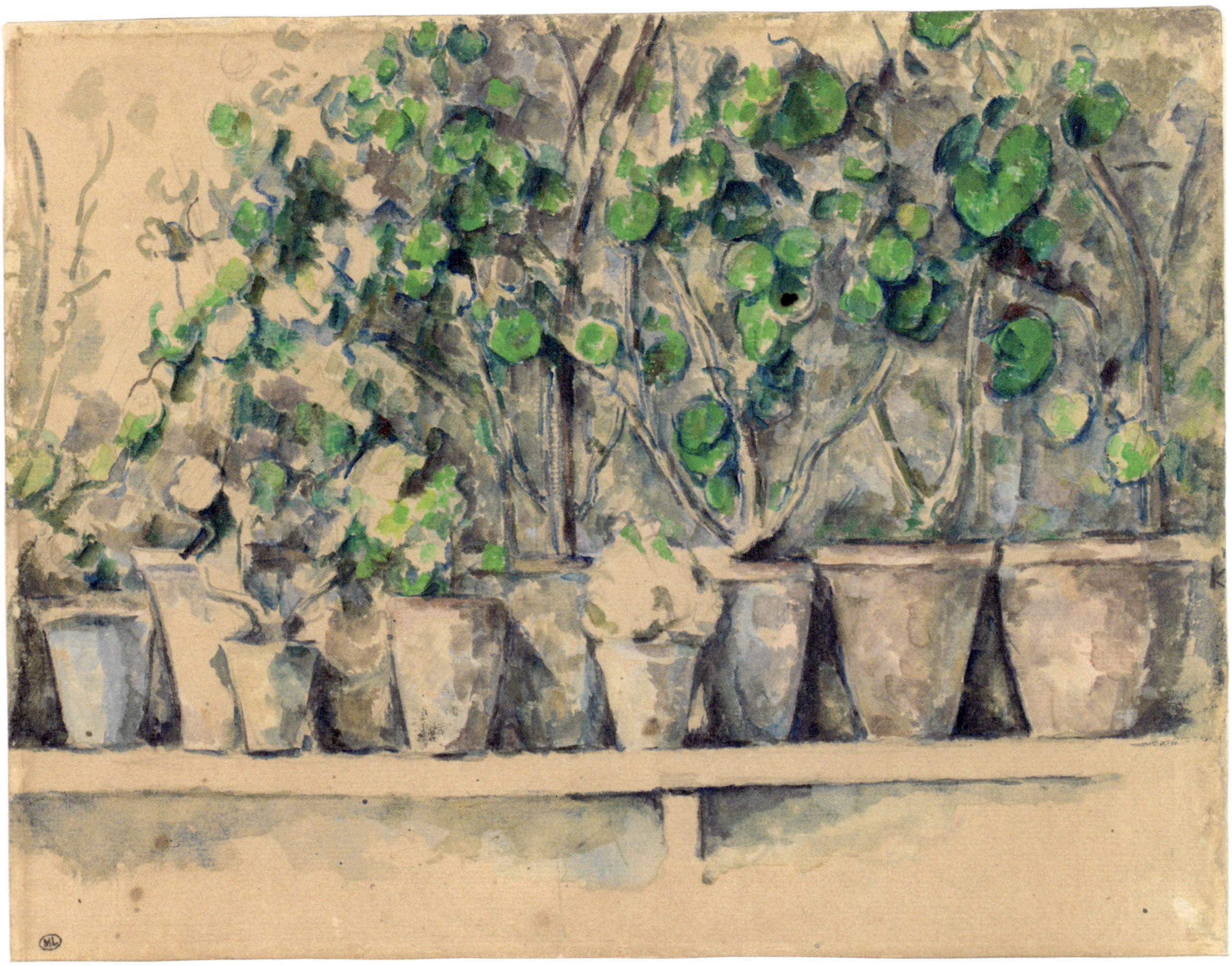

195 Paul Cézanne, *Les Pots de fleurs* (*Flower Pots*), c. 1883–1887
Watercolor on graphite on paper, 9 ¼ × 12 ⅟₁₆ in. (23.5 × 30.7 cm)

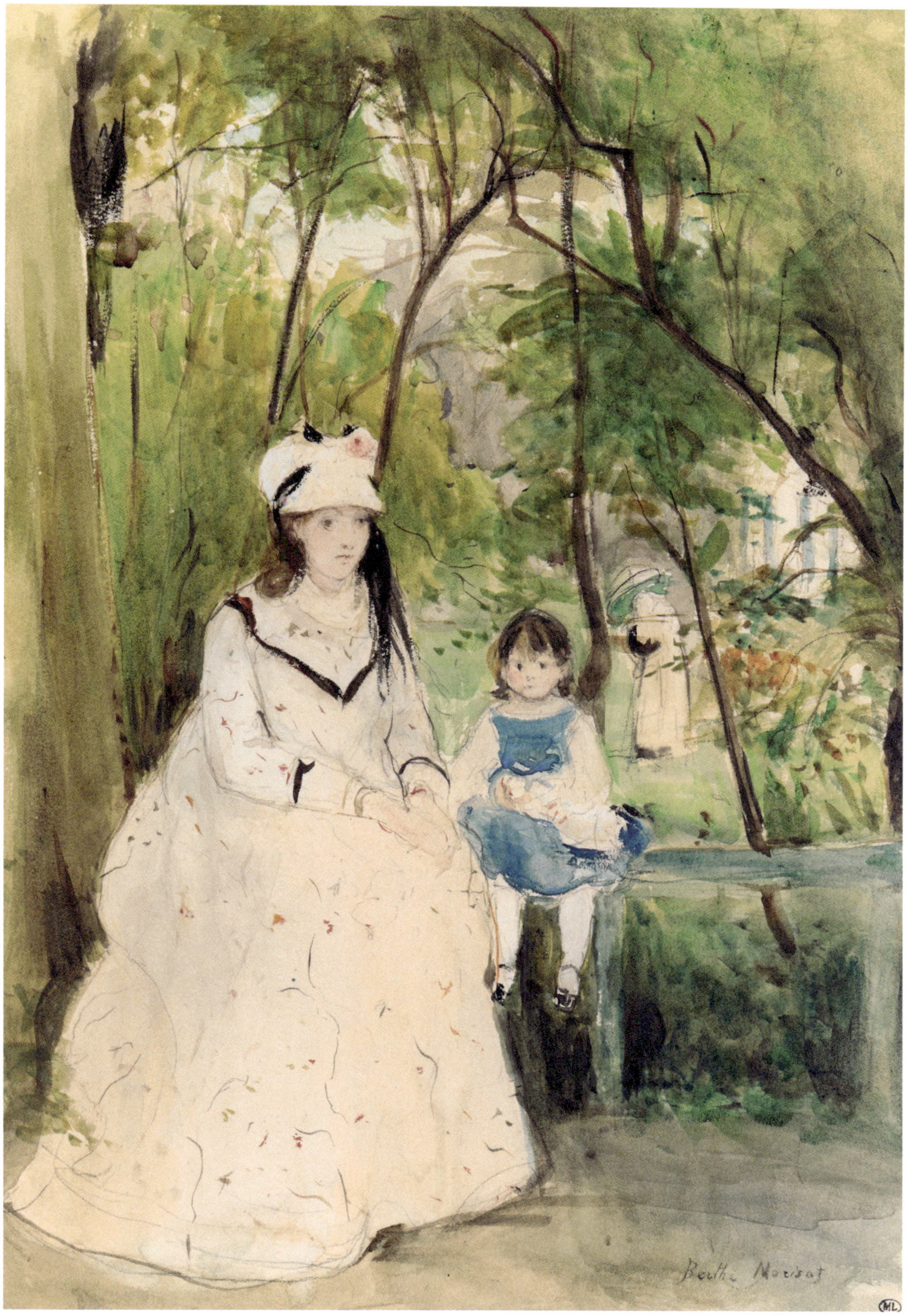

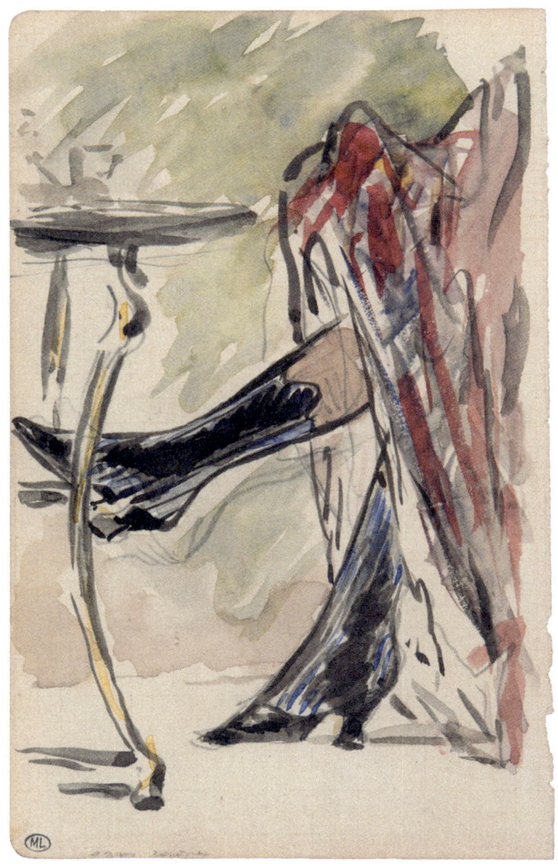

196 Left: Berthe Morisot, *Jeune femme dans un paysage* (*Young Woman in a Landscape*), 1872
Watercolor on paper, 13 × 9 1⁄16 in. (33 × 23 cm)

197 Right: Édouard Manet, *Deux jambes avec bottines sous une jupe rouge, devant un guéridon* (*At the Café, Study of Legs*), 1880
Watercolor, black wash, and graphite on squared paper, 7 5⁄16 × 4 3⁄4 in. (18.6 × 12 cm)

Paul Cézanne
The Curtains

Cézanne exhibited the watercolor *The Curtains* in his solo show organized by Ambroise Vollard in 1895. It was purchased by Isaac de Camondo, whose collection also featured other watercolors by the artist—*Flower Pots* (p. 212), *The Lime Kiln* (p. 240), and *The Green Jug* (c. 1885–1887)—all now held at the Musée d'Orsay thanks to his very significant bequest.

From the 1890s onward, Cézanne made ever-increasing use of "reserves" in his watercolors—that is, unpainted areas where the paper color is integral to the image. As Marie-Pierre Salé, chief curator of prints and drawings at the Musée du Louvre, writes, "these reserves give the impression of a very rapidly executed sketch, but at the same time these works … possess a classical perfection, in their intellectual arrangement of the subjects and their singularly formal, almost purist refinement." Brightly colored, luxurious draping curtains can often be seen as a background motif in the still lifes and portraits that Cézanne painted between 1885 and 1895, along with other interior decoration features such as folding screens, pieces of rococo furniture, and stenciled wallpapers. Here, the drapes become the actual subject matter of the watercolor. Revealing a view through to a door bathed in light—it is not clear whether the door is open or closed—they are drawn back by passementerie cords. The bright colors of their patterns recall the harmonies of greens, yellows, blues, and reds heightened by whites of those great colorists the Venetian Renaissance master Veronese and, more recently, Delacroix, both of whom Cézanne admired. L. J.

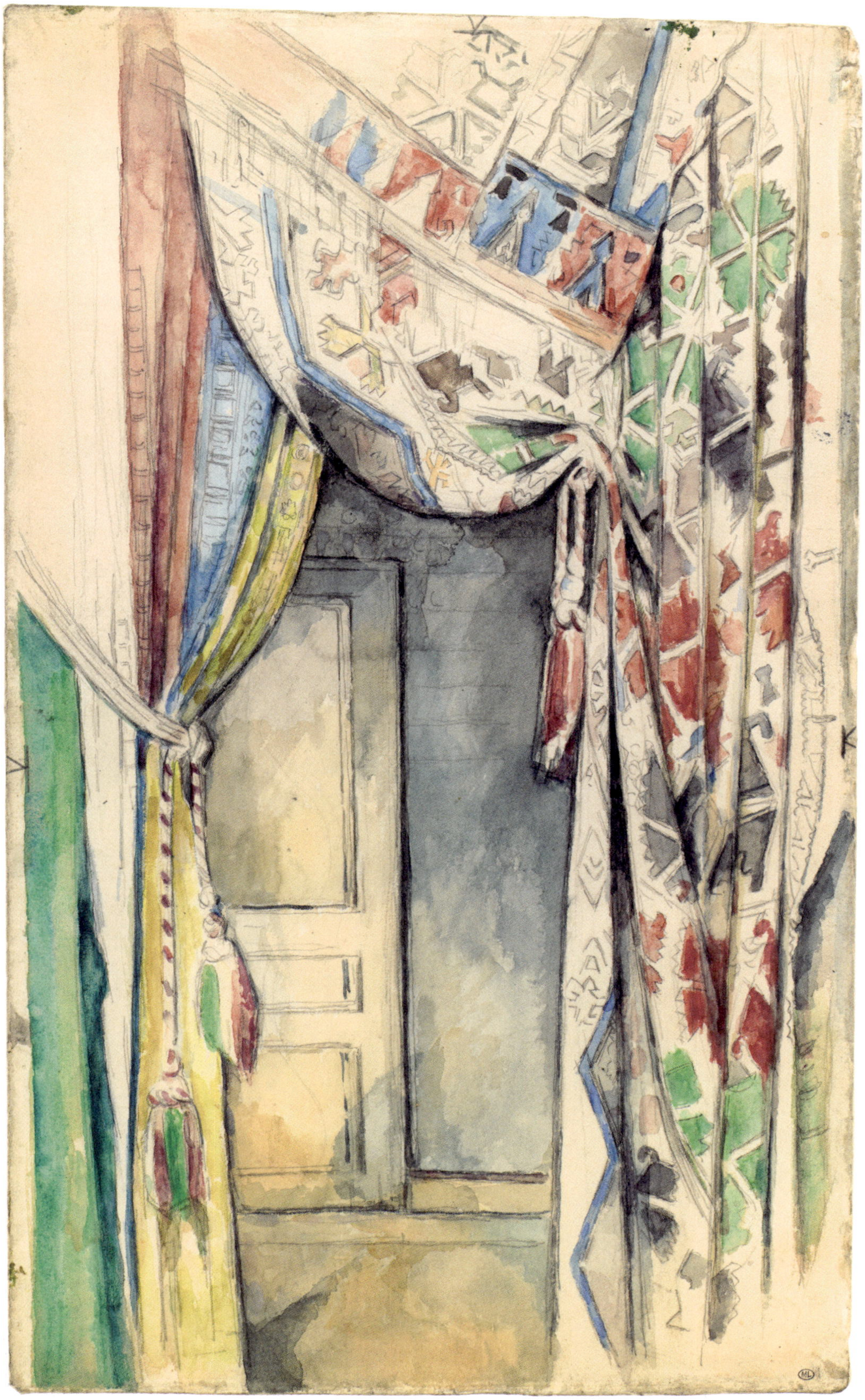

198 Paul Cézanne, *Les Rideaux* (*The Curtains*), c. 1885–1890
Watercolor over graphite sketch on paper, 19 5⁄16 × 12 1⁄16 in. (49 × 30.7 cm)

Cézanne and still life

Of all the "New Painting" protagonists, Cézanne would reveal himself to be the most attached to still life—a genre that made commercial sense for those who, like him, struggled to sell their figure paintings. It also offered the added advantage of obedient models and the comfort of being able to control both their staging and their pictorial transposition. The art historian Charles Sterling said artists would paint still lifes twice: first by arranging the objects physically, and then by transferring them to the canvas. The balance between the senses of something that has been happened across and of something that has been finely orchestrated varies from painting to painting. Even when not depicting the items commonly found in *vanitas* paintings (e.g. skulls, candles, open books), Cézanne would combine the solid with the fleeting, the eternal with the transient. Some of the paintings he produced alongside Pissarro exude rustic bliss. Apples, bottles of local wine, and associated accessories willingly fall into loose arrangements, sometimes enhanced by the presence of a kitchen table. Rarely, however, do we encounter a genuine invitation to share a meal. As the years went by, Cézanne was ever less afraid of allowing the organization that went into the image to be perceptible. Committed to "wrestling directly with the objects," assimilating their volume and texture into his vision and imagination, he always remained in control, whether the subject was a bowl or some pieces of fruit. Quiet and introverted—or, as the poet Rainer Maria Rilke put it, "miraculously absorbed" in themselves—these paintings belong to our world only in a distant, baroque sense. Cézanne's final compositions are full-blown visual surges that seem to reconcile the French baroque painter Nicolas Poussin with the Venetian Renaissance master Tintoretto. We know from a letter written by one of Cézanne's friends to another in 1866 that he had won over one of his eminent elders: "Cézanne has already written to you about his visit to Manet's; but he didn't tell you that Manet had seen his still lifes at Guillemet's; he found them perfectly handled; Cézanne is overjoyed, but, as usual, he doesn't go on about it, and barely even mentions it. Manet is due to pay him a visit." S. G.

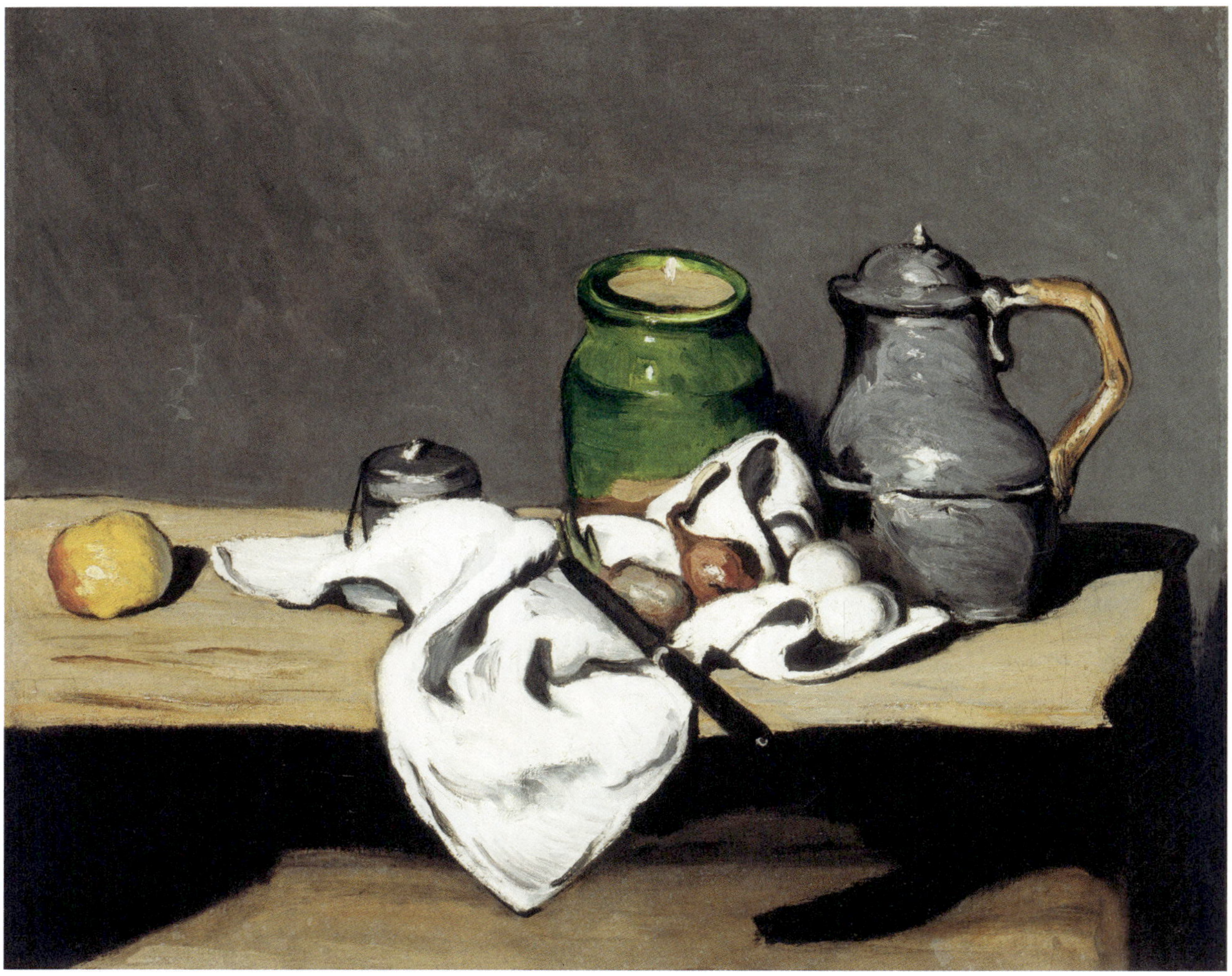

199 Paul Cézanne, *Nature morte à la bouilloire (Still Life with Kettle)*, 1867–1869
Oil on canvas, 25 ⅜ × 31 ⅞ in. (64.5 × 81 cm)

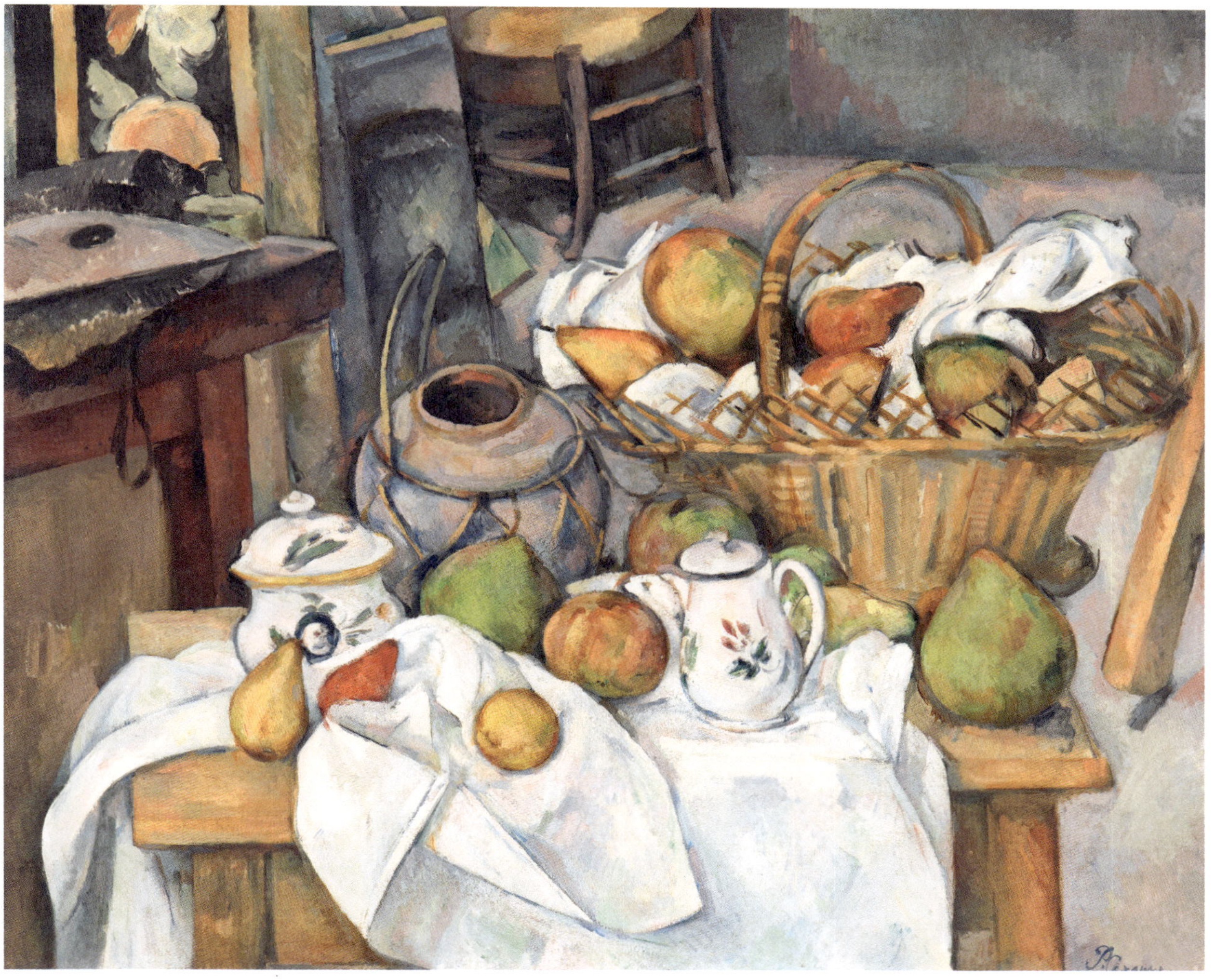

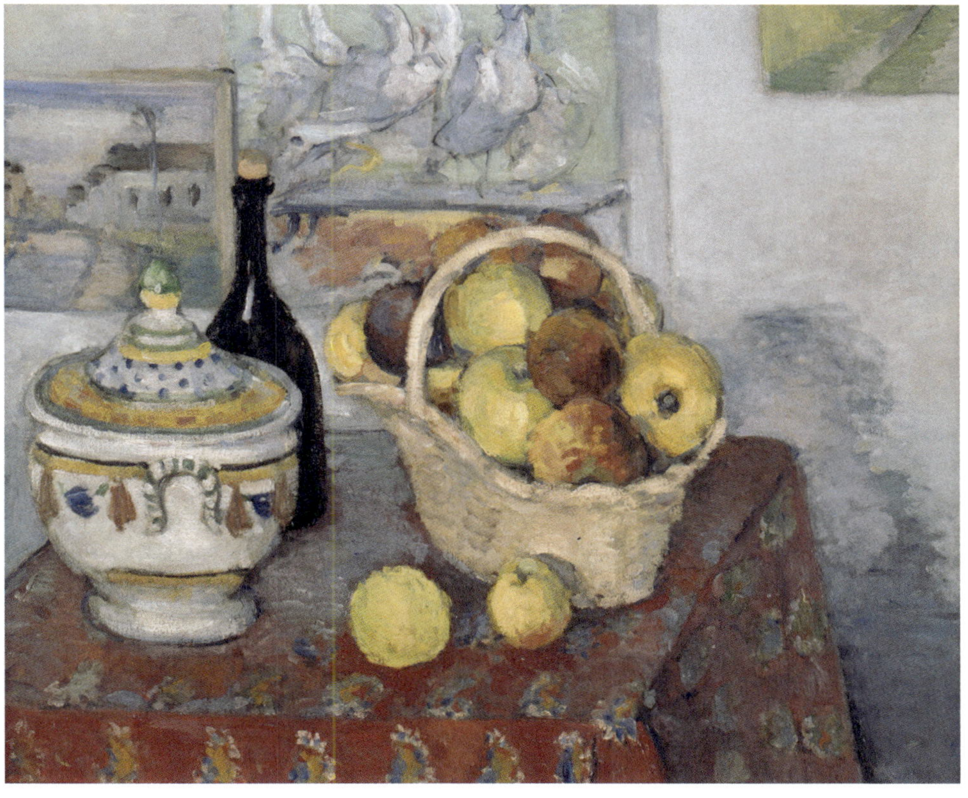

200 Top: Paul Cézanne, *La Table de cuisine* (*The Kitchen Table*), 1888–1890
Oil on canvas, 25 9⁄16 × 32 1⁄16 in. (65 × 81.5 cm)

201 Bottom: Paul Cézanne, *Nature morte à la soupière* (*Still Life with Soup Tureen*), c. 1877
Oil on canvas, 25 9⁄16 × 32 1⁄16 in. (65 × 81.5 cm)

Women at their toilet

Hygiene was big business in the late nineteenth century, and left countless images of its advances. At the same time, depictions of the age-old subject of women washing themselves became enormously popular. Despite his reputation as an incurable misogynist, Degas brought this theme to heights that have seldom been equaled. Among his many pictures of bathtubs and bathing is *Woman Getting Out of the Bath* (1876–1877; Musée d'Orsay, Paris), which he exhibited in 1877 at the third Impressionist exhibition. This small pastel adheres so little to standards of beauty that some of the press found it offensive, and it ended up in Caillebotte's collection. It also suspends any suspicion of banal voyeurism, through a sense of propriety that its artist would only ever abandon when dealing with brothel scenes. The model is treated entirely respectfully, despite the viewer's incursion. Even immodesty contains its opposite—the modesty of an accepted confrontation that was so familiar to Manet. His own bathing scene, probably painted in response to Degas, rejects any sense of "male dominance." Through just a glance, the model, who is difficult to identify, keeps us at a distance. Renoir did not trouble himself with these sorts of subtleties and scruples; he abandoned himself to his models' radiant beauty. The fact that the subject was not perceived at the time as inherently sexist is confirmed through Morisot's multiple images on the theme, treated with a grace that partly harks back to the eighteenth century. Her inclusion of cheval glasses adds a sensual element to her already charming paintings, pastels, and drawings. At the time of the posthumous retrospective of her work in 1896, the critic François Thiébault-Sisson summarized her output as "the poem of the modern woman, imagined and envisioned by a modern woman." Her daughter, Julie Manet, described one of her versions of the theme in that same year: "the beautifully modeled back lets the gown slip down; this woman is attending to her hair with a graceful gesture as she looks at her reflection in the [First] Empire cheval glass." Cassatt produced some similar images. S.G.

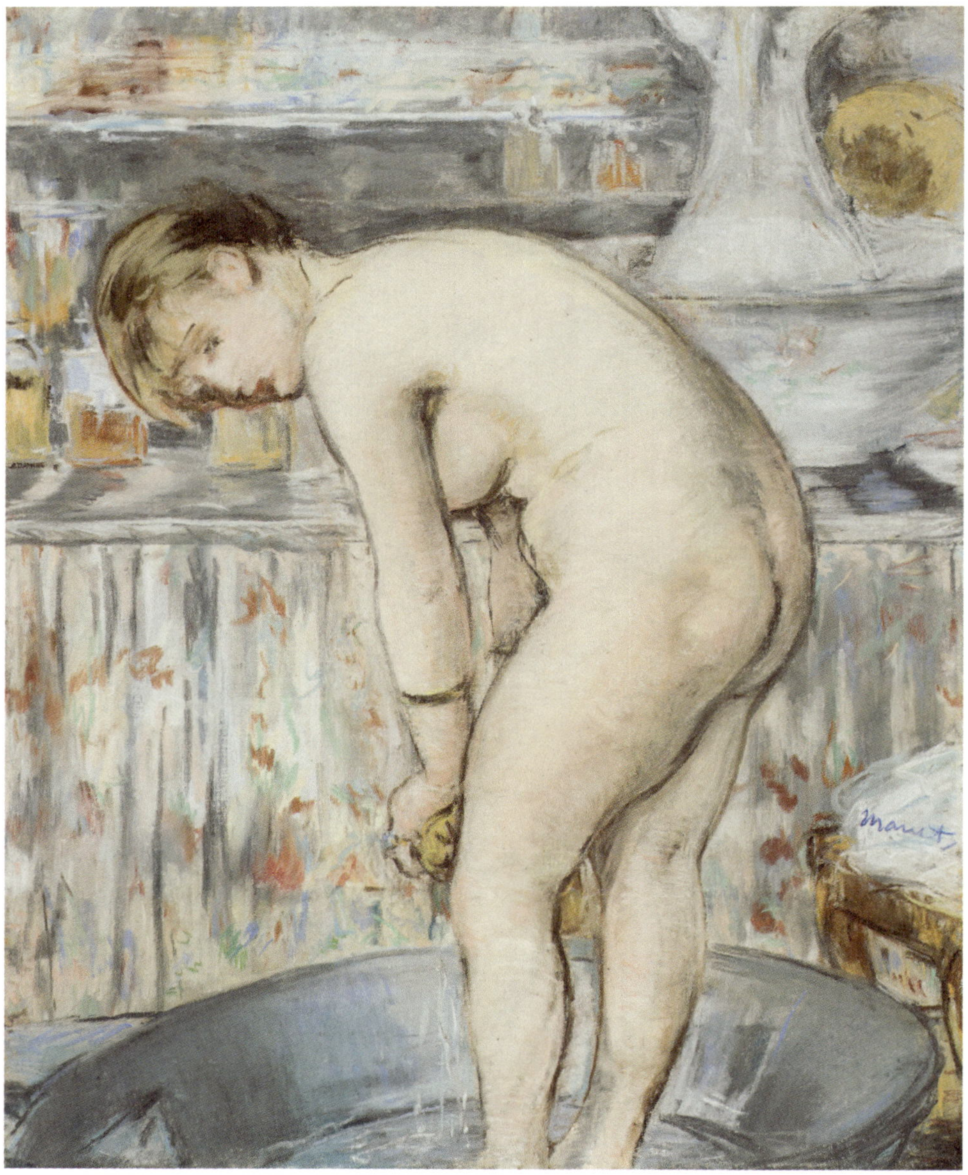

202 Édouard Manet, *Le Tub* (*The Tub*), 1878
Pastel on canvas, 21 ¼ × 17 ¹¹⁄₁₆ in. (54 × 45 cm)

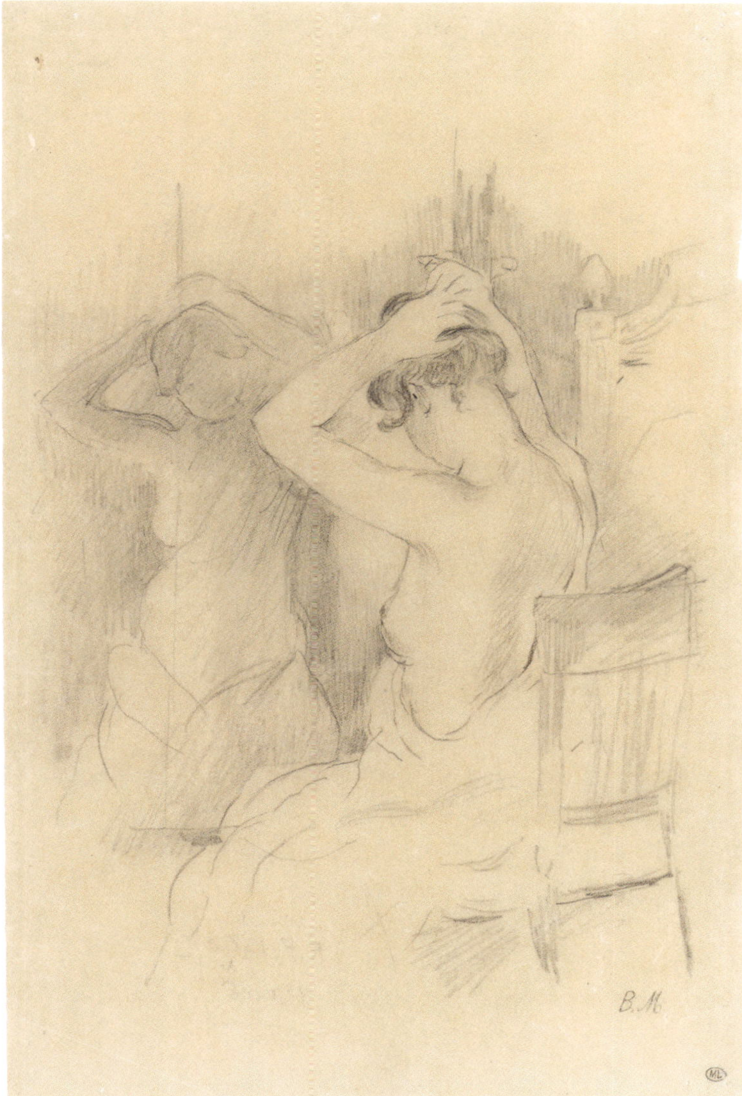

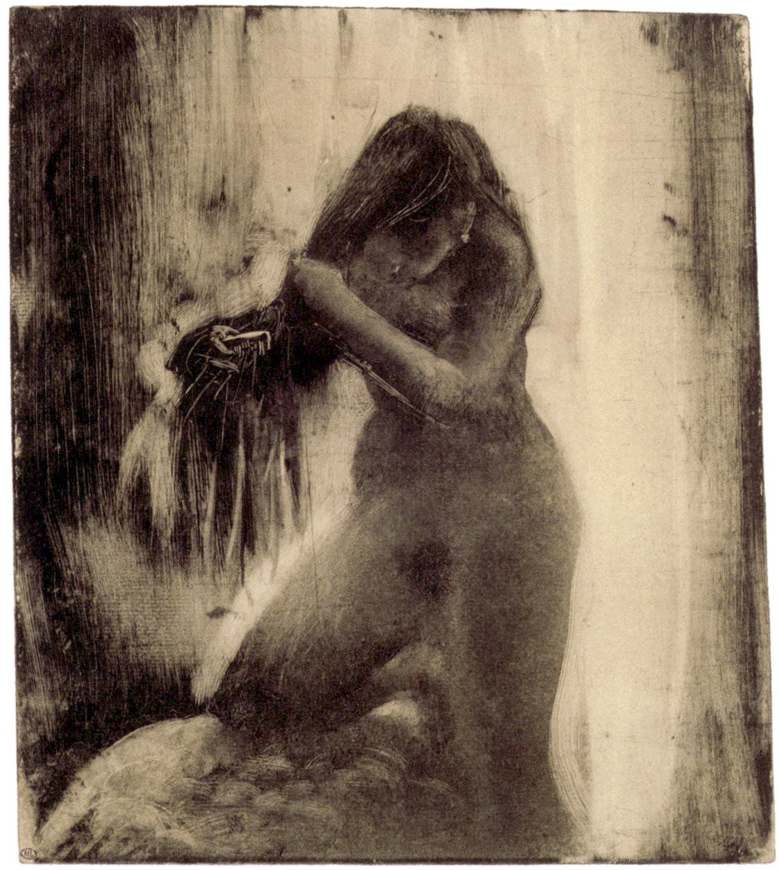

203 Left: Berthe Morisot, *Femme demie nue, vue de dos, se coiffant, une glace reflétant son corps* (*Half-Undressed Woman Seen from the Rear, Doing Her Hair, Her Body Reflected in a Mirror*), c. 1889–1890
Graphite on tracing paper, 12 × 8 ⅛ in. (30.5 × 20.7 cm)

204 Right: Edgar Degas, *Femme nue, se coiffant* (*Nude Woman Combing Her Hair*), 1879–1883
Black ink and monotype on cream paper, 12 ⅜ × 11 in. (31.5 × 28 cm)

Edgar Degas
Women at Their Toilet

Women's hair was victim to the decorum of the time. It was not generally permitted for a woman to be seen with her hair loose in public, other than in working-class contexts. Equally, when outdoors, a hat would keep the hair out of eyeshot. As the master of spontaneous or unsettling private moments, it is easy to understand why Degas so frequently constructed his images of modern women around manes of hair that were presented almost wildly to the viewer. We are never invited to revel in this forbidden space; Degas never portrayed these figures as being there for the purpose of our intrusion, comfortable to let us pore over them. On the contrary: their poses and the handling of the forms take on a certain brusqueness that explains why we react in such opposite ways to what we are seeing. Added to this ambiguity is the blurred quality typical of the monotype technique, more a feature of the printing than of the engraving process. The artist creates the image with printing ink on a metal plate, and is then limited in the number of pressings, the second print being considerably paler than the first. It was generally the second print that Degas would cover in pastel, to compensate for the lack of contrast. An admirer of Rembrandt, he could not imagine the world of boudoirs without the magical lighting that makes him the Northern master's equal. The background here evidences this, like a shadow play that drowns out the details of the young woman untangling her hair. The only thing we can distinguish is her teeth. Hair was a central subject in Degas's output, to the point that its fascinating and sometimes thunderous cascade dominates many of the scenes he depicts.   S.G.

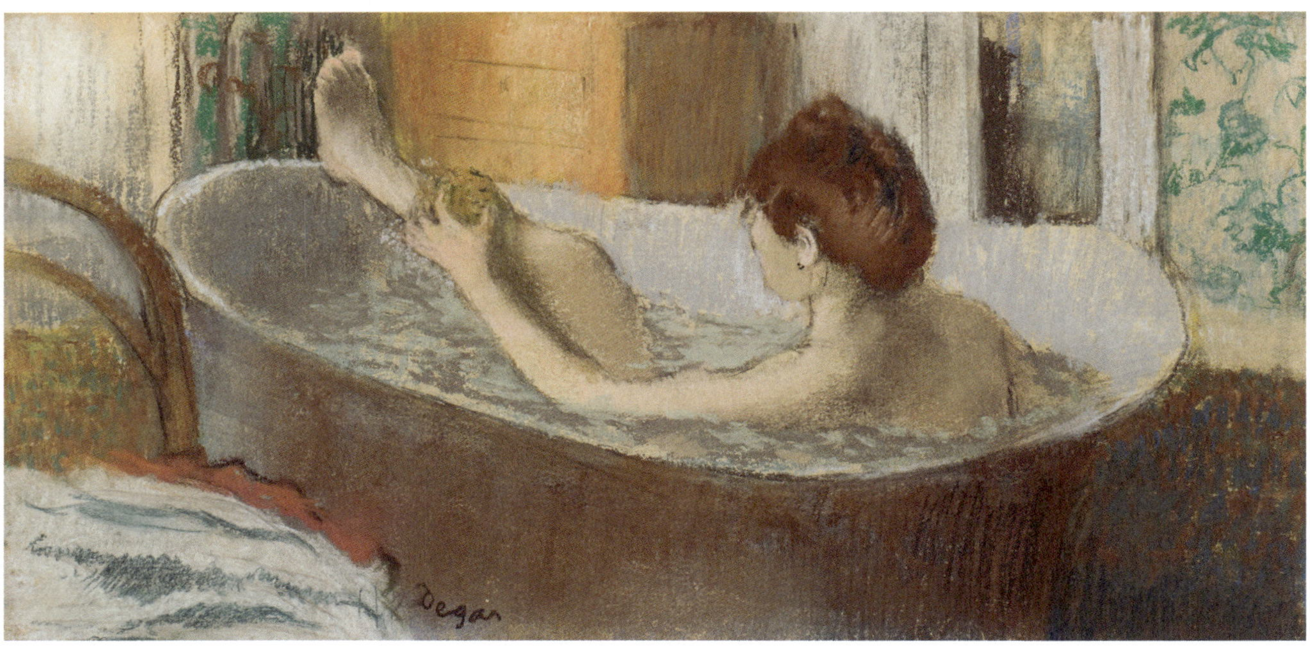

205 Edgar Degas, *Femme dans son bain s'épongeant la jambe (Woman in Her Bath, Sponging Down Her Leg)*, c. 1883
Pastel on monotype, 7 ¾ × 16 ⅛ in. (19.7 × 41 cm)

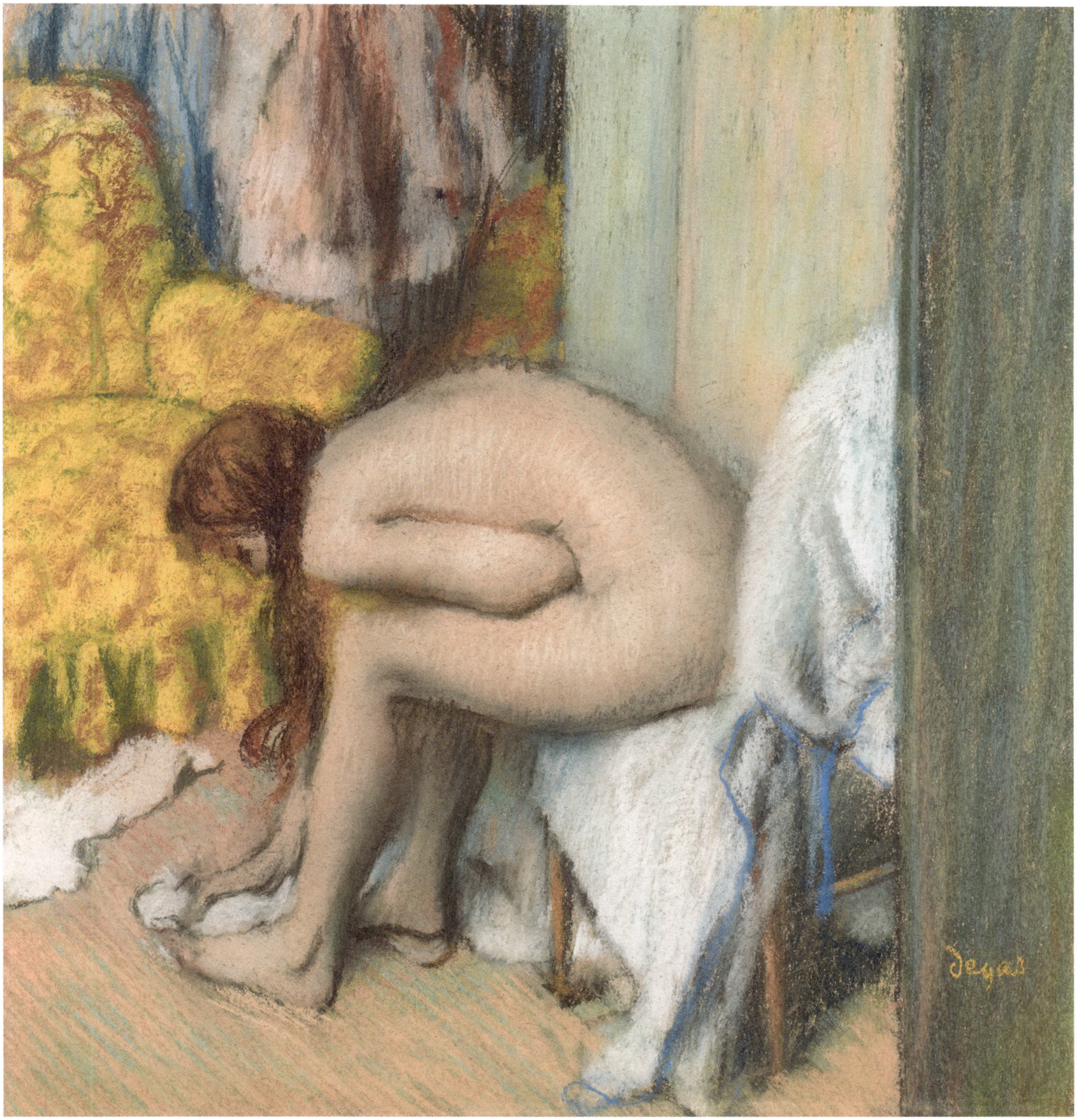

206 Edgar Degas, *Femme à sa toilette essuyant son pied gauche* (*Nude Wiping Her Left Foot*), 1886
Pastel on board, 21 ⅜ × 20 ⅝ in. (54.3 × 52.4 cm)

Edgar Degas
The Tub

Having studied in the wake of Ingres and been instilled with a love of ancient statuary, it was not long before Degas chose the female nude as one of his key sources of observation and imagination. This was not merely down to a fascination with studying the body itself, capturing its poses truthfully and accurately, and even the sense of the skin's warmth that the medium of pastel allows. The women he depicts are in their own personal worlds and engaged in various activities, all in socially or privately characterizable situations. Being less governed by petty moralism than the official Salons were, the Impressionist exhibitions allowed him to broach the subject of modern hygiene with a freedom that some commentators in 1877 found offensive, but which captivated the more emancipated collectors (such as Caillebotte). Less than a decade later, Degas's boldness knew no bounds: at the last group exhibition, in 1886, he showed a "series of female nudes bathing, washing, drying themselves, combing their hair, or having it combed." Of the ten pastels that made up this series, seven have been identified with near certainty; *The Tub* is one, and perhaps the most graceful. Echoes of the *Crouching Venus* (Musée du Louvre, Paris)—a Roman copy of a Greek original from the second century BCE that was discovered in France in the late 1820s—are certainly manifest here. A duality is created between sensual proximity and respectful distance, and the skewed perspective gives us the illusion of seeing through the insatiable artist's eyes. S. G.

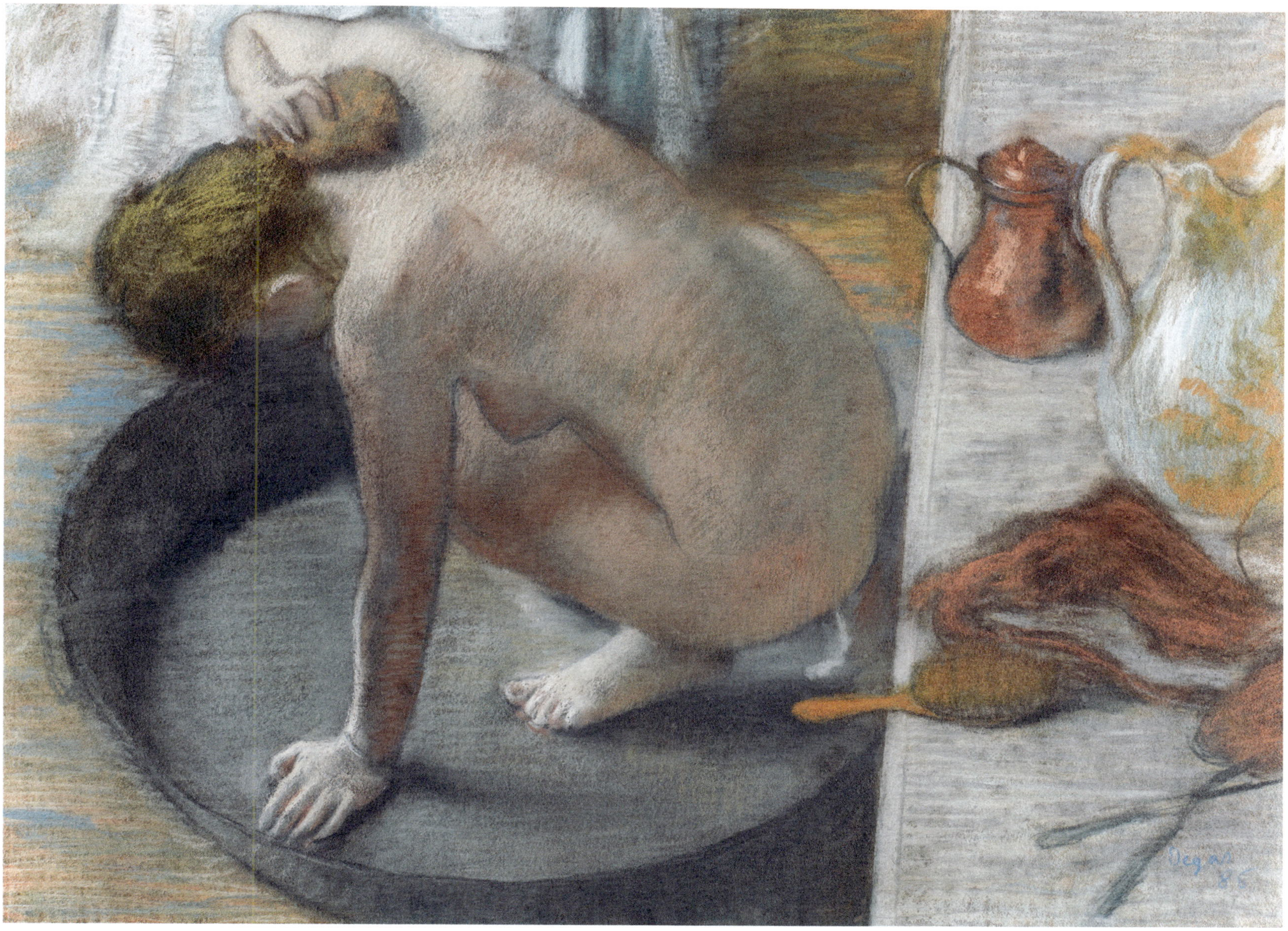

207 Edgar Degas, *Le Tub* (*The Tub*), 1886
Pastel on board, 23 ⅝ × 32 11⁄16 in. (60 × 83 cm)

Mary Cassatt
Woman and Child

Cassatt joined the Impressionists' ranks from the time of their fourth exhibition, in 1879, on Degas's invitation. In the following year, she started to address scenes of women and children, modernizing the Madonna and Child archetype by introducing a new, unconventional view of early childhood and of the relationship between women and children. She produced sketches from life recording the intimacy and physical contact between nurse, mother, grandmother, and child, although the exact relationship between the figures is not always clear. She favored pastel for its sensual, velvety qualities, its almost pure pigments being ideal to represent flesh and its subtle nuances. This technique also allowed her to work quickly, and to capture her young models' expressions as accurately as possible.

In this pastel, the pensive woman is holding a little child with a dreamy expression on its face. She clasps the child to her bosom, cheek to cheek, in a gesture that is tender but also firm and protective. The woman's braced arm contrasts with the child's chubby legs, which Cassatt emphasizes through black outlines, while the skin's silky-smoothness is suggested by a web of crosshatching and white and blue zigzags against a pink ground.

The pastel's first owner was Henri Rouart. Like Cassatt, he was close to Degas and had exhibited regularly with the Impressionists, although his works were outshone by theirs. C.C.-P.

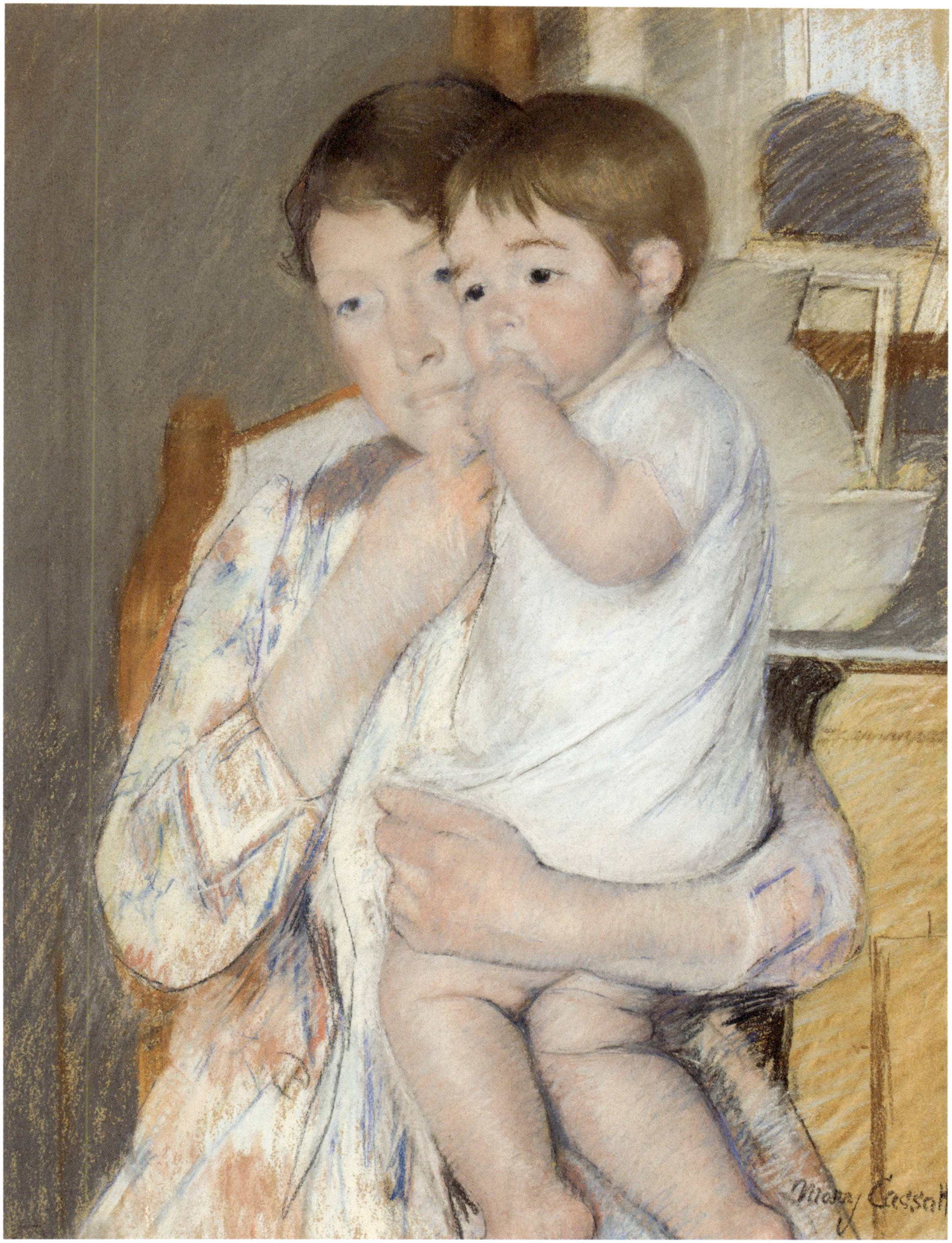

208 Mary Cassatt, *Femme et enfant devant une tablette où sont posés un broc et une cuvette* (*Woman and Child in Front of a Small Table Bearing a Wash Basin and Pitcher*), 1889
Pastel on beige paper mounted on canvas, 25 9⁄16 × 19 11⁄16 in. (65 × 50 cm)

Camille Pissarro
Woman with a Green Scarf

Pissarro painted this headscarfed woman during the winter of 1892–1893, at his home in Éragny-sur-Epte where he had been living for almost ten years. Diffuse light coming from high up in the room caresses the wallpaper, making the patterns dance; it also gives the model's face a golden glow, and she seems to turn away from it, dazzled. Although Pissarro focused mainly on landscapes, at Éragny in the 1880s he also painted large single figures: countryfolk either going about their tasks or resting. However, the woman he had pose for this work was different: at the time he had access to "a model who doesn't really look the type, but with the help of a headscarf ... she could be made into a countrywoman," he wrote to his son on November 20, 1892. The tight framing emphasizes the woman's graceful posture and gentle gesture. With its vibrant, rhythmic brushwork (recalling the artist's neo-Impressionist technique, developed a few years earlier) and thick surface, the painting seems to quiver in the raking light. This rich impasto was not unanimously well received. The art dealer Paul Durand-Ruel, who saw the painting shortly after its completion, found the woman's hand "too obviously flaked!"[37] Nevertheless, in February 1893 he did put it on show in his gallery, where it was bought by Cassatt, known as an eminent painter of female figures, and also a keen-eyed collector. A.R.

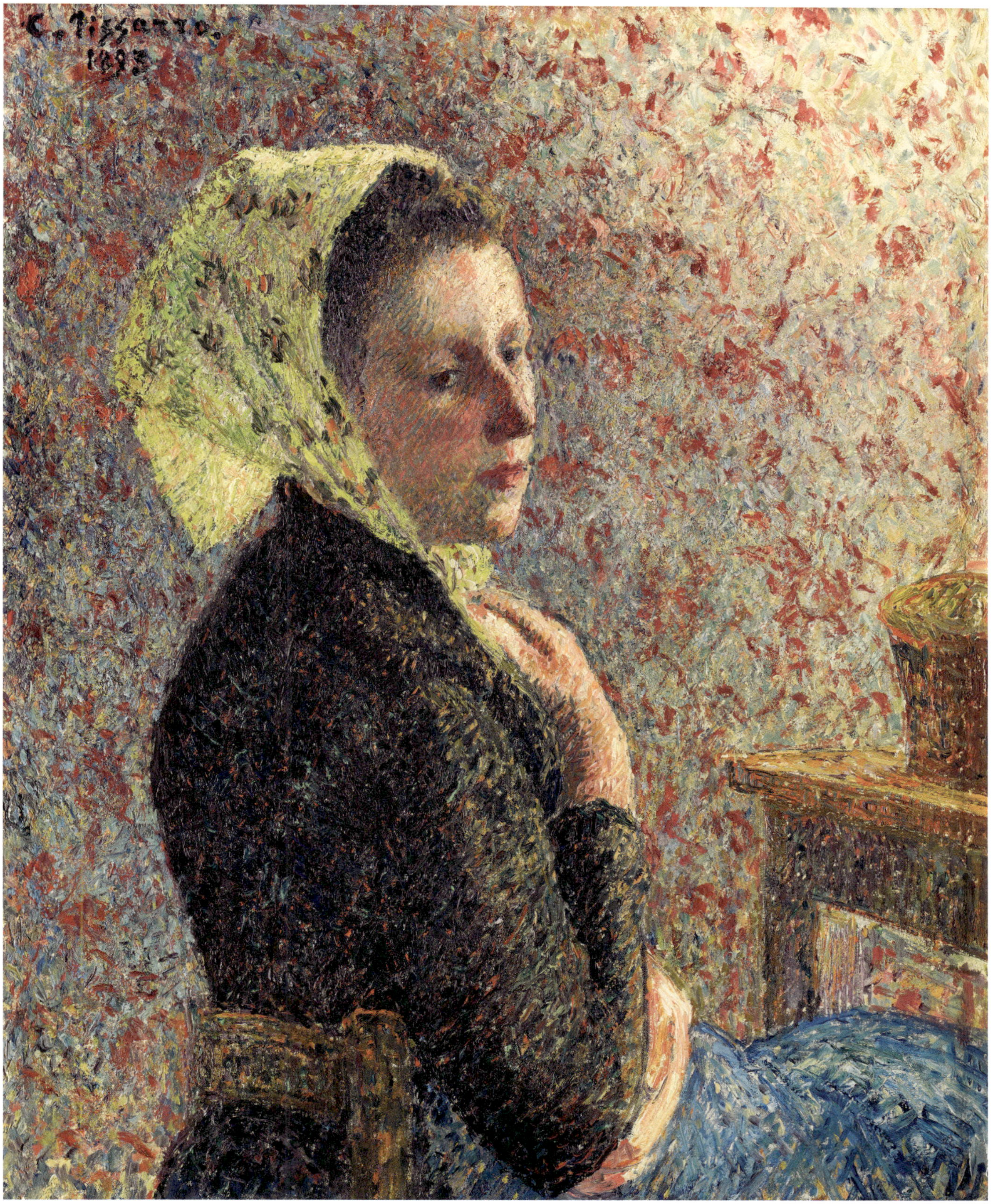

209 Camille Pissarro, *Femme au fichu vert* (*Woman with a Green Scarf*), 1893
Oil on canvas, 25 13/16 × 21 7/16 in. (65.5 × 54.5 cm)

Berthe Morisot
The Hydrangea

The Hydrangea is a fine example of Morisot's work as she approached the end of her life: she died suddenly just a few months after its completion. It is sometimes called *The Two Sisters*, underlining the family relationship between the two models, whom we know only by their forenames—Marthe and Jeanne-Marie—and their appearances in other paintings by Morisot from this period. They are presented face-on, in a private scene: the blonde girl, wearing a house dress, is putting up her sister's intense black hair. The latter sister's pink, shawl-collared gown may indicate that she is getting ready to go out.

Like Renoir in this period (p. 231), Morisot plays with the contrast between dark and blonde hair, and between cold colors and warmer golden yellows, applied with a very nimble brush. The combination of young women and flowers (no doubt the blonde-haired girl is attaching one in her sister's hair), and the prominence accorded to the potted hydrangea—a very fashionable flower in the 1890s, with blue ones the most on-trend of all according to the press of the time—which also references beauty, harmony, and a certain coldness or even chastity, all give this work a *fin-de-siècle*, Symbolist dimension. In the early 1890s, Morisot's painting changed course: atmospheres of suggestion and mystery rather than impression and immediacy (p. 213), and fluid brushwork rather than rapidity and fragmentation, evoke the Norwegian painter Edvard Munch's treatment of some interiors with figures around the same time. S. P.

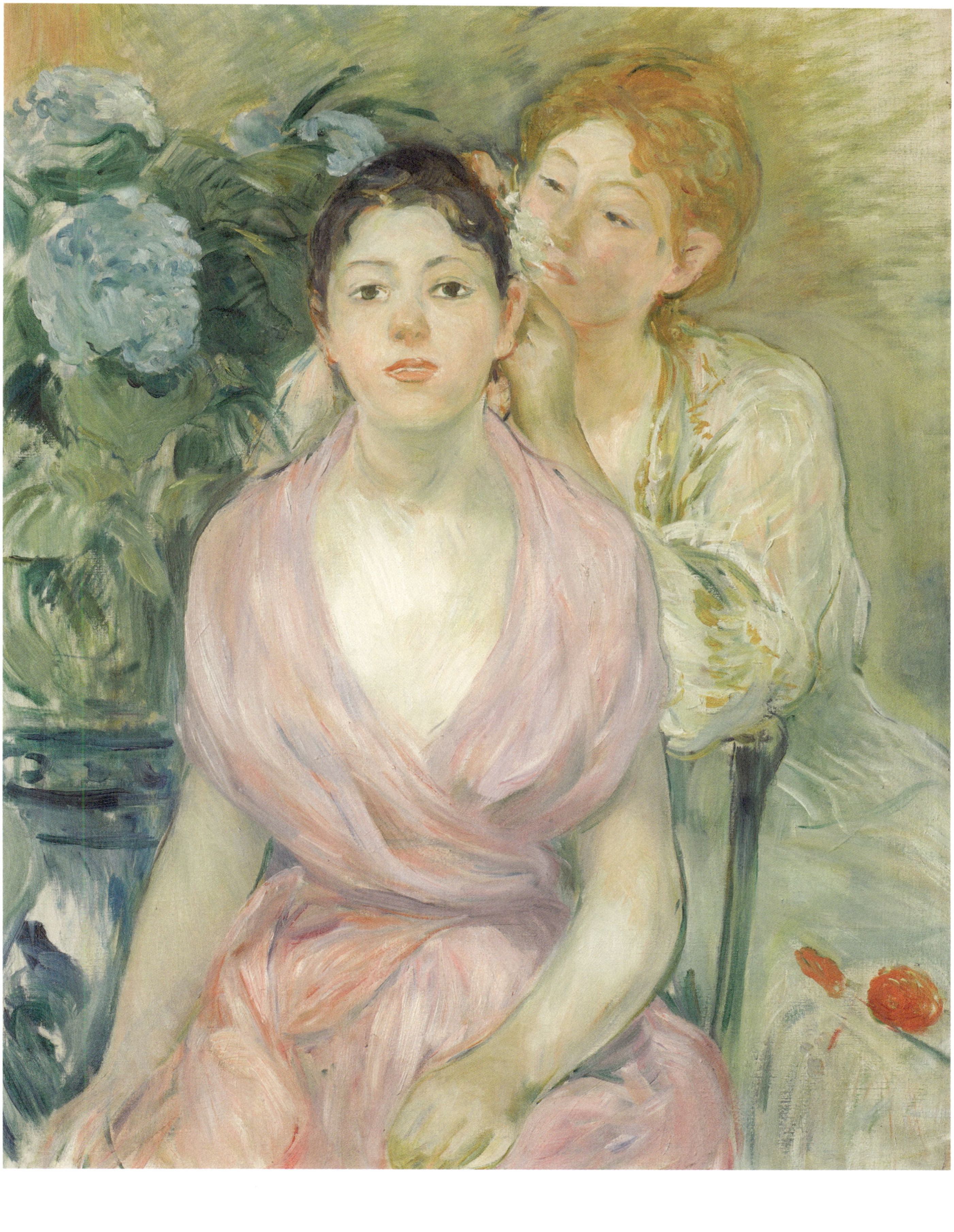

210 Berthe Morisot, *L'Hortensia* (*The Hydrangea*), 1894
Oil on canvas, 28 ¾ × 23 ¾ in. (73.1 × 60.4 cm)

1892

The State's first purchase from Renoir

Up to the 1890s, Sisley was the only Impressionist to have had a work of his bought by the State: *September Morning* (c. 1887–1888), in 1888. But that painting was promptly deposited in the Musée des Beaux-Arts in the city of Agen, where it remains to this day, and never reached the walls of Paris's prestigious Musée du Luxembourg, which was then devoted to contemporary art. Change came in 1892 following the appointment of Henry Roujon as new national Director of Fine Arts. His friend Mallarmé (who was also close to the Impressionists) convinced him to visit Monet and Renoir to buy a work from them, thus making up for the years of indifference and even hostility that the public authorities had displayed toward the Impressionists. Renoir, who was then in his fifties, prepared a new composition specially for the occasion: *Young Girls at the Piano*.

With its two girls playing music in a bourgeois interior, the picture is an ode to the beauty and lightheartedness of youth, to a sort of decorative opulence, and to the arts in general. The artist's palette is bright, dominated by contrasts between warm and cold pastel tones, which are blended into one another with a very soft brush. After his "Ingresque" works of much of the 1880s, Renoir "permanently reverted to [his] earlier soft, light style of painting," as he wrote in a letter to Durand-Ruel in November 1888. More dissatisfied and indecisive than ever, he worked relentlessly and produced several different versions, finally presenting this one to Roujon, who bought it for 4,000 francs, against the advice of the national museums' curators.

The painting was put on show at the Musée du Luxembourg at the end of the year; it was the first Impressionist work to be displayed there. In 1894, again thanks to Mallarmé, the State bought a painting by Morisot—*Young Woman in a Ball Gown* (p.177)—from the Théodore Duret sale. P.P.

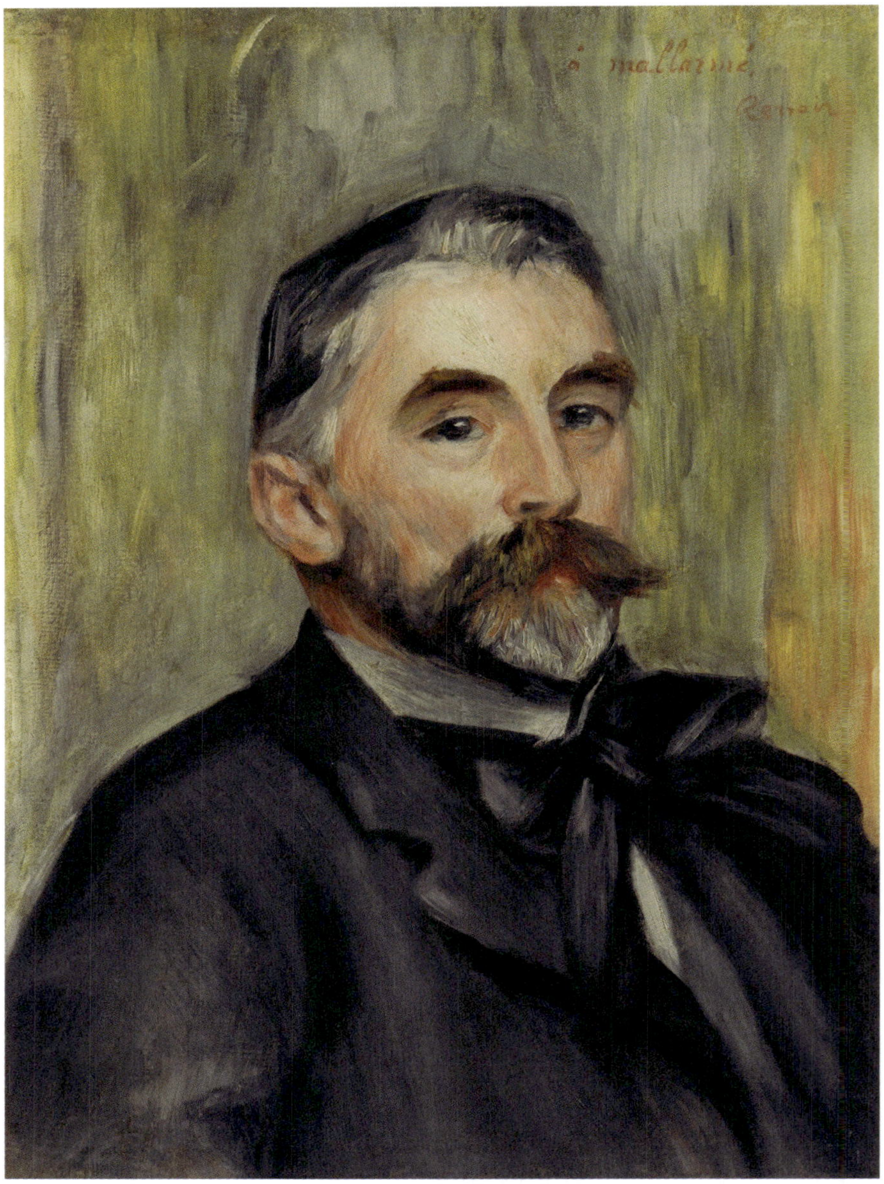

211 Auguste Renoir, *Portrait de Stéphane Mallarmé* (*Portrait of Stéphane Mallarmé*), 1892
Oil on canvas, 19 11⁄16 × 15 ¾ in. (50 × 40 cm)

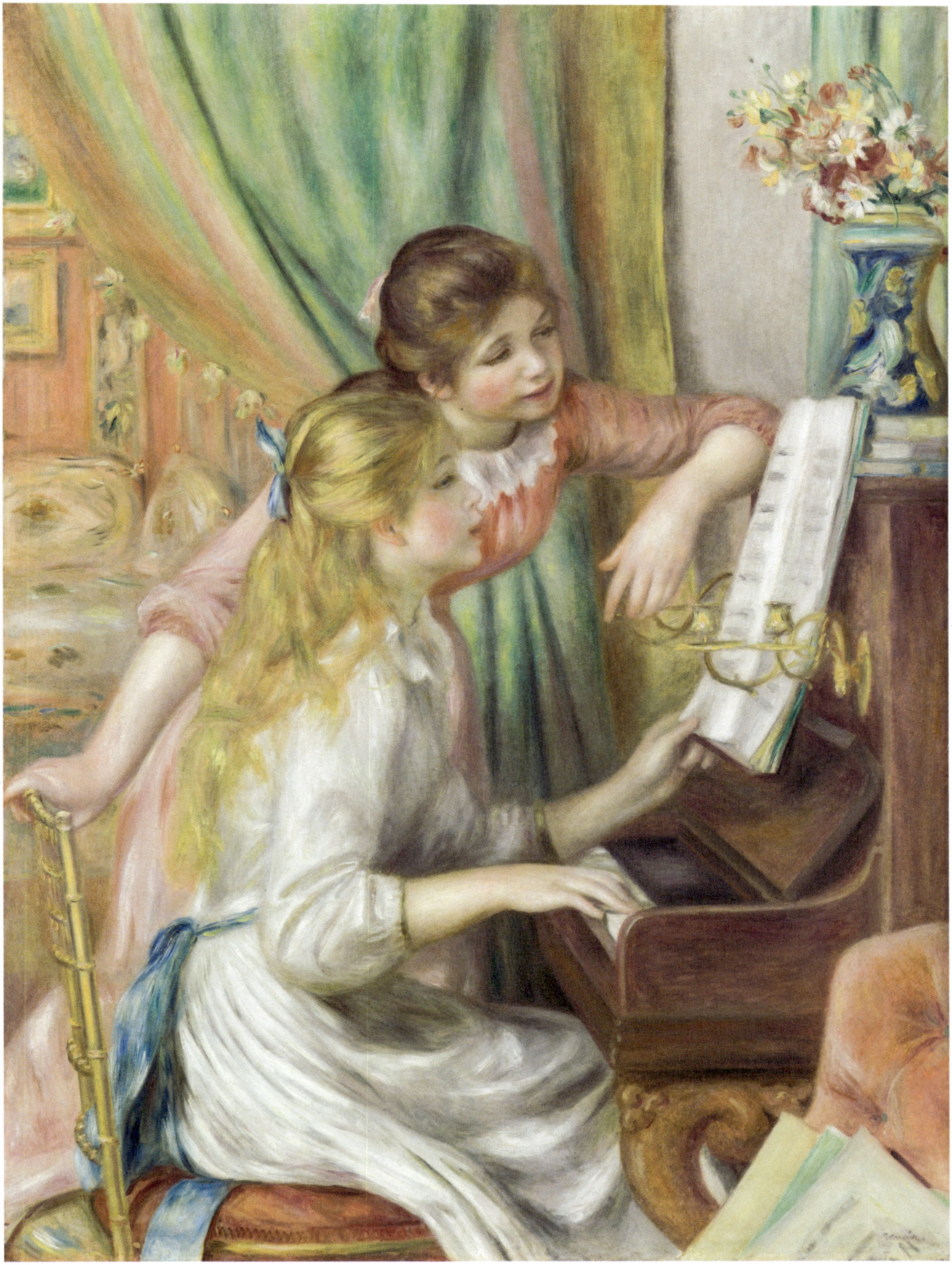

212 Auguste Renoir, *Jeunes filles au piano* (*Young Girls at the Piano*), 1892
Oil on canvas, 45 11⁄16 × 35 7⁄16 in. (116 × 90 cm)

Paul Cézanne
The Cardplayers

Having definitively moved back to the city where he was born, Aix-en-Provence, in the fall of 1890, Cézanne worked on several paintings of cardplayers, no doubt inspired by a work on the same subject that he had seen in the city's museum. He made numerous preparatory sketches, in pencil and watercolor or in oil on canvas, and completed five paintings in a range of formats, featuring between two and five figures. This canvas is one of three compositions that show only two cardplayers, facing each other across a table. A bottle standing between them catches the light, creating a pale line that reinforces the impression of a face-off between rivals, each absorbed in his game. Cézanne had agricultural workers from the Jas de Bouffan estate pose for the painting, no doubt in the farm on the property. After their day's work, they would entertain themselves by playing cards. Cézanne paid the man on the right, Paulin Paulet, five francs to pose for him. For each of his canvases on this theme, he sketched the models separately before bringing them together on the canvas itself, hence the feeling of isolation that each figure exudes. This restrained composition, stripped of any unnecessary detail, focuses our attention on the silent confrontation between the two men and their humble nobleness. The critic Roger Fry observed that the figures have "the gravity, the reserve and the weighty solemnity of some monument of antiquity," unequalled since the "Italian Primitives," and that "this little café becomes for us ... an epic scene...."[38] A.R.

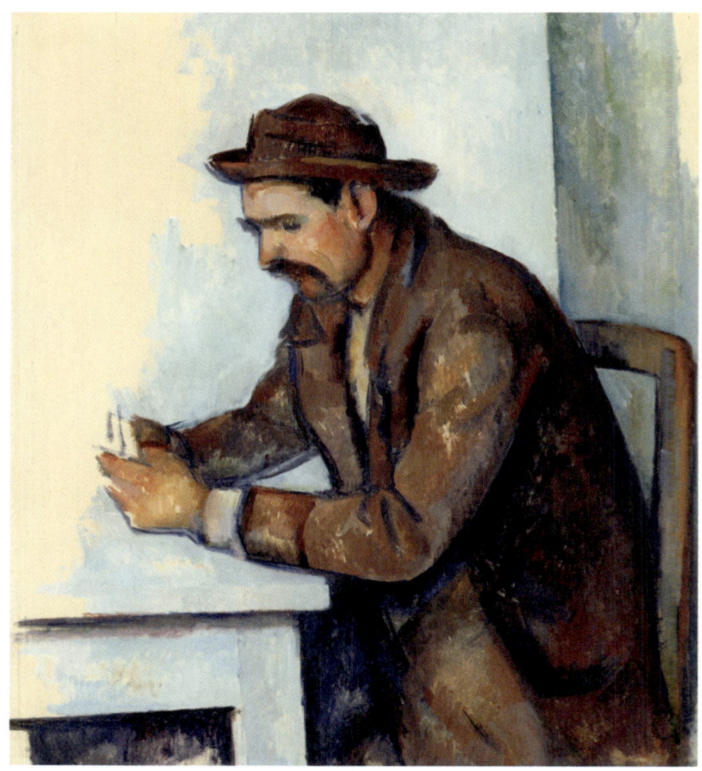

213 Paul Cézanne, *Le Joueur de cartes* (*The Cardplayer*), 1890–1892
Oil on canvas, 19 11⁄16 × 18 1⁄8 in. (50 × 46 cm)

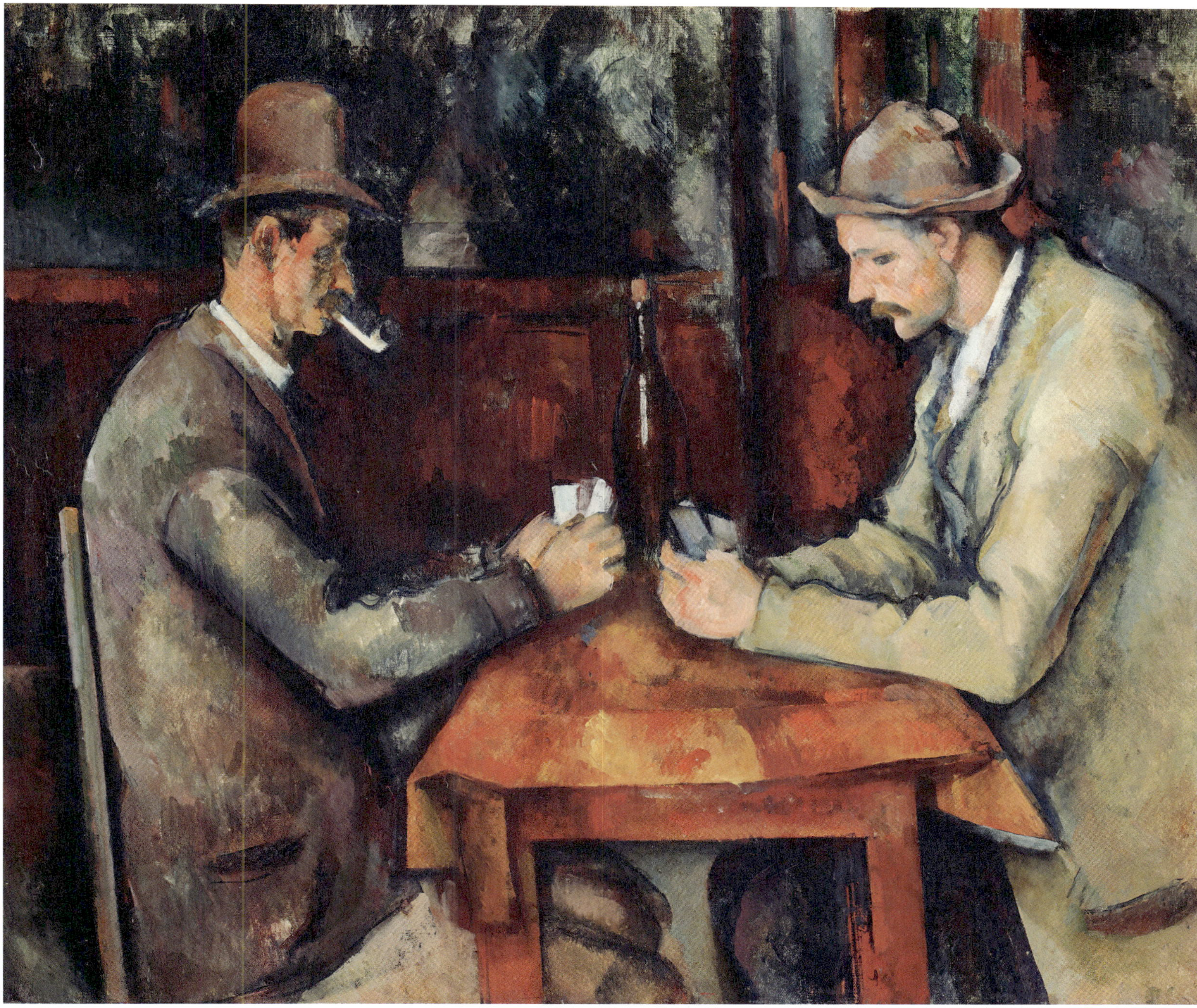

214 Paul Cézanne, *Les Joueurs de cartes* (*The Cardplayers*), 1893–1896
Oil on canvas, 18 ½ × 22 ¼ in. (47 × 56.5 cm)

Paul Cézanne
Woman with a Coffeepot

This woman's identity remains a mystery. She could perhaps be Madame Brémond—one of the Cézanne family's domestic employees at the Jas de Bouffan—or a cook whose name is now forgotten. Similarly to his portraits of agricultural laborers and nearby sharecroppers, Cézanne shows her at rest, but her "rough-hewn" face bears the marks of effort, and her sturdy hands speak of a life of labor. Although she is seated, she seems to loom up in front of us, "as solid as a mighty tower," ready to get back to work. Only the broken fold of her coutil dress, marking her bent knee, indicates that she is sitting. Just as Cézanne "lifts up" his landscapes to place them in front of us, parallel to the canvas, here he confronts us with this woman by straightening her out—an impression that is emphasized by the strong verticals of the selvage down the front of her dress, along with the straight lines of the coffeepot. Even the spoon standing in the cup points straight upward, echoing the geometry of the doors in the background. The woman has an inscrutable expression; rather than conveying the model's psychology, Cézanne analyses her relationship with the space around her. Her austere, imposing look gives her an extremely strong presence, like a Renaissance sculpture. The light sculpts the forms and builds up the figure's volumes. It creates a vibration of changing, transparent colors, especially on the skirt and the doors, as if being filtered through a stained-glass window. A.R.

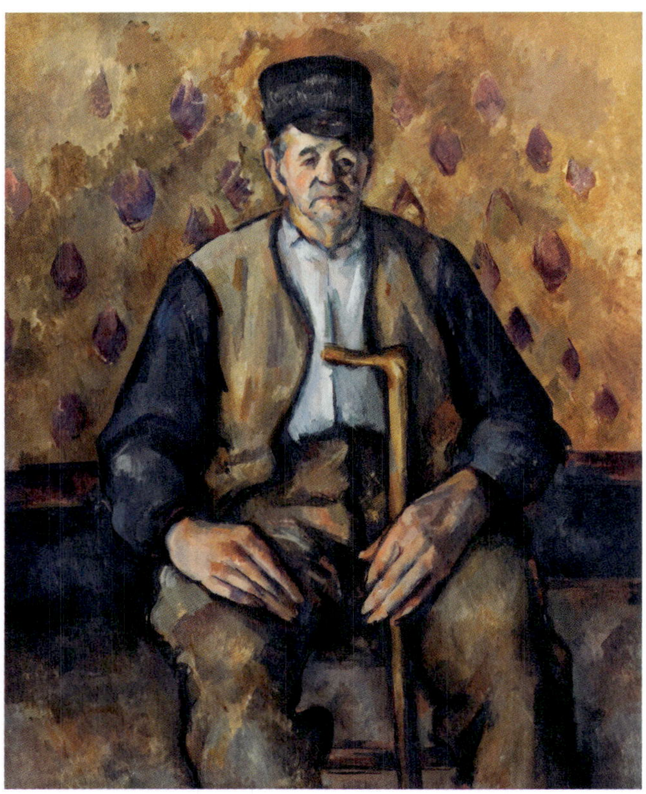

215 Paul Cézanne, *Paysan assis (Seated Peasant)*, c. 1900
Oil on canvas, 28 ⅞ × 23 ¾ in. (73.3 × 60.3 cm)

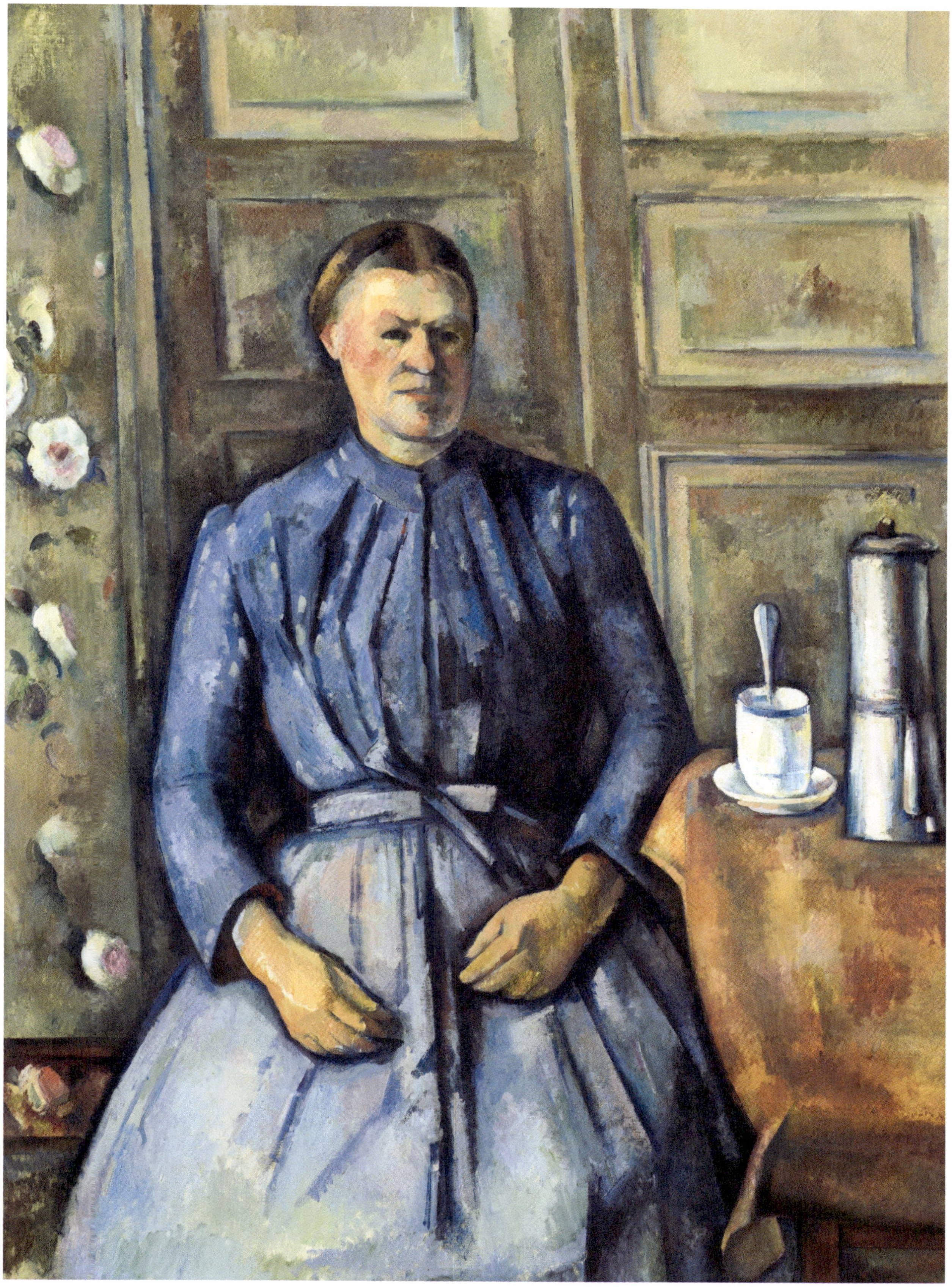

216 Paul Cézanne, *La Femme à la cafetière* (*Woman with a Coffeepot*), c. 1895
Oil on canvas, 51 ³⁄₁₆ × 38 ³⁄₁₆ in. (130 × 97 cm)

Bathers

"Bathers" started to appear at the Salon in the mid-nineteenth century, and met with resounding success. They allowed artists to paint large-scale nudes without resorting to mythological or historical pretexts. Some of them—such as the one in Manet's *Le Déjeuner sur l'herbe*, which at the time was titled *Bathing* (p. 15)—caused a scandal, but the subject gradually became a firm favorite, and more and more examples of it were painted. The Impressionists seized upon it—first Bazille and then Renoir, Degas, and Cézanne. They painted groups of male or female bathers, bathing scenes set in the countryside, the public baths along the banks of the Seine, and women at their toilet in the privacy of their homes. Relating simultaneously to the modern world of hygiene and leisure, and to the great tradition of the nude since Greco-Roman antiquity, the theme allowed artists to cleverly combine references to the past with social commentary on their own era.

It was with a painting on this subject that Seurat burst onto the artistic scene at the Salon des Indépendants in 1884 as a new talent to watch, with *Bathers at Asnières* (1884; National Gallery, London), which shows working-class people enjoying leisure time in suburban Paris. The subject is typical of the Impressionists, but Seurat uses his pointillist technique of dividing colors, and simplifies the figures' forms in a manner reminiscent of Pierre Puvis de Chavannes. In Pissarro's case, the theme is situated in a more rural context. This is no longer the Seine, with its pleasure boats and barges passing the bathers at close quarters, but a small watercourse in the countryside. At the center of the image is a nude with her back to us, whose pose recalls both classical statuary and figures from Ingres. Lastly, in a late pastel, Degas flouts all conventions on composition and perspective. The theme was not a pretext for him to paint graceful, poised nudes. Quite the opposite: he liked to show bodies in motion, in strange poses, and from novel viewpoints.   P. P.

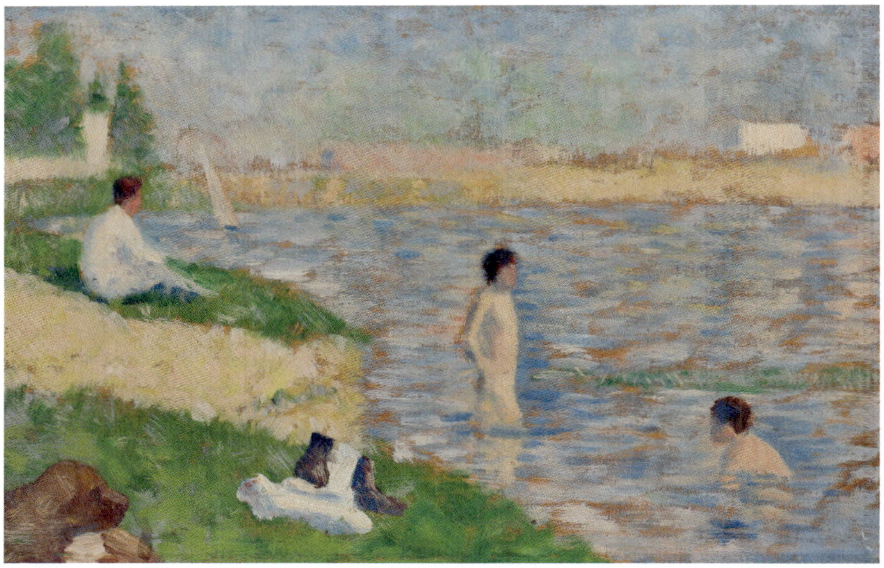

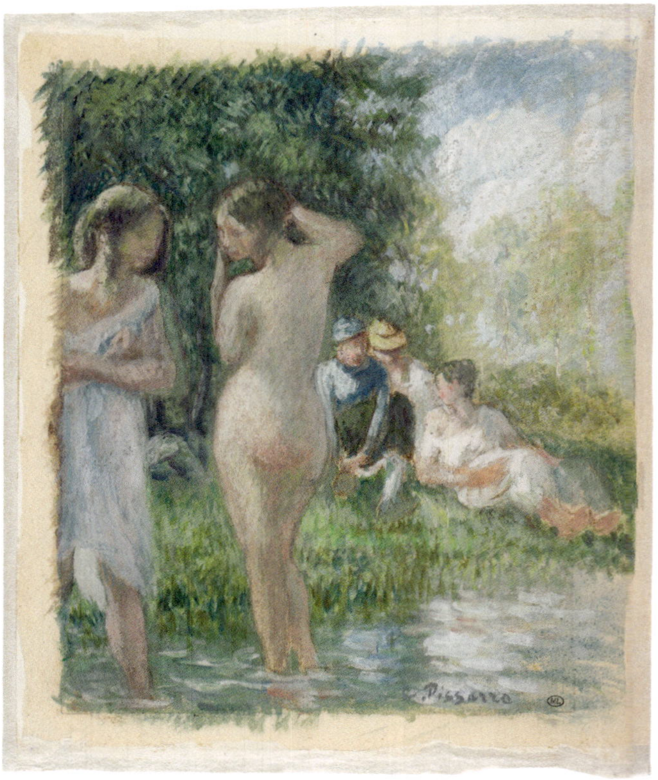

217 Left: Georges Seurat, Study for *Une baignade à Asnières (Bathers at Asnières)*, 1883
Oil on wood, 6 ⅛ × 9 ¹³⁄₁₆ in. (15.5 × 25 cm)

218 Right: Camille Pissarro, *Baigneuses au bord de l'eau (Bathers at the Water's Edge)*, 1894–1896
Gouache on silk, 10 ¹⁄₁₆ × 8 ⁹⁄₁₆ in. (25.6 × 21.7 cm)

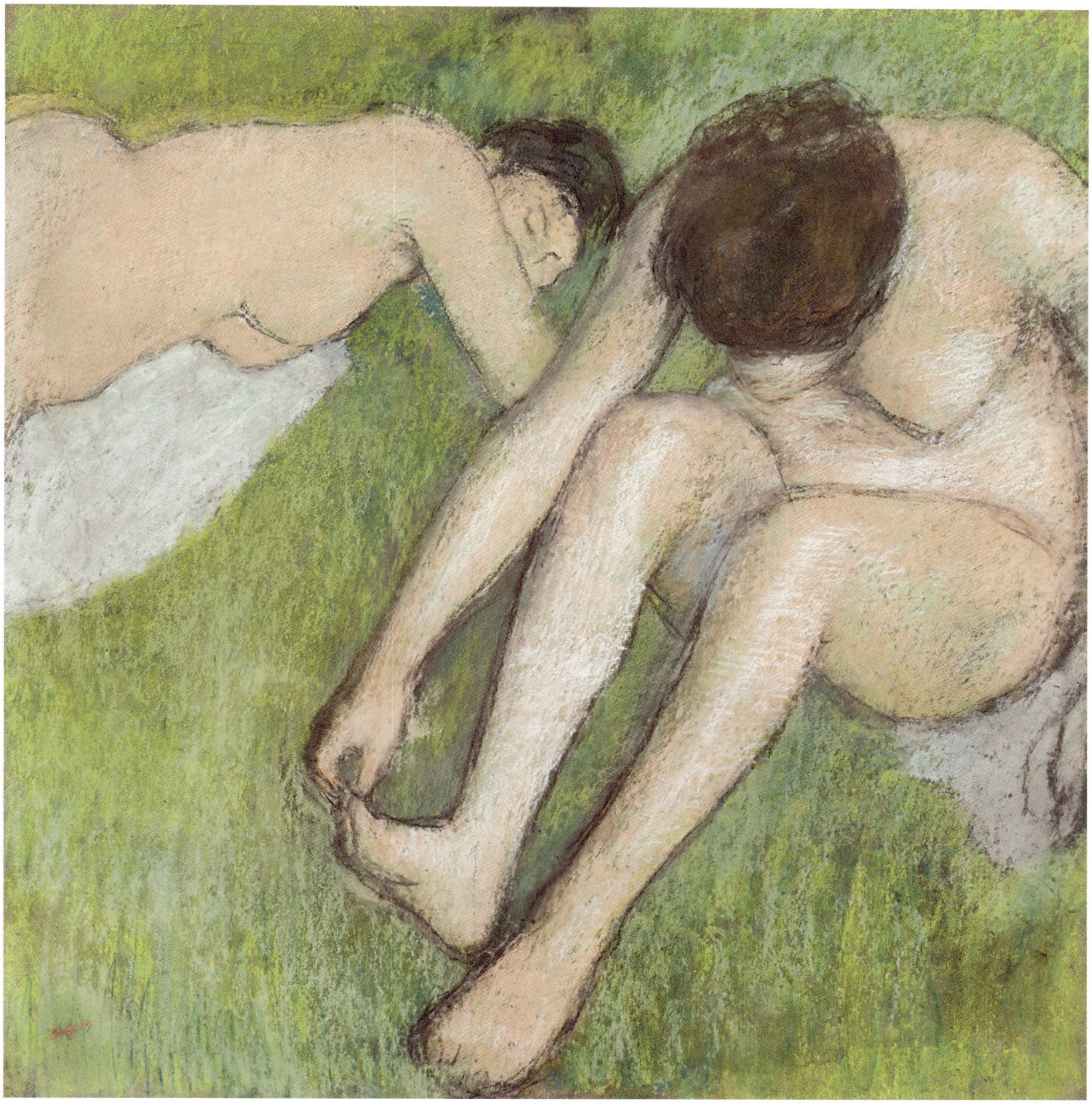

219 Edgar Degas, *Deux baigneuses sur l'herbe*
(*Two Bathers on the Grass*), 1886–1890
Pastel on brown paper, 27 $\frac{9}{16}$ × 27 $\frac{9}{16}$ in. (70 × 70 cm)

Paul Cézanne
Bathers

Nude bathers depicted on a riverbank became a major theme in Cézanne's work from the 1870s onward, culminating in large-scale works such as *Bathers at Rest* (1876–1877; The Barnes Foundation, Philadelphia), which was presented in 1877 at the third Impressionist exhibition (p. 132), and the three versions of *Large Bathers* (1894–1906). Chromatic variations on these highly structured compositions can be found in multiple sketches and small oils that vary the number and poses of the figures. Seven of these are held at the Musée d'Orsay.

The almost square format of *Three Bathers* demonstrates the attention paid by Cézanne to its composition: geometric, constructed through the straight lines in the landscape and the dynamic forms of the bodies. The figures' outstretched arms recall those of the *Bather and Rocks* (c. 1862–1869; Chrysler Museum of Art, Norfolk, Virginia) that he painted at the Jas de Bouffan, and of Courbet's *The Bathers* (1853; Musée Fabre, Montpellier), a copy of which Cézanne kept in his studio. However, what is striking about Cézanne's nudes is not any excessive realism, but instead the impasto and the bodies' unrealistic proportions: the woman on the right is contained within a perfect circle. Although the theme harks back to chaste depictions of Venus or the iconography of a woman surreptitiously caught bathing, Cézanne avoids any suggestion of narrative, so as to foreground the nude as a purely pictorial concern. This radicalism in his treatment of bathers appealed to other artists: Émile Bernard painted dozens of works on the same theme (including *Bathers with Water Lilies*, 1889; Musée d'Orsay, Paris), while Henri Matisse and then Pablo Picasso each acquired a version.

The group of figures in *Bathers*, one of the most finished versions, forms a frieze contained within an oval, enlivened by the sinuous or angular lines of the bodies. The one holding the piece of cloth may be a reference to a drawing by Luca Signorelli, of which Cézanne owned a reproduction. Conversely, *Five Bathers* shows the livelier brushwork that the artist developed at the end of his life. Painting without models, he relied on his imagination when working on these little Arcadias that are so full of freedom, light, and air. J.-R. T.

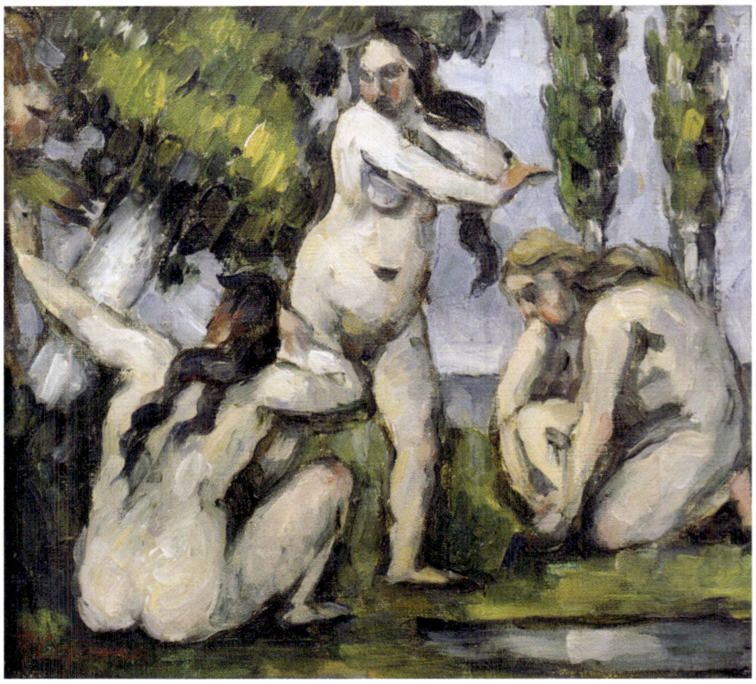

220 Paul Cézanne, *Trois baigneuses* (*Three Bathers*), c. 1874–1875
Oil on canvas, 7 11⁄16 × 8 7⁄8 in. (19.5 × 22.5 cm)

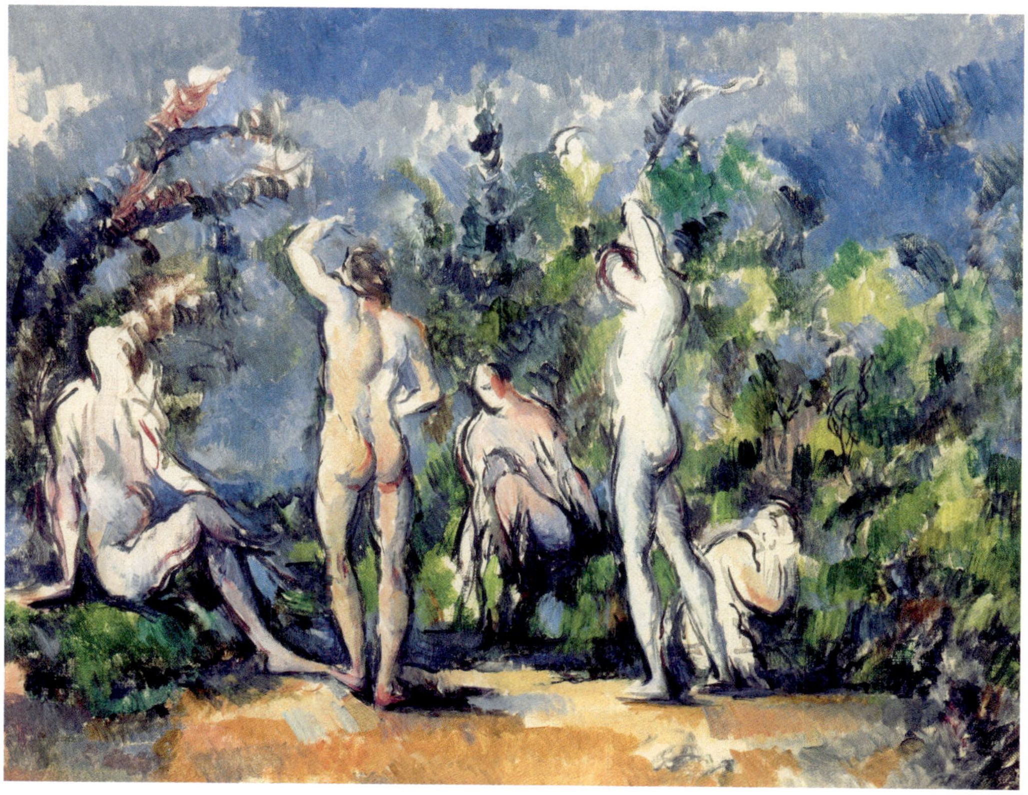

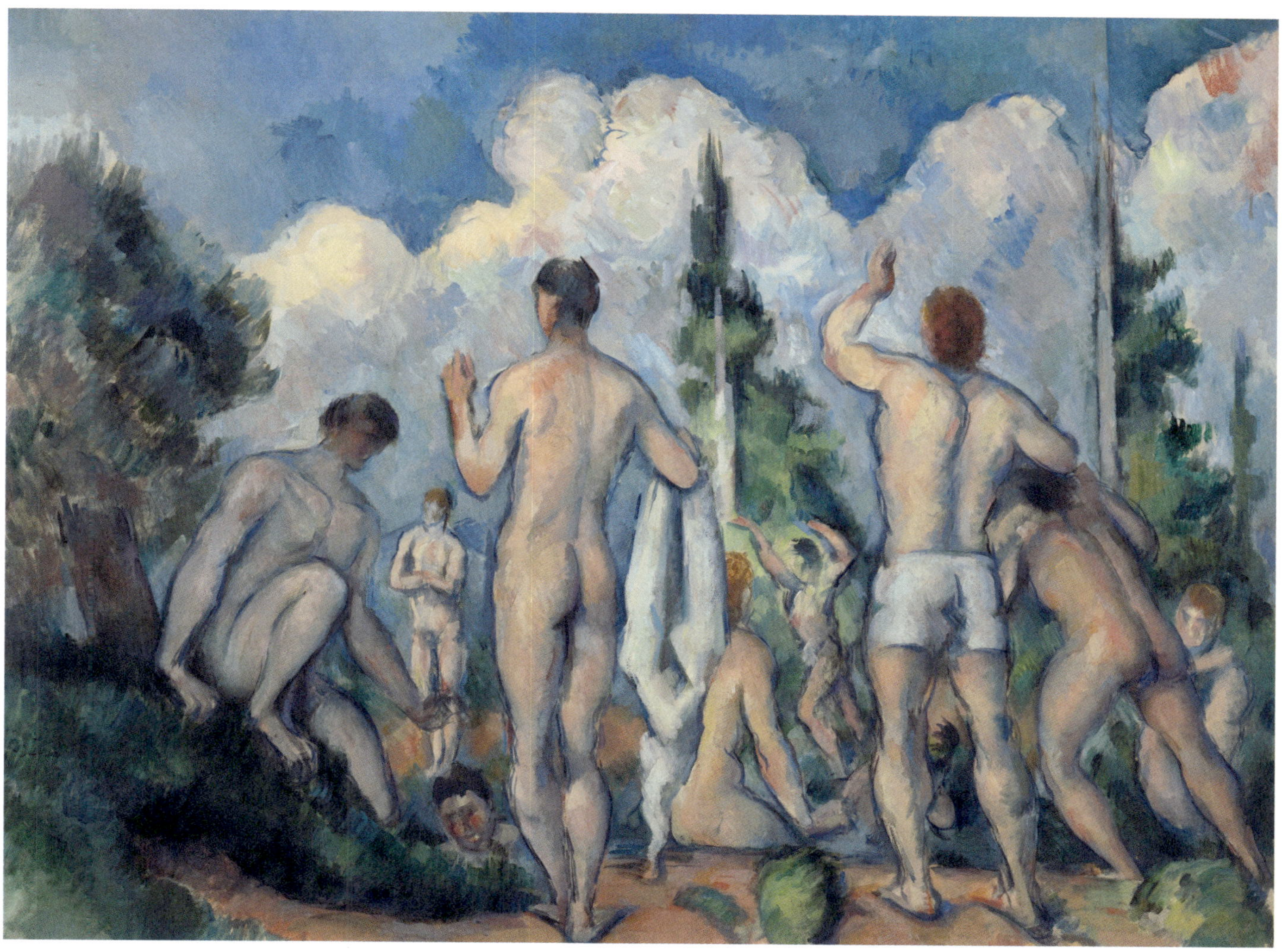

221 Top: Paul Cézanne, *Cinq baigneurs* (*Five Bathers*), between 1900 and 1904
Oil on canvas, 16 9⁄16 × 21 5⁄8 in. (42 × 55 cm)

222 Bottom: Paul Cézanne, *Baigneurs* (*Bathers*), c. 1890
Oil on canvas, 23 13⁄16 × 32 ½ in. (60.5 × 82.5 cm)

Paul Cézanne
Mont Sainte-Victoire

Over almost thirty years (1878–1906), Cézanne tirelessly painted the Mont Sainte-Victoire that looms up behind Aix-en-Provence, his birthplace. Whether working in oil or watercolor, he adopted a new viewpoint and new composition every time, sometimes changing position by only a few feet. The versions from the 1880s, when he was developing a so-called "classical" style, form calm, structured panoramas—perhaps sometimes slightly buffeted by the mistral. Cézanne nonetheless gradually asserted the predominance of colored brushwork until, after 1900, he was producing powerfully lyrical works in which the apparent unfinishedness and the depth of the blues destabilize representation. The watercolors held at the Musée d'Orsay show that Cézanne painted the mountain both from a distance, combining it with man-made structures, and at close range, focusing on its rocky summit and reinforcing the work's abstract dimension.

Mont Sainte-Victoire is clearly part of a group that was painted from Bellevue, the property of Cézanne's sister; in the foreground is what appears to be one of its parapets. The lush greenery, rendered with long brushstrokes, opens out into a V shape, beyond which the plain of the Arc river is scattered with miniature houses that melt into the vast panorama. According to the painter Émile Bernard, Cézanne's aim was to paint like Poussin, but from nature: he thus brings together Impressionism, direct observation *en plein air*, brightness, and a rigorous composition structured around masses and strong principal lines. Balancing out the upward sweep of the vegetation and the mountain are the overlaid horizontal lines of the parapet, the fields, and the viaduct, whose modern arches echo those of ancient viaducts. Grandeur and calm predominate, despite the lively brushwork and the richness of the palette—an array of ochres and greens, with soft violet accents to the mountain, and the sky a flash of blue. The effect of unfinishedness is particularly experimental, notably in the foreground, where streaks of pure color—blue and orange—seem to have been applied to the canvas in a split second. J.-R.T.

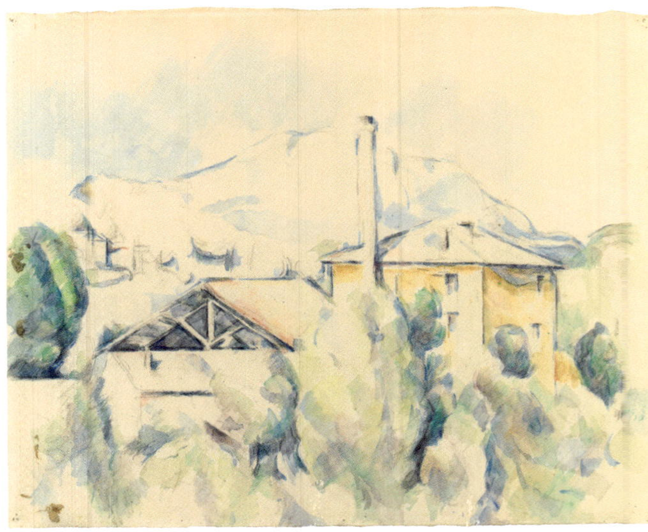

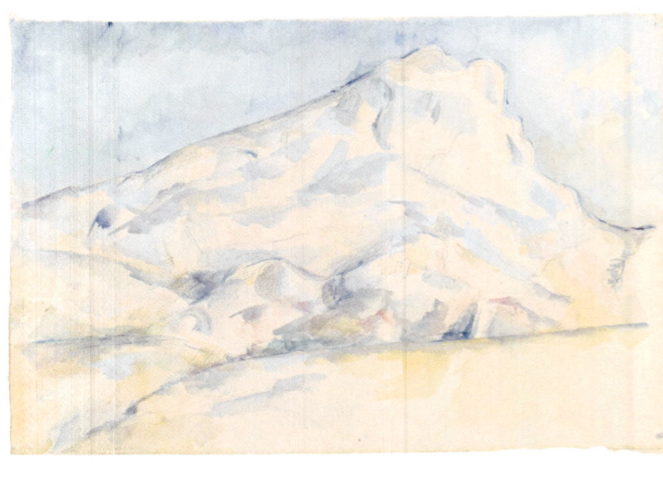

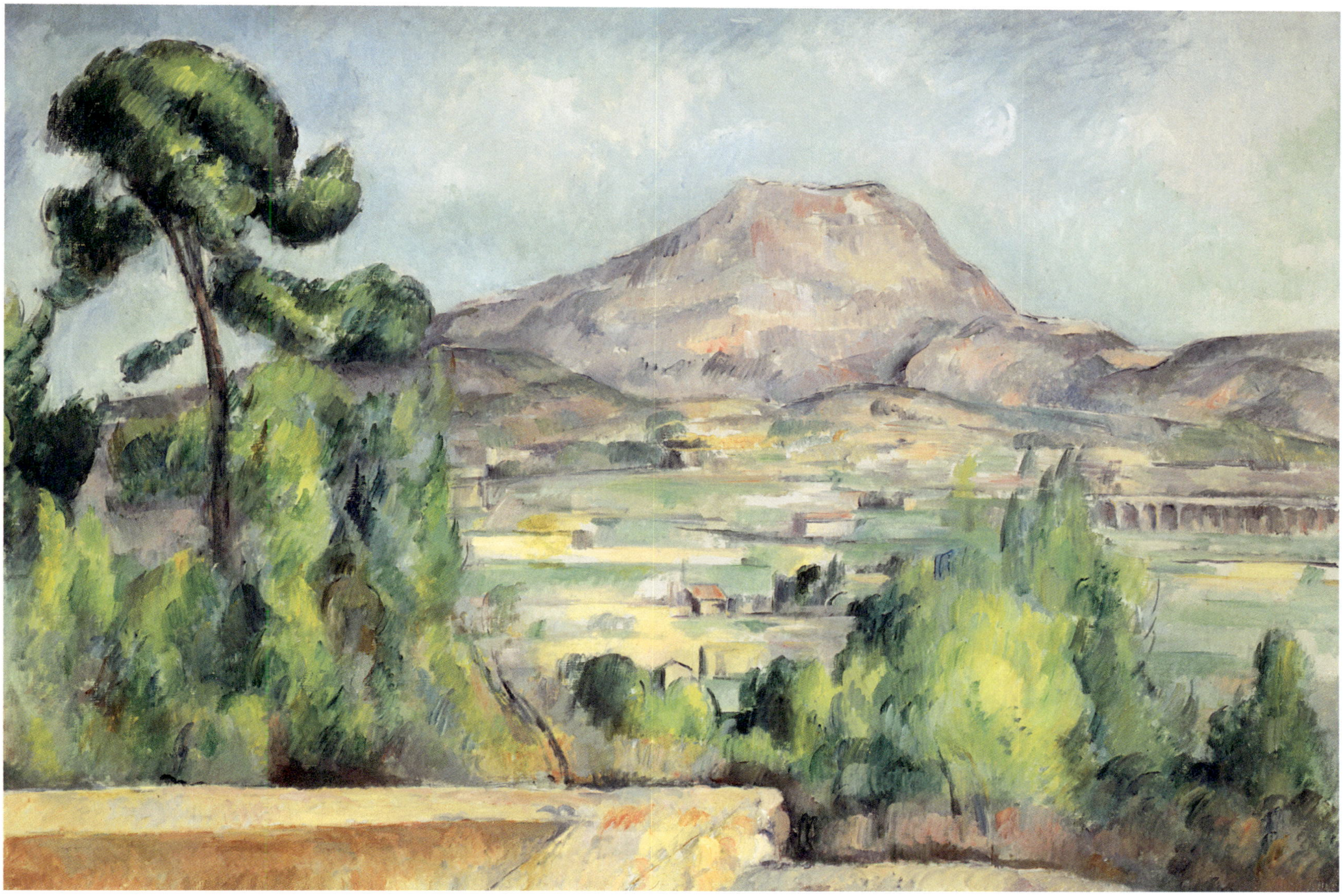

223 Facing page, top: Paul Cézanne,
Le Four à plâtre (*The Lime Kiln*), c. 1890–1894
Watercolor over black pencil sketch on thick cream vellum paper, 16 9⁄16 × 20 7⁄8 in. (42.1 × 53.1 cm)

224 Facing page, bottom: Paul Cézanne,
La Montagne Sainte-Victoire (*The Mont Sainte-Victoire*), c. 1900
Watercolor over graphite sketch on paper,
12 1⁄4 × 18 3⁄4 in. (31.1 × 47.7 cm)

225 Above: Paul Cézanne, *Montagne Sainte-Victoire* (*Mont Sainte-Victoire*), c. 1890
Oil on canvas, 25 9⁄16 × 37 1⁄2 in. (65 × 95.2 cm)

Monet and his series

In the early 1890s, Monet's work focused on Giverny and its environs. Thereafter he would hardly ever paint a subject just once, instead producing groups of paintings showing the same subject at different seasons and times of day, forming what he called "series." Patient, repeated observation was the method that enabled him to convey "effects." For what is considered his first true series, he chose an ordinary, familiar subject that was a typical feature of the French countryside and which had often appeared in paintings: the stacks of wheat or other grains that farmers would make after the harvest. Between the late summer of 1890 and the winter of 1891, he painted at least twenty-five canvases of them; "the further I get, the more I see that a lot of work has to be done in order to render what I'm looking for: 'instantaneity,' the 'envelope' above all, the same light spread over everything,"[39] he wrote to Gustave Geffroy on October 7, 1890. He exhibited fifteen of these in May 1891 under the title "*Série des meules,*" known in English as the *Haystacks*, or, more accurately, *Grainstacks* series. They proved a success, both financially and in the press. Soon afterward, Monet set up his easel on a boat on the Epte river at Giverny to execute some twenty canvases of poplar trees. He showed fifteen of these in 1892, this time unaccompanied by any other paintings, making his artistic approach fully clear. This second success heralded that of his 1895 *Rouen Cathedral* series (p. 244).

Monet often said that he sought above all to paint the feelings that the spectacle of nature inspired in him. From the 1890s onward, what he was expressing was not so much elements of the landscape as impalpable, intangible qualities such as light, color, and atmosphere, and fleeting aspects like the passage of time or the changing effects of light. His paintings appeared ever more like visions, memories or dreams, such as his hazy views of branches of the Seine and views of London. He was less interested in the Houses of Parliament's riverside silhouette than in the storm effects around it. Glints of yellow in the water reflect the agitated sky, in contrast to the calm scene presented by the same buildings at sunset. Monet took four years to finish this major series, and did not hesitate to paint some canvases entirely in his Giverny studio. When the series was put on show in 1904, it again proved successful. S. P.

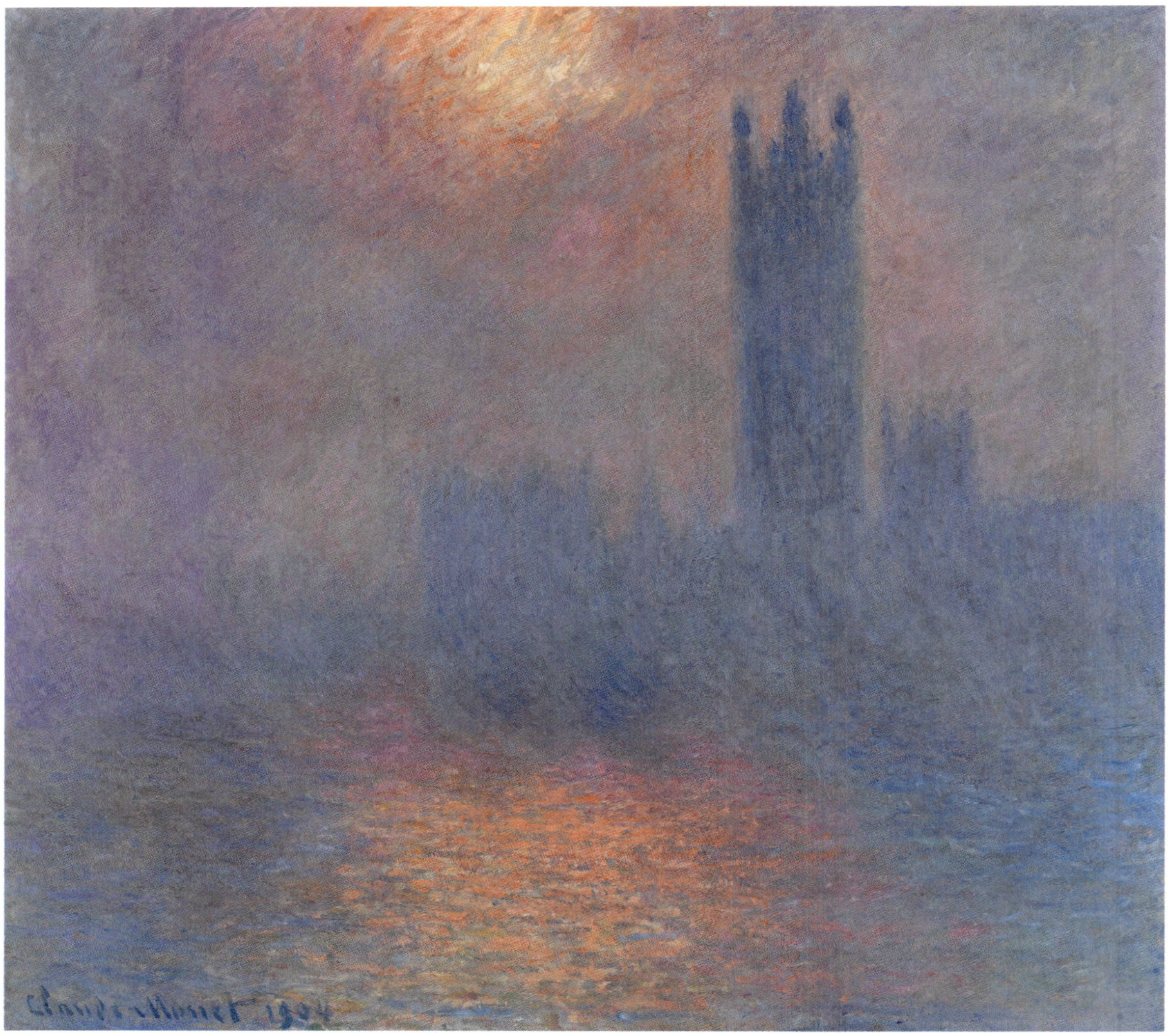

226 Claude Monet, *Londres, le Parlement. Trouée de soleil dans le brouillard (London, Houses of Parliament: Effect of Sunlight in the Fog)*, 1904
Oil on canvas, 32 1⁄16 × 36 7⁄16 in. (81.5 × 92.5 cm)

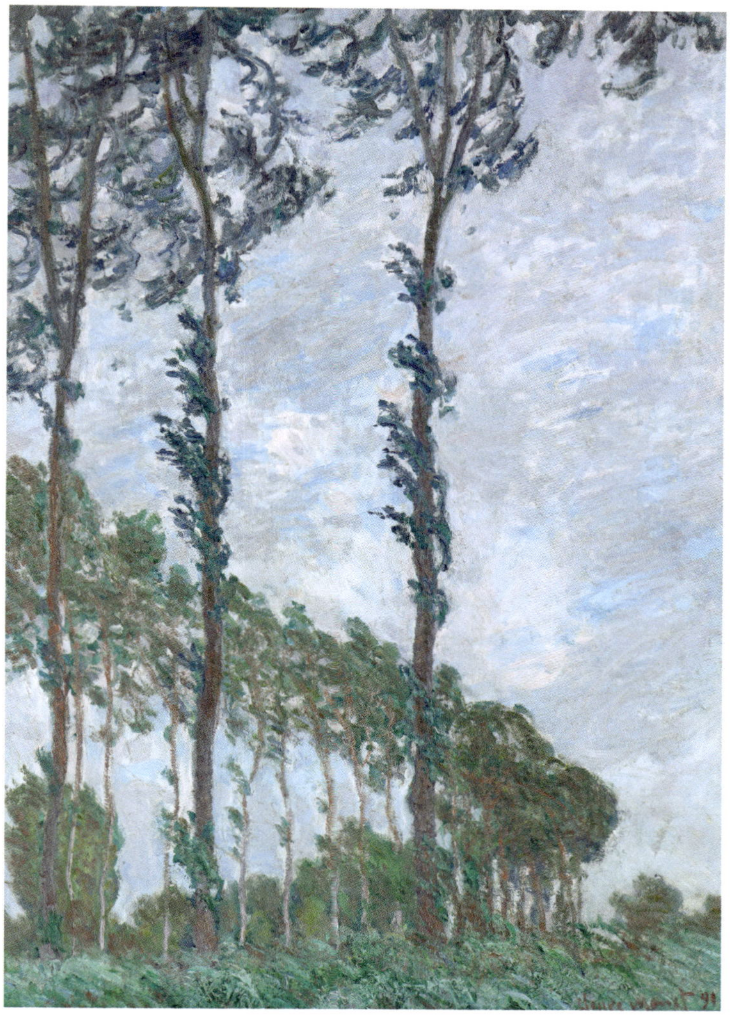

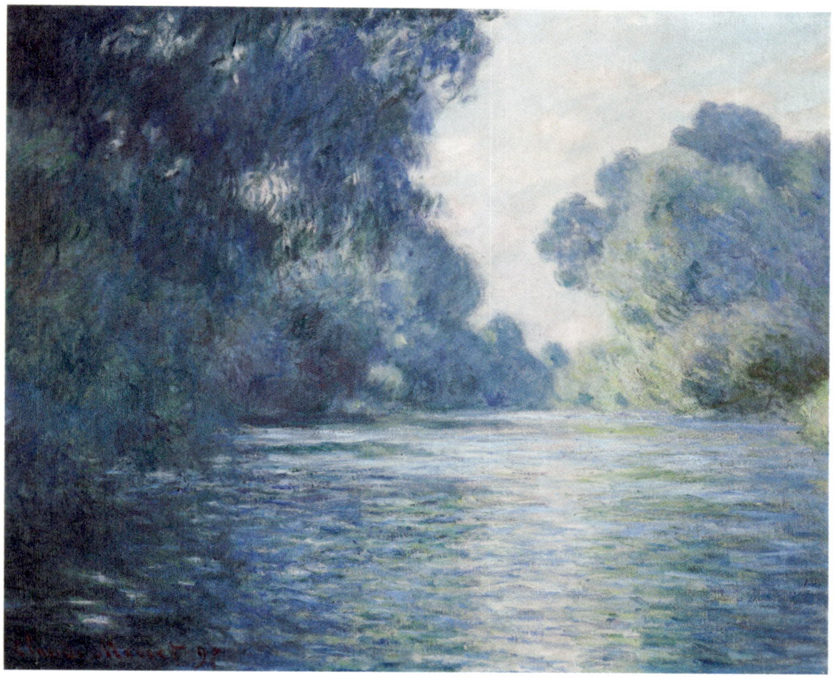

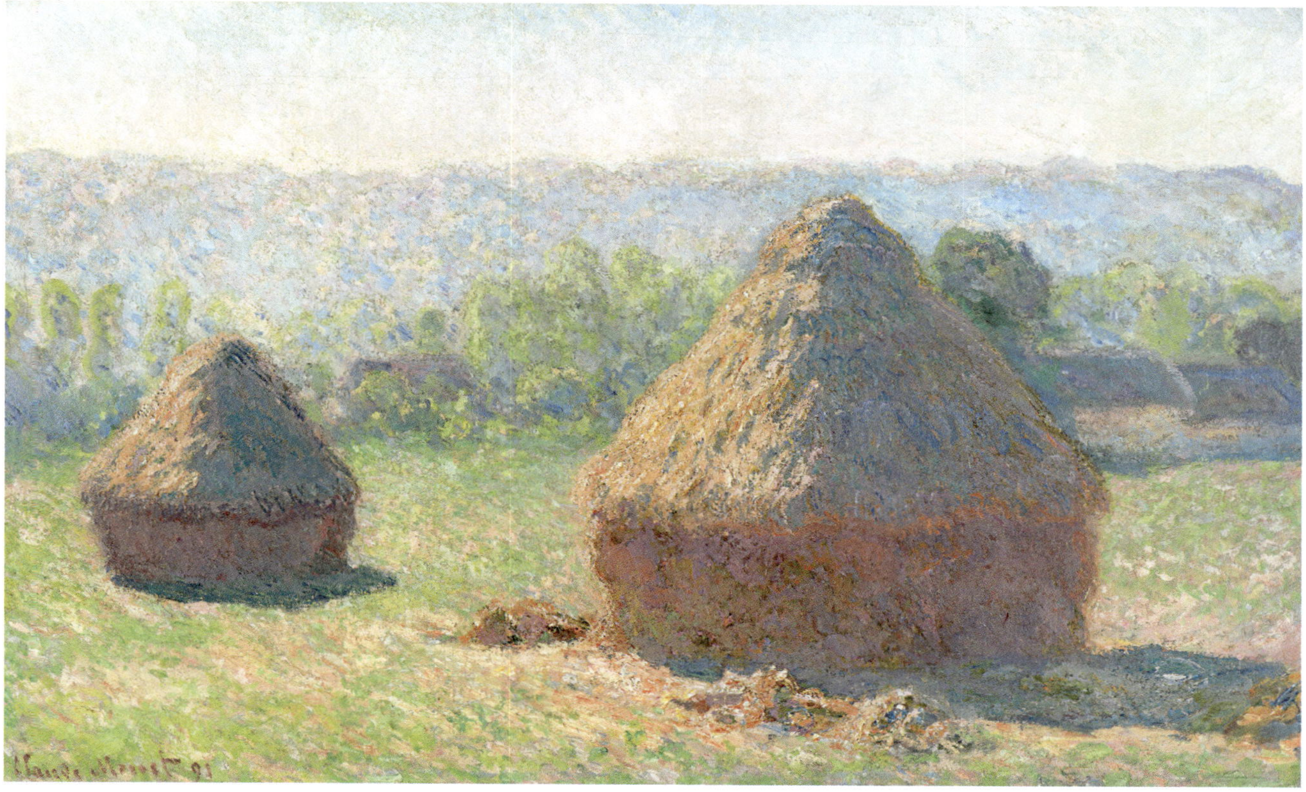

227 Top, left: Claude Monet, *Effet de vent, série des peupliers* (*Poplars: Wind Effect*), 1891. Oil on canvas, 39 ⅜ × 29 ⅛ in. (100 × 74 cm)

228 Top, right: Claude Monet, *Bras de Seine près de Giverny* (*Branch of the Seine near Giverny*), 1897. Oil on canvas, 28 13⁄16 × 36 ⅝ in. (73.2 × 93 cm)

229 Bottom: Claude Monet, *Meules, fin de l'été* (*Grainstacks, Late Summer*), 1891 Oil on canvas, 23 13⁄16 × 39 11⁄16 in. (60.5 × 100.8 cm)

Claude Monet
Rouen Cathedral

For an exhibition in May 1895 at Paul Durand-Ruel's gallery, Claude Monet chose twenty of the thirty views of Rouen Cathedral that he had painted in the winters of 1892 and 1893 from the vantage point of an apartment across the road from it. This group showed the public a single subject's metamorphoses, transformed by the atmosphere of the ambient light. Some critics were reserved in their response, but most hailed Monet's virtuosity and his determination to explore the effects of light through painting.

Although these works appear to be a series in the same manner as the grainstacks and poplars, Monet did not intend them to form an inextricably related, fixed set. Even before the 1895 exhibition, some of them had already been sold, and they were very soon dispersed around the world. Today, the thirty are shared out across fourteen museums and eight private collections, some alone, some in groups. The Musée d'Orsay has the largest set, with five, of which four are from the 1911 Isaac de Camondo bequest, while the other, *The Portal Seen from the Front*, was purchased by the State in 1907. They were brought together in 1947 when the Musée du Jeu de Paume opened to house the State collection of Impressionist works, and then taken to the Musée d'Orsay when it opened in 1986. Each one is distinctive in its viewpoint, format, brushwork, weather, and time of day, but when placed alongside each other they are striking in their shared creative dynamic, and offer a shifting, fluctuating vision of the cathedral. B. T.

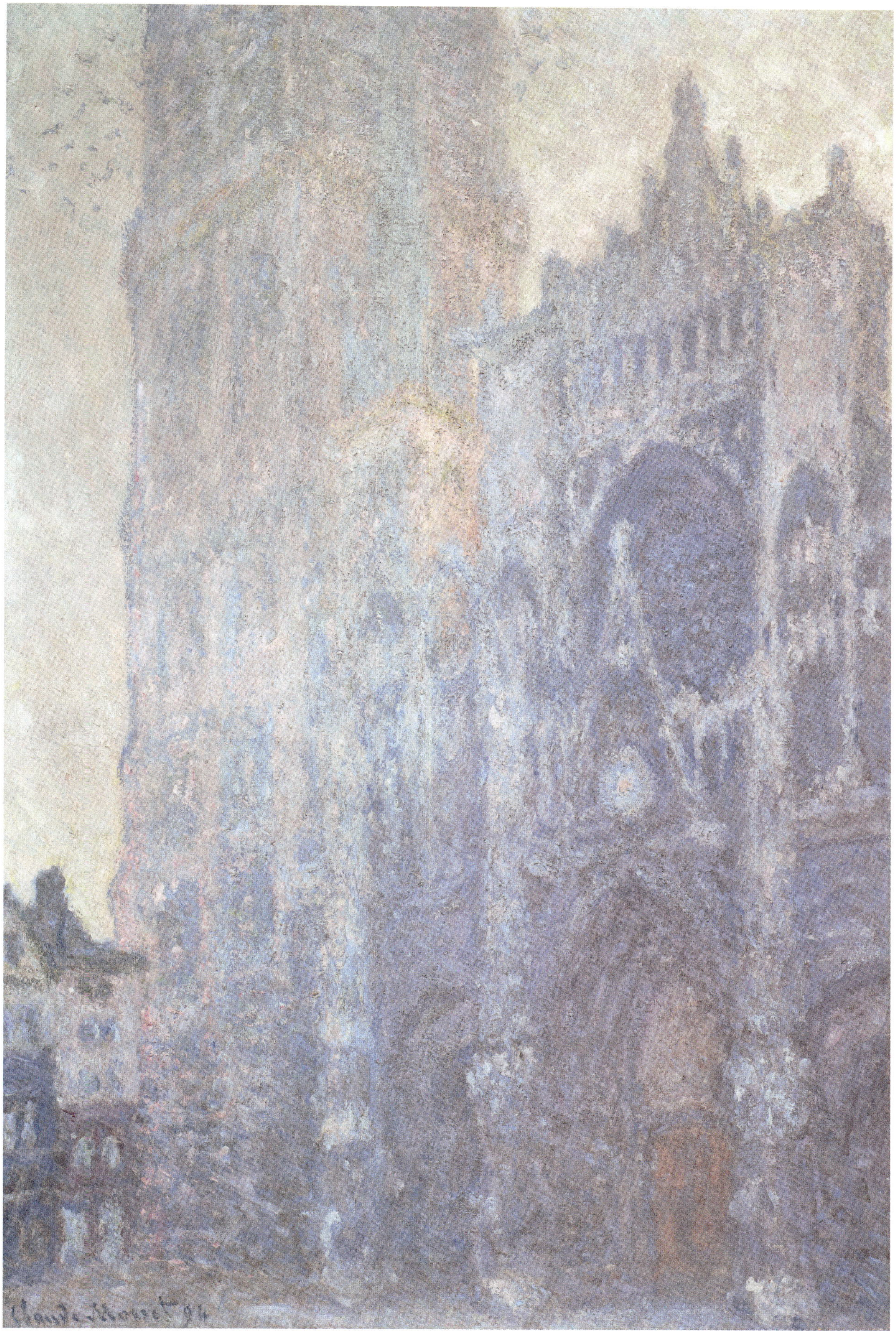

230 Claude Monet, *La Cathédrale de Rouen. Le Portail et la tour Saint-Romain, effet du matin* (*Rouen Cathedral: The Portal and the Saint-Romain Tower, Morning Sun*), 1893
Oil on canvas, 41 15⁄16 × 28 13⁄16 in. (106.5 × 73.2 cm)

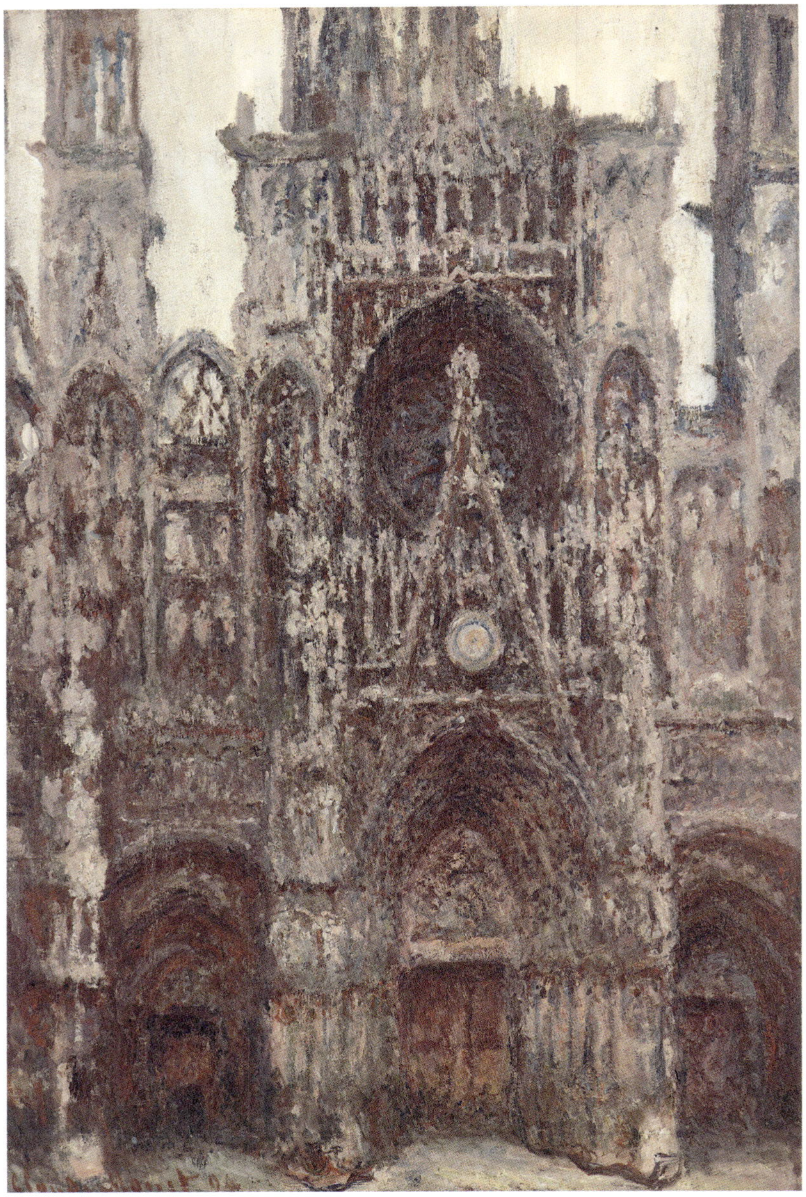

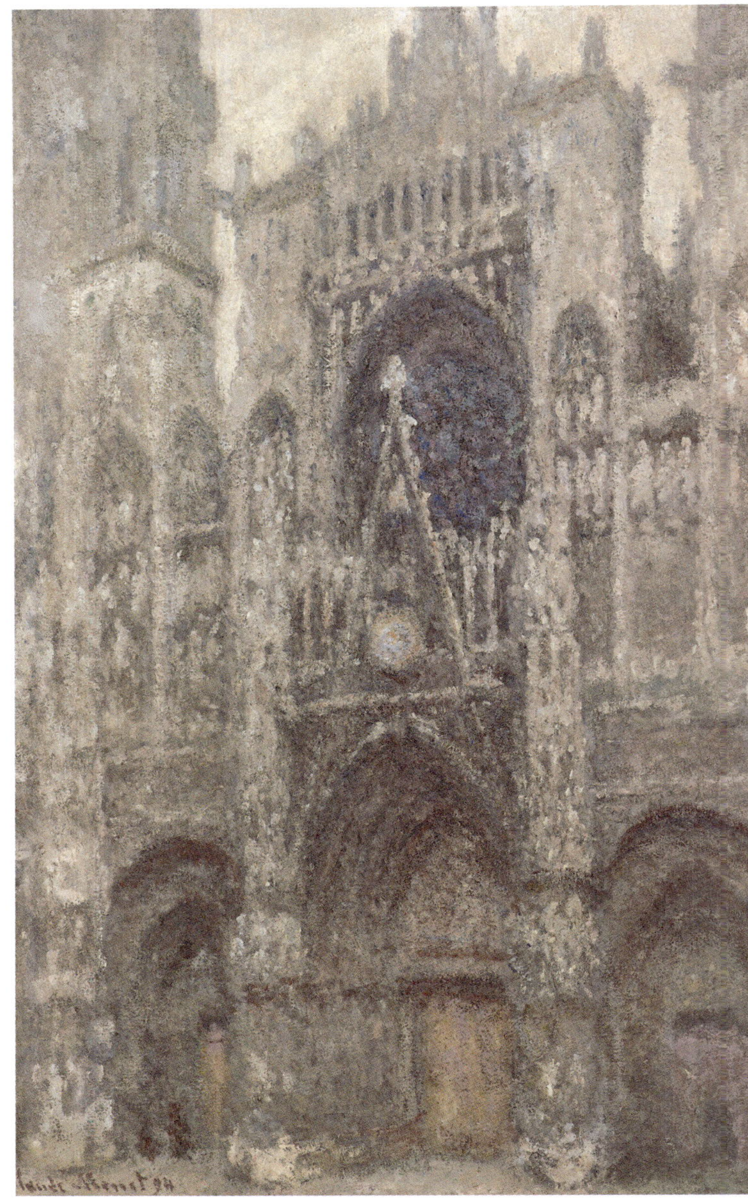

231 Left: Claude Monet, *La Cathédrale de Rouen. Le Portail vu de face* (*Rouen Cathedral: The Portal Seen from the Front*), 1892
Oil on canvas, 42 ⅛ × 29 ⅛ in. (107 × 74 cm)

232 Right: Claude Monet, *La Cathédrale de Rouen. Le Portail, temps gris* (*Rouen Cathedral: The Portal on a Gray Day*), 1892
Oil on canvas, 39 7/16 × 25 ¾ in. (100.2 × 65.4 cm)

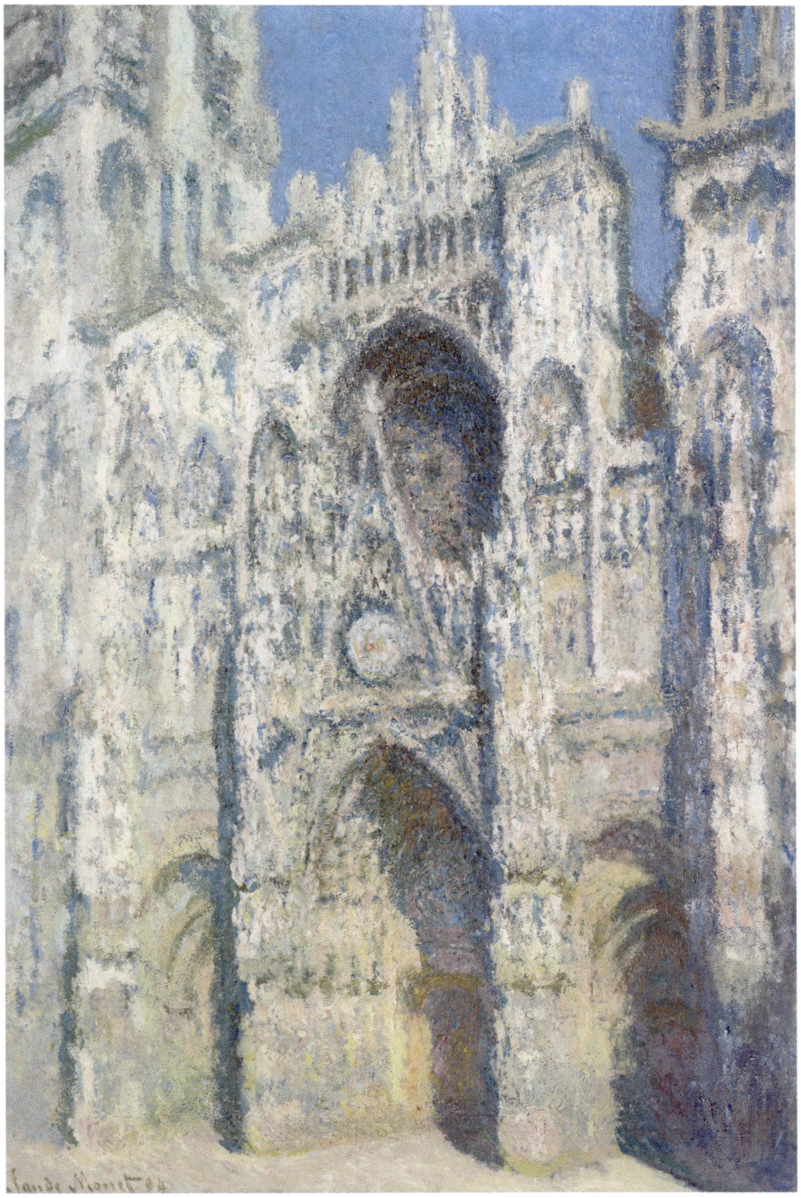

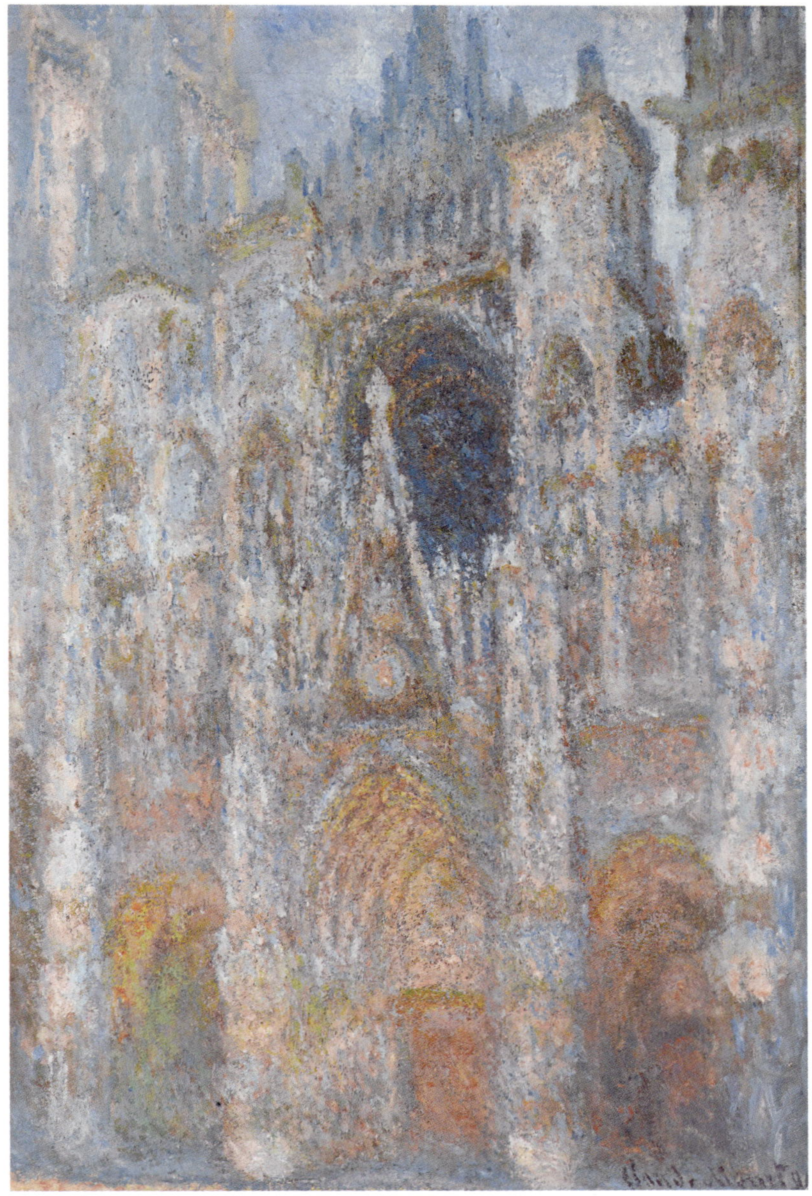

233 Left: Claude Monet, *La Cathédrale de Rouen. Le Portail et la tour Saint-Romain, plein soleil* (*Rouen Cathedral: The Portal and the Saint-Romain Tower in Full Sun*), 1893
Oil on canvas, 42 ⅛ × 29 ⅛ in. (107 × 73.5 cm)

234 Right: Claude Monet, *La Cathédrale de Rouen. Le Portail, soleil matinal* (*Rouen Cathedral: The Portal in the Morning Light*), 1893
Oil on canvas, 36 5⁄16 × 24 13⁄16 in. (92.2 × 63 cm)

Camille Pissarro
Ports

Pissarro first visited Rouen in 1883, and returned there in 1896 with the firm intention of bringing home twenty to thirty paintings. He had decided on their subjects in advance, having no shortage of confidence. However, the same could not be said for his finances, and so he rented modest lodgings at the Hôtel de Paris, between the Boïeldieu and Corneille bridges, where his room proved impossible to heat but he enjoyed "a splendid view of the harbor."[40] Claude Monet's brother Léon introduced him to François Depeaux, the most active local collector.

Another cause for his enthusiasm was the port activity, from the hubbub of people and cars, to the horizon that prickled with factory chimneys. The bridge itself, with its three steel arches and masonry piers, filled him with delight, especially when the fog wrapped around it, mingling vaporousness with solidity. He described it as "very lively" and "very hectic," but this was no socio-political criticism: here, work was a source of harmony. The image is wonderfully dynamic, along similar lines to examples by Monet and Caillebotte, and leads our gaze through to the new-built neighborhood of Saint-Sever, the subject of the second painting. In beautiful gray-black monochrome shades, this canvas suggests the coldness of winter. It has belonged to prominent collectors (Depeaux, Eduardo Mollard). The Rouen scenario was repeated in Dieppe in 1902, with the hyperactive bustle of the port captured from the high viewpoint of a hotel window, producing a panorama of broken lines that energize the painting and our perception of it—an explosion of color and brushwork. S.G.

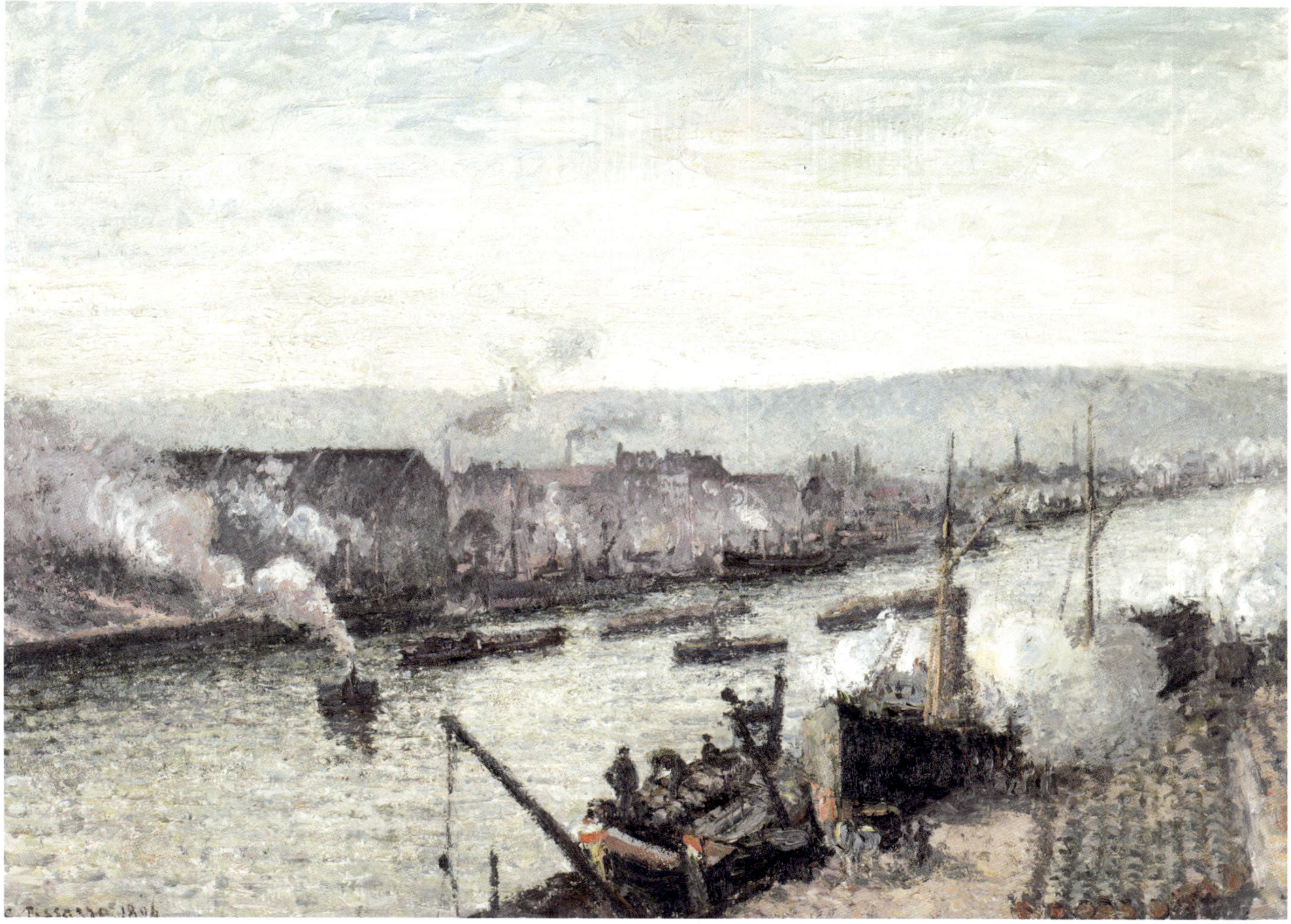

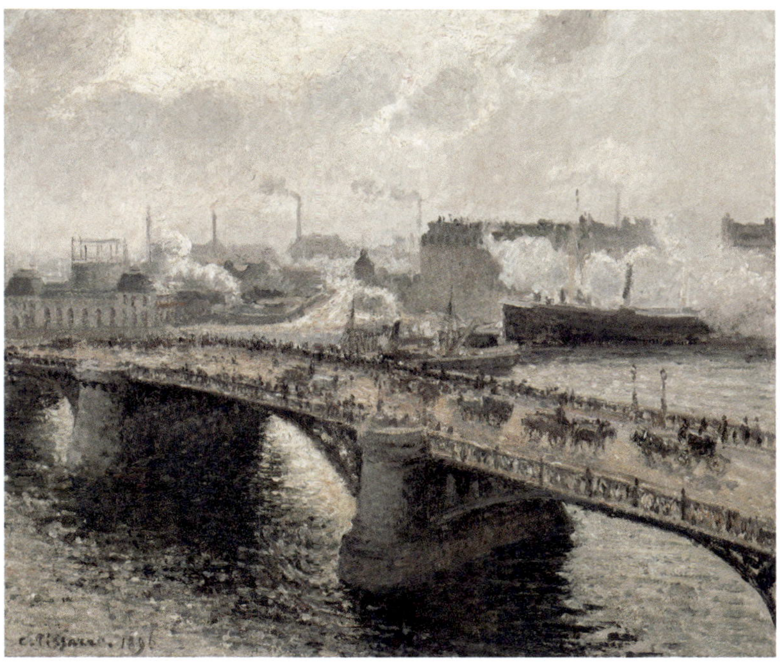

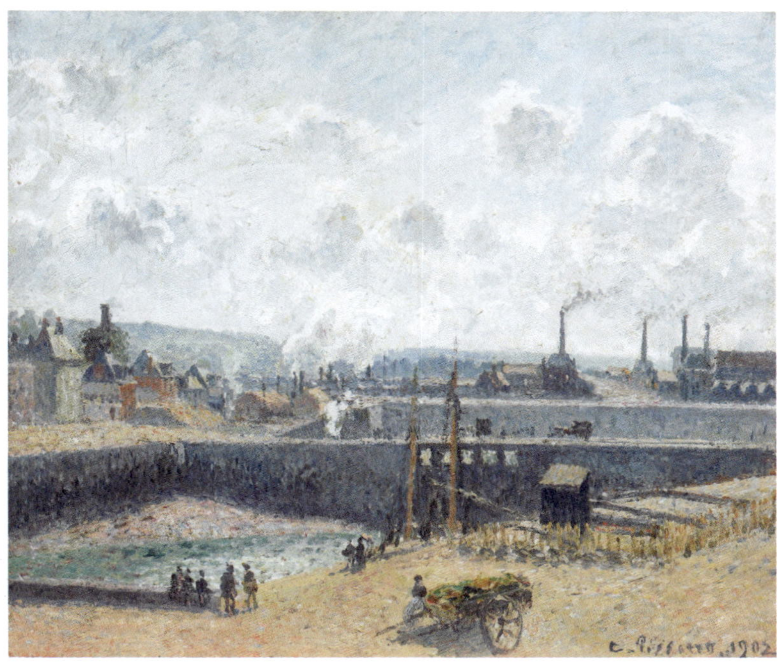

235 Top: Camille Pissarro, *Port de Rouen, Saint-Sever* (*The Port of Rouen, Saint-Sever*), 1896
Oil on canvas, 25 13/16 × 36 5/16 in.
(65.5 × 92.2 cm)

236 Bottom, left: Camille Pissarro, *Le Pont Boïeldieu à Rouen* (*The Boïeldieu Bridge, Rouen*), 1896
Oil on canvas, 21 1/4 × 25 9/16 in.
(54 × 65 cm)

237 Bottom, right: Camille Pissarro, *Dieppe, bassin Duquesne. Marée basse, soleil, matin* (*Dieppe, Duquesne Docks: Low Tide, Morning Sunlight*), 1902
Oil on canvas, 21 7/16 × 25 9/16 in.
(54.5 × 65 cm)

Degas and photography

Although no painter at the time was indifferent to the visual revolution that photography ushered in, few of them practiced the medium themselves. Among the Impressionists, Degas was the only one to take an interest in it, specifically at the moment when it was becoming more accessible and seeing competition from another invention: cinematography. Succumbing to a bout of photography fever that was as intense as it was brief (begun in March 1895 and reaching a peak over the following summer and winter), Degas first attempted to photograph the twilight and moonlight. He continued his experiments through nocturnal portraits of his closest friends: the painters Paule Gobillard, Henri Rouart, Jacques-Émile Blanche, and Henry Lerolle; Lerolle's daughters Yvonne and Christine; the playwright Ludovic Halévy and his wife Louise; and the poet Stéphane Mallarmé. He took these photographs after dinners that he organized at his home, or at his respective sitters' homes, but always indoors.

Running counter to his contemporaries' fascination with immediacy, the outdoors, and capturing movement, Degas recorded his models' expressions and bodies in interiors that were lit with electric lamps, where they had to hold their poses for several long minutes without moving. Through subtly playing with indirect light and reflections, the results are hieratic silhouettes that emerge from the darkness, often leaving the details of the room in deep shadow, though still inhabited by large mirrors, a bookcase, paintings, or an imposing sculpture. Conversely, the women's long dresses, the heavy wall hangings, the immaculate collar of a man's shirt, or the decorative upholstery of a chair absorb the lighting's glow. With this chiaroscuro treatment, Degas returned to the contrasts of white and black that he had already experimented with in his paintings, sculptures, and monotypes.

Within this opaque atmosphere—an echo of the Symbolist milieu that Degas frequented, notably at the Lerolles'—the subjects are immersed in thought or feign sleep. Degas also put himself in the frame, sometimes with others, sometimes alone. In one of these self-portraits, he presents himself in profile, leaning back in a rocking chair, his chin resting meditatively in his right hand. Prominently placed on a console table next to him are *Weeping Girl* and *The Angel of Light*, plaster statues that his friend Albert Bartholomé had just given to him. The former is crouching down, the latter lifting up a tombstone. These two figures of despair are studies for the grave in the Père-Lachaise cemetery that the sculptor was working on at the time, in memory of his beloved late wife, Prospérie. It was as an aging, solitary man that Degas passionately poured himself into photography, elevating it to the status of funerary art. M.R.

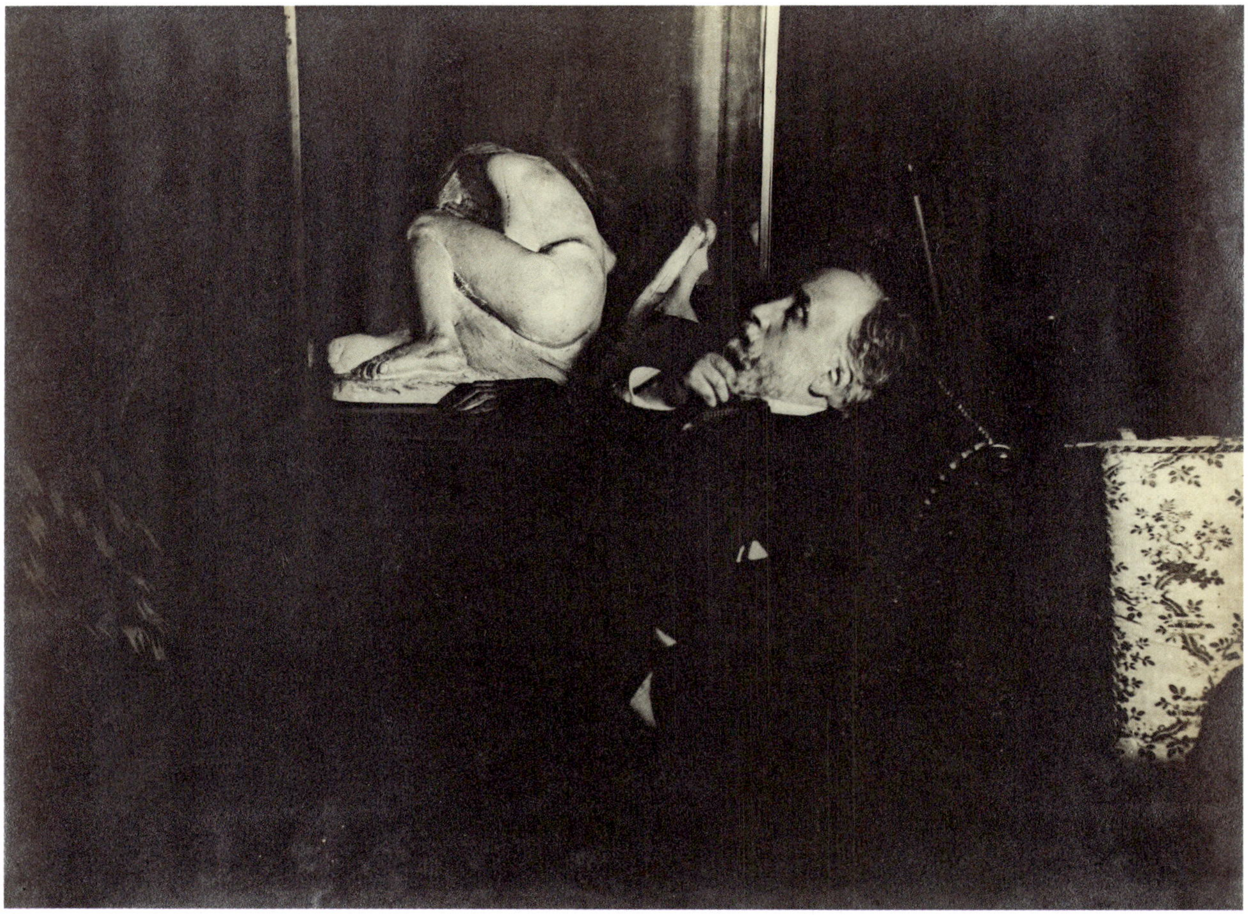

238 Edgar Degas, *Autoportrait à la statue de Bartholomé* (*Self-Portrait with Bartholomé Statue*), 1895
Silver print, 11 ¼ × 15 ½ in. (28.5 × 39.3 cm)

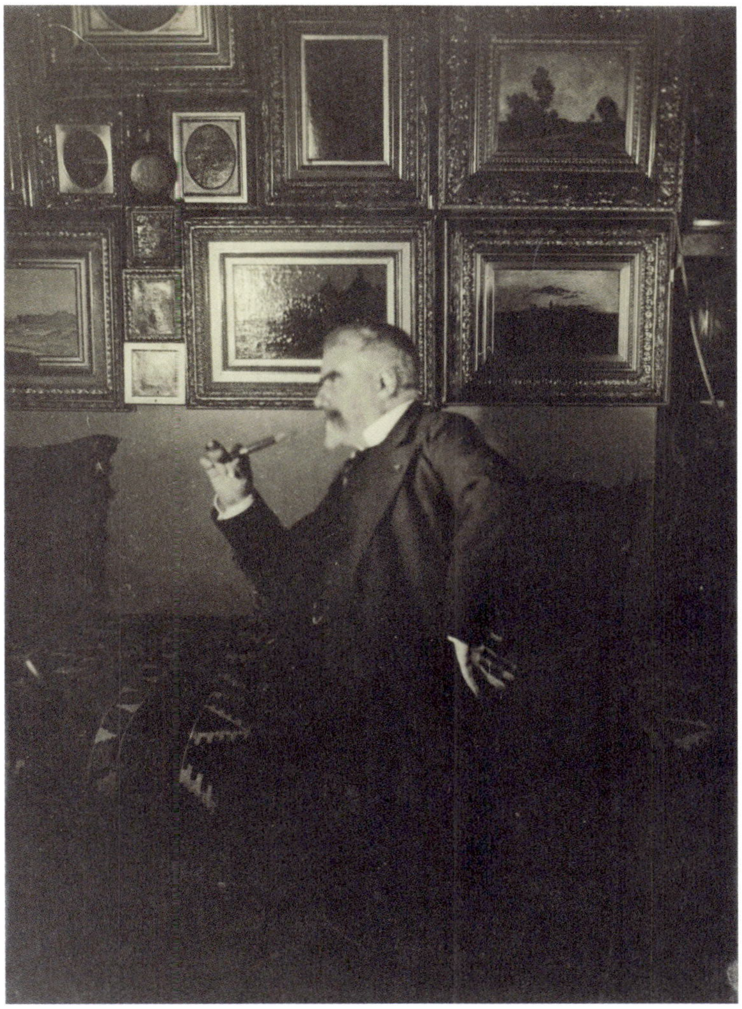

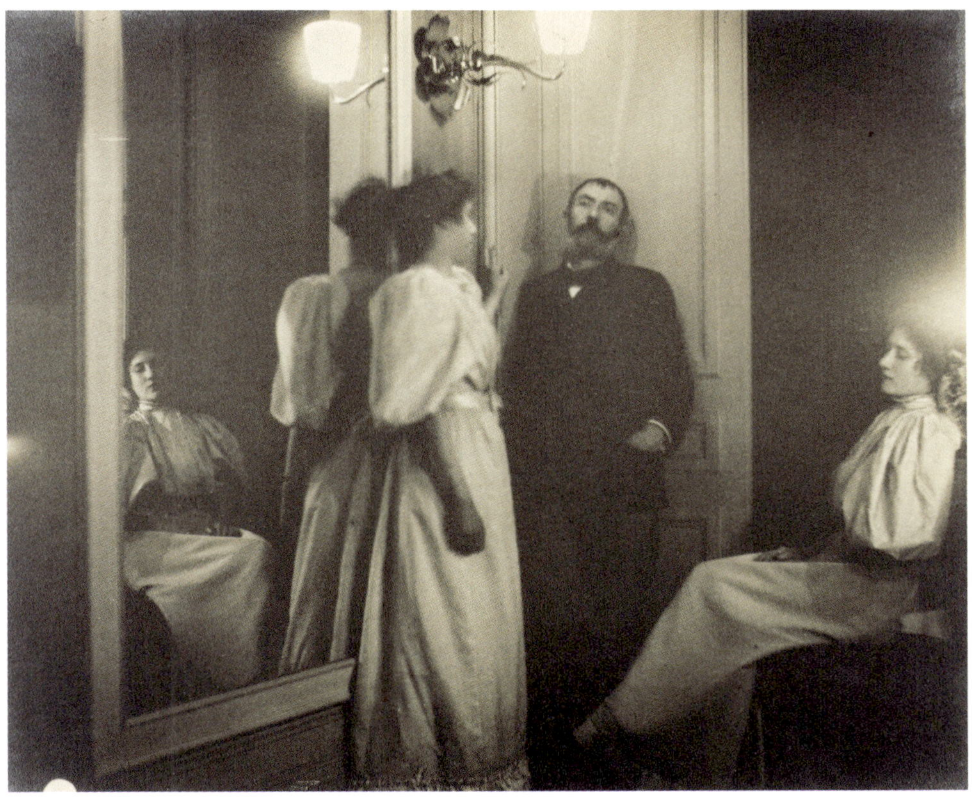

239 Top: Edgar Degas, *Henri Rouart (1833–1912), industriel et collectionneur, chez lui, devant ses tableaux* (*Henri Rouart, Industrialist and Collector (1833–1912), at Home, in Front of His Paintings*), 1895. Gelatin silver print from a glass negative, 14 ¾ × 10 ¹³⁄₁₆ in. (37.5 × 27.5 cm)

240 Bottom: Edgar Degas, *Portrait au miroir du peintre Henry Lerolle et de ses deux filles, Yvonne et Christine* (*Portrait of the Painter Henry Lerolle and His Two Daughters, Yvonne and Christine, with Mirror*), between 1895 and 1896. Gelatin silver print from a glass negative, 11 ⁷⁄₁₆ × 14 ¼ in. (29 × 36.2 cm)

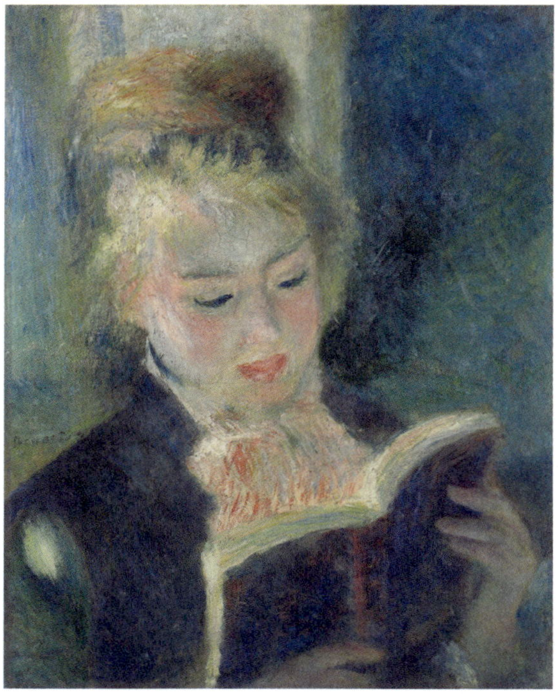

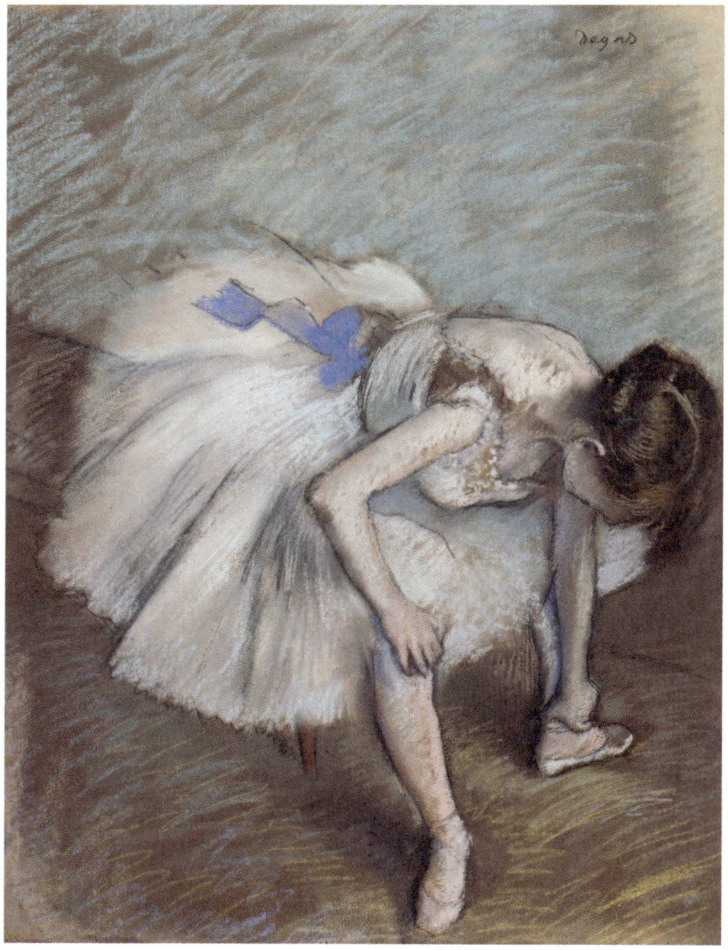

241 Top: Auguste Renoir, *La Liseuse* (*Woman Reading*), 1874–1876
Oil on canvas, 18 5⁄16 × 15 3⁄16 in. (46.5 × 38.5 cm)

242 Bottom: Edgar Degas, *Danseuse assise se massant le pied gauche* (*Seated Dancer Massaging Her Foot*), 1881–1883
Pastel on tan paper mounted on board, 24 7⁄16 × 19 5⁄16 in. (62 × 49 cm)

1897

The opening of the Caillebotte bequest room at the Musée du Luxembourg

Caillebotte came from a wealthy bourgeois family in Paris, and bought a large number of paintings from his friends. For him, it was both a matter of supporting them financially, and also amassing a collection that would one day find its place in a museum. In 1876, when he was just twenty-eight, he wrote his first will, in which he bequeathed his collection to the State, specifying that the works must all be exhibited at Paris's Musée du Luxembourg (then the "museum of living artists"), and later at the Louvre. On his death in 1894, his collection featured more than seventy works by Cézanne, Degas, Manet, Millet, Monet, Pissarro, Renoir, and Sisley, including some masterpieces such as *The Balcony* (p. 63), *The Gare Saint-Lazare* (p. 135), *The Star* (p. 145), and *Dance at the Moulin de la Galette* (p. 137). The two major omissions were Morisot and Cassatt, even though Caillebotte did recognize their merit.

The State initially accepted the bequest in its entirety as presented, but problems soon arose concerning the possibility of displaying all the works at the Musée du Luxembourg, which was too small, already full, and usually did not accept more than two or three works per artist (Caillebotte's bequest included sixteen paintings by Monet, for example). After lengthy discussions and heated debate in the press, a compromise was reached: the bequest would only consist of forty works, but all of them would be put on show. Monet, Pissarro, Renoir, and Sisley helped select the works and set aside some of their own paintings that they did not consider of sufficient quality. To ensure that Caillebotte would be as well represented in the museum as his friends, his brother Martial and Renoir, the executor of Caillebotte's will, chose two of his paintings to give to the State (*Floor Scrapers*, p. 121, and *View of Rooftops [Snow Effect]*, p. 158).

A new wing was built at the Musée du Luxembourg, and in February 1897 the Caillebotte room was opened to the public, despite objections from the Académie des Beaux-Arts. Having such a number of Impressionist works displayed together in a museum was unique in the world at the time. P. P.

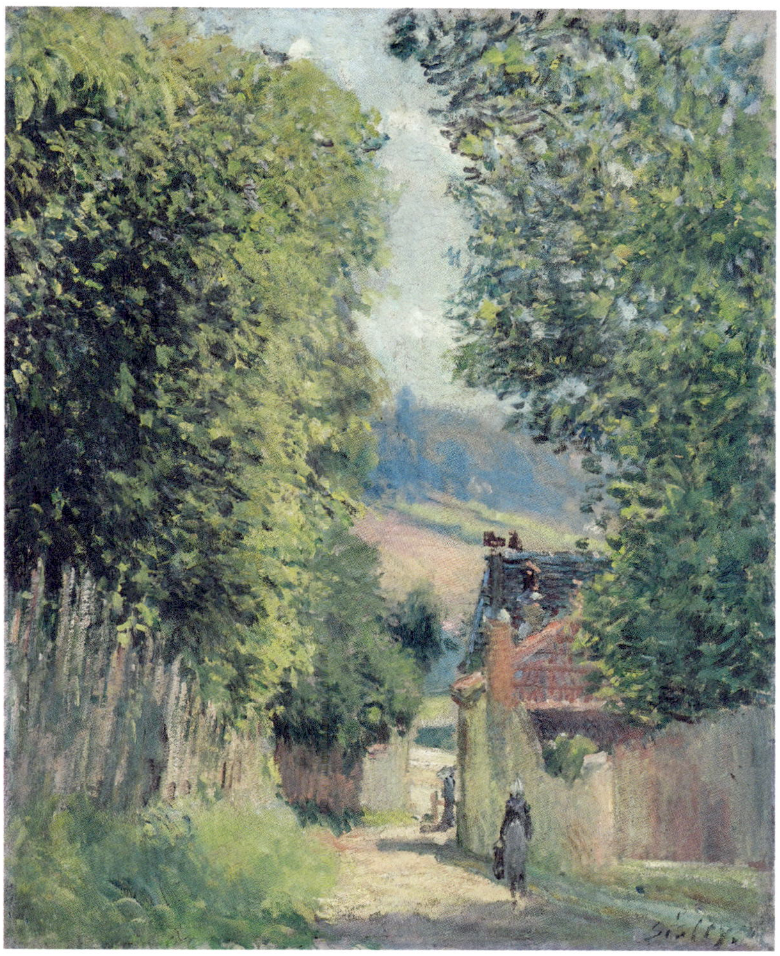

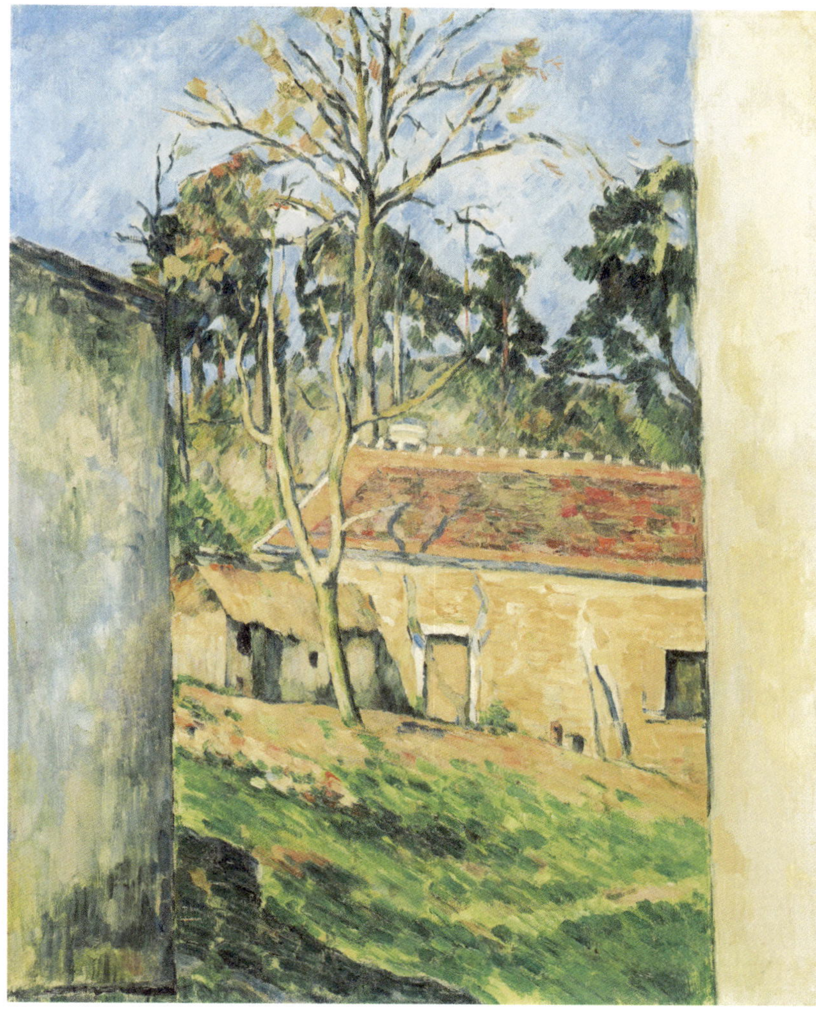

243 Left: Alfred Sisley,
Chemin de la briqueterie, Marly-le-Roi, c. 1876
Oil on canvas, 21 ⅝ × 18 ⅛ in. (55 × 46 cm)

244 Right: Paul Cézanne, *Cour d'une ferme* (*Farm Courtyard in Auvers*), c. 1879
Oil on canvas, 25 9⁄16 × 21 7⁄16 in. (65 × 54.4 cm)

Mary Cassatt
Mother and Child

Cassatt shared Degas's taste for experimental techniques, and preferred pastel for its versatility, ease of manipulation, and sensual qualities, which especially lend themselves to the subject matter that became her hallmark from the 1890s onward: women and children. This topic also enabled her to take her place within art-historical tradition and to transform the traditional theme of the Virgin and Child, which she had studied extensively in European museums, into a contemporary everyday subject.

The treatment of the pastel is particularly varied in this work. The green background is worked as pure flat color, and Cassatt makes the white of the infant's nightshirt light up this heart-warming, intimate scene of a woman cuddling a little baby. She applies the pastel smoothly, blending it to achieve the soft skin of the faces. The baby's round cheeks, whose redness suggests that it has just woken up or is teething, display the artist's observational talents and her ability to "embody" her models. For their clothes, she adopts incisive, energetic strokes, with crosshatching and zigzags leaving her artistic intervention and gestures visible, while playing with the aesthetic of unfinishedness around the work's edges.

Initially titled *Femme et enfant* (*Woman and Child*) when Cassatt donated it to the national collections in 1897, this pastel was swiftly renamed *Mother and Child*. The same was done to most of her works on this subject. C.C.-P.

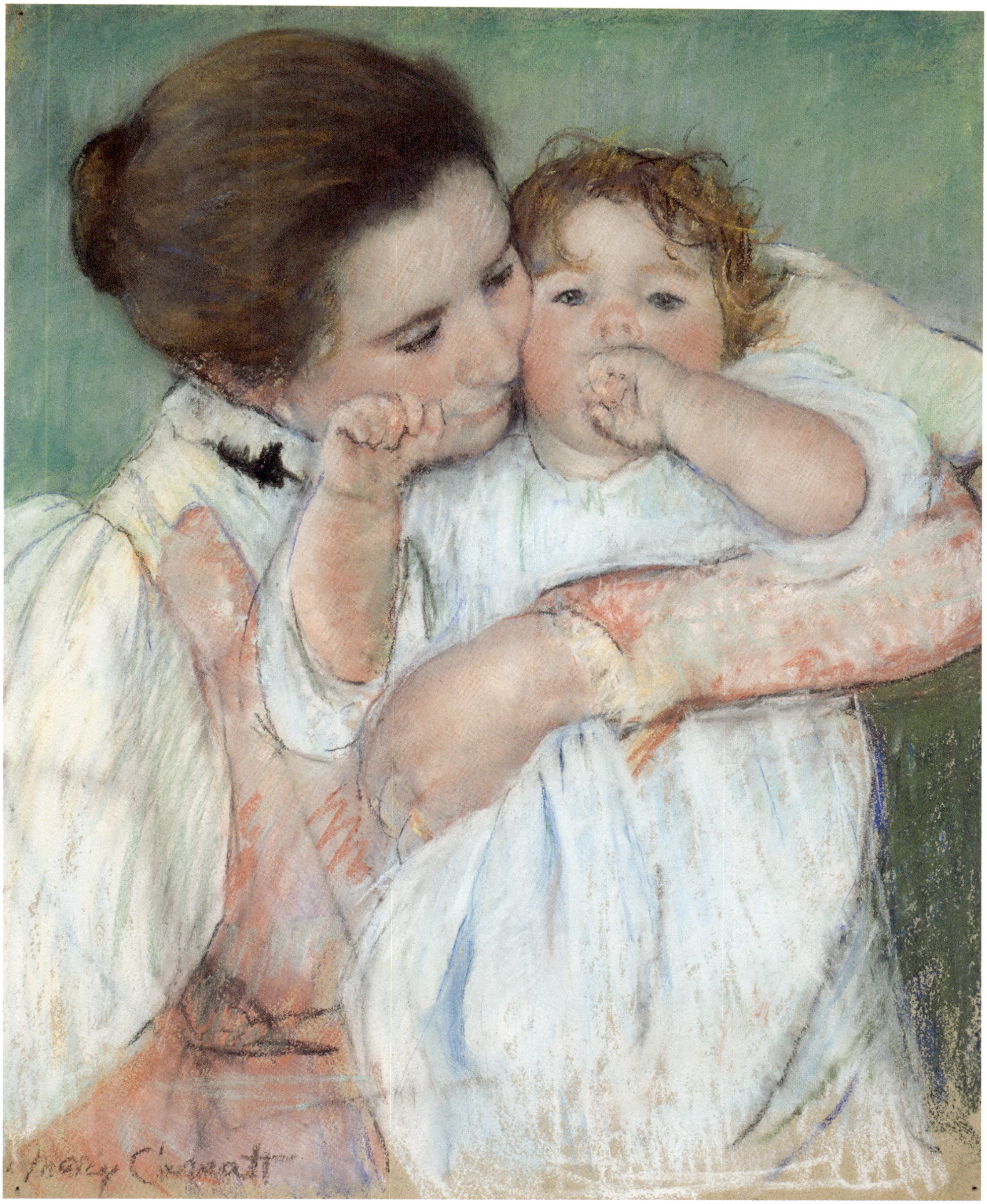

245 Mary Cassatt, *Mère et enfant sur fond vert* (*Mother and Child Against a Green Background*), 1897
Pastel on beige paper mounted on canvas, 21 5⁄8 × 18 1⁄8 in. (55 × 46 cm)

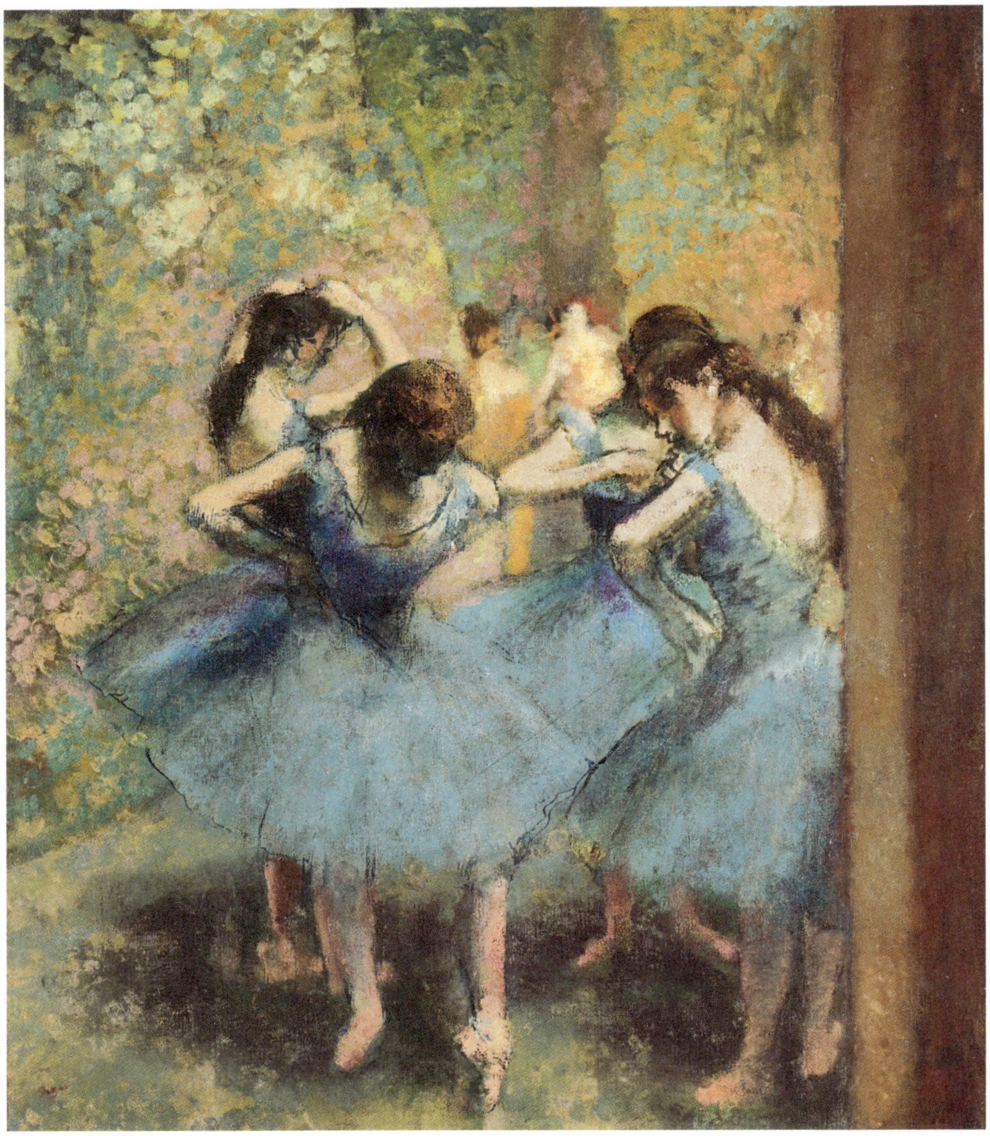

246 Edgar Degas, *Danseuses bleues* (*Blue Dancers*), c. 1890
Oil on canvas, 33 9⁄16 × 29 5⁄8 in. (85.3 × 75.3 cm)

The late style: The Impressionists in the twentieth century

After the deaths of their former colleagues Bazille and Morisot, the remaining major Impressionists—Monet, Degas, Cézanne, Pissarro, and Renoir—began the twentieth century with a conviction that a fresh approach to the aesthetic established in 1874 was needed, if not already underway. The fact that late works by Degas, who died in 1917, are so absent from French public collections proves by default how radical he was after 1886, the year of the final Impressionist group exhibition. Indeed, he was only connected to the group through vague collective strategies. From that time on, he opted for what André Masson called "close-up views," whether of milliners or of bathers glimpsed surreptitiously, portrayed perfectly respectfully and sometimes perfectly implausibly. The pact of realism was shattered. In 1895, Degas bought seven Cézannes from Vollard to add to his collection. As for Cézanne himself, his desire to escape strict empiricism grew ever stronger over the ten years immediately prior to his death in 1906. His obsession with the subject never faltered—indeed, it was what killed him. But he sought to transpose it more synthetically, with primitive accents that Pissarro would have described as Pompeiian. More than ever, the canvases were part of a rooted history and culture that was sheltered from the modern world. Cézanne's Provence was a familiar furrowed space, a private geography that he studied every day from life, in the light of his geologist friends such as Antoine-Fortuné Marion, who was obsessed by the slightest prehistoric trace. When a rockface took possession of the picture plane, stone, greenery, and a glimpse of the sky would all adopt a post-diluvial character. Renoir and Cézanne met regularly in the 1880s. It was at that time that Renoir, who was increasingly moving away from Impressionism, produced a flurry of images of women, where flesh and flowers come together in a Renaissance- or eighteenth-century-inspired dream. On November 29, 1919, four days before Renoir's death, the art critic and doctor Élie Faure noted: "This crippled old man makes painting a miraculous act.... And it is all the more admirable given that the gap between his waxing lyricism and his waning physical capacity is ever widening." S.G.

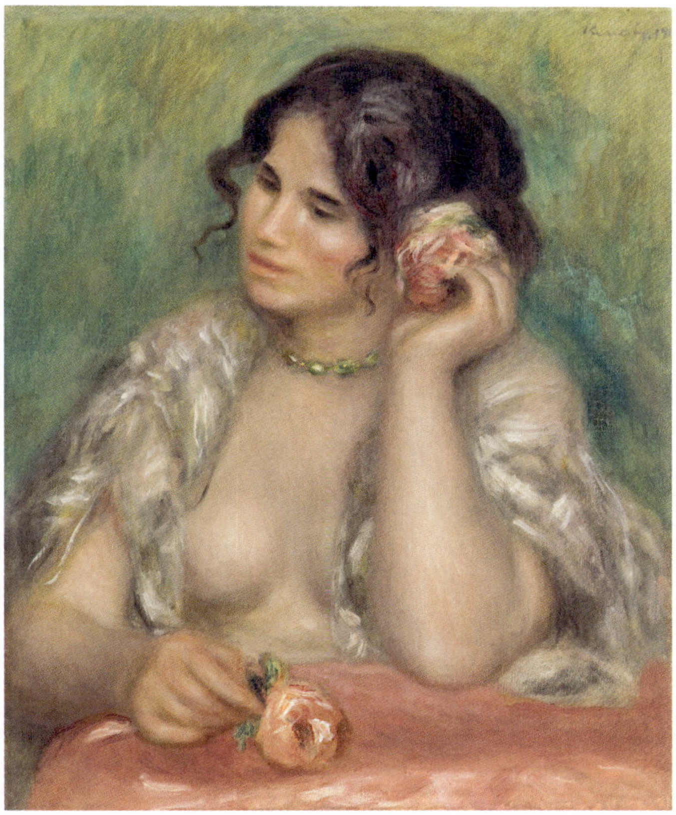

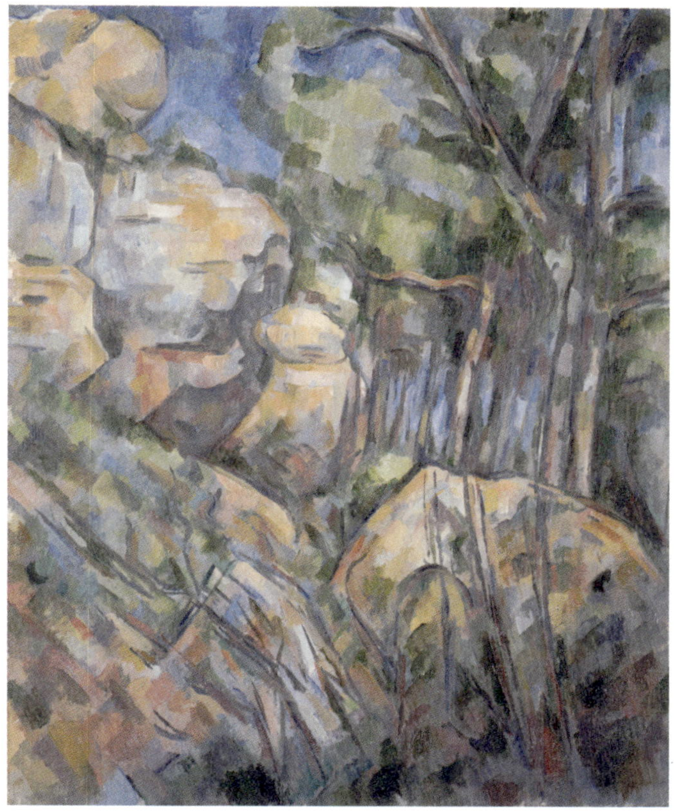

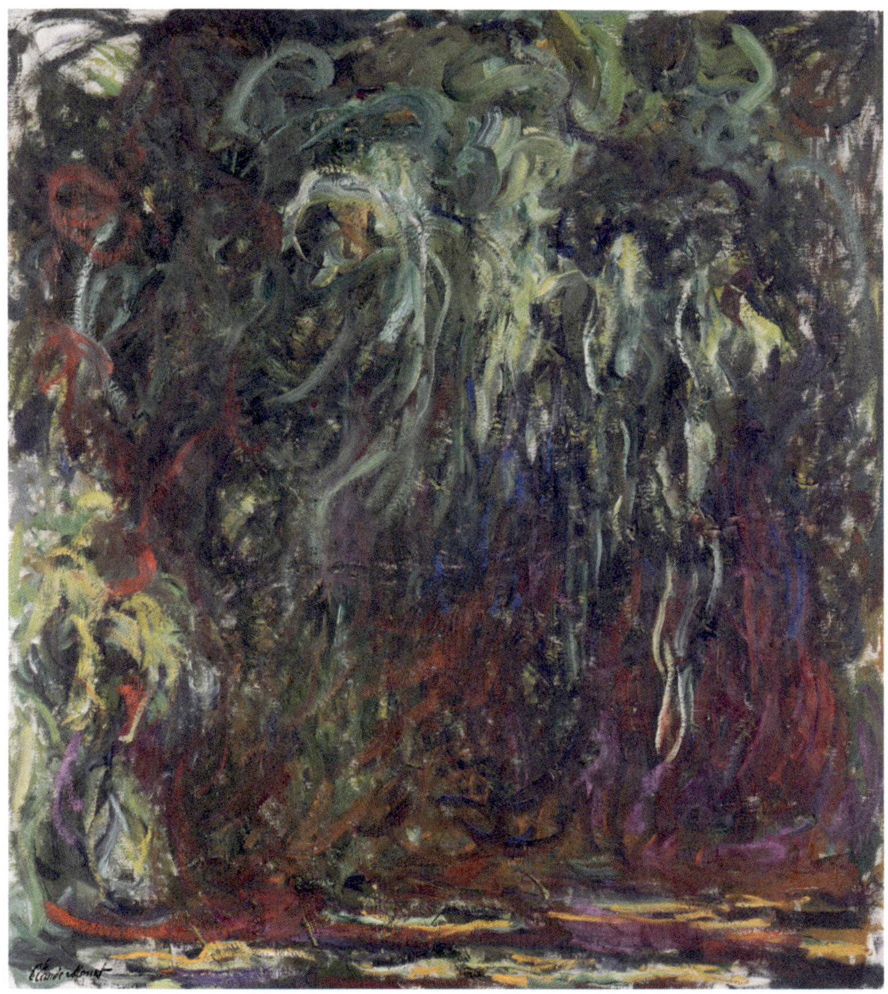

247 Left: Auguste Renoir, *Gabrielle à la rose* (*Gabrielle with a Rose*), 1911
Oil on canvas, 21 7/8 × 18 1/2 in. (55.5 × 47 cm)

248 Top, right: Paul Cézanne, *Rochers près des grottes au-dessus du Château-Noir* (*Rocks near the Caves Above the Château-Noir*), c. 1904
Oil on canvas, 25 13/16 × 21 7/16 in. (65.5 × 54.5 cm)

249 Bottom, right: Claude Monet, *Saule pleureur* (*Weeping Willow*), between 1920 and 1922. Oil on canvas, 43 5/16 × 39 3/8 in. (110 × 100 cm)

Auguste Renoir
Large Nude

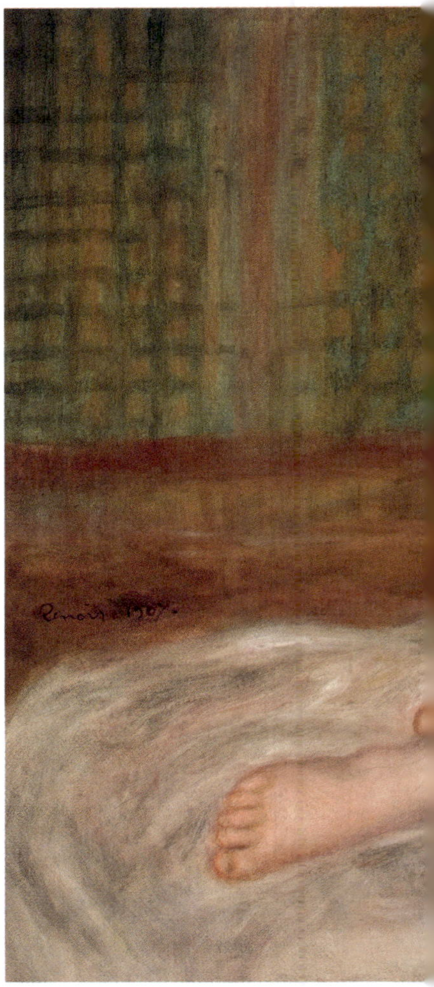

Given the poor reception of his attempts to shift away from Impressionism—his *Great Bathers* (1884–1887; Philadelphia Museum of Art), for instance, was severely criticized when first put on show in 1887—Renoir gradually abandoned his new, dry, flat style and from the late 1880s took up the "softer, lighter manner of before.... It's nothing new, it follows on from eighteenth-century paintings."[41]

Envisaging himself as the latest successor in a specific painting tradition, he visited Europe's major museums, and his efforts to measure up to his forebears—Rubens, Velázquez, Fragonard—became ever more explicit. This was notably the case for his female nudes, the subject matter of which was sourced from the Venetian Renaissance painters Giorgione and Titian. These became central to his work after 1900, and also allowed him to distance himself from modern subjects and focus instead on exploring light, form, and color, in a sensual, hedonistic approach to painting. Recalling the effect of seeing Titian's *Venus with an Organist and Cupid* (c. 1555) in Madrid's Prado Museum, he enthused: "You actually feel the joy he had in painting it."[42]

Large Nude is the last of a group of landscape-format paintings executed in the first decade of the twentieth century that show young women in an odalisque-like pose, lying back against cushions and with a flower in their hair, such as the two titled *Reclining Nude (Gabrielle)*, respectively of 1903 in the Museum of Fine Arts, Budapest, and of 1906 at the Musée de l'Orangerie, Paris. It demonstrates Renoir's mastery of rendering flesh onto canvas through transparent glazes in subtle hues that give the painting an intensely luminous quality. An array of textiles in warm, vibrant colors constitute the nude figure's setting. The full, rounded forms are patiently built up through soft, fluid brushstrokes. *Large Nude* is one of Renoir's most ambitious paintings from this turn-of-the-century period. P. P.

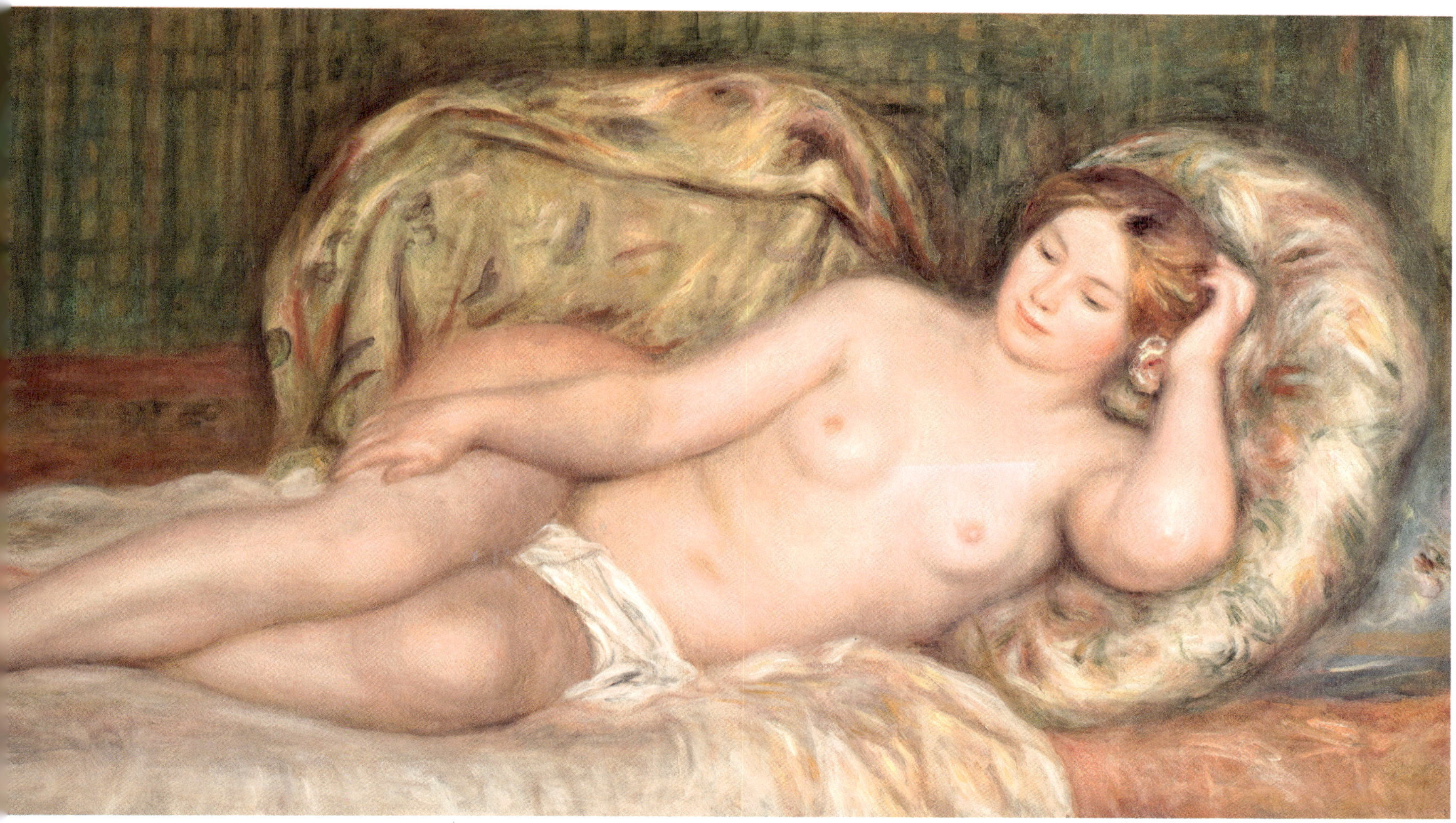

250 Auguste Renoir, *Grand nu* (*Large Nude*), 1907
Oil on canvas, 27 15⁄16 × 61 7⁄16 in. (71 × 156 cm)

Auguste Renoir
The Bathers

Renoir's health rapidly deteriorated in the early years of the new century. He suffered terrible rheumatic crises which left him severely disabled and, from 1912, completely unable to walk. No doubt in reaction to his physical suffering, he found his greatest outlet in the pleasure of painting, and devoted his time to producing powerfully sensual, comforting visions. The female nude became his main subject matter in his final years, and the bodies he depicted were increasingly rounded, with a redder hue to their skin, in line with his perceptions of youth and health.

The year before his death, Renoir seems to have set himself one final challenge by executing his last large-scale painting. The work was a homage to all the masters he had admired since his youth—Jean Goujon, Veronese, Titian, Rubens, Fragonard, Ingres, Courbet, etc.—and brought the Impressionists' quest to represent figures in outdoor settings to a final close. It was painted in a glazed studio built in Renoir's garden at Cagnes, which combined outdoor light with indoor comfort. The very dense composition is full of little touches of bright color that reflect the aging artist's idea of art's objective: "Painting's purpose is to decorate walls, is it not? So, it must be as rich as possible."[43] The colors are as transparent and fluid as watercolor, creating an interplay with the white primer underneath and sending the light bouncing off it.

From a more historical point of view, and similarly to Monet's *Water Lilies*, *The Bathers* is in its own way a celebration of the peace that had been reestablished on the signing of the Armistice in 1918. Regarded by many as Renoir's artistic testament—"He considered [*The Bathers*] the culmination of his life's work. He felt that in this picture he had summed up all his researches and prepared a springboard from which he could plunge into further researches"[44]—the painting was given to the State by the artist's sons after his death. P.P.

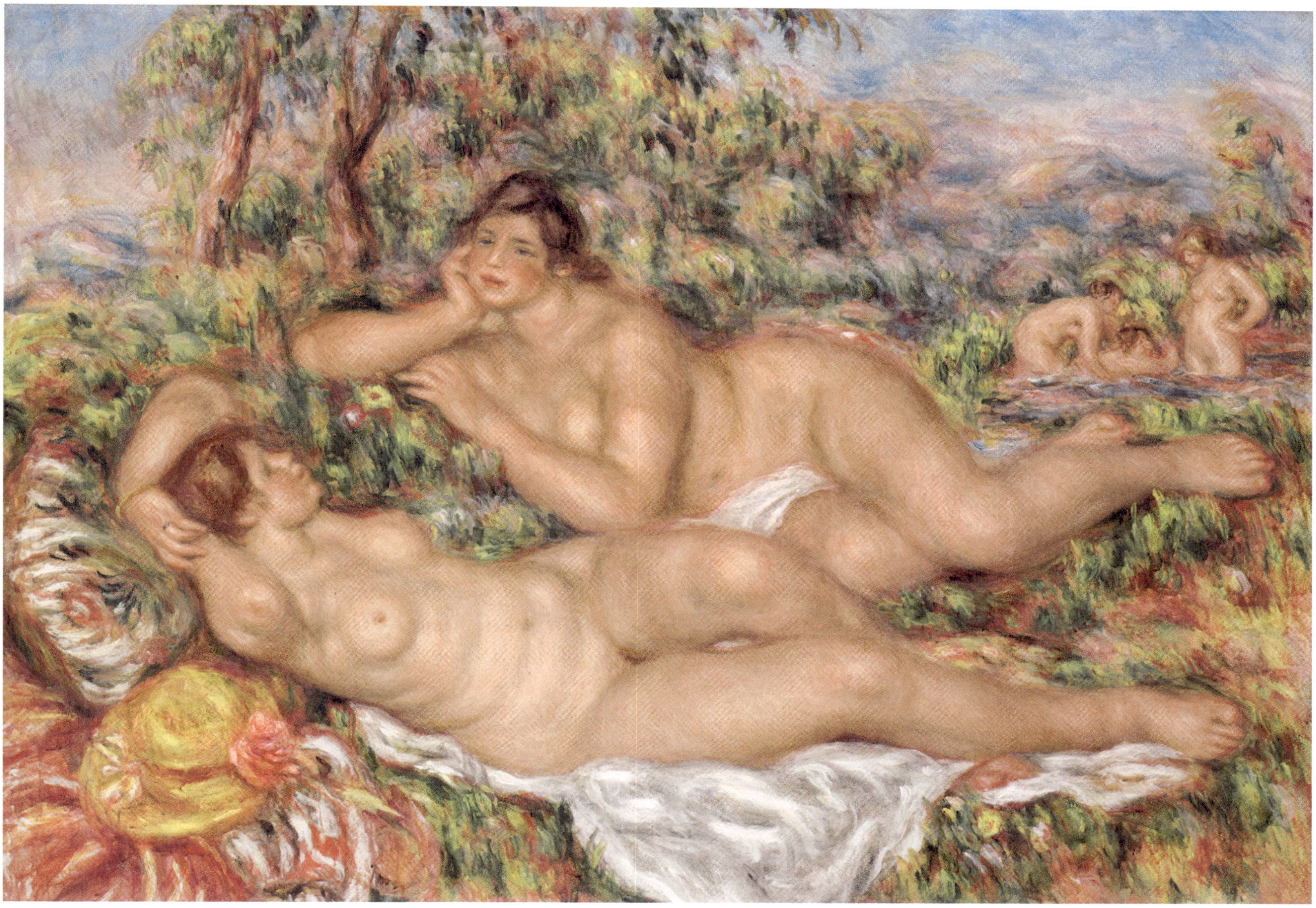

251 Auguste Renoir, *Les Baigneuses* (*The Bathers*), 1918–1919
Oil on canvas, 43 5⁄16 × 63 in. (110 × 160 cm)

Claude Monet
The Water-Lily Pond

Monet's unveiling of his first series inspired by his lily pond, at the Galerie Durand-Ruel in Paris from November 22 to December 15, 1900, was met with astonishment. Reactions varied, from his future biographer Arsène Alexandre's criticism of what he saw as their "rather simple subject" and "secondary interest," to admiration, such as from the collector Isaac de Camondo, who bought the two lily-pond paintings in the Orsay's collection. Very few people were aware that the "motifs for painting," as Monet had described them in 1893 to explain why he was creating a water-lily pond in his garden at Giverny, had become central subjects for his art.

It was not until the middle of the decade that he started to capture his water lilies in paint. In the summer of 1899, and again the following year, he set up his easel at the end of the pond, which was completely covered with sumptuous water lilies that he had carefully selected from a major plant nursery catalog. Adopting the same viewpoint and an unusual, almost square format for all eighteen of the series' canvases, which he painted partly *en plein air* and partly in his studio, Monet glorified a landscape that he had created from scratch. Both the bridge and the flowers were inspired by Japanese prints, which he collected. The abundant vegetation—willow foliage, irises, and rafts of water lilies—combines with infinitely varied reflections to saturate the surface of the painting like a tapestry, and give an unprecedented decorative power to the whole. As the poet Émile Verhaeren underlined, with this first water-lilies series Monet went beyond the "motif" to achieve a cosmic, poetic vision of nature. S.P.

252 Facing page, top: Claude Monet,
Le Bassin aux nymphéas, harmonie verte
(The Water-Lily Pond; Green Harmony), 1899
Oil on canvas, 35 ¼ × 36 7/16 in. (89.5 × 92.5 cm)

253 Facing page, bottom: Claude Monet,
Le Bassin aux nymphéas, harmonie rose
(The Water-Lily Pond; Pink Harmony), 1900
Oil on canvas, 35 7/16 × 39 9/16 in. (90 × 100.5 cm)

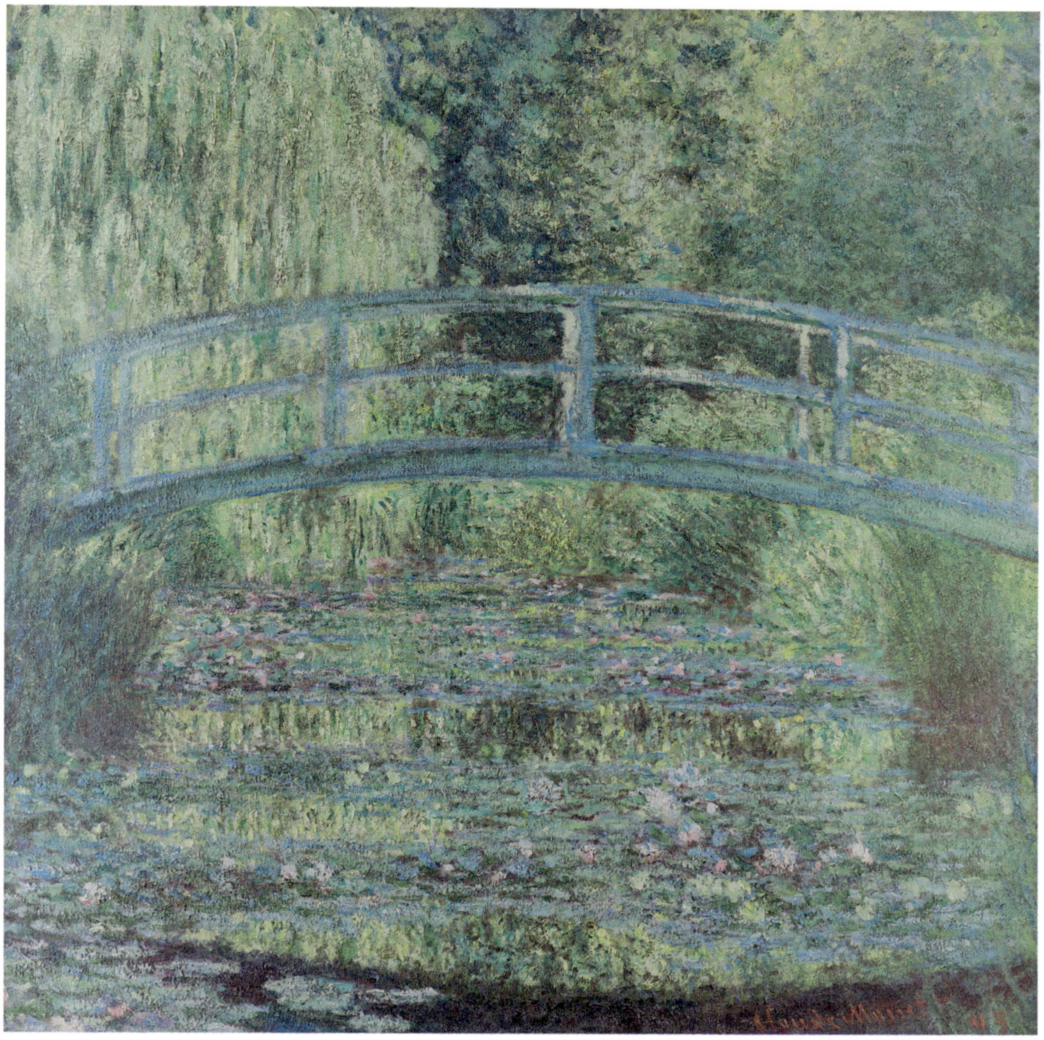

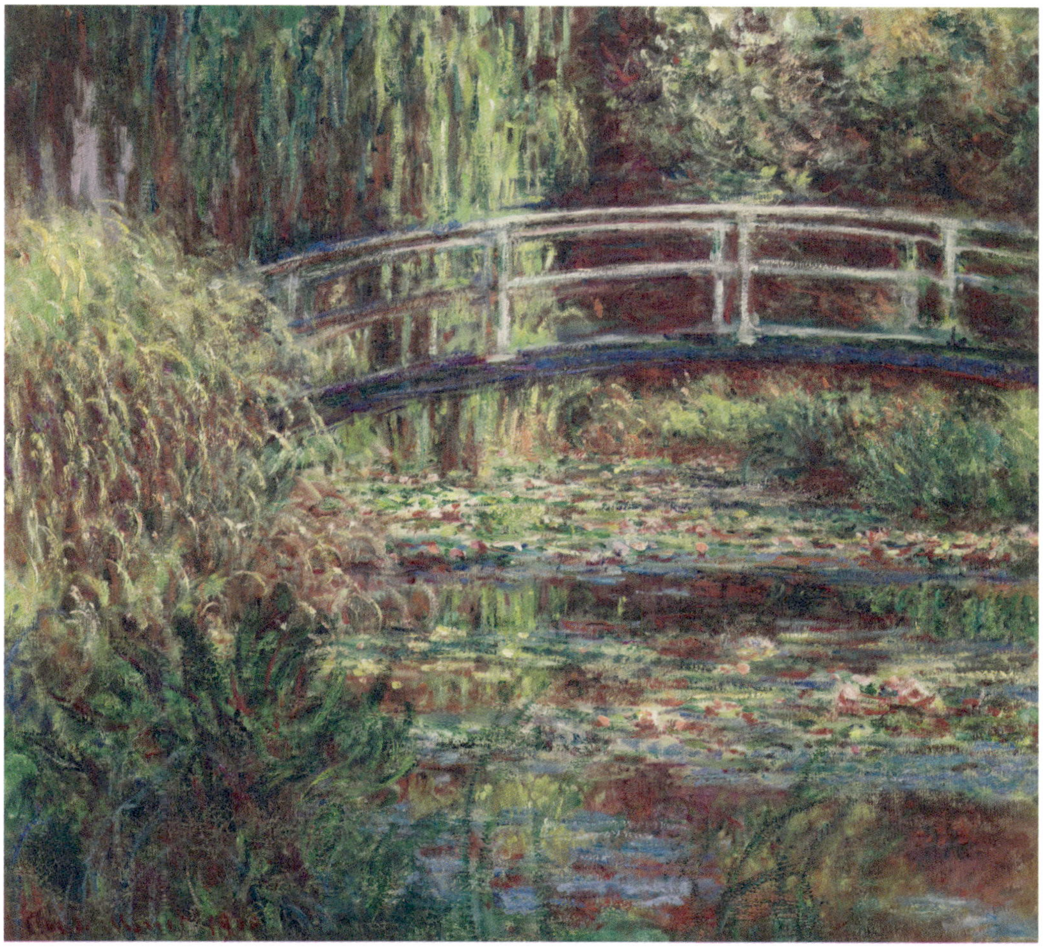

Claude Monet
Blue Water Lilies

When he commented on the lily-pond paintings (p. 263) in 1900, Émile Verhaeren noted that Monet had achieved a cosmic vision, and thus presaged the expansion and power of the *Water Lilies* in Monet's late output. In 1901, Monet tripled the size of his pond at Giverny and painted ever larger-scale "waterscapes." When World War I broke out in 1914, he took refuge in what would become, as he acknowledged, an "obsession" with water lilies. By then in his seventies, he set about his "*grandes décorations*" (great decorations)—panels largely more than six-and-a-half feet (two meters) tall and several times that in width, representing the flower-loaded surface of his water garden in close-up, changing through the seasons and times of day.

While in the late 1890s he had envisaged a décor for a dining room, the war and his friendship with Georges Clemenceau, France's prime minister and minister of war, gave this final project a historical and public dimension, as well as an unprecedented philosophical and artistic one. In the wake of the signature of the Armistice between France and Germany, the painter offered two panels to the French State, as a way of "taking part in the victory," in the words of his letter to Clemenceau of November 12, 1918. Ultimately no fewer than twenty-two panels would be installed in 1927 in Paris's Musée de l'Orangerie, in accordance with his wishes after his death in 1926. They can still be admired there today.

He completed this extraordinary undertaking, which haunted him for more than ten years, with his customary fluctuations between enthusiasm and despondency: its genesis was accompanied by more than a hundred other paintings of water lilies, including this study preserved at the Musée d'Orsay. *Blue Water Lilies* was definitely painted during the war, despite the difficulties in obtaining canvas and pigments. Most of those panels in which he tested and explored so many options—whether studies or finished works that did not make his final selection—never left his studio during his lifetime. It was only in the 1950s that they started to become immensely popular. At a time when Abstract Expressionism was triumphing in the United States, the "all-over" treatment of these water lilies—floating as they do across the entire surface of the canvas—was much appreciated, as was their gesturalism, which verges on abstraction while at the same time asserting the artist's supreme freedom and subjectivity. S.P.

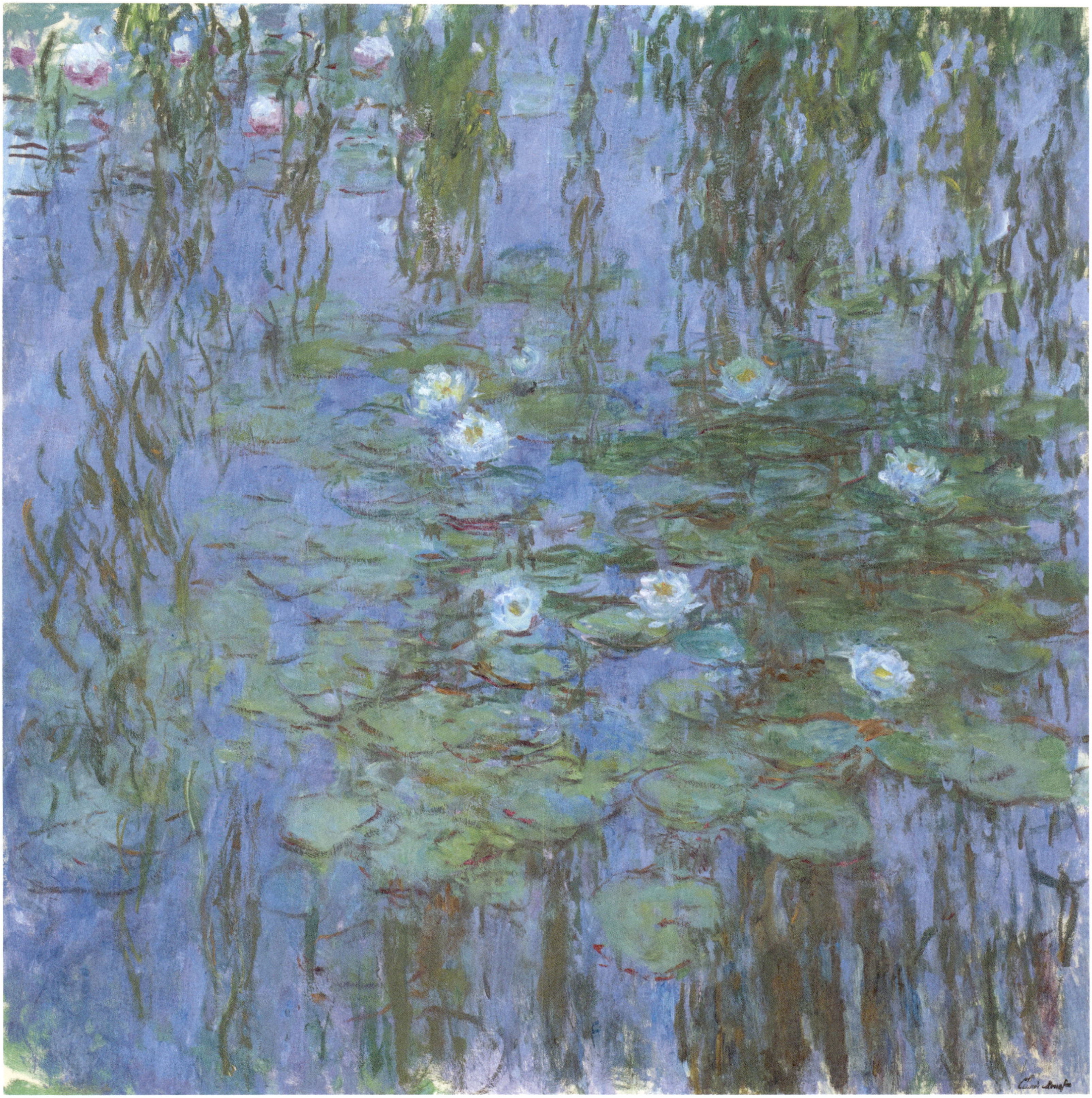

254 Claude Monet, *Nymphéas bleus* (*Blue Water Lilies*), 1916–1919
Oil on canvas, 80 5⁄16 × 78 3⁄4 in. (204 × 200 cm)

List of artworks

Frédéric Bazille
(Montpellier, France, 1841–
Beaune-la-Rolande, France, 1870)

Forêt de Fontainebleau
(Forest of Fontainebleau), 1865
Oil on canvas, 23 5/8 × 28 13/16 in.
(60 × 73.2 cm). Gift of Mme
Fantin-Latour, 1905; RF 2721;
16, p. 24

L'Ambulance improvisée
(The Improvised Field Hospital), 1865
Oil on canvas, 18 7/8 × 25 9/16 in.
(48 × 65 cm). Purchased 1967;
RF 1967 5; 17, p. 24

L'Atelier de Bazille (*Bazille's Studio*),
also known as *L'Atelier de la rue*
La Condamine (*The Studio*
on Rue La Condamine), 1869–1870
Oil on canvas, 38 9/16 × 50 5/8 in.
(98 × 128 cm). Bequest of Marc
Bazille, 1924; RF 2449; 57, p. 69

La Robe rose (*The Pink Dress*), 1864
Oil on canvas, 58 1/4 × 43 5/16 in.
(148 × 110 cm). Bequest of Marc
Bazille, 1924; RF 2450; 21, p. 30

Pierre Auguste Renoir, c. 1867–1869
Oil on canvas, 24 1/8 × 19 11/16 in.
(61.2 × 50 cm). Purchased 1935;
DL 1970 3; 2, p. 12

*Portraits de la famille**** (*Portraits*
*of the *** Family*), also known as
Réunion de famille (*The Family*
Gathering), 1867–1868
Oil on canvas, 59 13/16 × 90 9/16 in.
(152 × 230 cm). Purchased with
a contribution from Marc Bazille,
Frédéric Bazille's brother, 1905;
RF 2749; 25, p. 35

Study for *Portraits de famille****
(*Portraits of the *** Family*), 1867
Black pencil, charcoal, and graphite
on paper, 11 7/8 × 11 13/16 in.
(30.1 × 30 cm). Gift of André
Jourbin, 1921; RF 5257; 24, p. 34

Eugène Boudin
(Honfleur, France, 1824–
Deauville, France, 1898)

La Plage de Trouville
(The Beach at Trouville), 1865
Oil on board, 10 7/16 × 15 7/8 in.
(26.5 × 40.3 cm). Bequest of Eugène
Béjot, 1932; RF 3663; 41, p. 49

Soleil couchant ou ciel d'orage
(Setting Sun or Stormy Sky),
c. 1859–1860
Dry pastel on cream laid paper,
8 7/16 × 11 5/16 in. (21.5 × 28.7 cm)
Gift of Mme Asselain, daughter
of Claude Roger-Marx, 1978;
RF 36795; 72, p. 85

Marie Bracquemond
(Landunvez, France, 1840–
Sèvres, France, 1916)

La Dame en blanc
(The Lady in White), c. 1880
Oil on canvas, 71 1/16 × 41 5/16 in.
(180.5 × 105 cm). Purchased 1919;
RF 2751; 158, p. 173

Trois femmes aux ombrelles
(Three Ladies with Umbrellas), 1880
Oil on canvas, 55 5/8 × 35 1/4 in.
(141.3 × 89.5 cm). Bequest of
Gustave Geffroy, 1926; sans 194;
178, p. 195

Gustave Caillebotte
(Paris, France, 1848–
Gennevilliers, France, 1894)

Dans un café (*In a Café*), 1880
Oil on canvas, 61 × 45 1/4 in.
(155 × 115 cm). Purchased 1943;
RF 1943 70; 124, p. 139

Henri Cordier, 1883
Oil on canvas, 25 9/16 × 32 1/16 in.
(65 × 81.5 cm). Gift of Mme Henri
Cordier, 1926; RF 2729; 47, p. 56

Le Nageur (*The Swimmer*), 1877
Pastel on paper, 27 3/16 × 34 13/16 in.
(69 × 88.5 cm). Purchased 1946;
RF 1946 34; 71, p. 84

Les Soleils, jardin du Petit
Gennevilliers (Sunflowers,
Garden at Le Petit-
Gennevilliers), c. 1885
Oil on canvas, 51 3/8 × 41 5/8 in.
(130.5 × 105.8 cm). Accepted
in lieu of estate tax, 2022;
RF MO P 2022 4; 112, p. 124

Partie de bateau
(Boating Party), c. 1877–1878
Oil on canvas, 35 1/4 × 45 15/16 in.
(89.5 × 116.7 cm). Purchased thanks
to exclusive funding from LVMH,
Major Sponsor of the Musée
d'Orsay, 2022; RF MO P 2022 5;
146, p. 161

Portrait de Camille Daurelle dans
le parc de Yerres (*Portrait of Camille*
Daurelle in the Park at Yerres), 1877
Pastel on paper, 28 3/4 × 23 5/8 in.
(73 × 60 cm). Bequest of
Marie-Jeanne Daurelle, 2019;
RF MO AG 2019 5; 159, p. 173

Raboteurs de parquets
(Floor Scrapers), 1875
Oil on canvas, 40 3/16 × 57 7/8 in.
(102 × 147 cm). Gift of Caillebotte's
heirs, 1894; RF 2718; 107, p. 121

Vue de toits (Effet de neige)
(View of Rooftops [Snow Effect]), 1878
Oil on canvas, 25 3/8 × 31 7/8 in.
(64.5 × 81 cm). Gift of Martial
Caillebotte, 1894; RF 876; 144, p. 158

Mary Cassatt
(Pittsburgh, United States, 1844–
Le Mesnil-Théribus, France, 1926)

Femme et enfant devant une
tablette où sont posés un broc
et une cuvette (*Woman and Child*
in Front of a Small Table Bearing
a Wash Basin and Pitcher), 1889
Pastel on beige paper mounted
on canvas, 25 9/16 × 19 11/16 in.
(65 × 50 cm). Gift of Jean-Pierre
Hugot and Mlle Louis Hugot
with life interest retained, 1968;
RRF 31843; 208, p. 225

Jeune fille au jardin (*Young Girl*
in the Garden), 1880–1882
Oil on canvas, 36 7/16 × 25 9/16 in.
(92.5 × 65 cm)
Bequest of Antonin Personnaz,
1937; RF 1937 20; 162, p. 179

Mère et enfant sur fond vert
(Mother and Child Against
a Green Background), 1897
Pastel on beige paper mounted
on canvas, 21 5/8 × 18 1/8 in.
(55 × 46 cm)
Gift of Mary Cassatt, 1897;
RF 2051–1; 245, p. 255

Paul Cézanne
(Aix-en-Provence, France,
1839–1906)

Achille Emperaire, 1867–1868
Oil on canvas, 79 1/8 × 47 5/8 in.
(201 × 121 cm). Gift of Mme René
Lecomte and Mme Louis de
Chaisemartin, Auguste Pellerin's
daughter and granddaughter, 1964;
RF 1964 38; 55, p. 65

Apothéose de Delacroix (*Apotheosis*
of Delacroix), 1890–1894
Oil on canvas, 10 5/8 × 13 3/4 in.
(27 × 35 cm). Accepted in lieu of
estate tax, 1982; RF 1982 38; 8, p. 18

Baigneurs (*Bathers*), c. 1890
Oil on canvas, 23 13/16 × 32 1/2 in.
(60.5 × 82.5 cm). Gift of baronne
Eva Gebhard-Gourgaud, 1965;
RF 1965 3; 222, p. 239

Cinq baigneurs (*Five Bathers*),
between 1900 and 1904
Oil on canvas, 16 9/16 × 21 5/8 in.
(42 × 55 cm). Gift of Philippe Meyer
with life interest retained, 2000;
RF 2000 13; 221, p. 239

Cour d'une ferme (*Farm Courtyard*
in Auvers), c. 1879
Oil on canvas, 25 9/16 × 21 7/16 in.
(65 × 54.4 cm). Bequest of Gustave
Caillebotte, 1896; RF 2760;
244, p. 253

Gustave Geffroy, 1895–1896
Oil on canvas, 46 1/16 × 35 1/4 in.
(117 × 89.5 cm). Gift of Auguste
Pellerin's granddaughter with life
interest retained, 1969; RF 1969 29;
155, p. 169

La Femme à la cafetière
(Woman with a Coffeepot), c. 1895
Oil on canvas, 51 3/16 × 38 3/16 in.
(130 × 97 cm). Gift of M. and Mme
Jean-Victor Pellerin, 1956;
RF 1956 13; 216, p. 235

La Madeleine
(Mary Magdalene), c. 1869
Oil on plaster transferred
onto canvas, 66 1/8 × 39 9/16 in.
(168 × 126.4 cm). Purchased with
funds from an anonymous Canadian
donation, 1952; RF 1952 10; 11, p. 21

La Maison du pendu, Auvers-sur-Oise
(The House of the Hanged Man,
Auvers-sur-Oise), 1873
Oil on canvas, 21 7/8 × 26 1/8 in.
(55.5 × 66.3 cm). Bequest of comte
Isaac de Camondo, 1911; RF 1970;
86, p. 101

La Montagne Sainte-Victoire
(The Mont Sainte-Victoire), c. 1900
Watercolor over graphite sketch on
paper, 12 1/4 × 18 3/4 in. (31.1 × 47.7 cm)
Gift of Kojiro Matsukata, 1959;
RF 31171; 224, p. 240

La Table de cuisine
(The Kitchen Table), 1888–1890
Oil on canvas, 25 9/16 × 32 1/16 in.
(65 × 81.5 cm). Bequest of Auguste
Pellerin, 1929; RF 2819; 200, p. 217

Le Christ aux limbes
(Christ in Limbo), c. 1869
Oil on plaster transferred
onto canvas, 66 5/16 × 39 9/16 in.
(168.5 × 100.5 cm). Accepted
in lieu of estate tax, 2005;
RF 2005 3; 12, p. 21

Le Four à plâtre (*The Lime Kiln*),
c. 1890–1894
Watercolor over black pencil sketch
on thick cream vellum paper,
16 9/16 × 20 7/8 in. (42.1 × 53.1 cm).
Bequest of comte Isaac de
Camondo, 1911; RF 4031; 223, p. 240

Le Golfe de Marseille vu de l'Estaque
(The Gulf of Marseille seen
from L'Estaque), 1878
Oil on canvas, 23 7/16 × 28 3/4 in.
(59.5 × 73 cm). Bequest of Gustave
Caillebotte, 1896; RF 2761; 141, p. 155

Le Joueur de cartes
(The Cardplayer), 1890–1892
Oil on canvas, 19 11/16 × 18 1/8 in.
(50 × 46 cm). Gift of Heinz
Berggruen, 1997; RF 1997 54;
213, p. 232

Pont de Maincy
(The Bridge at Maincy), c. 1879
Oil on canvas, 23 × 28 1/2 in.
(58.4 × 72.4 cm). Purchased 1955;
RF 1955 20; 142, p. 157

Le Vase bleu (*The Blue Vase*),
1889–1890
Oil on canvas, 24 1/8 × 19 11/16 in.
(61.2 × 50 cm). Bequest of comte
Isaac de Camondo, 1911; RF 1973;
34, p. 43

Les Joueurs de cartes
(The Cardplayers), 1893–1896
Oil on canvas, 18 1/2 × 22 1/4 in.
(47 × 56.5 cm). Bequest of comte
Isaac de Camondo, 1911; RF 1969;
214, p. 233

Les Peupliers (*The Poplars*),
1879–1880
Oil on canvas, 25 9/16 × 32 1/16 in.
(65 × 81.5 cm). Bequest of Joseph
Reinach, 1921; RF 2324; 93, p. 110

Les Pots de fleurs
(Flower Pots), c. 1883–1887
Watercolor on graphite on paper,
9 1/4 × 12 1/16 in. (23.5 × 30.7 cm)
Bequest of comte Isaac de
Camondo, 1911; RF 4032; 195, p. 212

Les Rideaux (*The Curtains*),
c. 1885–1890
Watercolor over graphite
sketch on paper, 19 5/16 × 12 1/16 in.
(49 × 30.7 cm)
Bequest of comte Isaac de
Camondo, 1911; RF 4030; 198, p. 215

Montagne Sainte-Victoire
(Mont Sainte-Victoire), c. 1890
Oil on canvas, 25 9/16 × 37 1/2 in.
(65 × 95.2 cm). Gift of Auguste
Pellerin's granddaughter with life
interest retained, 1969; RF 1969 30;
225, p. 241

Nature morte à la bouilloire
(Still Life with Kettle), 1867–1869
Oil on canvas, 25 3/8 × 31 7/8 in.
(64.5 × 81 cm). Purchased by the
Musées Nationaux with installments
from a donation, 1963; RF 1964 37;
199, p. 216

Nature morte à la soupière
(Still Life with Soup Tureen), c. 1877
Oil on canvas, 25 9/16 × 32 1/16 in.
(65 × 81.5 cm). Bequest of Auguste
Pellerin, 1929; RF 2818; 201, p. 217

Pastorale (*Pastoral*), 1870
Oil on canvas, 25 9/16 × 32 1/16 in.
(65 × 81.5 cm). Accepted
in lieu of estate tax, 1982;
RF 1982 48; 104, p. 118

Paysan assis
(Seated Peasant), c. 1900
Oil on canvas, 28 7/8 × 23 3/4 in.
(73.3 × 60.3 cm). Accepted
in lieu of estate tax, 2009;
RF 2009 8; 215, p. 234

Portrait d'Achille Emperaire (*Portrait*
of Achille Emperaire), c. 1867–1870
Charcoal and graphite on
mounted buff paper, 19 × 12 1/8 in.
(48.2 × 30.8 cm)
Gift of Adrien Chappuis, 1967;
RF 31778; 54, p. 64

Rochers près des grottes
au-dessus du Château-Noir
(Rocks near the Caves Above the
Château-Noir), c. 1904
Oil on canvas, 25 13/16 × 21 7/16 in.
(65.5 × 54.5 cm). Accepted
in lieu of estate tax, 1978;
RF 1978 32; 248, p. 257

Trois baigneuses (*Three Bathers*),
c. 1874–1875
Oil on canvas, 7 11/16 × 8 7/8 in.
(19.5 × 22.5 cm). Accepted
in lieu of estate tax, 1982;
RF 1982 40; 220, p. 238

Une moderne Olympia
(A Modern Olympia), 1873–1874
Oil on canvas, 18 3/16 × 21 7/8 in.
(46.2 × 55.5 cm). Gift of Paul
Gachet, 1951; RF 1951 31; 82, p. 96

Edgar Degas
(Paris, France, 1834–1917)

Au café-concert des Ambassadeurs (At the Ambassadeurs Café-Concert), 1885
Pastel on monotype etching on paper, 10 7/16 × 11 5/8 in. (26.5 × 29.5 cm). Bequest of comte Isaac de Camondo, 1911; RF 4041; 127, p. 143

Autoportrait à la statue de Bartholomé (Self-Portrait with Bartholomé Statue), 1895
Silver print, 11 1/4 × 15 1/2 in. (28.5 × 39.3 cm). Gift of Alberto Martinez through the Société des Amis du Musée d'Orsay, 1992; PHO 1992 5; 238, p. 250

Ballet, also known as *L'Étoile (The Star*, or *Dancer on Stage)*, c. 1876–1877
Pastel on monotype on paper, 23 × 16 9/16 in. (58.4 × 42 cm)
Bequest of Gustave Caillebotte, 1896; RF 12258; 129, p. 145

Chez la modiste (At the Milliner's), 1882
Pastel on paper, 26 3/8 × 20 1/2 in. (67 × 52 cm). Gift of Philippe Meyer with life interest retained, 2000; RF 52075; 173, p. 189

Choristes (Chorus), 1876–1877
Pastel on monotype on paper, 10 11/16 × 12 11/16 in. (27.1 × 32.3 cm)
Bequest of Gustave Caillebotte, 1896; RF 12259; 128, p. 144

Dans un café (In a Café), also known as *L'Absinthe (The Absinthe Drinker)*, 1875–1876
Oil on canvas, 36 1/4 × 26 15/16 in. (92 × 68.5 cm). Bequest of comte Isaac de Camondo, 1911; RF 1984; 125, p. 139

Danseuse assise se massant le pied gauche (Seated Dancer Massaging Her Foot), 1881–1883
Pastel on tan paper mounted on board, 24 7/16 × 19 5/16 in. (62 × 49 cm). Bequest of Gustave Caillebotte, 1896; RF 22712; 242, p. 252

Danseuse, position de quatrième devant sur la jambe gauche, première étude (Dancer, Fourth Position on Left Leg, First Study), between 1896 and 1911
Wax on wooden base, 16 1/8 × 10 1/4 × 9 13/16 in. (41 × 26 × 25 cm)
Gift of Paul Mellon, 1956; RF 2770; 169, p. 185

Danseuse, vue de dos, les mains sur les hanches (Dancer, Hands on Hips, Viewed from Behind), c. 1873
Turpentine-thinned oil heightened with white on pink paper, 14 1/2 × 10 1/8 in. (36.8 × 25.7 cm)
Bequest of comte Isaac de Camondo, 1911; RF 4038; 134, p. 148

Danseuses bleues (Blue Dancers), c. 1890
Oil on canvas, 33 9/16 × 29 5/8 in. (85.3 × 75.3 cm)
Gift of Dr. and Mme Albert Charpentier, 1951; RF 1951 10; 246, p. 256

Danseuses montant un escalier (Dancers Climbing the Stairs), 1886–1890
Oil on canvas, 15 3/8 × 35 1/4 in. (39 × 89.5 cm). Bequest of comte Isaac de Camondo, 1911; RF 1979; 130, p. 146

Deux baigneuses sur l'herbe (Two Bathers on the Grass), 1886–1890
Pastel on brown paper, 27 9/16 × 27 9/16 in. (70 × 70 cm)
Purchased with funds from an anonymous Canadian donation, 1953; RF 29950; 219, p. 237

Deux danseuses (Two Dancers), 1878–1879
Fan; watercolor heightened with gold and silver on cream silk laid on card, 11 × 22 13/16 in. (28 × 58 cm)
Gift of the Kan family, 2026; RF MO AG 2026 2; 139, p. 153

Falaises au bord de la mer (Cliffs at the Seaside), 1869
Pastel on gray paper, 12 3/4 × 18 7/16 in. (32.4 × 46.9 cm). Gift of baronne Eva Gebhard-Gourgaud with life interest retained, 1965; RF 31199; 43, p. 53

Femme à sa toilette essuyant son pied gauche (Nude Wiping Her Left Foot), 1886
Pastel on board, 21 3/8 × 20 5/8 in. (54.3 × 52.4 cm). Bequest of comte Isaac de Camondo, 1911; RF 4045; 206, p. 221

Femme dans son bain s'épongeant la jambe (Woman in Her Bath, Sponging Down Her Leg), c. 1883
Pastel on monotype on paper, 7 3/4 × 16 1/8 in. (19.7 × 41 cm)
Bequest of comte Isaac de Camondo, 1911; RF 4043; 205, p. 220

Femme nue, couchée sur le dos (Nude Woman Lying on Her Back, study for *Scene of War in the Middle Ages)*, 1865
Black pencil on paper, 10 1/2 × 13 15/16 in. (26.7 × 35.3 cm)
Purchased 1918; RF 15519; 14, p. 22

Femme nue debout (Standing Female Nude), 1880–1883
Pastel and charcoal on blue-green paper, 19 1/2 × 12 1/16 in. (49.5 × 30.7 cm)
Purchased 1942; RF 29346; 135, p. 149

Femme, nue, se coiffant (Nude Woman Combing Her Hair), 1879–1883
Black ink and monotype on cream paper, 12 3/8 × 11 in. (31.5 × 28 cm)
Purchased 1922; RF 16724; 204, p. 219

Femmes à la terrasse d'un café, le soir (Women on a Café Terrace in the Evening), 1877
Pastel on monotype on paper, 16 1/8 × 23 5/8 in. (41 × 60 cm)
Bequest of Gustave Caillebotte, 1896; RF 12257; 126, p. 141

Fin d'arabesque (Finishing the Arabesque), 1876–1877
Turpentine-thinned oil and pastel on canvas, 29 9/16 × 14 15/16 in. (67.4 × 38 cm). Bequest of comte Isaac de Camondo, 1911; RF 4040; 118, p. 132

Henri Rouart (1833–1912) industriel et collectionneur, chez lui, devant ses tableaux (Henri Rouart, Industrialist and Collector (1833–1912), at Home, in Front of His Paintings), 1895
Gelatin silver print from a glass negative, 14 3/4 × 10 13/16 in. (37.5 × 27.5 cm). Purchased 2003; PHO 2003 7; 239, p. 251

L'Orchestre de l'Opéra (The Orchestra of the Opéra), c. 1870
Oil on canvas, 22 5/16 × 18 1/8 in. (56.6 × 46 cm). Purchased from Mlle Marie Dihau with life interest retained, 1923; RF 2417; 52, p. 61

La Classe de danse (The Dance Class), 1873–1876
Oil on canvas, 33 11/16 × 29 1/2 in. (85.5 × 75 cm). Bequest of comte Isaac de Camondo, 1911; RF 1976; 131, p. 147

La Femme à la potiche (Woman with Porcelain Vase), 1872
Oil on canvas, 25 9/16 × 21 1/4 in. (65 × 54 cm). Bequest of comte Isaac de Camondo, 1911; RF 1983; 62, p. 72

La Repasseuse (Woman Ironing), 1869
Charcoal, white chalk, and pastel on paper, 29 1/8 × 24 in. (74 × 61 cm)
Bequest of Antonin Personnaz, 1937; RF 28829; 84, p. 97

Le Champ de courses. Jockeys amateurs près d'une voiture (The Racecourse: Amateur Jockeys near a Carriage), 1876–1887
Oil on canvas, 25 11/16 × 31 15/16 in. (65.2 × 81.2 cm). Bequest of comte Isaac de Camondo, 1911; RF 1980; 137, p. 151

Le Défilé (The Parade, or *Racehorses Before the Stands)*, 1866–1868
Oil on paper mounted on canvas, 18 1/8 × 24 in. (46 × 61 cm)
Bequest of comte Isaac de Camondo, 1911; RF 1981; 136, p. 151

Le Tub (The Tub), 1886
Pastel on board, 23 5/8 × 32 11/16 in. (60 × 83 cm). Bequest of comte Isaac de Camondo, 1911; RF 4046; 207, p. 223

Ludovic Halévy et Albert Boulanger-Cavé dans les coulisses de l'Opéra (Portrait of Friends on the Stage, also known as *Portrait of Ludovic Halévy and Albert Boulanger-Cavé)*, 1879
Tempera and pastel on paper, 31 1/8 × 21 5/8 in. (79 × 55 cm)
Gift of Mme Halévy with life interest retained, 1958; RF 31140; 145, p. 159

Marine (Seascape), 1869
Pastel on buff paper, 12 3/8 × 18 7/16 in. (31.4 × 46.9 cm). Gift of baronne Eva Gebhard-Gourgaud with life interest retained, 1965; RF 31202; 44, p. 53

Marine (Seascape), 1869
Pastel on paper, 9 7/16 × 10 3/8 in. (24 × 26.3 cm). Bequest of M. and Mme Georges Morhange, 1990; RF 42993; 45, p. 53

Petite danseuse de quatorze ans (Little Fourteen-Year-Old Dancer), between 1878 and 1881 (model), between 1921 and 1931 (bronze)
Patinated bronze, tulle tutu, satin ribbon, wooden base, 40 7/8 × 19 3/16 × 19 11/16 in. (103.8 × 48.8 × 50 cm)
Purchased thanks to the generosity of Edgar Degas's heirs and the Hébrard family, 1931; RF 2137; 166, p. 183

Physionomie de criminel (Physiognomy of a Criminal), 1880–1881
Pastel and charcoal on paper mounted on artist's board, 18 13/16 × 24 15/16 (47.8 × 63.2 cm)
Purchased 2025; RF MO AG 2025 13 1; 165, p. 182

Portrait au miroir du peintre Henry Lerolle et de ses deux filles, Yvonne et Christine (Portrait of the Painter Henry Lerolle and His Two Daughters, Yvonne and Christine, with Mirror), between 1895 and 1896
Gelatin silver print from a glass negative, 11 7/16 × 14 1/4 in. (29 × 36.2 cm). Purchased 2004; PHO 2004 4; 240, p. 251

Portrait de famille (Family Portrait), also known as *La Famille Bellelli (The Bellelli Family)*, 1858–1869
Oil on canvas, 79 1/8 × 98 1/4 in. (201 × 249.5 cm). Purchased 1918; RF 2210; 51, p. 59

Portrait de Giulia Bellelli (Portrait of Giulia Bellelli), c. 1858
Black pencil, gray wash, turpentine, and white highlights on cream paper, 9 5/16 × 7 3/16 in. (23.6 × 19.6 cm)
Purchased at public auction, 1927; RF 11689; 50, p. 58

Portrait de René de Gas (Portrait of René de Gas), c. 1855–1856
Graphite on paper, 11 13/16 × 9 1/16 in. (30 × 23 cm). Purchased at public auction, 1994; RF 44320; 133, p. 148

Portraits à la bourse (Portraits at the Stock Exchange), 1878–1879
Oil on canvas, 39 9/16 × 32 1/16 in. (100.5 × 81.5 cm). Gift of Ernest May with life interest retained, 1923; RF 2444; 49, p. 57

Quatre études d'une danseuse (Four Studies of a Dancer), c. 1878–1879
Graphite with white highlights on pink paper, 19 5/16 × 12 5/8 in. (49 × 32 cm). Purchased at public auction, 1919; RF 4646; 164, p. 182

Repasseuses (Women Ironing), between 1884 and 1886
Oil on canvas, 29 15/16 × 32 1/16 in. (76 × 81.4 cm). Bequest of comte Isaac de Camondo, 1911; RF 1985; 110, p. 123

Répétition d'un ballet sur la scène (Ballet Rehearsal on Stage), 1874
Oil on canvas, 25 9/16 × 32 1/16 in. (65 × 81.5 cm). Bequest of comte Isaac de Camondo, 1911; RF 1978; 132, p. 147

Scène de guerre au Moyen Âge (Scene of War in the Middle Ages), c. 1865
Turpentine-thinned oil on paper pasted on canvas, 32 1/4 × 58 7/16 in. (83.5 × 148.5 cm). Purchased 1918; RF 2208; 15, p. 23

Sémiramis construisant Babylone (Semiramis Building Babylon), 1861
Oil on canvas, 59 5/8 × 101 9/16 in. (151.5 × 258 cm). Purchased 1918; RF 2207; 10, p 20

Henri Fantin-Latour
(Grenoble, France, 1836–Buré, France, 1904)

Hommage à Delacroix (Homage to Delacroix), 1864
Oil on canvas, 63 × 98 7/16 in. (160 × 250 cm). Gift of Étienne Moreau-Nélaton, 1906; RF 1664; 9, p. 19

Un atelier aux Batignolles (A Studio at Les Batignolles), 1870
Oil on canvas, 80 5/16 × 107 11/16 in. (204 × 273.5 cm). Purchased 1892; RF 729; 56, p. 67

Paul Gauguin
(Paris, France, 1848–Atuona, French Polynesia, 1903)

Nature morte aux oranges (Still Life with Oranges), c. 1881
Oil on canvas, 13 × 18 1/8 in. (33 × 46 cm)
Bequest of Ernest Chaplet, 1910; RF 2766; 171, p. 186

Nature morte. Vase de fleurs à la fenêtre (Still Life: Vase of Flowers at the Window), c. 1881
Oil on canvas, 7 1/2 × 10 5/8 in. (19 × 27 cm)
Bequest of Carle Dreyfus, 1953; RF 1953 6; 170, p. 186

Eva Gonzalès
(Paris, France, 1847–1883)

La Matinée rose (The Pink Morning Gown), 1874
Pastel on paper and stretched canvas, 36 15/16 × 29 1/4 in. (93.8 × 74.3 cm)
Purchased 1885; RF 12299; 69, p. 81

Une loge aux Italiens (A Box at the Théâtre des Italiens), c. 1874
Oil on canvas, 38 7/16 × 51 3/16 in. (97.7 × 130 cm)
Gift of Jean Guérard, 1927; RF 2643; 160, p. 175

Armand Guillaumin
(Paris, France, 1841–
Orly, France, 1927)

Femme nue couchée
(Reclining Nude), c. 1877
Oil on canvas, 19 5/16 × 25 9/16 in.
(49 × 65 cm)
Gift of Paul Gachet, 1951;
RF 1951 35; 105, p. 119

La Place Valhubert
(Place Valhubert), c. 1880
Oil on canvas, 25 ⅜ × 31 ⅞ in.
(64.5 × 81 cm). Bequest of Antonin
Personnaz, 1937; RF 1937 28;
157, p. 172

Les Pêcheurs (Fishing), c. 1885
Oil on canvas, 31 ⅞ × 26 in.
(81 × 66 cm). Bequest of Antonin
Personnaz, 1937; RF 1937 33;
189, p. 207

Soleil couchant à Ivry
(Setting Sun at Ivry), 1873
Oil on canvas, 25 9/16 × 31 ⅞ in.
(65 × 81 cm). Gift of Paul Gachet,
1951; RF 1951 34; 87, p. 103

Johan Barthold Jongkind
(Lattrop, Netherlands, 1819–
Saint-Egrève, France, 1891)

En Hollande, les barques près
du moulin (In Holland, Boats
near the Mill), 1868
Oil on canvas, 20 11/16 × 32 in.
(52.5 × 81.3 cm). Bequest of comte
Isaac de Camondo, 1911; RF 1990;
42, p. 51

Ruines du château de Rosemont
(Ruins of the Château
de Rosemont), 1861
Oil on canvas, 13 ⅜ × 22 ¼ in.
(34 × 56.5 cm)
Gift of Étienne Moreau-Nélaton,
1907; RF 1703; 4, p. 14

Stanislas Lépine
(Caen, France, 1835–
Paris, France, 1892)

Paysage (Landscape), 1869
Oil on canvas, 11 13/16 × 22 13/16 in.
(30 × 58 cm). Bequest of Enriqueta
Alsop in the name of Dr. Eduardo
Mollard, 1972; RF 1972 26; 83, p. 96

Édouard Manet
(Paris, France, 1832–1883)

Anguille et rouget
(Eel and Red Snapper), 1864
Oil on canvas, 14 15/16 × 18 ⅛ in.
(38 × 46 cm). Gift of Dr. and
Mme Albert Charpentier, 1951;
RF 1951 9; 31, p. 41

Berthe Morisot à l'éventail
(Berthe Morisot with a Fan), 1872
Oil on canvas, 23 ¾ × 17 13/16 in.
(60.4 × 45.2 cm). Gift of Étienne
Moreau-Nélaton, 1906; RF 1671;
66, p. 75

Berthe Morisot au bouquet
de violettes (Berthe Morisot with
a Bunch of Violets), 1872
Oil on canvas, 21 ⅞ × 15 15/16 in.
(55.5 × 40.5 cm). Purchased with
contributions from the Fonds du
Patrimoine, the Fondation Meyer,
the China Times Group, and
sponsorship coordinated by the
Japanese daily newspaper *Nikkei*,
1998; RF 1998 30; 65, p. 75

Branche de pivoines blanches et
sécateur (Branch of White Peonies
and Shears), 1864
Oil on canvas, 12 × 18 5/16 in.
(30.5 × 46.5 cm). Bequest of comte
Isaac de Camondo, 1911; RF 1995;
36, p. 44

Deux jambes avec bottines sous
une jupe rouge, devant un guéridon
(At the Café, Study of Legs), 1880
Watercolor, black wash, and
graphite on squared paper,
7 5/16 × 4 ¾ in. (18.6 × 12 cm)
Purchased 1954; RF 30521;
197, p. 213

Émile Zola, 1868
Oil on canvas, 57 ½ × 44 ⅞ in.
(146 × 114 cm). Gift of Mme Émile
Zola with life interest retained, 1918;
RF 2205; 29, p. 39

Fleurs dans un vase de cristal
(Flowers in a Crystal Vase), 1882
Oil on canvas, 21 7/16 × 13 ¾ in.
(54.5 × 35 cm). Gift of Philippe
Meyer with life interest retained,
2000; RF 2000 19; 35, p. 43

Georges Clemenceau, 1879–1880
Oil on canvas, 37 × 29 1/16 in.
(94 × 73.8 cm). Gift of M. Louisine
Havemeyer, 1927; RF 2641;
154, p. 169

La Dame aux éventails
(Lady with Fans), 1873
Oil on canvas, 44 ½ × 65 9/16 in.
(113 × 166.5 cm). Gift of M. and
Mme Ernest Rouart, 1930; RF 2850;
140, p. 153

L'Asperge (Asparagus), 1880
Oil on canvas, 6 ⅝ × 8 ⅝ in.
(16.9 × 21.9 cm). Gift of Sam Salz,
1959; RF 1959 18; 30, p. 40

L'Évasion de Rochefort
(Rochefort's Escape), c. 1881
Oil on canvas, 31 ⅛ × 28 ⅜ in.
(79 × 72 cm). Accepted in lieu
of estate tax, 1984; RF 1984 158;
156, p. 171

La Lecture (Reading), 1865–1873
Oil on canvas, 24 × 28 13/16 in.
(61 × 73.2 cm). Bequest of princesse
Edmond de Polignac, 1947;
RF 1944 17; 61, p. 72

La Serveuse de bocks (The Beer
Waitress), 1878–1879
Oil on canvas, 30 5/16 × 25 ⅜ in.
(77 × 64.5 cm). Entered the Louvre
in accordance with the French
peace treaty with Japan, 1959;
RF 1959 4; 123, p. 138

Le Balcon (The Balcony), 1868–1869
Oil on canvas, 66 15/16 × 49 3/16 in.
(170 × 125 cm). Bequest of Gustave
Caillebotte, 1896; RF 2772; 53, p. 63

Le Christ aux anges (The Dead Christ
with Angels), c. 1865–1867
Watercolor, pen and India ink,
gouache, and graphite on paper,
12 13/16 × 10 ⅝ in. (32.5 × 27 cm)
Bequest of Mme Émile Zola, 1918;
RF 4520; 13, p. 21

Le Déjeuner sur l'herbe
(Luncheon on the Grass), 1863
Oil on canvas, 81 ½ × 104 5/16 in.
(207 × 265 cm). Gift of Étienne
Moreau-Nélaton, 1906;
RF 1668; 5, p. 15

Le Fifre (The Fifer), 1866
Oil on canvas, 63 3/16 × 38 3/16 in.
(160.5 × 97 cm). Bequest of comte
Isaac de Camondo, 1911; RF 1992;
28, p. 37

Le Tub (The Tub), 1878
Pastel on canvas, 21 ¼ × 17 11/16 in.
(54 × 45 cm). Purchased 1973;
RF 35739; 202, p. 218

Lola de Valence, 1862
Oil on canvas, 48 7/16 × 36 ¼ in.
(123 × 92 cm). Bequest of comte
Isaac de Camondo, 1911; RF 1991;
26, p. 36

Olympia, 1863–1865
Oil on canvas, 51 ⅜ × 75 3/16 in.
(130.5 × 191 cm). Gift to the State
through public subscription
organized by Claude Monet, 1890;
RF 644; 7, p. 17

Portrait de Berthe Morisot
à l'éventail (Portrait of Berthe
Morisot with a Fan), 1874
Oil on canvas, 24 3/16 × 19 ⅞ in.
(61 × 50.5 cm). Accepted
in lieu of estate tax, 1999;
RF 1999 12; 64, p. 74

Portrait de Madame Édouard
Manet sur un canapé bleu
(Portrait of Madame Édouard
Manet on a Blue Sofa), 1874
Pastel on tan paper mounted
on canvas, 19 5/16 × 23 ⅝ in.
(49 × 60 cm). Purchased 1918;
RF 4507; 70, p. 83

Stéphane Mallarmé, 1876
Oil on canvas, 10 11/16 × 14 1/16 in.
(27.2 × 35.7 cm). Purchased through
the Société des Amis du Louvre
and D. David Weill, 1928; RF 2661;
152, p. 168

Study for *Olympia*, 1862–1863
Red chalk on paper, 9 ¾ × 17 15/16 in.
(24.7 × 45.6 cm). Purchased at
public auction, 1935; RF 24335;
6, p. 16

Sur la plage (On the Beach), 1873
Oil on canvas, 23 ⅝ × 28 15/16 in.
(60 × 73.5 cm). Gift of Jean-Édouard
Dubrujeaud, in memory of his uncle
Jacques Doucet, with life interest
retained, 1953; RF 1953 24; 46, p. 55

Une dame à sa fenêtre (étude)
(A Lady at Her Window [Study]), 1865
Oil on canvas, 36 ¼ × 28 15/16 in.
(92 × 73.5 cm). Bequest of Gustave
Caillebotte, 1896; RF 3664; 27, p. 36

Vase de pivoines sur piédouche
(Vase of Peonies on a Pedestal), 1864
Oil on canvas, 36 ¾ × 27 9/16 in.
(93.3 × 70 cm). Gift of Étienne
Moreau-Nélaton, 1906; RF 1669;
37, p. 45

Claude Monet
(Paris, France, 1840–
Giverny, France, 1926)

Bras de Seine près de Giverny
(Branch of the Seine near
Giverny), 1897
Oil on canvas, 28 13/16 × 36 ⅝ in.
(73.2 × 93 cm). Bequest of comte
Isaac de Camondo, 1911; RF 2003;
228, p. 243

Camille sur son lit de mort
(Camille on Her Deathbed), 1879
Oil on canvas, 35 7/16 × 26 ¾ in.
(90 × 68 cm). Gift of Mme Katia
Granoff, 1963; RF 1963 3; 151, p. 167

Champ de tulipes en Hollande
(Fields of Tulips in Holland), 1886
Oil on canvas, 25 13/16 × 32 1/16 in.
(65.5 × 81.5 cm). Bequest of
princesse Edmond de Polignac,
1947; RF 1944 19; 179, p. 196

Chrysanthèmes
(Chrysanthemums), 1878
Oil on canvas, 21 ⅜ × 25 11/16 in.
(54.3 × 65.2 cm). Gift of Paul
Gachet, 1951; RF 1951 36; 33, p. 42

Coquelicots (Poppies), 1873
Oil on canvas, 19 11/16 × 25 11/16 in.
(50 × 65.3 cm). Gift of Étienne
Moreau-Nélaton, 1906; RF 1676;
85, p. 99

Effet de neige à Vétheuil
(Snow Effect at Vétheuil), 1878–1879
Oil on canvas, 20 11/16 × 27 15/16 in.
(52.5 × 71 cm). Bequest of Gustave
Caillebotte, 1896; RF 3755;
150, p. 165

Effet de vent, série des peupliers
(Poplars: Wind Effect), 1891
Oil on canvas, 39 ⅜ × 29 ⅛ in.
(100 × 74 cm). Accepted in lieu
of estate tax, 2002; RF 2002 30;
227, p. 243

Essai de figure en plein-air:
femme à l'ombrelle tournée vers
la droite (Study of a Figure in the
Open Air: Woman with a Parasol
Facing Right), 1886
Oil on canvas, 51 ⅜ × 35 3/16 in.
(130.5 × 89.3 cm). Gift of Michel
Monet, 1927; RF 2620; 176, p. 193

Essai de figure en plein-air:
femme à l'ombrelle tournée vers
la gauche (Study of a Figure in
the Open Air: Woman with a Parasol
Facing Left), 1886
Oil on canvas, 51 9/16 × 34 15/16 in.
(131 × 88.7 cm). Gift of Michel
Monet, 1927; RF 2621; 177, p. 193

Étretat: la plage et la porte
d'Amont (Étretat: The Beach and
the Porte d'Amont), 1883
Oil on canvas, 26 × 31 15/16 in.
(66 × 81.2 cm). Bequest of Antonin
Personnaz, 1937; RF 1937 42;
38, p. 46

Femmes au jardin
(Women in the Garden), c. 1866
Oil on canvas, 100 ⅜ × 80 11/16 in.
(255 × 205 cm). Purchased 1921;
RF 2773; 23, p. 33

Hôtel des Roches Noires,
Trouville, 1870
Oil on canvas, 31 ⅞ × 22 13/16 in.
(81 × 58 cm). Gift of Jacques
Laroche with life interest retained,
1947; RF 1947 30; 40, p. 47

Intérieur d'appartement
(Apartment Interior), also known
as *Un coin d'appartement*
(Corner of an Apartment), 1875
Oil on canvas, 32 1/16 × 23 ⅝ in.
(81.5 × 60 cm). Bequest of Gustave
Caillebotte, 1896; RF 2776; 74, p. 87

La Cathédrale de Rouen: Le Portail
et la tour Saint-Romain, effet
du matin (Rouen Cathedral: The
Portal and the Saint-Romain Tower,
Morning Sun), 1893
Oil on canvas, 41 15/16 × 28 13/16 in.
(106.5 × 73.2 cm). Bequest of comte
Isaac de Camondo, 1911; RF 2001;
230, p. 245

La Cathédrale de Rouen:
Le Portail et la tour Saint-Romain,
plein soleil (Rouen Cathedral:
The Portal and the Saint-Romain
Tower in Full Sun), 1893
Oil on canvas, 42 ⅛ × 29 ⅛ in.
(107 × 73.5 cm). Bequest of comte
Isaac de Camondo, 1911; RF 2002;
233, p. 247

La Cathédrale de Rouen: Le Portail vu
de face (Rouen Cathedral: The Portal
Seen from the Front), 1892
Oil on canvas, 42 ⅛ × 29 ⅛ in.
(107 × 74 cm). Purchased from
Claude Monet, 1907; RF 2779;
231, p. 246

La Cathédrale de Rouen: Le Portail,
soleil matinal (Rouen Cathedral:
The Portal in the Morning Light), 1893
Oil on canvas, 36 5/16 × 24 13/16 in.
(92.2 × 63 cm). Bequest of comte
Isaac de Camondo, 1911; RF 2000;
234, p. 247

La Cathédrale de Rouen: Le Portail,
temps gris (Rouen Cathedral:
The Portal on a Gray Day), 1892
Oil on canvas, 39 7/16 × 25 ¾ in.
(100.2 × 65.4 cm). Bequest of comte
Isaac de Camondo, 1911; RF 1999;
232, p. 246

La Charrette. Route sous la neige
à Honfleur (The Cart: Snow-Covered
Road at Honfleur), c. 1867
Oil on canvas, 25 9/16 × 36 ⅝ in.
(65 × 93 cm). Bequest of comte
Isaac de Camondo, 1911; RF 2011;
19, p. 27

La Gare Saint-Lazare
(The Gare Saint-Lazare), 1877
Oil on canvas, 29 ½ × 41 5/16 in.
(75 × 105 cm). Bequest of Gustave
Caillebotte, 1896; RF 2775; 121, p. 135

La Pie (The Magpie), 1868–1869
Oil on canvas, 35 1/16 × 51 3/16 in.
(89 × 130 cm). Purchased 1984;
RF 1984 164; 20, p. 29

La Rue Montorgueil, à Paris: Fête du 30 juin 1878 (Rue Montorgueil, Paris: Festival of June 30, 1878), 1878
Oil on canvas, 31 ⅞ × 19 ¹¹⁄₁₆ in. (81 × 50 cm). Accepted in lieu of estate tax, 1982; RF 1982 71; 147, p. 163

La Seine à Vétheuil, effet de soleil après la pluie (The Seine at Vétheuil, Sun Effect After Rain), 1879
Oil on canvas, 23 ¹³⁄₁₆ × 32 ¹⁄₁₆ in. (60.5 × 81.5 cm). Bequest of comte Isaac de Camondo, 1911; RF 1998; 98, p. 113

Le Bassin aux nymphéas, harmonie rose (The Water-Lily Pond; Pink Harmony), 1900
Oil on canvas, 35 ⁷⁄₁₆ × 39 ⁹⁄₁₆ in. (90 × 100.5 cm). Bequest of comte Isaac de Camondo, 1911; RF 2005; 253, p. 263

Le Bassin aux nymphéas, harmonie verte (The Water-Lily Pond; Green Harmony), 1899
Oil on canvas, 35 ¼ × 36 ⁷⁄₁₆ in. (89.5 × 92.5 cm). Bequest of comte Isaac de Camondo, 1911; RF 2004; 252, p. 263

Le Bassin d'Argenteuil (The Dock at Argenteuil), c. 1872
Oil on canvas, 23 ⅝ × 31 ⅞ in. (60 × 81 cm). Bequest of comte Isaac de Camondo, 1911; RF 2010; 76, p. 89

Le Déjeuner sur l'herbe (Luncheon on the Grass), 1865–1866
Oil on canvas, 98 × 85 ¾ in. and 164 ½ × 59 in. (248.7 × 218 cm and 418 × 150 cm). Accepted in lieu of estate tax, 1987; RF 1987 12; RF 1957 7; 22, p. 31

Le Déjeuner. Panneau décoratif (The Luncheon: Decorative Panel), c. 1873
Oil on canvas, 63 × 79 ⅛ in. (160 × 201 cm). Bequest of Gustave Caillebotte, 1896; RF 2774; 102, p. 115

Le Jardin de l'artiste à Giverny (The Artist's Garden at Giverny), 1900
Oil on canvas, 32 ⅛ × 36 ⁷⁄₁₆ in. (81.6 × 92.6 cm). Accepted in lieu of estate tax, 1983; RF 226; 114, p. 125

Le Mont Kolsaas en Norvège (Kolsås Mountain, Norway), 1895
Oil on canvas, 25 ¹³⁄₁₆ × 39 ⁹⁄₁₆ in. (65.5 × 100.5 cm). Purchased 1967; RF 1967 7; 138, p. 152

Le Pavé de Chailly (The Pavé de Chailly), c. 1865
Oil on canvas, 17 ⅛ × 23 ⅜ in. (43.5 × 59.3 cm). Gift of Étienne Moreau-Nélaton, 1906; RF 1672; 18, p. 25

Le Pont d'Argenteuil (The Argenteuil Bridge), 1874
Oil on canvas, 23 ¾ × 31 ½ in. (60.3 × 80 cm). Bequest of Antonin Personnaz, 1937; RF 1937 41; 101, p. 114

Le Pont de Waterloo à Londres (Waterloo Bridge, London), c. 1899
Pastel on pinkish-beige paper, 12 ⁵⁄₁₆ × 19 ⅛ in. (31.3 × 48.5 cm). Bequest of baronne Eva Gebhard-Gourgaud with life interest retained, 1965; RF 31206; 73, p. 85

Le Pont du chemin de fer à Argenteuil (The Railway Bridge at Argenteuil), between 1873 and 1874
Oil on canvas, 21 ¼ × 27 ¹⁵⁄₁₆ in. (54 × 71 cm). Gift of Étienne Moreau-Nélaton, 1906; RF 1679; 78, p. 91

Les Déchargeurs de charbon (Unloading the Coal), c. 1875
Oil on canvas, 21 ¼ × 25 ¹³⁄₁₆ in. (54 × 65.5 cm). Accepted in lieu of estate tax, 1993; RF 1993 21; 111, p. 123

Les Dindons (The Turkeys), 1877
Oil on canvas, 68 ½ × 67 ¹⁵⁄₁₆ in. (174 × 172.5 cm). Bequest of princesse Edmond de Polignac, 1947; RF 1944 18; 117, p. 131

Les Glaçons (Ice Thawing on the Seine), 1880
Oil on canvas, 23 ¹³⁄₁₆ × 39 ³⁄₁₆ in. (60.5 × 99.5 cm). Gift of baronne Eva Gebhard-Gourgaud, 1965; RF 1965 10; 149, p. 165

Les Rochers de Belle-Île, la Côte sauvage (The Rocks of Belle-Île: The Wild Coast), 1886
Oil on canvas, 25 ¹³⁄₁₆ × 32 ¹⁄₁₆ in. (65.5 × 81.5 cm). Bequest of Gustave Caillebotte, 1896; RF 2777; 184, p. 199

Les Tuileries; esquisse (The Tuileries: Sketch), c. 1876
Oil on canvas, 19 ¹¹⁄₁₆ × 29 ¾ in. (50 × 75.5 cm). Bequest of Gustave Caillebotte, 1896; RF 2705; 120, p. 133

Les Villas à Bordighera (Villas at Bordighera), 1884
Oil on canvas, 45 ⅞ × 53 ¾ in. (116.5 × 136.5 cm). Unique acquisition arrangement, 2000; RF 2000 94; 181, p. 197

Lilas, temps gris (Lilacs, Gray Weather), 1872–1873
Oil on canvas, 19 ¾ × 25 ¹¹⁄₁₆ in. (50.2 × 65.2 cm). Gift of Étienne Moreau-Nélaton, 1906; RF 1680; 113, p. 125

Londres, le Parlement. Trouée de soleil dans le brouillard (London, Houses of Parliament: Effect of Sunlight in the Fog), 1904
Oil on canvas, 32 ¹⁄₁₆ × 36 ⁷⁄₁₆ in. (81.5 × 92.5 cm). Bequest of comte Isaac de Camondo, 1911; RF 2007; 226, p. 242

Madame Louis Joachim Gaudibert, 1868
Oil on canvas, 85 ¼ × 54 ½ in. (216.5 × 138.5 cm). Purchased with funds from an anonymous Canadian donation, 1951; RF 1951 20; 48, p. 57

Méditation. Madame Monet au canapé (Meditation: Madame Monet on the Sofa), c. 1871
Oil on canvas, 19 × 29 ⁵⁄₁₆ in. (48.2 × 74.5 cm). Bequest of M. and Mme Raymond Koechlin, 1931; RF 1951 20; 60, p. 71

Meules, fin de l'été (Grainstacks, Late Summer), 1891
Oil on canvas, 23 ¹³⁄₁₆ × 39 ¹¹⁄₁₆ in. (60.5 × 100.8 cm). Purchased with funds from an anonymous Canadian donation, 1975; RF 1975 3; 229, p. 243

Nature morte: le quartier de viande (Still Life: The Quarter of Meat), c. 1864
Oil on canvas, 9 ⁷⁄₁₆ × 13 in. (24 × 33 cm). Gift of Étienne Moreau-Nélaton, 1906; RF 1675; 32, p. 41

Nymphéas bleus (Blue Water Lilies), 1916–1919
Oil on canvas, 80 ⁵⁄₁₆ × 78 ¾ in. (204 × 200 cm). Purchased 1981; RF 1981 40; 254, p. 265

Régates à Argenteuil (The Regatta at Argenteuil), c. 1872
Oil on canvas, 18 ⅞ × 29 ⅝ in. (48 × 75.3 cm). Bequest of Gustave Caillebotte, 1896; RF 2778; 95, p. 111

Saule pleureur (Weeping Willow), between 1920 and 1922
Oil on canvas, 43 ⁵⁄₁₆ × 39 ⅜ in. (110 × 100 cm). Gift of Philippe Meyer with life interest retained, 2000; RF 2000 21; 249, p. 257

Tempête, côtes de Belle-Île (Storm off the Belle-Île Coast), 1886
Oil on canvas, 25 ¾ × 32 ¹⁄₁₆ in. (65.4 × 81.5 cm). Bequest of Gaston Migeon, 1932; RF 3163; 183, p. 199

Vétheuil, soleil couchant (Vétheuil, Setting Sun), c. 1900
Oil on canvas, 35 ⁷⁄₁₆ × 36 ⅝ in. (90 × 93 cm). Bequest of comte Isaac de Camondo, 1911; RF 2006; 148, p. 164

Zaandam, 1871
Oil on canvas, 18 ¹³⁄₁₆ × 28 ¾ in. (47.8 × 73 cm). Gift of Étienne Moreau-Nélaton, 1906; RF 1673; 58, p. 70

Berthe Morisot
(Bourges, France, 1841—Paris, France, 1895)

Chasse aux papillons (Chasing Butterflies), 1874
Oil on canvas, 18 ⅛ × 22 ¹⁄₁₆ in. (46 × 56 cm). Gift of Étienne Moreau-Nélaton, 1906; RF 1681; 115, p. 127

Dans les blés (In the Wheatfields), 1875
Oil on canvas, 18 ⁵⁄₁₆ × 27 ³⁄₁₆ in. (46.5 × 69 cm). Bequest of Antonin Personnaz, 1937; RF 1937 45; 90, p. 105

Femme demie nue, vue de dos, se coiffant, une glace reflétant son corps (Half-Undressed Woman Seen from the Rear, Doing Her Hair, Her Body Reflected in a Mirror), c. 1889–1890
Graphite on tracing paper, 12 × 8 ⅛ in. (30.5 × 20.7 cm)
Means of acquisition unknown, 1929; RF 12006; 203, p. 219

Jeune femme en toilette de bal (Young Woman a Ball Gown), 1879
Oil on canvas, 28 ⅛ × 21 ¼ in. (71.5 × 54 cm). Purchased 1894; RF 843; 161, p. 177

Jeune femme dans un paysage (Young Woman in a Landscape), 1872
Watercolor on paper, 13 × 9 ¹⁄₁₆ in. (33 × 23 cm). Gift of Étienne Moreau-Nélaton, 1907; RF 3393; 196, p. 213

Jeune femme se poudrant (Young Woman Powdering Her Face), 1877
Oil on canvas, 18 ⅛ × 15 ⅜ in. (46 × 39 cm). Bequest of Antonin Personnaz, 1937; RF 1937 44; 63, p. 73

L'Hortensia (The Hydrangea), 1894
Oil on canvas, 28 ¾ × 23 ¾ in. (73.1 × 60.4 cm). Gift of Ernest and Julie Rouart, 1920; RF 2268; 210, p. 229

Le Berceau (The Cradle), 1872
Oil on canvas, 22 ¹⁄₁₆ × 18 ⁵⁄₁₆ in. (56 × 46.5 cm). Purchased 1930; RF 2849; 68, p. 79

Portrait de Madame Edma Pontillon, née Edma Morisot, sœur de l'artiste (Portrait of Madame Edma Pontillon, née Edma Morisot, the Artist's Sister), 1871
Pastel on paper, 32 ¹⁄₁₆ × 25 ⅞ in. (81.5 × 65.8 cm). Bequest of Mme Pontillon, 1921; RF 5262; 67, p. 77

Sur la falaise (On the Cliff), 1873
Watercolor heightened by gouache over pencil lines on paper, 7 ¹⁄₁₆ × 9 ¹⁄₁₆ in. (18 × 23 cm)
Gift of Étienne Moreau-Nélaton, 1907; RF 3429; 39, p. 46

Sur un banc au bois de Boulogne (On a Bench in the Bois de Boulogne), 1894
Oil on canvas, 15 ¹⁄₁₆ × 21 ¾ in. (38.2 × 55.3 cm). Bequest of Nadia Boulanger, 1980; RF 1980 43; 96, p. 111

Camille Pissarro
(Charlotte Amalie, Danish West Indies [now US Virgin Islands], 1830—Paris, France, 1903)

Baigneuses au bord de l'eau (Bathers at the Water's Edge), 1894–1896
Gouache on silk, 10 ¹⁄₁₆ × 8 ⁹⁄₁₆ in. (25.6 × 21.7 cm). Purchased 1931; RF 16726; 218, p. 236

Champs au soleil (Fields in the Sunshine), c. 1886
Watercolor over graphite sketch on paper, 7 ¹⁄₁₆ × 8 ⅝ in. (18 × 21.9 cm). Gift of Mme Louis Léon Weill, 1981; RF 38837; 194, p. 211

Côte Saint-Denis à Pontoise (The Côte Saint-Denis at Pontoise), 1877
Oil on canvas, 21 ⁷⁄₁₆ × 25 ¹³⁄₁₆ in. (54.5 × 65.6 cm). Bequest of Gustave Caillebotte, 1896; RF 2735; 92, p. 109

Dieppe, bassin Duquesne: Marée basse, soleil, matin (Dieppe, Duquesne Docks: Low Tide, Morning Sunlight), 1902
Oil on canvas, 21 ⁷⁄₁₆ × 25 ⁹⁄₁₆ in. (54.5 × 65 cm). Bequest of Antonin Personnaz, 1937; RF 1937 55; 237, p. 249

Femme au fichu vert (Woman with a Green Scarf), 1893
Oil on canvas, 25 ¹³⁄₁₆ × 21 ⁷⁄₁₆ in. (65.5 × 54.5 cm)
Bequest of Enriqueta Alsop in the name of Dr. Eduardo Mollard, 1972; RF 1972 30; 209, p. 227

Femme dans un clos, soleil de printemps dans le pré à Éragny (Woman in a Field; Spring Sunshine in the Meadow at Éragny), 1887
Oil on canvas, 21 ⁷⁄₁₆ × 25 ⁹⁄₁₆ in. (54.5 × 65 cm). Bequest of Antonin Personnaz, 1937; RF 1937 47; 193, p. 209

Femme étendant du linge (Woman Hanging Laundry), 1887
Oil on canvas, 16 ⅛ × 13 in. (41 × 33 cm). Bequest of Enriqueta Alsop in the name of Dr. Eduardo Mollard, 1972; RF 1972 29; 192, p. 208

Gelée blanche (Hoarfrost), 1873
Oil on canvas, 25 ¹³⁄₁₆ × 36 ¹¹⁄₁₆ in. (65.5 × 93.2 cm). Bequest of Enriqueta Alsop in the name of Dr. Eduardo Mollard, 1972; RF 1972 27; 91, p. 107

Jardin potager à l'Hermitage, Pontoise (Vegetable Garden at L'Hermitage, Pontoise), 1879
Oil on canvas, 21 ⅝ × 25 ¹³⁄₁₆ in. (55 × 65.5 cm). Bequest of Antonin Personnaz, 1937; RF 1937 48; 88, p. 104

La Bergère (The Shepherdess), 1881
Oil on canvas, 31 ⅞ × 25 ½ in. (81 × 64.8 cm). Bequest of comte Isaac de Camondo, 1911; RF 2013; 163, p. 181

La Brouette, verger, le Valhermeil, Auvers-sur-Oise (Wheelbarrow in an Orchard at Le Valhermeil, Auvers-sur-Oise), c. 1879
Oil on canvas, 21 ¼ × 25 ⁹⁄₁₆ in. (54 × 65 cm). Bequest of Gustave Caillebotte, 1896; RF 2734; 188, p. 206

La Route de Sydenham, Londres (The Avenue, Sydenham, London), 1871
Gouache over pencil lines on paper, 5 ⅞ × 9 ¹¹⁄₁₆ in. (15 × 24.6 cm)
Bequest of Antonin Personnaz, 1937; RF 28798; 59, p. 71

Le Chemin des Mathurins montant à travers champs, Pontoise (The Chemin des Mathurins in Pontoise, Climbing Through Fields), 1879
Oil on canvas, 21 ¼ × 25 ⁹⁄₁₆ in. (54 × 65 cm). Bequest of Gustave Caillebotte, 1896; RF 2736; 172, p. 187

Le Pont Boïeldieu à Rouen (The Boïeldieu Bridge, Rouen), 1896
Oil on canvas, 21 ¼ × 25 ⁹⁄₁₆ in. (54 × 65 cm). Accepted in lieu of estate tax, 1983; RF 1983 7; 236, p. 249

Marché à Gisors (Market at Gisors), 1890
Gouache over charcoal lines on canvas, 18 ⅛ × 14 ¹⁵⁄₁₆ in. (46 × 38 cm).
Bequest of Antonin Personnaz, 1937; RF 1938 43; 109, p. 123

Port de Rouen, Saint-Sever (The Port of Rouen, Saint-Sever), 1896
Oil on canvas, 25 ¹³⁄₁₆ × 36 ⁵⁄₁₆ in. (65.5 × 92.2 cm)
Bequest of Enriqueta Alsop in the name of Dr. Eduardo Mollard, 1972; RF 1972 31; 235, p. 249

Port-Marly, 1872
Oil on canvas, 18 ⁵⁄₁₆ × 22 ¹⁄₁₆ in. (46.5 × 56 cm). Bequest of Gustave Caillebotte, 1896; RF 2732; 79, p. 93

Printemps. Pruniers en fleurs (Springtime: Plum Trees in Blossom), 1877
Oil on canvas, 25 ¹³⁄₁₆ × 31 ⅞ in. (65.5 × 81 cm). Bequest of Gustave Caillebotte, 1896; RF 2733; 143, p. 158

Auguste Renoir
(Limoges, France, 1841—Cagnes-sur-Mer, France, 1919)

Bal du Moulin de la Galette (Dance at the Moulin de la Galette), 1876
Oil on canvas, 51 ¾ × 69 ½ in. (131.5 × 176.5 cm). Bequest of Gustave Caillebotte, 1896; RF 2739; 122, p. 137

Champ de bananiers (Field of Banana Trees), 1881
Oil on canvas, 20 ¹⁄₁₆ × 24 ¹³⁄₁₆ in. (51 × 63 cm). Purchased with funds from an anonymous Canadian donation, 1959; RF 1959 1; 182, p. 197

Chemin montant dans les hautes herbes (Path Rising into Deep Grass), c. 1875
Oil on canvas, 23 ⅝ × 29 ⅛ in. (60 × 74 cm). Gift of Charles Comiot through the Société des Amis du Louvre, 1926; RF 2581; 94, p. 110

Claude Monet, 1875
Oil on canvas, 33 ¹⁄₁₆ × 23 ¹³⁄₁₆ in. (84 × 60.5 cm). Bequest of M. and Mme Raymond Koechlin, 1931; RF 3666; 100, p. 114

Danse à la campagne (Dance in the Country), 1883
Oil on canvas, 71 × 35 ⁷⁄₁₆ in. (180.3 × 90 cm). Purchased 1979; RF 1979 64; 174, p. 191

Danse à la ville (Dance in the City), 1883
Oil on canvas, 70 ¾ × 35 ¹⁄₁₆ in. (179.7 × 89.1 cm). Accepted in lieu of estate tax, 1978; RF 1978 13; 175, p. 191

Étude (Study), also known as *Torse, effet de soleil (Torso, Sunlight Effect)*, c. 1876
Oil on canvas, 31 ⅞ × 25 ⁹⁄₁₆ in. (81 × 65 cm). Bequest of Gustave Caillebotte, 1896; RF 2740; 103, p. 117

Frédéric Bazille, 1867
Oil on canvas, 41 ⁵⁄₁₆ × 28 ¹⁵⁄₁₆ in. (105 × 73.5 cm). Bequest of Marc Bazille, 1924; RF 2448; 3, p. 13

Gabrielle à la rose (Gabrielle with a Rose), 1911
Oil on canvas, 21 ⅞ × 18 ½ in. (55.5 × 47 cm)
Gift of Philippe Gangnat in memory of his father, 1925; RF 2491; 247, p. 257

Grand nu (Large Nude), 1907
Oil on canvas, 27 ¹⁵⁄₁₆ × 61 ⁷⁄₁₆ in. (71 × 156 cm). Accepted in lieu of estate tax, 2000; RF 1975 18; 250, pp. 258–59

Jeunes filles au piano (Young Girls at the Piano), 1892
Oil on canvas, 45 ¹¹⁄₁₆ × 35 ⁷⁄₁₆ in. (116 × 90 cm). Purchased from Auguste Renoir, 1892; RF 755; 212, p. 231

Julie Manet, 1887
Oil on canvas, 25 ¹³⁄₁₆ × 21 ¹⁄₁₆ in. (65.5 × 53.5 cm). Accepted in lieu of estate tax, 1999; RF 1999 13; 187, p. 205

La Balançoire (The Swing), 1876
Oil on canvas, 36 ¼ × 28 ¾ in. (92 × 73 cm). Bequest of Gustave Caillebotte, 1896; RF 2738; 116, p. 129

La Liseuse (Woman Reading), 1874–1876
Oil on canvas, 18 ⁵⁄₁₆ × 15 ³⁄₁₆ in. (46.5 × 38.5 cm). Bequest of Gustave Caillebotte, 1896; RF 3757; 241, p. 252

La Mosquée (The Mosque), 1881
Oil on canvas, 28 ¹⁵⁄₁₆ × 36 ⁷⁄₁₆ in. (73.5 × 92.5 cm). Gift of the Biddle Foundation in memory of Margaret Biddle, 1957; RF 1957 8; 180, p. 197

La Seine à Champrosay (The Seine at Champrosay), 1876
Oil on canvas, 21 ½ × 26 in. (54.6 × 66 cm). Bequest of Gustave Caillebotte, 1896; RF 2737; 119, p. 133

Le Garçon au chat (Boy with a Cat), 1868
Oil on canvas, 48 ⅝ × 26 in. (123.5 × 66 cm)
Purchased at public auction, 1992; RF 1992 409; 106, p. 119

Le Poirier d'Angleterre (The English Pear Tree), c. 1873
Oil on canvas, 26 ³⁄₁₆ × 32 ¹⁄₁₆ in. (66.5 × 81.5 cm). Accepted in lieu of estate tax, 2012; RF 2012 5; 89, p. 105

Les Baigneuses (The Bathers), 1918–1919
Oil on canvas, 43 ⁵⁄₁₆ × 63 in. (110 × 160 cm). Gift of Auguste Renoir's sons, 1923; RF 2795; 251, p. 261

Les Marronniers roses (Red Horse-Chestnut Trees), also known as *Pont de chemin de fer à Chatou (Railway Bridge at Chatou)*, 1881
Oil on canvas, 21 ⁷⁄₁₆ × 25 ¹³⁄₁₆ in. (54.5 × 65.5 cm). Bequest of Gustave Caillebotte, 1896; RF 3758; 75, p. 88

Madame Georges Charpentier, 1876–1877
Oil on canvas, 18 ⅛ × 14 ¹⁵⁄₁₆ in. (46 × 38 cm). Gift of the Société des Amis du Luxembourg with a contribution from Mme Tournon, née Georgette Charpentier, 1919; RF 2244; 153, p. 169

Maternité (Motherhood), 1885
Oil on canvas, 36 ¼ × 28 ⅜ in. (92 × 72 cm). Accepted in lieu of estate tax, 1998; RF 1998 35; 185, p. 201

Paysage algérien, le ravin de la femme sauvage (Algerian Landscape: The Ravine of the "Femme Sauvage"), 1881
Oil on canvas, 25 ⁹⁄₁₆ × 32 ¹⁄₁₆ in. (65 × 81.5 cm). Purchased 1943; RF 1943 62; 99, p. 113

Portrait de Stéphane Mallarmé (Portrait of Stéphane Mallarmé), 1892
Oil on canvas, 19 ¹¹⁄₁₆ × 15 ¾ in. (50 × 40 cm). Purchased 1950; RF 1950 44; 211, p. 230

Trois baigneuses au bord de l'eau (Three Bathers at the Water's Edge), study for *Baigneuses. Essai de peinture décorative (The Great Bathers)*, c. 1886
Black pencil with white and red chalk highlights on paper, 42 ½ × 63 ¾ in. (108 × 162 cm)
Gift of Jacques Laroche with life interest retained, 1947; RF 29660; 186, p. 203

Auguste Renoir
Richard Guino
(Girona, Spain, 1890—Antony, France, 1973)
Venus victrix, between 1914 and 1916
Patinated shellac-sealed plaster, 75 ⁹⁄₁₆ × 52 ¾ × 28 ¾ in. (192 × 134 × 73 cm). Purchased 2018; RF MO S 2018 3; 168, p. 185

Medardo Rosso
(Turin, Italy, 1858—Milan, Italy, 1928)

Aetas Aurea (The Golden Age), 1886
Bronze relief, 19 ¹¹⁄₁₆ × 14 ⅞ × 10 ⁷⁄₁₆ in. (50 × 37.8 × 26.5 cm). Purchased 1988; RF 4231; 167, p. 184

Georges Seurat
(Paris, France, 1859–1891)

Study for *Un dimanche après-midi à l'île de la Grande Jatte (A Sunday on La Grande Jatte)*, 1884–1886
Oil on wood panel, 6 ¼ × 9 ¹³⁄₁₆ in. (16 × 25 cm). Anonymous gift, 1930; RF 2828; 191, p. 207

Study for *Un dimanche après-midi à l'île de la Grande Jatte (A Sunday on La Grande Jatte)*, 1884
Oil on wood panel, 6 ⅛ × 9 ¹³⁄₁₆ in. (15.5 × 25 cm). Gift of Mlle Thérèse and Georges-Henri Rivière in memory of their parents, 1948; RF 1948 1; 190, p. 207

Study for *Une baignade à Asnières (Bathers at Asnières)*, 1883
Oil on wood, 6 ⅛ × 9 ¹³⁄₁₆ in. (15.5 × 25 cm). Gift of baronne Eva Gebhard-Gourgaud, 1965; RF 1965 13; 217, p. 236

Alfred Sisley
(Paris, France, 1839—Moret-sur-Loing, France, 1899)

Chemin de la briqueterie, Marly-le-Roi, c. 1876
Oil on canvas, 21 ⅝ × 18 ⅛ in. (55 × 46 cm). Bequest of Gustave Caillebotte, 1896; RF 2783; 243, p. 253

L'Inondation à Port-Marly (The Flood at Port-Marly), 1876
Oil on canvas, 23 ⅝ × 31 ⅞ in. (60 × 81 cm). Bequest of comte Isaac de Camondo, 1911; RF 2020; 80, p. 95

La Barque pendant l'inondation, Port-Marly (The Bark During the Flood, Port-Marly), 1876
Oil on canvas, 19 ¹³⁄₁₆ × 24 in. (50.4 × 61 cm). Bequest of comte Isaac de Camondo, 1911; RF 2021; 81, p. 95

La Forge à Marly-le-Roi (The Forge at Marly-le-Roi), 1875
Oil on canvas, 21 ⅝ × 28 ¾ in. (55 × 73 cm). Gift of Étienne Moreau-Nélaton, 1906; RF 1689; 108, p. 122

Le Héron aux ailes déployées (The Heron with Outstretched Wings), 1867
Oil on canvas, 31 ½ × 39 ⅜ in. (80 × 100 cm)
Gift of Mme Pierre Goujon with life interest retained, 1971; RF 1971 15; 1, p. 12

Passerelle d'Argenteuil (Footbridge at Argenteuil), 1872
Oil on canvas, 15 ⅜ × 23 ⅝ in. (39 × 60 cm). Gift of Étienne Moreau-Nélaton, 1906; RF 1688; 77, p. 89

Rue de la chaussée à Argenteuil (Rue de la Chaussée at Argenteuil), 1872
Oil on canvas, 18 ⁵⁄₁₆ × 25 ¹⁵⁄₁₆ in. (46.5 × 66 cm). Gift of Étienne Moreau-Nélaton, 1906; RF 1692; 97, p. 112

Endnotes

1. p. 28: Richard Kendall (ed.), with translations by Bridget Strevens Romer, *Monet By Himself: Paintings, Drawings, Pastels, Letter* (Macdonald Orbis, 1989), 26.

2. p. 32: Édouard Mortier, Duke of Treviso, "Le pèlerinage de Giverny," *Revue de l'Art ancien et moderne*, t. I (1927): 122.

3. p. 32: Émile Zola, "Mon Salon: Les actualistes," *L'Événement illustré* (May 24, 1868), 2. Republished in Émile Zola, *Écrits sur l'art* (Gallimard, 1991), 209.

4. p. 36: Juliet Wilson-Bareau (ed. and transl.), *Manet By Himself: Correspondence & Conversation; Paintings, Pastels, Prints and Drawings* (Little, Brown & Company, 1991), 41.

5. p. 36: Wilson-Bareau, *Manet By Himself*, 43.

6. p. 38: Wilson-Bareau, *Manet By Himself*, 38.

7. p. 38: Émile Zola, *Édouard Manet, étude biographique et critique* (E. Dentu, 1867), 24.

8. p. 40: George Heard Hamilton, *Manet and his Critics* (Yale University Press, 1954), 101.

9. p. 42: Wilson-Bareau, *Manet By Himself*, 32.

10. p. 60: Henri Loyrette, *Degas* (Fayard, 1991), 242.

11. p. 64: Marius Roux, "Chronique," *L'Événement illustré* (27 août, 1868), 1.

12. p. 82: Arsène Alexandre, "Essai sur Monsieur Degas," *Les Arts* 14, no. 166 (1918), 22.

13. p. 98: Philippe Burty, "Chronique du jour," *La République française* (April 16, 1874), 2.

14. p. 98: Jean Prouvaire [Mendès?], "L'exposition du Boulevard des Capucines," *Le Rappel* (April 20, 1874), 3.

15. p. 98: Jules-Antoine Castagnary, "Exposition du Boulevard des Capucines," *Le Siècle* (April 29, 1874), 3.

16. p. 100: Letter from Camille Pissarro to Antoine Guillemet (September 3, 1872).

17. p. 104: Émile Zola, "Mon Salon: Les naturalistes," *L'Évenement illustré* (19 May, 1868), 3.

18. p. 116: Albert Wolff, "Le calendrier parisien," *Le Figaro* (April 3, 1876), 1.

19. p. 116: Louis Enault, "Mouvement artistique," *Le Constitutionnel* (April 10, 1876), 2.

20. p. 126: Gérard de Nerval, "Les papillons," *Odelettes* (1853).

21. p. 128: Gaston Vassy, "La journée à Paris," *L'Événement* (April 6, 1877), 2.

22. p. 130: George Moore, *Confessions of a Young Man* (Swan Sonnenschein, Lowrey, & Co., 1888), 56.

23. p. 134: Jean Renoir, *Renoir, My Father*, trans. Randolph and Dorothy Weaver (Collins, 1962), 174.

24. p. 134: Émile Zola, "Notes parisiennes. Une exposition: les peintres impressionnistes," *Le Sémaphore de Marseille* (April 19, 1877), 1.

25. p. 152: Zola, *Édouard Manet, étude biographique et critique*, 24.

26. p. 152: Letter from Claude Monet to his daughter-in-law Blanche Hoschedé (1895).

27. p. 164: Letter from Claude Monet to Émile Zola, quoted in John Rewald, *The History of Impressionism*, (Museum of Modern Art, 1946), 291.

28. p. 166: Georges Clemenceau, *Claude Monet: Les Nymphéas* (Terrain Vague, 1990), 14.

29. p. 178: Gustave Geffroy, "Histoire de l'impressionnisme," *La Vie artistique* (E. Dentu, 1894).

30. p. 178: Gustave Geffroy, "Salon de 1886," *La Justice* (May 26, 1886), 2.

31. p. 188: Georges Jeanniot, "Souvenirs sur Degas," *Revue universelle*, no. 15 (November 1, 1933).

32. p. 188: Paul-André Lemoisne, *Degas et son œuvre* (Plon, 1954).

33. p. 192: Octave Mirbeau, "Claude Monet," *L'Art dans les deux mondes*, (March 7, 1891).

34. p. 200: Octave Mirbeau, "Impressions d'art," *Le Gaulois* (June 16, 1886), 1.

35. p. 202: Ambroise Vollard, *Renoir: An Intimate Record*, translated by Harold L. Van Doren and Randolph T. Weaver (Alfred A. Knopf, 1925), 118.

36. p. 204: Notebook of Berthe Morisot (January 11, 1886).

37. p. 226: John Rewald (ed.) with translations by Lionel Abel, *Camille Pissarro: Letters to his son Lucien Pissarro*, (Pantheon, 1943), 207.

38. p. 232: Roger Fry, Cézanne: *A Study of his Development*, (Noonday Press, [1927] 1958), 73.

39. p. 242: Kendall, *Monet By Himself*, 172.

40. p. 248: Rewald, *Camille Pissarro: Letters to his son Lucien Pissarro*, 280.

41. p. 258: Letter from Auguste Renoir to Paul Durand-Ruel (November 1888).

42. p. 258: Vollard, *Renoir: An Intimate Record*, 118.

43. p. 260: Albert André, *Renoir* (G. Crès, 1919).

44. p. 260: Renoir, *Renoir, My Father*, 456.

Authors

F.B. **François Blanchetière**
Senior Curator of Sculpture,
Musée d'Orsay

C.C.-P. **Caroline Corbeau-Parsons**
Curator of Painting and Works on Paper,
Musée d'Orsay

S.G. **Stéphane Guégan**
Scientific Advisor to the President,
Musée d'Orsay

L.J. **Leïla Jarbouai**
Senior Curator of Painting
and Works on Paper, Musée d'Orsay

S.P. **Sylvie Patry**
Delegate to the Musée d'Orsay's
and Musée de l'Orangerie's anniversary
celebrations, Senior Curator,
Musée d'Orsay

P.P. **Paul Perrin**
Chief Curator, Director of Curatorial Affairs
and Collections, Musée d'Orsay

I.P. **Isolde Pludermacher**
Senior Curator of Painting,
Musée d'Orsay

A.R. **Anne Robbins**
Senior Curator of Painting,
Musée d'Orsay

M.R. **Marie Robert**
Senior Curator of Photography
and Cinema, Musée d'Orsay

J.-R.T. **Jean-Rémi Touzet**
Curator of Painting,
Musée d'Orsay

B.T. **Bénédicte Trémolières**
Paintings Conservator

MUSÉE D'ORSAY

Publishing director
Marie-Caroline Dufayet
Editorial coordination and picture research
Virginie Berri, assisted by Angelina Andryushchenko

Copyediting and proofreading of the French
Alice Norasingh-Ertaud

FLAMMARION

Editorial directors
Kate Mascaro and Julie Rouart
Editorial administration manager
Delphine Montagne
Managing editor, French edition
Mélanie Puchault
Editors, English edition
Helen Adedotun and Eleanor Corbett
Translation from the French
Abigail Grater
Proofreading
Sarah Kane
Production
Élodie Habay-Conjat

Book design and typesetting
Brice Tourneux

Color separation
Quadrilaser, Orléans

Printed in Slovenia by Florjančič

This book is typeset in Moulin (Sandrine Nugue) and is printed on Magno Natural 140 g.

Simultaneously published in French as *L'impressionnisme au musée d'Orsay*

26 27 28 3 2 1
ISBN Musée d'Orsay: 978-2-35433-458-1
ISBN Flammarion: 978-2-08-044721-0
Legal deposit: 05/2026

Flammarion is actively committed to reducing the ecological footprint of its publications. The book you hold in your hands was printed on paper made from wood sourced from sustainably managed forests, using vegetable-based inks, by a printer committed to environmental protection. Send regulation (EU) 2023/988 inquiries to latelier@flammarion.fr

MIX
Paper | Supporting responsible forestry
FSC® C106954

Photographic credits

GrandPalaisRmn (musée d'Orsay)/Daniel Arnaudet: 1; Daniel Arnaudet, Jean Schomans: 169; Martine Beck-Coppola: 124, 180; Michèle Bellot: 35, 221, 249; Jean-Gilles Berizzi: 70, 84, 186; Gérard Blot: 4, 14, 60, 73, 97, 197, 211; Sylvie Chan-Liat: 120, 190, 191; Adrien Didierjean: 6, 27, 138, 153, 154, 164, 248; Thierry Le Mage: 13; Hervé Lewandowski: 8, 10–12, 18, 33, 34, 42–46, 48, 58, 69, 72, 80, 85, 86, 88, 93, 99, 105, 108, 110, 136, 148, 157, 158, 172, 185, 188, 189, 199, 213, 222, 228, 235–237, 239, 241, 243, 244, 253, 254; Stéphane Maréchalle: 90, 98, 250, 252; Tony Querrec: 24, 39, 50, 54, 55, 109, 195, 196, 198, 203, 223, 224; Franck Raux: 134, 144, 162, 167, 179, 209; Michel Urtado: 59, 194, 204, 217, 218.

MBA, Rennes, dist. GrandPalaisRmn/Adélaïde Beaudoin: 170, 171.

Musée d'Orsay, dist. GrandPalaisRmn/Alexis Brandt: 238; Sophie Crépy: 11, 75, 112, 146; Patrice Schmidt: cover, 2, 5, 7, 9, 15–17, 19, 21, 22, 23, 25, 26, 28–32, 36–38, 40, 41, 47, 49, 51-53, 56, 57, 61–68, 71, 74, 76–79, 81-83, 87, 89, 91, 92, 94–96, 100–104, 106, 107, 111, 113–119, 121–123, 125–133, 135, 137, 140–143, 145, 147, 149, 150–152, 155, 156, 159, 160, 161, 163, 166, 168, 173, 174–178, 181–184, 187, 192, 193, 200–202, 205–208, 210, 212, 214–216, 219, 220, 225–227, 229, 230-234, 240, 242, 245–247, 251; Laëtitia Striffling-Marcu: 3, 20, 139, 165.

Photo Agraci, Paris: 11 (top).

© Adagp, Paris, 2026: Richard Guino

Front cover: Claude Monet, *Le Jardin de l'artiste à Giverny* (*The Artist's Garden at Giverny*), 1900